THE
BLACKWELL PHILOSOPHER DICTIONARIES

A Hegel Dictionary

Michael Inwood

Copyright © Michael Inwood 1992

The right of Michael Inwood to be identified as author of this work has been
asserted in accordance with the Copyright, Designs and Patents Act 1988.

First published 1992
Reprinted 1993, 1995, 1996, 1997 (twice), 1998, 1999

Transferred to Digital print 2003

Blackwell Publishers Ltd
108 Cowley Road
Oxford OX4 1JF, UK

Blackwell Publishers Inc.
350 Main Street
Malden, Massachusetts 02148, USA

British Library Cataloguing in Publication Data
A CIP catalogue record for this book is available from the British Library

Library of Congress Cataloging in Publication Data
Inwood, M. J., 1944–
A Hegel dictionary / Michael James Inwood.
p. cm.
Includes bibliographical references and index.
ISBN 0–631–17532–6 (hard) — ISBN 0–631–17533–4
1. Hegel, Georg Wilhelm Friedrich, 1770–1831 — Dictionaries,
indexes, etc. I. Title
B2901.I58   1992   92–13463
193—dc20   CIP

Typeset in Baskerville on 10/11 pt
by Acorn Bookwork, Salisbury, Wilts.

This book is printed on acid-free paper

Contents

Preface · vii

Notes on the use of this book · 1

Hegel and his language · 5

Introducing Hegel · 19

DICTIONARY ENTRIES A–Z · 27

Bibliography · 315

Index of foreign-language terms · 329

General index · 339

Preface

I wish gratefully to acknowledge my debt to my colleagues at Trinity College, Oxford, for granting me sabbatical leave to complete this book and also for providing an incomparably congenial and stimulating environment for my research. I have benefited greatly from numerous discussions with them on various topics in this book. I am especially indebted to Chris Arthur, of Sussex University, for his learned and incisive comments on my manuscript. In dedicating the book to my wife, Christiana Sourvinou-Inwood, I express my gratitude for her constant help and advice.

M.I.
Trinity College, Oxford
February 1992

Notes on the use of this book

An article in this book usually deals with more than one English word and with their German (and sometimes Greek or Latin) counterparts. No single principle governs my grouping of words. Sometimes words are taken together, because Hegel treats them together (e.g. ACTION, DEED and RESPONSIBILITY) and none can be explained without reference to the others. Often this is because the words are, in Hegel's usage, contrasted with, and thus defined in terms of, each other (e.g. REASON and UNDERSTANDING). Sometimes relatively distinct concepts are treated in one article, for the reason that a single English word overlaps two or more German words (e.g. FORCE and POWER). I have attempted to indicate the English words dealt with by an article in the title of the article. But the General index at the end of the book supplies fuller information on this. The Index of foreign-language terms indicates the main discussions of foreign words.

For many significant German words there is no single, established English equivalent. Thus *aufheben* alone has been translated as 'SUBLATE', 'sublimate', 'annul', 'cancel', 'merge', 'integrate', etc. It would be impossible in a work of this type to record all the existing English renderings of all the German words mentioned in the book. But several of the more common alternative renderings are indicated by headings of the form: **cancel** *see* SUBLATION. Further information also appears in the General index.

Although each article is intended to be readable and intelligible in its own right, the systematic interconnectedness of Hegel's thought and vocabulary, along with the need to avoid excessive repetition, have required frequent cross-references. These are usually indicated by the capitalization of a word, or a variant of a word, which appears in the title of another article. Thus the occurrence of 'SUBLATE', in contrast to 'sublate', means: Consult the article whose title contains the word 'sublate' or (as in this case) a variant of it such as 'sublation'. (Where the word so referred to is not the first word in the title of the article where it is primarily discussed and thus does not appear in alphabetical order, consultation of the General index will reveal the whereabouts of the main discussion of it.) The word 'I' (unlike its German equivalent, *ich*) is capitalized and also appears in the title of the article 'I': cross-references to this are indicated by an asterisk appended to the word ('I*'). I use the same system of cross-referencing in my introductory essays.

Those of Hegel's works that were intended as textbooks to accompany his lectures, namely the *Encyclopaedia* and the *Philosophy of Right*, are divided into fairly brief numbered paragraphs: the numbers remain the same in all editions and translations. In references to these works, I usually cite the relevant paragraph number (in roman numerals). I have not distinguished, in my references, between the paragraphs themselves and the 'Remarks' that Hegel added to them, but I have indicated that the reference is to an 'Addition', i.e. an excerpt from Hegel's lectures added by his posthumous editors, by appending 'A.' to the paragraph number. Hegel's other works are divided into fairly long sections, chapters, etc., and the page numbers vary between different editions and translations. Thus my references to these works are usually fairly imprecise: I indicate the broad area of the work from which a quotation is drawn (indicated by § or §§), but do not cite the page numbers of an edition or translation, which, in any case, the reader is unlikely to have at hand. (My quotations are intended to be illustrative, rather than exhaustive.)

Abbreviations

In referring to works by Hegel, I use the following abbreviations:

CJP = *The Critical Journal of Philosophy*, edited by Hegel and Schelling, in which Hegel published many of his early essays and reviews (1801–3)
DFS = *Difference between the Systems of Fichte and Schelling* (1801)
Enc. I, II and III = *Encyclopaedia of the Philosophical Sciences*, vols I, II and III (1817, 1827, 1830)
ETW = *Early Theological Writings*, transl. T. M. Knox (1795–1800)
FK = *Faith and Knowledge* (1802)
GC = *The German Constitution* (1800–2) (in *PW*)
LA = *Lectures on Aesthetics*
LHP = *Lectures on the History of Philosophy* ('I', 'II' and 'III' indicate the volumes of the Haldane and Simson translation)
LPEG = *Lectures on the Proofs of the Existence of God*
LPH = *Lectures on the Philosophy of History*
LPR = *Lectures on the Philosophy of Religion*
NL = *Natural Law* (1802)
PCR = *The Positivity of the Christian Religion* (in *ETW*)
PP = *The Philosophical Propaedeutic* (1808–12)
PR = *The Philosophy of Right* (1821)
PS = *The Phenomenology of Spirit* (1807)
PW = *Hegel's Political Writings*, transl. T. M. Knox (1798–1831)
SCF = *The Spirit of Christianity and its Fate* (in *ETW*)
SL = *The Science of Logic* (1812–16)
'Logic', with an initial capital, refers not to a single work by Hegel, but to the versions of logic contained primarily in *Enc.* I and *SL*, when the differences between them can be ignored.
Accounts of most of these works are to be found in articles assigned to them or to works containing them. Further information appears in the Bibliography at the end of the book.

The following abbreviations are used for works by other authors:

ACR = J. G. Fichte, *Attempt at a Critique of all Revelation* (*Versuch einer Kritik aller Offenbarung*, 1792)

AE = F. Schiller, *On the Aesthetic Education of Man in a Series of Letters* (*Über die ästhetische Erziehung des Menschen in einer Reihe von Briefen*, 1795)

AGN = J. G. Fichte, *Addresses to the German Nation* (*Reden an die deutsche Nation*, 1808)

B = F. W. J. Schelling, *Bruno, or On the Natural and Divine Principle of Things* (*Bruno oder über das natürliche und gottliche Prinzip der Dinge*, 1802)

CJ = I. Kant, *Critique of Judgment* (*Kritik der Urteilskraft*, 1790)

CPR = I. Kant, *Critique of Pure Reason* (*Kritik der reinen Vernunft*, 1781, 1787) (references are to the pages of the first [A] and second [B] editions)

CPrR = I. Kant, *Critique of Practical Reason* (*Kritik der praktischen Vernunft*, 1788)

EHR = G. E. Lessing, *The Education of the Human Race* (*Erziehung des Menschengeschlechts*, 1780)

FMM = I. Kant, *Foundations of the Metaphysic of Morals* (*Grundlegung der Metaphysik der Sitten*, 1785)

FNR = J. G. Fichte, *Foundations of Natural Right* (*Grundlage des Naturrechts*, 1796)

G = J. G. Herder, *God: Some Conversations* (*Gott. Einige Gespräche*, 1787, 1800)

HARD = G. E. Lessing, *How the Ancients Represented Death* (*Wie die Alten den Tod gebildet*, 1769)

HARD2 = J. G. Herder, *How the Ancients Represented Death: A Supplement to Lessing's Essay of the same Title and Content* (*Wie die Alten den Tod gebildet. Ein Nachtrag zu Lessings Abhandlung desselben Titels und Inhalts*, 1769)

IPHM = J. G. Herder, *Ideas on the Philosophy of the History of Mankind* (*Ideen zur Philosophie der Geschichte der Menschheit*, 1784–91)

IPN = F. W. J. Schelling, *Ideas for a Philosophy of Nature* (*Ideen zu einer Philosophie der Natur*, 1797)

IUH = I. Kant, *Ideas for a Universal History with a Cosmopolitan Intent* (*Ideen zu einer allgemeinen Geschichte in weltbürgerlicher Absicht*, 1784)

MENS = I. Kant, *Metaphysical Elements of Natural Science* (*Metaphysische Anfangsgründe der Naturwissenschaft*, 1786)

MM = I. Kant, *Metaphysic of Morals* (*Metaphysik der Sitten*, 1797)

NO = J. H. Lambert, *New Organon, or Thoughts on the Investigation and Designation of the Truth and its Discrimination from Error and Illusion* (*Neues Organon oder Gedanken über die Erforschung und Bezeichnung des Wahren, und dessen Unterscheidung von Irrthum und Schein*, 1764)

OL = J. G. Herder, *On the Origin of Language* (*Über den Ursprung der Sprache*, 1772)

OPP = I. Kant, *On Perpetual Peace* (*Zum ewigen Frieden*, 1795)

PA = J. P. Richter, *Primer of Aesthetics* (*Vorschule der Ästhetik*, 1804)

RLR = I. Kant, *Religion Within the Limits of Reason Alone* (*Religion innerhalb der Grenzen der blossen Vernunft*, 1793)

RT = C. F. Wolff, *Rational Thoughts on God, the World, the Soul, and all Things*

3

in General (*Vernünftige Gedanken von Gott, der Welt und der Seele, auch allen Dingen überhaupt,* 1719)

SKW = J. G. Fichte, *Science of Knowledge* (*Wissenschaftslehre,* 1794)

STI = F. W. J. Schelling, *System of Transcendental Idealism* (*System des transzendentalen Idealismus,* 1800)

UE = J. G. Herder, *Understanding and Experience: a Metacritique on the Critique of Pure Reason* (*Verstand und Erfahrung, eine Metakritik zur Kritik der reinen Vernunft,* 1799)

VM = J. G. Fichte, *The Vocation of Man* (*Die Bestimmung des Menschen,* 1800)

WS = F. W. J. Schelling, *On the World Soul* (*Von der Weltseele,* 1798)

Page references to works by J. G. Fichte are to the posthumous collected edition of his works published by his son, I. H. Fichte, in 1845–6. The pagination of this edition reappears in most subsequent editions and translations.

Page references to works by F. W. J. Schelling are to the posthumous collected edition of his works published by his son, K. F. A. Schelling, from 1856 to 1861. The pagination of this edition is reproduced in most later editions and translations.

Hegel and his language

Hegel wrote and lectured in German. He did so at the end of a period in which the German language had become, in the hands of Goethe, Schiller, Lessing, etc., the vehicle of a great national literature, comparable to those of France, England and Italy, and in which it was used as never before for the expression of scientific, cultural and philosophical ideas. Hegel did not regard his philosophy as peculiarly German, in the sense that it is valid only for the German language or that it can be appropriately expressed only in German, but he held that it is crucial for the development of a people to possess literary and cultural products in its native tongue and that the structure and vocabulary of German are especially well suited for the expression of certain important truths: German has a 'speculative spirit' (*SL*, Pref. to 2nd edn). He thus aimed to 'teach philosophy to speak German', just as 'Luther made the Bible speak German, and you [Voss] have done the same for Homer'.[1]

In this essay, I first sketch some general features of the German language that need to be borne in mind both in reading Hegel and in using this book. Secondly, I consider some aspects of the development of German as a philosophical language, especially in the eighteenth century. Finally, I examine some of the peculiar features of Hegel's use of German and the general character of his contributions to philosophical German.

THE GERMAN LANGUAGE

Together with Frisian, Dutch and English, German belongs to the West Germanic group of languages and is thus closely related to English. But it differs from English in several crucial respects. Most notably, German is a highly inflected language: the grammatical structure of a German sentence is conveyed by the endings of nouns and verbs, as well as by word-order. Each noun (and pronoun) has four cases (nominative, accusative, genitive or possessive, and dative), usually indicated by the ending of the word and conveying the role of the noun in the sentence. (The subject of the sentence, e.g., is in the nominative case.) Again, every German noun is classified into one of three genders: masculine, feminine and neuter. The gender of a noun need not coincide with the sex of the object it denotes: thus *Mensch* ('man, human being') is masculine and *Frau* ('woman, wife') is feminine, but *Weib* ('woman, wife') and *Fräulein* ('young woman') are neuter, and *Kunst*

5

('skill, art') is feminine. The case-endings of nouns (and of the adjectives, articles, relative pronouns, etc. that accompany or qualify them) vary according to the gender of the noun. (These apparent complexities often enable German to avoid ambiguity more easily than English.)

All nouns (but not usually pronouns) in German begin with a capital letter. Thus the common practice of translating significant nouns by a word with an initial capital ('Reason', 'Notion', etc.) has no warrant in German, which does not distinguish between nouns in this way.

German, like English, has a definite article, *der*, etc. ('the'), and an indefinitive article, *ein*, etc. ('a(n)'). These vary according to the gender and case of the accompanying noun: thus, in the nominative case, it is *der Mensch, die Frau, die Kunst* and *das Weib*. The indefinite article, *ein*, also means 'one': thus *eine Frau* can mean 'a woman' or 'one woman'. Hegel sometimes adopted the common practice of distinguishing these senses by using a capital letter for the sense of 'one': *eine Frau*, is 'a woman', while *Eine Frau* is 'one woman'. (The occasional reproduction of this in English translations – 'One woman', etc. – has no justification.)

German, like English, has a variety of ways of turning another part of speech into a noun. Thus an adjective such as *schön* ('fine, beautiful') commonly appears (attributively) between the article and the noun ('the/a beautiful painting') or is predicated of a noun ('The painting was beautiful'). The addition of a suffix, especially *-heit* or *-keit*, turns the adjective into an abstract noun. Thus *die Schönheit* is 'beauty'. (German, unlike English, usually requires a definite article in such cases.) But German, like English, also converts an adjective into a noun more directly by simply adding an article to the appropriate form of the adjective. Thus the adjective *einzeln* means 'individual', but *der/ein Einzelne* is 'the/an individual'. More commonly, the article and the adjective are in the neuter: thus *das Schöne* is 'the beautiful', *das Allgemeine* 'the universal', *das Sinnliche* 'the sensory', *das Wahre* 'the true', and so on. Such expressions are ambiguous: e.g. *das Schöne* can refer to some particular beautiful item, to beautiful things in general ('The beautiful usually fetches a high price') or to the abstract quality of beauty ('The beautiful is distinct from the true').

Another part of speech that can be transformed into a noun is the verb. English often does this by adding the suffix '-ing' to the core of the verb: 'run' becomes 'running', etc. German similarly adds *-ung*: e.g. *erklären* ('to explain, define') becomes (*die*) *Erklärung* ('definition, explanation'), *aufheben* ('to cancel', etc.) becomes (*die*) *Aufhebung* ('cancellation', etc.), *bestimmen* ('to determine', etc.) becomes (*die*) *Bestimmung* ('determination', etc.), and so on. English also occasionally uses the infinitive as a noun-phrase: 'to be is to be perceived', 'to hear is to obey', etc. German, or at least Hegel's German, makes far more use of this device, by adding (usually) the neuter definite article to the infinitive form: *das Erklären* ('explaining, explanation (as an activity)', etc.), *das Aufheben* ('cancelling', etc.), *das Bestimmen* ('determining', etc.). Adjectives and adverbial phrases can be incorporated into such verbal nouns. Thus *bestimmt sein* is 'to be determined', and this becomes *das Bestimmtsein* ('being determined, to be determined'). *An und für sich sein* is 'to

6

be in and for itself', and in Hegel this becomes *das Anundfürsichsein* ('being-in-and-for-itself') or simply *das Anundfürsich* – though this can also mean 'that which is in and for itself', equivalent to *das Anundfürsichseiende*, where *seiend(e)* is the present participle of *sein*.

As this suggests, German has a greater facility than English (and a far greater facility than French) for combining words to form more complex words, often with meanings that cannot be readily inferred from the meanings of their constituents.[2] The most obvious sign of this is the great variety of compound verbs, verbs composed of a core verb preceded by a preposition or adverb. English examples are 'outdo', 'overcome'; but English more usually forms new verbs by a following adverb or preposition: 'put off, over, up with', etc. In German the simple verb *setzen* ('to put, set, posit', etc.), for example, forms the following compounds: *festsetzen* ('to set up, establish'), *entgegensetzen* ('to oppose, object'), *voraussetzen* ('to (pre)suppose, presume'), and many others. In sentences the core verb and its prefix are often separated from each other, with the prefix following the verb, often at some distance from it (e.g. *setzen . . . voraus*, rather than *voraussetzen*), but this does not, as in English (e.g. 'overcome' and 'outride', in contrast to 'come over' and 'ride out'), alter the meaning of the compound verb. These verbs, together with the fact that each constituent of the verb usually has a familiar meaning of its own, enable Hegel to draw connections between words that are not easily conveyed in English translation. Thus *voraus* means 'in front, in advance', and Hegel can suggest that to presuppose (*voraussetzen*) something is to posit it or set it up (*setzen*) in advance. Nouns too are often composed of simpler words. (*Der*) *Gegenstand* ('object (e.g. of consciousness)') is formed from *gegen* ('towards, against') and *Stand* ('standing, position', etc.) and is thus literally 'that which stands over against'. Simpler examples are *Kunstwerk* ('work of art'), *das Kunstschöne* ('artistic beauty, the beauty of art'), *das Naturschöne* ('natural beauty, the beauty of nature'), etc.

Connected with German's facility for composition is the fact (or supposed fact) that German, like ancient Greek, but unlike English and French, is an 'original (*ursprüngliche*)' language. This idea goes back to Vico, who claimed that German is a 'living heroic language', but it was popularized in Germany especially by Herder and by Fichte.[3] In its beginnings, the argument runs, language is governed by 'poetic logic' (Vico) and depends on concrete imagery and metaphor. The primitive man says not that he is angry, but that the blood boils in his heart. All languages originate in this way, but in some, such as English, the primitive roots of the language have been obscured by its later development, in particular by the importation of foreign words whose original meanings are not apparent to speakers of the language. For example, the English 'object' comes from the past participle, *objectum*, of the Latin verb *obicere* (*ob-icere*), 'to throw against', and thus meant originally 'that which is thrown over against', but this is not apparent to English speakers, since 'object' was taken as a whole from Latin, and *ob*, *ject*, and *icere* have no independent meanings in English. German, by contrast, has fewer foreign loan-words (especially since Germans have been less subject to foreign invasions than the English), and has thus preserved its primitive roots. Thus

7

it is apparent to a German that a *Gegenstand* is what stands against, since *gegen* and *Stand* both have familiar meanings in the language. Again, the original sense of *Augenblick* (literally 'eye-glance') is apparent to the German, while those of its English equivalents – 'moment', from the Latin *movere*, 'to move', and 'instant', from the Latin *instare*, 'to stand on' – are not readily accessible to English-speakers.

Nevertheless, as we shall see in the next section, German borrowed and retained many foreign, especially Latin, words. For example, in addition to *Gegenstand*, it has *Object* or, in its more Germanic form, *Objekt*. Some purists advocated the removal of such loan-words, and their replacement by native equivalents. But influential figures, such as Leibniz and Hegel, insisted that useful imports should be retained.[4] They are often assigned a slightly different sense from their native counterparts.

Despite the supposed originality of their language, Germans, including Hegel himself, often assigned incorrect etymologies even to native words. This happened, for example, in the case of the prefix *ur-*, which occurs in such words as *Urteil* ('judgment') and *Ursache* ('cause'). This, owing mainly to its presence in *Ursprung* ('origin') and *ursprünglich* ('original'), was taken to mean 'original, primeval, proto-', and several words were formed on this assumption: (*das*) *Urbild*, a seventeenth-century coinage for 'original, proto-type, archetype'; (*die*) *Urpflanze*, the 'proto-plant, archetypal plant', from which, on Goethe's view, all species of plant derive; (*das*) *Urphänomen*, the 'proto-phenomenon', the general, archetypal phenomenon, from which, on Goethe's view, more specific phenomena derive. In fact *ur-* is a form of *er-* (as in *Erscheinung*, 'APPEARANCE') and its original force was that of 'out of', 'forth' or 'from within'. The original sense of *Ursprung* was the 'springing forth', especially of water. Nevertheless, the widespread belief that German is an original language and that its primitive roots are transparent to the native speaker had a considerable influence on the use, interpretation and development of German in this period. Hegel's exploration and exploitation of etymologies, both real and imagined, will be a constant theme in this book.

THE DEVELOPMENT OF PHILOSOPHICAL GERMAN

Leibniz extolled the virtues of German and advocated its development and use for scholarly, scientific and philosophical purposes. But Leibniz, like most other German scholars of the late seventeenth century, wrote and published for the most part in French or Latin. German had fallen into disuse as a scholarly language.

Despite this, the formation of German philosophical terminology has a long history.[5] An important early figure is Notker (*c.* 950–1022), who translated into German the Latin versions of Aristotle's *Categories* and *De Interpretatione*, and Boethius' *De Consolatione Philosophiae*. He thus proposed Germanic equivalents for many Latin philosophical terms: some of his suggestions (e.g. *ewig* for *aeternus*, 'eternal') have survived, but others (e.g. *mitewist* for *accidens*, 'accident (of a substance)') have not. But the most important factor in the growth of philosophical German throughout the medieval period (when mainstream philosophy was, as elsewhere, normally written in Latin) was German mysticism, which owed as much to Neoplatonism[6] and to gnosticism as to Christianity. Its first major representative was the Dominican, Meister (Johann) Eckhart (*c*. 1260–1327). The aim of Eckhart, as of other mystics, was the unification of the soul with God, the vision of God in the depths of one's own soul. Before the creation God is 'nothing in nothing'. Only in the nature that he creates (*genaturte Natur*, i.e. *natura naturata*) does God become conscious of himself. Everything comes to be in and with God, and everything passes away again into God. The mystics developed a vocabulary for the expression of these views, and used several terms that have since established themselves: words ending in *-heit* such as *anderheit* ('otherness'), *menschheit* ('humanity'), and *würklicheit* ('actuality, reality'); and *eigenschaft*, but in the senses of 'possession' and 'peculiarity', rather than the modern sense of 'attribute, PROPERTY (of a THING)'.

Luther (1483–1546) had a massive impact on the growth of theological and philosophical terminology. Another figure who was influenced by mysticism, and himself influenced its subsequent development, is Paracelsus (1493–1541), a doctor who wrote on philosophical matters and also lectured in German on medicine at Basle *c*. 1526. Paracelsus used *Erfahrung* ('experience') to mean both the whole of the given as an object of cognition and the activity of cognition itself. He also established *Verstand* as the counterpart of the Latin *intellectus*, but (unlike Hegel) he placed it above *Vernunft* ('reason, the Latin *ratio*'). (Eckhart had used variants of *Verstand* such as *verstandnisse*, but not *Verstand* itself. The usual mystical word for the highest activity of the MIND is *gemuet*, i.e. *Gemüt*.)

Paracelsus influenced the thought of Jakob Böhme (1575–1624), a shoemaker and mystic, whom Hegel regarded as the 'first German philosopher', through whom 'philosophy emerged in Germany with a character of its own'. Böhme tended to pervert loan-words (e.g. *qualitas*, 'QUALITY') by associating them with etymologically unrelated native words (e.g. *Qual*, 'pain, torture'). But he also developed several philosophical words and concepts: e.g. *Zweck* for 'PURPOSE', and *Auswicklung* for 'DEVELOPMENT' (which was supplanted by *Entwicklung* only in the eighteenth century).

Leibniz thought highly of such mystics as Böhme, and recommended them as a source of German philosophical terminology. Böhme was also valued by the romantics, especially Novalis, and F. Schlegel affirmed that no one else was so 'rich in allegory and symbolic representation'. He exerted a strong influence on Schelling, and in particular on his philosophy of nature.

Although Leibniz wrote little in German, he made some contributions to German philosophical vocabulary. One that survived is the use of *Urteil* ('JUDGMENT') in the logical sense; one that did not is *Selbstand* (literally 'standing by itself') for the Latin *substantia* ('SUBSTANCE'). Leibniz held no university post and thus did not give lectures. Christian Thomasius (1655–1728), a lecturer at the University of Leipzig, created a stir in 1687 by announcing in the German language a course of lectures, which he then delivered in the German language. He was eventually driven out of Leipzig, in part because of his insistence on lecturing and publishing in German, and moved to the University of Halle, which raised no objection to this departure from tradition. In his published writings, Thomasius continued to use loan-words alongside native ones, and objected to artificial Germanic coinages to replace well-established loan-words.[7] Thus he uses both *Materie* and the native *Stoff*, both *Object* and *Gegenstand*.

The problem for the philosopher writing in German, however, was not primarily that native words (or acceptable loan-words) were not available for use, but that there was no settled and generally accepted philosophical vocabulary. Some writers retained Latin words; others translated them into native German. But there was as yet no agreement on the translations. Thomasius did little to remedy this, in part because his writings were still shot through with Latin borrowings, in part because his terminological proposals lacked the clarity, authority and consistency needed for widespread acceptance. The most significant step in this direction was taken by the foremost philosopher of the German Enlightenment, Christian Wolff (1679–1754).

Wolff was originally a mathematician and he believed that philosophy should be presented with mathematical clarity and rigour. When a term is introduced, it must, on his view, be clearly defined, and it must not be used subsequently in a sense other than that originally assigned to it. We must not use two or more terms synonymously: apparent synonyms must be given distinct, well-defined senses. Thus Wolff distinguishes between *Grund* ('ground, reason') and *Ursache* ('cause'): 'The ground is that by which one can understand why something is, and the cause is a thing that contains in itself the ground of another thing' (*RT* §29). And between a *Vermögen* ('ability, power') and a *Kraft* ('force, power'): 'The ability is only the possibility of doing something, whereas, since the force is a source of alterations, it must involve an endeavour to do something' (*RT* §117). Wolff wrote for the most part in German, and he provides a German equivalent for almost every Latin or Latinate word. The German word is only rarely his own creation, but he provides a stable and well-defined use for words that had previously lacked it. He gave to *Begriff*, e.g., its modern sense of 'concept', and attempts to distinguish it from *Vorstellung* ('representation', CONCEPTION'): concepts are the conceptions of genera and species of things (*RT* §273). (Wolff also seems to have coined some Latinate terms, which passed into German: *genetische Definition, Monist* and *Monismus, Teleologia*, etc.)

Owing to the clarity and simplicity of his style, Wolff's writings became immensely popular, and influenced literary as well as philosophical usage. The use of *Begriff* became widespread largely owing to his clarification and stabilization of it. Hegel had little time for Wolff as a philosopher, but he concedes in *LHP* that it was Wolff who 'first made thought in the form of thought into common property', 'made an immortal contribution to the development of the German intellect [*Verstand*, 'UNDERSTANDING']', and 'made philosophy a science that belongs to the German nation'.

Several philosophers in the tradition of Leibniz and Wolff made substantial contributions to philosophical German: Baumgarten gave us *Ästhetik*, etc.; Lambert coined *Phänomenologie*; and Tetens refined psychological vocabulary, distinguishing, e.g., an *Empfindung* ('sensation'), as a 'copy' of an object, from a *Gefühl* ('feeling'), as a perceived 'alteration in oneself'. The creative, but undisciplined, Herder gave a wider, more historical sense to *Kultur, Entwicklung* and *Fortschritt* ('progress'); while Jacobi introduced the contrast between *mechanisch* and *organisch*.

Kant (1724–1804) was not especially interested in language as such, but owing to the power, clarity and systematic nature of his thought, he had a lasting impact on German philosophical vocabulary and style, and conferred on many words what has since become their standard meaning.[8] Unlike Hegel, he did not for the most part challenge Wolff's usage, but refined, developed and extended it. He sometimes compares himself to a chemist, who analyses substances and separates what is confused. Thus he draws distinctions between words, e.g., between *Schein* ('ILLUSION') and *Erscheinung* ('APPEARANCE') and between *analytisch–synthetisch* and *a priori–a posteriori*. He often uses a foreign word alongside its native counterpart, but he tends to distinguish their senses: e.g. *Notio(n)* and *Begriff*, *Empirie* and *Erfahrung*, and *Phaenomenon* and *Erscheinung*. Kant was also thoroughly systematic, and presented his vocabulary in such orderly constructions as the table of categories. In Hegel's day the standard meaning of a philosophical term was usually the sense in which Kant had used it.

HEGEL'S LANGUAGE

The development of philosophical German in the hands of Wolff and Kant can be seen as the emergence of *Verstand*, the UNDERSTANDING, with its sharp clarity and analytical rigour, in the realm of terminology. Distinctions are drawn and clearly demarcated, between, e.g., a logical ground (*Grund*) and a real ground, between the objective and the subjective, and so on. The German idealists represent, by contrast, the reaction of dialectical REASON (*Vernunft*). While not wishing to supplant the understanding with sheer FEELING or to revert to the pre-Wolffian phase, they blur, or at least complicate, distinctions that hitherto seemed clear and precise. Functions of thought, such as *Idee* (IDEA), *Begriff* and reason become real active forces, involved in the world as much as in our thought about the world. The colloquial uses of terms intrude into their philosophical uses. There is a greater concern for the place of a thing, a concept or a word in the whole to which it belongs, and an insistence that words and concepts cannot be understood piecemeal, apart from their place in such a system. Ideally, Fichte argues, a fixed philosophical vocabulary is desirable, but that can come only at the end of the system, when reason has completed its work. For the present, he avoids a 'fixed terminology – [which is] the easiest way for literalists to rob a system of its spirit and transform it into a dry skeleton' (*W* 87). Terminology thus becomes more fluid and develops with his thought.

Fichte nevertheless has a distinctive vocabulary, marked, e.g., by the frequent use of *absolute(-s, -r)* ('ABSOLUTE') as an adjective distinguishing his use of a word from its common use: the absolute I, e.g., is distinct from, if related to, me, you and Fichte. *Wissenschaftslehre* ('doctrine of science, science of knowledge') is itself Fichte's recommended substitute for *Philosophie*, though he later admitted that it had not found much favour. To Fichte we owe the development of Kant's notion of *intellektuelle Anschauung* ('intellectual INTUITION'), the frequent and seemingly indiscriminate use of *setzen* ('to POSIT'), and the triad 'thesis–antithesis–synthesis', often wrongly attributed to Hegel.

Schelling, like Hegel, explicitly rejected the sharp antitheses which he took to be characteristic of previous philosophy. What is missing in modern philosophy is, he argues, 'mediating concepts' (*mittleren Begriffe*). In the absence of these we assume that if something is not, then it is nothing; that if it is not fully spiritual, it is crudely material; that if it is not ethically free, then it is mechanical; and if it is not intelligent, then it lacks understanding altogether. A special feature of Schelling's own terminology is his use of terms from the natural sciences for wider philosophical purposes: *Organismus* and *organisch*, *Polarität*, *Potenz* ('power (in mathematics), potency') and *potenzieren* ('to raise to a higher power, magnify'), and *Metamorphose*. Nature, especially the organic, is a source of analogies for the spiritual and the metaphysical. (Hegel criticizes this tendency, both as obfuscating and as assimilating the higher to the lower. But he is himself not wholly immune to it.)

But by far the most innovative and influential of the idealists is Hegel. He effected a radical transformation of philosophical German, which, though it has not supplanted the Wolffian–Kantian tradition, still influences much philosophical discourse, not only in German, but in other European languages. He did so not by coining new terms, but by exploiting the existing resources of German, both its native forms and its loan-words. German, he argues in the Preface to the 2nd edition of *SL*, contains a wealth of 'logical expressions', prepositions, etc., which can be used for philosophical purposes. (The best-known example is *an sich*, *für sich* and *an und für sich*, IN ITSELF, FOR ITSELF and IN AND FOR ITSELF.)

Thus any word that Hegel uses is likely to have, first, a use in ordinary discourse, and, second, a use, or rather a range and history of uses, in previous philosophers. Often enough, Hegel uses words in these ways, using, e.g., *an sich* unselfconsciously in its ordinary sense or, when he is discussing some past philosopher, using a word in the way in which that philosopher used it. But often he assigns to the word a relatively novel sense, related to, but distinct from, its ordinary and previous philosophical senses. Some general characteristics of Hegel's innovations are these:

Often different words and phrases have approximately the same sense. Thus in ordinary usage *an sich*, *für sich* and *an und für sich* do not differ in meaning sharply or clearly; *Sittlichkeit* ('ethics') and *Moralität* were, in Kant and other philosophers, approximate synonyms; *Dasein* ('existence, determinate BEING') is used interchangeably with *Existenz*; and so on. Hegel dislikes synonyms as much as Wolff and conducts a campaign of ruthless desynonymization.[9] Thus *Sittlichkeit* and *Moralität* are given different meanings, respectively 'ETHICAL LIFE, social morality' and 'individual MORALITY, the morality of conscience'. On the whole, however, Hegel assigns different senses to apparent synonyms, not for its own sake, but for the sake of some important conceptual distinction which the differentiation of senses enables him to draw. Thus he marks a distinction by differentiating *ideal* from *ideell* ('IDEAL'), but he sees no parallel distinction between *real* and *reell*, and tends to use them interchangeably. (Even when Hegel does differentiate words, he is not always careful or consistent in his use of them, especially, and understandably, in his lectures.)

The sense Hegel assigns to a word is never unrelated to its ordinary or previous philosophical uses. Often he sees a connection between the (real or supposed) etymology of a word, indicating its (real or supposed) past use, and the sense he assigns to it. Thus *Sittlichkeit* is related to the current word for 'custom', *Sitte*, and can thus be assumed to have originally meant 'customary' rather than 'individual' morality. Hegel is more inclined to explore the etymology of native words than of loan-words, since *Moralität* also derives from the Latin for 'custom', *mos* (plural: *mores*). But he appeals to foreign etymologies when the occasion arises. He stresses the derivation of *Existenz* ('EXISTENCE') from the Latin *existere*, 'to step, stand forth'.

When apparent synonyms are differentiated in this way, Hegel rarely supposes them to be merely different. They are usually systematically related in some way. Thus *an sich, für sich* and *an und für sich* are often, though not invariably, seen as marking three stages in the development of an entity. *Moralität* is often seen as a stage whose inadequacy leads to the growth or introduction of *Sittlichkeit*, and which persists as a phase within at least the modern form of *Sittlichkeit*. (If what Hegel has in mind is ancient Greek *Sittlichkeit*, the order is likely to be reversed.) Similarly, *Dasein* and *Existenz* are systematically related in the Logic, even if at some distance from each other. The interconnection of concepts, and thus of the words expressing them, into a SYSTEM is a central function of Hegel's dialectical method.

In ordinary usage, words often do not have a single clear meaning or use, but a range of loosely connected meanings, or even two or more fairly distinct meanings. Examples in German are *Begriff* ('concept', etc.); *Reflexion*; *Urteil* ('JUDGMENT'); *aufheben* ('to preserve, destroy, elevate', etc.); *wahr* ('true (e.g. judgment, friend, etc.)'); *Freiheit* ('FREEDOM'). The standard, especially Wolffian, philosophical response to this is to assign one clear meaning to the word in question, attempting to disregard its other uses and connotations, and henceforth to employ it exclusively in this sense. Hegel rejects this standard procedure. He does not replace it with any single procedure, but adopts different strategies in different cases. In the case of one ambiguous word, *aufheben*, Hegel avowedly and regularly uses it in two opposite senses simultaneously: 'to preserve and destroy, i.e. to SUBLATE'. Generally, when Hegel uses a word, even if on that occasion of its use one of the word's senses seems to dominate or even exclude its other senses, its other senses or uses are likely to influence Hegel's use of it. Nevertheless, it is not invariably the case that whenever Hegel uses a word, all its common senses and uses are in play to an *equal* extent. He treats ambiguities in the language available to him

13

in different ways. In the case of some ambiguous words, e.g. *Freiheit, Reflexion, Urteil*, etc., he attempts to relate systematically the different senses of the word, arguing, e.g., that a judgment in the sense of 'assessment' or 'verdict' is the highest type of judgment in the wider sense. Often he distinguishes different senses of the word by a preceding adjective, e.g. 'OBJECTIVE' and 'SUBJECTIVE' freedom, 'subjective, etc. SPIRIT (*Geist*)'. Sometimes he brusquely rejects one sense of a word, and favours and develops another of its senses: he argues, e.g., that a judgment cannot be true (only 'correct'), and assimilates his own use of *wahr* to its use in 'true friend'. Sometimes he distinguishes between a good or 'true' sense of a word and a bad or 'false' sense: e.g. true and bad INFINITY. The cases of 'truth' and 'infinity' differ in that while the expression 'true judgment' or 'true proposition (*Satz*)' plays virtually no role in Hegel's discourse, 'bad infinity' or 'the bad infinite' occur frequently, and the notion of bad infinity plays a crucial role in the emergence of the notion of true infinity. (Nevertheless, a version, or at least a close relative, of the correspondence definition of judgmental truth – that truth is the 'agreement of a concept with reality' – plays a part in Hegel's own account of truth.)

Thus, contrary to the Wolffian ideal, Hegel has no general interest in using a word in the same sense throughout his works or even in a single text. There are several reasons for this. Most obviously, since he is constantly concerned with HISTORY, and especially with the history of philosophy, a term must remain available for us in the senses in which past philosophers employed it, e.g. *Idee* ('IDEA') must be available in Plato's sense, as well as in Hegel's.

Secondly, the assignment of meaning to a word is no easy matter, and even if it were possible simply to assign wholly novel senses to old words, Hegel's belief that the philosopher should immerse himself in his SUBJECT-MATTER debars him from doing so: he must, as it were, watch words developing their own senses rather than arbitrarily declare that he intends to use them in such and such a way. Moreover, since philosophy has, on Hegel's view, no presuppositions, a word's acquisition of meaning is an integral part of philosophy, not a mere preliminary which we can assume to be complete when we begin to do philosophy. Standardly, then, Hegel begins by using a term in one or more of its already familiar senses and then develops his own sense or senses from it. The new sense of the word invariably involves, in a 'sublated' form, the earlier senses, since, on Hegel's view, the result of a temporal or logical process always contains the process that led up to it. (This is one reason why, however much a word is modified, it remains ready for use in previous senses.)

Thirdly, the meaning of a word does not depend on the word alone, but on its place in a system of words, in particular of words that contrast with it. (Hegel endorsed Spinoza's dictum 'DETERMINATION is NEGATION'.) To take a simple example from English, the meaning of 'man' varies as it contrasts with (1) 'beast' or 'animal', and perhaps 'God' and 'angel'; (2) 'woman'; (3) 'boy'; (4) 'officer', etc.; or (5) 'mouse'. This implies that a word such as *Sein* ('BEING'), the first word explicitly considered in the Logic, cannot retain exactly the same meaning as that first assigned to it once further terms are

14

introduced. The meaning of this, and of other words, develops as the system unfolds.

There are, finally, three Hegelian doctrines that imply that a word changes its meaning as his thought progresses:

(1) In a proposition such as 'God is being', 'God is eternal' or 'The actual is the universal', the subject-term ('God', etc.) has no fixed, independent meaning, but is assigned a meaning by the predicate-term ('being', etc.) (*PS*, Pref; *Enc.* I §31). The subject-term thus develops in meaning as we apply further predicates to it or, more generally, say more about it.

(2) Hegel's thought usually advances in TRIADS, the third term of which is a restoration of the first on a higher level. The same word is often used both for the first and for the third term of a triad, in distinct, but systematically related senses: see e.g. ABSOLUTE, IMMEDIACY, etc.

(3) The UNIVERSAL specifies itself into the universal, the PARTICULAR and the INDIVIDUAL. Thus the universal appears both as the genus and as a species of that genus. Thus the same word is often used in both a generic and a specific sense (*see* e.g. BEING, etc.).

Hegel's redefinition or 'reconstruction' of words involves a complex interplay between the standard or current sense(s) of a word (both in philosophy and in ordinary speech), the real or presumed literal sense(s) of the word, which is often a past sense (disclosed by the word's real or presumed etymology), and philosophical argument. Thus *unendlich*, 'infinite', has the core meaning of 'not (*un-*, in-) having an end or boundary (*Ende, finis*)'. It is standardly applied both to an infinite series (e.g. 1, 2, 3, etc.) or extent (boundless space, etc.) and to an infinite deity, distinct from the finite world. But these applications, Hegel argues, are at odds with its root meaning, since a God that is distinct from the finite is bounded by the finite, and we can handle an infinite series or expanse only by carving it into finite segments. ('1, 2, 3, etc.' is as finite and bounded as '1, 2, 3'.) Hegel also notes that to be endless or unbounded something need not, as we say, 'go on forever'. The circumference of a circle (or the surface of a sphere) does not have a boundary or come to an end. ('1, 2, 3, 1, 2, 3, 1, etc.' is unbounded in a way that '1, 2, 3, etc.' and '1, 2, 3.' are not.) Thus Hegel's reconstruction of 'infinity' uses philosophical argument to prise apart two layers of the meaning of *unendlich*, and to realign the word (along with its core or root meaning) to a new sense or application. He applies a similar procedure to many other words: *an sich* and *für sich*, and so on.

Hegel's exploitation of etymology has several sources. First, as we have seen above, to argue that a word should be used in one sense rather than another normally presupposes that the word in question has two or more levels of meaning, which can be played off against each other and be shown to involve a conflict or CONTRADICTION. The supposed root or original meaning of a word is one such layer of meaning, in potential conflict with the word's current uses. Moreover, Hegel believes, just as a result always contains the process that led up to it, so a word never wholly discards its past meanings; they are invariably involved in the current meaning of the word. He does not believe, however, that a word's earlier senses or original meaning are superior to its later ones. Such a belief would be wholly at odds with his view that the ESSENCE of a thing lies in its fully developed state rather than its initial state, in the oak tree rather than the acorn. Thus he conceives himself to be developing and perfecting language rather than restoring its beginnings. But to do this often requires an examination of its earlier states. Thus when he suggests (in both cases mistakenly) that *Urteil* means 'original division' (*Ur-teil*) or *wahrnehmen* ('to perceive') means 'to take truly, in truth' (*wahr-nehmen*), he is not attempting to recapture the original senses of these words, but drawing attention to potentialities for their further development implicit in their past, and thus also their present, meanings. That he often neglects the etymology of a word (e.g. *Moralität*) suggests that etymology concerns him only when it indicates a potentiality, which he wants to develop for philosophical rather than etymological reasons.

Hegel, like Schelling, was averse to the sharp oppositions characteristic of Wolff's philosophy and of the Enlightenment understanding (*Verstand*) generally. He saw the overcoming of such oppositions, between e.g. the understanding and the senses, as a central task of philosophy. He approaches different oppositions in different ways, but one typical strategy is to suggest that at their extreme points opposites change into each other. For example, if something is wholly 'INNER' (i.e. latent and undeveloped), then it is also wholly 'OUTER' (i.e. known only to an external observer). In general, he is reluctant to say that anything has a certain characteristic to the total exclusion of the opposite or negation of that characteristic. Thus he rejects such Wolffian–Kantian dichotomies as *a priori–a posteriori*, analytic–synthetic, etc., at least in so far as they require something to be *either a priori*, etc., *or a posteriori*, but not both together (e.g. *Enc.* I §12).

One of the dichotomies that Hegel seeks to overcome is that between SUBJECTIVITY and OBJECTIVITY or between THINKING and THINGS. Philosophy traditionally distinguishes between terms applicable to things ('being', 'causality', etc.) and terms applicable to our thoughts or discourse: 'TRUTH', 'DIALECTIC, 'CONTRADICTION', 'CONCEPT', 'JUDGMENT', 'INFERENCE', etc. One striking feature of Hegel's linguistic reconstruction is his comprehensive transference of subjective terms into the objective realm: things, as well as concepts, may be true, contradictory, judgments, etc. This transference has antecedents in e.g. Neoplatonism and Böhme, as well as in our everyday application of 'rational' (*vernünftig*) both to thoughts and to states of affairs. But Hegel carries it through far more systematically and self-consciously than any of his predecessors. It is a consequence of one central strand in his idealism, the belief that thought is not distinct from things, but is embedded in them and responsible for their nature and development.

CONCLUSION

The intricacies of Hegel's German are difficult for a German-speaker to unravel. But the difficulties are multiplied for the English-speaker. A significant German word often has a range of meaning and use to which no single English word exactly corresponds: thus *Bestimmung* ('determination') indicates both the present state of a thing and its future 'vocation' or 'destiny'. Even if a German word has an acceptable English equivalent, its history and (real or supposed) etymology are likely to differ from those of the English word: no translation can subject 'judge' and 'judgment' to the manoeuvres that *urteilen* and *Urteil* undergo in Hegel's hands. The case becomes even more complicated if the German word, whether or not it is directly derived from Latin or Greek, is influenced in its previous development and/or in Hegel's use of it by a Latin or Greek counterpart: one cannot understand, e.g.; Hegel's use of *Schicksal* ('FATE') without knowing something of a range of Greek words bearing on this concept. Thus in this book I frequently refer to the German words Hegel uses and to the uses he makes of them. I describe some aspects of their ordinary use, of their historical development, and of the history of their previous philosophical use, thus attempting to convey something of the layers of meaning that supply Hegel with the materials for his own development of them. Often too I consider the uses of a corresponding Latin or Greek term.[10] This information does not, of course, guarantee a full understanding of Hegel's texts, but it is usually a necessary precondition of it.

NOTES

1 Letter to Voss of 1805 (*Letters*, p. 107). Luther translated the Bible into German, and Voss translated the *Odyssey* (1781) and *Iliad* (1793).

2 Cf. W. Whewell, in *The Philosophy of the Inductive Sciences, founded upon their History* (2nd edn, London: Parker, 1847), II p. 486: 'Of modern European languages the German possesses the greatest facility of composition; and hence scientific authors in that language are able to invent terms which it is impossible to imitate in the other languages of Europe.'

3 *The New Science of Giambattista Vico*, translated from the third edition (1744) by T. G. Bergin and M. H. Fisch (Ithaca, NY and London: Cornell University Press, 1948), §445. Vico adds that German 'transforms almost all names from foreign languages into its own' (§445), that it is 'a mother language (because foreign nations never entered that country to rule over it)', in which 'the roots are all monosyllabic' (§452), and that it 'preserves its heroic origins intact – even to excess – and this is the reason ... why Greek compound words can be happily rendered in German, especially in poetry' (§471). The heroic stage of language is, on Vico's view, preceded by the 'divine' stage of 'mute' signs and 'natural symbols' – hieroglyphs or ideograms – and is followed by the 'human' stage, dominated by reason and convention. Herder discusses the originality of languages in, e.g., *OL*, especially III. In *AGN*, IV, Fichte argues that German, in contrast to the Romance languages, is an original language. See also I. Berlin, *Vico and Herder: Two Studies in the History of Ideas* (London: Hogarth, 1976).

4 Leibniz expressed his views in two essays written in German: 'Admonition to the Germans on the Improvement of their Understanding and Language, with an added Proposal for a Philogermanic Society' (1682–3, but published 1846), and 'Timely Thoughts concerning the Use and Improvement of the German Language' (1697, published 1717). Fichte, in *AGN*, IV, deplored the use of Latinate

words such as *Humanität, Popularität* and *Liberalität.* In the Preface to the second edition of *SL*, Hegel says that 'we should adopt from foreign languages some words that have through usage already acquired citizen rights in philosophy'. See also Blackall (1959), ch. I.

5   On this subject and elsewhere in this book, I have benefited from Hoffmeister (1955); Eucken (1879); G. Drosdowski, *Das Herkunftswörterbuch: Etymologie der deutschen Sprache*, Duden vol. VII (2nd edn, Mannheim, Vienna, New York: Duden, 1989); and, on eighteenth-century developments, Blackwell (1959).

6   On the Neoplatonists, Plato's late followers (though they were also heavily influenced by Aristotle), see especially TRIADS. See also A. C. Lloyd, *The Anatomy of Neoplatonism* (Oxford: Clarendon, 1990).

7   He rejects e.g. Phillip von Zesen's proposal of *Zeugemutter* (literally 'creative mother') for the Latinate *Natur,* and *Unterlage* ('what lies under, foundation, substratum') for the Latin *subjectum.*

8   Eucken (1879), pp. 139f, argues that Kant lacked an important motive for interest in philosophical language, since he rejected the Enlightenment belief (of e.g. Mendelssohn) that philosophical disputes are ultimately verbal, and held that there are substantial, non-verbal philosophical disagreements.

9   Some modern philosophers are also averse to synonymy. J. L. Austin, in *Sense and Sensibilia* (Oxford: Clarendon, 1962), IV, differentiates 'look', 'seem' and 'appear' by way of their etymology in a manner reminiscent of Hegel.

10 I have benefited from consulting F. E. Peters, *Greek Philosophical Terms: A Historical Lexicon* (New York and London: New York University Press, 1967); and J. O. Urmson, *The Greek Philosophical Vocabulary* (London: Duckworth, 1990).

Introducing Hegel

An introduction to a philosopher is usually felt to require an account of his life. But to introduce Hegel in this way might seem inappropriate. Not only was Hegel's life (like that of many philosophers) relatively uneventful, spent mostly in reading and writing, Hegel himself was disinclined, both by temperament and by conviction, to allow the peculiarities of his life and personality to intrude into his philosophical thought. By temperament he was supremely objective, devoting himself from boyhood to the study of other men's works and of the cultural tendencies of his time.[1] Only after an extensive and profound education, he believed, is it possible to make an original contribution of one's own. Hegel is thus one of the most learned of philosophers, with an immense knowledge of the art, literature, religion, philosophy, political life and sciences, both of his own and of previous ages.

But Hegel also believed that the philosopher, even after he has mastered his craft and acquired the knowledge needed for its exercise, should not strictly make a contribution of his own. His job is simply to watch the development of his SUBJECT-MATTER and to report his findings to the reader. In this way, Hegel believes, he can avoid error. For the subject-matter itself cannot err; only the idiosyncratic opinions of the philosopher can introduce error, and are thus to be excluded as far as possible. In criticizing the views of others, his aim is not to appear as a one-sided partisan, counterposing his own view to theirs, but to show how his opponent's view develops into his own and thus forms a part or phase of the UNIVERSAL or all-embracing view that Hegel purports to represent. Few of Hegel's readers have shared his beliefs that the subject-matter 'moves' or develops without his help, or that it is possible wholly to avoid partiality by integrating all reasonable views into a coherent whole. But most would agree that he succeeds to a remarkable extent in excluding his own personality from his works. Hegel is, as has been said of God and Shakespeare, both everyone and no one.[2] The detail of his life seems singularly irrelevant to his thought.

Nevertheless, Hegel also insists that no one can leap beyond his own age, and he, like any other philosopher, bears the marks of the time (and place) in which he lived. Even his ambition to master the totality of human knowledge locates him in the early nineteenth century rather than the twentieth. The political, cultural and intellectual situation in which he found himself also influenced the knowledge available to him, the manner of his approach to it and the direction in which he developed it.

19

Hegel's age was an age not only of political and cultural ferment, but also of prodigious philosophical achievement. This involved three main trends. First, during Hegel's childhood and youth, Immanuel Kant was producing his most important works. These inspired a host of young Germans to publish philosophical works of their own, expounding, developing and/or criticizing Kant. Philosophical systems, and critiques of philosophical systems, followed one another in rapid succession. Second, philosophical trends were, to a far greater extent than elsewhere in Europe, intertwined with literary and other cultural developments. The most obvious manifestations of this were the *Sturm und Drang* (literally 'storm and stress') movement[3] and, later, the ROMANTIC Circle. *Sturm und Drang* was a reaction against Enlightenment rationalism (of, among others, Kant) in literature, aesthetics, religion, history, etc. It stressed the need, as Hegel did later, to overcome the sharp dichotomies of the UNDERSTANDING: between, e.g., REASON and FEELING, and between thought and sensation. Most of its leading figures – Hamann, Herder, the young Goethe and, on its margins, Schiller – straddle the frontier between literature and philosophy. The romantics – F. von Schlegel, Novalis, etc. – were friends of Fichte and Schelling, and their writings were inspired by a philosophical vision and pregnant with philosophical significance. But many other writers who do not fit easily into either of these categories – Lessing, Hölderlin, etc. – also exemplify the tendency to combine philosophy with culture in general. Third, many earlier philosophers were, in this period, revived, edited, translated, reassessed or transformed: Plato,[4] Plotinus,[5] Proclus,[6] Böhme and the mystics,[7] and Spinoza[8] are only the most obvious examples. Germany in this period experienced a revival of classical learning comparable to the Italian Renaissance. Hegel's excellent command of Greek and Latin enabled him to take full advantage of this.

Georg Wilhelm Friedrich Hegel was born in 1770 in Stuttgart, the capital of the duchy of Württemberg, in Swabia in southern Germany and one of the many small states into which Germany was at that time divided. (Throughout his life he retained a strong Swabian accent and several features of the Swabian dialect.) He was the eldest child of a civil servant in the duke's employ, a descendant of Protestant refugees from Catholic Austria to Lutheran Württemberg. His devotion to his younger sister, Christiane, influenced, and was influenced by, his reading of Sophocles' *Antigone*. He was educated at the local Gymnasium or high school, and studied history, theology and classics. There he proved to be studious, methodical and retentive, but was not seen as exceptionally gifted.

In 1788 Hegel entered the theological seminary at Tübingen, with the aim of becoming a Lutheran pastor. There he formed close friendships with Hölderlin, one of the greatest (and most philosophical) of German poets, and with Schelling, who, though five years younger than Hegel, was far more precocious. Hegel's contemporaries called him 'the old man', owing to his ponderous and studious manner. But he was excited not only by the works of Kant, but also by the outbreak of the French Revolution in 1789 and joined Hölderlin and Schelling in planting (to the dismay of the authorities of the seminary) a 'liberty tree' to celebrate it. (He soon lost his revolutionary fervour, but, despite his critique of the Terror in *PS*, he believed throughout his life that the revolution was a necessary phase in the growth of the modern STATE, never to be wholly obliterated by the Restoration.) He also shared Hölderlin's enthusiasm for ancient Greek society, culture and philosophy, but, unlike Hölderlin – who went insane in the early 1800s – he later arrived at a more sober assessment of the prospects of reviving Greek ETHICAL LIFE in modern Germany.[9] He completed his theological studies, but decided that his true vocation lay in philosophy rather than the Church.[10]

On leaving the seminary in 1793, Hegel followed the common practice of seeking a post as house tutor. He found employment with an aristocratic family in the German Swiss city of Bern. He was not happy in this post and acquired an aversion to the Bernese aristocracy, but access to a good library enabled him to study Gibbon, Montesquieu, Kant, Herder, etc., and write some notes and essays on 'folk-RELIGION' and Christianity.[11] In 1796, he obtained a tutor's post at Frankfurt, with the help of Hölderlin, who also held a tutorial post in the city.[12] Here he deepened his Bern studies, producing in particular the substantial essay, *SCF*. (Apart from the writings mentioned in my article on *ETW*, Hegel wrote commentaries on Kant's ethics and on Sir James Steuart's *Inquiry into the Principles of Political Economy* (1767).[13])

In 1799 his father's death provided Hegel with a small legacy, which released him from tutoring. In the same year, Fichte was charged with atheism and forced to leave Jena for Berlin. Schelling succeeded to Fichte's professorship and was by now the rising star of German philosophy. In 1801, he helped Hegel to become a *Privatdozent* at Jena University, an unsalaried lecturer who charged a fee for attendance at his lectures. He obtained this post on the strength of his doctoral dissertation, the notorious *On the Orbits of the Planets* (1801), in which he supposedly attempted to prove that there are only seven planets.[14] In the same year he had published his first book, *DFS*, which won Schelling's approval as an account of his philosophy. Schelling secured his collaboration on *CJP*, and Hegel here published some significant essays and reviews.

At this time Hegel was a protégé of Schelling's and used much of the same vocabulary. Schelling and others thus tended to see him as Schelling's disciple and assistant.[15] But it soon became clear that this was not so. In particular, Hegel's lectures at Jena – on logic, natural RIGHT, history of philosophy, etc. – are considerably different in subject-matter, content and style from Schelling's work, and present the main outlines of his later system.[16] Relations between the two deteriorated, and in 1803 Schelling left for a chair at Würzburg.

Hegel became an associate professor in 1805, and remained in Jena to write *PS*. This was completed in 1806 at about the time of Napoleon's defeat of Prussia at Jena (and of Hegel's expulsion from his lodgings owing to his impregnation of his landlord's wife). But he had left Jena by the time of *PS*'s appearance in 1807. Hegel, like Goethe, regarded Napoleon, 'the world spirit on horseback', as a great liberator. When the university closed as a result of the French occupation, he went to Bamberg in Bavaria and, for a year, edited the *Bamberger Zeitung*, a pro-Napoleonic newspaper.[17] (Throughout his life Hegel read French and English, as well as German, newspapers, and wrote several articles on current affairs.)

In 1808, he was appointed headmaster of a Gymnasium in Nuremberg, and there gave the lectures on philosophy that are now published as *PP*. In 1811, he married an aristocratic girl twenty-two years younger than himself, Marie von Tucher. The marriage was a happy one, and their two sons had successful careers. (In 1817, they adopted Hegel's illegitimate son, Ludwig Fischer, who died in 1831.) Between 1812 and 1816, he published *SL*, which, in 1816, won him a full professorship at Heidelberg. There he published the first edition of *Enc*.

Hegel's concern for his students and for the administrative duties of his post, as well as his fame as a philosopher, led to the offer of the chair at the relatively new University of Berlin, which had been vacant since Fichte's death in 1814. Here Hegel published *PR*, an expanded edition of *Enc*. in 1827 and a third edition in 1830. But he mainly devoted himself to his increasing administrative duties and, above all, to lecturing, on logic, natural right, philosophy of nature, philosophy of MIND or SPIRIT, art, religion, history and the history of philosophy. (He also played cards, travelled and attended plays and operas.)

Hegel was not a dazzling lecturer: his slow, Swabian delivery was interrupted by constant throat-clearing and coughing, as he hunched over his manuscript. His pedagogical practice (like his theory) was non-Socratic. He did not invite questions or comments from his audience. They were expected to steep themselves, as he had done, in the subject-matter. Only at the end of a long and gruelling apprenticeship was a student in a position to ask sensible questions and make appropriate comments. But his deep intelligence, wide learning, evident passion for philosophy and frequent inspired improvizations secured him a large audience, often from other parts of Germany.[18]

Hegel published several essays during his years at Berlin. Apart from a long attack on the English Reform Bill of 1831,[19] these mainly appeared in the *Jahrbücher für wissenschaftliche Kritik* (*Yearbooks for Scientific Criticism*), produced by Hegel in collaboration with his friends, Gans, Marheineke, Forster, etc., from 1827 on. This provided him with an outlet for essays on W. von Humboldt, Solger and Hamann.[20]

Hegel died at the end of 1831 from the cholera then sweeping through Germany, and was buried in Berlin next to Fichte. He died at the height of his fame, widely regarded as the greatest philosopher in Germany. A few days after his death his family helped to form a 'Society of Friends of the Deceased (*Verein von Freunden des Verewigten*)', consisting of his pupils and followers, to edit his works, including the lectures, which, they felt, were needed to supplement the picture of his system conveyed by his published works. The edition appeared in 21 volumes, with various editors, between 1832 and 1845.

Even during his lifetime, however, Hegel had his critics, a/ proliferated after his death. The most interesting of them is Sche criticized Hegel's notion of the 'self-movement of the CONCEPT', anu claimed to have originated the method that Hegel employed. In 1841 Schelling was invited by the Prussian government to lecture in Berlin, in the hope that this would counteract the theological and political radicalism of the 'young' Hegelians. The lectures were on the 'philosophy of revelation' and Schelling argued that Hegel (like the young Schelling) had propounded a 'negative' philosophy, concerned only with the conceptual possibility ('the what (*das Was*)') of things. Schelling proposed to supplement this with a 'positive' philosophy, disclosing the EXISTENCE (*Existenz*) or 'the that (*das Dass*)' of things. The audience included Engels, Bakunin, Burckhardt, Savigny, Ranke and Kierkegaard. But the lectures were not a success and Schelling's audience soon drifted away, leaving him to endure an embittered old age until his death in 1854.[21]

Hegelianism soon lost its position in German universities, owing in part to the growing criticism of it, in part because its apparent claim to totality and finality seemed to be undermined by the rapid growth of the empirical, especially the natural, sciences, and in part because the increasing radicalism of its most gifted representatives, such as Feuerbach and Marx, disqualified them from obtaining university posts. For the followers of Hegel soon fell into disagreement over his ambiguous legacy, and divided into the 'old' or 'right' Hegelians (Göschel, etc.), the 'centre' (Rosenkranz, Erdmann, etc.) and the 'young' or 'left' Hegelians (Strauss, Michelet, Ruge, Vischer, etc.). The classification depended partly on whether Hegel was interpreted as a proponent of religious and political orthodoxy or not, and partly on whether the Hegelian was himself a political and religious conservative or not. The Right continued to publish in the *Yearbooks for Scientific Criticism* founded by Hegel, while the Left resorted to the *Hallischen Jahrbücher* (*Halle Yearbooks*), edited by Ruge and Echtermeyer from 1838.

Marx, the most renowned of Hegel's followers, transformed Hegelianism into historical materialism, arguing that with Hegel's system philosophy as such had come to an end. But Hegel's influence extended to other significant thinkers, who, though not full-blooded Hegelians, were indebted to him for crucial aspects of their thought. In Germany, Dilthey, a Hegel scholar who was also described as the 'greatest cultural historian since Hegel', made potent use of Hegel's notion of 'objective SPIRIT' in his account of cultural products, and shared the Hegelian belief that 'man finds out what he is only through history'.[22] But Hegel's impact was felt throughout Europe: in Italy especially (Croce, Gentile), but also Britain (Bradley, Bosanquet, McTaggart), Denmark (culminating in Kierkegaard, who bears the scars of his conflict with 'the (Hegelian) SYSTEM'), and France (Meyerson, Sartre). In the United States (W. T. Harris, Peirce, Royce) Hegel left his mark on pragmatism.

Few philosophers since Hegel's death have been unqualified adherents of his system, and it is now no more possible to be an unalloyed Hegelian than it is, on Hegel's view, to be a pure Platonist. But Hegel's thought, like

Plato's, has had a profound, and often surprising, effect both on his followers and on other philosophers, and also on practitioners of other disciplines, notably theology and the social and political sciences.

However, to appreciate fully Hegel's influence we need to understand Hegel himself. And to do this we need, among other things, to know something of the complexities of his language. Thus in this book I say relatively little about thinkers influenced by Hegel or the later history of the terms he used, and far more about thinkers (both German and non-German) who helped to shape his language and concepts, and about his own creative use of what he inherited from them. Hegel suggested that Plato's later works should be prefaced by the words that Dante placed above the entrance to Hell: 'Abandon all hope, you who enter here!' Hegel did not mean that we should not read these works: their philosophical value is, on his view, proportionate to their difficulty. Hegel's works are similarly difficult. But this book is written in the belief that the reader need not abandon all hope of understanding them, and can, like Dante, re-emerge from them enriched.

NOTES

1 Rudolf Haym, in what is still one of the best books on Hegel, *Hegel und seine Zeit* (Berlin: Gaertner, 1857), stresses Hegel's supreme and life-long objectivity.

2 J. L. Borges, 'Everything and nothing', in *Labyrinths* (Harmondsworth: Penguin Books, 1970), pp. 284–5.

3 See R. Pascal, *The German Sturm und Drang* (Manchester: Manchester University Press, 1953).

4 On the impact of Plato in this period, see J.-L. Vieillard-Baron, *Platon et l'idéalisme allemand (1770–1830)* (Paris: Beauchesne, 1979), and G. W. F. Hegel, *Leçons sur Platon. 1825–1826*, translated and introduced by J.-L. Vieillard-Baron (Paris: Aubier, 1976).

5 Hegel's friend and Heidelberg colleague, Creuzer, edited, translated and discussed parts of Plotinus. His complete edition appeared after Hegel's death, in 1835.

6 Proclus was edited by Creuzer (1820–5) and by another friend of Hegel's, Cousin (1820–7). Both editions contain dedications to Hegel and Schelling. In his autobiography Creuzer reported that Hegel helped him in his work on the edition. For more details, see E. Wind, *Pagan Mysteries in the Renaissance* (2nd edn, Oxford: Clarendon, 1980), pp. 192ff, and, in German, the pioneering work of W. Beierwaltes, *Platonismus und Idealismus* (Frankfurt am Main: Klostermann, 1972).

7 On Böhme and the mystics, see p. 9 above.

8 In his article on Spinoza in his *Dictionnaire historique et critique* (1696, 1702), Bayle had condemned him as an atheist. But many Germans of this period were attracted to Spinoza, whom they interpreted to suit their own purposes: Goethe, Lessing, Mendelssohn, F. H. Jacobi, Herder (in *G*) and Schelling. Novalis called Spinoza a 'God-intoxicated man'.

9 A classic account of German Hellenism in this period is E. M. Butler, *The*

Tyranny of Greece over Germany: A study of the influence exercised by Greek art and poetry over the great German writers of the eighteenth, nineteenth and twentieth centuries (Cambridge: Cambridge University Press, 1935). See also H. Hatfield, *Aesthetic Paganism in German Literature: From Winckelmann to the Death of Goethe* (Cambridge, Massachusetts: Harvard University Press, 1964). Nostalgia for Greece and Rome had more than a scholarly or a poetic significance: revolutionaries throughout Europe (and America) saw themselves as attempting to revive ancient republicanism.

10   The professor of logic and metaphysics at the seminary was a first-rate mathematical logician, G. Ploucquet. He lived until 1790, but had ceased to lecture in 1782 after a heart attack. Thus although Hegel later knew of his work (but disapproved of his logical calculus), it is doubtful whether he was taught by him.

11   These were published by H. Nohl in *Hegels theologische Jugendschriften* (Tübingen: Mohr, 1907) and are translated in *ETW* and in *Three Essays, 1793–1795*.

12   Hegel's tenure of his post was less eventful than Hölderlin's. In 1798 Hölderlin was dismissed by his employer, a banker, owing to his love-affair with the banker's much younger wife, Susette Gontard, who is immortalized in Hölderlin's works as 'Diotima'. Susette's death in 1802 hastened the onset of Hölderlin's insanity.

13   These manuscripts are now lost, but were available to K. Rosenkranz for his *Hegels Leben (Hegel's Life,* 1844).

14   The full title is: *Dissertatio philosophica de orbitis planetarum.* It appears in H. Glockner's *Jubiläumsausgabe* (Jubilee Edition: Stuttgart, 1927–39) of Hegel's works, vol. I. Krug, in his *Wörterbuch,* vol. V, p. 507, quotes Hegel's claim that there is no planet between Mars and Jupiter, and adds: 'And shortly afterwards four new planets were discovered there.' But it was asteroids, rather than planets, that were discovered: some 1500 bodies rotate round the sun between Mars and Jupiter, but none exceeds 300 miles in diameter. B. Beaumont, 'Hegel and the seven planets', *Mind* LXIII (1954), pp. 246–8, gives a sober account of the controversy.

15   A year or two earlier, Fichte's tendency to view *Schelling* as his assistant led to a stormy breach of relations between them.

16   The 1804–5 lectures on logic and metaphysics draw a distinction between 'logic' and 'METAPHYSICS', which disappears in *SL.*

17   Haym, in *Hegel und seine Zeit,* castigates Hegel for this unpatriotic episode, but praises his journalistic skill.

18   Between 1820 and 1831, when he was a *Privatdozent* (unsalaried lecturer) at Berlin, Schopenhauer fixed his lectures to coincide with Hegel's and never attracted more than three students.

19   *On the English Reform Bill* (1831), translated by T. M. Knox in *Political Writings.*

20   The review of Humboldt's *Über die unter dem Namen Bhagavad-Gita bekannte Episode des Mahabharata (On the Episode of the Mahabharata, familiar by the Name of Bhagavad-Gita,* 1826) appeared in 1827. (Humboldt did not disclose to Hegel his contempt for this review.) The review of *Solgers nachgelassene Schriften und Briefwechsel (Solger's Unpublished Writings and Correspondence,* 1826) appeared in 1828, as did that of *Hamanns Schriften (Hamann's Writings,* 1821–5). The *Jahrbücher* also contain Hegel's reviews of Göschel, Ohlert, Görres and of the two anonymous critiques of him (by Hülsemann and Schubart). These, like several of Hegel's other reviews (especially the 1817 review of the third volume of Jacobi's *Works),* are not yet translated.

21 Schelling's first public attack on Hegel appeared in his brilliant 'Munich Lectures' of 1827. He returned to the theme in his Foreword to the German translation of Cousin's *On French and German Philosophy* (1834).

22 Dilthey's *Jugendgeschichte Hegels* (*History of the Young Hegel*, 1905) was a pioneering work on the subject. Dilthey also had an important influence on Heidegger.

A

absolute The German *absolut* is an adjective or adverb, used in much the same ways as the English 'absolute(ly)'. It derives from the Latin *absolutus* ('loosened, detached, complete'), the past participle of *absolvere* ('to loosen [from], detach, complete'), and thus means: 'not dependent on, conditional on, relative to or restricted by anything else; self-contained, perfect, complete'. It first occurs as a noun in Nicholas of Cusa, who, in his *De docta ignorantia* (*On Learned Ignorance*, 1440), used *absolutum* to refer to God, as the being which is not conditioned by, limited by or comparable to anything else, and German philosophers after Kant regularly use *das Absolute* to refer to the ultimate, unconditioned reality. This may, but need not, have the features (personhood, etc.) traditionally associated with God. The account of 'the absolute' that most concerned Hegel was that of Schelling, who, though an early adherent of Fichte's idealism, soon abandoned it in favour of the view that the absolute is a neutral 'IDENTITY' that underlies both the SUBJECT (or mind) and the OBJECT (or nature) – a view that owed as much to Spinoza as to Kant and Fichte.

Hegel's response to Schelling (and Spinoza) is not to deny that the absolute exists: he was committed to granting that there is an absolute both by his belief that not everything is dependent on something else, and by his belief in God, for whom, on his view, 'the absolute' is the philosophical expression, shorn of its anthropomorphic presuppositions. The question is rather what the absolute (or for that matter God) is; unless we answer this question the claim that the absolute exists is empty. (In the Preface to *PS*, Schelling's absolute is described as the 'night in which all cows are black'.) His own view is this: A theory of the absolute postulates three types of entity: (1) the absolute; (2) the phenomenal world (rocks, trees, animals, etc.); (3) human knowledge of (1), of (2), and of the relationship between them. But this schema invites several criticisms:

1. Neither Spinoza nor Schelling gives an adequate account of how or why the absolute generates the phenomenal world. They implicitly appeal to an outside observer to whom the absolute appears in various guises, an observer who is inconsistently treated both as responsible for the absolute's manifestation of itself and as merely one of the absolute's manifestations.

2. The absolute alone, (1), cannot be the absolute, if it does not manifest itself in the form of (2) and (3). It is only the manifestation of the absolute that makes it the absolute (as it is only the development, *ceteris paribus*, of a

27

tadpole into a frog that entitles us to classify it as a tadpole). So the absolute, (1), depends on its manifestations, as much as they depend on it. Thus (1) alone, since it depends on (2) and (3), is not the absolute; the absolute is rather (1), (2) and (3) together.

3. The true nature of an entity is that entity's fully developed rather than its embryonic state (the frog rather than the tadpole): hence the true absolute is (1) as developed into (2) and (3) rather than (1) alone.

4. The absolute, (1), is not epistemically absolute or unconditioned: our knowledge of it is not (as Schelling's theory of 'intellectual INTUITION' implies) immediate and unconditioned; it involves a long process of inquiry, both for the individual and for humanity as a whole. The absolute cannot remain simple and static, but must mirror the development of our knowledge of it, (3), since this knowledge is (by 3 above) not distinct from the absolute, but its highest phase.

5. The absolute in its original sense, (1), is superfluous: a proposition such as 'The absolute is (a/the) substance' (unlike 'The chef is angry') does not have a subject-term that is intelligible apart from the concept we apply to it. So we may as well omit it altogether and concentrate only on such concepts as substance, concepts which we apply to the phenomenal world, (2), and to ourselves, (3), and which constitute the ESSENCE of these realms, since neither we nor the phenomenal world could exist unless such concepts were applicable to them. Hegel concludes that the absolute is not something underlying the phenomenal world, but the conceptual system embedded in it. Since this conceptual system is not static, but develops, manifesting itself both at successively higher levels of nature and in the advance of human knowledge over history, the absolute is not static, but developing, and reaches its final stage in Hegel's own philosophy.

6. What is absolute is not exclusively immediate or unconditioned, but has conditions and mediations which it sublates into immediacy. For example, philosophy, the highest phase of the absolute and itself 'absolute knowledge', depends on a certain natural and cultural environment. But it frees itself of this environment by, say, doubting its existence, by focusing on pure, non-empirical concepts, or by conceptualizing this environment. Similarly, human beings in general sublate the natural environment on which they depend by their cognitive and practical activities ('SPIRIT'). Both for this reason, and because the conceptual system that structures nature and history forms the core of the human MIND, the absolute is spirit.

Hegel also uses 'absolute' as an adjective. *PS* culminates in 'absolute KNOWLEDGE' – in contrast to reason, spirit and religion; *SL* concludes with the 'absolute idea' – in contrast to life and the idea of cognition; and the climax of the whole SYSTEM, in *Enc.* III, is 'absolute spirit' – in contrast to subjective spirit and objective spirit. *SL* also refers to 'absolute DIFFERENCE' – in contrast to diversity and OPPOSITION; to 'the absolute GROUND' – in contrast to the determinate ground and the condition; to the absolute unconditioned – in contrast to the relative unconditioned; to the 'absolute RELATION' – in contrast to the essential relation, the absolute, and actuality; and to 'absolute NECESSITY' – in contrast to formal and relative necessity.

Usually, the item characterized as absolute comes at the end of a series of items: absolute spirit comes after, and is in some sense higher than, subjective and objective spirits. But this is not invariably so: absolute difference comes before diversity and opposition, and the absolute ground comes before the determinate ground and the condition – suggesting that what is 'absolute' is in some sense inferior to what succeeds it. This difference corresponds to a difference between two senses of 'absolute': in one sense to be 'absolute' is to exclude mediation and conditions, while in another sense it is to have sublated mediation and conditions. An uneducated child is absolute in the first sense, while an educated adult who sublates his education (perhaps by linguistic or scientific innovation) is absolute in the second sense.

abstract and concrete In the sixteenth century *abstrahieren* ('to abstract') was borrowed from the Latin *abstrahere*, literally 'to draw away, remove (something from something else)'. The past participle of *abstrahere*, *abstractus*, gave rise, in the eighteenth century, to *abstrakt* and *das Abstrakte* ('the abstract') to characterize the products of such abstraction (*Abstraktion*). Similarly, *konkret* and *das Konkrete*, derive from the past participle, *concretus* ('grown together, condensed'), of the Latin *concrescere* ('to grow together, condense').

The abstract is usually regarded as a THOUGHT, CONCEPT or UNIVERSAL, which we abstract from the concrete, the perceptible reality. But Kant, in many of his writings, insisted that *abstrahieren* should be used intransitively, to say, that is, not that we abstract something (especially a concept), but that the concept itself, or we in using a concept, abstract from (i.e. disregard) something, especially the inessential, contingent features of the concrete. Hegel too often uses *abstrahieren* intransitively, to say e.g. that the WILL, or the I*, abstracts (itself) from its concrete desires, etc. (*PR* §5).

Another feature of Hegel's usage is that, in line with the noncommittal etymology of *abstrakt* and *konkret*, a sensory item or a PARTICULAR, as well as a thought or a universal, may be abstract (viz. cut off from a thought or from other sensory items), and a universal may be concrete (viz. 'grown together' with other universals or with the sensory concrete), as well as abstract. (But Hegel also tends to see any item, whether sensory or intellectual, that is cut off, or abstracted, from other things as (abstractly) *universal*: see e.g. *PS*, I, on sensory certainty.)

From the eighteenth century, German philosophers objected to the abstraction characteristic of the Enlightenment. Anticipating Nietzsche, as well as Hegel, Herder in *UE* criticized Kant's separation of the *a priori* from the *a posteriori*, of the FORM of our cognition from its MATTER. The abstract was associated with the meagre, the dependent, the universal, the conceptual and the lifeless. The mischief wrought by abstraction was detected in theology, science and history, as well as philosophy. Hegel was sympathetic to this strand in German thought, and in *ETW* he tended to skirt REASON, the UNDERSTANDING and the conceptual in favour of the concreteness of LIFE and love. In his mature works, however, he does not reject the abstract for immersion in the concrete, but works his way from the abstract through to

29

the concrete: 'The life of the spirit is not the life that balks at DEATH and keeps its distance from devastation, but the life that endures death and maintains itself in it' (*PS*, Preface).

Thoughts, such as BEING, CAUSALITY or universality – the subject of the Logic – are, he concedes, abstract, in contrast both to perceptible entities and to REPRESENTATIONS, such as the conception of a house, a tree or a cow. They are not, however, derived by abstraction from perceptible entities or from representations, in the sense that we *first* perceive things and form low-level conceptions of them, and *then* abstract from the conceptions (or directly from things) their common features, so as to form general thoughts or concepts. If this were so, then the abstract would be inferior to the concrete, since concepts formed in this way would contain (as *Merkmale*, marks or criteria) only those features of things that happen to strike our attention and enable us to recognize things as of a certain type when we encounter them. But the thoughts with which Logic deals are, first, of the ESSENCE of things – there could be nothing, for example, to which the concept of being was not applicable, or which was not an individual – and, second, they are so basic as to be presupposed by any such process of abstraction: one could not, for example, abstract the thought of NEGATION without already possessing the thought of what is *not* negation. (Hegel also doubts whether such conceptions as that of a horse are formed in this way, since e.g. in abstracting the conception we would at least have to ignore deformed and defective horses.) Thus while it is true that when we do logic and think about pure thoughts we abstract from the concrete and its inessential features, these abstract thoughts are not formed by abstraction from the concrete. Nor, since they form the essential features of the concrete, are they in any clear sense inferior to it.

There is another sense of 'abstract' in which thoughts are not abstract. If concepts are formed, as Hegel sometimes allows they can be, by abstraction from things or representations, they are usually abstract in the sense of sharply and fixedly separated *from each other*, with none of the fluid relationships between concepts that he discloses in his Logic. (Hegel believed, e.g., that the types of syllogism in Aristotle's logic were presented 'empirically' or 'historically', and were to that extent products of the 'abstract (i.e. abstracting) understanding (*Verstand*)'.) In Hegel's treatment by contrast, thoughts are derived from each other and thus shown to form a concrete system rather than a discrete and abstract aggregate. One of his reasons for believing that our concepts must be unifiable in this way is that such concepts (or 'the concept') form the core or essence of the human mind, which would lack an appropriate unity, if its concepts were a simple aggregate.

Thus when Hegel speaks of the 'concrete concept' and of 'concrete universality' he usually has at least two points in mind: that concepts or universals are not sharply separate from the perceptible concrete – since, e.g., they form the essence of the concrete – and that they are not sharply separate from each other, that, e.g., the concept of universality is not sharply distinct from those of particularity and INDIVIDUALITY. But Hegel is also opposing the tendency to view all concepts or universals as on a par with, say, redness, where the redness of a thing need not significantly affect either its nature or its relationships with other red things: a red object can easily become (or be imagined to be) some other colour without changing its other qualities, and red objects may have little else in common. By contrast, a universal such as life constitutes, in part, the essence of living things, directing their internal articulation, and living things are essentially related to each other in virtue of their life: different species feed off, and occasionally support, each other, and species reproduce themselves. Thus we have a science of life, while it would be absurd to propose a science of red objects. (Hegel regarded spirit and God as similarly concrete.) Again, Hegel was averse to the idea that such concrete and historically developing phenomena as punishment and monarchy can be captured in a single, simple definition.

It is, however, similarly difficult to define the word 'abstract', and many of Hegel's uses of it are intelligible only in the context in which they occur: It is thinking abstractly, he says in a short essay 'Who thinks abstractly?' (1807), to 'see in the murderer nothing but this abstraction, that he is a murderer, and to efface the rest of the human essence in him.' Money is or expresses the abstract value of other goods. The first work of art, the Egyptian or Greek temple, is the abstract work of art, in contrast to the increasingly self-conscious living, and then spiritual, works of art of later Greece. Abstract RIGHT – in contrast to MORALITY and ETHICAL LIFE – concerns the rights of individuals against each other, primarily the rights of PROPERTY, contract and non-interference, and is characteristic of highly – and abstractly – individualist societies such as imperial Rome, but also an essential element in modern society. But Hegel is averse to the reckless application of such 'abstractions' as freedom, equality and fraternity to concrete ACTUALITY, and believes that it destroys it.

The notions of the abstract and the concrete thus pervade the whole of Hegel's thought. In general, his view is that the abstract is an essential element: in logic, we abstract from the perceptible concrete, and concepts are seen initially, though not ultimately, as distinct rather than as an undifferentiated mass. In the histories of humanity, of art, of religion and of philosophy the abstract and the concentration on it is an essential phase. In modern society, abstract right, abstract principles and the abstract individual are an essential feature, alongside the concrete richness of personal, customary and ethical relationships.

action, deed and responsibility   Non-human entities, as well as humans, act and react on each other, and are active in various ways. For 'active' and 'activity' in this general sense, Hegel uses the words *tätig* and *Tätigkeit*. The usual word for a human action is *Handlung*, from the verb *handeln*, 'to act' (literally 'to handle' or 'to grasp with the hands'). Hegel usually considers action in the context of objective SPIRIT and, more specifically, MORALITY. Action, especially moral action, is seen as an attempt by the WILL to realize itself in a way appropriate to its essential UNIVERSALITY.

An action presupposes an external environment that is as yet independent of my will and of which I have more or less incomplete knowledge. Suppose,

31

e.g., that I am in a clearing in a forest. I then deliberately set light to a tuft of grass, the fire spreads, and the forest and a nearby village burn down. Setting light to the grass was, in Hegel's terminology, my *Vorsatz*, my design or purpose. The burning of the forest and the village, together with whatever other consequences ensue, and whether or not they were foreseen or intended by me, is my *Tat* or deed. But how much of my deed is to be imputed to me as my responsibility (*Schuld*), and regarded as *my action* (*Handlung*)? The burning of the forest and the village, or only the lighting of the grass? A first move is to say that my action coincides with the realization of my *design*, namely to burn the grass. But this is unsatisfactory. I may have intended the wider confla-gration (or some part of it), and even if I did not intend it, I may (and should) have been aware of the probable, if not inevitable, consequences of lighting the grass. The next move, then, is to say that I am responsible for, that my action includes, that part of my deed that corresponds to my *Absicht* or intention. *Absicht* derives from the verb *absehen* (literally 'to look away'), and, Hegel says, it 'implies ABSTRACTION, either the form of universality or the extraction of a PARTICULAR aspect of the CONCRETE thing' (*PR* §119). That is, in ascribing an intentional action to an agent, we do not ascribe the whole of the deed with all its manifold features and consequences nor do we ascribe only the individual act involved in the *Vorsatz*, but some essential, 'universal' feature of the deed intended by the agent: 'arson' or 'burning a forest' – a description which is universal both in the sense that it is applicable to indefinitely many actions performed on different occasions, and in the sense that on a given occasion it embraces a multiplicity of events and not simply the realization of the agent's *Vorsatz*. In so far as the agent intended his action, he must have seen it as contributing to his or others' *welfare*, as satisfying needs, interests or purposes, and Hegel regards such satisfaction as an essential ingredient even in actions that are not primarily motivated by it. (He was scornful of attempts to debunk great deeds and great men by disclosing their self-interested motives, and was fond of saying, 'No one is a hero to his valet – not because he's not a hero, but because the valet is a valet.')

Intention and welfare, however, do not provide adequate guidance for either the performance or the assessment of actions. *Any* action can be justified by the intention and welfare of the agent: burning a forest, for example, by my desire to cook sausages or to release land for development. Nor does the welfare of others, even of all others, much improve matters: 'When St Crispin stole leather to make shoes for the poor, his action was moral, but wrong and so inadmissible' and 'it is one of the commonest blunders of abstract thinking to make private rights and private welfare count as *absolute* in opposition to the universality of the state' (*PR* §126). Although Hegel turns from intention and welfare to an account of the good, that is, individual morality as portrayed by Kant and his successors, he felt that it too provided no solution to the problem of action and its assessment. For the 'moral world-view' too allows that any act is justified as long as it results from a good intention or a 'good heart'. We are responsible, Hegel argues, for many, if not all, of even the unforeseen or unintended consequences of our actions, since to act at all is essentially to take one's chances with an external reality that is not fully in one's own power or foreknowledge. (He cites an old proverb: 'A flung stone is the devil's'.) Thus although he concedes that we must take some account of a person's intentions – today we would not hold Oedipus responsible for patricide and incest – his general view is that the 'truth of the intention is the deed itself'.

A notable feature of Hegel's thought is his tendency to assimilate action and COGNITION, practical and theoretical MIND or spirit. Initially, we conceive action as quite different from cognition, since, while cognition is concerned with what *is* the case, action is motivated by the belief that I OUGHT, for whatever reason, to introduce an alteration into an alien, EXTERNAL reality. Hegel seeks to undermine this view of action. The environment in which I act is in general already moulded by *others*, and contains a variety of norms and institutions which guide my actions, and which my actions help to sustain rather than alter – as my use of a language in general sustains the language, and alters it only gradually and peripherally. That other people share this environment, and acknowledge, interpret and respond to my actions, is also, on Hegel's view, an essential feature of action. (In post-Kantian German philosophy in general, *other* people are considered under the heading of moral rather than theoretical philosophy.) Hence the ABSOLUTE idea is seen as the 'identity of the theoretical and the practical' ideas, the identity, that is, of the ideas of 'the true' (cognition) and of 'the good' (moral activity) which immediately precede it in the Logic.

For this reason (and also because Hegel's system is historical and retro-spective), Kierkegaard argued that Hegel's SYSTEM excludes a proper account of action, especially of those actions that require a decision that is not prescribed by, and may conflict with, generally accepted norms and prac-tices: 'most systematizers are like a man who builds an enormous castle and lives in a shack close by.' Hegel can accommodate the dissident choices of figures such as Antigone and the revolutionary deeds of 'world-historical' individuals such as Caesar, Alexander and Napoleon, for they represent an aspect of the value-system of their age. But he has little regard for the wholly idiosyncratic and non-rational adoption of a creed or a way of life that Kierkegaard had in mind. A rational agent will, on Hegel's view, conform to the norms and institutions of his society, just as a rational knower will surrender himself to the object of cognition.

actuality The word *wirklich* ('actual') is connected, both etymologically and in Hegel's thought, with *wirken*, 'to be active or effective', *wirksam*, 'effective', and *Wirkung*, 'effect': 'What is actual can take effect (*wirken*).' Its uses are similar to those of 'actual' and 'real': an actual or real detective is contrasted with a fictitious, imaginary or merely possible detective, such as Sherlock Holmes or the detective who is at present sitting next to me; with a simulated detective, a wax-work model, say, or an impostor; with a substan-dard, bungling detective; and with a merely potential detective, a novice who has the capacity to become a detective, but has not yet actualized or realized this capacity. In each case the actual detective can have an effect in a way that his unreal counterpart cannot.

Philosophers such as Kant generally used 'actual' in the first of these ways, as a synonym for 'what is' or 'exists', with a stress on the sensorily perceptible and in contrast to what is merely possible, thought or imaginary. Hegel dissents from this usage and tends to deny actuality not only to what is merely possible, but also to ontologically low-grade and contingent entities, and to entities that are substandard or undeveloped with respect to their type, to, e.g., bad or tyrannical STATES and to infants who have not yet realized their potentiality to become rational human beings. This is why actuality is said to be the unity of the INNER and the OUTER (or of ESSENCE and EXISTENCE) – categories which precede actuality in the Logic: a low-grade entity, such as a rainbow, is contingent in the sense that its existence is not the product of its own inner nature or essence but is solely dependent on other entities; a tyrannical state is a perversion of the nature of a state; an infant has not yet realized its inner nature (and is also, to that extent, dependent on others for its present survival and future development).

But it is characteristic of Hegel that he does not simply stipulate his own use of 'actual': he develops it out of an examination of other uses. Beginning with the idea that the actual contrasts with what is merely possible or consistently thinkable, he argues that the actual in this sense is what is contingent, that is, capable of not being, as well as of being, since it is grounded not in itself, but in something else. But contingent entities, the *immediate* actualities, form the conditions of a *developed* actuality, which is also necessary, both because all the conditions of its realization are present and because its conditions are sublated or absorbed into it, so that it is in a sense independent and self-determining. A 'developed actuality' is an entity such as a living organism that absorbs the chance objects in its environment, so as to foster its own growth according to a pattern prescribed by its inner nature; a rational agent who uses whatever he encounters to fulfil a foreordained plan; or a society which converts the materials and forces in its environment into purposive structures. But Hegel often equates the truly actual with *God*, and suggests that God (or the world SPIRIT) steers the contingencies of this world towards the fulfilment of a divine plan by the 'cunning of REASON'. (This is not unlike Adam Smith's 'Invisible Hand'.)

In the Preface to *PR* Hegel said: 'what is rational is actual and what is actual is rational.' Usually, we contrast what is real or actual with ideas or thoughts. We can then play off actuality and ideas against each other, claiming that something is merely an idea and not real or realizable, or, alternatively, that actuality is at fault, since it is at odds with our ideas or IDEALS. Hegel wants to undermine this opposition. Thoughts, he argues, and especially 'the IDEA', are not primarily SUBJECTIVE entities, but are immanent in actuality. This doctrine has several senses:

(1)   an ontological sense: things could not be unless they were structured in accordance with the thoughts of the Logic (causally ordered, actual, etc.);

34

(2)   a theological sense: things fulfil a divine plan;

(3)   an epistemological sense: things are fully intelligible and knowable;

(4)   an evaluative sense: things are reasonable and conform to rational standards.

(Different interpreters of Hegel stress different aspects of the doctrine, but Hegel plainly had them all in mind.) The implication of the doctrine for the study of politics and history is that it should not criticize present or past states of affairs or recommend changes, but attempt solely to understand them and to discern their rationality, that is, both their intelligibility and their ultimate justification. Our 'ideas' and proposals are inevitably superficial in comparison to the ideas embedded in the nature of things. (This attitude first appears in *GC*: 'if we see that it [viz. what exists] is as it must be, that it is not arbitrary or accidental, then we see too that it should be as it is.')

The doctrine was attacked by Hegel's critics, and understood to prohibit criticism or reform of *any practice, institution or ruler*. (If the doctrine applies to *everything* that happens, it is also self-stultifying, unless Hegel refrains from criticizing those who criticize the status quo, and from proposing that they cease to do so.) So in the second edition of *Enc.* (1827), he insists that he does not regard everything as actual, and that some things that exist (the contingent, brain-waves, error, evil, and what has merely 'stunted and transient existence') are APPEARANCE (*Erscheinung*) rather than actuality (*Enc.* I §6). (Those reluctant to see theology in Hegel can interpret his further claim, that only *God* is truly actual, as meaning that only the logical structure of things is actual.) On this view, a tyrannical or ineffectual state is not (an) actual (state), and is not exempt from criticism and reform. Hegel was a realist with respect to concepts, and thus believes himself immune to the objection that, say, an unreal *state* may nevertheless be a real or actual *tyranny*. But he supplies no clear criterion for distinguishing the actual from the apparent: not even the best of states is faultless or everlasting.

The doctrine that the actual is rational is not simply a product of Hegel's conservatism. (He was, however, conservative in the sense that he more or less accepted the current state of affairs, not in the sense that he regarded it as desirable or practicable to restore the *old* order overthrown by the French Revolution.) It also represents a stoic and Spinozist strand in his thought, the belief that it is better to comprehend and contemplate things than to fret over them or alter them, and that FREEDOM consists in the understanding of necessity, in that such understanding enables us to accept the world as it is rather than to change it.

alienation and estrangement   Hegel uses two words for 'alienation':

1. *Entfremdung* corresponds to *entfremden* ('to make alien'), from *fremd* ('alien'). In Middle High German (i.e. from the twelfth to the fifteenth century) it referred to taking or stealing a person's goods and also to mental alienation, especially a coma or stupor. But later it primarily indicated the estrangement of persons from one another.

35

2. *Entäusserung* corresponds to *entäussern*, 'to make OUTER or external (*ausser*)', and means 'surrender' or 'divestiture'. (Hegel uses *Entäusserung*, but not *Entfremdung*, to refer to the alienation, i.e. voluntary disposal, of one's own property: *PR* §§65ff.)

Other words in the same area are: *Entzweiung* (from *zwei*, 'two'), 'bifurcation', 'disunion'; *Zerrissenheit* (from *zerreissen*, 'to tear, rend, dismember, disconnect'), 'dismemberment', 'disjointedness'; *Zwiespalt* (also from *zwei*), 'discord', 'conflict', 'discrepancy'; *Diremtion*; and *Trennung*, 'separation' (from *trennen*, 'to separate').

Alienation for Hegel is the stage of disunion which emerges from a simple unity and is subsequently reconciled in a higher, differentiated unity. His concept of alienation, though substantially original, owes much to previous thinkers: to Rousseau's idea that the social contract requires each person to surrender himself to the community; to Fichte's suggestion, in *ACR*, that the 'idea of God as a lawgiver, through the moral law in us, is based on an *Entäusserung* of what is ours, on translating something subjective into a being outside us; and this *Entäusserung* is the real principle of religion, in so far as religion is to be used for determining the will', and to his claim in *SKW* that the I* or SUBJECT produces the phenomenal world by a process of *Entäusserung*, of self-alienation or -externalization; to Schiller's argument in *AE* that the advance of culture has fragmented the original harmony of the ancient Greek with his own essential nature, with other men, with his society and with nature – a disunion which on Schiller's view (but not Hegel's) can only be repaired by art; and to Diderot's portrayal, in *Rameau's Nephew* (Goethe's translation of which appeared in 1805), of the servile, self-aware cynic, who plays a thousand parts to curry favour with power and wealth, and is, in *PS*, VI.B, a paradigm of the 'rent (*zerrissene*) consciousness' and the 'self-alienated (*sich entfremdete*) spirit'.

Hegel does not use the word *Entfremdung* before *PS*, but several of his earlier writings foreshadow his later views: In the fragment on 'Love' (in *ETW*), 'LIFE' (like, in *PS*, 'SPIRIT') undergoes a process of immature unity, opposition and final reunion. Love restores unity between individuals, and between the individual and the world, but without entirely annihilating the individual. In *SCF*, he, like Schiller, regards the discord within us between intellect and feeling as a necessary phase of spiritual development, but argues that reunion can only be achieved by religion, conceived as 'reflection and love united'. In the 'Fragment of a System' (in *ETW*), religion enables man to transcend his finite or restricted life and to unite himself with the 'infinite life' or 'spirit' that pervades the world.

In *DFS*, it is philosophy as REASON (in contrast to UNDERSTANDING), rather than religion (or ART), that can reconcile the *Entzweiung* involved in the development of culture. Such an *Entzweiung* – 'the emergence of consciousness out of the totality, the bifurcation into being and non-being, into concept and being, into finitude and infinity' – is one of the two 'presuppositions' of philosophy, the other being the 'absolute itself . . . the goal that is sought, but is already present': 'The task of philosophy is to unify these presuppositions, to install being in non-being – as becoming, bifurcation in the absolute – as appearance, the finite in the infinite – as life.' One aspect of the overcoming of alienation is the reconciliation (*Versöhnung*) with ACTUALITY in *GC*.

PS contains two striking portrayals of alienation. One is the near-Feuerbachian account of the 'unhappy, internally divided (*entzweite*) CONSCIOUSNESS' of early and medieval Christianity, which regards itself as variable and inessential, and projects its universal, essential and invariable aspect onto a transcendent being with whom it seeks reunion (IV.B). (*SCF* had described the religion of Abraham in similar terms.) The other occurs in *PS*, VI, especially B.I, where the unalienated ETHICAL LIFE of ancient Greece declines, first into the atomism of the right-endowed individuals of the Roman Empire, and then into the 'world of the self-estranged (*sich entfremdete*) spirit'. This world (which Hegel traces from the fall of Rome to the French Revolution) is marked by separation: between the actual world and a world beyond, which is represented by FAITH (*Glaube*) as the ESSENCE of the actual world; between the SELF-CONSCIOUS individual and the social SUBSTANCE; and between state-power and wealth. Each of these elements is both alien to and yet dependent on the others. The interplay between them occurs in the form of CULTURE (*Bildung*): a person sheds or alienates his merely natural self and has value only in proportion to his acquired cultivation.

R. Schacht, in *Alienation* (1971), pp. 37ff, argues that in *PS*, VI Hegel uses *Entfremdung* for two distinct phenomena: (1) the fact that the social substance is alien to the individual; (2) the individual's alienation or surrender of his particular self and identification with the universal substance. (*Entfremdung* in sense (2), but not in sense (1), is, Schacht argues, interchangeable with *Entäusserung*.) Schacht also argues that the individual's alienation (2) of himself by the acquisition of culture is, on Hegel's view, the solution to alienation (1). But this is incorrect. Culture is as much the possession of the 'base', alienated individual (Rameau's nephew) as of anyone else: culture is the medium in which alienation (1) is played out, not the solution to it. Alienation (2) cannot resolve alienation (1), for two reasons:

1. Alienation (2) involves a genuine loss of individual integrity and independence, not simply a restoration of one's universal essence or real self: alienation (2) is only required of the individual in virtue of alienation (1), and the alienated (2) individual is a stranger to himself. Culture in general, Hegel believes, involves self-alienation in a strong sense, e.g. the mastering of alien languages, not simply of one's native language.

2. At this stage the social substance presents no stable, coherent set of institutions or values with which an individual can identify: if he devotes himself to the STATE to the exclusion of wealth, the state power turns, i.e. alienates (2) itself, into an individual (the monarch) and a dispenser of wealth – hence the 'heroism of service' turns into the 'heroism of flattery'; wealth and state power may alternately be seen as good or bad depending on whether one views the state as sustaining the universal good or as alien and repressive, and wealth as serving one's own fleeting pleasures or rather the good of all.

Thus while Hegel ultimately hoped for a reconciliation of the individual with the social substance that leaves the individual's integrity unimpaired, he does not believe that this was possible in the alienated society of Louis XIV's France, and his immediate sympathy is with the supremely alienated Rameau, who sees through and unashamedly mimics the alienated and shifting values and institutions of his society. The solution to this alienation (1), Hegel argues, was not an immediate identification with the social substance, but the *intensification* of alienation – enlightenment and revolution.

'Alienation' occurs in several other contexts. Hegel speaks, both in the Preface and at the end of the *PS*, of God's *Entfremdung* and spirit's *Entäusserung* in NATURE and of the overcoming of this in HISTORY. In *PS*, VI, he regards LANGUAGE, especially the use of such UNIVERSAL words as 'I*', as involving the *Entfremdung* or *Entäusserung* of the PARTICULAR (in contrast to the universal) self to a greater degree than either ACTION or 'physiognomical expression'. In the Preface he suggests that EXPERIENCE requires the object to alienate itself and then return to itself from this alienation (*Entfremdung*): we can, e.g., comprehend phenomena only by invoking abstractions which initially seem remote from the phenomena themselves.

Alienation is most vividly portrayed in *PS*, but both the words and the idea(s) are important in Hegel's later works. But their importance, and even their presence, was hardly noticed by Hegel scholars until the appearance of Marx's discussions of *Entfremdung* and *Entäusserung* in his 'Philosophical Manuscripts' of 1844, but first published in German in 1932, and in English in 1959.

annul, annulment *see* SUBLATION

appearance, illusion and shining German has two words for appearance: *Schein*, with the verb *scheinen*, and *Erscheinung*, with the verb *erscheinen*. (1) *Scheinen* has two distinct senses: (a) 'to shine, glow'; (b) 'to appear, seem'. Correspondingly, *Schein* means: (a) 'shine, glow'; (b) 'appearance, semblance, illusion'. (2) *Erscheinen* and *Erscheinung* also mean 'to appear' and 'appearance or phenomenon', but, unlike *Schein* and *scheinen*, both may be used of the appearance, i.e. publication, of a book, or of putting in an appearance, where there is no suggestion that things are other than they appear.

In eighteenth-century philosophy, *Schein* tended to be equated either with *Täuschung* ('deception, illusion') or with *Erscheinung*. But Kant drew a distinction between them: *Erscheinung* is a perceptible 'phenomenon', what we perceive an object to be in accordance with our forms of sensibility and understanding, in contrast to the 'noumenon', the supra-sensible reality or the object as it is in itself. (Unlike Fichte, who held phenomena to be products of the activity of the I*, Kant argued that an appearance implies something that appears and that is not itself an appearance.) *Schein*, by contrast, is an illusion resulting in a false judgment either about phenomena or about supra-sensible matters. *Schein* also has a use in aesthetics: Both Herder, in his *Plastik*, and Kant, in *CJ*, distinguish painting as the art of sensuous *Schein* from sculpture and architecture as the arts of sensuous truth, since painting gives only the *illusion* of three-dimensionality. But Schiller regarded *Schein* (in the sense of aesthetic 'semblance', not of 'deception') as a characteristic of *all* art (in contrast to reality), and also of any object in so far as it is viewed aesthetically.

Hegel rejects *Kant's* distinction between *Schein* and *Erscheinung*, just as he rejects the unknowable THING-in-itself and the (on Hegel's view) subjective IDEALISM of Kant and Fichte, on which Kant's distinction rests. (Phenomena, as conceived by Kant, are, Hegel believes, *Schein* rather than *Erscheinung*.) But the terms are for Hegel distinct. *Schein* is correlative to *Wesen* ('essence'): ESSENCE shows or appears (*scheint*), but itself remains hidden behind a veil of *Schein*. In that case, *Sein* ('BEING', i.e. what we are immediately acquainted with) is *Schein*, both in the sense that it is dependent on something else, an essence, and in the sense that it does not fully manifest that essence. (*Sein* and *Schein* are phonetically similar, but etymologically remote.) But *Schein* and *scheinen* retain for Hegel the sense of 'shine' or 'glow'. (They are closely associated with the similarly ambiguous REFLECTION.) Thus Hegel speaks of the essence as 'shining' within or into itself, as if essence itself and its distinctness from *Schein* is constituted by a process similar to that by which it 'shows' itself externally: it is only by projecting an appearance (shining outwardly) – e.g. the bubbles on a boiling liquid – and then withdrawing that appearance (shining inwardly), that an essence constitutes itself as an essence. Hegel also employs this notion of a double *Schein* in connection with other pairs of correlative terms: e.g. in so far as the universal shines into itself, it is strictly universal or generic (e.g. 'colour' in relation to 'red', etc.), while in so far as it shines outwardly, it becomes specific or particular in contrast to the 'other' into which it shines (e.g. 'colour' in relation to 'shape' or 'sound'). (Here *Schein* is interchangeable with *Reflexion*.) Hegel, like Schiller, believes that art involves *Schein*: he distinguishes *Schein* from *Täuschung*, and associates it with the phonetically similar (and etymologically related) *schön* ('beautiful').

In Hegel's usage, *Erscheinung* and *erscheinen* differ from *Schein* and *scheinen* in several respects: (1) *Erscheinung* is also the appearance of an essence, but the essence fully discloses itself in *Erscheinung* and keeps nothing hidden. (The original force of the prefix *er-* was 'from within', which led to the idea of 'transition' or 'resultant state', and hence to that of 'obtaining or attaining to'.) (2) An *Erscheinung* is, like *Schein*, transient and dependent, but what it depends on and succumbs to is not, immediately at least, an essence but another *Erscheinung*. Hence *Erscheinung*, in contrast to *Schein*, is a diverse, interdependent and fluctuating WHOLE or world. (3) *Erscheinung* contrasts primarily not with 'essence', but with 'CONCEPT' or 'ACTUALITY' (as what fully embodies the concept), and is contingent and fleeting rather than necessary, rational and stable: e.g. empirical psychology considers only the *Erscheinung* of MIND, and metaphysical psychology considers only its concept, while the correct approach, Hegel believes, is to see how the concept of the mind realizes itself in *Erscheinung*; and, whereas a crime is merely *Schein* since it is in conflict with RIGHT and right restores itself by NEGATING (viz. PUNISHING) this

39

Schein, a particular contract is *Erscheinung* since, while not in conflict with right, it is only a contingent manifestation of it (*PR* §82). (*Erscheinung* – and *Schein* – is apt to change its application, depending on what Hegel regards, in a given context, as the concept or rational structure that it contrasts with.)

Both in *PS* and in *SL*, the world of *Erscheinung* generates another world, a world that is essential or IN ITSELF and is the reverse (*Verkehrung*) of the world of appearance. The interplay of appearance is governed by LAWS (*Gesetze*, which Hegel associates with the idea that any appearance is *gesetzt*, POSITED or produced, by another appearance). The laws explain changes in the realm of appearance. But since these changes are reversals (what is hot becomes cold, etc.), the laws must specify that what in the world of appearance is, say, hot, is *essentially* or *in itself* cold, and so on. This suggests the idea of a world that is the reverse of the world of appearance, in which everything that has, in our world, a certain quality, has, in the world in itself, the opposite quality.

The significance of this inverted world is not clear. Is Hegel claiming that two such worlds would be indistinguishable? Some of his examples (e.g. the opposite poles of magnets, and positive and negative electricity) imply that they would be indistinguishable, while others (e.g. black and white) do not. Are we to think of the human subject as inhabiting each of these worlds and as undergoing a corresponding reversal, or rather as transcending both worlds and holding them together in thought (which would imply that he at least is not mere *Erscheinung*)? But some things are clear. First, the idea has a variety of sources and meanings for Hegel: he was, like Schelling, intrigued by the polarity of magnets and electricity; but it also has ethical and religious significance, in, e.g., the reversal of good and evil. (*See* ALIENATION in *PS*, VI.B.) Second, similar reversals occur throughout his works, e.g., the alienated social world after the fall of Rome generates a similarly inverted world of FAITH. Third, despite his interest in the inverted world and his belief that our world is a world of appearance, Hegel rejects both the belief in, and the longing for, a world 'beyond' (*Jenseits*) that were common among his contemporaries (Kant, Herder, Schelling, etc.). The essence or logical structure (which Hegel does not hesitate to call 'GOD') of the world of appearance is fully manifest in its interplay and reversals. (Some scholars, e.g., Shklar, *Freedom and Independence* (1976), link the inverted world with the world of Plato's FORMS. But Plato's forms are an idealization, not an inversion, of the phenomenal world.)

arbitrary, arbitrariness *see* WILL AND WILFULNESS

art, beauty and aesthetics (*Die*) Kunst ('art, skill, craft', from *können*, 'can, to be able') originally had, like the Greek *technē*, no special connection with beauty (*Schönheit*) or with what came to be known in the eighteenth century as the 'fine arts' (*die schönen Künste*) – in contrast to (1) the seven medieval liberal arts (including astronomy, mathematics and philosophy), and (2) a craft, skill or profession. (*Kunst*, unlike 'art', has no special association with painting.) The *concept* of fine art, covering architecture, sculpture, music, painting and poetry, goes back to Plato. But art and beauty were treated separately by Plato (beauty in, e.g., the *Symposium* and art in, e.g. the *Republic*) and by Aristotle (in his *Poetics*).

For Plato and Aristotle, art, when it was not simply a craft, involved primarily the imitation of nature and of human affairs. The Neoplatonists, especially Plotinus, first compared the artist to the world-creator (especially the divine demiurge of Plato's *Timaeus*, who embodies the IDEAS in matter). Thus the artist imitates not the products of nature, but nature's productive activity: in works of art he realizes the idea in perceptible material. In the seventeenth and eighteenth centuries art was still widely regarded as imitation, but this view was rejected by Goethe, Hegel and especially Schelling, who placed the creativity of the artist on a par with that of nature.

Plotinus brought together the concepts of art and of beauty (*Enneads*, V. viii, 1). On Hegel's view, works of art are essentially *schön*, 'beautiful'. In earlier writers, e.g. Burke and Kant (especially in *Observations on the Feeling of the Beautiful and the Sublime*, 1764), the sublime (*das Erhabene*) is an aesthetic category co-ordinate with the beautiful (*das Schöne*). (The sublime first appears in a work of the first century AD attributed to Longinus, *peri hypsous*, *On the Sublime*.) But Hegel's aversion to the intellectually intractable and especially to bad INFINITY means that sublimity plays a subdued role in *LA* and is more or less confined to the aesthetically unsatisfactory pre-classical symbolic art, in which FORM and CONTENT are not in harmony. But *schön* is a wider term than 'beautiful', occurring in such contexts as 'a *fine* piece of work' and 'making a *good* job of something'. *Schönheit* for Hegel accommodates significant dissonances and even ugliness.

The term 'aesthetics' (from the Greek *aisthēsis*, *aisthanesthai*, 'perception', 'to perceive', and thus literally the 'study of perception') was first used for the 'study of sensory beauty' (including the beauty of nature, as well as of art) by a follower of Leibniz, A. G. Baumgarten, especially in his *Aesthetica* (1750–8). In *CPR* Kant objected to this usage and to Baumgarten's hope of 'bringing the critical assessment of the beautiful under principles of reason, and raising its rules to SCIENCE' (A21, B35f). He retains the word in its original sense, for the study of the conditions of perception. But in *CJ* he uses it in Baumgarten's sense, while still insisting that 'there is no science of the beautiful, but only a critique, nor beautiful science, but only beautiful art' (§44). In *LA*, Hegel criticizes the term *Ästhetik* for its stress on the SENSORY and FEELING, but retains it in the title of his lectures. (He rejects another proposed term, *Kallistik* ('the study of beauty' – from the Greek *kalos*, *kallos*, 'beautiful', 'beauty'), since it covers beauty in general, and is not restricted to the beauty of art.)

In Hegel's Germany, aesthetics was dominated by Kant's *CJ*. He argued (in opposition to utilitarian, hedonistic and intellectualist accounts) that the beautiful gives rise to a 'disinterested' pleasure, stemming from the free play of our imagination; it is 'non-conceptual'; it has 'the form of PURPOSIVENESS without the representation of the end'; and it is the 'object of a universal pleasure'. It arises from the faculty of JUDGMENT (*Urteilskraft*) in association with feeling. We import our idea of beauty into a world that is not intrinsically beautiful, and we regard beauty as a symbol of the MORAL good.

After Kant, aesthetics moved to the centre of German philosophy. In the first place, Schiller argued, especially in *AE* (a work much admired by Hegel), that beauty is objective and that the contemplation of it will repair the ALIENATION that afflicts modern man, the fissures between man and nature, man and man, and reason and desire. Second, Fichte's doctrine that the phenomenal world is produced solely by the (FREE, and yet NECESSARY) activity of the I*, suggested a parallel with the creative activity of the artist. Schelling, in particular, developed this parallel and argued, in *STI*, that the 'key-stone' of philosophy is the philosophy of art: art mediates mind and nature, since artistic activity combines the free, purposeful creativity of mind with the necessary, unconscious creativity of nature. The German idealists' account of art thus differed from Kant's in several interrelated respects:

(1) Beauty is objective; it is the revelation of SPIRIT, the IDEA, and the divine in the world of appearance.

(2) While Kant was interested only in the subjective judgment of taste, they were more interested in the artist and his products.

(3) Kant was as ready to see beauty in nature as in art, but his successors devalued the beauty of nature. For Schelling, NATURE, like MIND, is imbued with spirit and the IDEAL, but it is inferior in beauty to art, which unites mind and nature. For Hegel, spirit evolves out of nature, which is inferior in beauty to the products of spirit, and is only seen as beautiful in the light of such products.

(4) Kant was indifferent to the HISTORY of art (and of taste), but the idealists gave a central place to history.

In part Hegel's account of art brings to fruition a programme that he shared with Schelling and Fichte. In *PS*, VII.B, art is considered under the heading, not of 'SPIRIT', but of 'RELIGION': the 'religion of art' (Greece) appears between 'natural religion' (Persia, India and Egypt) and 'revealed religion' (Christianity). But in *Enc*. III, art forms, together with religion and PHILOSOPHY, a part of 'ABSOLUTE spirit', the spirit, that is, which presupposes the individual psychology of SUBJECTIVE spirit and the social institutions of *objective* spirit, but transcends them both. Art, like religion and philosophy, has a rational, cognitive value: it progressively reveals the nature of the world, of man and the relationship between them (the absolute) in a sensuous form or the form of INTUITION (*Anschauung*), while religion does so in the form of figurative REPRESENTATION (*Vorstellung*), and philosophy in the form of THOUGHT or the CONCEPT. In *LA* Hegel combines a systematic account of art with an account of its unfolding over history. Art is divided, first, into three main styles – symbolic, classical and romantic – and, second, into genres – architecture, sculpture and painting, music and poetry. Histori- cally, art falls into three main periods: the ancient Orient (especially Egypt), Greek and Roman antiquity, and Christian modernity. (These divisions, and their more detailed subdivisions, are intended to be conceptually, rather than empirically, grounded, and to depend ultimately on the conceptual system presented in the Logic. But Hegel supports them with a wealth of empirical material.) A genre of art, while it occurs in all periods, is dominant in one period and is associated with a particular style: architecture, e.g., is the symbolic art-form and was dominant in Egypt; later architecture is transposed into the classical or the romantic style, but is not the dominant genre of those periods, does not, that is, give to the absolute the highest artistic expression of which it is capable in those periods.

Hegel lived in an age of great artists, some of whom (e.g. Goethe and Hölderlin) were his friends. But he denies to art the supreme position that Schelling (and many of his other contemporaries) gave to it. First, art in general expresses the absolute less adequately than do religion and philosophy, since intuition is a medium inferior to conception and thought. (Philosophy, for example, can comprehend art, but art cannot comprehend philosophy.) Second, in modern times art cannot express our view of the absolute as adequately as it expressed the views of earlier times. Greek art expressed the Greek world-view with supreme aptness and elegance — more so perhaps than did Greek philosophy; ROMANTIC art can barely express such conceptions as the Trinity — in so far as it does so, it transcends the realm of art and forgoes the harmony and beauty of classical art. Schelling agreed that Greek art had not as yet been surpassed or even equalled in modern times, but he expected this to happen in the future, after the creation of a modern mythology comparable to that of Homer. But Hegel believed that art could no longer capture the complexity of our world-view, and had no future as a primary vehicle for the expression of the absolute.

Hegel's doctrine of the end of art is connected with his view of modern society. Both Hegel and Schelling held that art, though the immediate product of individuals of talent or genius, is in a wider sense the product of the cultivated society or people (*Volk*) to which they belong. (It is because art does not depend only on the native talent of the artist that art has a history.) Schelling believed that society or the state can and should be a work of art. Hegel, by contrast, while he agreed that Greek society had the harmony and cohesion characteristic of art, did not believe, in his maturity, that this aesthetic ideal can be restored in modern society. Modern men are too reflective and self-aware, and too dispersed in the complex economic life of CIVIL SOCIETY, to constitute an aesthetically coherent whole. Great works of art cannot arise in such unaesthetic surroundings.

B

being, nothing and becoming   The infinitive of the verb 'to be' in German is *sein*. Like other German infinitives, it can be used as a noun, *(das) Sein*, 'being'. Unlike the verb 'to be', *sein* has a distinct present participle, *seiend*, which is used as an adjective ('which is' or 'existent') or as a noun-phrase, *das Seiende*, 'that which is'. Used as a verb, *sein* can be predicative, identifying or existential in force. As a noun, *Sein* refers to the being or existence of things in general, in contrast to their DETERMINATE being or character *(Dasein)*. In the history of philosophy, Hegel associates being especially with Parmenides, who argued that since what *is* cannot not-be, being excludes all NEGATION, determinacy and becoming.

The negation of *Sein* is strictly *Nichtsein*, 'non-being', but Hegel rejects this in favour of *nichts*, 'nothing', or the noun formed from it, *(das) Nichts*, since the concept of non-being is, or may be taken to be, mediated, that is, generated by the negation of *Sein*, rather than immediate or primitive in the way that *Sein* is. (*Nichts* is itself the genitive of the Middle High German *niht*, 'nothing' (from *ni-wiht*' 'not a whit'), and *nicht*, 'not', is the accusative. But this complex mediation is not apparent in modern German.)

Das Werden, 'becoming', is formed from *werden*, 'to become'. (*Werden* is also used as an auxiliary verb in future tense and passive verbs: thus *ich werde fahren* is 'I shall drive' and *geliebt werden* is 'to be loved'.) Becoming is associated for Hegel with Heraclitus, who held that everything is involved not in being, but in continual becoming and conflict. Plato endorsed this doctrine with respect to the phenomenal world, and argued, in the *Timaeus*, that the word 'being' should be used only of the unchanging FORMS or IDEAS, while only 'becoming' should be applied to the degenerate world of APPEARANCE. Later Greek philosophers shared, for the most part, Plato's preference for being over becoming. German thinkers, by contrast, tended to prefer *becoming* to the rigidity of *being*, and applied 'becoming' to the self-unfolding, but arduous and conflict-ridden, DEVELOPMENT of HISTORY and of LIFE. Eckhart regarded becoming as the ESSENCE of God. Goethe, whose maxim 'Become what you are!' was repeated by Nietzsche in *Also sprach Zarathustra* (1883/4), assigns what *is becoming* to REASON ('which enjoys development'), and what *has become*, and thus *is*, to the UNDERSTANDING ('which wants to hold everything fast, so that it can use it'). As Nietzsche wrote in *The Gay Science* (1882): 'We Germans are Hegelians even if there never had been any Hegel, in so far as we (in contrast to all Latins) instinctively assign a deeper sense and richer value to becoming, to develop-

44

ment, than to what "is"; we hardly believe in the justification of the concept "being".'

Like Heraclitus, Hegel saw opposition and conflict as essential to becoming. He also saw the world itself, and the concepts by which we categorize it, as becoming, rather than as statically being. The ABSOLUTE is not an unchanging entity that underlies our attempts to comprehend it, but the very development of these attempts. Similarly, SCIENCE is not a set of results independent of the process by which we arrive at them, but essentially involves this process. But Hegel did not, like Nietzsche and (on Hegel's interpretation) Heraclitus, abandon being altogether in favour of unremitting flux. Interludes of relatively stable being, the province of the understanding rather than of reason, are essential to the world, to the conceptual system of the Logic, and to our social and political life.

Hegel's central account of being, nothing and becoming appears in his Logic. Here 'being' is used in two main ways. First, in contrast to 'essence' and the 'CONCEPT', it denotes the subject-matter of the first of the three main sections of the Logic ('The Doctrine of Being'), namely, the 'immediate', surface features of things, both qualitative and quantitative, in contrast to their inner essence and their conceptual structure. Both in the Logic and elsewhere (in e.g. *LPEG*) Hegel continues to use 'being' as the antithesis of 'THINKING' and the 'concept'.

Second, within 'The Doctrine of Being', '(pure) being' denotes the first, 'immediate' category with which the Logic begins. Being is the appropriate beginning, since, unlike *Dasein* ('determinate being'), it involves no such inner complexity as to require development within logic: to apply 'being' to anything is simply to say that it is, without ascribing to it any qualitative determinacy. (Hegel argues in *PS*, I, that sensory certainty amounts to the ascription of such 'empty' being.) Since it is wholly indeterminate, being amounts to, or 'becomes', nothing. But conversely, nothing, since it too is blankly indeterminate, is or becomes being. Thus being and nothing each become the other, and so constitute the concept of becoming. (Becoming also involves, or is the 'unity' of, both being and nothing, in that becoming is either the coming to *be* of what was *not*, or the ceasing to be of what was.) But becoming too is unstable, since it contradictorily contains both being and nothing, and it collapses into *Dasein*.

This episode has exercised Hegel's interpreters and critics – among them Feuerbach – since its first appearance. Is the thought of pure being a genuine thought? Is it immediate, or does it presuppose an anticipation of the end of the Logic, the absolute idea? How can concepts become, or pass into (*übergehen*), each other, rather than being statically related by identity, or difference (or some more complex relation of identity-in-difference)? Why is becoming the uniquely appropriate outcome of the instability of being and nothing? Some of these difficulties may be partially relieved, if we remember the context of theological and metaphysical debate in which Hegel wrote and to which he refers in this passage of the Logic. Hegel's contemporaries were apt to make such claims as 'God (or the absolute) is (or is pure being)' or 'The absolute is pure indifference/identity'. (Hegel believes that 'absolute identity', or any other expression, is equivalent to 'being', if it expresses a concept that is immediate.) But, Hegel argues, if nothing is true (or knowable) of GOD or the ABSOLUTE except that it *is*, these claims do not differ from the claim that God or the absolute is nothing or is not. But conversely, the claim that God is not or is nothing is similarly unstable, and amounts to saying that he *is*. (An atheist might dispute this step, but Hegel believes that any conceptual claim about reality is a claim about God or the absolute, and involves at least a minimal theism.) The only way out of this instability is to develop and fill out the concepts that we apply to the absolute.

Hegel argues that the concept of pure being is implicit in the 'is' of the predicative judgment, which he discusses in 'The Doctrine of the Concept'. He does not, in the opening section of the Logic, distinguish between the 'is' of predication, of identity and of existence. One reason for this is his tendency, in the account of the judgment, to conflate predication and identification. Another, but perhaps related, reason is that such distinctions can only be drawn if we introduce more concrete concepts than that of being: the distinction between 'Thera is rugged', 'Thera is Santorini' and 'Thera is/exists' cannot be drawn unless we deploy such concepts as 'INDIVIDUAL' and 'QUALITY', exemplified by 'Thera' and 'rugged'. But this is forbidden at the stage of pure being: more concrete concepts must be logically reconstructed and not presupposed at the start. Similarly, the emptiness of the claim 'God is', and its equivalence to 'God is being' (as well as to 'God is not(hing)'), stems from Hegel's denial of any content to the term 'God', apart from that available at this stage of the Logic, namely, being.

belief, faith and opinion   German, like English, has a variety of words for types and degrees of belief. The most significant, in Hegel, are *Glaube(n)* and *Meinung*. *Glaube* comes from *glauben* ('to believe', etc.), which originally meant 'to hold dear (*lieb*), approve (of)'. It was used by pre-Christian Germans for one's trust in a deity, and it later expressed the Christian's relationship to God. It was then weakened to mean 'believe'.

Thus like the cognate 'belief', *Glaube* indicates: (1) trust or confidence (*Vertrauen*) in a person, a thing or God; (2) acceptance of something as true (*Fürwahrhalten*); (3) what is believed. But *Glaube* is narrower than 'belief', in that it implies a stronger conviction and less reliance on sensory and rational evidence than 'belief' does. (The verb *glauben*, however, does not exclude reliance on evidence.) Thus *Glaube* amounts to 'faith': Hegel often associates it with 'immediate certainty (*Gewissheit*)' – a subjective certainty that does not entail truth – and contrasts it with REASON, THINKING and the CONCEPT. The German for 'superstition' is formed from *Glaube*: *Aberglaube*, 'perverse belief' – but the exact sense of *Aber-* is uncertain. (The possibly Hegelian 'Oldest System-Programme of German Idealism' (1796 or 1797) uses *After-glaube* instead of *Aberglaube*.)

Hegel associates *Glaube* not with ancient religion – the Greeks were, on his view, too immersed in their own society and its religious beliefs and practices to have 'faith' or 'trust' ('it is one thing to be a pagan, another to *believe* in a pagan religion', *PR* §147) – but with Christianity, since *Glaube* implies

46

separation from God or the ABSOLUTE and a REFLECTIVE attitude to it. Hegel is especially concerned with *Glaube* in *ETW*. In these writings, especially *PCR* and *SCF*, he attempts to answer the question how Christianity became a 'positive' religion, involving, among other things, a 'positive faith', that is, a 'system of religious propositions that is supposed to have truth for us, because it is required of us by an authority, to which we cannot refuse to submit our faith'. This conception of faith is that of the Catholic Church: faith is the supernatural virtue by which, with the help of God's grace, we accept as true what God has revealed, solely on God's authority, and not because we have discerned its truth by the natural light of reason.

Hegel, by contrast, endorsed the Lutheran conception, that faith is less a matter of belief in certain historical facts than of confidence in God, of receiving God's promise. It is this conception of *Glaube* that he attributes to Christ and the early Christians, faith not as an acceptance of something as true, but in its original meaning of trust or confidence in the divine: 'Faith in the divine is possible only because there is in the believer himself a divine element, which rediscovers itself, its own nature, in the object of its faith. . . . The intermediate state between, on the one hand, the darkness, remoteness from the divine, captivity to actuality, and, on the other, one's own wholly divine life, a confidence in oneself, is faith in the divine; faith is the presentiment, the cognition, of the divine and the longing for unification with it.'

Later, Hegel was averse to any conception of *Glaube*, whether Catholic or Protestant, that counterposed it to reason and conceptual thought. First, under the influence of the Enlightenment, he could not allow that certain doctrines must simply be accepted on authority. Doctrines, if they are to be accepted, must be attested by a person's own 'insight' (*Einsicht*), not received on the authority of Church or state. Second, he rejected any two-world view, any world 'beyond' postulated by faith as a refuge from the world of mundane, secularized reality. His youthful ideal was the Greek city-state, in which the citizen was wholly at home with his city and with the gods who, as it were, resided within it. He soon abandoned this ideal, realizing that such 'yearning' (*Sehnsucht*) was only another version of faith in a world beyond, but he retained his aversion to dualism. Third, Hegel disliked the modern dilution of the rich faith of early and medieval Christianity into a meagre faith in an 'absolute ESSENCE (*Wesen*)' or a god conceived only as e.g. pure being. Such a faith is both intellectually empty and incapable of providing any focus for a popular faith or of revitalizing an increasingly secularized reality, conceived in terms of mechanism and utility. This impoverishment of faith has, Hegel believes, several sources: the Protestant stress on SUBJECTI-VITY, the spirit and intensity of belief, at the expense of OBJECTIVITY, the content of belief; the related individualism of Protestantism, the stress on personal conviction and devotion at the expense of public authority and communal worship; the encroachment of Newtonian science on areas pre-viously reserved for faith; the struggle of the Enlightenment against *Aber-glaube*; and the self-seeking individualism associated with the rise of CIVIL SOCIETY.

47

This process was mirrored in the thought of Kant and his followers, especially Jacobi and Fichte, as Hegel records in *FK*. Kant supposed that he had demolished the theoretical arguments for religious doctrines in *CPR*, arguing that he had 'destroyed knowledge in order to make room for faith' – a faith for which he later attempted to provide a basis in MORALITY. But Hegel saw the outcome as an attenuated faith wholly detached from the world of KNOWLEDGE (*Wissen*). The doyen, in Hegel's eyes, of the philosophy of faith was Jacobi, who spoke of the *salto mortale* of faith required to cross the gulf between philosophical cognition (*Erkennen*) and religious truth. Jacobi used a variety of terms for what was involved in this mortal leap: 'faith', 'immediate knowledge' (*Wissen*, in contrast to *Erkennen*), 'FEELING' and 'INTUITION'. Hegel saw little difference between these terms: in view of their shared *immediacy*, they amount to the same thing. But the immediacy of Jacobi's faith accounts for its central deficiency, that, in contrast to Christian faith, its content is vanishingly thin, supplying at most the lowest common denominator of all religions. Another factor contributing to the attenuation of *Glaube* is its application to mundane matters: Jacobi claimed, e.g., that I know of the existence of external objects, and of my own body, by *Glaube*. Hegel argues, in his account of sensory certainty, that the rich content of the external world cannot be captured by immediate knowledge or faith (*PS*, I). On his view, a cognitive state must be as complex and mediated as its object.

Hegel believed that in the complex mediations involved in his Logic, philosophy of religion and philosophy of right he had given the best possible reconciliation of the apparently conflicting demands of a modern faith: (1) to preserve the rich and weighty content of the Christian faith; (2) to satisfy the individual's right rationally to assess and endorse the views that he is required to adopt; and (3) to embody this faith in our society, our lives and our conception of this world rather than assign it to a world beyond.

Glaube and *glauben* are distinct from *Meinung* ('opinion, view') and *meinen* ('to think, believe, opine'). Kant defined *Meinung* as 'an acceptance as true [*Fürwahrhalten*] that is consciously insufficient both subjectively and objectively. If the acceptance as true is only subjectively sufficient, but is held to be objectively insufficient, then it is faith. Finally, acceptance as true that is sufficient both subjectively and objectively is knowledge' (*CPR* B850). Hegel associates *Meinung* with (the etymologically unrelated) *mein* ('mine') and thus with idiosyncrasy: it is 'a subjective REPRESENTATION [*Vorstellung*], a random thought, a fancy, which I can form in any way I like, while someone else can do it differently. A *Meinung* is *mein*; it is not an intrinsically universal thought that is IN AND FOR ITSELF. But philosophy is objective SCIENCE of truth, science of its necessity, conceptual cognition, not opining and spinning out opinions' (*LHP*, Introduction). In *PS*, I, and elsewhere, Hegel contrasts my *Meinung* and what I *meine* with what I *say*: what I *meine*, my particular *Meinung*, cannot be expressed in the universal words available in language. (Hegel invariably champions the rationality of language and depreciates *Meinung*.) Here *meinen* and *Meinung* amount to 'mean, intend' and 'meaning, intention', but always in the sense of what a person means or intends by an expression or utterance, rather than *the* meaning of a word.

Öffentliche Meinung, a term that came into fashion shortly before the French Revolution, means 'public opinion'. Public opinion, Hegel argues, is an expression of the modern principle of subjective FREEDOM, according to which rational norms and political structures cannot be imposed by FORCE or by custom and tradition, but only by convincing the citizen of their merits. Hence public opinion involves a paradoxical combination of public and authoritative rationality with the privacy, contingency and perversity of *Meinung*. Thus 'independence of public opinion is the first formal condition of anything great and rational in life as in science . . . . Public opinion contains all kinds of falsity and truth, but it takes a great man to find the truth in it' (*PR* §316–18).

C

---

cancel, cancellation *see* SUBLATION

category *see* DETERMINATION AND DETERMINATENESS; THINKING AND THOUGHT

causality and reciprocity   German has two words for causality: (1) *Kausalität*, with the adjective *kausal* deriving from the Latin *causa*; *causa* was also used by some German philosophers for 'cause', but not by Hegel except in discussing other philosophers. (2) *Ursache* is the native German for 'cause', and derives from *ur-* ('from out of', hence 'original') and *Sache* ('THING, matter', originally 'case in dispute, legal case'); like *causa*, it was originally a legal term, for the 'original occasion for a judicial action', but was generalized to mean 'cause'. *Ursache* gives rise to the adjective *ursächlich* ('causal') and the noun *Ursächlichkeit* ('causality'), but the verb *verursachen* ('to cause, occasion, produce') rarely occurs in Hegel's accounts of causality.

The correlative of *Ursache* is *Wirkung* ('(an) effect'), from the verb *wirken* ('to work, cause, operate, act (on), affect'). But *Wirkung* is ambiguous: it can mean either what is effected or produced (*gewirkte*), or the effecting of it, efficacy, action (*Wirksamkeit*). Hence it is also used in the expressions *Wirkung und Gegenwirkung* ('action and reaction') and *Wechselwirkung* ('reciprocity', the interaction of two or more substances). Hegel's usual term for a cause's *producing* an effect is *setzen*, to 'POSIT', but his use of it is not restricted to causality.

Hegel makes no distinction between *Kausalität* and *Ursächlichkeit*. But like other philosophers, he distinguishes them from other, similar RELATIONS, such as that of *Grund* and *Folge* ('GROUND' and 'consequent'), *Bedingung* and *Bedingte* ('CONDITION' and 'conditioned') and *Kraft* and *Äusserung* ('FORCE' and its 'expression'). Both *Grund* and *Bedingung*, e.g., have a 'logical', as well as a 'real' use: they refer to the entailment of one proposition by another, as well as to the dependence of one event on another. Moreover, *Grund*, in Leibniz's usage, includes the PURPOSE, or final cause, of a thing, while *Ursache* does not. (Hegel occasionally uses *Endursache* for 'final cause', but he distinguishes this sharply from the 'efficient' or 'mechanical' causes which form the subject-matter of his account of *Ursache*.) Both of these relations are thus, on Hegel's view, of wider application than causality. A force, unlike a cause, is conceived as general rather than as a particular event, and as underlying or hidden rather than overt: my flicking a switch *causes* a light to go on, while electricity is the force which underlies, makes possible, and is expressed in, the production of this effect, but which is also involved in many other events of diverse types.

50

In his Logic, especially *SL*, Hegel develops the concept of causality out of that of SUBSTANCE: the substance, the 'original thing or matter' (*Ur-sache*) passes over into its accidents, and thus produces or 'posits' an effect. But cause and effect are implicitly identical. For there is, Hegel argues, nothing in the cause that is not also in the effect, and conversely nothing in the effect that is not also in the cause. Thus what was first the effect is itslf a cause, and has an effect of its own; while conversely what was first the cause is itself an effect and has a further cause of its own. Hence we move from the single substance producing its accidents to an endless series of causes and effects. Another route by which he reaches the same conclusion is this: when the cause produces its effect, the cause disappears entirely into the effect. The effect is thus not simply an effect, but is itself the 'original matter', that is the *Ursache* or cause which produces an effect. The ambiguity of *Wirkung*, denoting not simply a passive effect, but also activity or production, also plays a part here, as does the connection that Hegel sees between *Wirkung* and *Wirklichkeit* ('ACTUALITY'): the effect, once produced, is an independent actuality, capable of generating effects of its own.

The doctrine that neither the cause nor the effect contains anything that the other does not is interpreted by Hegel in two distinct ways.

1. In virtue of the very concepts of a cause and of an effect, a cause is not a cause unless it has an effect, and an effect is not an effect unless it is the effect of some cause. The concepts of a cause and of an effect are thus logically inseparable.

2. There is, Hegel argues, a non-logical or real identity between the cause and its effect; e.g., when rain makes the ground wet, the wetness of the ground is not distinct from the rain that produced it: it is simply the rain in a different form. Cause and effect are the same matter or *Sache*, e.g., moisture, first in an original form, and then in the form of 'positedness'. Indeed, the very distinction between a cause and its effect is the work of a 'subjective UNDERSTANDING', a distinction introduced by *us* into an essentially homogeneous continuum. Causal propositions such as 'Rain makes things wet' are not, he infers, synthetic, as Kant believed, but analytic propositions or tautologies. This inference is faulty: it is not inconceivable that rain should make, or leave, things dry. In virtue of Hegel's principle that an effect has the same content as its cause, the dryness would not count as an *effect* of the rain, but the rain would still not have made things wet. Thus what might be claimed to be analytic is not 'Rain makes things wet', but 'If rain has any effect, then it makes things wet'. But even this claim will encounter the difficulty that the principle that cause and effect have the same content is, at best, vague. Hegel agrees that such cases as a person's painting a canvas or the propulsion of one moving object by another are less favourable to the principle, since, unlike rain, a painter and a moving object contain many features that do not pass over into their effects. But the painter and the object are only causes, he argues, in respect of those of their features that *do* reappear in the effect.

The principle that cause and effect have the same content has two consequences for Hegel's account of causality. First, he does not, like Kant, regard the causation of one event by another as dependent on a causal LAW or rule: since cause and effect are not distinct, but at bottom the same, no rule or law is required to govern their connection. Thus laws figure in Hegel's account of APPEARANCE (*Erscheinung*) rather than of causality. Second, causality does not apply to all phenomena: in particular, it does not apply to living or to spiritual entities. Nutrition is not the cause of blood, and Caesar's ambition was not the cause of the fall of the Roman Republic. For living and spiritual entities do 'not admit another original entity into themselves or let a cause continue into them, but break it off and transform it'. Hegel here makes two distinct points. First, what a living organism, a mind or a society makes of some external impact on it differs too much in content from the external object itself to count as an *effect* of that object: the pearl is not the effect of the grain of sand. Second, in the case of minds and societies, if not of living organisms generally, such an external impact is neither a necessary nor a sufficient condition of what results from it: a person or a society may, in view of its creative inner nature, respond in different ways to any given impact, and it may make use of different events or objects in order to achieve the same result. Thus an impact is at most an 'occasion' (*Veranlassung*) or an external 'stimulus' (*Erregung*), and it is made into an occasion by the 'inner SPIRIT' of a person or a society. Caesar's ambition or Cleopatra's nose did not *cause* the fall of the Republic: the Republic made the ambition or the nose the *occasion* of its downfall, as it might have used other objects or events to the same end, had these not been available.

Cause and effect are inseparable. Thus in producing an effect, the cause makes itself into a cause and is thus, in a sense, the cause of itself and also the effect of itself. Cause and effect thus reverse their roles: the effect is a cause, since only its occurrence makes the cause a cause, and conversely the cause is an effect, since it is made a cause by its effect. But the understanding attempts (contradictorily) to separate the cause and effect as distinct events. When they are thus separated, the reciprocal relation of cause and effect expresses itself as an infinite regress and an infinite progression: any cause is the effect not of its own effect, but of some further cause, and any effect is the cause not of its own cause, but of some further effect. This false or bad INFINITY is unstable – one cannot, e.g., fully explain an event if its causal antecedents regress to infinity – and gives way to the relation of action and reaction, or, more explicitly, of reciprocity, in which two or more substances interact in such a way that the states of the one are both the cause and the effect of the states of the other. Cause and effect are thus brought into the intimate, reciprocal relation that their formal or logical relation requires, a relation closer to the circularity of true infinity than to the bad infinite regress.

The logical superiority of reciprocity makes it, on Hegel's view, more suitable for the understanding of higher, viz. biological and social, phenomena than is unidirectional causality. It is more likely that the different organs of an animal, or the customs and the political constitution of a PEOPLE, reciprocally affect each other, than that one is simply the effect of the other. But to explain x in terms of y, and y in terms of x, though correct as far as it goes, cannot provide a satisfactory explanation of either x or y. What is required for this is a third entity which embraces both x and y, viz. the CONCEPT of the entity, e.g., the organism or society, of which x and y are aspects.

civil society   The German is *bürgerliche Gesellschaft*:

1. A *Bürger* was originally a defender of a castle (*Burg*), hence, from the twelfth century on, a town-dweller or townsman. It also means a 'citizen', but it retains its association with the French *bourgeois*, and suggests a contrast with the nobility and the clergy. *Bourgeois* comes from the cognate *bourg*, a 'market town' or 'borough'. It is distinct from *citoyen* (from the Latin *civis*), which Hegel uses when he wishes to specify the sense of a 'citizen' of a STATE. The adjective *bürgerlich* thus means 'civil, civic' (as in 'civil law, rights' and 'civic duty') and also 'middle-class, bourgeois'. In *bürgerliche Gesellschaft*, both senses are in play, but with a stress on the latter.

2. *Gesellschaft* ('society') comes from *Geselle*, originally someone who shared one's dwelling space, later a 'companion, friend', etc., but also a 'journey-man'. A *Gesellschaft* is any amicable association, whether temporary (e.g. a 'party') or enduring (e.g. a commercial 'company'). Since the fifteenth century it has been used for the 'social order'. (*Gesellschaftswissenschaft* is the same as *Soziologie*, but both words postdate Hegel.) Tönnies later distinguished *Gesellschaft*, a mechanical association based on self-interest, from *Gemeinschaft* (from *gemein*, 'common'), an organic community based on shared values, affection, etc. (*Gemeinschaft und Gesellschaft*, 1887. Cf. Durkheim's distinction between 'mechanical' and 'organic solidarity'.) Hegel's usage prefigures this distinction: civil society is not a *Gemeinschaft*, while a religious community is not a *Gesellschaft*, but a *Gemein(d)e* ('community', also from *gemein*).

Hegel, in *PR* §§181–256, recognizes *bürgerliche Gesellschaft* as a distinct area of ETHICAL LIFE, in contrast to, and MEDIATING between, the FAMILY and the state. It includes the economic life of the community, together with the legal, policing and social arrangements that ensure its smooth working. No earlier writer distinguishes as clearly as Hegel between civil society and the state. There are three reasons for this:

(1)   The economy and the economic were not clearly distinguished from the family or household. 'Economy' (*Ökonomie*) comes from the Greek *oikonomia* (the 'running of a household', from *oikos*, 'family, household'), which Aristotle in his *Politics* divides into the relations of master and slave, of husband and wife, and of parent and child, with money-making as an afterthought. (The native German, *Wirtschaft*, also originally meant 'house-keeping', and only later acquired the sense of 'economy'.) People of significance, i.e. adult male citizens, were to devote their time to public affairs rather than to money-making. Aristotle *implicitly* recognized an economy transcending the household: he argued that the purpose of the state (*polis*) cannot be to facilitate trade, since separate states have commercial treaties, with legal arrangements to prevent injustice. But an adequate conceptualization of the

53

area had to await the growth of societies too large for all citizens to participate in public life, the significant growth of the economy beyond the household, and the emergence of the expression 'political (i.e. non-household) economy' (*Nationalökonomie*). (The phrase *politikē oikonomia* occurs in the pseudo-Aristotelian *Oeconomica*, but it bore little fruit at the time.)

(2) The political could not be adequately disentangled from the social, until the rise of centralized monarchical or revolutionary states that were clearly distinct from the social life of their subjects.

(3) Many political theorists, especially contract theorists, held (in contrast to Aristotle, as well as to Hegel) that the purpose of the state is simply to facilitate social, and especially commercial, relations by preventing injustice among citizens. This too obscures the distinction between the political and the socio-economic, since enforceable regulations are essential to economic intercourse, even between members of different states.

Thus Aristotle's expression, *koinōnia politikē*, and its descendants (*civitas, respublica*, Aquinas' *communitas civilis sive* ('or') *politica*, Locke's 'civil or political society') refer to the political state and draw no distinction between 'political' and 'civil'. The expression *bürgerliche Gesellschaft*, which owed its popularity in Germany to Ferguson's *Essay on the History of Civil Society* (1767, translated into German in 1768), had a similar use in, e.g., *ETW* and in Kant's *CJ* §83.

Hegel's extrication of civil society from both the family and the state thus has two sources: (1) his discovery of the economy from his study of, e.g., Adam Smith, Steuart and Ferguson during his Jena years, an influence that is especially marked in his 1805–6 Jena lectures on philosophy of SPIRIT; and (2) his growing conviction that the state has a higher purpose than the regulation of relations between citizens. Civil society makes one a *Bürger*; the state makes one a *citoyen*, a citizen of France or of Prussia, and not simply a trader, who does business with Frenchmen as well as with Prussians.

Hegel's account of civil society falls into three sections:

1. The SYSTEM of needs (*Bedürfnisse*). This is the economy proper, in which individuals exchange goods and services to satisfy their needs, needs which multiply as the system develops. Individuals are related by self-interest, not by love and trust as in the family, but their interests are interdependent and give rise to a division of labour. Thus 'estates' or classes (*Stände*) emerge: an agricultural class, a business class and a 'UNIVERSAL' class of civil servants. These provide their members with a status, a right to RECOGNITION and a professional ethic.

2. The administration of justice (*Rechtspflege*). ABSTRACT RIGHT is codified in LAWS that are definite, promulgated and known, and are designed to protect individuals against injury. In this realm, Hegel argues, a 'man counts as a man in virtue of his manhood alone, not because he is a Jew, Catholic, Protestant, German, Italian, etc.' (*PR* §209).

3. The police and corporation. *Polizei* (from the Greek *politeia*, 'constitution', via Latin) is wider than our 'police'. From the fifteenth to the

eighteenth century it was used for 'government, public administration'. Hegel still equates it with *öffentliche Macht* ('public POWER, authority'). Thus it covers not only law enforcement, but also the fixing of the prices of necessities, control of the quality of goods, the provision of public alms-houses, hospitals, street-lighting, etc. Hegel was not opposed to private charity, but argued that 'public social conditions are to be viewed as all the more perfect, the less is left for an individual to do by himself as his private inclination directs' (*PR* §242). He was disturbed by the growth of an impoverished and resentful 'rabble' (*Pöbel*), especially in Britain. The aboli-tion of poverty is 'one of the most disturbing problems that agitate modern society' (*PR* §244A.). But he has no obvious solution to it: to support the rabble at the expense of the rich would violate the 'principle of civil society' and the self-respect of individual members of the rabble. To provide work for them worsens the problem, which arises from the excess of production over the needs of productively employed consumers (*PR* §245). Thus civil society is driven by its DIALECTIC to seek markets, and thus its means of subsistence, in other, poorer countries (*PR* §246).

Korporation originated in workmen's guilds in ancient Rome. It is not a 'trade union', since it embraces employers as well as employees, and in Hegel's usage also covers religious bodies, learned societies and town coun-cils. Like the estates, the corporations mitigate the competitive individualism of the system of needs and educate their members for life in the state.

Hegel sees the economic market as a central and inevitable feature of the modern state, but believes that its workings depend on a significant degree of public regulation and support, and on the inculcation of non-competitive values. Thus he includes in the realm of civil society much that is assigned to the state by other writers.

classification   Hegel's interest in classification has two aspects. First, there are the procedures by which we group together individuals, notably plants and animals, into species, and these species in turn into wider genera. Interest in these procedures began with Plato and especially Aristotle, himself a distinguished biologist and responsible for many of our ideas concerning species and genera, and classification in general. Second, Ger-man philosophers, notably Kant, were concerned that their thought and writing should not proceed haphazardly from one topic to the next, but should form a carefully articulated system. Hegel in particular stressed that philosophy must be systematic, and one consequence of this is that his works usually proceed by first presenting a general concept of the subject-matter, then dividing this concept into three segments, and each of these in turn into three subsegments, and so on until the subject-matter is, for his purposes, exhausted. The principles of these successive divisions and of the resulting structure were of great importance to Hegel and occupied his attention throughout his career.

The native German word for 'classification' (in contrast to the Latin-derived *Klassifikation* or *Klassifizierung*) is *Enteilung*, from *enteilen* ('to divide, classify'). It is used by Hegel to indicate both biological or other types of empirical classification and the division of a concept in philosophy. Classification involves three things: (1) A genus (*Gattung*) or generic concept that is to be divided – e.g., *animal(s)*; (2) a principle of classification (*Enteilungsgrund* – e.g., whether the animal's customary habitation is land, water or air; and (3) the terms or members of the classification (*Enteilungsglied, -er*) that result from the application of the principle of division to the genus – e.g., land-animals, birds, fish. These subclasses are commonly called 'species' (*Art, -en*). But *Gattung* and *Art* are relative terms: a class is regarded as a genus in relation to the species subordinate to it, but as a species in relation to the wider class of which it, along with other co-ordinate species, is a subdivision. (German, like English, supplies a variety of terms for classes and subclasses, but *Gattung* and *Art* are those most commonly used by Hegel.) The feature that differentiates a species from other species of the same genus is a 'specific difference' (*Artsunterschied*), but this is often referred to as a *Merkmal*, a distinguishing mark or feature. Traditionally, the definition of a species refers both to the genus to which it belongs, and to its specific difference: a fish, e.g., is an aquatic animal.

Hegel discusses such classification in several places, but most notably in *SL*, under the headings of 'the disjunctive JUDGMENT' and of 'synthetic COGNITION (*Erkennen*)'. The problems that vexed him are these: Classification can proceed in either of two ways. We can, first, proceed empirically or *a posteriori*: examining the features of one individual after another, deriving inductively from our observations species into which we group these individuals, and finally classifying together groups of species into higher genera. Or, second, we can proceed *a priori* in the opposite direction: starting with a generic concept, which we divide into species by an assumed principle of division, and then fitting such individuals as we encounter into our classificatory scheme. Hegel saw difficulties in both procedures. If we proceed purely *a posteriori*, we will give the same weight to our observations of damaged or defective individuals as to those of sound ones, and so we might conclude that the horse is not a quadruped, since not all horses have four legs. (Still less does every 'circle' we encounter conform to Euclid's definition 15: 'a plane figure contained by one line such that all the straight lines falling upon it from one point among those lying within the figure are equal to one another'.) Or again, we may observe that all men, in contrast to other creatures, have earlobes. (Hegel attributes this claim to J. F. Blumenbach.) What is to prevent us from treating this trivial feature as the specific difference of a human being, rather than some more essential characteristic such as his capacity for thought?

If, conversely, we proceed *a priori*, we may again select a principle of division (the possession of earlobes) that is not essential to our subject-matter. Moreover, the procedure will be empirical to the extent that the principle of division that we select is not determined by the genus that we are dividing: the genus *animal* alone, does not tell us whether to divide it into aquatic and non-aquatic or into vertebrate and invertebrate.

Hegel's response to these difficulties is this: Our approach to biological classification can be neither purely empirical nor purely *a priori*. To ensure that, as far as possible, our classifications correspond to the essential natures of our subject-matter, we should base them on the ways in which individuals group themselves into species and distinguish *themselves* from individuals of other species, namely the sexual organs by which members of the same species reproduce themselves, and their weapons of attack and defence ('teeth and claws') against other species.

His general principle here is that entities, whether individuals or species, define themselves by conflict with other entities. But he does not invariably follow this principle: although he believes that *individual* political states define themselves in conflict with other states, he does not argue that *types* of state (e.g. monarchies, aristocracies and democracies) define themselves in conflict with each other; different types of state are often historically successive rather than contemporaneous, and, even when they are contemporaneous, a state is as likely to wage war against another state of the same type as against one of a different type. The classification of states must, on Hegel's view, proceed both empirically and *a priori*. The division into democracy, aristocracy and monarchy, though indispensable, should not obscure the existence of degenerate versions of these 'pure forms' (ochlocracy, e.g., is a perversion of democracy) or of earlier transitional forms: oriental despotism and feudal monarchy share with genuine constitutional monarchy the abstract feature that 'the will of one individual stands at the head of the state', but differ from it in essential respects.

The divisions involved in Hegel's own works are intended to be, so far as possible, non-empirical, both in the sense that at least the broad outlines of the division are based not on empirical observation of the subject-matter, but on the *a priori* divisions of logic, and in the sense that the way in which a generic CONCEPT is divided is determined by the concept itself. One way in which he attempts to achieve this is by arguing that the UNIVERSAL concept that is to be divided is itself one of its own subdivisions, that it is both generic and specific. This idea derives from Aristotle, who argued that the three types of soul, the souls of a plant, an animal and a man, are not co-ordinate, but form a series proceeding from the universal plant-soul, which possesses only the powers of nutrition and reproduction common to all types of soul, to the animal-soul, which is further specified by the additional capacity of perception, and finally to the human soul, which has the capacity for thought in addition to the other two: the plant-soul is thus both a universal, containing the highest common factor of all types of soul, and a particular type of soul.

Hegel generalizes this idea by arguing that the very concept of a universal implicitly contains the concepts of a PARTICULAR and of an INDIVIDUAL – since, for example, a universal concept is a *particular* type of concept, co-ordinate with the particular and the individual concept – and thus the universal is *both* a genus *and* one of three species into which the generic universal 'particularizes' itself. This explains in part why Hegel's divisions (unlike Plato's dichotomies) are generally TRIADIC, why each term of the division is higher than its predecessor, and why the title of a section of a work is often also the title of its first subsection (e.g. BEING). He hoped in this way to show that a generic concept DEVELOPS or successively particularizes itself without the introduction of an external principle of division. The development of the concept in the Logic is not temporal or historical, but he often illustrates it with temporal examples, e.g., of a plant that develops from a seed conceived as universal or indeterminate. In the case of entities that develop over history, Hegel believes that they evolve from simpler, 'universal' forms into more specific forms. Political constitutions become differentiated and articulated only in the modern world; those of the Greeks were simple and universal (*PR* §279A.). The self-particularization of the universal thus has application to history as well as to Hegel's system.

concept   The verb *begreifen* comes from *greifen* (literally 'to grasp, seize') and means 'to comprehend', both in the sense of 'include, comprise' and in that of 'understand, conceive, conceptualize', but it has a narrower application than *verstehen* ('to UNDERSTAND') and implies an effort to grasp or to encompass. (The past participle is also used in the expression *begriffen sein in*, to be doing, or engaged in, something.) Among other compounds of *greifen*, Hegel uses *übergreifen*, 'to overlap, encroach (on), overreach, outflank': the concept overreaches its OTHER, since, e.g., the concept of what is other than a concept, an OBJECT, is itself a concept.

The noun *Begriff* means both 'concept' and 'conception', especially in the sense of 'ability to conceive'. (The expression *im Begriff sein* means 'to be about to do, on the point of doing', something.) Eckhart used it for the Latin *conceptus* or *notio*; and Wolff used it in the sense of a 'REPRESENTATION of a thing in thoughts', but its meaning was stabilized by Kant: in contrast to 'INTUITION (*Anschauung*)', the *Begriff* ('concept') is a 'UNIVERSAL representation [*Vorstellung*] or a representation of that which is common to several objects' (*Logic* I, i §1). *Begriff* in Hegel is often translated as 'Notion', since, for Hegel, a *Begriff* is neither exclusively universal nor a *Vorstellung* nor indicative of what objects have in common. But this rendering obscures its links with *begreifen* and also with the standard use of *Begriff*, which Hegel did not simply reject, but reflectively developed or SUBLATED.

In early works, especially *SCF*, Hegel contrasts the ABSTRACT concept with LIFE and love, and regards it as expressing only the common features of things, not their inner essence. But in Jena he came to believe that philosophy must be conceptual, rather than intuitive or impassioned. He declared this belief in the Preface to *PS* and never abandoned it. The belief that conceptual thought should capture, rather than sidestep, the wealth of empirical, emotional and religious experience is a central motive for his transformation of the standard view of the concept.

In the Logic, *Begriff* contrasts with several ranges of terms:

(1)   It contrasts with INTUITION or the SENSORY (*das Sinnliche*), and with the representation (*Vorstellung*): a *Begriff* is not, as it was for Wolff and Kant, a type of *Vorstellung*; an empirical conception (of e.g. redness, a house, or a man), which we form by reflection on objects, is distinct from a concept.

(2)   *Begriff*, as the subject-matter of the third main part of the Logic, contrasts with BEING and with ESSENCE, the subjects of the first two parts.

58

(3)   It contrasts with the OBJECT or OBJECTIVITY, which realizes or actualizes it, and with the IDEA, which is the union of the concept and its object.
(4)   It contrasts with the JUDGMENT, into which it bifurcates, and with the INFERENCE, which reunites the concept with itself.

Each of these contrasts brings out a different aspect of *Begriff*, but the central feature of Hegel's account is his rejection of the following view of concepts and conceptual thought: The I* or the UNDERSTANDING (for Kant, the faculty of concepts, in contrast to REASON, the faculty of *ideas*) is confronted by a world of objects, accessible to it through intuition. To deal with these objects, it abstracts from them (or from sensory intuition) a range of concepts that it uses in its subsequent dealings with objects. Concepts are distinct from the I that deploys them, from the objects to which it applies them, and from each other. Hegel challenges each of these distinctions:

1. Concepts are not sharply distinct from the I: to say that they are 'means used by the understanding in thinking' is like saying that 'chewing and swallowing food is merely a means to eating, as if the understanding did a lot of other things besides thinking' (letter to Niethammer of 10 October 1811). Without concepts, there could be no I or understanding, and without concepts I could not ABSTRACT concepts or conceptions from sensory data. Hegel also has other reasons for identifying the I with a (or *the*) concept: The I (and SPIRIT) forms a peculiarly intimate unity which cannot be explained by the mechanistic categories of CAUSALITY or RECIPROCITY, but only conceptually. Moreover, the I is *both* wholly universal or indeterminate – if I think of myself as simply a Cartesian ego, bereft of a body and of empirical content – *and* PARTICULAR, in that it cannot exist without a corporeal embodiment and a determinate CONSCIOUSNESS of objects other than itself. Thus the structure of the I mirrors that of the concept, which is at once universal, particular and INDIVIDUAL, and which, like the I, embraces ('comprehends') or overreaches (*übergreift*) what is other than itself. But the identification of the I with the concept does not entail that all men at all times deploy the same concepts: for Hegel, unlike Kant, different categorical concepts become successively available over HISTORY.

2. Concepts are not sharply distinct from objects. Hegel has several arguments for this:
(a)   The general concepts considered in the Logic *constitute*, rather than simply qualify, the objects that exemplify them: no object can be wholly indeterminate, and no object that is, e.g., a THING with properties could fail to be a thing with properties.
(b)   The very contrast between concepts and external objects is itself a concept or a conceptual construction: the concept bifurcates into the concept of a concept and the concept of an object (as well as the concept of the I), just as the universal particularizes itself into the universal, the particular and the individual; the concept overreaches what is other than itself.
(c)   The I has no non-conceptual access to objects: intuition and percep-

tion, though distinct from conceptual thought, are deeply concept-laden.

(d) Relatively self-developing unities, such as minds, organisms and societies, both grow and cohere in virtue of the concept embedded in them (or encoded in the seed), not as a result solely of external impacts. Such concepts as that of a plant (or of a rose) are relatively specific and empirical, but, unlike the conceptions *we* form, they are active and develop, by a process that Hegel regards as a *judgment*. (Hence he rejects Kant's view that the existence of something cannot be derived from its concept.) Since the parts of such an entity are so closely united, and the entity is relatively immune to impacts from its environment, which it overreaches and employs rather than simply endures, Hegel associates the concept with FREEDOM, in contrast not to NECESSITY as such, but to the external necessity involved in causality and reciprocity. Since concepts are not formed by abstraction from empirical reality, an object need not fully fit its concept. Concepts are, for Hegel (as for Plato), normative ideals: a damaged or defective horse is not fully a horse, and an infant or a seed are only 'in concept' and have not yet fully realized their concept. (Thus *Begriff* in Hegel often refers to the initial stage of an entity in contrast to its developed form.) In the case of categorical concepts, a low-level entity, such as a rock, does not fully match *the* concept, but only a low-level fragment of it, such as the concept of a thing with properties.

3. Concepts are not sharply distinct from each other. They form a dialectically interwoven SYSTEM that cannot be acquired by piecemeal abstraction. Thus there is at bottom only one concept, the concept that unfolds itself in the Logic, and forms the essence both of the world and of the I.

Hegel often assimilates the concept to GOD, whose creation of the world from nothing expresses the self-realization of the concept into an object that is other than, yet identical to, itself. What he means is this: The concept applies to FINITE entities within the world, but no such entity fully matches the concept; even those that are relatively self-determining also depend on external input. But the world as a whole depends on nothing other than itself for its nature and development: it must therefore fully accord with its concept. The world is fully determined by the concept in a way that, among finite entities, is best exemplified by the MIND. Thus Hegel is inclined to believe that it is possible to infer at least the broad outlines of the world from a consideration of the concept, but he admits a realm of CONTINGENCY, the nature and extent of which he does not fully explain. His works on specific areas (e.g. *PR, LA, LPR*) open with an account of the relevant concept (such as the concept of right, of beauty, or of religion), which, he suggests, develops into a more specific account of the subject-matter (the structure of modern society, artistic styles and genres, types of religion, etc.) in considerable independence of the 'external' introduction of empirical content.

But the extent to which, on Hegel's view, the nature of the world is determined by, and is derivable *a priori* from, the logical concept (or idea) is controversial: Interpretations form a spectrum ranging from the view that the Logic simply 'reconstructs' and clarifies concepts, which Hegel then uses to organize and illuminate empirical content (e.g. M. J. Petry, K. Hartmann), to the view that he believes the world to 'emanate' from the concept in the tradition of Neoplatonism. These differences reflect the ambiguity and complexity intrinsic to Hegel's thought.

consciousness and self-consciousness   *Bewusst*, a technical term in philosophy and psychology since the eighteenth century, means 'conscious'. It is used to distinguish conscious mental states and events from unconscious ones, but in philosophy it primarily indicates intentional consciousness or consciousness of an OBJECT (*Gegenstand*). *Bewusstsein* ('consciousness', literally 'BEING conscious') was coined by Wolff for the Latin *conscientia*, and it tended to replace Leibniz's *Apperzeption*, but this is still used by Kant alongside *Bewusstsein*. Kant and Hegel use *das Bewusstsein* to denote not only a subject's consciousness, but the conscious SUBJECT himself, in contrast to the object of which he is conscious.

The addition of the pronoun *selbst* ('self') gives *selbstbewusst* and *Selbstbewusstsein*, which indicate consciousness, knowledge or awareness of oneself. This concept first appeared explicitly in Plotinus' expression *synaisthēsis hautou*, 'self-perception'. In the standard sense of eighteenth-century psychology and philosophy, *Selbstbewusstsein* was knowledge of one's own changing conscious states and of the processes occurring in oneself, together with an awareness that one's own I* or self is the bearer of these states and processes; that one has/is only one I; that this I persists throughout, and independently of, the varying succession of one's experiences; and that one's I stands in contrast to an external world of objects, from which it distinguishes itself as a subject that persists identically throughout the changes in the objects of which it is conscious. But Kant argued that self-consciousness in this sense is not, as this account implies, wholly independent of the character of my experience and of the objects I am aware of. My intuitions, if they are to be *my* experiences and experiences of objects distinct from myself, must be 'synthesized' in accordance with certain categories, such as causality (e.g. *CPR* A107, B144). This synthesis is, on Kant's view, performed by the I itself.

This doctrine – together with the doctrine of the Neoplatonists and of Böhme that the self and the world are reciprocally related and that knowledge of the one affords knowledge of the other – led the German idealists to conceive of the self not as sharply distinct from other objects, but as permeating and embracing them. Correspondingly, to be fully self-conscious is not simply to be conscious of oneself in contrast to objects, but to see the external world as the product, the possession, or the mirror-image of one's own self. Hegel's use of *selbstbewusst* and *Selbstbewusstsein* depends on these considerations. But it also depends on the colloquial sense of these words ('self-confident, -assured', etc.), which is quite different from that of their English counterparts ('embarrassed', etc.).

Hegel's two main accounts of consciousness and self-consciousness occur in *PS*, IV.A. and *Enc*. III §§413ff. In both texts, the account of consciousness is followed by those of self-consciousness and of REASON (*Vernunft*). (*Bewusst-sein* is also used in a wide sense, covering self-consciousness and reason, as well as consciousness 'as such'.) In *Enc.* III, but not *PS*, the account of consciousness is preceded by that of the SOUL (*Seele*), which is aware, in its higher phases, of its own sensory states, but not of objects other than itself. Since consciousness essentially involves an object other than itself, it is 'APPEARING' or 'apparent' (*erscheinend*, not, that is, 'illusory', but 'displaying itself in, and thus dependent on, an other'), in contrast both to the soul, which has not yet procured an object, and to reason and SPIRIT, which eliminate the otherness of the object. In both texts, consciousness successively takes three FORMS or 'shapes' (*Gestalten*): SENSORY CERTAINTY or consciousness (IMMEDIATE knowledge of sensory items, seen simply as individuals to be referred or pointed to); PERCEPTION (mediated knowledge of sensory items as THINGS with properties); and UNDERSTANDING (knowledge of things as manifestations of FORCES and as appearance – *Erscheinung* – governed by LAWS).

Hegel is not committed to saying either that objects produce consciousness or that consciousness produces its objects. The terms are correlative. Thus consciousness is not a uniform medium that remains unaltered while its objects vary: the character of the consciousness varies with that of its objects. A form of conciousness is not yet *self*-consciousness, but it is aware of itself, as well as its objects: its awareness of a discrepancy between itself and its object brings about the advance to a new form, whose object is the previous form of consciousness. For example, sensory consciousness uses UNIVERSAL terms, such as 'this', to denote its putatively individual objects; such universals become the avowedly universal properties of a thing, the object of perception. But no form of consciousness knows that this is how it arose; only 'we' philosophers know that. (Fichte too, in *SKW*, distinguishes between *our* knowledge and that of the I at the stage under consideration. Fichte, like Hegel, aims to trace the development of the I until its knowledge coincides with *ours*.)

The advance to self-consciousness occurs when consciousness as understanding deploys conceptions that involve a 'distinction which is no distinction' (such as the opposite poles of a magnet or of electricity): it sees both that the inner ESSENCE of things, conceptualized in terms of a vanishing distinction, is its own product, and that the concept of such a distinction is applicable to its own relation to its object. This gives the simplest form of self-consciousness: the I is conscious of itself, namely the I. But this phase of self-consciousness is deficient, since in contrast to the external world, the self-conscious I is vanishingly thin and elusive. It thus attempts by a series of manoeuvres both to remove the alien otherness of external objects and, *ipso facto*, to acquire objective content for itself. These manoeuvres are more practical than cognitive: desire (an endless process of consuming sensory objects); a struggle for RECOGNITION by another self-consciousness and the enslavement of the vanquished by the victor; and, in *PS*, disregarding the external world (STOICISM), denying its existence (SCEPTICISM), and projecting the essential features of oneself and the world into a transcendent realm (the unhappy consciousness), but, in *Enc.* III, the advance to *universal* self-conciousness, the mutual recognition of self-conscious individuals coexisting in an ethical community.

But the advance of self-consciousness does not end there. Hegel proceeds to an account of reason, the unification of consciousness (knowledge of an object seen as other than myself) and self-consciousness (knowledge of myself seen as other than the object): reason regards the DETERMINATIONS of the self as belonging also to the object. In fact self-consciousness advances both throughout HISTORY and throughout Hegel's own SYSTEM, which is, on his view, the culmination of human self-consciousness.

Hegel's account of self-conciousness has three notable features. First, self-consciousness is not an all-or-nothing matter, but proceeds through increasingly adequate stages. Second, it is essentially interpersonal and requires the reciprocal recognition of self-conscious beings: it is 'an I that is a we, and a we that is an I' (*PS*, IV). Third, it is practical as well as cognitive: finding oneself in the other, the appropriation of the alien other, in which self-consciousness consists, involves the establishment and operation of social institutions, as well as scientific and philosophical inquiry. Elements of these features appear in his predecessors, especially Schelling, but Hegel's view as a whole is substantially original.

contradiction The verb *widersprechen* (literally 'to speak against') and the noun *Widerspruch* are exact equivalents of 'to contradict (a person or a thing)' and 'contradiction'. In logic, 'contradiction' has two senses: (1) a narrower sense, in which two propositions or concepts contradict each other if, and only if, one is the negation of the other (e.g. 'red' and 'not red'); (2) a wider sense, in which two propositions or concepts contradict each other if they are logically incompatible (e.g. 'square' and 'circle', or 'red' and 'blue'). The LAW (in German, the *Satz*, 'PROPOSITION') of contradiction was regarded, since its first formulation by Aristotle, as the supreme 'law of THOUGHT' (*Denkgesetz*). It was formulated in various ways: 'It is impossible for the same thing both to belong and not to belong to something at the same time' (Aristotle); 'A is not non-A' (Leibniz); 'A predicate belongs to no thing that it contradicts' (Kant). Kant saw contradiction as a *negative* criterion of TRUTH: no two contradictory propositions are both true and no single self-contradictory proposition is true, but both of two propositions that do not contradict each other, or a proposition that is not self-contradictory, may yet be false.

From the earliest times some philosophers claimed that not only our thought, but the world itself, involves OPPOSITIONS or contradictions. Aristotle's paradigm of this was Heraclitus, who, though he had no word for 'contradiction', describes the world in oppositional or contradictory ways; the world, moreover, is governed by the *logos* ('word, REASON', etc.), so that no sharp distinction is drawn between the contradictions involved in his own thought or discourse and those in the world itself. Böhme too, though not using the word *Widerspruch*, saw *Gegenwurf* or opposition in the world. Evil, as well as good, is in everything, and without it there would be no life or movement; all things are a Yes and No; the No is the *Gegenwurf* of the Yes or of the truth. Novalis, who was largely responsible for Böhme's revival in this

63

period, wrote: 'It is perhaps the highest task of the higher logic to annihilate the law of contradiction.'

Early on, Hegel saw a conflict between the law of contradiction and the truths of RELIGION. In *SCF*, he argues (with reference to the opening of John's Gospel: 'In the beginning *was* the Logos; the Logos *was with* God; and God *was* the Logos; in him *was* life') that 'everything expressed about the divine in the language of reflection is *eo ipso* contradictory', and concludes that 'what is a contradiction in the realm of the dead is not one in the realm of life'. From the early 1800s he attempted to devise a logic that could accommodate religion and LIFE, as well as the insights of traditional logic.

The view of contradiction that Hegel eventually reached is this: We can, provisionally, distinguish between subjective contradictions, contradictions in our thoughts, and objective contradictions, contradictions in things. Traditional logic acknowledges the occurrence of subjective contradictions: Kant held that in reasoning about the world as a whole we inevitably fall into contradictions or 'antinomies'. But, Hegel argued, such contradictions are far more widespread and significant than Kant believed. Any FINITE thought or conception, taken in isolation, involves a contradiction. (Such a contradiction lies primarily in a concept, such as CAUSALITY, but it also infects propositions, such as 'The world is a causal order'.) Thinking, or the thought itself, has an impulse (*Trieb*) to overcome the contradiction. It often attempts to do so, initially, by resorting to an INFINITE regress (e.g. of causes and effects), but the appropriate solution is to move to a new, higher concept, which is intrinsically related to the first and removes the contradiction in it. The new concept usually involves a contradiction of its own, and so thought proceeds by successively revealing and overcoming contradictions, until it arrives at the (infinite) absolute IDEA, which is free of the sort of contradiction that generates further movement. The absolute idea is appropriate for the conceptualization of entities, such as God, that elude the rigid conceptions of the UNDERSTANDING. It, and the claims licensed by it (e.g. that God is both a GROUND and a consequence, that he is mediated but sublates his MEDIATION into immediacy), *seem* contradictory to the understanding, but this is because the understanding isolates aspects of the absolute idea in ways that have been shown to be illegitimate.

Traditional logicians, notably Kant, excluded the possibility of *objective* contradictions. But Hegel argued that finite things, like finite thoughts, involve contradictions. Just as finite thoughts have an impulse to overcome contradiction, and thus move on to other thoughts, so finite things have such an impulse that leads them to move and change. But finite things, unlike the MIND, cannot sustain contradictions: they ultimately perish. The world as a whole, by contrast, does not perish, since it is free of the contradictory finitude of the entities that it embraces.

Hence the law of contradiction is a 'law of thought' neither in the sense that contradictions are unthinkable (or unintelligible) nor in the sense that contradictions cannot occur in the world. Hegel accepts it only in so far as he holds that contradictions, both objective and subjective, must be overcome, and that a contradictory thought or entity is not *true* (in Hegel's sense of 'true').

Hegel saw the contradictions that he postulated in thoughts and in things as contradictions in the traditional sense. But there is room for doubt whether this is so. He occasionally flatly rejects notions, such as that of a 'composite concept', by describing them not as contradictory, but as 'wooden iron' (viz. a 'square circle' or a contradiction in terms). In the Logic, his account of contradiction follows those of DIFFERENCE and of opposition, suggesting that he sees a contradiction as an intense opposition: no formal logician need deny that the world contains intense oppositions. Moreover, his examples, especially of objective contradictions, often bear little resemblance to formal logical contradictions. Objective contradictions are, for the most part, inner conflicts produced by a thing's entanglements with other things. Subjective contradictions are often the result of an attempt to keep distinct concepts, such as those of cause and of effect, that are conceptually interdependent. But occasionally a finite, truncated conceptual system gives rise to a more interesting 'contradiction': if I deploy only terms for determinate qualities belonging to ranges whose members are mutually exclusive (e.g. red, green, etc.; flat, round, etc.), then, since I am aware, both simultaneously and successively, of several such qualities, I can describe *myself* or my own consciousness in such terms only contradictorily (e.g. 'I am both red and green (and *neither* red *nor* green'); to avoid this, I must introduce, as Hegel does in the Logic, the concept of being FOR ITSELF, which transcends the determinacy of *Dasein* ('DETERMINATE BEING').

Subjective contradictions are thus more palatable than objective ones. But for Hegel both are intrinsically interdependent. There is, on his view, no sharp distinction between thought and the world. Thoughts and concepts are embedded in the world, and many of the concepts reserved by traditional logic for the description of our thought and discourse – 'NEGATION', 'truth', 'JUDGMENT', 'INFERENCE', etc. – have, for Hegel, an objective sense in which they are applicable to things. That finite things embody finite concepts and their contradictions is thus a central feature of Hegel's IDEALISM. (The traditional view that a contradictory proposition entails any proposition whatsoever, often advanced in criticism of Hegel, is now rejected by 'relevance logic'.)

Critical Journal of Philosophy (Kritisches Journal der Philosophie)

(CJP) The intellectual ferment of the late eighteenth century gave rise to several periodicals edited by distinguished figures: Fichte and F. I. Niethammer edited the *Philosophical Journal* (1795–1800); Schiller edited *Die Horen* (*The Seasons*) (1795–7); and A. W. and F. Schlegel edited the *Athenäum* (1798–1800). The *CJP* was Schelling's conception. He originally hoped to edit it with Fichte, but when Fichte, owing to his awareness of differences between himself and Schelling (especially after Schelling's *STI*) rejected the suggestion, Schelling recruited Hegel (in August 1801) as co-editor of the journal. Hegel, who had come to Jena early in 1801, was then virtually unknown. But the appearance in August 1801 of his first book, *DFS*, initiated the serious discussion of the differences between Fichte and Schelling, and won Schelling's approval.

Kritik originally means 'assessment, judgment' and need not involve the exposure of faults. Kant contrasted *Kritik* and *Kritizismus*, the attempt to find the conditions, range and limits of our COGNITIVE powers, with *Dogmatismus*, the assumption that reason alone, by means of mere concepts, can arrive at knowledge of reality. A reader of *CJP* would naturally think of Kant's use of *kritisches*. But *CJP* is not critical in Kant's sense: it criticizes, for the most part, not our intellectual and practical faculties, but other philosophers, and it often criticizes them more in the sense of finding fault than of exposing their presuppositions and limitations. This is because the aim of Hegel (who wrote most of *CJP*) and Schelling was to clear away dross or 'unphilosophy' (*Unphilosophie*) as a preparation for genuine philosophy. The philosophies (and unphilosophies) criticized, such as Krug's common sense and Schulze's scepticism, are mostly developments of Kant's critical philosophy.

CJP appeared between January 1802 and June 1803 in two volumes each with three issues. The main contents are these:

1. 'Introduction. On the Essence of Philosophical Criticism in general and its Relation to the Present State of Philosophy in particular' (Hegel with revision by Schelling, I,1: January 1802). This explores the notion of the criticism of one philosopher by another, a crucial issue in view of the proliferation of philosophical systems in the wake of Kant. (Hegel compares it with the proliferation of philosophies in ancient Greece.) Criticism, it argues, presupposes a standard that is not simply that of the critic or that of the object of criticism. In the case of philosophy, such a standard is supplied by the 'IDEA of philosophy', of which a particular philosophy embodies a particular aspect. But unphilosophy (e.g. common sense masquerading as philosophy) and the philosophical critic have nothing in common to which both can appeal. Hence the criticism of unphilosophy is negative and polemical. Hegel also attacks the popularization of philosophy: 'Philosophy is by its very nature esoteric . . . It is only philosophy in virtue of being at odds with the UNDERSTANDING and still more with plain common sense (which amounts to the local and temporal limitations of a breed of men); in relation to common sense the world of philosophy is a wholly and intrinsically inverted world.' In later works, such as *PS*, Hegel is still troubled by the problem how one can criticize another view without begging the question. He continues to downgrade common sense and the understanding, but attempts to find a place for the understanding in his system and also for popular beliefs: e.g. he takes himself to be justifying the most developed of religions, Lutheranism.

2. 'On the System of Absolute Identity and its Relation to the most recent Dualism (Reinhold's)' (Schelling, I,1: January 1802).

3. 'How Plain Common Sense Takes Philosophy, as shown in the Works of Krug' (Hegel, I,1: 1802). Wilhelm Traugott Krug was a clear-headed Kantian of little originality and prodigious industry. In 1805 he succeeded Kant in the chair at Königsberg. He was a staunch liberal and wrote several pamphlets in support of the 1821 Greek uprising against the Turks. Thus in later works he criticized Hegel's dictum that everything ACTUAL is rational,

as well as predicting that if Hegel did not write more clearly he would soon cease to be read. *Krug* means 'jug, tankard', which gave Hegel an occasion for what Krug described as 'beer-bench humour'.

Hegel reviews three books by Krug: (1) *Letters on the Science of Knowledge* (1800), a critique of Fichte's idealism; (2) *Letters on the Latest Idealism* (1801), a critique of Schelling's *STI*; (3) *Sketch of a New Organon of Philosophy or Essay on the Principles of Philosophical Cognition* (1801), which argues for a system that is neither exclusively idealist, starting from the I*, nor exclusively realist, starting from the object, but both: we must set out from the 'facts (*Tatsachen*) of CONSCIOUSNESS', which embraces both SUBJECT and OBJECT. The most interesting episodes in the review relate to (2):

(a) Krug challenged Schelling to 'deduce' the moon, a rose, etc., or even the pen he was writing with. Hegel replies that the moon can be deduced, in the philosophy of NATURE, in the context of the whole solar system. But he gives no satisfactory response to the problem of the pen. In *PS*, he argues (against SENSORY CERTAINTY, but probably with Krug in mind) that philosophy is not concerned with, since it cannot uniquely refer to, an individual entity. (Any pen may be referred to as 'this pen'.) But even if this argument were sound, the questions would remain whether Hegel (or Schelling) is, or should be, able to deduce pens in general, and if not, why not.

(b) Krug cannot conceive of 'an action or activity without a BEING [*Sein*, viz. a substratum]', which the idealist concept of the I involves.

(c) Krug fails to see that 'philosophical REFLECTION' involves the 'supersession (or SUBLATION) and retention of CONSCIOUSNESS in a single act'.

3. 'Relation of Scepticism to Philosophy, Exposition of its different Modifications and Comparison of the Latest with the Ancient Version' (Hegel, I,2: March 1802). This is a review of G. E. Schulze's *Critique of Theoretical Philosophy* (1801). Schulze had adopted the name of an ancient sceptic for his *Aenesidemus or On the Foundations of K. L. Reinhold's 'Elements of Philosophy', with a Defence of Scepticism against the Presumptions of the Critique of Reason* (1792). (This was reviewed by Fichte.) Schulze's SCEPTICISM persists in the later work, which gives an historical account of scepticism and a clear-headed critique of post-Cartesian philosophy, especially Kant's system. His scepticism concerns PHILOSOPHY rather than everyday perceptual matters, and he presented an argument that vexed Hegel throughout his career: How can we rationally choose one among so many conflicting, but equally well-justified and coherent, philosophies? Hegel criticizes (not always correctly) Schulze's account of ancient scepticism, and argues that it is superior to the modern version, since it is more thoroughly sceptical, extending to the 'facts of consciousness', as well as to philosophy. In 1810, Schulze took up the chair at Göttingen, where he taught philosophy to Schopenhauer.

4. 'Ruckert and Weiss, or the Philosophy that requires no Thought or Knowledge' (Schelling, I,2: March 1802).

5. 'On the Relation of Philosophy of Nature to Philosophy in general' (Schelling, possibly with help from Hegel, I,3: printed Spring, issued Nov./Dec. 1802).

6. 'On Construction in Philosophy' (Schelling, I,3).

7. 'Faith and Knowledge [*Wissen*] or the Reflective Philosophy of Subjectivity in the Entirety of its Forms as Kant's, Jacobi's, and Fichte's Philosophy' (Hegel, II,1: July 1802). This long essay concerns the conflict between FAITH and reason in the ALIENATED CULTURE of the time and its reflection in philosophy. Hegel is far more respectful of Kant, Jacobi and Fichte than of Krug and Schulze. His account of Kant is more subtle and sympathetic than his later accounts.

8. 'On the Scientific Ways of Treating Natural Right, its Place in Practical Philosophy and its Relation to the Positive Sciences of Right' (Hegel, II,2: Nov./Dec. 1802, continued in II,3: May/June 1803). In this long essay, Hegel argues against the atomistic and egalitarian liberal conception of human nature. He constructs a tripartite organic STATE on the model of Plato's *Republic*. The ETHICAL LIFE of the nation is distinguished from private individual MORALITY: 'The absolute ethical whole is nothing more, and nothing less, than the nation [i.e. not the individual].'

9. 'On Dante with Respect to Philosophy' (Schelling, May/June 1803).

CJP ceased publication owing to Schelling's departure from Jena in May 1803. Other possible factors in its demise were the editors' growing awareness of their differences and the fact that Hegel's longer pieces, 7 and 8, transcend the polemical aim of the journal. But *CJP* had served its purpose of enabling Hegel to come to grips with contemporary philosophy and to develop some of the themes and concepts that reappear in *PS*. He was influenced more than he acknowledged by the philosophers he attacks, not only by the problems they posed for his solution (he returns to Krug's pen in *Enc*. III §250), but also by their positive doctrines: e.g. *PS*'s account of the development of consciousness, together with its objects, bears some resemblance to the programme of Krug's *Sketch for a New Organon of Philosophy*.

culture and education   German has two common words for 'to educate' and 'education': *bilden* and *erziehen*, and *Bildung* and *Erziehung*. *Bilden* also means 'to form, shape, fashion, cultivate', and, earlier, *Bildung* denoted only the physical formation of an entity; in the eighteenth century J. Moser gave it the sense of 'education, cultivation, culture', both as a process and as a result. But *bilden* and *Bildung* stress the result of education, *erziehen* and *Erziehung* the process. Thus *Erziehung*, unlike *Bildung*, does not mean 'culture'.

Hegel's interest in culture and education has several sources:

1. Rousseau's *Emile or On Education* (1762), which sees proper education as the removal of obstacles to the natural development of a child's abilities, especially by isolating it from ordinary civilized life, had a great impact on German thought. Against Rousseau, Hegel argued that education involves overcoming nature and making 'the ETHICAL [*das Sittliche*] into the individual's second nature'. He endorses a Pythagorean's advice on education: 'Make him a citizen of a state with good laws' (*PR* §153).

2. The defeat of Prussia by France in 1806–7 led to a movement for educational reform. Fichte, in *AGN*, proposed a wide-ranging plan for

educational reform as a remedy for national humiliation and disunity. Fichte derived some of his ideas – especially on education as a socially regenerative force – from the Swiss educationalist, J. H. Pestalozzi. Schelling also made a contribution to this debate in *On University Studies* (1803).

3. The interest of Herder and others in language as the vehicle of a national culture merged with a long-standing movement for the development and use of German as a language of literature, science and scholarship. Fichte was not alone in proposing the extrusion of foreign loan-words, such as *Humanität*, from German, to make the Germans a fully cultivated PEOPLE (*gebildete Volk*). Hegel tolerated well-established loan-words, but shared the aim of cultivating the Germans.

4. This movement achieved one of its aims in the creation, especially by Goethe and Schiller, of a literature comparable to that of other European nations. One popular genre was the *Bildungsroman*, the novel of culture or education, in which the protagonist acquires an education in a series of experiences and encounters. The masterpiece of the genre is Goethe's *Wilhelm Meisters Lehrjahre* (*Wilhelm Meister's Apprenticeship*, 1795–6); Novalis's *Henry von Ofterding* (1802) is a lesser example. The *Bildungsroman* influenced, and was influenced by, philosophical works, which often had a similar form and purpose: Novalis studied Fichte's *SKW*; and Hegel's *PS*, which bears some resemblance to *Wilhelm Meister* (e.g. both works give an account of the 'beautiful SOUL' (*schöne Seele*)), is a 'history of the *Bildung* of consciousness to science' (*PS*, Preface).

5. Growing historical awareness led to an interest in different cultures or *Bildungen*, and also to the idea that mankind as a whole has undergone (and is still undergoing) a process of education comparable to that of an individual. Lessing's *EHR* argued that religion played a crucial part in this education, and that 'revelation is to the whole human race what education [*Erziehung*] is to the individual man' (§1). Schiller assigned a similar role to art in *AE*, and anticipates Hegel's view that culture involves ALIENATION and OPPOSITION: 'The only way to develop the manifold potentialities in man was to set them in opposition to each other. This antagonism of forces is the great instrument of culture [*Kultur*]' (*AE*, VI).

Hegel was a teacher and, as such, mildly, but not excessively, interested in the process and technique of education. He was a historian, who saw the development of culture(s) as essentially, if circuitously, progressive. And he was a philosopher, aware of the cultural presuppositions of philosophy, and of the cultural context and significance of his own thought. His view of education and culture, whether of an individual, a people, or mankind as a whole, differs from both the Enlightenment and from Goethe's classical humanism. For the Enlightenment, education is a smooth, unilinear perfection of the individual and of society by the gradual supplanting of FAITH by reason. For Goethe education is a similarly regular shaping of the individual towards an ideal of aesthetic harmony. Hegel, by contrast, saw education (and DEVELOPMENT in general) as a progression from a stage of primitive, natural unity to a stage of alienation and estrangement, and then to a stage of harmonious reconciliation (*Versöhnung*). The Enlightenment contrast of faith

69

and reason is itself a feature of alienation, which is to be overcome in the stage of reconciliation.

Thus in his Nuremberg speech of 29 September 1809, Hegel argues that education involves an estrangement of the mind from its 'natural essence and state', and this is best achieved by the study of the ancient world and its languages. These are sufficiently alien to 'separate' us from our natural state, but sufficiently close to our own language and world for us to 'find ourselves again (*wiederfinden*)' in them, no longer ourselves in our natural state, but 'in conformity with the genuine, universal essence of the mind'. We become reconciled too to our own language and world, but now with a deeper appreciation of its structure and significance. (Hegel also stresses that states that neglect the 'inner citadel in the soul of their citizens' and seek only profit and utility are liable to decay and destruction.) This pattern of estrangement from a natural unity, and later reconciliation with it, occurs at every phase of education: The infant's self-absorption is disrupted by its awareness of an external world, which, at first strange and alien, becomes increasingly familiar with further exploration. Its natural inclinations are subjected to ethical and social norms, which, at first alien and repressive, eventually become a second nature. The study of logic alienates us from the familiar (*bekannte*) forms of our native tongue, but we return to them with an enriched understanding. The youth loses the child's naive contentment with his social environment and rebels against it; he is eventually reconciled to it in a more reflective contentment. The disruption of primitive unity is often harsh and difficult, and requires effort and discipline (*Zucht*). But the end-product, the cultivated man, though he has fully absorbed the culture of his society, has more independence of thought and action than the child or the youth owing to his stock of 'universal conceptions'.

The education of a people or of mankind as a whole, by contrast, has no established IDEAL of the culture to be achieved and no external educator to raise them towards such an ideal. It depends on teachers, such as Luther, who themselves belong to the people and to mankind, and on the inner DIALECTIC of thought and SELF-CONSCIOUSNESS. But it too follows the pattern of simple unity – estrangement – reconciliation. The culture of the Greeks was, on Hegel's view as on Schiller's, relatively harmonious. But the later development of culture generated a variety of estrangements and oppositions, between the individual and his society, between wealth and power, between faith and reason, and so on. *DFS* and *FK* argue that these oppositions require a philosophy that will resolve them, a philosophy that Hegel later attempted to supply.

D

death and immortality Death was a topic of vital interest in Hegel's Germany. Some of the ROMANTICS, especially Kleist and Novalis, saw death as inextricably intertwined with LIFE, and one's death as the supreme climax of one's life. Belief in immortality was widespread among sober philosophers such as Mendelssohn, who reworked the arguments for immortality presented in Plato's *Phaedo*, as well as more exuberant thinkers such as Herder, who endorsed the doctrines of palingenesis or reincarnation (*Wiederentstehung*) and metempsychosis (*Seelenwanderung*). Kant regarded immortality not as a theoretically sustainable doctrine, but as a 'postulate of pure practical reason': since our will cannot become wholly adequate to the moral law in this life, it must become so by a progress to INFINITY, which requires eternal life. In a similar, though less egalitarian, vein, Goethe argued that great men (such as himself) cannot expect their activity to be cut short by death: nature must provide for its continuance in an afterlife. Another feature of the period is a growing awareness that attitudes to death vary over HISTORY. Lessing argued, in *HARD*, that the Greeks feared death less than moderns do: they represented death not as a skeleton, but as a benign spirit, the 'brother of sleep'. In *HARD2*, Herder responded that such benign portrayals of death were the Greeks' attempt to cope with their fear of it. But he broadly supported Lessing's view, as did Schiller in his poem 'The Gods of Greece'. In his Bern writings Hegel too argued that the ancients were less afraid of death, and that this derives from their close identification with the city-state.

In these early writings, Hegel tended to contrast death (*Tod*) and the dead (*das Tote*) sharply with life and the living, especially in metaphorical characterizations of, e.g., the Jewish law as 'dead' in contrast to the 'living' love and FAITH advocated by Christ. But later he came to regard death and the confrontation with death as an essential ingredient of life itself: death is SUBLATED in life. This is apparent in his metaphorical uses of 'death' in, e.g., the Preface to *PS*: the philosopher must take account of the 'dead' ABSTRACTIONS of the UNDERSTANDING, and not simply discard them, since 'the life of the spirit is not the life that shies at death and keeps clear of devastation, but the life that endures death and maintains itself in it.' It is apparent also in his literal treatment of death. Like the STOICS, especially Seneca, Hegel, both in *NL* and in *Enc.* III, saw man's capacity to die as conferring on him a FREEDOM from compulsion that he would otherwise lack. In *PS*, IV.A., the combatant in the struggle for RECOGNITION displays and confirms his SELF-CONSCIOUSNESS, his bare self-awareness in contrast to the contingencies of life and existence, by his risk of death, and subsequently the defeated slave derives a similar benefit from his fear of death at the hands of his master.

In *PS*, *LA* and *LPR*, Hegel regards death and the rites associated with it as conferring a significant *universality* on the mundane life of the dead individual. An apparent exception to this is the 'terror' of the French Revolution, the 'meaningless [*bedeutungslose*] death, the pure terror of the negative, that contains nothing positive, nothing that fills it out'. Hegel regards the guillotine as the only resolution of the conflict that afflicted revolutionary France, between the 'universal WILL' and self-enclosed, atomic individuals: 'The sole work and deed of universal freedom is therefore death, and indeed a death that has no inner depth and filling; for what is negated is the unfilled point of the absolutely free self; it is thus the coldest, tritest of deaths, with no more significance than cutting off a head of cabbage or taking a gulp of water.' But first, this bare, pointless death is appropriate to the bare individuals who succumb to it. And second, the fear of this death, the 'absolute lord', makes possible both the restoration of a differentiated order that followed the revolution in France, and the turn to Kantian MORALITY that emerged in Germany. Death is sublated into life.

Hegel was especially interested in the dramatic deaths of great men. Hölderlin had been engrossed by the death of Empedocles, who was reputed to have thrown himself into the crater of Etna to give the impression that he had risen up among the gods – a plan that was betrayed by the emergence of one of his shoes from the volcano. But Hegel was primarily concerned with the deaths of Christ and of Socrates. (Socrates' enigmatic last words, 'We owe a cock to Asclepius' – that is, we owe an offering to the god of healing for the cure effected by death of our bodily affliction – fascinated Hegel from his schooldays.) To the unbeliever, these deaths are similar: a martyr's death unjustly inflicted on a wise man. But Christ's death, Hegel argues, has a theological and metaphysical significance that Socrates' death lacks. It presents in an intuitive form the reconciliation of the dichotomy between God and the world. On the one hand, God appears in a finite form and undergoes a painful death, which reveals that God himself involves FINITUDE and NEGATION. On the other hand, his undergoing and then overcoming death – to which all men are subject – shows that man's SPIRIT can triumph over death, his finite and contingent individuality being sublated or trans-figured into godlike universality. Hegel anticipates Nietzsche in saying 'God is dead' (the words also occur in a Lutheran hymn, '*O Traurigkeit, O Herzeleid*' (O sorrowing, O heartfelt sadness), by Johann Rist), but adds that God's survival of death is the 'death of death'. 'Death' refers here *both* to death in the literal sense and its significance for our lives, *and* to the 'negative' in general, the death of death standing for the 'negation of the negation', which spirit is. Spirit involves the overcoming or sublation of our natural and immediate will and consciousness – an overcoming which is both a metapho-rical death and in part effected by the prospect of actual death; but the SUBJECTIVE spirit survives this 'death' to ascend to the essential universality of OBJECTIVE spirit (social and political life) and ABSOLUTE spirit (art, religion and philosophy) – the death of death.

Hegel's account of Christ's death suggests that he believed men to be immortal. He gives some space, in *LPR*, to the immortality of the SOUL (*Seele*) in non-Christian religions, affirming that their views of God and of immortality go hand in hand. He says, in *LPR*, that the spirit (*Geist*) is immortal, but adds that it is not of endless duration, as mountains are, but eternal. Otherwise, Hegel barely mentions immortality, and, even if he believed in it, plainly had little interest in it. Some of his followers, e.g. C. F. Göschel (in *On the Proofs of Immortality*, 1835) and McTaggart, argue that individual immortality is a consequence of Hegel's system; but others, such as Feuerbach (in *Thoughts on Death and Immortality*, 1830) and Kojève, argue that it is at odds with his system. (Kojève accepts Hegel's linking of God with immortality and argues that Hegel rejects both, while Feuerbach agrees with McTaggart that God and immortality are distinct issues, and argues that personal immortality conflicts with Hegel's theism.)

There are several reasons for doubting that individual immortality is compatible with Hegel's system:

1. Hegel did not (like McTaggart) believe TIME to be unreal, but he suggests that atemporal ETERNITY (*Ewigkeit*) is in some sense prior to time and that the essence of things is eternal rather than temporal. But if men survive death, what survives is usually regarded as what is essential to them. This, on Hegel's view, will be eternal rather than of endless duration. But genuine immortality requires persistence in time rather than durationless eternity. The immortality in the sense of eternity that Hegel claims for spirit amounts only to man's ability to abstract from his spatio-temporal position and study such non-temporal subjects as logic, and to the universal, spiritual significance that a person achieves by his death.

2. Significant and valuable immortality is excluded by Hegel's aversion to bad INFINITY. A life cannot acquire import from the indefinite postponement of its ending, but only from a significant ending, an ending that raises the life, with all its individual contingencies, to spiritual universality. This involves not only the death itself, but the funeral rites and memorials by which the living (e.g. Antigone, Achilles) honour their dead (e.g. Polyneikes, Patroklos).

3. On Hegel's view, conflict and OPPOSITION are required to keep human beings alive and awake: SELF-CONSCIOUSNESS emerges from conflict; men die when they become too contented with their environment; nations die when they are reluctant to wage WAR; and perpetual peace among states would mean the death of the STATE. If there is a Hegelian afterlife, it must involve more conflict than the traditional Christian heaven.

4. A person's death is, on Hegel's view, deeply connected with the course of his life: a person is responsible for his death, not only if he dies of sophisticated contentment with his surroundings, but even if he dies of an apparently contingent illness or accident. (This depends in part on his belief that CAUSES cannot have an effect on healthy living or spiritual creatures. He also argues that the death of states or societies is invariably the result of internal decline rather than of external impacts.) Death completes one's life;

it does not cut short a flourishing life or prevent one from doing things, since one dies only when one has nothing more to do. And nothing more to do in an afterlife, either.

5. On most views of it, the afterlife is not a simple continuation of this life, but releases us from dependence on material factors, and gives us more free space for our activities – thought, love, moral improvement, etc. Hegel rejects this sharp contrast between the material and the spiritual realms. The material realm and our dependence on it is sublated and idealized by the realms of objective and of absolute spirit, which mediate the sharp dichotomy between soul and body, or reason and desire, characteristic of Platonic and of Kantian philosophy. Spirit is not hampered by matter and has, in this life, all the free play required for its activities.

6. Personal immortality presupposes that an individual is sufficiently distinct from its social context, for its survival outside that (and perhaps any other) social context to be conceivable, valuable and significant. Hegel was not an individualist. Such subjective FREEDOM as he allows must be embedded in a culture and overseen by a state if it is to be meaningful or valuable. Detached from all society, one would be barely human – unable to think, speak or act in a recognizably human way. Thus the survival of a human being bereft of all trace or memory of a human society is hardly desirable or even intelligible.

7. Hegel's historicism is at odds with immortality. His doctrine that no one can leap beyond his age, which forbids us to speak in any detail, whether prophetically or prescriptively, about the future, would also exclude significant discourse about an afterlife. A person is too deeply embedded in and moulded by his historical situation to be reincarnated into a different historical situation or to persist outside HISTORY in a community of pure spirits. He allows the possibility of *pure* THINKING, in which I* ABSTRACT myself from my historical and social context in order to engage in logic, in timeless thought about the nature of things. But in doing so, I lose all sense of myself as a distinct individual whose survival is possible or desirable. What matters for Hegel is the persistence not of individuals, but of the interpersonal structures of objective and of absolute SPIRIT, to which individuals make their contribution and then die when they have no more to offer.

definition   Kant complained that the 'German language has only one word for the [Latinate] terms *Exposition, Explikation, Deklaration* and *Definition*: *Erklärung* (*CPR* B758). Wolff used *Erklärung* (from *erklären*, 'to clarify, explain, declare') to translate the latinate *Definition*, but the word is also used for 'EXPLANATION'. Hegel regularly reserves *Erklärung* for 'explanation', and for 'definition' uses *Definition* or, occasionally, *Bestimmung* ('DETERMINATION').

Hegel discusses definition explicitly in two main contexts: First, he argues that the 'determinations' or 'categories' considered in the Logic (or at least the first and third member of each TRIAD) may be seen as 'definitions of the ABSOLUTE, as metaphysical definitions of God', e.g. BEING supplies the definition 'The absolute (or God) is being' (*Enc.* I §§85, 86). (He regards this way of viewing the categories as misleading, since the terms 'God' and 'the absolute' are either empty, and given a sense only by the predicate of the definitional PROPOSITION, or they carry over into logic the pictorial REPRESEN-TATIONS usually associated with them.) A definition in this sense is not a definition of the expression 'God' or 'the absolute', but a specification of it in terms of THOUGHT.

Second, he considers definition, in *SL*, as the first stage of 'synthetic COGNITION'. (The other two stages are CLASSIFICATION and the theorem (*Lehrsatz*)). Here he considers the definition of three types of entity:

1. *Artefacts* can be defined straightforwardly in terms of the PURPOSE (*Zweck*) for which they are intended and of the features required for the fulfilment of this purpose.

2. Mathematical entities are abstractions produced by us and can be defined in terms of what we put into them. Hegel, unlike Kant, regards a definition such as 'A straight line is the shortest distance between two points' as a *stipulative* definition and thus as an analytic proposition.

3. CONCRETE natural and spiritual entities are more problematic. Their definition, on the view of cognition that Hegel is presenting, involves three elements: (a) the genus, or the UNIVERSAL element; (b) the specific difference, or the PARTICULAR element; and (c) the object itself, the INDIVIDUAL element, which lies outside the definition, but instantiates the genus and the specific difference. Tetens had anticipated Wittgenstein in objecting, in *On the Origin of Languages and Writing* (1772), pp. 52–3, that many words are not open to such a definition, since there is no single feature common and peculiar to, say, all species of animal; different animal species resemble each other, but in different respects. Hegel does not raise this objection, in part because he is thinking of an empirical scientist's attempt to form concepts of the objects he encounters, rather than of the definition of established words. The problem is rather that, initially at least, we lack any criterion for selecting as the specific difference of a species a feature that is essential, a feature, that is, on which the overall character of the species depends, and we typically choose some relatively superficial distinguishing mark, on the strength of its possession by all or most members of the species, and its persistence throughout their careers. Hegel concludes that such a definition, especially in view of the occurrence of deformed and defective individuals that lack the distinguishing mark of their species, cannot justify the 'NECESSITY' of its content.

Kant held that philosophical definitions cannot, like biological definitions, proceed by genus and differentia, nor, like mathematical definitions, construct a concept; they give an analysis and exposition or explanation (*Erklärung*) of an already existing concept. It follows, he argued, that, unlike mathematics, philosophers should not, like Spinoza, begin with definitions: the final definitions come at the end, not at the beginning (*CPR* B758–9). Hegel agrees with this in some respects, but not in others:

(1) Most philosophical CONCEPTS are not susceptible to definition by genus and differentia.

(2) Even if such a definition is possible, it does not show the 'necessity' of the concept or of the definition given of it.

(3) This can be shown only by deriving or 'deducing' the concept from other concepts, as, e.g., the concept of RECIPROCITY is derived from that of CAUSALITY.

(4) But the account of such a concept does not *conclude* with a clear definition of it, since the concept evolves throughout Hegel's treatment of it and eventually passes over into a different concept, as causality passes over into reciprocity. The definition of the concept is the account of the whole course of its DEVELOPMENT rather than any single phase of it. Hegel was also loath to begin his Logic with a definition of logic, believing that such a definition would amount only to a survey of current CONCEPTIONS (*Vorstellungen*) of logic. To find out what logic (or, for that matter, mathematics) is, we must follow the course of it. Consistently with this, he argued that the definitions (and axioms) with which Spinoza's *Ethics* begins do not become intelligible until we see what is derived from them.

(5) Philosophy neither constructs its concepts nor analyses pre-given concepts. It does not analyse an established conception or assess its account of a concept by its conformity to such a conception, to etymology or to the 'facts of consciousness' (viz. intuitive self-evidence – the phrase was popular at the time, especially with J. F. Fries). It simply shows the degree of conformity to common conceptions of such concepts as it derives and 'reconstructs'.

In a discussion of definition in *PR* §2, Hegel notes that Roman jurists warned that 'every definition is dangerous', since a clear definition of a concept may expose the 'CONTRADICTORY' features of existing institutions. A definition of man, e.g., would either (improbably) exclude slaves from the scope of the concept or else reveal that slaves, though men, were treated in ways that contravene the concept of man. This coheres with Hegel's view that a concept, and thus a definition, does not simply record the features common to everything that falls under it. Things, e.g. a slave, often fall short of the concept, e.g. that of a man, that primarily applies to them. While a fully fledged man is free FOR HIMSELF, a slave is free only IN HIMSELF. An ancient defender of slavery, such as Aristotle, would have replied that some men are 'natural slaves', since they think only at a low level and thus do not fulfil the qualification for full humanity, viz. rational thought: a degenerate member of a type need not receive the treatment appropriate to its non-degenerate members. To this Hegel might respond: (1) It is unlikely that any existing system of slavery enslaved all those, and only those, who are, on Aristotle's account, natural slaves; (2) there are no natural slaves, since (our capacity for) thought is intrinsically developing and cannot be frozen by nature at a low level; but (3) since slaves may, owing to circumstances, think only at a low level – and also because of Hegel's reluctance to criticize ACTUALITY – (1) and (2) do not entail that slavery, whenever and wherever it exists, OUGHT to be abolished at a stroke. It is not clear that definitions *alone* are as dangerous as the jurists believed.

Hegel's view of definition can be usefully compared with Nietzsche's remark on PUNISHMENT: 'all concepts in which a whole process is semiotically concentrated elude definition.'

determination and determinateness   The verb *bestimmen* originally meant 'to name, designate, establish with the voice (*Stimme*)', hence 'to fix, arrange'. It has a variety of ordinary senses: to fix, settle, appoint, decide (on) (e.g. a price), induce ('The weather induced me to stay indoors'), determine ('The space available will determine the number of guests'), ordain (of a power or law), define (a concept), destine, intend (e.g. a person for an office). In eighteenth-century logic, it came to mean 'to determine' in the sense of delimiting, demarcating or defining a concept by giving the features that distinguish it from other concepts. In Fichte's *SKW*, the I* POSITS itself as determined or affected (*bestimmt*) by the non-I, and the non-I as determined by the I. The theoretical *Wissenschaftslehre* is based on the first of these positions, the practical *Wissenschaftslehre* on the second.

The past participle, *bestimmt*, is also used as an adjective or adverb, 'determinate(ly), definite(ly), specific(ally)', but with a range of senses corresponding roughly to those of the verb. This gives rise to the noun *Bestimmtheit*, 'determinedness, determinacy, definiteness', what distinguishes a thing or concept from any other thing or concept. But it refers ambiguously either to the fact that something is determinate (e.g. the fact that (the concept of) a vertebrate is determinate in contrast to (that of) an animal) or to the feature in virtue of which it is determinate (e.g. having a backbone).

The (seventeenth-century) noun *Bestimmung* denotes both the process of determining something (in all senses of *bestimmen*) and the result of the process. (In the latter sense *Bestimmung* is often hard to distinguish from *Bestimmtheit* in the sense of a 'determinate feature'.) But *Bestimmung* has another ambiguity, and has two broad meanings:

1. 'Determination', in such senses as (a) 'delimitation, DEFINITION'; (b) making a concept or a thing more determinate by adding features to it, or the feature(s) so added; (c) finding out the position of something; (d) (in the plural) legal provisions or regulations. The addition of *selbst* ('self') gives *Selbstbestimmung*, 'self-determination', the autonomous DEVELOPMENT or operation of something, e.g. the WILL, in contrast to its determination by external forces. (*Bestimmung*, like other *bestimmen* words, never means 'resoluteness' or 'fixity of purpose'.)

2. 'Destination, destiny, calling, vocation'. To have a *Bestimmung* for high office, a person must not only be on the way to or aiming at high office, but also designed for it, so that achievement of the goal expresses his true NATURE. The '*Bestimmung* of man' is thus the final PURPOSE or *destiny* of man in general, which confers meaning on his existence. Several works of the period bore this title, most notably Fichte's *VM*. *Bestimmung* thus has religious undertones.

Hegel uses *bestimmen* words throughout his works, and in a variety of contexts and senses. In *SL*, '*Bestimmtheit* (*Qualität*)' is the title of the first section of the 'Doctrine of BEING'; here *Bestimmtheit* is a general term for 'qualitative determinacy', in contrast to 'QUANTITY' and to 'MEASURE', the titles respectively of the second and third sections. Hegel endorses Spinoza's claim that 'determination is NEGATION' (Spinoza, Letter 50), that is, that a thing or concept is determinate only in virtue of a contrast with other things or concepts, which are determined in a way that it is not. (In a typical move, Hegel argues that the indeterminacy (*Unbestimmtheit*) of being, with which the section begins, is itself a sort of determinacy, since being's indeterminacy contrasts with, and distinguishes it from, the determinacy of QUALITY.)

In this section, Hegel distinguishes the terms *Bestimmtheit*, *Bestimmung* and *Beschaffenheit* ('condition, quality, constitution, the way a thing is created or made'). His discussion is complex, in part because he is attempting to combine both main senses of *Bestimmung* in a single concept. The connection of *Bestimmtheit* with negation nevertheless allows us to distinguish between what a thing is IN ITSELF (*an sich*) and what it is *in it* (*an ihm*), that is, between its INNER nature or potentiality and its OUTER, explicit qualities, which are both *its* qualities and its RELATIONS to other things, revealing its inner nature to other things and enabling it to interact with them, e.g., a man is *an sich* thinking, that is, he has inner thoughts (or perhaps the capacity for thought). Conceived just as *an sich*, thinking is the *Bestimmtheit* of man: it is what distinguishes him from other creatures. But if *an sich* thinking is conceived as something that should be and is *an ihm*, expressed in thoughtful discourse and conduct, then thinking is the *Bestimmung* of man, a *Bestimmung* that may or may not be fulfilled (*erfüllen*, ambiguously 'fill' and 'fulfil'). The fulfilled *Bestimmung*, overtly rational conduct, is also a *Bestimmtheit*, but it is so solely in virtue of its determinate existence and not in virtue of its relationship to the inner state or potentiality.

A man also has many features which depend not on his inner nature, but on his 'natural' and 'sensory' aspects and on his contingent encounters with other things. These are his *Beschaffenheit*, his superficial and variable features in contrast to his unvarying inner nature. They are too, in a general sense, a *Bestimmtheit*, but not, initially at least, his *Bestimmung*. But the fulfilment of his *Bestimmung* involves the absorption of his *Beschaffenheit* into it: a man can imbue his natural and sensory aspects with thought, and to some extent control his encounters with other entities or make use of them for his own rational purposes.

Hegel also relates the distinction between *Bestimmtheit* and *Bestimmung* to two uses of 'real (*reell*)' and 'REALITY': a 'real man' is both something that, in contrast to, say, a statue, has the defining features or *Bestimmtheit* of a man, and a man who fulfils the *Bestimmung* (or CONCEPT) of a man, namely one who thinks and acts rationally.

Not only men have a *Bestimmung*: The *Bestimmung* of FINITE things (in contrast to man) is their end. The *Bestimmung*, e.g., of an acid, in contrast to its current *Bestimmtheit*, is to be neutralized by an alkali. In particular, Hegel's usual term for the concepts considered in the Logic is *Bestimmungen* or *Denkbestimmungen* ('THOUGHT-determinations'). The primary sense of this term is that these are ways in which thought determines itself, in contrast to remaining indeterminate. But a secondary sense, which Hegel occasionally exploits, is that such a thought-determination is *destined* to pass into another thought-determination. *Bestimmung* is often equivalent to 'concept (*Begriff*)': if something (including a thought-determination) fulfils its *Bestimmung*, it also fulfils its concept. But 'concept' is often contrasted with *Bestimmtheit*; e.g., *LPR* opens with the *concept* of religion, proceeds to determinate (*bestimmte*) religion, that is, specific historical religions, and concludes with complete or consummate (*vollendete*) RELIGION, viz. Christianity. The concept is relatively indeterminate, but its *Bestimmung* is to determine itself, and finally to return to its initial UNIVERSALITY, enriched by the determinacy acquired on its journey.

development The usual word for 'development' is *Entwicklung*, from the verb (*sich*) *entwickeln* ('to unravel, unfold, develop (itself), evolve, explain', etc.), but *Entfaltung* ('unfolding') is also used. Until the eighteenth century, it applied primarily to the logical activity of unfolding or explicating a concept, so as to reveal its content, scope and relationships to other concepts. But it was also used to express the Neoplatonist conception that the world is the self-development or self-unfolding of God. In the Renaissance, development was conceived as the self-development or -unfolding of LIFE, both life as a whole and the life of an individual. All three strands of thought come together in Hegel and in such thinkers as Herder, Goethe, Schelling: development is conceived as (1) the self-unfolding of the divine in the world; (2) the self-development of life, especially human life, towards the divine; and (3) the development of our conception of the cosmic process involved in (1) and (2).

Hegel's main accounts of development appear in the Introductions to *LPH* (C.a) and *LHP* (A.2.a). As the word *Entwicklung* implies, the development of something involves the unfolding of its inner potentiality (the IN ITSELF) into explicit ACTUALITY (the FOR ITSELF). Thus Hegel's paradigm of development is the growth of a plant from a seed. A seed requires water, nutrition and sunlight if it is to develop into, e.g., a rose. But it is determinate and relatively self-developing, in that, given appropriate conditions, it becomes a rose and no variation in the conditions will make it become a geranium or a lion instead. The potentiality of a seed differs from that of a block of marble, which can be carved by a sculptor into a variety of shapes. The seed is thus implicitly CONCRETE, but Hegel rejects the theory of preformation, developed by Leibniz and Bonnet, and endorsed by Malebranche, according to which a seed or egg contains a complete organism, with all its parts, actual but invisible, so that its development consists only in the enlargement of these parts (*Enc.* I §161). (The theory was called *Einschachtelung, Emboîtement* or 'boxes-within-boxes', since it implies that any seed or egg contains the 'germs' of all future generations on an ever smaller scale.) One objection to this theory is that, by Hegel's account of MEASURE, the shape of an organism, and the relative sizes of its parts, cannot remain unaltered while its size varies. On Hegel's view, the seed develops from potentiality to actuality, since as merely potential it involves a CONTRADICTION and thus an impulse to develop. The final stage (the IN AND FOR ITSELF) is reached when the plant returns to its original simplicity by producing new seeds.

Nature as a whole does not, on Hegel's view, develop or evolve: its changes are periodic and repetitive. What evolves or develops, both as a whole and in the individual, is SPIRIT or MIND. Like a plant, it does so by moving from simple, but concrete, potentiality (the theory of innate IDEAS, like the preformation theory, is rejected by Hegel) to explicit actuality, and then returns to its simple state in 'coming to itself (*Zusich(selbst)kommen*)' and 'being at home with itself (*Beisichsein*)', a stage of SELF-CONSCIOUSNESS and FREEDOM. (The individual, like the plant, produces offspring, but this is only a secondary aspect of spirit's return to itself.) Spirit's development, unlike a plant's, involves ALIENATION, OPPOSITION and conflict. Spirit develops when it becomes for itself what it is in itself, but in the case of spirit, unlike the plant, this means that it becomes *aware* of what it is *implicitly*, e.g., man is FREE in himself or implicitly. But in antiquity many men were not actually free, but slaves. When men became aware that they were *implicitly* free, a conflict arose between this awareness and slavery, a conflict that was resolved eventually by the abolition of slavery, so that men were free both in and for themselves. The same TRIADIC process is repeated both in HISTORY and in the development of the individual.

Hegel believes that philosophical concepts develop out of each other in a similar way. The formal structure of this development is exhibited in the Logic, but the development also occurs over time in the history of philosophy: the logical IDEA unfolds by becoming for itself or aware, at any given stage, of what it implicitly or in itself was at the previous stage, and then resolving the conflict between the in itself and its awareness of it. This pattern, Hegel agrees, is not always easy to discern in logic and history, but it is his most general answer to the question why they develop.

Things develop, on Hegel's view, owing to a drive to realize their CONCEPT, and he often equates the 'in itself' of, e.g., a plant with its concept, encoded in the seed, which strives to realize itself in the plant. Thus in the Logic development is especially associated with the third phase, the Doctrine of the Concept. In the first phase, the Doctrine of BEING, categories 'pass over' (*übergehen*) into others; in the second phase, the Doctrine of ESSENCE, they 'shine' or APPEAR (*scheinen*) in(to) each other; but in the third phase, the concept *develops* by POSITING only what is already implicit in it (*Enc.* I §161A.). Thus while the logical idea as a whole develops, the relationship of a given logical category to other categories reflects the character of the things to which the category applies. For example, since a SUBSTANCE does not develop into its accidents, but appears or shines in(to) them, the category of substance similarly appears in that of an accident. But the logical *concept* develops, positing what is implicit in it, in a way corresponding to the development of an entity that embodies a concept, such as a seed. This twofold approach to the development of the logical idea reflects the double role that Hegel assigns to it: On the one hand, the logical idea is the concept embedded in the world as a whole, as well as in aspects of it such as the history of philosophy: as such, the logical idea as a whole develops. (At, e.g.,

Enc. I §114, being and essence are said to develop.) On the other hand, the logical idea involves various FINITE categories applicable to finite entities within the world: as such, only the categories of the Doctrine of the Concept develop conceptually; the inferior categories of the Doctrine of Being and of Essence do not.

dialectic *Dialektik* derives from the Greek *dialektikē* (*technē*), which comes from *dialegesthai*, 'to converse', and was originally the 'art of conversation', but is used by Plato for the correct philosophical method. (Plato favours different methods at different times, but he usually regards his currently preferred method as 'dialectic'.) In antiquity Zeno of Elea was regarded as the founder of dialectic, by reason of his indirect proofs of, e.g., the impossibility of motion by deriving absurdities or CONTRADICTIONS from the supposition that motion occurs. Socrates' dialectic, as portrayed in Plato's early dialogues, tends to take a destructive form: Socrates interrogates someone about the definition of some concept that he has employed (e.g. 'virtue') and derives contradictions from the successive answers given. But in later dialogues, which owe more to Plato himself than to Socrates, dialectic is a positive method, designed to produce knowledge of the FORMS or IDEAS and of the relations between them. In these dialogues, the dialogue-form tends to become relatively unimportant and dialectic loses its link with conversation (except in so far as thinking is regarded as a dialogue with *oneself*). For Hegel, dialectic does not involve a dialogue either between two thinkers or between a thinker and his subject-matter. It is conceived as the autonomous self-criticism and self-DEVELOPMENT of the SUBJECT-MATTER, of, e.g., a form of CONSCIOUSNESS or a concept.

'Dialectic' also acquired a pejorative sense from its association with the so-called 'sophists' or professional 'teachers of wisdom', who, though opposed by Socrates, often used near-Socratic methods to discredit received concepts and doctrines. They thus acquired a reputation for hair-splitting and 'sophistry'. Kant uses 'dialectic' in this pejorative sense when he defines it as the 'logic of ILLUSION (*Schein*)', the illusion, especially, of attempting to derive truths that transcend our EXPERIENCE from concepts and formal principles alone; but he uses it in a favourable sense when he says that his own 'transcendental dialectic' is a 'critique of dialectical illusion' (*CPR* B86). An aspect of Kant's dialectic that impressed Hegel is the derivation of antinomies, of two incompatible answers to a question (whether, for example, the world has a beginning in time or not) that transcends our experience. Fichte's three-step procedure of a thesis (the I* POSITS itself), an antithesis (the I posits a non-I), and a synthesis (the I posits in the I a divisible non-I in opposition to the divisible I) also influenced Hegel's dialectic. (But Hegel uses the terms 'thesis', 'antithesis', 'synthesis' *only* in his account of Kant.)

In a wide sense, Hegel's dialectic involves three steps: (1) One or more concepts or categories are taken as fixed, sharply defined and distinct from each other. This is the stage of UNDERSTANDING. (2) When we reflect on such categories, one or more contradictions emerge in them. This is the stage of

81

dialectic proper, or of dialectical or negative REASON. (3) The result of this dialectic is a new, higher category, which embraces the earlier categories and resolves the contradiction involved in them. This is the stage of SPECULATION or positive reason (*Enc.* I §§79–82). Hegel suggests that this new category is a 'unity of OPPOSITES', a description that fits some cases (e.g. BEING, NOTHING and BECOMING) more readily than others (e.g. MECHANISM, CHEMISM and TELEOLOGY). Hegel holds that opposites, in the case both of thoughts and of things, change into each other when they are intensified, e.g. a being whose power is so great that he annihilates all resistance, lapses into impotence, since he no longer has an opponent to test, reveal and sustain his power.

This method is applied not only in the Logic, but throughout Hegel's systematic works. *PR*, for example, proceeds in a similar way from the FAMILY to CIVIL SOCIETY, and then to the STATE. But dialectic is not only a feature of concepts, but also of real things and processes. An acid and an alkali, for example, (1) are initially separate and distinct; (2) dissolve into each other and lose their individual properties, when they are brought together; and (3) result in a neutral salt, with new properties. Or the EDUCATION of a person involves ALIENATION from his natural state, to which he is later restored or reconciled on a higher plain. Hegel holds that the SPIRIT can endure contradictions, while they result in the destruction of other, unqualifiedly FINITE, entities. This is connected with a further difference between spirit and NATURE. The dialectic of natural things and events does not mirror the dialectic of our thought about them: our thought advances dialectically from lower to higher stages of nature (e.g. from mechanical to organic nature), while the dissolution of a natural entity results in an entity of the same or a similar type (a new seed, say, of the same plant), not in a transition to a higher stage of nature. Spirit, by contrast, has a progressive history (e.g. the destruction of a state often results in a new type of state, not simply a new state of the same type), and thus its development often, though not invariably, corresponds to the advance of our thought about it.

Hegel distinguishes INTERNAL from EXTERNAL dialectic. The dialectic of objective things must be internal to them, since they can only grow and perish in virtue of contradictions actually present in them. But dialectic may be applied externally to concepts, finding flaws in them that they do not really contain. This, on Hegel's view, is sophistry. Proper dialectic, by contrast, is internal to concepts or categories: it radically develops the flaws that they contain and makes them 'pass over' (*übergehen*) into another concept or category. Hegel often speaks as if it is the concepts themselves, rather than the thinker, that conduct this operation, and that they change and break down autonomously, in the way that things do, except that their 'dialectical movement (*Bewegung*)' is non-temporal. (Schelling and Kierkegaard criticized him for speaking of the 'movement' of concepts.) He may simply mean that the thinker follows the natural grain of the concepts in exposing their contradictions and proposing solutions to them, but he nevertheless held that there is a parallel between the development of thoughts or concepts and the development of things that implies that dialectic is internal to both. On this account, dialectic is not a *method*, in the sense of a procedure that the thinker applies to his subject-matter, but the intrinsic structure and development of the subject-matter itself.

Dialectic, on Hegel's view, accounts for all movement and change, both in the world and in our thought about it. It also explains why things, as well as our thoughts, systematically cohere with each other. But the transience of finite things and the elevation (*Erhebung*) above the finite effected by dialectical thought also has a religious significance for him, and he is inclined to assimilate dialectic in the negative sense to the POWER (*Macht*) of God.

E

Early Theological Writings (Theologische Jugendschriften) (ETW) This is the title of a collection of Hegel's early unpublished manuscripts, edited by H. Nohl in 1907 and translated in part by T. M. Knox in 1948. These writings differ greatly in both style and content from Hegel's later writings, but they show his later thought and some of his central concepts emerging from his early preoccupation with RELIGION.

The writings involve three main conceptions of religion:

1. Folk religion (*Volksreligion*), a concepton that owes much to Herder and to Hölderlin. The paradigm of a folk religion is ancient Greek religion. Greek religion was not, on Hegel's view, a universalistic religion, like Christianity, but was intrinsically bound up with the life of a particular PEOPLE. It imposed no creed, dogmas, rules, rites or ecclesiastical institutions that were felt as alien by its adherents, but was intertwined with the life of the people, with its CUSTOMS and festivals. It appealed not to any single faculty, such as REASON, but to the whole person, his emotions and IMAGINATION, as well as his reason. The religion was simply and naturally accepted by all, and required no special act of FAITH or reason. The gods were not regarded as transcendent, mysterious or imperious, but as benevolent deities inhabiting and protecting the city. This religion was closely connected with the political FREEDOM of the Greeks, with their virtue, the beauty of their art, and the harmony and serenity of their lives. In his youth, Hegel yearned for the restoration of this IDEAL, but he began to see its impracticability during his years at Bern (1793–6).

2. Positive religion. Everything historical, Hegel concedes, is 'positive' in that it is not purely 'rational', but in a narrower sense a religion is positive if it lays down dogmas, rituals and rules that are to be accepted simply because they are prescribed by earthly or divine authority, and not because they cohere with the life and customs of its adherents or can be seen to be rationally justified. (Thus 'positive' in this sense contrasts with 'rational', not with 'NEGATIVE'.) Hegel's paradigm of positive religion is Judaism; he cor.nects its positivity with its belief in a transcendent, inscrutable and alien deity, who demands unconditional service (*Dienst*), and with the political oppression to which the Jewish people were subjected.

3. Rational religion, especially the religion of MORALITY that Kant developed in *CPrR* and *RLR*. The dogmas of religion can, on Kant's view, be justified only in so far as they are required by, express and sustain a morality

84

of universal, rational and self-imposed moral imperatives. He attempted to interpret Christianity in this light, dismissing intractable elements as merely historical and not purely religious. Hegel at first endorsed Kant's view, but soon came to see it as sharing one of the faults of Judaism: Kantian morality and religion appeals to and satisfies not the whole man, but only his reason. It sets up an OPPOSITION between duty and inclination, reason and the heart, is and OUGHT. These oppositions, Hegel came to believe, can only be repaired by a religion of *love*.

ETW consists of the following items:

(a) 'Fragments on Folk-Religion and Christianity' (1793–4). (The title was given by Nohl.) These are a preparation for the larger works, but contain interesting discussions of folk religion, under the influence especially of Herder.

(b) *The Life of Jesus* (1795) presents Jesus as a teacher of Kant's purely moral religion, with no mention of miracles or of the transfiguration. This conflicts with the view of (a) and of (c), *PCR*, that Christ, unlike Socrates, introduced a positive element into his teaching, such as the requirement of baptism and of faith in his own person. But (c) presupposes the (b)-view of Christ, if not his teaching, that he was rational and more or less Kantian.

(c) *The Positivity of the Christian Religion* (1795–6, with a revised version of the opening sections from 1800). Hegel asks how Christianity (Catholicism primarily, but also Lutheranism) came to be a positive religion, in view of Christ's opposition to the authoritarian positivity of Judaism, and how it supplanted the folk religions of antiquity. His answers are that Christ had to compromise with Judaism to make his message palatable, appealing to God's will and miracles, and that the Roman Empire destroyed the free communities of Greece and the Roman Republic, turning their citizens into self-seeking individuals ruled from above, who thus became receptive to an authoritarian religion: 'God's OBJECTIVITY is a counterpart to the corruption and slavery of man.'

(d) Some fragments on religion and love from 1797–8, including one on love, which argues that love can heal the oppositions characteristic of modernity and of positive Christianity.

(e) *The Spirit of Christianity and its Fate (Schicksal)*(1798–1800). Hegel criticizes not only the positivity of Judaism, but also Kantian morality: the difference between the adherents of a positive religion and a dutiful moralist is simply that the 'former have their lord outside themselves, while the latter carries his lord in himself, yet is at the same time his own slave.' The Sermon on the Mount, Hegel argues, 'does not teach reverence for the laws; … it exhibits that which fulfils the law but annuls it as law, and so is something higher than obedience to law and makes law superfluous. … This congruence of law and inclination is life, and as the relation of differents to one another it is love.' LIFE and love play the reconciling role that Hegel later assigns to SPIRIT. But love alone, he argues, was insufficient to convert all mankind, and this reintroduced positivity: it is Christianity's 'FATE that church and state, worship and life, piety and virtue, spiritual and worldly action, can never dissolve into one.'

(f)   'Fragment of a System of 1800' (Nohl's title). The two surviving pages of this manuscript deal with the unification of such opposites as FINITE and INFINITE, God and man, and SUBJECT and OBJECT. The solution, Hegel argues, is life, the 'union (*Verbindung*) of union and non-union' or of 'synthesis and antithesis': God is infinite life, in which men, as living beings, share and to which they elevate themselves in religion. Reflective conceptual thought can play only a preparatory role: 'Philosophy must cease where religion begins, since it is a type of THINKING, and thus implies an opposition between thinking and non-thinking, between the thinker and what is thought; it has to disclose the finitude in everything finite and to require the completion of the finite by reason; in particular, it has to recognize the illusions stemming from its own [concept of the] infinite and so to locate the true infinite outside its confines.'

In these writings, Hegel moves from the hostility to (ecclesiastical) Christianity, as compared with folk religion, expressed in (a) and (c), to a deep sympathy with Christianity and an acceptance of the inevitability of the positivity of the Church in (e) and to the elaboration of an erotic and vitalistic pantheism in (d) and (f). The concern to overcome ALIENATION and opposition persist in his later works, but conceptual thought there plays the dominant role.

ego *see* I

Encyclopaedia of the Philosophical Sciences in Outline (*Enzyklopädie der philosophischen Wissenschaften im Grundrisse*) (*Enc.*) (1817, 1827, 1830, 1840–5)   The word 'encyclopaedia' was formed in the second half of the sixteenth century from the Greek *enkyklios* ('circular' or 'in circulation, i.e. customary') *paideia* ('education') and thus means either 'circular, viz. all-embracing' or 'customary education', and more particularly a survey either of all arts and sciences or of a particular field in systematic or alphabetical order. The best-known encyclopaedias in Hegel's day were Bayle's *Dictionnaire historique et critique* (1695–7) and Diderot's *Encyclopédie, ou dictionnaire raisonné des sciences, des arts et métiers* (1751–80). But Hegel's choice of the title may have been influenced by the Bavarian educational regulations of 1808, which prescribed instruction in a 'philosophical encyclopaedia' (a course that Hegel gave as rector of the Nuremberg Gymnasium), and by G. E. Schulze's *Encyclopaedia of the Philosophical Sciences, for use with his Lectures* (1814).

Hegel's *Encyclopaedia* too was intended as a textbook to accompany his lectures. The entries appear in numbered paragraphs which were to be explained and expanded in the lectures. The main paragraphs are thus often extremely brief and obscure. On the other hand, since the work was also published for a wider readership, Hegel added to the paragraphs 'Remarks', which often contain empirical material, which is only loosely connected to the main paragraph. Successive editions of the work increased both the number and length of these Remarks: the second edition is nearly twice as long as the first; the third is slightly longer than the second; the posthumous fourth edition, published by his followers, appends to many paragraphs 'Additions', excerpts from notes on his lectures.

Like other encyclopaedias, Hegel's purports to give only an outline of the sciences and not a complete account of them. In particular, the systematic connections between successive entries are not presented as fully as in some of Hegel's other works. The first part, for example, 'The Science of Logic', is far less detailed (but often clearer) than *SL*. Thus *Enc.* does not present the finished version of Hegel's SYSTEM, though it is our main source for certain parts of it, especially his philosophy of NATURE. On the other hand, Hegel's *Encyclopaedia* differs from others, in that it does not present an 'aggregate of sciences' or 'a mere collection of information', but presents them in their 'logical connection'.

The 1830 edition of the *Encyclopaedia* falls into the following segments:

(1) Prefaces to all three editions. The first claims that the work presents a 'new treatment of philosophy in accordance with a method which will yet, I hope, be recognized as the only true method, as the method that is identical with the content.' In the second and third Prefaces he defends the right of philosophy to discuss religion and argues that PHILOSOPHY and RELIGION are ultimately identical.

(2) An Introduction, which discusses the nature of philosophy, the 'THINKING consideration of OBJECTS [*Gegenstände*]', and of the *Encyclopaedia*.

(3) A 'Preliminary Concept (*Vorbegriff*)', which discusses the general status and nature of logic, the 'science of the pure IDEA, that is, of the idea in the abstract element of thinking.'

(4) A critical account of three 'attitudes of thought to objectivity', which, like *PS*, serves as an introduction to SCIENCE. The first 'attitude' is that of pre-Kantian rationalists, who attempt to discern the truth about GOD, the SOUL and the world by thinking. Their failure, Hegel argues, was to neglect the CONTRADICTORY, DIALECTICAL nature of thought. The second is that of the empiricists and Kant, who argued that the nature of things is not accessible to thought alone, or indeed to cognition in general. The third is that of F. H. Jacobi, who held that the nature of things, both earthly and divine, is accessible not to thought or COGNITION, but to IMMEDIATE FAITH or KNOWLEDGE.

(5) A brief account of the three aspects of logic, the UNDERSTANDING, the DIALECTICal and the SPECULATIVE, together with the division of logic into the Doctrines of BEING, ESSENCE and the CONCEPT.

(6) The Logic itself, in its three divisions, proceeds, like *SL*, from pure being to the absolute idea, but differs from it somewhat in content and arrangement. The idea finally 'resolves to let the MOMENT of its PARTICULARITY or of the first determining and other-being, the immediate idea as its REFLECTION, go forth freely from itself as nature' (I §244). Hegel

believes that this 'resolve' marks a return to the beginning of logic, namely to being, since nature is the 'idea that has being'.

(7) The second Part of *Enc.*, the *Philosophy of Nature*, proceeds through the stages of NATURE, beginning with space and concluding with the animal organism. The stages of nature are correlated, more or less, with the categories of logic, so that the *Philosophy of Nature* is a replay of the idea, but in the realm of nature rather than of thought. The DEATH of the animal, the passage of the individual into the UNIVERSALITY of its genus, supplies the transition to SPIRIT.

(8) The third Part, the *Philosophy of Spirit*, has, like the other Parts, three subdivisions: I. The Subjective SPIRIT; II. The Objective Spirit; III. The Absolute Spirit. Each of these has three further subdivisions: 'The Subjective Spirit' is divided into: A. 'Anthropology [i.e. 'the study of man', not, as now, 'ethnology']. The Soul' is an account of the primitive, non-intentional levels of the human SOUL (*Seele*), that does not, for the most part, appear elsewhere in Hegel's published works; B. 'The Phenomenology of Spirit. Consciousness' is an account of intentional CONSCIOUSNESS that is a brief replay of sections A and B of *PS*; C. 'Psychology. The Spirit' is an account of our intellectual and practical faculties, in isolation from the objects on which they are directed. This too is not found in Hegel's other published works. Each of these divisions is again divided, and usually subdivided, into three. These stages or levels of subjective spirit form, like those of nature, an ascending hierarchy, and the transitions between them are underpinned by logic. But unlike the stages of nature, they DEVELOP, to some extent at least, over time. For example, the anthropological stages occur alone in infants; they are more prominent in primitive than in civilized peoples; in cultivated adults they are overlayed and controlled by higher phases, but re-establish their dominance in sleep and in pathological states.

'Objective Spirit' is divided into RIGHT, MORALITY and ETHICAL LIFE. It is a briefer version of *PR*. 'Absolute Spirit' is divided into ART, revealed RELIGION and PHILOSOPHY. It corresponds, but only roughly, to the end of *PS*: VII. 'Religion' and VIII. 'Absolute Knowledge'.

The second and third Parts both return, like the Logic, to its beginning. But *Enc. as a whole* is seen as returning to its beginning, since logic, philosophy of nature and philosophy of spirit are respectively the sciences of the idea IN AND FOR ITSELF, in its otherness, and in its return to itself out of its otherness. (The last phase of spirit, philosophy, itself begins with logic.) *Enc.* thus portrays philosophy as a 'circle of circles' (*Enc.* I §15), and provides a 'circular education'.

end *see* PURPOSE AND PURPOSIVENESS; LIMIT, RESTRICTION AND FINITUDE

essence The Middle High German verb *wesen* ('to be') had become obsolete by Hegel's time, but it still supplied the past tenses of the verb *sein* ('to be'), especially its past participle, *gewesen*, and the verbal noun (*das*) *Wesen*. The most important uses of *Wesen* are these: (1) a being, creature or entity, especially a living one (e.g. 'God is the supreme *Wesen*', 'Man is a finite *Wesen*'); (2) the essence, nature or character of an individual entity, its being thus and so (*Sosein*) in contrast to its EXISTENCE (*Dasein*); (3) the permanent, dominant nature of a thing, that underlies its varying outer states or APPEARANCE (*Erscheinung*); (4) the actual or essential nature of a thing in contrast to how it *seems* or its appearance (*Schein*); (5) the essential or UNIVERSAL features of a group of entities, in contrast to their individual variations; (6) in compounds such as *Postwesen* (the 'Post Office' or 'postal system'), a system or complex. (Hegel argues that this use of the word is close to his own, since it implies that things are to be taken as a complex and in their 'diverse [and overt] relationships', *Enc.* I §112A.)

Wesen gives rise to an adjective, *wesentlich* ('essential'), contrasting with *unwesentlich* ('inessential'), and these can form noun-phrases, 'the essential' and 'the inessential'. It also gives rise to another noun, *Wesenheit* ('essentiality'), which is that which constitutes the essence of a thing, in contrast to *Wesentlichkeit* ('essentialness'), which is the quality of being essential. Hegel uses the plural *Wesenheiten* as equivalent to *Reflexionsbestimmungen*, 'DETERMINATIONS of REFLECTION', namely those determinations that constitute the essence of things and are generated by, and/or accessible to, reflection, and are considered in the Doctrine of Essence, the second section of the Logic.

In *PS*, essence is considered in the third section of 'CONSCIOUSNESS' (*PS*, III), where it is correlative to the UNDERSTANDING. In the fuller account of the Logic, especially *SL*, 'essence', like 'BEING', has a wide and a narrow use: it *both* covers all the concepts or determinations of reflection in the Doctrine of Essence, *and* refers to the first and most general of these determinations. The transition from being (in the wide use) to essence (in the narrow use) is this: In the Doctrine of Being, we met with QUALITIES, QUANTITIES and the complex interplay between qualities and quantities in MEASURE. These determinations and their alterations are IMMEDIATE, in the sense that they are not seen as belonging to a single entity (*Wesen*) or as explicable by an underlying, persistent essence (*Wesen*). Hegel's express reason for the move to *Wesen* is that the false INFINITE regress of variations of quantity, punctuated by qualitative changes, gives way to the truly infinite reciprocal transformation of quality and quantity into each other, which gives rise to a substratum that is, as such, neither qualitative nor quantitative. There are other, underlying, reasons for his belief: (1) The I* or SUBJECT requires an OBJECT distinct from itself, and such objectivity requires the possession of qualities and quantities by a relatively persistent entity. (2) An entity's possession of diverse and variable features in turn requires the explicability of these features and of their coherence with each other in terms of the essence of the entity. (3) The subject itself must be more than a series of such variable features, if it is to be aware either of them or of itself: it must be a persistent entity underlying its varying states. (One reason for Hegel's omission of such arguments is his belief that quantity, quality and measure pass of themselves into essence, and that essence is not simply introduced by our 'external reflection' to solve the problems they raise.)

The *Wesen* of a thing is initially contrasted, as the essential, with the inessential, the immediate surface features that were previously *Sein*. But this pair of terms is inadequate, both because the essential depends on its contrast with the inessential as much as the inessential depends on the essential, and because, as a consequence of this, the characterization of one of the terms, rather than the other, as essential, requires an external observer. (Hegel's arguments here, and in the Doctrine of Essence generally, are similar to his arguments on the ABSOLUTE.)

Next, then, *Wesen* is contrasted with *Schein* ('APPEARANCE'). What was previously *Sein* ('being') has become a simple, indeterminate *Wesen*: being RECOLLECTS or internalizes itself into essence. (Here Hegel stresses *Wesen*'s link with the past: 'the essence is being that is past (*vergangene*), but timelessly past'.) But what was previously *Sein*, immediate surface features, still persists as *Schein*, apparent features MEDIATED by the activity of essence. *Wesen* and *Schein* now have a relation other than that of mere contrast or 'otherness': *Schein* is generated by essence's appearing (*scheinen*). But *Schein* and *scheinen*, like the notion of REFLECTION introduced later in the section, are ambiguous:

1. They are associated with appearance, seeming and illusion, with what seems or appears to an observer. But the observer is aware not only of *Schein*, but also of *Wesen*: his thought reflects back from *Schein* on(to) the *Wesen* at its source. Thus essence moves from dominance of *Schein* to parity with it: it acquires implicit determinacy, in contrast to the simplicity with which it began, and is as much a product of the human mind as (according to some IDEALISTS) *Schein* is.

2. They are associated with the shining of light. The idea of a simple, persistent source of light that expands into a varied glow fits well with the idea of a simple essence that generates a wealth of surface features. *Schein*, on this model, is the product of essence itself, not simply of an outside observer: essence shines within itself. But it also shines into itself. For light, when it strikes a surface, is reflected back towards its source. Hence *Wesen* and *Schein* come to be reciprocally related by shining, each shining into the other. In this way too, *Wesen* becomes as determinate as the *Schein* it generates, containing IN ITSELF all the variety it is required to explain.

The other determinations of reflection are developments of the notion of essence. For example, IDENTITY derives from the self-identity of essence, and DIFFERENCE from its self-differentiation into *Schein*. The determinations, unlike those of being, form pairs (e.g. identity and difference), the terms of which are related by *shining* (*scheinen*) into each other. Hegel contrasts such shining with the passing, or transition, into each other characteristic of the determinations of being and with the DEVELOPMENT of the determinations of the CONCEPT. But he also speaks of the development of essence (and of being) as a whole. This development proceeds from essence conceived as a hidden substratum to essence conceived as the overt logical structure and interrelatedness of phenomena, that is, from essence that merely shines, by way of its emergence into appearance (*Erscheinung*), to ordered and articulated ACTUALITY.

It is not wholly clear what Hegel means by associating *Wesen* with the past(-tense):

(1) He is unlikely to share the view of Sartre, in *Baudelaire* (1947): 'What I am is what I was, since my present freedom always puts in question the nature that I have acquired.' I do, on Hegel's view, transcend or SUBLATE my past states, but I do not do so with the SUBJECTIVE FREEDOM that Sartre has in mind, and I do not transcend my general essence as an I* or a THINKING being.

(2) Often the point seems to be that the essence of something emerges (temporally, outside logic) from its past state(s) and is not explicit from the start: e.g. 'by this reflection into itself, SPIRIT completes its liberation from the form of mere being [of the "natural SOUL"], gives itself the form of essence and becomes I*' (*Enc.* III §412A.).

(3) Sometimes the point seems to be that the essence of a present entity is the whole past process of which it is the result: 'every blade of grass, every tree has ... its HISTORY. ... This is still more the case in the sphere of the SPIRIT; as actual spirit in its appearance it can only be portrayed exhaustively ... as such a course of history' (*LA*). (This is close to Nietzsche's view of the definition of PUNISHMENT.)

The ambiguities of *Wesen* and associated words, as well as the generality intrinsic to logic, mean that Hegel is not concerned with only one use of 'essence', but with a whole range of uses, in theology, metaphysics, empirical science and informal discourse.

ethical life and custom The word *Sittlichkeit*, usually translated in Hegel's works as 'ethical life', but occasionally as '(social or customary) morality', etc., derives from *Sitte*, the native German for a 'custom', a mode of conduct habitually practised by a social group such as a nation, a class or a family, and regarded as a norm of decent behaviour. (A *Sitte* is never a deliberately chosen, individual custom, as in 'It is my custom to ...') In *PCR*, Hegel shows some disdain for customs instituted by the Church, in that, e.g., customs concerning mourning for dead relatives prescribe the manifestation of more grief than most people actually feel. But in *NL*, he argued that customs, mediating between the individual and the LAWS of his society, are essential to the vitality of a PEOPLE; successful legislation presupposes customs to which it must conform. In *PS*, he affirmed that 'wisdom and virtue consist in living in conformity to the customs of one's people'. He never abandoned these beliefs.

In the usage of other philosophers, the plural *Sitten* tends to be equated with 'ethics' and 'MORALITY'. (These words too derive from the words for 'custom' in Greek and Latin, respectively.) Thus Kant's *Metaphysik der Sitten* (*MM*) deals with ethics in general, not with customs, and for Fichte *Sittenlehre* (literally the 'doctrine of customs') is equivalent to 'moral philosophy'. Other words derived from *Sitte* moved in the same direction: a *Sittengesetz* is an ethical law or norm, especially, for Kant, one certified by reason, not by custom, and, though it is valid for all rational beings, by the individual, not by the community. The adjective *sittlich* is equated with 'moral' or 'ethical', and the abstract noun *Sittlichkeit* with 'morality'.

Hegel often uses *Sitte*-words in these senses, when discussing the views of other writers. But from early on, he distinguishes between *Sittlichkeit* and *Moralität*: *Moralität* is individual morality, arrived at by one's own reason, conscience or FEELINGS. *Sittlichkeit* is the ethical norms embodied in the customs and institutions of one's society. These notions are not simply contrasted with each other, but systematically related: In the ideal state, modelled on Plato's *Republic*, which Hegel sketched in *NL*, *Moralität*, as private, bourgeois morality, is assigned to the commercial and wealth-producing class, while *Sittlichkeit* is the preserve of the ruling, warrior class. But in later works, especially *PS*, *PR* and *Enc*. III, the relation between them is this: In all three works, the account of *Sittlichkeit* is preceded by an account of Kantian *Moralität*. But this corresponds to their logical order (or, in *PS*, to the order in which they occur to a reader of Rousseau and Kant), not to the order of their appearance in HISTORY. Historically, the *Sittlichkeit* of the Greek city-state preceded the emergence of individualist morality. (The Greek city-state was not the first political formation in history: it was preceded by a variety of non-individualist oriental societies, and in *LA* Hegel argues that Greek mythology depicts the emergence of Greek civilization from them and the taming of the natural forces that they represent.) Greek *Sittlichkeit*, on Hegel's view, involved, initially at least, complete harmony between the individual and his society. The individual could not say 'Doing so-and-so contravenes customary values, but it may still be morally right', or 'It is worth doing, since it is in my self-interest'. (That Hegel's account, though idealized, is not wholly misguided is suggested by the story that the fifth-century Athenian Alcibiades was widely criticized for acquiring a private art collection.) Private morality had no place in such a community, which Hegel often describes as 'ethical SUBSTANCE'. Its members had objective, but not subjective, FREEDOM.

Hegel gives a variety of reasons for the breakdown of Greek *Sittlichkeit*:

(1) In *PS* it is ascribed to the unresolvable conflict, portrayed especially in Sophocles' *Antigone*, between the laws of the gods of the nether world, governing the FAMILY and administered by the woman, and the laws of the Olympian gods, governing STATE power and administered by the man. (King Creon forbids the burial of Antigone's traitorous brother, but she is obliged to bury him.) The conflict is not initially between the individual and the state, but between different aspects of ethical life; but the conflicting demands on the individual give rise, on Hegel's view, to individualism.

(2) Hegel often assigns a central role in the breakdown of Greek *Sittlichkeit* to Socrates' questioning of customary values. He sees Plato's *Republic* not as an IDEAL, but as a vain attempt to restore harmonious *Sittlichkeit*.

(3) The conquests of Alexander the Great and of the Roman emperors created much larger societies, whose subjects were inevitably remote from their rulers and thrown back on their own resources.

Sittlichkeit in the Greek sense cannot be restored. But in a wider sense, any stable society requires *Sittlichkeit*, a system of customary norms accepted by its members. Rational *Moralität* presupposes such norms, if it is to have any definite content, and self-interest alone will not hold a society together. (Socially appropriate conduct cannot be secured by FORCE alone, unless the wielders of force at least are motivated and guided by *Sittlichkeit*.) But modern *Sittlichkeit* must accommodate the moral SUBJECTIVITY and the self-interested PARTICULARITY, to which intervening history has given rise. It thus differs from the ancient version in three respects. First, like ancient *Sittlichkeit*, it involves the family and the state. But to these it adds CIVIL SOCIETY, a realm of self-seeking economic activity that is overseen by the state, but considerably more independent of it than ancient economic life was. Second, it grants the individual certain RIGHTS, such as the choice of a mate and of a career. (Hegel mistakenly inferred, from his reading of Plato, that these rights were denied to most Greeks.) Third, the cultivated member of a modern state does not, like the Greek, unreflectively accept the norms and institutions of his society. He accepts them because he has reflected on the rational justification for them. (To provide such a justification was a central aim of Hegel's philosophy.) Thus modern *Sittlichkeit* allows room for the SUBJECT, as well as for substance, and for subjective, as well as objective, freedom.

existence, reality and determinate being   German has a variety of words in this area. Hegel attempted, to a greater extent than most earlier philosophers, to distinguish them from each other. The most general of them, on his view, is *sein* ('BEING'): it carries minimal ontological baggage and applies to everything. *Sein* and the adverb *da* ('there', 'here', etc.) gives *dasein* ('to be there, be present, exist') and, in the seventeenth century, the verbal noun (*das*) *Dasein* ('being there, presence, existence (especially in space and time)'). *Dasein* was used by Leibniz and Wolff for the Latin *existentia*, the existence of a thing in contrast to its character. For Kant, *Dasein* was the contrary of *Nichtsein* ('non-being'), and he uses it for the existence of anything, including God. (Hegel too often uses it for the existence of GOD, but this is either a concession to traditional usage or implies a special contrast with the CONCEPT of God.) The Heideggerian association of *Dasein* with human being in time occasionally appears in this period, but it has little significance for either Hegel or other philosophers.

   The Latin *res* ('thing') gave rise to *realis* ('real' – probably first in Abelard) and *realitas* ('reality' – first used by Duns Scotus). In German these become *real*, with the French-derived variant *reell*, and *Realität*. Like their English equivalents, the force of these words depends on their context and especially on the expression contrasted with them. The central contrast is with IDEAL (or *ideell*) and *Idealität*, in the common (but non-Hegelian) sense of present only in thought or imagination. But the expression *ideale* or *ideelle Realität* occurs, in philosophy, for the actual presence of something in thought, and, in Hegel, for that aspect of OBJECTIVITY that, in contrast to EXTERNAL (*äusserliche*) reality, corresponds to the concept. *Realität* is often equated with 'ACTUALITY' (*Wirklichkeit*) and 'objectivity', but for Hegel these are distinct

93

concepts: *ideale Realität* is close to *Wirklichkeit*, but *Realität* as such is associated with *Dasein*.

The classical Latin *exsistere* ('to step forth') gave rise to the medieval Latin *existentia*, the existence of something in contrast to its *essentia* or nature. These become, in German, *existieren* ('to exist', but retaining, in Hegel and other philosophers, its implication of stepping forth or emerging) and *Existenz*.

Dasein, Hegel says, is being (*Sein*) with a DETERMINACY (*Bestimmtheit*), an IMMEDIATE determinacy (in contrast to an underlying ESSENCE), that is, a QUALITY. (Hence *Dasein*, in this context, is usually translated as 'determinate being'.) A determinate entity is *ein Daseiendes* (a noun formed from the present participle, *daseiend*) or a 'something' (*Etwas*, a nominalization of the pronoun *etwas*, 'something'). *Dasein* has emerged from the collapse of BECOMING, the reciprocal passage of being and NOTHING into each other. Hence *Dasein* involves NEGATION: a *Daseiendes* has a determinate character only in virtue of a contrast with other somethings with different characters. Hegel often illustrates *Dasein* with examples of things that have more than one quality and which can change their qualities without ceasing to exist, but a *Daseiendes* (like a patch of colour projected onto a screen) is at this stage coterminous with its quality: it cannot have more than one quality or survive a change of quality. This does not prevent us from speaking of the *Dasein* of more complex, changing entities, but such entities are not complex and changing in virtue of *Dasein* alone. It does mean that Hegel is reluctant to assign *Dasein* more than a very subordinate role in the constitution of SPIRIT, for, on Hegel's view (as on Heidegger's and Sartre's), human beings, unless sick or deranged, are not dominated or 'penetrated' by their qualities (their passions or characters) in the way that THINGS are. (Spirit is more appropriately characterized as being-FOR-ITSELF.) For this reason, and also because *Dasein* implies the existence of something else, distinct from and contrasting with the *Daseiendes*, *Dasein* is not strictly attributable to God or to the ABSOLUTE. But *Dasein* is often used in contrast to 'CONCEPT': a concept is said, e.g., to 'step forth' or 'emerge' (*hervorgehen, hervortreten*) into *Dasein*. In this sense (where Hegel's usage is not simply traditional) the *Dasein* of God is the real world, and the *Dasein* of spirit is the concrete activities and products in which it manifests itself. But *Dasein* in this sense is still thought of as involving contingencies and imperfections, not as fully corresponding to the concept, in the way that actuality does.

Realität, in Hegel, has two senses. First, corresponding to the customary contrast with *ideal*, it is associated with *Dasein*, and is close to 'quality', except that it contrasts with 'negation', though, like a quality, it essentially involves negation. In this sense, Hegel argues, we can speak of the reality or realization of a plan or intention, of the body as the reality of the soul, of RIGHT as the reality of FREEDOM, and of the world as the reality of the divine concept. (*Realität* is here close to *Dasein*.) Second, *Realität* has an evaluative sense, as in 'a real philosopher'; here it is not equivalent to *Dasein*, and does not contrast with *ideal*: it indicates the 'agreement of a *Daseiendes* with its concept', and is close to 'actuality' (*Enc.* I §91A.).

Existenz, on Hegel's account, is a DETERMINATION of essence. In the Logic, it follows the category of GROUND: the notion of a ground develops into that of a condition (a *sine qua non*), and when the totality of conditions is realized the THING or matter (*Sache*) emerges into existence. The existent (*das Existierendes*) is a thing (*Ding*) with many properties. What enables it, unlike the 'something', to have or combine several properties is its emergence from a ground. But the ground or essence is not hidden beneath the properties of the thing; it is fully SUBLATED in the existent. Just as the something belongs to a system of differently qualified somethings, the existent belongs to a system of existents, each of which is a condition of the others, and what properties a thing has depends in part on its contrastive interactions with other things.

The notion of *Existenz*, in contrast to REASON, the concept and the IDEA, later became a rallying call for such opponents of Hegel as Schelling, Kierkegaard and Ranke. (Hamann and Jacobi too had invoked it against the rationalist systems of Kant and other Enlightenment philosophers.) Their criticisms were, first, that Hegel deals with the concept of existence, not with actual existence, and, second, that in so far as he does deal with actual existence, his rationalist systematization of it does not do justice to the complexity and particularity of religious, historical and human existence. But these charges cannot be assessed in terms of *Existenz*, which has been pre-empted by Hegel for his own specialized purposes. Like *Dasein*, *Existenz* is not, for Hegel, associated with human existence, whose adequate conceptualization requires more advanced categories. *See* ACTION.

experience and the empirical Hegel uses the Greek-derived *Empirie* ('experience'), *empirisch* ('empirical(ly)') and *Empirismus* ('empiricism'), but his native German words for 'to experience' and 'experience' are *erfahren* and *Erfahrung*. (The words *erleben* and *Erlebnis* ('lived experience') became important only in the twentieth century.) *Erfahren* comes from the prefix *er-* (*see* APPEARANCE) and *fahren*, originally 'to fare, go, wander', hence 'to get on, fare (e.g. well)', and 'to travel or go on a voyage or journey'. Thus the root meaning of *erfahren* is 'to set out on a journey to explore or get to know something'. *Erfahrung* refers either to this process or to its result.

Erfahrung was first used by Paracelsus for the Latin *experientia*. It contrasts with what is merely THOUGHT and with what is accepted on authority or tradition. Kant argued, in *CPR*, that all our knowledge begins with *Erfahrung*, but that it does not all arise from *Erfahrung*, since *Erfahrung* is the joint product of our sensory INTUITIONS and of the forms of intuition (space and time) and categories of the UNDERSTANDING that we contribute to such intuitions. We cannot have COGNITION, on Kant's view, of what transcends such experience, that is, of THINGS-in-themselves and of such entities as GOD, the SOUL and FREEDOM.

Hegel uses *Erfahrung* in more than one way. In *PS*, it is not associated with any particular FORM of CONSCIOUSNESS, but is the experience undergone by consciousness on its way to SCIENCE. Here the suggestion of a voyage of discovery is in play. Moreover, consciousness's experience is not specifically empirical: *Erfahrung* contrasts not with 'thought' (though Hegel distinguishes the experiences of consciousness from logic), but indicates what consciousness undergoes or finds out for itself in contrast to what we onlookers know about it. 'Experience' in this sense differs from its usual sense, in that consciousness discovers the inadequacy of one of its forms and proceeds to the next, not by encountering some *other* object in its experience, but by experiencing the internal incoherence between its OBJECT and its conception of that object and the transformation of that conception into its next object.

The idea that *Erfahrung* is essentially one's *own* experience persists in Hegel's later accounts of empirical experience, especially in the introductory sections of *Enc.* I. For a merit of empiricism, he argues, apart from its provision of cognitive support for its claims, is its insistence that a man should accept only what he has experienced for himself. This leads him to assimilate, e.g., F. H. Jacobi's immediate KNOWLEDGE of, or FAITH in, such entities as God to the empiricism of Hume and of natural scientists. But another source of this assimilation is the indeterminacy of the relationship between experience and thought. This indeterminacy occasionally appears in Kant, but it is most obvious in Hume, where experience is equivocally both of impressions, which require no conceptual or imaginative processing for their apprehension, and of objects, which are a conceptual and imaginative construct. (Hume also equivocates over whether experience is one's own experience or that of men in general: it is not my personal experience, but that of humanity in general, that, e.g., dead men do not rise again.) Thus *Erfahrung* in Hegel has three broad senses:

(1) It is, especially in accounts of Hume, raw sensory material, unprocessed by thought. (Hegel believed that he had refuted the empiricism that appeals to experience in this sense in his account of sensory certainty in *PS*, I.)

(2) It is sensory material that has undergone some conceptual processing. Hegel's usual view is that *Erfahrung* in this sense goes beyond PERCEPTION in that it involves empirical LAWS, but it does not see the NECESSITY of such laws.

(3) In a wide sense entities such as God are objects of experience. This sense has a variety of sources: the *PS* sense of 'experience' as undergone with any object of consciousness, for example, and Goethe's claim that although 'experience (*Empirie*)' usually contrasts with 'theory (*Theorie*)', there is a refined type of experience that so intimately identifies with its object that it ascends to the level of theory. But Hegel's central argument is this: Hume and Kant distinguish between the legitimate conceptualization of sensory material involved in the natural sciences and the application of concepts to transcendent entities such as GOD. But this distinction is arbitrary. God is presented as transcendent by rationalist theologians, who postulate a gulf between God and the mundane world. If we reject this incoherent view, to experience God is just to apply more thoughts or concepts to our experience of the world. Kant and the empiricists seek to impose an arbitrary limit on our thought.

Despite this extension of the notion of experience, experience is, for Hegel, still distinct from thinking, especially ABSTRACT philosophical thinking, since experience in all three senses involves experience in sense (1) in a way that pure thought does not. Thought presupposes experience if it is not to be, like early philosophy, impoverished and stunted. It presupposes not primarily the philosopher's own experience, but the work of empirical scientists, historians, theologians, etc., who process empirical material into experience in sense (2), and sometimes (3), so as to meet the philosopher half-way. The philosopher then takes over the results of the empirical sciences (*Erfahrungswissenschaften*), and shows them to be *a priori* and necessary, much as Greek geometers took over the results of earlier empirical geometers and embodied them in an *a priori* system. In general, once something has been discovered *a posteriori*, but not before, the philosopher can establish it *a priori*. Since empirical scientists deploy thoughts or categories that are the concern of logic, the philosopher can also criticize their account of experience if they misconstrue or misapply categories. (Hegel is alive to the fact that what passes for empirical observation is often simply the application of an oversimple *a priori* conceptual schema to the neglect of recalcitrant empirical data.)

Hegel often regards what would normally be regarded as conceptual or *a priori* disciplines as empirical, if they proceed haphazardly and unsystematically. For example, traditional logic, arithmetic and Kant's transcendental logic are compared to empirical sciences, not because their subject-matter is inherently experiential, but because it is derived, developed and presented not systematically but 'empirically' (*empirisch*) or 'HISTORICALLY' (*historisch* – in this context, a derogatory synonym of *empirisch*).

explicit(ly) and implicit(ly) *see* IN, FOR, AND IN AND FOR ITSELF, HIMSELF, ETC.; POSITING AND PRESUPPOSITION

F

family and women *Familie* was taken in the sixteenth century from the Latin *familia*, which comes from *famulus* ('servant'), and hence originally meant one's 'domestics', but came to refer to the whole household, both free and slave, under the tutelage of the *pater familias*. In Hegel's day, as now, *Familie* meant (1) a 'community of parents and children', but also (2) a wider, blood-related 'kinship group'. But the relevant sense, for Hegel, is (1).

Hegel held that the family is the sphere of the woman, and that women should be excluded from activities associated with CIVIL SOCIETY and the STATE. This view was shared by most philosophers both of his time and earlier. The main exception is Plato, who argued, in the *Republic*, that the family should be abolished (at least for the class of guardians or rulers) and that women should receive the same EDUCATION as men and be promoted to the status of guardian, should they prove suitable. (He did not believe that they are as likely to be suitable as men are.) In *LHP*, Hegel discusses the abolition of the family, but neglects Plato's views on women. The Neoplatonists included several women among their adherents, especially Hypatia (daughter of the mathematician Theon), who lectured on philosophy at Alexandria and is said to have been torn to pieces by a Christian mob. (She is the subject of Charles Kingsley's *Hypatia*.) Hypatia is not mentioned by Hegel, unsurprisingly, since nothing is known of her specific doctrines. The only woman to whom he refers (in *LA*) as having made a significant cultural contribution is the lyric poet Sappho.

The French Revolution generated an interest in women's RIGHTS. The revolutionary Condorcet wrote an essay on *The Admission of Women to the Rights of Citizenship* (1790). But the liberal Krug, like Hegel, associates women with feeling, affection and instinct, rather than reason or understanding, and thus regards their place as the home, rearing and educating children. Women are to have human rights (*Menschenrechte*), but not civic or citizen rights (*Bürgerrechte*). Apart from Plato, Krug mentions three contemporary dissenters: (1) Mary Wollstonecraft, *Vindication of the Rights of Woman* (1792, translated into German, 1793–4); (2) G. F. C. Weissenborn, who translated (1) and wrote *Letters on the Civil Independence of Women* (1806); and (3) Wm. Thomson, *Appeal of one half of the human race, Women, against the pretentions of the other half, Men, to retain them in political, and thence in civil and domestic slavery* (1825). None of these is mentioned by Hegel. Other works listed by Krug, including the Hegelian Karl Rosenkranz's *The Emancipation of*

Woman, considered from the standpoint of Psychology (1836), appeared after Hegel's death.

Women achieved a large degree of social and sexual emancipation in late eighteenth- and early nineteenth-century Germany, especially in the ROMANTIC Circle. (F. Schlegel's *Dialogue on Poetry* (1799–1800) reveals something of the intellectual role of women in the circle.) But the romantics stressed love rather than civic rights, and held that marriage loses its meaning when love ends. This view was expressed in F. Schlegel's novel *Lucinde* (1799) and Schleiermacher's *Intimate Letters on Lucinde* (1800), written in defence of Schlegel (cf. *PR* §164A.). In *ETW*, Hegel is influenced by the romantics' view of love and the cosmic significance they assigned to it. But his later works subordinate love to rationality: marriage originates in love, but as a rational, social institution it should transcend and outlast the contingencies of passion (*PR* §§162ff).

Hegel considers women and the family in two main contexts:

1. *PS*, VI.A.a, considers, under the heading of SPIRIT, Greek ETHICAL LIFE as reflected in Greek tragedy, especially his favourite play, Sophocles' *Antigone*. Greek society, on Hegel's view, was governed by two types of law:
   (a) The unwritten LAW of the nether gods, which 'is not of yesterday or today, but everlasting, though no one knows whence it came'. (Antigone's words are often quoted by Hegel.) This is the sacred law of the family, which binds the living with the dead. It prescribes the spiritualization of DEATH by appropriate funeral rites. The observance of this law, and the safeguarding of the family in general, is assigned to the woman. (In fact, in Sophocles' Athens the disposal of the dead, especially the war dead, was not simply a private, family concern.)
   (b) Public, human law, the law of the state, sanctioned by the Olympian gods. This is assigned to men, in this case the ruler, Creon, who has forbidden the burial of Antigone's rebellious brother, Polyneikes.
Neither law overrides the other. Hence a tragic conflict arises.

Neither Hegel nor Sophocles' Greek audience saw this as a conflict between the state and the INDIVIDUAL. It is, on Hegel's view, a conflict between POWERS, represented by individuals: individualism arose only later, in part as a result of such conflicts. His interpretation of the play is controversial, but it has the merit of taking seriously Creon's position, as well as Antigone's. (Creon is not simply a tyrant, but a statesman attempting to restore the order on which civilized life depends.)

2. At *PR* §§158–81, the family is considered as the first, IMMEDIATE phase of ethical life, which SUBLATES raw, sensual urges into the institution of marriage and prepares the individual for participation in civil society and the state. The family is the sphere of the woman, who 'has her substantive destiny in the family, and to be imbued with family piety is her ethical frame of mind' (§166).

Hegel's view of the husband–wife relationship is sometimes associated with his account of the master–slave relation in *PS*, IV.A., implying that

Hegel saw the wife as her husband's slave or servant, and perhaps that she, like the slave, may find fulfilment and/or liberation in the work she does for him. This association, with any inferences drawn from it, is incorrect:

(1) Domestic service was widespread in Hegel's day, and women of Hegel's class were not expected to work in the house: 'Antigone did not do her own washing-up' (W. H. Walsh).

(2) The differentiation of the husband–wife relation from the master–servant relation goes back to Aristotle, for whom the husband's 'rule' over his wife is like the rule of a citizen over his fellow citizens, and thus quite different from a master's 'despotic' rule over his slaves. There is no evidence that Hegel sanctioned a radical departure from this tradition.

(3) German, like Greek and Latin, has two words for 'man': *Mensch*, which applies to all humans, and *Mann*, which means both 'adult male' and 'husband'. But the German for 'Mr, Sir, gentleman', *Herr*, also means 'lord, master'. But the fact that Mr (*Herr*) Hegel is also the master (*Herr*) of his household does not entail that he is the master of Mrs Hegel. (The lord of the manor does not lord it over his wife. His status reflects onto her and she is the lady of the manor.) *Herr*, like many words, enters into several contrasts: as 'master', it contrasts with *Knecht* or *Diener* ('servant, slave'); as 'Mr', with *Frau* ('Mrs', but also 'woman, wife'); and, as 'gentleman', with the similarly respectful *Dame* ('lady').

(4) Antigone, Hegel's ideal woman, was nobody's slave or servant. Hegel knew several intelligent and socially active women (including the novelist Caroline Paulus), but he would probably have disapproved of a modern Antigone, believing that such conduct (like comparable male conduct) is appropriate to ancient, heroic times, but not to the modern bourgeois state.

A. W. Wood plausibly argues that the exclusion of women (and peasants) from public life is a symptom of a conflict between three ideas espoused by Hegel:

(1) Social life requires SUBSTANCE as well as SUBJECTIVITY and REFLECTION. But these principles can be reconciled only if they are assigned to different people, respectively to women and to men.

(2) One cannot, in the modern world, fully actualize one's human nature without subjective FREEDOM, i.e. without becoming a PERSON and a SUBJECT in civil society.

(3) All human individuals are persons and subjects (*Hegel's Ethical Thought*, pp. 245f).

Wood suggests that, while the substantive principle (the 'foundation of the ethical in feelings, dispositions, and personal relationships') and the reflective principle are both essential to Hegel's theory, (1) might be modified so that their reconciliation can be effected not only by their assignment to different groups, e.g. sexes, but also, more acceptably, by their integration 'within each human personality' (p. 246). This may, as Wood argues, be difficult in practice, but it should be possible in principle, since no one is unremittingly reflective and subjective. Philosophers and statesmen not only emerge from substance as children and, on Hegel's view, return to it in DEATH, they usually return to substance in the evening. It is thus hard to see why anyone need be exclusively substantial.

fate, destiny and providence   German has several words for 'fate' or 'destiny':

(1)   *Bestimmung* (DETERMINATION) is one's 'destiny' or 'destination', in so far as this depends on one's inner nature.

(2)   (*Das*) *Geschick* ('fate', and now also 'skill') comes from *schicken* (originally 'to cause to happen', now 'to send'), which is in turn cognate with (*ge*)*schehen* ('to happen'). *Geschick* now refers to the events themselves, rather than the power that determines them.

(3)   (*Das*) *Schicksal* also comes from *schicken*. It refers both to events and to the power determining them, but it is used only with reference to human beings, not to things. It can be used either unqualifiedly or for the fate or destiny *of* something, e.g. of Christianity. It is Hegel's usual word for 'fate' or 'destiny'.

(4)   *Das Fatum* comes from the Latin *fari*, 'to express, make known', and thus refers originally to the decree of a deity. Leibniz, in his *Theodicy* (1710), distinguished (a) 'Mohammedan' *Fatum*, which is inscrutable and inescapable; (b) STOIC *Fatum*, which we can understand and thereby achieve inner tranquillity; and (c) Christian *Fatum*, which should be borne gladly, since it is sent by a benign deity. Hegel sometimes distinguishes *Fatum* from *Schicksal*: *Fatum* is wholly blind necessity, indifferent to justice and injustice, while *Schicksal* is recognized, in Greek (especially Sophoclean) tragedy, as true justice. But often they are synonymous, as in his report of Napoleon's remark to Goethe that we no longer have a *Schicksal* to which men are subject and the old *Fatum* has been replaced by politics. (In *LPH*, Hegel applies this dictum to imperial Rome, rather than the modern world.)

(5)   (*Das*) *Verhängnis*, *from verhängen* ('to let (something) hang, let happen'), was used in the Reformation for divine 'dispensation', and in the Enlightenment as an equivalent of *Schicksal*. It now means an 'untoward fate, doom'.

Hegel is also influenced by the Greek concept(s) of fate, especially *moira* ('allotted portion (especially of death), fate', also personified as *Moirai*, 'the Fates'), which appears in epic, tragedy and, especially in the guise of *ananke* ('NECESSITY'), in pre-Socratic philosophers (especially Heraclitus). The gods, especially Zeus, are often dispensers of fate, sometimes superior to it, and sometimes constrained by it. Zeus and fate somehow determine events, but men have free will: fate exploits the character of men to maintain cosmic order. In the fourth century BC, *heimarmene* ('fate', but also 'chain' of causes) supplanted *moira*, and astrologers and STOICISM attempted to resolve the paradoxes of earlier belief. The Stoics identified fate with *logos* ('reason'), *pronoia* ('providence') and Zeus. Irrational fate and rational determinism (*ananke*, 'necessity') converge in *heimarmene*. In later Greek philosophy, God becomes more transcendent and thus God and *heimarmene* are separated again. Often, Hegel sees fate as a single, indeterminate, UNIVERSAL power above the diversity and PARTICULARITY of the gods. In his account of MEASURE in *SL*, he equates *Schicksal* with Nemesis, divine indignation at, and retribution for, human presumption (hubris) , the transgression of due bounds or measures (cf. *Enc.* I §107A.).

Schicksal plays a part in native German mythology and popular belief, but Hegel, like Hölderlin and Schelling, derived his interest in it from Greek tragedy. Schelling, in *STI*, associated fate especially with antiquity: HISTORY is the self-disclosing revelation of the ABSOLUTE, and falls into three periods. In the first, *Schicksal*, a wholly blind power, holds sway and is responsible for the destruction of the Greek world; in the second, beginning with the expansion of Rome, nature is dominant and the obscure LAW of fate becomes the clear law of nature; the third, which is yet to begin, will be that of providence (*Vorsehung*), when what appeared earlier as fate and nature will be seen to have been the beginning of a self-revealing providence (*STI*, III.604). In *On University Studies*, viii, Schelling presents the three periods in the order: nature, fate, providence. The Greeks are in harmony with nature; then a rift opens up between freedom and fate as necessity (the 'Fall of Man'); finally, Christianity begins the reign of providence. In his lectures on the philosophy of art (1801 and 1804), Schelling gives a more refined account of the role of fate in various literary genres and of the differences between ancient and modern conceptions of fate.

Fate involves four elements:

(1) Individuals to whom things happen.
(2) Events that are not planned or intended by the individuals to whom they happen, and are not easily avoided. Thus they require:
(3) A POWER, external to the individual(s), that is (held) responsible for these events.
(4) The relationship between 1 and 3, which brings about 2.

Hegel's account of fate can be considered in terms of these elements:

1. Things happen to non-human individuals owing to external forces, and Hegel, in *SL* (under the heading of blind MECHANISM), concedes that the fate of a LIVING ORGANISM is its genus (*Gattung*), i.e. its dissolution into the genus by DEATH. But simply as OBJECTS (*Objekte*), living creatures have no fate, since it is their very nature or CONCEPT to be determined from without. Thus external DETERMINATION is, in a sense, their own *self*-determination. Only in the case of humans and human groups is there a suitable contrast between an individual that can, to some degree, determine its own career or 'fate' and events that happen to it outside its control. To have a fate, an individual must be more or less SELF-CONSCIOUS, able to draw a contrast between itself as a free I* that has wishes and plans of its own, together with some capacity for fulfilling them, and external events or an external power that it sees as ALIEN

to itself. But not all human beings are self-conscious to the same degree. An ancient Greek was sufficiently self-conscious to distinguish between himself and the external world and thus to be subject to fate. But if his fate was untoward, he did not, like the Christian, protest that things were not as they OUGHT to be and require some consolation (*Trost*) for his disappointment, since he had no well-developed contrast between 'is' and 'ought'. For him, things were more or less as they should be, and he simply accepted his fate with a resigned 'It is so' (*Enc.* I §147A.).

2. Events are attributed to fate or are seen as *the* fate of an individual or group. While the Greeks were most interested in the fate of individuals, Hegel is, from a wider historical perspective, also concerned about the fate of PEOPLES and civilizations, especially the fate of Greek civilization itself.

3. The power that produces fateful events must, on Hegel's view, be more or less inscrutable and blind in its workings. It cannot work in intelligible ways for the realization of a PURPOSE that is known to us. (In *SCF*, he discusses the differences between PUNISHMENT under human laws and punishment as fate.) Fate may, as in Sophocles, serve justice. But its conception of justice must remain more or less obscure, thus leaving no room for complaints or for demands for consolation. To the extent that fate serves an ascertainable purpose, it becomes providence (*pronoia, Vorsehung*).

4. To be exposed to fate, Hegel argues in *SL*, one must perform a DEED (*Tat*), which leaves a 'side open for the communication of one's ESTRANGEd (*entfremdeten*) ESSENCE': 'A PEOPLE [*Volk*] without deeds [*tatlose*] is without blame [*tadellos*].' Thus at some level one is always responsible for one's fate. But this can be conceived in different ways. In *LA*, he argues that in drama a character creates his own fate, by his pursuit of his aim in circumstances known to him, while in epic his fate is made for him, since 'the situation is too great for the individuals'. Again, in Greek tragedy, an individual's fate emerges from his ACTION, while in romantic drama (e.g. *Macbeth*) his fate is also 'an inner growth, a development of his *character*'. Hegel's own view is that one's fate is an 'evolution of oneself' and thus one's own responsibility (*Enc.* I §147A.). Accidents happen, but it is up to us whether or not we turn stones into pearls. On the large scale, what happens to us is directed by the providence of the world-SPIRIT rather than by blind fate.

Hegel's view of fate is the end-result of a TRIADIC movement: (1) naive (Greek) acceptance of fate; (2) modern (post-Greek) resistance to fate and demand for consolation, especially in an afterlife; (3) sophisticated (Hegelian) reconciliation (*Versöhnung*) to fate, based on a deeper conception of the human being and his relation to the world spirit.

feeling and sensation   German has two common words for 'feeling': (1) *Empfindung* ('sensation, feeling') is from *empfinden* ('to sense, feel') and it carries a suggestion of 'what one finds (*findet*) in oneself'. An *Empfindung* involves sensitivity to and awareness of a stimulus: it is associated with the sense organs, and also with pain and aesthetic experience. (2) *Gefühl*, from *fühlen* ('to feel'), also has a wide range of meaning, which coincides only

103

partially with that of *Empfindung*. It originally referred to the sense of touch, but by Hegel's day it had acquired most of the senses of our 'feeling'.

German usage drew no stable, generally accepted distinction between *Empfindung* and *Gefühl*. But they differ in two respects. First, *Gefühl* stresses subjective feelings, while *Empfindung* stresses sensitivity to an objective stimulus. Thus Kant agrees that *Empfindung* can denote *both* the sensation of an objective quality, such as the green colour of a meadow, *and* the subjective sensation of pleasure one derives from the sight of the meadow, but he reserves *Gefühl* for the latter (*CJ*, I §3). Second, a *Gefühl* is more closely interwoven with the whole psyche, while an *Empfindung* is more localized and fleeting. Hegel argues that since common usage admits the expressions '*Gefühl* of RIGHT' and *Selbstgefühl* ('self-feeling', viz. obscure self-awareness, but also 'self-esteem'), but not '*Empfindung* of right' or *Selbstempfindung*, and since it connects *Empfindung* with *Empfindsamkeit* ('sensitiveness'), *Empfindung* stresses passivity or finding, while *Gefühl* stresses selfhood or selfishness (*Selbstischkeit*) (*Enc*. III §402).

Thus in Hegel's main account of feeling (*Enc*. III §§399–412) *Empfindung* is the final stage of the 'natural SOUL' and refers to discrete and fleeting sensations, which, though semi-conscious, are not CONSCIOUS in the sense that they are directed towards external OBJECTS, since the natural soul has not yet developed a distinction between itself and the external world. The next phase, the 'feeling (*fühlende*) SOUL', also has no consciousness of an external world, nor, consequently, of itself in contrast to such a world. But *Gefühl* forms a bridge between the wholly self-enclosed natural soul and the consciousness that has a view of the world as a whole and of its own place in it. Sensations and feelings play a part in developed consciousness, but a subordinate part: we are conscious of large tracts of the world only by having heard or read about them and not from direct SENSORY contact.

The feeling soul has three stages: (1) The feeling soul in its IMMEDIACY, or life-feeling (*Gefühlsleben* or *Lebensgefühl*), a vague awareness of one's total bodily condition, which Hegel associates primarily with life in the womb. (2) Self-feeling, a vague awareness of oneself as an individual in contrast to, but absorbed in, one's particular feelings. Hegel associates this primarily with infancy and its *Selbstischkeit* ('selfishness' or 'self-absorption'), which is quite different from reflective self-awareness or -consciousness. (3) Habit (*Gewohnheit*), in which by constant repetition sensations and feelings become familiar and thus less obtrusive. Habit liberates and distances us from our feelings and sensations. In particular, one's body is habituated to the effortless expression of feelings, so that it becomes a pliable, unresisting instrument: feelings are thus externalized and disengaged from the self. This leads to the third phase of soul, the 'ACTUAL soul', in which the complete habituation of the body forms the transition to conciousness.

These stages of feeling are primarily associated with our early life, but they persist, sometimes pathologically, into adulthood. Life-feeling, for example, is dominant in dreams; it underlies our less than fully rational attachments to particular places and people; it constitutes the deep levels of our character and personality that account for our particular responses to external events, and, when we reflect and reason, for the types of consideration and argument to which we are susceptible; and it becomes dominant in various pathological states such as somnambulism. In the 'Remarks' of *Enc.* III, and in his accompanying lectures, Hegel attempted to illuminate the feeling states of infancy and, by way of contrast, the nature of rational SELF-CONSCIOUSNESS by examining the pathological states that afflict some adults, such as obsessive delusions. He held that madness (*Verrücktheit*, literally, 'displacement' or 'dislocation') involves not a complete loss of reason, but a CONTRADICTION between rational (self-)consciousness and a more primitive level of the psyche that is not properly subsumed or SUBLATED under it.

Feeling appears, however, not only in these simple guises. Like other lower stages of spirit, it can provide a FORM for content derived from higher stages. An adult, unlike an infant, can sense or feel that stealing is wrong or that God exists. Thus some philosophers, notably F. H. Jacobi, argued that the truths of religion and morality are discerned by feeling (or FAITH) rather than thought or reason. Hegel criticized this doctrine on several counts:

(1) Feelings can have a bad or false, as well as a good or true, CONTENT. One might feel that stealing is right. Hence a feeling as such does not validate the content of the feeling. (He makes the same criticism of appeals to conscience.)

(2) The content of the feeling is in these cases supplied by THOUGHT and REPRESENTATION rather than feeling itself. It is thus mediated, rather than simple and immediate, and thinking is therefore the appropriate way to develop and validate such content. (The experienced mathematician just feels that $13 \times 17 = 221$, but this truth is not ultimately derived from, or based on, this feeling.)

(3) The appeal to feeling tends to dilute the content of religious doctrine to an abstraction, the lowest common denominator of all religious belief. In an attack on his colleague at Berlin, Schleiermacher, Hegel says that animals too would have a religion if it consisted in a feeling of dependence.

Some philosophers, notably Pascal, tried to base religion and morality (and even such truths as the three-dimensionality and the infinity of space) on the heart (*Herz*), traditionally seen as the seat of feelings. In *PS* ('The Law of the Heart and the Frenzy of Self-conceit') Hegel argues that the law of the heart (Pascal's *ordre du coeur*) leads to subjectivism. If universalized to become the 'law of all hearts', it degenerates into a law under which everyone seeks to fulfil his selfish individuality. This conflicts both with the original ideal of the law of the heart and with a stable social order.

finite, finitude *see* LIMIT, RESTRICTION AND FINITUDE

force and power Hegel uses three main terms for 'force' or 'power'.

1. *Macht* is primarily the power held by persons in virtue of an institutional position (of power) that enables them to influence and control people, things

105

and events. It can be attributed to things, e.g. to love, music or FATE. A person or thing that has *Macht* may also be called a *Macht*. For example, God and Germany both have power and are powers.

2. *Gewalt* is the power to force (rather than influence) people to do what one wants. It is often, but not always, equivalent to 'violence' (*Gewalttätigkeit*, literally '*Gewalt*-activity'). More than *Macht*, it suggests the application of force or power: thus in *SL*, *Gewalt* is the APPEARANCE (*Erscheinung*) of *Macht*, or *Macht* as external. It too can be attributed to music, love, storms, etc., if their power is irresistible. But *Gewalt* also means legitimate power, and then refers to the specific organs of state-power and to the power wielded by officials of these organs. Thus the constitutional division of powers is the distribution of functions between distinct *Gewalten*, between, in *PR* §273, the legislative *Gewalt*, the governing or executive *Gewalt* and the princely *Gewalt*.

3. *Kraft* ('force, energy, vigour, strength', etc.), when applied to a person, means his individual physical, intellectual or moral power to effect things. *Kraft* is not primarily institutional or political power, nor is it essentially power over someone or something. Its main philosophical uses are these: it is a natural force, such as gravity, electricity or magnetism. German philosophers tended to reject the view that matter or substances simply *have* forces, and to argue instead that they *are* forces, with no independent substratum underlying the force itself. Their view of the world is dynamic: things are activities or at least the potentiality for activities. Leibniz saw a force as a capacity for action, which is actualized when certain conditions are fulfilled: a SUBSTANCE, on his view, is essentially a force. Wolff attributed to the elements of nature two forces, a force of inertia and a motive or moving force: in contrast to a *Vermögen* ('ability, capacity'), which is a mere possibility of doing or undergoing something, a *Kraft* has an intrinsic tendency to express or actualize itself. Kant argued, in *MENS*, that MATTER is constituted by a force of attraction and a force of repulsion. (In the Logic, Hegel assesses this doctrine of Kant's in his section on being-FOR-SELF.) Herder, in *G*, saw God as a supreme force, and the whole world as 'an expression of his ever-living, ever-acting forces'. Another common use of *Kraft* is to denote the powers or faculties of the MIND. *Vermögen* is also used in this sense.

In Hegel these terms conform on the whole to traditional usage, but he often takes issue with the doctrines they are used to express:

1. *Macht* is used in a political sense, but has no special political significance for him. He also speaks, in the Logic, of the *Macht* of substance and of the CONCEPT and the UNIVERSAL, cases where there is no resistance to be overcome. In *LA*, he discusses the 'universal powers of acting', which are the general institutions (FAMILY, nation, STATE, Church) and motivating forces (fame, friendship, honour, love) that drive the individual to act; in tragic situations, these powers come into collision with each other in the conflicting actions of the individuals who represent them. In so far as they result in action and conflict these powers are also *Gewalten* ('forces').

2. For several reasons, Hegel assigns *Gewalt* ('force') a limited role in internal political life: (a) A person with FREEDOM of WILL cannot be forced to

106

do things that he does not want to do: he can choose to resist or evade force, in the last resort by DEATH. (b) A citizen is initiated into the state by EDUCATION and the customs of ETHICAL LIFE. Hence (c) the state is an organic, rather a mechanistic whole: the citizen is more like a player in an orchestra than a billiard ball. (d) The state confers benefits that most people want, such as safe highways, and is not primarily an oppressive or restrictive institution. Force may play a large part in the foundation of states, but not in their subsequent operation. Hegel favours a division of powers (*Gewalten*) in the state, but only if these articulate the state-ORGANISM, and not if they are designed to limit or restrict each other – an arrangement that leads to political breakdown or inertia (*PR* §272).

3. Hegel endorses the view that things are at bottom activities rather than solid lumps, but holds that the notion of *Kraft* is of limited use in this regard: (a) Although *Kraft* is introduced in the Logic to give unity to the diverse parts of a thing, a force usually inheres in a substratum which it does not constitute: magnetic force presupposes a bar of metal that has other properties, e.g., a colour, not explained by the force. (b) A force does not express or realize itself automatically: it needs to be 'solicited' by another force. We thus have an INFINITE regress of forces or the interaction of two forces, each soliciting the other. A force differs in this from a PURPOSE, which realizes itself of its own accord. (c) There is a diversity not only of particular forces, but of types of force: gravity, magnetism, electricity, etc. To attempt to reduce these to a single force results in an empty abstraction. (d) The operation of a force is blind, and, unlike purpose, cannot account for the orderly nature of the world.

Thus force is a FINITE category: a given force has a restricted content, and presupposes both other forces and entities of a higher type, if it is to operate. Hence it is inappropriate to see God or the world as a whole as a force or forces. Force lacks the required INFINITY or self-explanatoriness. It is also mistaken to see the mind as a collection of forces, of *Vermögen*, or even of activities: (a) The mind is not a solid substratum, like a bar of iron. (b) It is relatively self-realizing and self-determining. (c) Above all, our faculties are not simply distinct from each other, as different forces are: the faculties form an ordered hierarchy, but THOUGHT controls and permeates all the others. For example, FEELING in its raw, primitive forms retires into the background in a healthy rational adult, and thought supplies the content of higher types of feeling.

Hegel rejects the view that we can only know the expression (*Äusserung*) of a *Kraft*, not the force itself. There is, he argues, no more to be known about a force than its diverse expressions: its INNER and OUTER coincide.

form, matter and content   German has two words for 'form':

1. *Gestalt* is a native German word, originally from *stellen* ('to put, set up, arrange, form', etc.), but generating a verb of its own, *gestalten* ('to form, shape'), and hence the noun *Gestaltung* for the process or product of such forming. A *Gestalt* is not an abstract shape or form that may be shared by

several things, but the form or shape of an individual. Thus it can refer also to the formed or shaped individual itself. Unlike *Form*, *Gestalt* does not usually imply a contrast with 'matter' or 'content'. Objects that have a *Gestalt* (e.g. plants, musical works, cultures) are thought of as ORGANIC unities, appreciable only as a whole, not by the piecemeal consideration of their parts.

2. The Latin-derived *Form* usually indicates an ABSTRACT form shared by several individuals: unlike *Gestalt*, it can refer to, e.g., the sonnet-form in general, though, like *Gestalt*, it can also refer to the form of a particular sonnet. Thus it usually contrasts with 'matter' or 'content'. In aesthetics, the *Form* of a work of art is its perceptible, outer APPEARANCE (*Schein*), in contrast to its inner content. (The *Form*, but not the *Gestalt*, of the work may be inadequate to its content.) In the Aristotelian tradition, by contrast, the *Form* (Greek: *eidos*) of a thing, as distinct from its matter, is often seen as its inner ESSENCE, which determines the outer form. The notion of an essential, inner form appears in Herder, Goethe, and Hegel (*see* CONCEPT). The adjective *formal* or *formell* applies to whatever pertains to the form and abstracts from the content, and *Formalismus* is an excessive concentration on the form at the expense of content.

In Hegel's Logic, *Form* is contrasted with 'essence', but more centrally with 'matter' and 'content':

1. *Materie*, like 'matter', has two main uses in philosophy:
(a) It denotes physical matter, in contrast not primarily to 'form', but to MIND or SPIRIT and to the IDEAL or abstract. *Materie* in this sense is equivalent to *Stoff* ('stuff', matter'). These words also occur in the plural, especially when Hegel discusses the theory that the properties of a THING are matters or stuffs (e.g. heat is 'caloric matter'), but 'porous' stuffs that can permeate each other, so that the thing can be, e.g., both hot and sweet throughout. But in the singular, *Materie* can denote the neutral, homogeneous matter of which, according to Newtonian physics, everything consists. Hegel (like Berkeley) regarded *Materie* of this type as an empty abstraction.
(b) In the Aristotelian tradition, the matter of an entity contrasts with its form. But 'matter' in this sense is also ambiguous: it refers to (i) the formless matter out of which the formed thing emerges, e.g. the block of marble from which the statue is made; and (ii) the formed matter that is contemporaneous with the formed thing, e.g. the shaped marble of which the statue consists. There are four further complications: First, matter in sense (b) is usually also matter or material in sense (a), but it need not be: the matter of, e.g., a painting may be either the materials (e.g. paint, canvas, etc.) used to make it or the theme or message of the painting. (Hegel more commonly uses *Inhalt*, 'content', for 'matter' in the latter sense.) Second, in the case of a statue, form and matter are relatively independent or 'indifferent' (*gleichgültig*): marble, or a given block of marble, can be made into other things than statues, and a statue of the same form can be

made of a different material, e.g. bronze. But in the case of such entities as living organisms, matter and form are not so indifferent: flesh, unlike marble, cannot exist before the entities made of it, it must constitute the particular animal that consists of it; conversely, an animal can only consist of flesh. Third, the marble, from which a statue is made and of which it then consists, or the flesh of which an animal consists, are formless relatively to the statue or the animal. But they in turn have a form that makes them different from, say, flint or blood, and consist of more elementary matter, which in turn has a form and consists of still simpler matter, and so on. There are then two alternatives: (i) any matter is analysable into form and matter, *ad infinitum*; (ii) the regress ends in 'prime matter', matter with no form, the ultimate, simple matter of which everything consists. This prime matter is not unlike the physicist's basic matter. (One might also argue that (iii) there are several ultimate matters, not further analysable into form and matter: the elements.) Finally, Aristotelians held that the series of entities constituted by the successive imposition of higher forms ends in pure form, form with no matter, viz. God.

2. There are two words for 'content': *Inhalt* and *Gehalt*. *Gehalt* differs from *Inhalt* in that, first, it implies that the content is more unified than does *Inhalt* (hence we might use 'content' for *Gehalt*, 'contents' for *Inhalt*), and, second, it implies more strongly the value of the content (hence *Gehalt* suggests 'import'). For both these reasons, the *Gehalt* of something is more closely intertwined with its *Form*, and Hegel, though he uses both words, usually contrasts *Form* with *Inhalt*. *Inhalt* differs from *Materie* in two ways. First, *Inhalt* is logically correlative to *Form*, and the *Inhalt* cannot exist before the formed thing. Second, *Inhalt* carries no suggestion of physical materiality. For both reasons, the content of a work of art is its theme, not the materials of which it is made.

Hegel uses all these words in the full range of their significance. He uses *Gestalt* in *PS* for the forms or shapes of CONSCIOUSNESS, for the forms or shapes of natural objects such as crystals, and especially for the shapes and forms of works of art. *Form* and *Inhalt* or *Materie* recur throughout his works. He stresses in particular the following points:

(1) *Form* and *Inhalt/Materie* can denote a variety of distinct contrasts: e.g. the material of which a book is made, viz. paper and leather, is its external *Form*, in contrast to its inner, literary form, and to its *Inhalt* (in two corresponding senses). How 'indifferent' form and content are, and which of the pair is seen as more essential and 'active', will depend on which contrast we have in mind.

(2) Even in the case of a single contrast, either of the contrasting terms may be seen as *Form*, and the other as *Inhalt*, depending on our point of view: e.g. the pure THOUGHTS involved in, or the logical structure of, a piece of discourse (in contrast to its empirical content), may be seen either as its *Form* or as its *Inhalt* (its 'nub').

(3) In living organisms and ideal works of art, *Form* and *Inhalt* are inseparably intertwined.

(4) There is no wholly formless matter or content, since what is formless relative to one form is 'informed' by another form: formless marble has the form of marble.

(5) Conversely, there is no wholly contentless form: e.g. the logical forms of two sentences can differ from each other only in virtue of a difference in their respective contents. Most crucially, what is at one level *Form* or *formell*, a thought or a logical form, can be the *content* of a higher (or meta-) thought: e.g. the thought BEING is part of the form of the sentence 'Roses are red', but part of the content of 'Being becomes nothing'. Thus pure thought or the 'logical IDEA', though in a sense pure *form*, is not exclusively formal, but has itself as its own content.

Pure, contentless form and pure, formless matter are, on Hegel's view, the same: a wholly indeterminate abstraction.

freedom *Freiheit* and *frei* correspond closely to 'freedom' and 'free'. They refer both to freedom of the WILL and to freedom in all its social and political senses. Thus 'freedom' contrasts with 'slavery', 'dependence', 'compulsion', 'NECESSITY', etc. Hegel attempts to interconnect this variety of senses into a single theory of freedom.

The core notion of freedom is this: something, especially a person, is free if, and only if, it is independent and self-DETERMINING, not determined by or dependent on something other than itself. But this formula raises three questions:

1. Where does the boundary lie between something and its other? For example, (a) I* have certain (b) thoughts; I have (c) perceptions, desires and a body; I inhabit (d) a social and political environment; and I dwell in (e) a natural world that surrounds and pervades my social environment and myself. Does the boundary between myself and the other lie between (a), on the one hand, and (b), (c), (d) and (e), on the other; between (a)–(b) and (c)–(d)–(e); between (a)–(b)–(c) and (d)–(e); or between (a)–(b)–(c)–(d) and (e)? What it is for me to be self-determining, rather than determined by an other, will differ according to which of these views we take.

2. How is the relation of determining or dependency to be specified? Is it, for example, causal determination, physical compulsion or restriction (e.g. imprisonment), threats, slavery (i.e. ownership by another person), voluntary acceptance of another's political, moral or doctrinal authority, etc?

3. How is freedom secured? There are three possibilities: (i) The relation of determination or dependency is severed, despite the persistence of both terms of the relation and of their otherness: e.g. I cease to care about my imprisonment or enslavement and retreat into myself. (ii) The relation of determination is severed by the elimination of one of its terms: e.g. I am released from slavery or imprisonment, or, conceivably, I attain freedom by my own DEATH. (iii) The two terms cease to be, or to seem, other than each other, because one or the other, or both, takes over or SUBLATES the other: e.g.

my captor and I fall in love, so that we cease to seem (or to be) alien to each other and I cease to feel obedience to his will as a constraint on my freedom.

Hegel's theory of freedom turns on the answers given to these questions:

1. The boundary between oneself and the other is not fixed or permanent, either in the life of the individual or throughout HISTORY. Nor is the content of the self fixed or permanent. What one is depends on one's SELF-CONSCIOUSNESS. An initially plausible view is that I am my thoughts, perceptions, desires and body ((a)–(b)–(c) above), and that I am free in so far as these and my pursuit of them are not other-determined (in one or more senses). But my desires, Hegel argues, are determined from without, and, especially in infancy, not easily controlled by me. It is easy to feel that one's bodily desires, and perhaps one's sense-perceptions, are alien to oneself, and to locate one's true self in the I ((a) above) or one's thought or reason ((b) above). Then one will suppose, like Plato, the Stoics and religious ascetics, that freedom consists not in satisfying one's desires, but in ignoring, repressing, controlling or eliminating them. A version of this was espoused by Kant: freedom from the intrusions of nature is to be attained by submission to MORAL laws endorsed and imposed by reason alone. Such a view also implies freedom from external natural, social and political constraints, since it is usually by way of one's desires and aversions that such external factors impinge on one. (But Kant, unlike many proponents of this view, was intensely concerned about political liberty.)

Hegel was sympathetic to this view, but felt that one's desires and the external world cannot be so easily disposed of, both because the sheer repression of one's desires by REASON is itself a type of enslavement, and because one's reason alone cannot give guidance for life or action. On Hegel's view, our desires are not, in the civilized adult, raw urges, wholly alien to oneself, but are imbued with THOUGHT by CULTURE and ETHICAL LIFE. But this means that the boundary between oneself and the other shifts, so that the self includes a good deal of the social environment that was previously supposed to be other than oneself. The paradigm of such an extension of the self to include one's society (or, conversely, of the absorption of oneself by one's society) was, for Hegel, Greek ethical life. This conferred OBJECTIVE freedom, but neglected SUBJECTIVE freedom, the freedom to pursue one's desires and to reflect rationally on traditional codes and doctrines.

2. Hegel considers several types of other-determination, and responds to them in different ways. Slavery, for example, his paradigm of socio-political unfreedom, has rightly been simply abolished since it is at odds with the ESSENCE of man. CAUSAL determination by nature, more prominent in the life of infants and primitive peoples, is gradually reduced by culture. (Hegel argues against causal determinism in a variety of ways, especially in *PS*, V, and *Enc.* III.) Social and political control is never eliminated, but, first, the modern STATE allows more subjective freedom than the ancient; and, second, ethical life is, and in philosophy is seen to be, an expression of the rationality that lies at the core of oneself, and thus not wholly other than oneself.

3. In the Logic the transition from necessity to the freedom of the CONCEPT

111

occurs when the necessity with which one thing determines another becomes so intense that they cease to be distinct. Freedom internalizes, rather than supplants, necessity. Usually, then, Hegel's thought on a type of freedom takes the following route: the attempt to sever one's relation to the constraining other by ignoring it (STOICISM, etc.) or by abolishing it (in their various ways SCEPTICISM, revolutionary Jacobinism, etc.) are, though historically fruitful, unsuccessful. Freedom lies rather in the IDENTITY of the other with oneself. The identity need not be the close identity of the Greek city-state, but the differentiated identity of the modern state that accommodates elements of the rejected or SUBLATED solutions, such as critical REFLECTION and pursuit of self-interest.

The identification of the other with oneself involves three distinct aspects: (1) Man *makes* the other less alien by his practical activities on it; he reforms his society, cultivates nature, etc. (2) He *discovers* that it is not wholly *other* by his theoretical activities: empirical and philosophical studies of society, nature, etc. reveal that they embody universal thoughts. (3) He makes it less alien by his theoretical activities on it: to reveal the thoughts involved in one's society, etc., is not only to discover, but to enhance, its affinity to oneself. These processes occur over history, which is for Hegel the realization of freedom. Since self-consciousness too consists in seeing the affinity of the other to oneself and in thus enriching one's conception of oneself, freedom and self-consciousness advance together.

G

God and Christianity   Like most of his contemporaries, Hegel claimed to believe in the existence of God. But the notions of BELIEF, EXISTENCE and God are all problematic:

1. At the level of FAITH, Hegel believed in the personal deity of the Lutheran Church. But he was not content simply to accept this doctrine without attempting to comprehend and justify it rationally. However, the rational comprehension and justification of the pictorial REPRESENTATIONS of faith does not leave them unchanged. Philosophical cognition transforms these conceptions into thoughts. In doing this, philosophers have usually altered the content of faith, diluting the personal God of Christianity, for example, into a 'necessary being'. Medieval philosophers appealed to the doctrine of 'double truth', the truth of faith and the truth of reason, which may not only not coincide, but even conflict. But one of Hegel's aims is to overcome the opposition, like other oppositions, between the wealth of traditional faith and the poverty of philosophical reason. Thus his philosophy is intended to have the same content as Christianity, while differing from it in FORM.

2. The notion of the existence of God presents several difficulties. One is that the readily available terms for 'being' or 'existence' tend to imply that God is a FINITE entity alongside other finite entities, existing in the way that they exist. Another is that when we speak of the existence of something, we usually imply a contrast with its CONCEPT: the concept of a lion is one thing, its existence is another. But, Hegel argues, God is not distinct from the concept of God, as a lion is distinct from the concept of a lion, since God is INFINITE rather than finite.

3. Another difficulty in ascribing existence to God is this: A faith such as Lutheranism supplies a rich conception of God as well as affirming his existence. (One might share this conception of him while doubting or denying his existence.) But philosophy can assume such a conception no more than his existence. It asks 'What is God?' as well as 'Does God exist?' At most it assumes the lowest common denominator of any conception of God, that he or it is (the) ABSOLUTE, which is the conception of God shorn of its pictorial anthropomorphism and transposed into the form of pure thought. Thus 'God' in Hegel is often equivalent to 'the absolute', and similar arguments apply to both concepts. The traditional PROOFS of God's existence are seen as filling out our notion of God, not simply as establishing

113

the existence of something of which we already have a clear conception. (Kant, in *CJ*, saw the proofs in a similar light.)

Since 'God', like 'the absolute', is an all but empty expression, and since therefore an answer to the question 'What is God?' (such as 'God is ESSENCE') amounts to little more than a readiness to employ the concept thus predicated of God (e.g. the concept of essence), it is barely possible to be an atheist: atheism would be simply a complete incapacity for thought. (Schopenhauer, who believed the ultimate reality to be WILL, and Nietzsche, who held it to be will-to-power, both saw themselves as atheists. Hegel would see them as theists who mistakenly, and emptily, believed God to be will or will-to-power.) But there is still room for at least two theological failings: (a) One may apply to God, or to the universe, only a relatively primitive thought, such as BEING or essence, stopping short of more advanced and appropriate thoughts such as the absolute IDEA or SPIRIT. (b) One may postulate an inappropriate RELATION between God and the world. This defect is connected to the first, in that to see God in terms of a certain thought implies a certain type of relation between him and the world. If, for example, God is a determinate being or EXISTENCE (a *Daseiendes*), then he must be other than, and limited by, the world; if he is an essence, the world must be an APPEARANCE (*Schein*). Only if he is seen in terms of the absolute idea or spirit is he related to the world in an appropriate way.

At first sight, God might be related to the world in three alternative ways: (1) God is distinct from the world. (2) God is identical to the world, but in such a way that only the world really exists, and God does not. This is the version of pantheism that, e.g., Bayle attributed to Spinoza. (3) God is identical to the world, but in such a way that only God really exists, and the world does not. This is the version of pantheism that Hegel calls *Akosmismus* ('acosmism', 'denial of the world') and holds to be Spinoza's real view. Although Hegel prefers (3) to (1) and (2), he holds all three to be inadequate: (1), because it makes God as finite as the world, and supplies no ultimate explanation of either; (2), because it leaves only the finite world; and (3), because it supplies no adequate account of the appearance of a finite world, especially of the philosophizing SUBJECT himself.

Hegel's own view of the relationship (which is akin to that of mystics such as Böhme) is this: God is a Trinity, consisting of father, son and holy spirit. His relation to the world is neither sheer identity nor sheer difference. The world of NATURE and of spirit are rather phases or MOMENTs of God: he (the father) achieves consciousness in nature (the son) and rises to SELF-CONSCIOUSNESS in the human spirit (the holy spirit, which includes awareness and worship of God in the religious community, but much else besides). These three phases are involved in the notion of spirit itself. This view is presented in terms of RELIGION in *LPR*. But it is presented in terms of philosophical thought in Hegel's whole system, since God the father is the logical idea, the conceptual system presented in the Logic, and the philosophies of nature and of spirit present the son and the holy spirit respectively. This identity-in-difference of God and the world is, on Hegel's view, symbolized by the incarnation and DEATH of Christ. (The 'son of God' has three meanings in Hegel: (1) the historical Jesus; (2) the natural world; (3) the 'eternal son' immanent in the father, the *logos* of St John's Gospel. (2) and (3) involve otherness and differentiation, but (1) represents reunification and reconciliation.)

The existence of God does not, on this view, require proof in the traditional sense, since God is the logical structure of the world and the world itself. Hence Hegel regards the proofs as recording man's 'elevation' (*Erhebung*) to God, an expression that ambiguously suggests *both* man's becoming aware of God *and* his becoming God(like). The suggestion that man becomes God is implicit in the view that the development of man's spirit is God's becoming self-conscious, and Hegel rejects the view that man is inescapably finite in contrast to the infinity of God. Thus he also rejects the view that God is in any way unknowable.

Hegel's religious thought raises several questions. One that divided his own pupils is: Is he a theist, a pantheist or an atheist? Some, such as Göschel (the 'right'-Hegelians), held him to be an orthodox believer, others, such as Strauss (the 'left'-Hegelians), took the contrary view. This question involves three subsidiary ones: (1) Is Hegel's philosophical system, however accurately it mirrors (in a different form) the structure of Christianity, an adequate translation of it, such that one who accepts the system can be said to be *ipso facto* a Christian? (2) Does Hegel's translation distort the content of Christianity too much (e.g. in assimilating man to God) to be a version of Christianity? (3) Should Hegel's frequent professions of faith in Christianity override the inadequacies of his philosophical translation of it? The complexity of such notions as 'belief', 'existence', 'God' and 'Christianity' exclude definitive answers to these questions. But Hegel's belief that opposites change into each other when they reach their highest pitch implies that if he arrived at atheism, he did so by stretching theism to its logical limits.

ground, condition and explanation The root meaning of *Grund* is 'ground, bottom, basis', with the implication that it supports what rests on it. Hegel exploits its occurrence in several colloquial expressions: *zu Grunde gehen* (literally 'to go to ground', hence, of a ship, 'to sink', and, of persons, etc., 'to be ruined, perish'); *zu Grunde richten* ('to send or direct to ground', hence 'to sink, ruin, destroy' a thing or person); *auf den Grund gehen* ('to get to the bottom' of something); *im Grunde* ('at bottom, fundamentally, strictly speaking'); and *von Grund aus* ('from the bottom up, thoroughly, radically'). *Grund* also means (a) reason (for an action, belief, or emotion)' and '(the) reason (for an occurrence)'. It enters into several compounds (e.g. *Grundsatz*, 'principle, axiom') and supplies two verbs, *gründen* (*auf*) ('to found, establish, base (ideas) on') and *begründen* ('to found, establish, consolidate, substantiate, give reasons for'). The correlative of *Grund* is *Folge* ('consequence, result', from *folgen*, 'to follow') or *das Begründete* ('the grounded').

Grund was used by mystics such as Eckhart for the deepest ESSENCE of the SOUL, where it is in contact with God. Eckhart also speaks of the *Abgrund* ('abyss') of God and of the soul, and later mystics introduce *Ungrund* ('non-ground') and *Urgrund* ('original ground'). For Böhme, the *Ungrund* is the first stage of the divine process, the ungrounded, self-enclosed unity, which then generates *Grund*, the second stage. Schelling too referred to the 'absolute IDENTITY', which precedes all grounds and existence, as the *Urgrund* or *Ungrund*.

The standard philosophical uses of *Grund* are these: a *Grund* is (1) a proposition that implies a second proposition; (2) a reason for believing something; (3) *one's* reason for believing something; (4) the event or state of affairs responsible for another event or state of affairs; (5) *a* reason for (or against) doing something; (6) *one's* reason for doing something (a *Beweggrund*, 'motive'). In each of these cases the *Grund* may (or may not) be sufficient (*zureichend*), in which case it fully explains, entails or grounds the occurrence, proposition, etc., whose ground it is. Hence Leibniz set up the 'principle of sufficient reason': 'Nothing happens without a cause or at least a determining reason.' This was regarded by Leibniz, and such followers as Wolff, as applying to propositions, as well as to events and states of affairs: no proposition is true unless there is a sufficient reason for it, even if the reason is not known to us. Hegel gives this principle a novel interpretation; namely, that everything is to be regarded not simply in its surface IMMEDIACY, but also as posited by something else, its ground. But to view things simply as grounded is not, for Hegel, ultimately satisfactory. He rejected the principle both as an explanatory principle and as an epistemological principle; he endorsed Leibniz's use of TELEOLOGICAL explanations, but held that this went beyond the notion of a ground to those of the CONCEPT and of PURPOSE.

In his main account of *Grund*, in *SL*, Hegel uses the word with a wide range of meaning. He first associates what is grounded with FORM and the ground with essence, matter and content. This is the ABSOLUTE ground: it begins by being a mere *Grundlage*, a 'bottom layer or stratum, a basis, a foundation', which does not require or determine any particular type of form or super-structure; but it ends by acquiring a content of its own, so that it is determinate ground, the ground of a particular (type of) phenomenon.

If the ground acquires content that fully mirrors the content of the phenomenon that it grounds, it is a 'formal' ground and it fully explains the phenomenon. But such an explanation (*Erklärung* – also 'DEFINITION') is, on Hegel's view, 'tautologous': it explains why opium sends one to sleep in terms of its soporific power, that is, it simply redescribes the phenomenon to be explained. In *PS*, as well as *SL*, Hegel had argued that explanations of phenomena in terms of, e.g., a force of attraction are tautological and represent CONSCIOUSNESS's 'communing with itself'. Such a ground not only grounds the phenomenon, but is also grounded by it: the content of the ground is wholly derived from, epistemically grounded in, the content of the phenomenon.

At the next stage, that of real ground, the ground is distinct in content from the phenomenon. Hegel here considers two types of case. First, there are scientific grounds, such as gravity (and theological grounds, such as God), which differ in content from any particular phenomenon in virtue of the great diversity of phenomena that they supposedly ground. But such a ground, though not tautological, fails to explain any particular phenomenon, just because it purports to explain too many: it cannot explain why the phenomenon as a whole is of one type (e.g. the movement of the planets) rather than another (e.g. tides). Second, one aspect of a phenomenon is often selected as its essential aspect, which supposedly grounds the phenomenon as a whole, with all its other aspects. For example, the deterrence aspect of PUNISHMENT is taken as the ground of, or reason for, punishment. But the selection of such an aspect is arbitrary, and the relationship of this aspect to other aspects remains CONTINGENT and external, unless we go beyond the category of ground and consider the concept of the whole phenomenon. Under this heading, Hegel also considers '*Räsonnement* [a pejorative word for "(sophistical) arguing"] from grounds', that is, looking for reasons for or against actions or beliefs. Such reasons are never conclusive: preservation of one's life, for example, is *a* reason for stealing or for deserting the battlefield, but a reason of this type is only one of many pros and cons, and it cannot justify the action in question.

Now that a gap has emerged between the ground and its consequence, the ground requires certain *conditions* if it is to take effect. A *Bedingung* ('condition') was originally a legal reservation or proviso, and hence it is a logically necessary condition, a proposition that must be true if another proposition is to be true, and also a causally necessary condition. The verb *bedingen* means both 'to stipulate, postulate, demand (as a condition of success)' and 'to cause, produce (as a result of certain conditions)'.

A condition differs from a ground. Hunger, for example, is the ground of my eating. It both supplies a reason for eating, and tends to result in eating if nothing else hinders it. But hunger alone will not result in my eating unless conditions are fulfilled, e.g., some fruit is available. Unlike my hunger, the fruit is an overt, independent entity, intrinsically unrelated to my eating: of itself the fruit gives no reason to eat and has no tendency to result in eating. The fruit is not intrinsically a condition of (my) eating, but is made a condition of it by my hunger for it: the fruit is conditioned by my hunger to become a condition of my eating. But once the fruit has been so conditioned and integrated into the sphere of my hunger, it is on a par with my hunger: the fruit *as hungered for* gives a reason for, and tends to result in, eating. My hunger and the fruit hungered for are two conditions of my eating, each alone merely a necessary condition, but together the *Totalität* ('TOTALITY') of conditions and thus sufficient to produce the fact or THING (*Sache*), eating. As I eat, the conditions of my eating, fruit and hunger, disappear: they are absorbed or SUBLATED into the eating they ground or MEDIATE, which is thus, in a sense, unconditioned. Since conditions are sublated, Hegel disagrees with Schelling's (early) view that something has conditions or is conditioned (*bedingt*) only if it is a THING (*Ding*).

In COGNITION, as well as in the world, Hegel believes, ground and conditions are sublated into what they ground and condition: e.g. a philosophical system and a developed political STATE absorb their extraneous material conditions, and their ground or basis is their overt logical structure, not a principle from which they begin or an underlying essence.

117

H

history   German has two words for 'history':

1. The Greek *historia* ('inquiry; knowledge, science; a written account of inquiries, narrative, history of events', from *historein*, 'to inquire, explore') entered German, via Latin, in the thirteenth century as *Historie*. From the eighteenth century the use and development of the word was repressed by that of *Geschichte*, but the adjective *historisch* and the noun *Historiker* ('historian') flourished. The original sense of *Historie* is close to that of *Erfahrung* ('EXPERIENCE'), and Hegel tends to use it for *Empirie*, rather than for specifically historical experience and events. He also speaks derogatively of *Historismus* in theology, historical erudition about religious opinions and institutions at the expense of conceptual inquiry into religious truths.

2. *Geschichte* ('story; affair, business; history') is a native German word, deriving from *geschehen* ('to be done, happen, occur'), and thus originally 'an event, a sequence of events'. But from the fifteenth century it was equated with *Historie* and used for a narrative or report. With the growth of historical research and awareness in the eighteenth century, it came to mean, especially in Herder, 'history' as the systematic investigation of past events. It is Hegel's usual word for 'history'. His use of the word is influenced by its kinship with *Geschick* and *Schicksal* ('FATE') and its similarity to *Schicht* ('stratum, layer').

'History', then, has two senses: the sequence of historical events and an account or study of such events. 'Philosophy of history' thus has two corresponding senses: philosophical REFLECTION, first, on the course of historical events, and, second, on the nature and methods of accounts of historical events. Philosophy of history before Hegel was of the first type rather than the second: The founder of the subject, Vico, argued, in his *Principles of a New Science of the Common Nature of Peoples* (1725), that all peoples pass through a divine, a heroic and a human stage, progressively developing from sensory thought to abstract thought, from the heroic ethic to MORALITY, and from privilege to equality of rights. (Hegel nowhere mentions Vico.) Voltaire (who coined the expression *philosophie de l'histoire*) described history, in his *Essay on the Customs and Spirit of Nations* (1756), as man's struggle for culture and progress. Herder, in *IPHM*, saw human history as a development towards 'humanity'; it is a continuation of the development of nature and proceeds in accordance with the same laws; the order and lawfulness of the world express the power and reason of God. Kant wrote two reviews of Herder's *Ideas*, and several essays on history, especially *IUH*, in which he argued that, despite free will, human actions are determined by universal laws and at least in the large may display to the historian a regular pattern; the goal of history is a perfectly just and rational STATE, which will secure the freedom necessary for the full development of human capacities, and remain in perpetual PEACE with other, similarly organized states. History was often seen, by e.g. Lessing and Fichte, as the realization of divine PROVIDENCE, of God's plan for the EDUCATION of the human race, which will ultimately result in its perfection.

Hegel's main account of history is in *LPH*. It has, in contrast to those of his predecessors, two distinctive features.

First, he was sceptical of the claims of philosophical historians to supply information about the end (or the beginning) of history that eluded empirical historians. History, for Hegel, ends with the present. While he often describes the present in terms (e.g. as the full realization of FREEDOM and SELF-CONSCIOUSNESS) which seem to leave little to happen in the future, he allows that there is more history to come, perhaps in America. But this is not the concern of the historian.

Second, Hegel regards philosophical history as a second-order enterprise, which makes essential use of the results of other historians. The ambiguity of *Geschichte* is not an accident: history as the narration of events emerges at the same time as strictly historical deeds and events. Societies that do not write history do not have a history: historical deeds and events require a self-consciousness that reveals itself in historical writing. (NATURE too does not, on Hegel's view, have a history: it develops and changes only in cyclical and repetitive ways.) Historical writing takes three main forms:

(1) 'Original' history, that of the chronicler, records the deeds of a people and a time to which he belongs and whose SPIRIT he shares.
(2) 'Reflective' history records the deeds of the past, but embodies the spirit of a later age and interprets the past in terms of it. Reflective history is of four types:
    (a) 'Universal' history records the whole history of a PEOPLE, a country or the world, on the basis of the work of original historians.
    (b) 'Pragmatic' history attempts to assimilate the past to the present and to derive lessons for the present from it. Hegel's belief that history involves DEVELOPMENT and that any phase of history sublates the conditions of its own emergence, commits him to the view that past historical periods are of no direct relevance to the present. He disapproves of the explanation of historic deeds in terms of trivial motives that are specific to no historical period (*Enc.* I §.140A.). He thus rejects pragmatic history as a genre.
    (c) 'Critical' history assesses the sources and plausibility of other historical accounts: it is a 'history of history'.
    (d) Histories of specific fields, such as ART, RIGHT, RELIGION or

119

PHILOSOPHY. Hegel sees the assumption of such a 'universal point of view' as forming a transition from reflective history to:

(3) Philosophical history. The philosophical historian uses the results of original and reflective historians to interpret history as the rational development of spirit in time, something that eludes both historical agents and other historians. The world-spirit, which embodies the IDEA, is carried forward by the passions of individuals, especially 'world-historical individuals' or heroes, such as Alexander, Caesar and Napoleon, who, with only a dim awareness of their historic purpose, but guided by the 'cunning of reason', forcibly bring about a new epoch, embodying a new and higher stage of spirit, of freedom and of self-consciousness. Unlike, e.g., Kant and Voltaire, Hegel held that such 'heroes' are not to be assessed by common moral or ethical codes.

Hegel gave lectures not only on world history, but on the histories of art, religion and philosophy. But his deeply historical outlook is manifest in all his works, and coheres with several features of his thought: (1) The individual is subordinate to the structures of objective and absolute spirit, which develop over history more obviously than individuals as such. (Thus pragmatic history needs to resort to petty, personal motives.) (2) The past stages of an entity are sublated in its present state, so that a full understanding of the present requires a knowledge of the past: 'what we are, we are at the same time historically' (*LHP*). (3) But one cannot understand something solely by knowing its history. Philosophical or, e.g., theological understanding involves more than simply recording past philosophical or religious beliefs. We must also discern the rationality of them and of their development. (4) The past stages of humanity are radically different from its present state: men in the past thought and acted in systematically different ways. (5) But past forms of thought and action are related to our own in ways that are rationally intelligible, not in traditional logic, but in Hegel's logic of conflict and development. (6) Since the historical process is rational, the historical fate of a doctrine or a way of life reflects its ultimate intellectual or ethical value; 'World-history is the judgment of the world [viz. the Last Judgment]' (*PR* §340; *Enc.* III §548). (This is a line adapted from Schiller's poem 'resignation'.)

I

I In ordinary German, *ich* ('I') is the first person singular pronoun, and contrasts with *du* ('you'), *er* ('he'), etc. But it can also form a substantive, *das Ich* ('the I, self, ego'), and then refers to a person's INDIVIDUALITY or ego (in contrast to the non-ego (*das Nicht-Ich*)), or to one part of his individuality such as his 'better self' (*besseres Ich*). 'The I' no longer contrasts with 'you', 'he', etc., since I can speak of 'your I' and 'his I' as well as of 'my own I'; it also has a plural, and one can say, for example, that everyone has two I's (e.g. an ordinary I and a better one).

Properties, states and activities are ascribed to animals and inanimate objects, as well as to humans. But only humans above a certain age can ascribe properties, etc., to themselves by the use of 'I'. Even ancient Greeks were able to do this, but the I, on Hegel's view, became an explicit theme of philosophy only with Descartes' *Cogito, ergo sum*. The I does not, on Descartes' view, embrace all the features which one can ascribe to oneself by using the word 'I', but only one's thought, including mental states of whose occurrence one can be immediately certain, but not one's bodily states, etc. Thus Descartes inferred that I am a thinking thing (*res cogitans*), to which such features as substantiality and immortality can be ascribed. Hume's failure to detect a *res cogitans* when he looked inside himself, or any impression corresponding to the I, led him to reject not only the *res cogitans* but the I as such (the *cogito*). But Kant argued that, though the I is not a substantial entity, the I or the 'I think' is a presupposition of all our REPRESENTATIONS (*Vorstellungen* in the wide sense), and must be able to accompany all of them. The I now excludes all mental, as well as physical, states, since it is solely the subject of EXPERIENCE. Anything that I ascribe to myself by using 'I' is *ipso facto* a predicate or object of the I, not the I itself. The I in this sense forms the starting-point of Fichte's (and Schelling's) 'theory of knowledge'. But now the I is not, initially, contrasted either with the I's of other individuals nor with a non-I: it precedes the differentiation between the I and the non-I, as well as between distinct individuals. It is a creative force that generates a non-I and the very distinction between 'I' and 'you'; but it does so in virtue of the logical difficulties involved in such an all-embracing, non-contrastive I. The I is referred to by Fichte, and often by Hegel, as the 'I = I', both because self-identity is all that can be ascribed to it, and because it is essentially self-reflexive: it exists only in virtue of, and produces itself by, its awareness of itself.

Hegel rejected the view that philosophy, in particular logic, should begin with the ABSOLUTE I: either the I = I requires explanatory MEDIATION or, if taken as immediate, is equivalent to pure BEING (*Enc.* I §86). But he regarded the uniquely human ability to ABSTRACT from all one's determinate features and concentrate one's existence into a bare point of being-FOR-SELF by saying 'I' as of supreme importance. Our FREEDOM of WILL and SELF-CONSCIOUSNESS are rooted in this capacity. But I-awareness, awareness of one's bare self-identity, is only the beginning of self-consciousness and of SPIRIT: full self-consciousness requires awareness of oneself as one inhabitant among others of a world informed by spirit.

The I has, on Hegel's view, several special features:

(1) The I is essentially self-reflexive: I-awareness is both necessary and sufficient for one to be (or have) an I. Thus the I is not a THING or SUBSTANCE.

(2) The I as such is UNIVERSAL in the sense that it is wholly indeterminate: I-awareness and 'I'-saying abstract from every determinate feature of one's mind, body and physical environment. 'I' shares this feature with 'this' and 'that', whose use also abstracts from every determinate feature of the human or non-human objects so referred to (*PS*, I. 'CONSCIOUSNESS'). But non-human objects do not apply these words to themselves, and we cannot, for example, conceive them to retain their identity through the drastic qualitative changes to which we can, in imagination, subject both ourselves and other human beings.

(3) The I is universal in the distinct, but related, sense that I-awareness and the use of 'I' as such do not succeed, except in 'meaning' or OPINION (*Meinung*), in picking out one particular individual among others: everyone is an 'I' or 'this particular individual'. This feature too 'I' shares with 'this'. The universality of 'this' is significant for Hegel: it enables him to reject the raw EXPERIENCE of SENSORY CERTAINTY and the challenge to deduce the existence of individual objects (*PS*, I, and *CJP*). But the universality of 'I' has an extra significance: I share a core of rational THOUGHT with all other men, and when I focus on this alone, abstracting from my mental and physical idiosyncrasies, I lose all sense of myself as a particular individual and, in doing logic especially, I become wholly absorbed in my SUBJECT-MATTER.

(4) But no one can be solely a self-aware I: I-awareness involves a body of some definite type. It also entails, and is entailed by, consciousness of a world distinct from itself, a world which the I, in company with other I's, must sublate and then return to itself as spirit. The I is thus an active universal that essentially involves PARTICULARITY and INDIVIDUA-LITY, a CONCRETE universal (in one sense of this expression).

Since the I is thus wholly universal and yet requires an other out of whose sublation it returns to itself, Hegel assimilates the I to the CONCEPT, which is also wholly universal and yet develops into particularity and individuality. But the assimilation depends not only on Hegel's belief that the I best exemplifies the concept (better, for example, than the seed of a plant), but also on his belief that the I is at bottom identical to the universal thoughts or concepts that it deploys: I cannot coherently distance myself from my thoughts, as I can from my desires and perceptions – by supposing, for example, that they might be wholly other than they are or by viewing them as alien forces that hold me in their power – since I-awareness itself and the act of distancing myself from what is viewed as not-I involve the thought of I and other thoughts such as that of difference. Thus the development of the I out of consciousness to full self-consciousness supplies Hegel with a model for the structure of the world portrayed in his SYSTEM: The concept or the logical idea is counterposed to nature, which at its lower levels is relatively alien to thought, but advances by stages up to the level of man's spirit, which gradually comprehends nature and eventually, in philosophy, comes to an awareness of the concept or logical idea. Hegel tends to equate this cosmic I and its development with GOD.

idea *Idee*, from the Greek *idea* ('image, form, shape, aspect or appearance (of a thing)'), corresponds closely to 'idea': it can be equivalent to '(a) thought', 'concept', 'conception', 'notion', 'image', 'belief', 'fancy', or 'plan' (in the ordinary, not the Hegelian, senses of these words). But it has also acquired a variety of philosophical senses over its complex history.

For Plato, an idea or FORM (*eidos*) is an ideal exemplar which, in contrast to the phenomena that 'imitate' or 'participate in' it, is fully existent, unchanging, perfect and universal: e.g. the idea of beauty is supremely and permanently beautiful, and is responsible for the fleeting and imperfect beauty of perceptible particulars. An idea is not a mental (or a physical) entity, but our dim awareness of it enables us to think about particulars and the goal of philosophy is to ascend by DIALECTIC to the non-empirical contemplation of ideas. Ideas form a hierarchical system with (in the *Republic*) the idea of the good at its summit. 'Idea', in this sense, is not contrasted with 'real' or 'reality', since the ideas, unlike particulars, are fully real. Despite Aristotle's view that forms or universals are inherent in particulars rather than transcendent, the doctrine persisted into Neoplatonism and into the Middle Ages, when 'realism' denoted the doctrine that universals are prior to and separate from particulars.

In early modern English and French philosophy 'idea' and *idée* came to denote a mental entity and was assimilated to 'REPRESENTATION'. But Kant used it in a sense close to Plato's: Ideas are concepts of REASON. No object corresponding to them is given in EXPERIENCE, but they are necessary and non-arbitrary. Ideas are either pure and transcendental (e.g. the ideas of FREEDOM, GOD, the world as a whole) or derivative and partly empirical (e.g. the ideas of virtue, of the perfect STATE, of philosophy). Theoretical reason cannot infer the existence of transcendent objects corresponding to pure ideas; such ideas as freedom, God and IMMORTALITY can only be substantiated by practical reason and have an essentially practical use. But both types of idea, though they do not, like the concepts of the UNDERSTANDING, *constitute* our experience, have a *regulative* use for our theoretical understanding: The idea of God, e.g., enables us to view the world as an ordered SYSTEM, and the idea of PURPOSE guides our understanding of living creatures.

Kant's successors welcomed his revival of Platonic ideas. Schiller speaks, e.g., of the 'idea of humanity', in the sense of a concept of reason that is yet to be fully realized; Schelling viewed them as 'supernatural powers' governing nature and ART; and Schopenhauer saw them as the prototypes that art imitates.

Hegel's use of *Idee* has several distinctive features:

(1)   An idea is not a subjective or mental entity: it is thus distinct from a representation, and does not contrast with 'REALITY' or 'ACTUALITY', except in so far as these are inferior categories which it involves or SUBLATES. An idea is the full realization or actualization of a CONCEPT (which, too, is not a mental entity): an idea is thus true or the TRUTH.

(2)   An idea is not transcendent and separate from particulars: it is fully realized in certain types of particular. Despite his respect for Plato, Hegel rejects any two-world view (*see* APPEARANCE) and inclines more to Aristotle's view that ideas are in things.

(3)   An idea is not an IDEAL that we OUGHT to realize: it is actual in the present. Hence ideas are not practical in Kant's sense.

(4)   Ideas are rational, but they do not simply regulate our understanding of the world: the idea of LIFE, e.g., involves purposiveness, just as much as MECHANISTIC systems involve CAUSALITY.

Hegel's view that an idea is a fully actualized concept has roots in Kant. Unlike a sensory OBJECT, an object corresponding to a pure idea is fully determined by its idea or concept, since no extra SENSORY material is required for its existence or for our knowledge of its existence. Such an object (e.g. God, the world as a whole) is thus unconditioned: it depends on nothing other than its own nature, its concept, for its existence. Hence the primary idea for Hegel is the world as a whole, which, unlike particular entities within it, depends on nothing external to itself and is thus wholly in accord with its concept. But the world does not entirely lack CONDITIONS, and to say that it is fully determined by its concept does not mean that it emerges at a stroke. For Hegel revises the notion of the unconditioned: what is unconditioned does not lack conditions altogether, but sublates such conditions as it has. Thus the world is a process, each phase of which conditions, but is sublated by, the next phase. Of its main phases, for example, the logical idea conditions NATURE, which in turn conditions SPIRIT, which then conditions the logical idea; the world is a circle of successively sublated conditions.

But this notion of a WHOLE, which is determined by its own concept, and sublates its external conditions, is transferred by Hegel to items within the world. Life is the IMMEDIATE idea: a living organism is relatively self-determined, i.e. determined by the concept encoded in it; it absorbs external conditions into itself and utilizes them in accordance with its concept.

The notion of the idea develops, in the Logic, and the idea of life is only its first phase. A living organism is in immediate accord with its environment, but in the next phase, the idea of COGNITION, there is a rift between the concept and an initially alien objective realm which the concept strives to overcome. The concept here is not so much a plan encoded in a seed or germ, but the I* and its conceptual resources. This idea subdivides into the idea of the true, or COGNITION proper, and the idea of the good, or MORALITY. The I strives to comprehend its environment in a systematic way, and then to transform it in accordance with its idea of the good. The idea in this case is not the already realized accord between the concept and OBJECTIVITY, but an idea in one of Kant's senses: an IDEAL of full accord between concept and objectivity that is to be striven for but may never be attained. (*LA* introduces the idea of beauty, which is also an ideal that ART, the sensuous portrayal of the absolute idea, strives to realize.)

The inadequacies of the idea in this sense lead to the ABSOLUTE idea, the final phase of Logic. The absolute idea is, first, simply the subject-matter of logic, the idea IN AND FOR ITSELF. This embraces within itself and thus sublates the dichotomies that beset the idea of cognition, between, e.g., SUBJECTIVITY and objectivity. It is a self-determining and self-differentiating whole: logic ABSTRACTS from its environmental and historical conditions and derives THOUGHTS from other thoughts without recourse to empirical phenomena. There is no rift between logic and its subject-matter: since logic is simply thinking about thinking or thoughts about thoughts, the concept is in full accord with its object, and truth is attained.

The idea then reappears in the realm of nature, as the idea in its otherness, and in that of spirit, as the idea returning to itself out of otherness. But it also appears in various relatively elevated entities within the world, in, e.g., the ETHICAL LIFE of the STATE. In such cases Hegel has in mind a variety of points: (1) The state, if it fulfils its idea, is as it ought to be: the individual is at home in it and there is no misfit between his ideals and the ethical world he inhabits. (2) The state is a relatively self-determining and self-differentiating organic whole. (3) Thus it moulds and forms the individuals who constitute it. The individuals are not independent of it. If they become so, and lose respect for their ethical and political institutions, the state becomes dead, like a body that has lost its soul. (4) The state exemplifies and overcomes a variety of dichotomies: it is, e.g., UNIVERSAL, PARTICULAR and INDIVIDUAL.

Idee in Hegel has a variety of applications and significances. This reflects the complexity of his notion of a concept: The concept is an initial plan (in a seed), an inner determining force (the soul, both literal and metaphorical, of a body), a normative ideal, a conceptual system and the cognizing I. The significance of the contrasting term ('reality', 'objectivity', etc.), and of the 'realization' of the concept, varies accordingly. Hegel's *Idee* (like Plato's *idea*) is the product of an attempt to fuse ontology, epistemology, evaluation, etc., into a single set of concepts.

ideal   In German, as in English, 'ideal' is both (1) a noun (*das Ideal*) and (2) an adjective (*ideal*). The adjective has a French-derived near-equivalent, (3) *ideell*. It generates another noun, (4) (*die*) *Idealität* ('ideality, the characteristic of being ideal') and a verb (5) *idealisieren* ('to idealize').

1. In ordinary usage an ideal is a goal or model in any sphere of human endeavour: education, politics, art, science, etc. An ideal may be an abstract conception such as perfect justice, or an imaginary individual (e.g. Plato's ideal STATE) or an existing individual (e.g. Socrates) regarded as embodying such a conception. One can rationally pursue an ideal even if one does not believe that one can fully realize it or even that it is realizable at all, as long as one believes that the pursuit will lead one closer to the ideal. For Kant, an *Ideal* is an individual conceived as fully conforming to an IDEA. Thus there are pure ideals (e.g. God, the highest good) and empirical ideals (e.g. perfect beauty, perfect happiness). Such ideals have no objective reality, but they regulate our cognitive and practical endeavours.

Hegel uses *das Ideal* in a similarly wide sense in early works (e.g. Christ as a personified ideal) and in discussing the views of others. But his own preference is to give *Ideal* an exclusively aesthetic sense. It need not refer only to art, but also, e.g., to the beauty of the body as an expression of the SPIRIT, but it is used most frequently in *LA*. The point of this restriction is this. For Hegel, as for Kant, an *Ideal* is the embodiment of an idea (*Idee*) in an individual. But actual individuals such as the STATE can embody the idea and do not involve the misfit between idea and reality suggested by *Ideal*, and Hegel, unlike Kant, was averse to imaginary ideal entities that are not, but ought to be, realized. (He saw Plato's state as a description of the Greek city-state, not an ideal.) But a work of art, such as a statue, (a) is an actual sensory individual and thus not a mere ideal; (b) portrays a sensory individual, e.g. a human body, that is ideal with respect to any existing individual of its type, since it lacks defects that any existing individual has; and (c) not only represents the absolute idea in sensory form, but itself exemplifies the idea, since it is a relatively self-contained whole, which SUBLATES the material CONDITIONS of its production and whose FORM and CONTENT are in full accord. Thus Hegel equates the idea of beauty, the idea in sensory form, with the *Ideal*.

2. The adjective *ideal* ('pertaining to an *Idee* or *Ideal*') has three senses: (a) 'ideal, exemplary, model'; (b) in contrast to *real*, 'not material, not sense perceptible, etc.'; (c) in contrast to *real* in another sense, 'not existing except in thought or imagination'. Hegel uses *ideal* in sense (b) in discussing the views of others, but his preferred sense is (a), restricted, like *Ideal*, to aesthetics and especially art: 'pertaining to the ideal or to the idea of beauty'.

3. In ordinary German *ideell* differs little from *ideal*, except that it is less likely to be used in sense (a) of *ideal* ('exemplary, model'). For Hegel, by contrast, *ideell* is distinct from *ideal*: *ideell* is connected with *Idee* ('IDEA') rather than *Ideal*, and, of the ordinary senses of *ideal*, it comes closest to (b). Since *ideell* contrasts, at least initially, with *real* or *reell* (Hegel draws no corresponding distinction between these words), it does not mean simply 'being or embodying a or the idea'. For the idea does not contrast with the real, but is the unity of the ideal and the real (*Enc*. I §214). Thus in the Logic Hegel first

introduces the *ideell* in connection not with the idea, but with being-FOR-ITSELF and INFINITY. The relation of the *ideell* to the *Idee* is this: the idea is the unity of the CONCEPT and its reality. The concept (e.g. the seed, the SOUL) is an intrinsic unity, but is nevertheless CONCRETE, involving diverse aspects or MOMENTS which are not yet posited in their full distinctness. The reality (e.g. the plant, the body) is a unity in virtue of the unifying power of the concept, but its diverse aspects are explicitly differentiated. All these items are *ideell* in different, but related ways:

(a) The concept as a whole is intrinsically *ideell* in contrast to its reality. It is not made *ideell* by anything else, but is *ideell* in virtue of its dependence only on itself. The I*, for example, is *ideell*, since it exists only in virtue of its awareness of itself.

(b) An aspect of the concept is *ideell*, both because it is only an aspect, not the whole concept, and because it is not yet realized: e.g. in the seed, blood is only *ideell*.

(c) The reality is *ideell* in virtue of its dependence on the concept or it is made *ideell* by the concept. It does not thereby cease to be real: its reality is SUBLATED in its ideality.

(d) An aspect of the reality is *ideell* in virtue of both its dependence on the concept and its dependence on the WHOLE of which it is a part: e.g. a severed limb cannot survive as a living organ.

Hegel often equates the *ideell* with what is sublated: reality and its parts are sublated by the concept. He also associates it with INFINITY: the FINITE parts of reality are sublated into the self-contained whole pervaded by the concept. The notion of the *ideell* applies to anything that exemplifies the idea: the world as whole, large phases of the world such as the logical idea, and items within the world such as LIFE, the MIND and the state. It is the central concept of Hegel's IDEALISM. (Occasionally Hegel uses *ideell* in a sense that has no clear relation to his sense of *Idee*: e.g. space and time are *ideell*, in contrast to bodies, in virtue of their lack of solidity, though they are not thereby non-existent or merely subjective.)

4. *Idealität* in philosophy is the characteristic of being ideal, but in contrast to 'real' and 'reality', not in the sense of 'exemplary'. Thus for Kant to believe that the existence of external objects is doubtful is to ascribe *Idealität* to them and constitutes (one type of) idealism with respect to them. He ascribes 'transcendental *Idealität*' to space and time, and thus endorses transcendental idealism with respect to them. For Hegel *Idealität* is the characteristic of being *ideell*, usually in Hegel's preferred sense, and to ascribe ideality to a type of entity constitutes idealism with respect to it.

5. Hegel occasionally uses *idealisieren* or *Idealisierung* ('idealizing'), and often employs the concept without using the word. It does not have the usual sense of treating or regarding something as ideal or exemplary, but that of making something *ideell*. The idea is a continuous process of idealizing or making things ideal, rather than a static result. Thus the I or the mind, in its intellectual and practical encounters with the objective world, makes it ideal. Even in the case of a living creature the soul or concept is continually at work making or keeping the body and its parts *ideell*; the creature dies if this

activity ceases. This exemplifies Hegel's belief that the world and significant items within it, notably humans, are in (or simply *are*) unremitting tension and activity, a belief that goes back to Heraclitus, but persisted in Neoplatonism.

idealism Idealism (*Idealismus*) is in general the doctrine that IDEAS or the IDEAL are ontologically and/or epistemologically prior to THINGS or the REAL. But idealism varies according to (among other things) the senses assigned to 'idea' and 'ideal', and the type of priority ascribed to them.

Plato's idealism affirmed the priority of ideal, mind-independent prototypes, but with the modern equation of an idea with a mental REPRESENTATION 'idealism' came to refer to the belief that objects as such or objects as we (can) know them are simply my (or our) ideas or constructions out of, or projections of, my (or our) ideas. The idealism of this type that overshadowed Hegel's age was the 'critical' or 'transcendental' idealism of Kant: there are mind-independent things in themselves, but we can know only their APPEARANCES, i.e. the ideas (*Vorstellungen*, not *Ideen*) that are the joint product of their effect on our senses, and the forms of our UNDERSTANDING (the categories) and our sensibility (space and TIME). Kant's idealism involved a dualism or OPPOSITION, between phenomena and the thing-IN-ITSELF and between concepts and sensory material, which his successors attempted to eliminate. Thus Fichte regarded the external world as a whole as the product of the ABSOLUTE I*. Fichte opposed idealism to 'dogmatism' or realism, especially that of Spinoza. But Schelling (like Hegel) saw idealism as essentially involving realism: the external world and the world of SPIRIT are two sides of the same coin, complementary manifestations of a single, neutral absolute. (For Hegel, 'dogmatic' means 'one-sided', so that idealism, as well as realism, can be dogmatic.)

Fichte's (and implicitly Kant's) idealism has three aspects: (1) ontological or metaphysical: the I produces the world; (2) epistemological: the I, unlike external objects, is immediately and certainly knowable, and we can deduce the main features of the world from it; (3) practical: not only does idealism accommodate FREEDOM of WILL in a way that realism does not, it prescribes a course of conduct: the FINITE I enmeshed in the world is to strive to purify itself and thus to return to the INFINITE I. Thus this idealism involves moral *ideals*, as well as *ideas*. Hegel constantly criticizes this idealism: He saw Kant, e.g., as a SUBJECTIVE idealist and rejected his claim that we could have knowledge of mere appearances; he rejected the thing-in-itself, which he detected in Fichte's non-I, as well as in Kant; and he rejected any ideal that we OUGHT to attain. But Hegel's idealism too involves the three aspects of ontology, epistemology and practice.

Hegel is not a subjective idealist: he did not believe that objects as such, or as known to us, are produced by, or are, my or our sensory representations. Such a doctrine cannot do justice to the dependence of finite spirit on nature. But above all it is an empty doctrine: it tells us about the ontological status of objects and ideas, but nothing about their content. He is, by contrast, an absolute idealist. This has several aspects:

128

1. In a minimal sense, idealism is the doctrine that finite entities are IDEAL (*ideell*): they depend not on themselves for their existence but on some larger self-sustaining entity that underlies or embraces them. What they depend on need not, at this stage, be a MIND or spirit. It may be, e.g., MATTER, so that even a materialist is in this sense an idealist. Although, on this account, any finite entity is ideal, certain finite entities are especially so, since they belong to relatively self-developing wholes within the world: e.g., the parts of a living ORGANISM or the citizens of a STATE are ideal in relation to the WHOLE to which they belong. Such finite, organic wholes within the world supply Hegel with a partial model for the world as a whole. So far idealism involves no specific reference to the mind or spirit, and idealism could be true even of a world that contained no minds.

2. The materialist sees matter as mind-independent stuff, but this, Hegel argues, is not so: since it is indeterminate, UNIVERSAL and accessible to thought alone, not to PERCEPTION, matter is a THOUGHT and not simply something corresponding to a thought. This means not that matter is simply read into the sensible world by me (or us), but that it belongs to an impersonal system of thoughts that constitute the core both of the mind and of nature. Idealism now refers to the mind, but it suggests that the world is mind-like, rather than that it is mind-dependent.

3. That nature is mind-like becomes clearer when we see that it cannot be adequately conceptualized in terms of anything so rudimentary as matter. Matter as such cannot explain its own proliferation into a world of finite entities: it presupposes an agency that induces it to do so. By such arguments as this, Hegel reaches the conclusion that the world can be adequately conceptualized only in terms of the absolute idea. This introduces more spiritual elements into idealism:

(a) Unlike, e.g., matter, the absolute idea provides for the adequate conceptualization of mind, as well as nature.

(b) It involves not only such relatively objective thoughts as that of matter, but also thoughts that are usually associated only with our thinking, not with the external world, such as the CONCEPT and the forms of JUDGMENT and of INFERENCE.

(c) The thoughts are at this stage explicitly seen as thoughts, not as objective entities, as the materialist regards matter. Nature is thus seen as mind-like and thought-ridden to a higher degree than at stage 2.

4. Nature is not only mind-like; it is also dominated or SUBLATED by mind. For nature develops into the human mind, which by degrees idealizes nature by its cognitive and practical activities. Nature is, independently of human activity, ideal in itself: mind or spirit makes it ideal FOR ITSELF. The historical process in which human beings collectively do this and, concurrently, reach ever higher phases of SELF-CONSCIOUSNESS, is itself mind-like and, at a higher level than nature, embodies REASON. Eventually men become aware of the system of thoughts with which we began, the logical idea.

5. Mind or spirit is not only the dominant phase of the world-process; the process as a whole is, or is analogous to, a mind, the absolute spirit. The

three main phases of the world-process – the logical idea, nature and mind – correspond to the three phases of finite spirit: I or me, the object of my CONSCIOUSNESS, and my return to self-consciousness from the object. Since the world-process, unlike the finite spirit, is wholly self-contained and requires no external input, there is thus a sense in which nature is wholly dependent on mind, and not simply like, or dominated by, mind – though the mind on which it depends is no individual, finite mind.

Hegel's idealism, like his belief in GOD, is ambiguous: Claim 5, e.g., might be interpreted as a thoroughgoing spiritualistic doctrine or as a relatively modest doctrine concerning the conceptual structure of the world and humanity's historical development. (The bridge between the two interpretations may be that, on Hegel's view, the core of the self just *is* a system of concepts.) Although Hegel often presents idealism as consisting in, or involving, the view that finite things, since they pass away, are merely APPEARANCE (*Schein*) and not ACTUAL, his idealism is compatible with, and even entails, realism, at least with respect to such elevated entities as living organisms and the state. His reluctance to distinguish, like Kant, between a mind-independent sensory given and a conceptual, mind-dependent element, or between things as they are in themselves and as they are for us, means that he occupies no half-way position between idealism and realism, but pushes each to their limit so that they veer into each other. Some specific difficulties in his idealism are these:

(a) The world-spirit, which is the world-process as a whole, is modelled on, and contains as a phase of itself, the finite spirit within the world. There is, on Hegel's view, no stark gulf between finite spirit and world-spirit; the world-spirit is simply the highest development of the human spirit, philosophy itself, which, in becoming aware of the logical idea, initiates, in a circular way, the world-process that begins (in some non-temporal sense) with the logical idea and leads eventually to its own emergence.

(b) Hegel implies that ideality is an absolute notion, when it is in fact relative: The members of an organism are ideal with respect to the organism itself; the organism is ideal with respect to its species; and the species is ideal with respect to the world as a whole. Similarly citizens are ideal in relation to their state, which is itself ideal in relation to world history. Thus idealism is inherently a many-tiered doctrine, concerning both several levels of reality within the world and the world as a whole.

(c) It is often unclear whether Hegel believes that something, e.g. nature, is (as in (1) above) mind-independently ideal, or (as in (4) above) idealized by spirit. The parts of organisms are ideal independently of us, while in, e.g., gardens nature is idealized by us. This ambiguity can be resolved in several ways: Since ideality is relative, what is independently ideal in one respect (e.g. the leg of a living pig) may be *idealized* by us in another respect (e.g. a leg of pork forming an integral part of a meal). Or what is independently ideal in itself or potentially (e.g. thought-ridden nature) may be made ideal for itself or actually (e.g. in our theories about it). Finally (and less plausibly), Hegel might invoke the circularity of the world-process: the members of an organism are *both* independently ideal, since they are ideal before mind comes on the scene, *and* idealized by mind, since the circularity of the process means they are also ideal *after*, and thus dependently on, the emergence of mind.

identity, difference and otherness   The common German expression for 'the same' is *der-, die-, dasselbe*. It indicates both numerical and qualitative identity. (German, like English, resorts to periphrases, such as *ein und derselbe*, 'one and the same', to distinguish numerical and qualitative sameness.) Contrasting with it is *ander* ('other'), which is used for both numerical and qualitative difference. Hegel often uses *derselbe*, etc., but does not discuss it in his Logic. He discusses qualitative otherness under the heading of 'DETERMI-NATE BEING', where 'the other' contrasts with 'the something' (*das Etwas*), and numerical otherness under the heading of 'being-FOR-ITSELF', where 'the other' contrasts with 'the one' (*das Eins*). But 'the other' and 'otherness' (*Anderssein*) are important throughout the Logic, and his system as a whole, e.g., SELF-CONSCIOUSNESS and FREEDOM consist primarily in overcoming other-ness.

Hegel's main account of identity occurs in the 'doctrine of ESSENCE' in the Logic. Here he introduces *Identität* (from the Latin *idem*, 'the same') with the adjective *identisch*. This indicates primarily numerical sameness, though in Hegel's hands it also comes to indicate qualitative sameness, since for him the very distinction between numerical and qualitative identity is problematic and fluid. Hegel often prefers to use *Einheit* ('unity, oneness', from *ein*, 'one' and also the indefinite article 'a(n)'), since he tends to associate *Identität* with the ABSTRACT identity of the UNDERSTANDING. The primary contrast with *Identität* is *Unterschied*, the most general word for 'difference' or 'distinction'. This comes from *unterscheiden* ('to distinguish, discriminate, discern'), which in turn comes from *scheiden* ('to separate, divide, etc.'). Since this has a reflexive form, *sich unterscheiden* ('to differ', but literally 'to distinguish or differentiate itself or themselves'), Hegel thinks of an *Unterschied* as the result of a process of *self*-differentiation. *Unterschied* can refer either to numerical or to qualitative difference. Hegel distinguishes *Unterschied* from the similar words, *verschieden* ('different, diverse') and *Verschiedenheit* ('difference, diversi-ty'). These also derive from *scheiden*, but the corresponding verb *verscheiden* has come to mean only 'to pass away, decease' (*scheiden* also means 'to depart (e.g. from life)'). Hence *Verschiedenheit* is more passive in flavour than *Unterschied*; it involves no active self-differentiation. It suggests qualitative, not simply numerical, difference.

Occasionally, Hegel uses the Latin-derived *Differenz*. This is more active than *Verschiedenheit*, since it generates a verb *differenzieren* ('to differentiate') and also contrasts with *indifferent*, which, like its English counterpart, has the flavour of 'making or discerning no (important) difference'. *Differenz* thus suggests a difference that makes a difference, primarily to the items differen-tiated. The ordinary German for 'indifferent' (both in 'It is indifferent

131

whether...' and in 'I am indifferent...') is *gleichgültig* (literally 'equally valid'). The distinguishing feature of *Verschiedenheit*, Hegel argues, is that the different items are indifferent (*gleichgültig*) to the difference between them. This leads him to consider the word *gleich* ('equal, (a)like'). This also expresses indifference, in the idiom 'It's all *gleich* ('the same') to me', but it mainly indicates the equality or qualitative identity of two or more things, or at least that they are more than approximately similar (*ähnlich*). (*Gleichheit* ('likeness') and *gleich* are also used for human and political 'equality'.) *Gleich* generates *gleichen* ('to equal, be like'), but more significant for Hegel is the verb *vergleichen* ('to liken, compare'). If the different items are indifferent to their diversity, likeness and unlikeness, then diversity, etc., are ascribed to them by an external observer who *compares* them. But not all differences between things are of this type: e.g. animal species, religions and political parties actively differentiate themselves from each other. Thus the CLASSIFICATION of animals requires not external comparison, but the recording of the ways in which species differentiate themselves. The differences in such cases are neither insignificant nor very great, such as that between a pen and a camel: they are specific differences on a background of generic identity. This is a DETERMINATE distinction (*bestimmter Unterschied*). This, finally, is heightened to OPPOSITION: each opposite (e.g. north and south) essentially depends on its other, and thus returns to a type of identity.

In this account Hegel has in mind three issues:

(1)　The 'LAWS of thought' of formal logic, especially the law of identity ('Everything is identical with itself' or 'A = A'), and Leibniz's law of *Verschiedenheit* or of the identity of indiscernibles ('Everything is qualitatively different from everything else' or 'No two things are exactly alike').

(2)　Theological or metaphysical doctrines of the identity or unity of the world: e.g. the Neoplatonist doctrine that the diverse world emanates from an original unity, Schelling's postulation of a neutral identity or indifference underlying nature and mind, and pantheism or the view that GOD is identical with the world.

(3)　The scientific classification of species, chemical elements, etc.

1. Hegel is averse to the abstract identity of traditional logic and to the law of identity. Some of his objections to it (e.g. that it confines us to statements of the type 'A planet is a planet' and that an identity claim of the form 'A = A' or 'A = B' *ipso facto* involves *two* entities (viz. two linguistic tokens)) are misconceived. His basic objections are these;

(a)　He has difficulty in seeing how a thing can have a RELATION (*Beziehung*) to itself without thereby reduplicating itself. One factor here is that the German for 'to be related (to)' is reflexive, *sich beziehen* (*auf*) ('apply, relate (oneself) to'), with a suggestion of active self-relating not conveyed by the English. Another is that the paradigm of self-identity for Hegel and other German idealists is the identity of the I*, the I = I, which does seem to involve a sort of self-duplication.

(b) He takes the claim that a thing is abstractly self-identical to mean that it is wholly self-enclosed and that it involves no inner self-differentiation. But a thing of this type would be wholly empty and indeterminate. It is only by actively relating itself to, and differentiating itself from, other things, and in the process differentiating itself from itself, that an entity acquires a determinate nature. Again, his model is the I: the I = I as such is empty; it acquires content by returning to itself from the other.

Hegel also objects to the law of *Verschiedenheit* in so far as it sees diversity as merely indifferent to the diverse items and not as the result of active self-differentiation.

2. Theological and metaphysical doctrines of unity require more than the abstract identity and abstract difference of the understanding. They require a type of identity or unity that differentiates itself into plurality, or a type of identity that enables us to say not simply that God is flatly identical with the world or flatly distinct from it, but that he is related to it by a self-developing identity-in-difference. What Hegel has in mind is not so much the identity ascribed to an entity differently described (e.g. 'Cicero = Tully') or identity over time (e.g. 'Octavian = Augustus'), as the identity of entities apparently belonging to distinct ontological levels (e.g. 'The soul = the body' or 'The mind = the brain'). This type of identity involves NEGATION, and Hegel often speaks of it as 'negative unity'.

3. Hegel's view of classification, both in the empirical sciences and especially in his own system, involves an identity or unity that differentiates itself and a difference that results from self-differentiation. In the Logic, his account of identity, difference, etc., itself exemplifies such a classificatory process. The concept of identity, for example, proceeds DIALECTICALLY into that of *Unterschied*, and is thus neither flatly distinct from it nor flatly identical to it.

in, for, and in and for, itself, himself, etc. The third person reflexive pronoun in German is *sich*. It is both singular and plural, and covers all three genders. It thus means 'one-, him-, her-, itself; themselves; each other'. It can be either accusative or dative, but not nominative or genitive. It accompanies German's numerous reflexive verbs, and can also be preceded by several prepositions. For example, *für sich* (literally 'for oneself', etc.) occurs in such contexts as 'He needs a room *for himself*', 'She lives *by herself*', and 'That is a problem *in itself*, viz. apart from its connections with other matters'. In ordinary usage, *an sich* ('in itself', etc.) often differs little from *für sich*: to consider a matter *an sich* is also to consider it apart from its connections with anything else, and if something is certain *an sich*, its certainty is IMMEDIATE and not dependent on anything else. In both these contexts, *an und für sich* ('in and for itself') is simply a more emphatic equivalent of *an sich*. Other expressions of this type used by Hegel are *in sich* ('within, into, in oneself', etc.) and, more crucially, *bei sich* ('(at one, at home) with oneself', etc.), which occurs in such contexts as 'to keep *to oneself*', but sometimes contrasts with *ausser sich* ('outside, beside oneself (with grief, etc.)').

In ordinary German, then, an expression of this type does not usually have a single well-defined use, but a range of uses overlapping that of other expressions. The only one that had acquired a settled philosophical use by Hegel's day was *an sich*, which was used by Wolff for Aristotle's *kath' hauto* ('in itself'), and means '(the thing) as such, ABSOLUTELY, apart from its relation to anything else'; e.g. a horse gallops *an sich* or *kath' hauto*, but its rider gallops only derivatively. *An sich* was also used to translate one of Plato's expressions for the FORM or IDEA: the form of, e.g., beauty is 'the beautiful *itself* or *an sich*'. For Kant, a THING *an sich* is a thing apart from its relation to our COGNITION and the way it appears to us: things in themselves exist 'outside us *für sich* (independently or on their own)'. Thus *an sich* in this sense contrasts not with *für sich*, but with *in uns* ('in us') or *für uns* ('for us').

Hegel often uses *sich*-expressions in their ordinary senses, drawing no special distinction, for example, between *an sich* and *für sich*. But often he uses them in special senses, in which *an sich* and *für sich* contrast with each other, and also with *an und für sich*. His reinterpretation and realignment of these expressions sets out from the philosophical use of *an sich*. A FINITE thing has a DETERMINATE nature only in virtue of its RELATIONS with other things, its NEGATION of, and by, them. This is true not only of items within the world, but also of Kant's thing-in-itself, since it too, if it is cut off, and distinct, from our cognition, is finite. Thus a thing as it is *an sich* has no overt determinate character: at most it has a potential character which will be actualized only by its relations to other things. An infant, e.g., is *an sich* rational, but its rationality is merely potential, not actual and 'for another' or 'in it' (*an ihm*). *An sich* in this sense does not contrast with *für uns*: the infant's rationality *is* for us, since we can see, from such actual features as it has, that it is potentially rational. Thus Hegel often uses the expression *an sich oder für uns* ('in itself or for us') to indicate that what something is only potentially and unknown to itself is known to us philosophers or outside observers. (That we can know what the infant is *an sich* implies that it is not – like Kant's thing in itself – wholly *an sich*, but has some actual features from which we can infer its potentialities. But this is because the infant is not wholly cut off from relations with other things.)

For Hegel, unlike Kant, *an sich* is not equivalent to *für sich*: *für sich* contrasts with *an sich*. But *Fürsichsein* ('being-for-(it)self') is a complex notion, in part because it contrasts not only with *Ansichsein* ('being-in-itself'), but also with *Sein-für-Anderes* ('being-for-another'). In *SL*, Hegel links it with the common expression *was für ein* (e.g. *Ding ist das?*), 'what sort/kind of (e.g. thing is that?)', but literally 'what for a (thing is that?)' and thus suggesting that to ask of what sort something is is to ask what it is for itself. Being-for-self involves, either together or in different contexts, several ideas:

1. A thing, e.g. an adult person, may be, e.g., a tinker, a tailor, a soldier or a sailor. But his being, e.g., a tailor depends in a variety of ways on *others*: tailoring must be a recognized occupation, there must be other occupations to contrast with it (if everyone is a tailor, no one is a tailor), and he must be acknowledged as a tailor. Thus his being a tailor involves his being for

another. But he is also a tailor *an sich*, not in the sense of being merely a potential tailor, but of having certain internal skills that suit him for this role and of having certain overt features which make it the case that he is a tailor rather than, e.g., a sailor. Being a tailor thus involves an interplay between being *an sich* and being for another. But a person is not simply a role-occupant. He is also an individual I, and as such he can distance himself from his role and think of himself just as *me* or *I**. When he does this, he is no longer for others, but *for himself*, since, although his SELF-CONSCIOUSNESS may presuppose RECOGNITION by others, an I is not one of a system of contrasting roles: everyone is an I. An I has, in a sense, no determinate character: its being consists solely in its being for itself, in the sense of being aware of itself and of being withdrawn or isolated from others. In the Logic, Hegel exemplifies being-for-self not only by the I, but also by the 'one', the unit or atom which differs from other units or atoms, in virtue not of any determinate quality, but only of its numerical distinctness, its independent being-for-self.

2. The idea that if something is for itself, it is aware of itself leads to the further idea that an entity may have *in itself* certain characteristics that are not *for itself*. An infant is rational in itself, but not for itself, since it is not aware that it is rational; a slave is, as a man, FREE in himself, but he may not be free for himself.

3. Often, if a person has a characteristic of which he is unaware, the characteristic is not fully developed or actualized. An infant's ignorance of its rationality is due to the immaturity of its rationality; the slave's ignorance of his freedom may be due to his state of slavery. Hence *an sich* and *für sich* come to mean 'potential' and 'actual', and may be applied to, e.g., the DEVELOPMENT of a plant, where there is no question of awareness or ignorance. (*An sich* in this sense often contrasts with 'POSITED' (*gesetzt*) rather than with *für sich*.) Characteristically, a fully developed, actual entity, in contrast to an acorn or an infant, has enough internal articulation and stability to exist 'by itself' or *für sich*, independent to some degree of relations to other entities.

4. In case 2, when a person becomes for himself what he is in himself, he usually recognizes what he is for himself as an adequate expression of what he is in himself. (Though he may feel that his actual condition of slavery or his limited powers of reasoning – which are also in a sense *for himself* – are out of accord with his *an sich* freedom or rationality.) But this is not always the case. He may come to be for himself, in an accurate portrayal of him by others or in a work of his own that amply expresses his personality, but not recognize himself in it. One reason why he might fail to do so is that such a portrayal or work is likely not only to bring before him what he is intrinsically, but also to actualize thoughts, feelings and traits that *in him* are merely potential or inchoate. An artist, e.g., does not usually have a fully worked out plan of his work in his mind before he sets to work: the work of art develops, as well as externalizes, his thoughts, etc. Hegel generalizes this idea: a person (or a group of persons) may produce a work or have an object, which makes him for himself, but which requires further activity, cognitive or practical, if he is to see himself or his *Ansich* (his 'in itself' or 'ESSENCE') in it. Paradoxical-

135

ly, in view of 1 above, the I as such is often seen as merely *an sich*: In itself, it is undeveloped and elusive; it becomes *für sich* only in its product or object.

Each of these ideas leaves room for a third stage, that of *Anundfürsichsein*, which brings together the *an sich* and the *für sich*:

(1) The retreat of the I into itself leaves the manifold external world unchanged. The tailor who distances himself from his role and thinks of himself as I can take the further step of reconciling himself to his job or of finding a job in which he is 'at home' (*bei sich*).

(2) The slave and the child can attempt to bring their current condition of slavery or of imperfect rationality into accord with their *Ansich*, their 'in-itself' or essence.

(3) Aristotle distinguished two grades of potentiality, as well as full actuality:

    (a) The infant who has not yet learnt a language is a potential speaker.

    (b) The person who knows a language, but is not now speaking, is a potential speaker in a higher sense, and an actual speaker in contrast to (a).

    (c) The person now speaking is a fully actual speaker.

But this is inapplicable to, e.g., a plant, and Hegel does not usually exploit it for his TRIADIC patterns. Development, for Hegel, involves a return to the begining or *Ansich*. Plants eventually produce seeds again. Old age is a return from the conflict characteristic of youth to a sophisticated version of the infant's familiarity and contentment with the world.

(4) *Anundfürsichsein* ('being-in-and-for-self') is often seen as being at home with oneself (*Beisichsein*), or coming to oneself (*zu sich*), in the OTHER. It is thus similar to INFINITY.

In general Hegel's use of *sich*-expressions is more fluid and diverse than accounts of his system often suggest.

inference, syllogism and conclusion The verb *schliessen* means 'to shut, close, conclude, draw a conclusion, infer'. A noun derived from it, *Schluss* ('close, closure, end, conclusion, inference'), was used by Böhme for the Latin *conclusio*, and by Leibniz and Wolff for the process of inference. Hegel exploits this link between 'closing' and 'inferring', and also the fact that *schliessen* forms, with the prefix *zusammen* ('together'), *zusammenschliessen* ('to unite, combine, connect').

The Greek *syllogismos*, from the verb *syllogizesthai* ('to infer'), is also associated with the ideas of concluding and combining or 'putting two and two together'. Hence Hegel's usual word for 'inference', *Schluss* – he uses *Syllogismus* only occasionally – is often translated as 'syllogism'. The disad-. vantage of this rendering is that while *syllogismos* originally meant 'inference', it has come to refer only to those inferences recognized as valid by Aristotle and to similar inferences added by logicians in the Aristotelian tradition. While most of the types of inference considered in Hegel's Logic fall more or less under this heading, some, notably the inductive inference, do not. (Aristotle recognized induction, but not as a valid form of syllogism.)

Hegel, like Kant, held that formal logic had made no significant progress since Aristotle. In fact, eighteenth- and early nineteenth-century logic contained several STOIC and medieval additions to Aristotle's logic. For example, Aristotle recognized only syllogisms whose premisses and conclusion take one of these forms: (1) Universal affirmative: 'All A's are B'; (2) Universal negative: 'No A's are B'; (3) Particular affirmative: 'Some A's are B'; (4) Particular negative: 'Some A's are not B'. But the logic of Kant's and Hegel's time added to these the INDIVIDUAL judgment forms: (5) 'This A (e.g. Socrates) is B'; (6) 'This A is not B'. An Aristotelian syllogism has two premisses and a conclusion. For example;

1 All men are mortal
2 All Greeks are men
3 All Greeks are mortal

1 is the major premiss (in German, *der Obersatz*), 2 is the minor premiss (*der Untersatz*), and 3 is the conclusion (*der Schlusssatz*). It also involves three terms or concepts, here 'man', 'Greek' and 'mortal'. The term that appears in both premisses, here 'man', is the middle term (in Hegel, often just *die Mitte*, 'the middle, mean'); the other two terms are the 'extremes'; the extreme in the major premiss, here 'mortal', is the major term, that in the minor premiss, 'Greek', is the minor term. Aristotle divides the syllogism into three schemata or figures (a fourth was added later, supposedly by Galen), which differ according to the positions of the middle, major and minor terms. The above example is in the first figure, since the terms occur in the following positions: 1 Middle–Major; 2 Minor–Middle; 3 Minor–Major. The two (or three) other figures vary the order of the terms in the premisses (though not in the conclusion). Each figure is then divided into several moods, according to the propositional form of the premisses and conclusion. Thus the above syllogism is in the first mood (of the first figure) since its premisses and conclusion are all universal and affirmative.

Hegel's account of the inference, in his Logic, considerably alters both Aristotle's logic and the formal logic of his own day. Aristotle was concerned with the ways in which a proposition can be validly derived from two other propositions. But, in accordance with his reinterpretation of the JUDGMENT as an original division of the CONCEPT into the UNIVERSAL, PARTICULAR and INDIVIDUAL, Hegel reinterprets the forms of inference as successively more adequate ways of restoring the unity of the concept. Thus it is crucial for Hegel that an inference should contain a universal, a particular and an individual term. For example, an inference of EXISTENCE (*Dasein*) in the first figure is this;

1 All *men* are *mortal*
2 *Caius* is a *man*
3 *Caius* is *mortal*

Here, the middle term, 'man', is particular; the major term, 'mortal', is universal; and the minor term, 'Caius', is individual. The individual term is combined with the universal by the MEDIATION of the particular (U–P–I). The second figure of the inference of *Dasein* differs from the first, in that it unites the universal with the particular, by way of the individual (P–I–U); and the third figure unites the individual with the particular by way of the universal (I–U–P). (The terms of the less significant fourth figure, the 'mathematical inference', are all universal.)

Hegel rejects Aristotle's moods as an unnecessary complication, and proceeds from the inference of *Dasein*, in which the terms are 'EXTERNAL' to each other and contingently connected, to the inference of REFLECTION, in which the terms are more closely connected. The first form is the inference of 'allness' (*Allheit*), an improved version of the first figure of the inference of *Dasein*. The second is the inference of induction, which unites the particular with the universal by way of individuals, and the third, the inference of analogy, unites the individual with the particular by the universal.

Finally, in the inference of NECESSITY, the relation between the terms is even closer: The categorical inference, a further improved version of the first figure of *Dasein*, unites an individual with its genus by way of its species (I–P–U). The hypothetical inference unites the species with the genus by way of the individual (P–I–U): e.g. 'If Fido is a dog, then Fido is an animal; Fido is a dog; so Fido is an animal.' Finally, the disjunctive inference unites the individual with the species, by way of the genus (I–U–P), which is exhaustively divided into its subordinate species: e.g. 'Fido, being an animal, is either a dog or a cat or a horse, etc.; he is not a cat or a horse, etc.; so he is a dog.' This inference, on Hegel's view, fully restores the unity of the concept, and we can now turn to the realm of OBJECTIVITY.

Unlike Aristotle, Hegel sees each type of inference, except the last, as having defects which can be resolved only by moving to the next type of inference. For example, the first figure of *Dasein* (I–P–U), exemplified above, has these defects:

(1) It is entirely contingent that we pick 'man', 'mortal' and 'Caius' as our terms. We could have deduced Caius' mortality from different pre-misses (e.g. 'All farmers are mortal' and 'Caius is a farmer'). This defect is resolved, on Hegel's view, by the ever closer relation between the terms in successive types of inference.

(2) The premisses of the inference, 'All men are mortal' and 'Caius is a man', are not yet demonstrated, and cannot be demonstrated in the first figure. Hegel, like J. S. Mill, even objects that the syllogism involves a *petitio principii*, since we cannot know that all men are mortal, unless we already know the conclusion, that Caius is mortal. This motivates the introduction, within each main type of inference, of the second and third figures (P–I–U) and I–U–P), since these can de-monstrate the premisses of the first figure. But what he requires is not an INFINITE regress, in which the premisses of any inference are demons-trated by two further inferences, but a circle of inferences, in which any two figures demonstrate the premisses of the third.

But Hegel's main deviation from Aristotelian orthodoxy is this: That inferences appear as a way of arguing from two propositions to a third is only their 'subjective form'. Inferences of *Dasein*, owing to the contingency of their terms, are more susceptible to this subjective reading than are higher types of inference. But all inferences have also an 'objective meaning' – the unification of universality, particularity and individuality – which is not essentially or primarily propositional. Nor is the inference, as Aristotle held, essentially or primarily a form taken by our subjective thinking. On Hegel's view, *everything* is an inference. Most basically, everything is an individual of a particular species and a universal genus. But a self-contained totality, such as the solar system (sun–planets–moons), the STATE, or the universe as a whole, are circular systems of three mutually supporting inferences, with a universal, particular and individual element each serving to unite the other two. The state, for example, involves the individual person (I), his needs (P) and a government (U), and each unites the other two. Similarly the universe involves the logical idea (U), nature (P) and spirit (I): in his system, Hegel presents them in the order U–P–I, but any order would be equally appropriate, since each term mediates the other two.

Hegel's objectification of the inference is a part of his systematic transposition of terms traditionally associated with subjective thinking (e.g. REASON, judgment, concept, CONTRADICTION, TRUTH) into the objective realm. Since, for example, reason is traditionally associated with the inference, and things, as well as thinking, can be rational and true, it is natural to suppose that things are also inferences. The motivation for the transposition is this: Thoroughgoing IDEALISM requires that things be not simply static projections of THOUGHT, but that they embody the processes of thought as well. But in accordance with Hegel's principle of OPPOSITES, the doctrine is also an extreme realism, since things fully conform to our thoughts and thought-forms.

A natural objection to the doctrine is that even if, e.g., the state does exhibit such a threefold structure, its relation to the inference is one of superficial analogy rather than of deep kinship.

infinity *Unendlichkeit* ('infinity') and *unendlich* ('infinite') contrast with *Endlichkeit* ('FINITUDE') and *endlich* ('finite'), and indicate the absence of an end (*Ende*) or LIMIT. The Greek equivalent, *to apeiron*, first occurs in Anaximander, where it refers to the basic stuff of which everything consists and probably has the sense of 'indefinite, indeterminate' rather than 'endless in space or time'. The atomists, Leucippus and Democritus, regarded atoms as infinite in number, and located them in an infinite space and infinite time. But in general the *apeiron* was seen as intellectually intractable and evaluatively disreputable: The Pythagoreans began their table of OPPOSITES with the limited and the unlimited, corresponding to the good and the bad. 'Unlimited' here still carries the sense of 'indeterminate', as well as 'infinite', and this persists in Plato's *Philebus*, where the limit (*peras*) and the unlimited are seen as two principles of being, presided over by a cosmic reason which mixes them together in everything. Aristotle, for whom the *apeiron* is more definitely the 'infinite', attempted to see the cosmos as finite in both time and space. When infinity seemed unavoidable, he argued that it was merely potential, not ACTUAL: e.g. a line can be divided indefinitely, but it does not consist of, and cannot be divided into, an actual infinity of parts. An ordered cosmos is felt to exclude unqualified infinity.

Ancient Greek gods were thus not infinite. But Philo of Alexandria (who combined Platonism with Judaism) saw God as infinite, not, that is, end-lessly extended in space or time, but containing in a concentrated form everything that can occur in space and time. The infinite is thus no longer defective, but complete and perfect. Early and medieval Christian philo-sophers retained the Greek idea that the world is finite, but reversed the valuation of it: the finite world is an imperfect product of an infinite God.

The view that the world is simply finite was challenged from two direc-tions. First, mystics such as Eckhart argued that since the human soul derives its essence from God and seeks union with him, it cannot be unqualifiedly finite. Second, Nicholas of Cusa (whom Hegel surprisingly never mentions) argued that, since the world explicitly extends in space and time what is implicitly concentrated in God, it too must be spatio-temporally infinite. This doctrine was developed by Copernicus and Giordano Bruno. Kant too was attracted by the idea that the infinite power of God was expressed in the unending DEVELOPMENT of his creation.

After Newton's and Leibniz's discovery of the infinitesimal calculus, mathematicians attempted to give a coherent account of the infinitely small, as well as of the infinitely large. The subject (to which Hegel devotes a long section of SL) was still unsettled in his day, but mathematicians were tending to the near-Aristotelian view that the infinitely small is merely potential, i.e. that lines, etc., can be made as small as we like, but there are no actual infinitely small lines. The infinitely large was also felt to be paradoxical: it is equal in size or number to a proper part of itself, e.g. the series 2, 4, 6, 8, etc., has as many terms as the series 1, 2, 3, 4, etc. But space and time, as well as numbers, seemed to require an infinitely large that was actual, not merely potential.

Schelling and Hegel saw two central problems in infinity. First, if the infinite is distinct from the finite, it is *limited* by the finite and is thus finite rather than infinite. If, e.g., GOD is distinct from the world, he is finite. Thus they, like Fichte, held that the infinite is not distinct from the finite but involves the finite as an aspect or 'MOMENT' of itself. Second, an infinite regress or an infinite progress(ion) is vicious, intellectually incoherent and practically self-defeating. (Schelling illustrated bad infinity by the English national debt, old loans being repaid by new loans indefinitely.) Thus they objected to Kant's and Fichte's idea that humanity has a goal which it OUGHT to strive for, but will not attain in a finite time. Schelling and Hegel do not, in general, distinguish between a series that tends to a limit (like Kant's, and e.g. $1 + \frac{1}{2} + \frac{1}{4} + \frac{1}{8} + \ldots$) and one that does not (e.g. $1 + 1 + 1 + 1 + \ldots$ or $1 - 1 + 1 - 1 + 1 \ldots$).

These two problems are distinct: God's infinity does not consist primarily in an infinite regress, even if rationalist theologians argued that he is, e.g., powerful to an infinite degree and can perform inferences of infinite length. Conversely, an infinite series contains its finite terms and is not sharply distinct from them. But in both cases, Hegel felt, the infinite is not genuinely infinite: in proceeding through an infinite series we only ever reach a finite segment of it, never the infinite itself. (One might also argue that a deity distinct from his creation, and thus finite, requires a further deity to explain *his* existence, and so on *ad infinitum*.)

Spinoza had distinguished between the (endless) infinity of the imagination and the (self-enclosed) infinity of the intellect. Hegel too distinguishes the bad (*schlecht*) infinite of the UNDERSTANDING from the TRUE infinite of REASON, which involves the finite, rather than contrasting with it, and does not go on forever. The bad infinite is represented by a straight line, infinitely extended at either end, the true infinite by a circle, which is, we might say, 'finite, but unbounded'. He applies this idea to any relatively self-contained reciprocal or circular structure in contrast to an endless advance from one thing to another: e.g. three mutually supporting INFERENCES in contrast to a bad infinite series of inferences; the reciprocal involvement of CAUSE and effect in contrast to an infinite series of causes and effects; the SPIRIT or SELF-CONSCIOUSNESS that is not limited by its other, but at home (*bei sich*) in it; and logic itself, in which THOUGHT has itself as its object and does not depend on a limiting other. True infinity is often associated with the NEGATION of the negation: the finite is the negative, which is in turn negated so as to produce an affirmative.

The central application of true infinity is to the universe as a whole: God cannot be distinct from the world, since they would then be two finite entities, which could not be self-sustaining or self-explanatory. Equally the world cannot go forward and backwards forever: it must have a self-contained circular form. Again, thought about the world cannot be distinct from the world, for then thought and being would each limit the other and be two finite, non-self-supporting entities. Hence thought is identical to (but also different from) the world, and it too is circular. The CONCEPT is thus as infinite as the world. True infinity thus explains several features of Hegel's system: e.g. why God must be the logical structure of the world, and why forms of thought, such as the inference, must be embedded in the world.

Hegel attempts to restore, on a higher plane, the self-enclosed finite world of Aristotle, in contrast to the open-ended world of the Enlightenment and of Newtonian science, burdened with oppositions between the self, God and the world, and with various indigestible infinities. But such infinities are hard to eliminate: Hegel implies that SPACE and TIME are (bad) infinities. He did not suggest, as he might have done, that space is circular, so that movement in a straight line would eventually return us to our starting-point. Nor did he, like Nietzsche, revive the Pythagorean idea that time is circular, involving the endless recurrence of exactly similar, or even numerically identical, events. Eternal recurrence would be at odds with Hegel's belief that HISTORY progresses towards a goal, but his neglect of it leaves him wavering equivocally between the view that history comes (or has come) to an end and the view that it goes on to (bad) infinity, even if we cannot know how it will continue and must confine ourselves to the true infinity of the present.

inner and outer, internal and external   The prepositions *aus* ('from, out of', etc.), *ausser* ('outside', etc.) and *in* ('in, into'), and the adverb *inne(n)* ('inside') give rise to several words in this area:

1. The adjectives *innerlich* ('internal, inward') and *äusserlich* (external, outward') are commonly used to distinguish what is on the surface from what is below it, in such expressions as 'an *äusserliche*, viz. superficial, wound', '*outward* calm, in contrast to *inner* turmoil', etc. The noun *Innerlichkeit* ('inwardness') derives from the German mystics and has two main senses; (a) the ESSENCE of a thing; (b) the self-composure, self-reliance, withdrawal into self, of a person. *Äusserlichkeit* ('outwardness, externality') was coined in the eighteenth century to indicate what is inessential to a thing or person.

Hegel uses both the nouns and the adjectives in a variety of contexts, and not always in contrast with each other: the *Äusserlichkeit* of a FORCE (its 'external manifestation') is identical with its *Innerlichkeit*. If two things are *äusserlich*, they are indifferent to each other, intrinsically unconnected and independently variable, like the shape of a thing and its colour. NATURE is OTHER and *äusserlich* to SPIRIT, and is consequently other and *äusserlich* to itself, viz. spread out in space and time. Thus the main uses of *Innerlichkeit* concern the realm of spirit. The *Innerlichkeit* ('inner life') of the spirit is contrasted with its DETERMINATE BEING (*Dasein*), viz. its bodily exterior (*PS*, VII.A.). But the *Innerlichkeit* of the mind is also contrasted with the *Äusserlichkeit* of the external world. The *innerlich* is sometimes equated with the IN ITSELF, which needs to be realized and revealed: great men bring to CONSCIOUSNESS the unconscious *Innerlichkeit* of their contemporaries. But more commonly *Innerlichkeit* is conscious; it may be the inner life characteristic of all men, or the especially self-conscious or SUBJECTIVE *Innerlichkeit* associated with Socrates, Protestantism, Descartes and ROMANTICISM. *Innerlichkeit* in this sense is similar to *Innigkeit* ('inwardness, intimacy'), which suggests inner intensity, especially when applied to such relationships as love and friendship. Hegel sees it as a special characteristic of the German people. In *LA*, *Äusserlichkeit* refers to the material FORM in which the aesthetic IDEAL is embodied, to the external environment of the individual, and to the presentation of the work to the public.

2. The adjectives *äusser* ('outer') and *inner* ('inner') are commonly used in such contexts as 'the inner/outer quadrangle', 'the inner (i.e. intimate) family circle', 'inner (i.e. intrinsic) value', 'outward appearances', 'internal/external (i.e. foreign) affairs'. The adjectival nouns, *das Innere* ('the inside') and *das Äussere* ('the outside') are common in ordinary German.

Hegel often uses *das Innere* for the internal essence of a thing and *das Äussere* for its outward appearance, and also for the inner life of a person in contrast to his body, actions and speech. His discussion of the concepts in his Logic develops out of his account of FORCE and its externalization (*Äusserung*). His argument is as follows: 'Inner' and 'outer' are correlative OPPOSITES. Thus each logically involves the other. He takes this to imply that in the case of actual things their inner or essence must correspond to or have the same CONTENT as their outer or APPEARANCE. But 'the inner' has two different senses in respect of actual things, and signifies:

(a) the undeveloped potentiality of a thing, e.g. the plant is merely inner in the seed, the rationality of the infant is merely inner, and so too is that of a defective person such as a criminal;

(b) the inner core or essence of something that is fully developed, e.g. the essence of nature or the inner purposes, etc., of an agent.

The principle of the identity of inner and outer applies differently to these two types of case:

(a) The external features of the seed do not reflect its inner potentiality. But since its nature is merely inner, the seed itself is merely external: a blank, unarticulated lump of matter, which in contrast to a plant is passive and a prey to external attacks. Similarly, the infant's body is relatively ill-coordinated and inexpressive, while an adult's body expresses his developed inner life. Moreover, the rational and cultural forms that constitute its inner nature are wholly external to it, embodied in its parents. Similarly, the social forms which the criminal has inadequately internalized seem to him to be alien impositions (in the form of PUNISHMENT), rather than expressions of his own WILL. The principle here is that the outer surface of the individual is merely 'external' to the same degree as its inner is merely inner, and that the externality that does express its inner lies at a distance from the individual corresponding to the depth at which its inner is buried.

(b) Hegel, like Goethe, held that the inner of a fully developed entity such as NATURE cannot differ from its outer. Its inner may lie at some distance from its surface, but it is in principle accessible to observation and thought. If we suppose that nature has an inner that differs from its outer, we find on REFLECTION that its postulated inner lies in *us*, the external observer, i.e. that, as in case (a), the inner is external to nature to a degree corresponding to its supposed depth within nature.

In particular, Hegel is averse to the view that a person's outer (his ACTIONS, works, etc.) does not reflect his inner (his intentions, etc.), either in the sense that a man's admirable deeds might result from petty or vicious motives (a claim which he associates with 'pragmatic' HISTORY) or that a person whose acts and works are worthless or harmful might have had good intentions, great talent, etc.: 'A man is what he does' (*Enc.* I §140A.). Well-layed plans may occasionally go wrong and great deeds can conceal hypocrisy. But in the long run and to the careful observer the inner will reveal itself in the outer.

In fact, the logical correlativity of 'inner' and 'outer' does not entail that the outer always accurately reflects the inner, since an *actual* inner and outer need not be as closely related as the *concepts* of inner and outer. Hegel's arguments in case (a) are either tautological (e.g. that if a thing's nature is inner, i.e. merely *potential*, its outer form is merely external, i.e. does not

143

express its inner) or play fast and loose with the notions of inner and outer. His conclusions in case (b) depend less on the logic of 'inner' and 'outer' than on the epistemological and explanatory difficulties of ascribing to a thing or person an inner that is wholly at odds with its outer, and on a preference for the outer over the inner in the evaluation of persons. But Hegel also assimilates case (b) to case (a): inner intentions, etc., are merely potential in that they lack a fully determinate character apart from their outer manifestation. Thus if a person's intentions are wholly base, they must reveal their baseness in outer conduct. But it is still conceivable that a man who makes glorious history has base intentions, etc., which reveal themselves only in his private life.

3. The verb *äussern* ('to utter, express'), especially in the reflexive form, *sich äussern* ('to express, manifest, show it-, oneself') is used, e.g., of a force. *Äusserung* is the 'expression' of, e.g., a force. Since there is no corresponding verb *innern* or noun *Innerung*, Hegel generally uses a different noun (e.g. *Rückkehr*, 'return') or verb (e.g. *zurückkehren*, 'to return') to convey the withdrawal of, e.g., a force into itself after it has had its effect. But he often uses the verb (*sich*) *erinnern* ('to RECOLLECT (itself)') in this sense, contrasting it with (*sich*) *entäussern* ('to ALIENATE (oneself)', etc.). *Ausdruck* and *ausdrucken* (literally 'pressing out' and 'to press out') are also used for verbal, bodily and artistic expression.

4. Hegel often uses the adverb *aussereinander* ('outside one another'), especially as a noun, *das Aussereinander* ('the/being outside one another'), to express the idea that the SENSORY (unlike THOUGHT and REPRESENTATION) and NATURE (unlike SPIRIT) are self-external or outside themselves, i.e. spread out in space and time, not simply external to the human being.

intuition, perception, sensation and the sensory The most notable words in this area are these:

1. *Anschauung* ('intuition') is by origin a visual word, from *anschauen* ('to intuit, look, view') and *schauen* ('to see, view, look'). It often means a 'view' or 'conception' (hence *Weltanschauung*, 'world-view'). But it entered philosophical German with Eckhart for the Latin *contemplatio*, in the sense of the activity or result of contemplating something, especially the eternal and divine. *Anschauung* implies immediate, non-discursive contact with the OBJECT, and the total absorption of the SUBJECT in it.

In later philosophy, *Anschauung* has two broad senses: first, intellectual contemplation, e.g. of Platonic IDEAS (the Greek *theōria*, 'contemplation, SPECULATION'); second, sensory impression or sensation. Kant argued that all human *Anschauung* is sensory (*sinnlich*): thought requires objects, and objects can be 'given' only by intuitions. But the UNDERSTANDING with its CONCEPTS can only 'think' intuitions and objects, not provide them. They can be given only by objects' affecting our senses. Kant allowed the *possibility* of an *intellektuelle Anschauung*, which supplies an object without sensory assistance. But intellectual intuition, which amounts to creating an object simply by thinking of it, is, on Kant's view, reserved for God alone.

Kant's attempt to confine *Anschauung* to the sensory was challenged from two directions. First, critics such as Hamann and Herder attacked his sharp separation of intuition and concepts. Goethe speaks of an 'intuition (*Anschauen*) of inner creative nature' which attains to the 'prototype' or the IDEA (*Intuitive Judgment*, 1817). Such intuition apprehends a phenomenon as a whole together with the interrelations of its parts. It does not dispense with concepts, but it is contrasted with analytical conceptual thought. Second, Fichte argued that the philosopher becomes aware of the pure I* by an act of intellectual intuition. Schelling adopted this idea, and when his ABSOLUTE ceased to be the I and became a neutral IDENTITY, that too, he held, is grasped by intellectual intuition.

Sensory intuition, on Hegel's view, involves the transformation of what is sensed (*das Empfundene*) into an external object (*Enc.* III §448A.). ART presents the absolute in the FORM of sensory intuition, in contrast to CONCEPTION (*Vorstellung*), the form of RELIGION, and to THOUGHT, the form of PHILOSOPHY. In early works, especially *DFS*, Hegel espoused Schelling's idea of a 'transcendental' intuition that unites OPPOSITES, such as NATURE and SPIRIT. But later he criticized intellectual intuition, because it is IMMEDIATE, and, unlike conceptual COGNITION, does not display the logical presuppositions and structure of the object. Intuition, even of Goethe's type, though it enables us to see things as a whole, rather than piecemeal, can only be a prelude to cognition (e.g. *Enc.* III §449A.). Nevertheless, Hegel's logic, since it is non-empirical thought about thoughts, somewhat resembles intellectual intuition in Kant's sense. Unlike Kant, Hegel has no qualms about assimilating man to GOD.

2. *Empfindung* ('sensation, FEELING') is close to sensory *Anschauung*. But it is more subjective in flavour and does not necessarily involve awareness of an object. Hence in *Enc.* III *Empfindung* belongs to the 'feeling SOUL', but *Anschauung* to the 'theoretical spirit'.

3. *Sinn* has a wide range of meanings corresponding roughly, but not exactly, to those of 'sense': a 'sense' (e.g. for music, of history or of humour), the five 'senses', 'mind' (e.g. an idea came into my 'mind'; out of one's, or in one's right, 'mind'; we are of one 'mind'), the 'sense, point, meaning' of a word, a remark, a work of art, an action, (a) life, etc. (*Sinn* in this last sense is more subjective than *Bedeutung* ('meaning'): *Sinn* refers to the sense of a word in a context, not to the sense(s) given in a dictionary.) The adjective *sinnlich* and the abstract noun *Sinnlichkeit* (introduce by Wolff for the Latin *sensibilitas*, *sensualitas*) correspond to only some of the meanings of *Sinn*: what is *sinnlich* is perceptible by the senses, 'sensory', 'sensuous'. Applied to a person or an aspect of a person, it means 'dominated by the sensory or by physical, especially erotic, desires'. Hegel often uses *das Sinnliche* ('the sensuous, sensory') in contrast to 'REPRESENTATION', 'thought', etc. *Sinnlichkeit* is: (a) the capacity to receive sensory stimuli from objects, by which, on Kant's view, intuitions, and thus objects, are given to us; (b) our EXPERIENCE or our nature, in so far as it involves sense experience and physical feelings, desires, etc. in contrast to thought, REASON, etc.

Since *sinnlich* and its derivatives contrast with 'thought', and thought can

145

either be pure or involve sensory material, *sinnlich* in Hegel can signify either raw sensory material or conceptualized sensory material. Correspondingly, *übersinnlich* ('supersensible') can mean either what wholly transcends the sensory and is accessible to thought alone or, as in *PS*, III, the sensory conceptualized so that it becomes APPEARANCE (*Erscheinung*). (Hegel's claim that 'the supersensible is the TRUTH of the sensible and perceptible, viz. to be appearance' also depends on the force of the prefix *über-*, 'over, beyond', but also 'excessively', rather than 'non-' or 'un-'.)

4. *Wahrnehmung* ('perception') is the sensory CONSCIOUSNESS of external objects (and derivatively of our inner states and processes). (In ordinary usage it also means 'observation' and thus 'care, protection (e.g. of one's interests)', and *wahrnehmen* means 'to observe, make use of, seize (e.g. an opportunity), protect, exercise (a role or function)' as well as 'to perceive'.) Thus, in contrast to *das Sinnliche, Empfindung*, and (in Kant's sense) *Anschauung*, it essentially involves a conceptual element. For Hegel, while *sinnliche Gewissheit* ('sensory CERTAINTY') is the non-conceptual apprehension (*Auffassen*) of sensory particulars, *Wahrnehmung* takes them as UNIVERSAL, as THINGS with universal properties (*PS*, I, II). *Wahrnehmung*, he argues, takes the truth or takes things as they are in truth (viz. the universal), deriving *wahrnehmen* ('to perceive') from *wahr* ('true') and *nehmen* ('to take'). This derivation is incorrect: *wahr-* in *wahrnehmen* is not etymologically related to *wahr*, 'true', but to the English 'aware'.

A central difficulty in Hegel's thought is this: Did he, like Kant, believe that the world and our experience of it involves a sensory element not reducible to or derivative of thought? There are several reasons for thinking that he did not: (1) He regularly attacks Kant's dualist doctrine. (2) The theology to which his system corresponds involves God's creating the world from nothing, not, as in Greek thought and early Judaism, the shaping of a primeval chaos; this implies that pure thought requires no sensory or material addition. (3) We cannot pick out a raw sensory element, free of conceptual contamination (*PS*, I), or a purely material factor with no FORM. But Hegel does not simply argue that thought and the sensory (or form and MATTER) are inextricably interwoven: the Logic attempts to extricate thought (and the relatively formal) from the sensuous (and the relatively material). The question how pure thought is related to the sensory (or to NATURE) is not satisfactorily answered. (The fact that a purely sensory element cannot be picked out independently of thought does not entail that there is no such element.)

irony and romanticism Hegel rarely uses the word 'irony' except to criticize the views of others, and, unlike Fichte and Schelling, he was not close to the Romantic Circle. But his interest in irony appears in many of his works: *PS* VII.B.c; *PR* §140; *Enc.* III §571; *LA*, Intro. (on romantic irony); *LPH* (especially on Socratic irony); and his 1828 review of Solger's *Posthumous Writing and Correspondence*.

Ironie was borrowed in the eighteenth century from the Greek *eirōneia* (via the Latin *ironia*), which meant 'dissimulation, pretended ignorance', and was seen as a fault. (An early English translation of *ironia* was 'Drie Mock'.) In Plato's *Republic*, Thrasymachus refers accusingly to Socrates' 'customary *eirōneia*'. When one of his interlocutors uses a term such as 'virtue', Socrates characteristically professes not to know what is meant by it and elicits from his opponent a definition which is then shown to involve fatal difficulties. Socrates' irony, Hegel argues, consists not only in his profession of ignorance but in his accepting his opponent's claim at face value and letting it refute itself. Irony is thus akin to DIALECTIC: dialectic gives things enough rope to hang *themselves*, and is thus the 'universal irony of the world' (*LHP*, I).

The seventeenth-century borrowing from the French *romantique, romantisch*, originally meant 'in the spirit of the medieval romance of chivalry', but, like the eighteenth-century *Romantik* ('romanticism'), it acquired all the connotations of its English counterpart, and especially came to refer to styles and epochs of ART, in contrast to the Enlightenment and the classical. (In German, *Romantik* is also associated with the novel, the *Roman*.) Since the 'classical' (*das Klassische*) is associated both with Graeco-Roman antiquity and with the (neo-)classical style of, e.g., Lessing and Goethe, 'romantic(ism)' is used (e.g. by Hegel) *both* for the period from the early Middle Ages to the present *and* for the romantic reaction to Goethe's classicism, represented especially by F. von Schlegel, his brother A. W. von Schlegel, Novalis, Tieck and Solger. (But Goethe is often presented as the supremely UNIVERSAL poet, who combines classicism and romanticism.)

The German romantics were devotees of *Ironie*, though *Ironie* varies in sense from author to author, and also within each author. F. Schlegel links romantic *Ironie* with Socrates' *eirōneia*:

> [Socratic irony] involves and arouses a sense of the irreconcilable conflict between the absolute and the relative, between the necessity of complete communication and its impossibility. It is the freest of all liberties, since it allows one to rise above oneself. ... It is all the better if harmonious dolts do not know what to make of this constant self-parody, if they waver endlessly between belief and disbelief until they get dizzy and take a joke for gravity and gravity for a joke. (*Lyceum Fragments*, 108 (1797))

Hegel argues that the two types of irony differ, since, e.g., Socrates was ironical towards people, while romantic irony is directed at ideas and values (*PR* §140).

Romantic irony is aloof, reflective and critical with respect to the world, its values, oneself and one's art. Irony 'surveys everything, raises itself infinitely above everything CONDITIONED, even above one's own art, virtue or genius' (F. Schlegel). The ironist espouses neither of two OPPOSITE positions, but reflects upon both and toys with each in turn: 'If you are infatuated with the absolute and cannot get rid of it, the only thing to do is to contradict yourself constantly and combine opposites' (F. Schlegel). He reflects upon his own reflection: 'We are close to waking when we dream about dreaming' (Novalis). The romantics disapproved of literary works whose author champions

147

one character against the rest, and favoured those (e.g. Shakespeare's) whose characters are all presented with impartial sympathy, and also those (e.g. Diderot's *Jacques le Fataliste* and Tieck's *Puss-in-Boots*), whose authors self-consciously play with their characters, and, by introducing themselves into the work, induce reflection on their own artistry and artistic conventions. Passion must be relieved by irony, 'a sort of confession, interwoven into the portrayal itself . . . of its overheated onesidedness in matters of fancy and feeling, which restores equilibrium once more' (A. W. Schlegel). Irony is also the 'recognition that the world is essentially paradoxical and that only an ambivalent attitude can grasp its contradictory totality' (F. Schlegel). God is often seen as an ironist: 'Supreme irony reigns in the conduct of God as he creates men and their life. In mundane art irony means this: God-like conduct' and true irony 'begins with the contemplation of the world's FATE in the large' (Solger). (The comparison of God to a dramatist runs from Plotinus' *Enneads*, III.ii.17, to Schelling's *STI*, III. 602–4).

'The three greatest tendencies of the age are the French revolution, Fichte's *Wissenschaftslehre* and Goethe's *Wilhelm Meister*' (F. Schlegel). Thus romantic irony, Hegel argues in *LA* (Intro.), is, in part, Fichte's philosophy applied to ART. (It is not an application of which Fichte – an advocate of decisive, patriotic action – approved.) Three Fichtean doctrines are relevant. The ambiguity of the doctrines – as to whether, e.g., the I* produces things, cognitively recognizes their existence, and/or endorses their value – is implicit in the romantics' use of Fichte:

(1)   The I is the principle of all knowledge, and it remains 'abstract and formal' and intrinsically simple, unaffected by the knowledge, etc., that it produces or acquires.

(2)   (a) All determinate CONTENT is negated in the I: everything is submerged in the abstract freedom and unity of the I. And conversely, (b) everything that has value or validity for the I is posited and recognized by the I itself. But what I bring about, I can just as easily annihilate.

1 and 2 imply that nothing has subsistence or worth, except in so far as it is produced by the SUBJECTIVITY of the I. The I is master over everything. ETHICAL LIFE, justice, religion, etc., has first to be posited by the I and can thus be annihilated by it. Everything is a mere show or ILLUSION (*Schein*), dependent on the I, which is free to dispose of it as it will.

(3)   The I is a living, active INDIVIDUAL (*Individuum*), and must thus assert its individuality both for itself and for others by expressing or EXTERNALIZING itself and emerging into APPEARANCE (*Erscheinung*).

With regard to art and beauty, 3 implies that one must live as an artist and shape one's life artistically. But on Schlegel's principle, I live as an artist only if all my action and expression, along with its content, is for me a mere show or illusion and its shape is wholly in my power. I cannot take this content or its expression seriously. Seriousness (*Ernst*) requires a substantial interest, a worthwhile cause, truth, ethical life, etc., a content that is essential for me, so that I am only essential for myself in so far as I immerse myself in it and conform to it in my action and knowledge. But the ironical artist cannot identify himself with anything of that sort: he ascribes SUBSTANCE and value only to his positing and destructive I.

Others may take me seriously, but only because they cannot understand or attain my elevated standpoint. Thus not everyone is as free as I am; for most men, RIGHT, ethical life, etc., are obligatory and essential. The ironical artist conceives himself as a God-like genius, whose ability to create and destroy is denied to most mortals. As a solitary genius, he regards his relations with others with the same ironical detachment as he does the rest of the world.

The divine irony of genius is a concentration of the I into itself: all its bonds are broken and it can live only in the bliss of self-enjoyment. Everything is vain except the I itself. But the I too is vain (*eitel, Eitelkeit* mean both 'empty, emptiness' and 'conceit(ed)'), since it cannot identify with any substantial content. Thus it finds no satisfaction in self-enjoyment (since there is nothing to enjoy in the I) and wants to attach itself to some OBJECTIVE cause, but cannot do so, since this would undermine its freedom. It thus succumbs to hopeless yearning (*Sehnsucht*), and becomes the beautiful SOUL, which can espouse no definite action for fear of compromising its inner harmony and purity. (F. Schlegel, like other romantics, later opted for Catholicism and conservatism.)

Irony governs not only the life of the ironist, but also his works of art. They are designed to show the divine as ironical. Worthy causes and objective values are shown to be vain and worthless by the fact that in the individuals who embody them they contradict and annihilate themselves and are thus ironical at their own expense. (Irony verges on comedy, but comedy trivializes the intrinsically trivial, which assumes an air of importance, while irony trivializes everything.) The ironist's characters betray the values they espouse. Thus the ironist can portray only weak, fickle characters, not strong ones, such as Antigone or Cato, whose whole being consists in the PURPOSE and values they represent. They are indecisive and hypocritical or else plagued by yearning and unresolved contradictions. Thus ironical art is insubstantial and trivial. Later, in *LA*, Hegel associates such irony with the works of Kleist, Hoffmann, Tieck and F. Schlegel. He finds an ironical detachment not in Homer's men, but in Homer's gods, who dabble in human affairs by taking sides, but then return to the serenity of Olympus. Shakespeare's characters, he maintains (against such critics as Tieck), are taut and decisive: even Hamlet was 'not doubtful about *what* he was to do, but only *how*'. But at the 'end of the romantic form of art', with the intensification of subjectivity characteristic of modernity, the artist becomes as the romantics conceive him: a '*tabula rasa*', with no FAITH or allegiance, using art as 'a free instrument' to portray anything and everything.

Hegel found elements of dialectic in irony, especially in Solger's stress on the 'IDEA's activity of negating itself as the INFINITE and UNIVERSAL, so as to become FINITUDE and PARTICULARITY, and then SUBLATING this negativity again and restoring the universal and infinite in the finite and particular' (*LA*, Intro.). But this 'dialectical unrest and dissolution' is only one MOMENT in the idea, not, as Solger believed, the whole of it. Like F. Schlegel, Hegel holds that we should embrace both limbs of an opposition, espousing neither to the exclusion of the other; that the I or SPIRIT constantly transcends and surveys its present position; and that philosophy itself should become 'the subject-matter of philosophy' (Schlegel). But the Hegelian does not remain aloof; he immerses himself in the SUBJECT-MATTER (*Sache*). When the I, SUBJECT or CONSCIOUSNESS is explicitly in play, as in *PS*, it does not remain empty and uncontaminated by its subject-matter, but is progressively enriched by it. For Schlegel, the infinitely deep and diverse world eludes our comprehension and we can only gesture towards it in CONTRADICTIONS and paradoxes. For Hegel, the world makes good sense, if we think these paradoxes through.

Romantic irony is comparable to SCEPTICISM and to revolutionary Jacobinism (*PS*, VI.B.III): it plays a similar, SUBLATED role in Hegel's thought. Kierkegaard was as intrigued by irony as Hegel, and his master's dissertation was *On the Concept of Irony with Constant Reference to Socrates* (1841). Romantic irony influenced his conception of the 'aesthetic', especially in *Either/Or*, I (1843). Nietzsche too owes much to irony, as does the Baudelaire portrayed in Sartre's *Baudelaire* (1947).

J

judgment and proposition Two words need to be distinguished:

1. *Urteil* ('judgment'), from *urteilen* ('to judge'). Here *ur-* does not mean 'original, primitive', but amounts to *er-* (*see* APPEARANCE), as in *erteilen* ('to give, award'). Hence *urteilen* was originally 'to give, allot' and an *Urteil* something given or allotted. *Urteil* was later restricted to a legal 'judgment, verdict, sentence', and it remained a legal word until the seventeenth century, when Leibniz gave it the sense of a propositional 'judgment'. Wolff defined it as the logical combination or separation of two or more CONCEPTS. Thus an *Urteil* is a logical, rather than a grammatical, entity, and is distinct from a sentence. In ordinary German *Urteil*, *urteilen* and the similar *beurteilen* ('to judge, criticize') retain the flavour of assessment or evaluation.

Leibniz also introduced into philosophy the recently coined *Urteilskraft* ('(power or faculty of) judgment'). Kant defined this as (in contrast to the UNDERSTANDING, the faculty of rules) the faculty of subsuming things under rules, i.e. of deciding whether the rule applies or not. If the rule is given, then the judgment is DETERMINING (*bestimmend*), but if only the particular is given and the task is to find a rule to apply to it, judgment is REFLECTIVE (*reflektierend*). Kant saw the power of judgment as crucial for the appreciation of works of ART and living creatures, which require respectively AESTHETIC (*ästhetische*) and teleological (*teleologische*) judgment.

Propositional judgments were classified by the scholastics and by Kant as follows:

(a) In quantity, judgments are UNIVERSAL ('All men are wise'), PARTICULAR ('Some men are wise') and INDIVIDUAL ('Socrates is wise').

(b) In quality, they are affirmative, negative and infinite or indefinite (*unendlich*) or *limitative*. For Kant an infinite judgment is one that is affirmative in form, but negative in sense, e.g., 'God is immortal (or non-mortal)' in contrast to 'God is not mortal'. Hegel gives a different account: The subject of a negative judgment, e.g. 'This rose is not red', has some quality belonging to the same range as the quality denied of it: the rose is some other *colour*, e.g. yellow. The subject of a (negative) infinite judgment, e.g. 'The mind is not red', has no quality in the range of the quality denied of it: the mind is not coloured. Here Hegel comes close to Ryle's notion of a category mistake.

(c) In *relation*, they are categorical (A is B), hypothetical (If A is, then B is) and disjunctive (A is B or C).

(d)   In modality, they are problematic (Possibly A is B), assertoric (A is B), and necessary (Necessarily A is B).

Kant derived his categories from these forms of judgment (e.g. ground or CAUSALITY from the hypothetical judgment), a procedure which Hegel often criticizes. He also classifies judgments as analytic or synthetic, but Hegel has little interest in this distinction. (He has more to say about the analytic and synthetic methods of COGNITION, but the connection between this distinction and the distinction of analytic and synthetic judgments is remote.)

2. *Satz* derives from *setzen* ('to make sit, set, put, POSIT', etc.), and is thus something put down or set out. It has a variety of senses (e.g. 'sediment, dregs'), but its common meaning, in philosophy and ordinary usage, is 'sentence, proposition'. While an *Urteil* consists of concepts, a *Satz* consists of words: it is an *Urteil* expressed in words. But it is often closer to 'proposition' than to 'sentence': e.g. what we call the 'LAW' or 'principle' of (non-) CONTRADICTION is, in German, the *Satz* of contradiction. Hegel drew a distinction between a *Satz* and an *Urteil* in respect of their content: An *Urteil* has a subject and a predicate; the subject must be either individual (e.g. 'Socrates') or particular (e.g. '(Some/All) Greeks'); if it is individual, the predicate is either particular (e.g. 'Greek') or universal (e.g. 'man'), while if it is particular, the predicate is universal. This suggests two reasons why a *Satz* may fail to be an *Urteil*:

(a)   The predicate may be of the same logical type as the subject. *SL* gives a case in which the predicate, as well as the subject, is individual: 'Aristotle died at 72, in the 4th year of the 115th Olympiad.' Since it is unclear that the predicate here is individual (others may have died at 72 in that year), a better case is the statement of IDENTITY, e.g. 'Cicero is Tully', 'BEING is nothing', or 'GOD is being'.

(b)   The subject is not genuinely distinct from the predicate: e.g. in 'The ABSOLUTE/God is being/eternal', we do not know what God/the absolute is independently of the predicate applied to it (*Enc.* I §31). By contrast, we know who Aristotle was without knowing when he died, and perhaps who Socrates was without knowing that he was Greek (but surely not without knowing that he was a man).

Hegel adds a third criterion that depends on *Urteil*'s suggestion of 'assessment':

(c)   An *Urteil*, unlike a *Satz*, implies some uncertainty that is resolved by an appeal to evidence: 'Your friend has died' is an *Urteil* only if there is doubt whether he is really dead or, e.g., only in a coma.

These criteria do not coincide and their application is uncertain.

Hegel accepted the widespread view that *Urteil* and *urteilen* derive from *ur-* ('original') and *teilen* ('divide'), and thus signify an 'original division'. Hölderlin, in his fragment *Judgment and Being* (1795), had argued that *Urteil* is the 'original separation of OBJECT and SUBJECT which are most deeply united in intellectual INTUITION. . . . "I am I" is the most fitting example of this concept.' For Hegel, the judgment is the original division or 'diremption' of the CONCEPT into its 'moments' of universality, particularity and individuality. This has several implications:

(a)   Hegel rejects the orthodox view that judgment involves the combining of concepts.

(b)   Just as the concept is not simply an abstract logical entity, but is embedded in the mind and in the world, so the forms of judgment have an 'objective meaning (*Bedeutung*)': e.g. the growth of a plant from its seed is a judgment, and all FINITE things are, in virtue of the misfit between their concept and their reality, a judgment. (Here Hegel has in mind the 'sentence' or judgment of death to which all finite things succumb.)

(c)   The four types of judgment, though they result from the division of the concept, are successively more adequate ways of restoring the unity of the concept. Each type has three sub-types:

   (i)   Judgments of DETERMINATE BEING, i.e. the positive, negative and infinite judgment, predicate a contingent quality.

   (ii)   Judgments of REFLECTION are the individual, particular and universal judgments.

   (iii) Judgments of NECESSITY (categorical, hypothetical and disjunctive) predicate a feature essential to the subject.

   (iv)   Judgments of the concept (assertoric, problematic and apodictic (viz. necessary)) judge the subject to be good or bad, viz. in, or out of, accord with its concept. The apodictic judgment assigns a predicate on the basis of a reason involved in the subject itself and thus verges on the INFERENCE, to which Hegel next turns. (The three main types of inference and their subdivisions correspond to the first three types of judgment. But there is no inference of the concept, perhaps because Hegel could not accommodate the modal syllogism and because *Schluss* ('inference') lacks the evaluative connotation of *Urteil*.)

(d)   Hegel takes the 'is' in, e.g., 'Socrates is wise' to assert the identity of subject and predicate, and to imply 'The individual is the universal'. This claim is 'one-sided' and thus requires a countervailing negative judgment: 'The individual is not the universal.' Hegel mistakes the logical *form* of a judgment ('the I is U') for a proposition implied by it. But his belief that the 'is' is one of identity stems too from his doctrine that the judgment attempts to restore the identity of the concept.

Hegel held that the *Urteil* and *Satz* are unsuited to SPECULATIVE doctrines, for two reasons: (1) In a *Satz* such as 'God is eternal', the subject-term is fully explained by the predicate, and is thus superfluous. (2) A *Satz* or *Urteil* is 'one-sided': it can say only, e.g., 'being is nothing' or 'being is not nothing', and cannot express the identity-in-difference of being and nothing. This reflects in part Hegel's dependence on a traditional logic, which, as he is aware, cannot do justice to his *own* sentences (or to much of non-Hegelian philosophical and non-philosophical discourse). But it also stems from his belief that the judgment involves an essential division that is at odds with the ultimate TRUTH about (or 'of') the universe.

153

K

knowledge, cognition and certainty No single German word corresponds in range to 'know', but a variety of words overlap it:

1. *Wissen* is 'to know, not be ignorant of', close to the French *savoir*. It can be followed by a noun (e.g. 'the right way'), 'of' (*von*), 'about' (*um*), 'how to', or a that-clause (*dass*). The verbal noun (*das*) *Wissen* ('knowledge, learning') is used in set phrases (e.g. 'to the best of my knowledge'), for knowledge of something or in a particular field, and for knowledge in general (e.g. 'Knowledge is power'). It is used by Hegel for 'ABSOLUTE knowledge'. It generates *Wissenschaft* ('SCIENCE').

2. The verb *kennen* (like the French *connaître*) is 'to know, be familiar with': in 'I do not know her, but I know about her', *kennen* translates the first 'know', *wissen* the second. The noun *Kenntnis* is 'cognizance, awareness' of a particular fact. The plural, *Kenntnisse*, is 'items of knowledge'. (*Wissen*, by contrast, has no plural and does not suggest items of knowledge.)

3. The verb *erkennen* means (a) 'to know again, RECOGNIZE' something previously encountered; (b) 'to recognize, realize, come to know, see', e.g. a truth, one's error or that one was mistaken; (c) 'to give a judgment or verdict', e.g. 'to *find* him guilty, *condemn* him to death'. The most important sense in Hegel is (b): he contrasts what is merely *bekannt* ('familiar, well-known') with what is *erkannt* ('systematically cognized, understood, known'): e.g. before one does logic, one's language and particular words and constructions are *bekannt*, afterwards they are also *erkannt*. (*Die*) *Erkenntnis* is philosophical or scientific knowledge. The plural, *Erkenntnisse*, means 'items of knowledge, cognitions'. Translators often distinguish 'cognition(s)' (*Erkenntnis(se)*) from 'knowledge' (*Wissen*). The verbal noun (*das*) *Erkennen* ('knowing, cognizing') is also common.

4. *Einsehen* (literally 'to see into, look into') is close to *erkennen* in sense (b): 'to come to realize, understand, know' a thing or that something is so. Hegel often uses the noun *Einsicht* ('insight'): in *PS*, it contrasts with FAITH (*Glaube*) and is associated with the rationalism of the Enlightenment. Unlike *Glaube*, it is conceptual, rational and individual; to have insight into things contrasts with simply accepting them. Hence, although one may accept, e.g., a religion into which one has insight, insight has tended to conflict with RELIGION.

5. *Wissen* is cognate with *gewiss* ('certain') and *Gewissheit* ('certainty'), in both an objective ('That's certain') and a subjective ('I am certain of it') sense. In Hegel the words usually have an subjective sense, and he constantly

154

stresses that certainty does not guarantee TRUTH in either the usual or Hegel's sense: SENSORY certainty is contrasted with the truth apprehended by PERCEPTION. (Sometimes this feature of *gewiss* is transferred to *wissen*, so that a person may 'know' for certain what is false.) Certainty in Hegel is IMMEDIATE rather than derived, and this is one reason why truth eludes it. It may be involved in religious faith. Self-certainty (*Selbstgewissheit*), Cartesian self-awareness, but also, in Hegel, self-assuredness, is a primitive version of SELF-CONSCIOUSNESS. *Gewissen* ('conscience') also derives from *wissen*. Originally *Gewissen* meant 'consciousness' (as does the word for 'conscience' in many European languages). But in *PS* and *PR*, Hegel stresses the connection of conscience with (self-)certainty, and its consequent fallibility.

Wissen was originally a past tense, meaning 'to have perceived'. Hence *Wissen* can be immediate, involving, unlike *Erkennen*, no process of coming to know. Thus Hegel often contrasts *Wissen* unfavourably with *Erkennen*, as a direct or immediate knowledge that cannot grasp CONCRETE interrelations. (In philosophical cognition, the steps by which we arrive at a result are involved in the structure of the result.) He cites the dictum 'we *wissen* that God is, but we do not *erkennen* God [viz. his actual concrete nature]' (*Enc.* III §445A.). Again, Jacobi's doctrine that we immediately know God's existence, etc., is a doctrine of immediate *Wissen*; *Erkennen*, by contrast, is inevitably mediated (*Enc.* I §§61ff). But *Wissen* is not always compared unfavourably to *Erkennen*: e.g. 'absolute knowledge' in *PS* is *das absolutes Wissen*. There are two reasons for this: (1) *Wissen* is drawn towards the invariably favourable *Wissenschaft* ('SCIENCE'), and away from the usually pejorative *Gewissheit*. (2) Since the result of cognition SUBLATES the steps by which we reached it, the result is immediate in a higher sense, and is thus *Wissen* as much as *Erkennen*.

Hegel examines *Erkennen* (but not *Wissen*), viz. the FINITE cognition of the natural and mathematical sciences, in the Logic: cognition is either analytic or synthetic. These notions (which have no close connection with analytic and synthetic JUDGMENT) derive from a Greek mathematician, Pappus: analysis (or the regressive method) and synthesis (the progressive method) are two procedures used, often complementarily, in geometry. If we have a problem to solve or a theorem whose truth-value is unknown, analysis starts by assuming the problem solved or the truth of the theorem and then derives consequences from this assumption. We assume, e.g., the truth of theorem A, then derive B from A, and C from B, until we reach a theorem, say M, whose truth-value is already known. If M is false, then A is now known to be false. If M is true, then synthesis works back from M (deductively in mathematics, but, e.g., inductively in the natural sciences) to prove the truth of A. Analysis thus proceeds from the unknown to the known, synthesis from the known to the (hitherto) unknown.

Hegel (unlike Kant) failed to see how cognition could proceed from the unknown to the known, and he thus associates analysis with mathematics in general, since it splits things up into quantities that are EXTERNALLY related (in *SL*), with the extraction of universal LAWS, FORCES and GENERA from concrete phenomena, and with the analysis of a substance into its chemical constituents (*Enc.* I §227 and A.). His much longer account of synthesis deals with DEFINITION, CLASSIFICATION and the theorem.

Hegel believes that his own cognitive procedure is both analytic and synthetic. This is true in one sense: he does not simply synthesize, e.g., the logical IDEA or RIGHT into a single whole or simply analyse them into their constituent elements, but presents them as unified, but articulated, WHOLES. But it is not true in Pappus' sense: Hegel never (officially at least) proceeds by working back from his intended result to what is required in order to reach it, but always by advancing from what is already known towards an as yet unknown result. (In *PS*, 'we' philosophers already occupy the standpoint of absolute knowledge, but we only observe, and do not assist, the development of CONSCIOUSNESS to this standpoint.) But the circularity of his system implies that progress is also regress towards the beginning: the conditions sublated in the result eventually re-emerge from it, and are fully understood only when the cycle is complete. There is thus another sense in which Hegel's cognition is both analytic and synthetic.

Hegel and his contemporaries were vexed by the threat of SCEPTICISM to both *Erkennen* and *Wissen*. He argued, against what he took to be Kant's view, that the problem cannot be met by *first* examining cognition, since if our cognitive powers are good enough for that task, they are good enough for direct application to the world: Kant's procedure is like trying to learn to swim without entering the water (*PS*, Intro.). But Hegel did not disdain epistemology: Not only *PS* (with its examination not of the world, but of forms of consciousness), but his whole system, is shaped in part as a response to scepticism. This response involves the reshaping or re-evaluation of several other concepts, besides that of knowledge: 'certainty', 'truth', 'PROOF', 'immediate', etc.

L

language Most of Hegel's works contain comments on language, and above all his writing is marked by a self-consciousness about his own language, and its relationship to ordinary speech, which we do not find in Kant. (Herder and Hamann criticized Kant's neglect of language.) But language has a relatively minor *explicit* place in Hegel's system. There are several reasons for this: (1) Language, like dialectic (to which Hegel also devotes little explicit attention), pertains to the whole of philosophy, and is thus not easily assigned to a special part of it. (2) A question that interested many philosophers (Rousseau, Herder, Fichte, etc.), viz. how language originated, was not, on Hegel's view, answerable, since HISTORY presupposes historical writing, and this presupposes language. History is concerned with the historical products of SPIRIT, not with language, the immediate expression of spirit involved in them all. (3) Another question of current interest, viz. the differences and affinities of languages, was not a dominant concern of Hegel's, both because it is a matter for empirical research (like that of W. von Humboldt), and because he was more interested in the logical categories that are embodied, more or less fully and explicitly, in all languages.

Language is considered in *Enc.* III §§458–64 under the headings of IMAGINATION and MEMORY: Language emerges (but not necessarily in history) from the attempt of the INNER, the dark 'pit' (*Schacht*) of the intelligence (*Intelligenz*), to find an appropriate objective, OUTER embodiment for its universal REPRESENTATIONS or conceptions, which does not involve constant dependence on the INDIVIDUALITY of sensory INTUITION. Imagination (*Phantasie*), which MEDIATES between conception and intuition, supplies images (*Bild*), which, though they give the intelligence some independence of intuition, are fleeting and subjective, as well as involving an essential sensory element. The next step is to represent a conception by a symbol (*Symbol*). The entity chosen to symbolize a conception retains an essential empirical feature that makes it appropriate to serve as a symbol: e.g. strength, or the strength of Jupiter, may be symbolized by an eagle, since the eagle is (regarded as) strong, but not, e.g., by a dove. Still greater liberation from intuition is conferred by the adoption of a sign (*Zeichen*), which is wholly conventional: e.g. a flag must have *some* empirical features, but its features are not determined by what it signifies. Hegel represents (or *symbolizes*) the sign by the pyramid, which contains an 'alien soul', viz. a mummy, to which it bears no resemblance (*Enc.* III §458). This soul is comparable to the meaning (*Bedeutung*) of a sign. The final step is the production of sounds to signify conceptions: not only are the empirical features of the sounds purely conventional with respect to their meaning, but sounds are themselves temporal and fleeting rather than spatial and persistent. This represents a further downgrading of sensory intuition.

The name is an intuition produced by the intelligence, combined with its meaning. At first, this combination is a transitory individual and the combination is correspondingly 'external'. But MEMORY internalizes or RE-COLLECTS this externality: It makes the individual combination into a universal and permanent one. The name ceases to be an intuition (viz. a token) and becomes a conception (viz. a type), whose meaning is also a conception. The two conceptions, that of the thing and that of the name, are thus fused together. We need no image or intuition to think about a lion: 'It is in names that we think' (§462). Thus the intelligence is both fully internalized (it relies only on its own abstract product, the name, and dispenses with empirical material) and fully externalized (it has direct access to objects, unmediated by sensory, psychological entities). (This exemplifies the DIALECTIC of INNER AND OUTER.)

So far words are grouped together according to our current sensations, conceptions or thoughts. But now, finally, they are arranged in a formal system, independently of their references to external objects. Language thus becomes 'external' to the intelligence that produced it, which transforms itself into the 'universal space of names as such ... the power over the various names, the empty bond that fixes series of names in itself and keeps them in firm order' (*Enc.* III §463). Hegel here has several things in view: the fact that in relation to any given speaker a language is an objective system to be learnt and conformed to; our ability, when words and their meanings are thoroughly familiar to us, to deploy them in disregard, and even contravention, of their meanings; and the advantages of rote-learning, which divests the mind of its private contents and prepares it for the reception of objective matters. (EDUCATION involves ALIENATION.)

In conformity with the correlativity of the inner and outer, Hegel denies that we can think without words: 'We know of our thoughts, we have determinate, actual thoughts, only when we give them the form of objectivity, of distinctness from our inwardness, thus give them the shape of externality, and of such an externality as bears the stamp of the highest inwardness' (*Enc.* III §462A.).

In *Enc.* III §459 Hegel discusses speech and writing. Articulate sound (*Ton*) is speech (*Rede*), and the system of speech is language (*Sprache*, from *sprechen*, 'to speak'). Language involves two aspects:

1. Phonetic material may derive originally from the imitation of natural sounds such as rustling and creaking, but this has no relevance to a developed language. Its elementary material depends on the 'gesture' (*Gebärde*) that we produce by the movements of our lips, palate and tongue. Any original meaning that these phonetic features, and vowels and consonants, once had is suppressed by their use in signs.

2. In contrast to phonetic material, the formal aspect, grammar, is the

product of the UNDERSTANDING, which introduces its categories into language. This 'logical instinct' has been at work from the very beginnings, since the languages of less civilized peoples have a more developed grammar, conveying distinctions that are lacking in those of more civilized peoples. He cites Humboldt's *Über den Dualis* (*On the Dual*, 1828) in support of this (essentially correct) view. (Vico and Herder had argued that primitive languages are simple.)

In his account of written language Hegel argues that an alphabetic script, whose characters are signs of the elements of the auditory signs of spoken language, is superior to a hieroglyphic script, which directly represents conceptions. This was a question of contemporary relevance, since Leibniz had proposed a script that would directly present ideas and the relations between them, constructed on hieroglyphic principles. (Leibniz was influenced by Chinese, rather than Egyptian, script.) Hegel's objections to such a script are these:

(a) Leibniz believed that such a language would serve the purpose not only of logical perspicuity, but of easier communication between peoples and especially scholars. But history suggests that alphabetic scripts were introduced because they facilitate everyday communication.

(b) If the sign for a conception is to embody an analysis of it, we shall need to change our signs whenever we change our analysis of conceptions. This occurs even in the case of chemical substances (which *are* named on hieroglyphic principles), but it would occur more frequently in the case of spiritual conceptions. Hieroglyphs are appropriate only for static societies such as China.

(c) Alphabetic script affects the spoken language, helping to simplify and systematize its articulation. A hieroglyphic script cannot have this effect; thus spoken Chinese is grotesquely complex, containing many near homonyms distinguishable only by differences of accentuation or tone that are barely discernible to a foreigner.

(d) Alphabetic, unlike hieroglyphic, script enables us to *reflect* on the spoken word: we can see from its written counterpart how it is constructed from a few simple elements. Hegel also ascribes pedagogical advantages to the learning of a formal system such as an alphabet.

(e) Alphabetic script, like spoken language, preserves the unity of the word, which is thus a *name*, since it connotes a certain conception *as a whole*, and not in virtue of the meanings of its constituent parts. A word is, for the ordinary speaker, a simple entity, not a collection of other words. As such, it refers directly to *things*, while on hieroglyphic principles our access and references to things are mediated by conceptions. Hegel's point would also apply to Mill's view that a word such as 'horse' denotes horses in virtue of connoting features that belong to all, and only, horses, and to Russell's view that a name such as 'Hegel' denotes Hegel in virtue of its association with a definite description that applies uniquely to Hegel.

(f) The meaning of a word can be analysed, but its logical features and their interrelations cannot be adequately represented by the external spatial relationships of hieroglyphs or of logical and mathematical symbolisms. In this connection, Hegel often attacks the Pythagorean view that mathematics provides a language appropriate for philosophy.

Derrida, in 'The pit and the pyramid', criticizes Hegel's beliefs that language is essential to thought, that spoken language is prior to written language and that alphabetic scripts are superior to hieroglyphs. Hegel's thought is oriented towards language, especially spoken language: he appeared at his best in lectures rather than books. He was also unappreciative of, e.g., musical thinking and of music without a content expressible in words. Nevertheless he downgrades the purely sensory features of language and argues, e.g., that poetry can be translated without much loss.

law and rule 'Law' may translate several German words: e.g. *Recht* ('RIGHT, law (in general, not in the sense of a particular law)'), *Bestimmung(en)* ('DETERMINATIONS, regulations, legal provisions'). But the main word for 'law' is *Gesetz*, from *setzen* ('to POSIT, lay down', etc.), and thus something laid down. Like 'law', *Gesetz* refers both to the laws of a community and to laws of NATURE. (The German for 'law of nature' is *Naturgesetz* or *Gesetz der Natur*, contrasting with *Gesetz des Rechts*, 'law of the land'. 'Natural law', in the sense of an ethical or social code implicit in the nature of man or the cosmos, is *Naturrecht*, in contrast to *positive Recht*.) This ambiguity is of long standing: Heraclitus suggests that the cosmos is governed by divine law (*nomos*), in a way comparable to that in which human societies are governed by human laws, and this is a central doctrine of the STOICS. The expression 'laws of nature' (*leges naturae*) occurs in Lucretius, with no literal theological or ethical associations.

There are also moral or ethical laws, which determine our duties whether or not they are also embodied in the law of the land. Kant distinguishes these from external (*äussere*) laws (viz. of the land), some of which can be known *a priori* to be binding, independently of actual legislation (external, but natural (*natürliche*) laws), while others are binding only in virtue of external legislation (*positive* laws). In Kant's day the term *Denkgesetz(e)* ('law(s) of THOUGHT') was applied to the laws or principles of IDENTITY, of (non-) CONTRADICTION, of the excluded middle and sometimes of sufficient reason or GROUND. Hegel rejects this title, since he believes it to be both easy and legitimate to think in contravention of these laws.

A *Regel* ('rule', in both a theoretical and a practical sense) differs from a law in that it admits exceptions ('As a rule ...', 'rules of etiquette', etc.). Hegel uses *Regel* mainly in connection with MEASURE (*Mass*), where it is a standard or criterion (*Massstab*, literally a 'measuring stick, rod'), a fixed unit of measurement embodied in a material entity (e.g. a ruler), whose repeated application to another entity determines its size. In *LA*, Hegel distinguishes *Regelmässigkeit* ('regularity') from *Gesetzmässigkeit* ('lawfulness'). Rule involves undifferentiated uniformity; thus regularity, which is closely related to symmetry, appears in, e.g., a series of parallel lines of equal length, a crystal and a circle. Law consists in a necessary connection between distinct features; thus lawfulness appears in the irregular movements of the planets, the irregular oval and the 'waving' line extolled by Hogarth in his *Analysis of Beauty* (1753). Regularity has a place in architecture and music, but is undesirable in sculpture and in general aesthetically inferior to lawfulness.

Hegel often assimilates the two main types of law, referring to laws of nature as a *Reich* ('kingdom, realm') of laws (in contrast to the realm of APPEARANCE) and introducing PUNISHMENT into a discussion of laws of nature (*PS*, III; *Enc*. III §422A.). But he distinguishes them at *PR*, Pref. A.: Laws of nature are not propositions formulated by us, but objective facts, which we can discover and cannot encroach on. Laws of the land are also, for the individual citizen, objective facts, which he needs to discover, and the positive study of law gives an objective account of them, similar to the scientist's account of the laws of nature. But the laws of the land are posited by men, and are not absolute, since they vary from society to society. Hence a rift can emerge between the laws and the citizen's private conscience. *PR* attempts to reconcile (*versöhnen*) us to the rationality of our laws, while the natural scientist does not try or need to reconcile us to the laws of nature. At *Enc*. III §529 and *PR* §211 the difference is said to be that stars and animals do not know (*wissen*) the laws that govern their conduct, while men do. (Hegel will not say that things actually conform to laws of nature, while men OUGHT to obey the laws of the land: a law that is not generally obeyed is a dead or defunct law.)

References to both main types of law occur throughout Hegel's works. His view of them is as follows:

1. In *ETW*, he often compares laws, both ethical and political, unfavourably to love, but he comes to the view that no stable society can dispense with laws. In early phases of HISTORY, state laws were not distinguished from divine or religious laws: *PS*, VI.A., considers the conflict between human and divine laws in Greek tragedy and society.

PR §211ff and *Enc*. III §529ff consider laws in modern society. The administration of law is assigned to CIVIL SOCIETY rather than the STATE: the state or its legislative POWER makes laws, but any large-scale human interaction requires a framework of law, not simply activity within the boundaries of the nation-state. Laws must be UNIVERSAL in form, clearly and definitely formulated, known to the citizens, authoritatively laid down, fairly administered and effectively enforced, with punishment for offences against them. Laws should refine, clarify and develop pre-existing CUSTOMS; laws that wholly contravene customs will not be enforceable. Since laws are universal, it is a 'tautology' that citizens are equal before the law, in the sense that laws apply impartially to all citizens (*Enc*. III §539). But 'as regards the concrete, citizens ... are equal before the law only in respects in which they are already equal outside the law.' In so far as citizens are relevantly different, the law assigns them different duties and entitlements.

The content of laws may be irrational. But even when laws are not irrational, it is often necessary for them to decide points of detail in an arbitrary way: the prohibition and punishment of theft is rationally justifiable, but a penalty of, say, ten years' imprisonment, rather than nine or eleven, is not. To say that a law is 'positive' can thus mean three things: that the law (a) contravenes REASON and is thus a bad law; (b) rationally and justifiably makes a ruling that is not rationally justifiable; or (c) though rationally justifiable and making a rationally justifiable ruling, is nevertheless a law posited by an authority. But laws are not simply an external imposition: obedience as such is an essential stage in the formation of one's character, and to obey the law is to conform to what is, in virtue of its universality, an expression of one's own essential rationality and WILL. Thus Hegel prefers a legal to a merely customary order, not simply because it regulates our conduct more effectively, but because it raises us to a higher level of SELF-CONSCIOUSNESS.

2. At *PS*, III, the consideration of FORCE (*Kraft*) leads to the introduction of laws, since the inner ESSENCE must be sufficiently differentiated to account for the diversity of appearance. A law relates distinct features of appearance, e.g., the distance traversed, and the time taken, by a falling body. But unlike appearance, laws do not change: the realm of laws is a 'static image [*Bild*, or copy, *Abbild*) of inconstant appearance (*Erscheinung*)'. But this does not mean that laws are any less objective than forces: they are the 'determinations of the UNDERSTANDING inherent in the world itself' (*Enc.* III §422A.). Initially Hegel considers the laws of motion, and finds two main problems in them: (a) Since a law purports to unify phenomena, laws should not be simply distinct from each other, but ultimately reducible to a single law. But attempts to reduce the number of laws tends (as in Newton) to result in an empty tautology, where everything depends on the antecedent conditions in which the law applies. (b) Laws do not fully GROUND phenomena: they explain only what happens *if* certain conditions are fulfilled, but not the fulfilment of these conditions. His reflection on these problems leads to a consideration of laws that involve polar OPPOSITES, such as laws of magnetism and electricity. This suggests the idea that the realm of laws is a reversal or mirror-image of the realm of appearance.

In *PS*, V.A., Hegel turns to 'observing (*beobachtende*) REASON', and considers laws concerning organic LIFE, and also logical and psychological laws, in particular laws supposedly correlating a person's psychological traits with his facial features ('physiognomy') or with the shape of his skull (*Schädellehre*, 'craniology, phrenology'). Hegel doubts the possibility of such laws: organisms are too unified and self-determining for there to be significant laws correlating their states with states of their environment. The MIND is similarly unified and cannot be split up into distinct traits or faculties, each corresponding to a distinct physical feature. It is even less susceptible than plants and animals to external CAUSES. In addition, once a person comes to *know* of an alleged law governing his thought or conduct, he can set out to evade or exploit its operation. Such laws (but not *inner* lawfulness, *Gesetzmässigkeit*) are thus more appropriate to MECHANISM than to higher types of organization.

Hegel did not substantially alter his views on these matters in later works.

Lectures on Aesthetics (*Vorlesungen über die Ästhetik*) (LA)   Hegel
lectured on AESTHETICS at Heidelberg and also at Berlin in the winter of 1820–1, the summers of 1823 and 1826, and the winter of 1828–9. H. G. Hotho edited *LA* in three volumes for the *Works* in 1835, and, with revisions, in 1842. The lectures altered over the years, but Hotho put together Hegel's notes and students' transcripts of the lectures of 1823, 1826 and 1828–9. *LA* is often given the title or subtitle 'Lectures on Fine Art', which, though not the title used by Hegel for his lectures, reflects their contents more accurately.

Unlike Kant, Hegel saw ART as a having a HISTORY, and was as interested in the CONTENT of art as its FORM. But in both respects his enterprise had antecedents. Herder, in his response to *CJ*, *Kalligone* (1800), had criticized Kant for focusing on the form of art at the expense of its content or SPIRIT. Herder stressed that poetry springs from the RELIGION, language, customs, etc., of a PEOPLE, and developed the genetic or historical approach to literary criticism. Art, like everything human, is historical: thus there are no ahistorical rules for evaluating art, and BEAUTY is 'historical', not 'absolute'. But the history of art was initiated by Winckelmann, especially in his *History of the Art of Antiquity* (1764). He argued that art falls into three phases: childhood, maturity and ageing. The phase of maturity is that of Greek art, which occupies most of the work. Hegel (like Herder) had a high regard for Winckelmann, and shared his admiration for Greek art, while rejecting his exaltation of it at the expense of all other art. A. W. Schlegel gave lectures on art (published as *Lectures on Fine [schöne] Literature and Art*, 1801–4). These were consulted by Schelling for his lectures on the philosophy of art in 1802–3, in which he attempts to give a 'historical construction' both of the content of art and of its forms. Schelling was less learned than Hegel, but his account of art and of its place in philosophy is similar to Hegel's. (Unlike Hegel, he placed art at the pinnacle of philosophy.)

LA begins with a general Introduction. The subject of aesthetics, Hegel argues, is fine art. Art, as a product of spirit, is superior to NATURE. Natural objects may be beautiful, but their beauty is parasitic on art: only the MIND or spirit is capable of TRUTH and beauty. Moreover, only the beauty of art can be studied scientifically. (*Kunst*, like 'art', contrasts with 'SCIENCE' (*Wissenschaft*). But German, unlike English, readily speaks of the 'science' or systematic study of art.) As a thing of beauty, e.g., the sun is an isolated entity, inferior to mind, while if we consider it scientifically, in its RELATIONS (*Zusammenhang*) to other entities, it is not considered by itself or, therefore, as beautiful.

It has been objected that art is too trivial, diverse and illusory to be the subject of a science, or again that an abstract scientific treatment will ignore the rich sensory and emotional content of art. Hegel replies that art is not primarily decorative, but (unlike nature) expresses 'the divine nature, the deepest interests of humanity and the most comprehensive truths of the spirit'. It is not illusion or deception; it 'liberates the real import [*Gehalt*] of APPEARANCES [*Erscheinungen*] from the semblance [*Schein*] and deception (*Täuschung*) of this bad and fleeting world, and imparts to them a higher ACTUALITY, born of spirit'. Thus art deserves a scientific treatment. And since art is essentially spiritual and not exclusively sensory, it invites philosophical reflection. Our age is an age of thoughtful REFLECTION, in which 'art no longer affords that satisfaction of spiritual needs that earlier epochs and peoples sought in it'; thus the science of art is 'a much more pressing need in our day'.

There are two traditional approaches to aesthetics. One approach starts from actual works of art. This includes, on Hegel's view, not only art-scholarship, which considers the whole range of works in their historical context, but attempts (e.g. Horace's), usually based on a narrow range of works, to formulate rules for the production of art or rules for its appreciation, rules of taste. Hegel argues that neither the production nor the assessment of art conforms to simple rules, and thus welcomed the recent opposing stress on the artist as a genius, whose creativity depends on no rules and breaks any rules prescribed to it. This, Hegel believes, underrates the knowledge and technical skill required of the artist, but it led to a widening of our aesthetic sensibility to include alien, e.g. Indian, art. The second approach, exemplified by Plato, is to examine the abstract concept of beauty. Neither approach is, on Hegel's view, adequate. We should develop a CONCEPT of beauty that is sufficiently CONCRETE to explain the emergence of particular types and works of art.

Ideally this concept emerges systematically from the preceding phase of philosophy, but here Hegel develops the concept from some common CONCEPTIONS about art. These fall under three headings:

1. *Art is a product of human activity.* Hegel argues that (a) art results neither from the application of rules, nor from genius and inspiration alone; (b) it is a higher revelation of GOD than nature is; and (c) it results from 'man's rational need to exalt the INNER and OUTER world into a spiritual CONSCIOUSNESS for himself, as an OBJECT [*Gegenstand*] in which he recognizes his own self.'

2. *Art is made for man, and is more or less borrowed from the SENSORY and addressed to man's sense.* Here he argues: (a) Art does not essentially express or arouse FEELINGS (*Gefühle*) or emotions (*Empfindungen*): feelings (e.g. fear, which can take *anything* as its object) are too indeterminate and coarse-grained to do justice to the rich detail of art. (b) It does not depend on a special feeling or sense of beauty (or 'taste'): taste is concerned only with the superficial trimmings of art and neglects its spiritual depths. (c) A work of art, e.g. a painting of fruit, does not, if viewed properly, arouse desire for the object portrayed. (d) It does not invite theoretical or conceptual analysis of the object portrayed, e.g. of the chemical or biological properties of the fruit. (e) Art thus gives the semblance (*Schein*), not the material presence, of the sensory. Hence it appeals to the 'theoretical' senses of sight and hearing, not

to the bodily senses of taste, smell and touch. (f) Thus the sensory is processed by the mind of the artist. A work of art has an inner meaning (*Bedeutung*), expressed by its outer FORM, as the SOUL or mind is expressed by the body. But the artist does not *first* conceive the meaning in prosaic terms and *then* embody it in a sensory form. Form and content are intrinsically intertwined, rather than externally combined. Thus the artist needs IMAGINATION (*Phantasie*).

3. *Art has an end or* PURPOSE. Hegel argues: (a) Its purpose is not merely imitation of nature. Such imitation is, e.g., superfluous. (b) Its essential purpose is not to present to us the whole range of possible human experience and emotion. This would mean that the content of art was a matter of complete indifference. (c) Art liberates us from our desires and passions (the sensory) by presenting them or their objects in an objective form, inviting contemplation rather than indulgence in them. But its inner significance involves more than this. (d) Art may purify the passions and morally improve us. But (i) it is not always easy to see how this can be achieved: 'the portrayal of Mary Magdalene, the beautiful sinner who later repented, has seduced many into sin, because art makes it look so beautiful to repent, and you must sin before you can repent.' (ii) Art essentially overcomes the OPPOSITIONS involved in MORALITY, between, e.g., the sensory and the conceptual, desire and reason. (iii) The purpose of art cannot be to serve some purpose external to itself, which might be served by other means. A work of art is an end in itself. Its aim is to reveal the truth in a sensuous form and to present the reconciliation of opposition. (Its meaning can be expressed by other means, e.g. in prose, only later, if at all.) This end, unlike, e.g., teaching, moral improvement, fame or money, is intrinsic to its concept.

The Introduction concludes with a 'Historical Deduction of the True Concept of Art', which considers Kant, Schiller, Winckelmann, Schelling and romantic IRONY. It is followed by an account of the 'Division' (or CLASSIFICATION) of aesthetics, which summarizes the contents of *LA*. This division follows, Hegel believes, from the concept of art. Art presents the IDEA in sensory images. This entails three requirements: (1) The content must be appropriate to artistic representation. (2) Thus the content must not be sheerly ABSTRACT, e.g. God conceived as a bare unity, but, like the Christian God, CONCRETE and representable. (The concreteness of the content involves the tendency of, e.g., the Christian God and especially the Greek gods to appear in a perceptible form.) (3) The sensory form of this content must itself be (a) concrete and (b) exist 'only for our mind (*Gemüt*) and spirit'. For, unlike natural beauties, the 'work of art has not such a naive, self-centred being, but is essentially a question, an address to the responsive heart, an appeal to minds and spirits.'

But some contents, or conceptions of the idea, can be expressed by art more adequately than others. The Greek gods can be fully represented in human form, while the Christian God, with his inner spiritual depth, eludes wholly adequate sensory portrayal. The excellence of art depends on the intimacy with which the idea and its shape combine. This supplies a principle of division, for art must traverse various stages of adequacy in this union of idea and form or shape. The division is this:

(1) A UNIVERSAL part, which considers the universal idea of beauty (the IDEAL), and its relations to nature and to artistic production.

(2) A PARTICULAR part, which considers the particular world-views (*Weltanschauungen*) that are expressed in art. These give rise to the symbolic form of art, in which the content is too meagre and abstract to be adequately expressed; the classical form, in which the expression of the content is wholly adequate; and the romantic (i.e. Christian) form, in which the content is too rich and SUBJECTIVE to find adequate expression in art.

(3) A part which considers the particular arts, but which is seen as INDIVIDUAL, since individual works of art emerge at this stage. These are distinguished primarily by the sensory medium employed: architecture, sculpture, painting, music, poetry. The items in (2) are, Hegel agrees, distinct from those in (3). But since a sensory material 'has the idea potentially for its inner soul, the particular sensory materials [of (3)] have a close affinity and secret accord with the spiritual distinctions and types of art presentation [of (2)]'.

The rest of the 'Division' fills out this schema, and *LA* does so at great length. Each of the items in (2) is seen as developing into the next, and similarly each item in (3) develops into its successor. The idea of beauty unfolds itself into (2) and (3) and finds its full expression only in the TOTALITY of (2) and (3). But poetry is the universal art, which restores the unity of the idea, since it idealizes or SUBLATES the sensory to a higher degree than other arts and thus essentially requires the imagination which all art involves. With poetry, 'art transcends itself, since it abandons the medium of a harmonious embodiment of spirit in the sensory and passes from the poetry of REPRESENTATION to the prose of THINKING.'

Lectures on the History of Philosophy (*Vorlesungen über die Geschichte der Philosophie*) (*LHP*) Hegel lectured on the history of philosophy at Jena (Winter 1805–6), Heidelberg (Winter 1816–17 and 1817–18) and Berlin (Summer 1819, Winter 1820–1, 1823–4, 1825–6, 1827–8, 1829–30). K. L. Michelet edited these lectures for the posthumous edition of Hegel's works, and they appeared in three volumes in 1833–6. Michelet put together material from different years, using Hegel's manuscripts and his students' transcripts. Some of this material has now been lost, but several transcripts, and Hegel's own versions of the Introductions to the lectures of 1816 and 1820, survive.

Ancient philosophers were interested in the history of philosophy only incidentally, in so far as it was relevant to the refutation of opposing doctrines and the statement of their own. Aristotle (like Hegel) held that the true view must explain and embody what is true in all significant views, and thus he often (especially in *Metaphysics* A.) prefaces his own view with an account of the views of his predecessors. In late antiquity several works appeared which recorded the main doctrines of philosophers and philosophical sects. The most famous of these is by Diogenes Laertius. For the most part these works show little historical or philosophical insight, but they often quote original documents at length and supply useful information about philosophers whose works do not survive in bulk.

In eighteenth- and nineteenth-century Germany, history of philosophy, like history in general, was taken more seriously, though before Hegel it was not treated at length by a philosopher or seen as an integral part of philosophy itself. The main history in the eighteenth century was Brucker's *Historia critica philosophiae* (1742–4), which ends with an account of Wolff. Brucker held Wolff's view that a philosophy is essentially a SYSTEM, in the sense of an architectonically ordered series of theses, and he attempted to extract such a system from the works of any given philosopher. On Hegel's view, the doctrines he attributes to past philosophers are phrased in Wolffian terms; he ascribes to a philosopher not only what he actually said, but all the supposed consequences and premises of what he said. Usually such systems fall short of Wolff's system and thus exhibit the follies of past philosophers. We should not, Hegel argues, attribute to a past philosopher what he was not explicitly conscious of: the history of philosophy consists in the emergence into CONSCIOUSNESS of what was merely implicit in previous thinkers.

In the late eighteenth century more thought was given to such theoretical questions as these: (1) How can the historian decide what is to count as philosophy? (2) Does his decision require that he espouse some particular philosophy? (3) Does the historian's espousal of some particular philosophy impair or enhance his work as a historian? (4) Is the history of philosophy anything more than a haphazard succession of beliefs, or does it have an underlying unity? (5) If it has a unity, does this consist in a cyclical repetition of the same themes and doctrines, or in an evolutionary DEVELOPMENT?

In the 1780s Gurlitt and Bardili argued that CONCEPTS, as well as opinions, develop over time and that history of philosophy presupposes a study of the development of metaphysical concepts, not only in philosophy, but in ordinary language, poetry and religion. In his essay *On the Concept of the History of Philosophy* (1791), Reinhold argued that the tendency to see the history of philosophy as a 'history of human folly' or a collection of 'sects' arose from the lack of an adequate 'comprehensive concept' (*Inbegriff*) of philosophy, so that either the form of some favoured contemporary philosophy was imposed on *all* philosophies, or all thinking was indiscriminately regarded as philosophy. Reinhold's version of Kant's philosophy supplies him with such a concept, a standard for assessing past philosophies and a goal at which they are regarded as aiming. Other Kantians attempted to explain the emergence of philosophies in terms of Kant's analysis of the human mind. But in general, Kantianism failed to support an adequate history of philosophy, both because its conception of philosophy is too narrow to embrace all historical philosophies and because it regards human faculties and fundamental concepts as the same at all times and places, and thus tends to see the history of philosophy as repetitive rather than developing.

Three monumental histories appeared in the 1790s:

D. Tiedemann, *Spirit of Speculative Philosophy* (1791–7), which, Hegel felt, showed little appreciation of philosophical SPECULATION.

J. G. Buhle, *Textbook of the History of Philosophy* (1796–1804), and his *History of Modern Philosophy* (1800–4) which starts with the Renaissance. Buhle was a Kantian and more open-minded than Tiedemann, and Hegel preferred him, but found him too brief on ancient philosophy.

W. G. Tennemann, *History of Philosophy* (1798–1819). Tennemann was a follower of Reinhold and viewed past philosophies in Kantian–Reinholdian terms. Hegel far prefers him to Brucker, Tiedemann and Buhle, but regards his philosophical equipment as inadequate for the understanding of ancient philosophy: one understands Aristotle better if one believes the opposite of what Tennemann says about him.

A pupil of Schleiermacher and follower of Schelling, F. Ast, wrote an *Outline of a History of Philosophy* (1807), which, Hegel said, was 'one of the better compendia. It is written in a good spirit.' Like Hegel, he saw the unity of philosophy, and of cultural history in general, as a product of SPIRIT: 'all systems, ideas and opinions are revelations of one spirit, and internally bound together by this. Their unity is thus not imposed on them externally and by some concept, but is immediately intrinsic to them.' Ast compares the unity and development of spirit with those of an ORGANISM.

Hegel regarded the history of philosophy not only as a good introduction to philosophy, but as the climax of philosophy itself, since it portrays the realization of the highest phase of ABSOLUTE spirit in history. Unlike, e.g., Kant or Fichte, he was deeply aware of the historical sources of his own ideas and saw history of philosophy as a process of RECOLLECTION (*Erinnerung*), an essential phase of one's self-knowledge.

Hegel's own philosophy was equipped to do justice to the unity, diversity and development of the history of philosophy. Like Ast, he sees it as the development of a single spirit. This advances circuitously towards full SELF-CONSCIOUSNESS by successively reflecting on its current state and thus moving beyond it. The advance of spirit is structured in terms of logic, which proceeds from simpler concepts to more complex ones that SUBLATE and contain their predecessors: 'the succession of the systems of philosophy in history is the same as the succession in the logical derivation of the concept-DETERMINATIONS of the IDEA.' Thus, e.g., Parmenides' philosophy corresponds to the concept of BEING, Heraclitus' to that of BECOMING, etc. Hegel's own philosophy corresponds to the absolute idea, which sublates all the THOUGHTS of the Logic. Philosophy, like logic, develops from the simple to the complex, and returns at last to the differentiated unity of Hegel's philosophy, which makes possible the reflection of philosophy on the whole of its own past.

In this way, past philosophers need not be interpreted anachronistically, and yet their thought is of relevance to modern philosophy, since it is an essential ingredient in it. Past philosophies are not viewed simply as bare stages on the way to the truth, artificially forced into abstract logical schemata. For:

(1)   The ultimate unity into which thoughts and philosophies are drawn is designed to give them (like the citizens of a modern STATE) free rein for their independent development.

(2)   Each philosophy (or group of philosophies) is regarded as the TRUTH of the age in which it appears. It epitomizes the thought and practice of the age, and thus has a historical value, apart from its merit as ABSTRACT philosophy.

(3)   In practice Hegel does not stick as closely to his logical ground-plan as his programmatic remarks suggest, and, conversely, the structure of his Logic is influenced by the history of philosophy.

(4)   Hegel read very widely in the history of philosophy, and his interest in past philosophers, especially the Greeks, goes beyond their significance for his own system.

In his Introductions Hegel discusses the nature of philosophy and its history, and the methodological principles of his inquiry. After a brief account of oriental (Chinese and Indian) philosophy, he discusses Greek philosophy from its beginnings (Thales) to its end (Proclus). (Greek philosophy occupies more than half the lectures.) A briefer account of medieval and Renaissance philosophy is followed by modern philosophy from Bacon to Schelling. Hegel himself does not figure by name, but a final section entitled 'Result' surveys the whole history of philosophy and thus implicitly presents him as the culmination of the whole history of philosophy, especially of the German idealism of Jacobi, Kant, Fichte and Schelling. (Only Schelling survived to contest this view.)

Hegel's preferences are not universally shared: e.g. he devotes far more space to Böhme and to Jacobi than to Hume, and neglects the seminal, if chaotic, Herder. (He nowhere mentions Vico or Nicholas of Cusa.) But in the main his approach to the history of philosophy (as to everything else) is OBJECTIVE and free of idiosyncrasy. He, e.g., abandoned the traditional view, propagated by Plato and persisting in, e.g., Tennemann, that the Greek sophists were immoral charlatans with no proper place in the history of philosophy, and saw them as DIALECTICAL thinkers, who, in contrast to the objectivism of earlier philosophers, developed the principle of SUBJECTIVITY and thus prepared the way for Socrates. This view, and Hegel's general approach, greatly influenced later historians of philosophy, especially Zeller.

Lectures on the Philosophy of History (*Vorlesungen über die Philosophie der Geschichte*) (*LPH*)   From the winter of 1822–3 to that of 1830–1, Hegel lectured biennially on the 'philosophy of world history'. The content of the lectures changed as he acquired new material. His son, Karl Hegel, says that the 1822–3 series concentrated on the 'DEVELOPMENT of the philosophical CONCEPT, and showed how it constitutes the real kernel of history and the moving SOUL of the world-historical peoples.' It illustrated this with a long account of China and India, dwelt at length on the Greeks, but dealt briefly with Roman, medieval and modern times. But later series gave less space to the Orient and also to philosophical material, and more to the medieval and modern periods. Gans says that only the 1830–1 series gave a full account of later history.

In his 1837 edition of *LPH* for the posthumous *Works*, Gans attempted to reconstruct the 1830–1 series from Hegel's notes and students' transcripts. (Hegel announced the 1830–1 series as 'The Philosophy of World History: Part One', since his material now exceeded the confines of a single lecture series. But according to Gans, and Karl Hegel, the series covered the whole of history.) In 1840 Karl Hegel re-edited the lectures with the aim of taking more account of the earlier series, especially those of 1822–3 and 1824–5, which he regarded as superior to the later series. But he does not distinguish material from different years or different hands. The most recent attempt to do this was made by Hoffmeister, whose edition of the Introduction to the lectures is much fuller than earlier versions and prints material from Hegel's manuscripts in italics. This Introduction is translated by Nisbet. So far the only complete translation of *LPH* is that of Sibree, who translated Karl Hegel's edition.

The contents of *LPH* are as follows:

1. The Introduction, often entitled or subtitled 'Reason in History'. The contents of this, in Hoffmeister's edition, are:

(a) A 'First Draft' of the Introduction, given the title 'Varieties of Historical Writing', which Hegel delivered in 1822 and 1828. This considers 'philosophical history' as the culmination of a series of types of historiography, beginning with 'original HISTORY'. This forms the basis for G. D. O'Brien's view, in *Hegel on Reason and History* (1975), that Hegel aims to produce a 'history of historical consciousness' rather than a SPECULATIVE account of world history as such.

(b) A longer 'Second Draft' of the Introduction, delivered in 1830. This has little to say about varieties of historiography and thus cannot be easily interpreted as a 'history of historical consciousness'. Hegel opposes *a priori* speculation about, e.g., the origins of the human race, but insists that philosophy presupposes that 'REASON governs the world and that world history is thus a rational process'. The course of history, he argues, is governed by a single world SPIRIT, which uses human interests and passions for the fulfilment of its divine plan. Schematically, spirit proceeds by reflecting on its current state and thus advancing beyond it, while yet retaining and SUBLATING its earlier phases. Spirit, viz. mankind, thus progresses to ever greater SELF-CONSCIOUSNESS and FREEDOM.

(c) An 'Appendix' containing:

(i) 'The natural context or the geographical basis of world-history'. In this Hegel excludes large parts of the world from world history. Africa is 'the land of childhood, removed from the light of self-conscious history and wrapped in the dark mantle of night'. Asia, after a promising beginning, has remained static. The centre of world history is Europe.

(ii)   A brief account of 'The Phases of World History'. (Sibree entitles this 'Classification of Historic Data.)

(iii)   Some 'Additions from the winter semester of 1826–7'.

2. 'The Oriental World'. China, with its despotism, and India, with its caste system, lack real freedom. The Persian empire, whose religion of light struggling with darkness represents spirit's overcoming of NATURE, is the first genuine world-historical stage. In Karl Hegel's edition, Hegel follows Herodotus in treating Syria, Egypt, etc., as parts of the Persian empire.

3. 'The Greek World'. Hegel sees Greek history as beginning and ending with the death of a young warrior, respectively Achilles and Alexander. Alexander's conquests hellenized the Persian empire for several centuries, but the centre of world history moved to the West.

4. 'The Roman World'. Hegel underrates the Roman contribution to world history in contrast to the Greek. Their main achievement is the formation of the legal PERSONALITY. Their exclusion from government made them receptive to Christianity.

5. 'The Germanic (*germanische*) World'. The Roman empire in the West was overrun by Germanic tribes, which had resisted conquest by the empire. They were marked more by *Gemüt* ('heart' – *see* MIND) than by civilization, but adopted the Christianity of the native peoples. The principle of universal freedom announced by Christianity is gradually realized in social institutions. The period falls into three phases:

(a)   'The Elements of the Christian–Germanic World', viz. the barbarian invasions, the rise of Islam and the Arab conquests, and the empire of Charlemagne.

(b)   'The Middle Ages', especially feudalism, the Crusades, the rise of absolute monarchy and the Renaissance of art and science.

(c)   'The Modern Period', especially the Reformation, the rise of the modern state, and the Enlightenment and French Revolution.

LPH concludes with a reaffirmation of the view that philosophy discerns in history the development of the 'self-actualizing IDEA, and indeed of the idea of freedom, which only exists as CONSCIOUSNESS of freedom'. To see history in this way and as the 'progress of spirit' is to supply a 'theodicy', a 'justification of GOD in history', which 'reconciles spirit with world history and ACTUALITY', showing it to be the 'work of God'.

Hegel sometimes speaks as if this view of history represents not an objective fact about history, but a view that we must hold and project onto history, if we are to make sense of it and engage in coherent historiography: 'if you look at history rationally, it will look rationally back at you.' His belief that only PEOPLES with written history figure in the advance of the world spirit might also be taken to imply that he is concerned with our view of history, with events as reworked by historians, rather than with historical events as such. This need not mean that the historian imposes PURPOSE and rationality on a history that is IN ITSELF purposeless and irrational, but rather that what the historian makes of events is the TRUTH, the real significance, of those events – in much the way that the truth of natural phenomena lies in the scientist's thought about them, rather than in raw, unconceptualized phenomena. But given Hegel's insistence that the historian's account should be factually accurate and his hostility to historical fictions, it is more likely that he believes that history is in fact, and not simply in the historian's view, the realization of the divine plan, etc. Historians' accounts of events, especially their eventual recognition of the divine plan as a whole, are an essential part of this plan, and it could not be realized without them. But it does not follow from this that the plan, etc., lies only in these accounts, and not in the events themselves.

Hegel's claim that only events recorded in written history belong to history proper has more than one sense:

(1)   Events that were not recorded at the time cannot figure in history proper, simply because they were not recorded at the time.
(2)   Events of which no contemporary record now survives cannot figure in history, simply because no record of them *survives*.
(3)   Events which were not recorded at the time cannot figure in history, not only because they went unrecorded, but because they cannot have been appropriately significant events.

Hegel conflates all three senses by arguing that historically significant events are events in the life of a STATE; that a state makes sure that such events are properly recorded; and that historical records of significant events do not perish. Whatever its precise interpretation, Hegel's claim would exclude from history events and societies (such as Minoan and Mycenaean Crete) which, though they involved a high degree of political centralization and organization, are known to us only from archaeological remains. Such archaeological remains as were known in Hegel's day were assigned to the history of ART, not to world history.

Nevertheless *LPH* testifies to Hegel's immense erudition. It forms a valuable commentary on, e.g., the historical sections of *PS*.

Lectures on the Philosophy of Religion (*Vorlesungen über die Philosophie der Religion*) (*LPR*)

Hegel lectured on RELIGION in 1821, 1824, 1827 and 1831. The lecture series differ from each other more markedly than the series of Hegel's other lectures. But K. P. Marheineke, who edited the lectures for the posthumous *Works* in 1832, combined materials from different series, concentrating most heavily on the 1831 series. In 1840, B. Bauer produced a second edition that made more use of materials for the earlier series. Some of these materials are now lost; what survives is Hegel's manuscript for the 1821 series, various transcripts of the 1824 and 1827 series, and D. F. Strauss's excerpts from a transcript of the 1831 series. These materials, together with the older editions, have now been used by W. Jaeschke to reconstruct the different lecture series and thus to reveal the changes in the form and content of Hegel's lectures. Jaeschke's edition is translated by P. C. Hodgson et al. (*see* BIBLIOGRAPHY).

The HISTORY of religion was initiated by J. L. von Mosheim's *Institutiones historiae ecclesiasticae novi testamenti* (1737), to which Hegel refers in *PCR*. It was developed by a pupil of Herder's and orientalist, J. F. Kleuker, and by F. L. Graf zu Stolberg, who wrote a *History of the Religion of Jesus Christ* (1806–18). Schleiermacher gave an impetus to the discipline, when he said, in his *Speeches on Religion to its Cultivated Despisers* (1799), that we must 'give up the vain and fruitless wish that there should be only one religion' and 'approach as impartially as possible all those religions that have already developed'.

Hegel was interested in religion from his youth, but the immediate occasion for his decision to lecture on it may have been the prospective publication of the first part of Schleiermacher's *The Christian Faith* (1821). (Hegel strongly preferred his Heidelberg colleague, F. Creuzer, who, besides editing Plotinus and Proclus, wrote *Symbolism and Mythology of Ancient Peoples, especially the Greeks* (1810–12), to his Berlin colleague, Schleiermacher, who translated Plato and also made a significant impact on Protestant thought.) His most explicit attack on Schleiermacher's attempt to base religion on FEELING appears in the 1824 series. Contemporary religious controversies explain in part the changes in Hegel's lectures, e.g. from the mid-1820s F. A. G. Tholuck, an orientalist and neo-pietist, challenged the central place of the Trinity in Christianity, regarding it as a borrowing from Greek, oriental and Islamic theology, and also charged Hegel with pantheism. Hegel deals with these matters more thoroughly in the 1827 and 1831 courses than earlier. But the changes in the lectures also reflect Hegel's attempts to organize his material in accordance with the conceptual forms of the Logic; to assimilate new sources of information on religions; and to rethink the philosophical significance of such Christian doctrines as the Eucharist.

Each lecture series consists of four parts, but the contents of each part differs from series to series:

1. The 'Introduction' discusses the nature of religion in general, its relationship to PHILOSOPHY, and the nature of, and need for, a philosophy of religion. The Introduction then argues for the division of the subject-matter into (a) the CONCEPT of religion; (b) the DEVELOPMENT of the concept or DETERMINATE (*bestimmte*) religion; and (c) the consummation or completion (*Vollendung*) of the concept, or revelatory or manifest (*offenbare*) religion, or consummate (*vollendete*) religion.

2. 'The Concept of Religion' discusses, e.g., (a) GOD or religion in general, (b) the 'religious RELATION (*Verhältnis*)', and (c) the cult. Under (b), Hegel discusses our cognitive attitudes to God, and the role of feeling, FAITH, IMMEDIATE KNOWLEDGE (F. H. Jacobi), REPRESENTATION (*Vorstellung*) and THOUGHT. (c) is conceived as a unification of the rift between God and man, and it includes an account of the relationship of religion to the STATE.

3. Determinate religion. In 1821, 1824 and 1827, this consists of (a) Nature religion, i.e. primitive and oriental religion; (b) Religion of spiritual individuality, i.e. Judaism and Greek religion; (c) Religion of PURPOSIVENESS, i.e. Roman religion. (Imperial Roman religion, like Roman culture as a whole, is conceived as utilitarian in spirit.) In 1831, it consists of: (a) Unity, i.e. primitive religion; (b) Bifurcation (*Entzweiung*), i.e. oriental, including

Jewish, religion; (iii) Reconciliation (*Versöhnung*), i.e. Greek and Roman religion.

4. Consummate or 'absolute' religion, i.e. Christianity. Hegel discusses, with variations between the series, God the father, the son and the holy SPIRIT. Christianity is conceived not as merely one religion among others, but as the 'return of the concept to itself' out of the development involved in determinate religion, and as fulfilling the concept of religion in a way that other religions do not. It is the TRUTH of, and SUBLATES what is true in, other religions, just as Hegel's philosophy sublates other philosophies.

Unlike, e.g., Kant, Hegel was genuinely interested in the details of religious belief and practice. But his account is adapted to the end of showing that Christianity coincides with philosophy. Thus he interprets Christianity (not unreasonably) so as to stress its convergence with philosophy, and does not invariably live up to his profession of orthodox Lutheranism. The convergence is not always close: e.g. the religious significance of Christ, the son or God-man, is man's unification with God, but in Hegel's system, the son represents NATURE, the OTHERNESS or ALIENATION of the logical IDEA.

He also wants to show that in their historical emergence religions have advanced, albeit circuitously, towards Christianity. Thus he pays little attention to Islam, a philosophy which is, on his view, inferior to Christianity and yet emerged later. Differences between lecture series arise in part from the fact that religions do not form such a clear chronological sequence as, e.g., philosophies.

Marheineke appended to *LPR* the *Vorlesungen über die Beweise vom Dasein Gottes* (*LPEG*), which Hegel gave in 1829 as a supplement to his lectures on logic and which he planned to prepare for publication in the winter of 1831-2. The manuscript (now lost) was virtually complete. These lectures are closer to logic than to philosophy of religion: they attempt to defend the PROOFS against Kant's attack on them by reinterpreting them in terms of Hegel's logic.

life and the living organism   The verb *leben* means 'to live' in two main senses: (1) 'to be alive', i.e. not dead; (2) 'to live' in a certain way, e.g. alone or dangerously. Similarly (*das*) *Leben* means (1) 'biological life, being alive'; (2) '(a, my) life'. The adjective *lebendig* and the abstract noun *Lebendigkeit*, for 'alive, vital' and 'vitality' both literally and metaphorically, are common in Hegel.

A living organism is seen as a special sort of unity. Aristotle held, for example, that if, say, a hand is cut off, it is no longer a hand in the strict sense. Unlike a part removed from a machine, a severed hand cannot survive for long, nor can it (until recently) be sewn on or transplanted from one organism to another. Life also involves constant activity. Some activity must continue even in sleep if life is not to cease. In *CJ*, Kant argued against the Cartesian and Enlightenment mechanistic view of life. The parts of a machine may depend on each other for their operation, but they do not produce and sustain each other in the way that living organs do. Life can be understood only in terms of TELEOLOGY: each organ is both an end or PURPOSE and a means in relation to the others. An organism cannot be understood piecemeal, in terms of its parts, but only from a conception of it as a WHOLE.

Schelling, in his philosophy of NATURE, views life as a continuous struggle against the threat of DEATH: Life is the 'process of separation and combination of opposed principles: complete separation, as well as complete combination, is the beginning of death'. With the advance of age, our organs become increasingly individualized and unresponsive to each other; this breaks the continuity of the life-functions and results in death (*WS*). But life is also a tendency towards death: 'Life-activity is the cause of its own extinction. It expires as soon as it begins to be independent of outer nature and unresponsive to external stimuli. Thus life itself is only the bridge to death.' Life is a heightened state of natural forces and is in continuous CONTRADICTION and conflict with external nature, viz. the same forces in a lower 'potency'. It succumbs to nature eventually, not because it is overwhelmed by it, but because it wins its battle against it and becomes insufficiently responsive to it. The forces that sustained it then return from their heightened state to 'universal indifference'. 'Even in its cessation the phenomenon of life is paradoxical' (*First Sketch of a System of Philosophy of Nature*, 1799).

Hegel's view of life (and death) lies in this non-mechanistic tradition. In *ETW*, life plays a role similar to that later assigned to SPIRIT: there is an INFINITE living unity of all things, in which human life shares after striving to fulfil its nature. Life is felt to elude conceptual thought: 'In the case of life absolutely all of thinking's thoughts give out: the omnipresence of the simple in the manifold externality is for reflection an absolute contradiction, an incomprehensible mystery' (*Jena Logic*). In *PS*, IV, the fluid self-differentiation and self-obliteration of life, which is nevertheless articulated into stable genera, forms the transition to SELF-CONSCIOUSNESS, since (1) it supplies a primitive model of self-consciousness; (2) its genera require an external consciousness to exist *explicitly* as genera; and (3) a living entity is the object of the desire by which the individual initially affirms his self-consciousness. *PS*, V.A.a gives an account of life, which, in its essentials, recurs in *SL* and *Enc.* 1 §§216–22.

Life resists the finite categories of the UNDERSTANDING, but not those of REASON. The living organism involves a SOUL (its INNER) and a body (its OUTER). Owing to the organism's peculiar unity, the soul is seen as a CONCEPT that is realized in the body. It is the soul's simple unity or self-relating UNIVERSALITY that unifies the organism. But the soul also PARTICULARIZES the body, since the differentiations of the body must correspond to the implicit differentiation of the soul. The organism is an INDIVIDUAL in virtue of the interplay between its body and its soul: the separate organs develop, but are brought back into unity, dependence and interdependence by the soul. They are reciprocally both ends and means. Since the organism is FINITE, body and soul are separable, and this separation constitutes death. But body and soul are not two *constituents* of the organism. (That is, losing one's soul or life is

175

more like losing one's shape than losing one's umbrella: the umbrella persists after its loss, the shape and the soul do not.)

Life involves three processes (in the Logic, three 'INFERENCES'):

1. Internally the organism (which, in the Logic, here appears as a SUBJECT or concept) has three functions:
   (a) *Sensibility* is not the capacity to sense or perceive external objects, but to sense or feel one's whole body.
   (b) *Irritability* is responsiveness to stimuli, and, in the case of animals, muscular reaction.
   (c) *Reproduction* is not the production of other organisms of the same species, but the self-maintenance of a single organism by the physiological regeneration of its organs.

These three functions are related thus: In (a) the organism is at one with itself; (b) disrupts or 'dirempts' (*dirimiert*) it; and (c) restores its unity.

2. The organism has inorganic nature outside it. (In the Logic, this is the JUDGMENT, i.e. division, of the concept.) Since this inorganic environment is an essential element in life itself, it appears in the organism as a want or lack (*Mangel*). The organism overcomes and consumes inorganic nature, and assimilates it to itself, since nature is IN ITSELF what the organism is FOR ITSELF. Thus the organism comes together with itself in the OTHER. But when it dies, these 'elemental powers of objectivity begin their play. . . . They are constantly on the alert to begin their process in the organic body, and life is the unremitting struggle against them' (*Enc.* I. §219A.).

3. The organism is *in itself* a member of a genus or species (*Gattung*). (Hegel prefers *Gattung* here: unlike *Art* ('species'), it is etymologically related to the notion of generation or 'begetting'. *See* CLASSIFICATION.) Its encounter with another member of the same genus, but the opposite sex, makes it *for itself* a member of the genus. The generic process has two aspects: the generation of a new member of the genus and the death of the organism by its dissolution into the genus. The living creature involves the CONTRADICTION that it is in itself the genus, but exists as an individual. Thus at the climax of its life, the generic process, it dies. At *Enc.* II §376 and A., Hegel argues that animals, like men, die of a 'processless habit (*Gewohnheit*) of life', in which they lose their active tension and become ossified.

In the Logic, life is the first stage of the IDEA. It is followed by the idea as COGNITION, in which the genus becomes explicit or *for itself*. In the fuller account at *Enc.* II §§337–76, plants and animals (and also the earth, which is an organism, but not itself alive: §§338ff) are described separately. Here too the death of the animal does not simply lead to a bad INFINITE regress of births and deaths, but passes over into SPIRIT, where universality or the genus is for itself.

Hegel affirms spirit to be IMMORTAL. But this does not mean that men do not die. Their lives, like those of animals, involve tension and activity, and they too die when life becomes a habit. But unlike animals, men are not interchangeable members of a genus. (1) The members of an animal genus do not, on Hegel's view, change from one generation to the next, but men

176

have a significant HISTORY. (2) An animal species is not, apart from differences of sex and age, articulated and differentiated within itself: it differentiates itself, by its teeth and claws, etc., from other species. Men, by contrast, divide themselves into significant, non-biological groups, and thus, unlike most animal species, fight *each other* to the death. (3) Thus the life and death of a person has, unlike that of an animal, an individual (and not merely generic) historical and social significance. Even the simplest group, the FAMILY, confers on its members and their ancestors an individual significance that goes beyond their significance as replaceable occupants of biological roles. Wider groupings, such as corporations and the STATE, do the same for at least their more distinguished members. Hence it is not only the human species and its subgroups that, like the animal genus, survive the death of individuals; the individual retains a significance after his death.

Despite its inferiority to spirit, life is for Hegel a potent metaphor for the active unification of diversity and diversification of unity involved in spirit and its forms. Dialectical logic is alive, in contrast to the dead logic of the understanding. The state is a living organism, a self-articulating WHOLE that allows its citizens much free reign, but IDEALIZES them and draws them into itself in time of WAR. A state that neglects this and allows its members the exclusive pursuit of their private interests is dead.

In *SL*, Hegel does not say of life (as he does of CHEMISM) that it is a general category, applicable beyond the realm of biology. But it presumably occurs in the Logic not only because it exemplifies the idea, but because 'life' and 'living' apply in the realm of spirit, as well as in nature, to the life of the state, of the mind, life in Hegel's Germany, etc. Nevertheless, some of the features ascribed to life in *SL* (especially the generic process) seem exclusively biological, with no obvious spiritual analogue.

limit, restriction and finitude What has or comes to an end (*Ende*) is *endlich* ('finite'). (This also means 'final, ultimate' and, as an adverb, 'finally, at last'.) *Endlichkeit* is 'finitude, finiteness'. The finite has a limit or bound (ary), for which German has two words:

1. *Grenze* ('limit, boundary, border, extreme point') generates two verbs: (a) *grenzen (an)*, 'to border (on)' both literally and figuratively; (b) *begrenzen*, 'to bound, limit, form the boundary of': e.g. a wall *limits* our view, a narrow-minded or illiberal person is *limited* (*begrenzt*), the possibilities are *unlimited* (*unbegrenzt*).

2. *Schranke* ('barrier', and, especially in the plural, *Schranken*, 'bounds, limits', as in 'to keep within *bounds*') also generates verbs, especially *beschränken* ('to confine, limit, restrict, prevent from exceeding a certain limit'); Hegel uses the noun *Beschränkung* for, e.g., the '*restriction*' or restraint of our impulses by society and the state. The suggestion of restriction is more prominent in *Schranke* than in *Grenze*.

In non-Hegelian philosophy, *Grenze* and *Schranke* are not usually distinguished. Either may be used for, e.g., the limits of human cognition, but *Grenze(n)* is more common. For Kant, a *Grenzbegriff* ('limiting or boundary

177

concept') is a concept that marks the boundary beyond which real concepts cease to be applicable. The concept of a *noumenon* ('intelligible') or of a THING IN ITSELF is a *Grenzbegriff*; it makes no definite claim about what lies beyond the limits of our experience, but serves as a 'Keep Out' notice. The concept of a *Grenze* and the absolute I*'s self-limitation to become a finite I is important in Fichte's *SKW*. In mathematics, a *Grenze* or *Grenzwert* ('limiting value') is the value which the terms of an infinite series approach ever closer, but never reach: e.g. the limit of the series 2, $1\frac{1}{2}$, $1\frac{1}{4}$, $1\frac{1}{8}$, ... is 1. Hegel discusses this notion in his account of the INFINITELY small in *SL*.

Hegel distinguishes *Grenze* and *Schranke*, and translators use distinct English words: respectively, e.g., 'limit' and 'limitation' (Miller)', 'limit' (or 'boundary') and 'barrier' (or 'check') (Wallace), or 'limit(ing)' and 'restriction, -ing' (Knox). The distinction is this:

1. A finite entity has a *Grenze*. Usually, it has a QUALITATIVE limit, as well as a QUANTITATIVE limit. A field of one acre has a quantitative limit in virtue of which it is one acre, but also a qualitative limit in virtue of which it is a field rather than a wood or a pond. Each type of limit is a NEGATION: it is one acre only in virtue of *not* extending beyond its boundaries, and it is a field only in virtue of not being a wood, a pond, etc. But the relation of the field to its limit is different in each case. The quantitative limit is EXTERNAL or indifferent (*gleichgültig*): if the field is enlarged in area, this will not affect the part of the field lying within its original boundaries, nor, if it is reduced in size, will this affect what remains of the field. But its qualitative limit is internal to the field: if it is flooded to form a reservoir, this will alter the field through and through. Because, and only because, the field is limited it is liable to change. Owing to its qualitative limit, it has one definite character (*Beschaffenheit*) among a range of possible characters, so that it is at least logically possible for it to acquire a different character. Owing to its quantitative limit, it has *other* entities beyond its boundaries, which *may* have different characters (e.g. rivers) and indeed must have different characters if it is to be marked off from neighbouring fields by such items as hedgerows and streams. These other entities interact with it: it is only in virtue of such interaction that it is a field of one acre. But they also encroach on it, so that eventually a change in its character will occur, e.g., it will be flooded, so as to form a pond. Such a change (*Veränderung*, from (*sich*) *verändern*, 'to alter, make or become OTHER') may, and eventually will, involve the field's passing away (*Vergehen*, from *vergehen*, 'to pass away'). Thus in virtue of its qualitative and quantitative finitude, the field is also temporally finite and will come to an end: 'the being of finite things involves the seed of their passing away as their being-within-self (*Insichsein*); the hour of their birth is the hour of their death' (*SL*).

2. The limit of a thing need not confine or restrict it. The field is indifferent to its limits and has no tendency to transgress them. But a seed has a tendency to transgress the limit that makes it a seed, and a human being may be aware of his limit as a restriction to be overcome: a person may (or may not) feel his intellectual limitations as requiring to be surmounted. Then the

limit is a *Schranke*. Hegel links the notion of a *Schranke* with that of *Sollen* ('OUGHT'), since a *Schranke* is a *Grenze* that in some sense ought to be overcome, and, conversely, to say that something ought to happen implies that the current state of affairs is a *Schranke*. The state at which an entity aims and its tendency to aim at it is its DETERMINATION or destiny (*Bestimmung*).

Hegel gives two accounts of the finite: (a) The finite is constituted by its limit. (b) The finite falls short of its CONCEPT: e.g. the living ORGANISM dies because it is only an individual, while its genus is a UNIVERSAL (*Enc.* I §221A.). The two accounts are connected. An infinite entity, viz. GOD, has all, and only, those features that are embodied in its concept, since there is nothing outside it to explain the absence of such features or the presence of extra ones. Moreover, the concept of an infinite entity is itself an infinite concept: it is not limited by, and does not contrast with, other concepts; thus it does not have a limited content, but contains all possibilities. Thus even if there were anything to make God change, there would be nothing for him to change to. God is thus IDENTICAL with his concept. It does not follow that God or his concept involves no limits or restrictions: it sets up internal limits which it then transcends DIALECTICALLY. A finite entity, by contrast, is entangled in RELATIONS with other entities and thus not fully determined by its concept: it has features that are not, and often lacks features that are, embodied in its concept. Its concept, moreover, is a finite concept, limited by, and contrasting with, other concepts: concepts such as 'field' or 'animal', and also pure concepts such as 'thing', which are limited by other concepts within the logical IDEA. Such finite concepts are thus appropriate for finite entities, but there can never be a full accord between the concept and the entity.

Even finite entities, at least of higher types, transcend certain of their limits or restrictions. Hunger, thirst and pain, e.g., are felt by animals as restrictions, but are overcome by them short of death. But animals cannot become aware of, let alone overcome, all of the limits that make them what they are. Man or SPIRIT, however, is a special case. For man can become aware of every limit that confines and constitutes him. In particular, Kant had argued that there are limits to human COGNITION, and attempted to specify those limits. But this, Hegel argues, is impossible: If there is a limit, there is something beyond the limit, and if I am aware of a limit (i.e. elevate it to a restriction), I must be aware of something beyond the limit. So in assigning a limit to my cognitive powers, I am already beyond the limit (*Enc.* I §60). Ultimately, spirit is not finite: it does not have a specific nature, limited by the natures of other things; it embraces and overreaches (*übergreift*) other entities, and finds itself at home in them. It becomes fully SELF-CONSCIOUS and perspicuous to itself, and thus conforms entirely to its (infinite) concept. It does not succumb to DEATH in the same way as other creatures.

Hegel's acount has two main flaws:

1. He conflates conceptual and physical limitation: If something is conceptually limited in being, e.g., a field, and not a wood, pond, etc., this does not entail that it is physically limited (and constituted, or even affected) by what

it is not, i.e. by woods, ponds, etc. It is not inconceivable that the earth's surface should be a uniform desert; it would then be conceptually limited, but not physically limited (at least by anything else on the earth's surface). Our ability to conceptualize and describe entities does require physical limitation and variety. But an entity's physical neighbours, by which it is physically bounded and with which it interacts, need not be its closest conceptual neighbours: lions interact with grass, rain and antelopes, not usually with such close conceptual relatives as tigers.

2. The doctrine that to assign, or to be aware of, a limit is to transcend that limit involves four errors. (a) It conflates the notions of a *boundary* and a *limit*: That a field or a body of knowledge has a (current) boundary implies that there is something beyond the boundary. But that there is a limit to successive reductions of the boundary of a field (e.g. by halving its area), viz. an unextended point, need not imply the existence of anything beyond the limit. (Even successive doublings terminate in the whole surface of the earth, on which there is nothing beyond the limit.) (b) Awareness of a limit need not entail a conception of what is beyond the limit. We know that the field cannot become smaller than a point, without any clear conception of what it would be for it to be smaller than a point. The speed of light is known to be the *limiting* velocity from the fact that the mass of a body travelling at the speed of light would be infinite, not from a clear conception of bodies that *exceed* the speed of light. (c) Even if we can *conceive* of what lies beyond a limit of which we are aware, this does not entail that we *know* there to be something beyond the limit; we must perhaps conceive of things in themselves, but we need not thereby know that there are any. (d) Even if we know that there is *something* beyond the limit, we may not know *what* it is (like).

The doctrines that the interrelations of things mirror the interrelations of concepts and that awareness of a limit involves transcending it are central to Hegel's IDEALISM.

logic, logical *see* SCIENCE OF LOGIC

M

---

matter, material *see* FORM, MATTER AND CONTENT

mechanism, chemism and teleology   In the Logic, the account of the subjective concept or SUBJECTIVITY (i.e. CONCEPT, JUDGMENT and INFERENCE) is followed by an account of OBJECTIVITY or the OBJECT. (Subjectivity and objectivity are later united in the IDEA.) Objectivity takes three successively higher forms: (1) *Mechanismus*; (2) *Chemismus*; and (3) *Teleologie* or *Zweckmäs-sigkeit* ('PURPOSIVENESS').

1. *Mechanismus* derives from the Greek *mechanē* ('device, means, machine, instrument') and means (a) an/the arrangement and interaction of objects on mechanical principles, i.e. the type of principles on which machines operated (at least in Hegel's day), and (b) the doctrine that apparently non-mechanical entities, especially living creatures, operate on mechanical principles. Hegel uses the term in sense (a), and rejects the mechanistic interpretation of LIFE and MIND. The briefer account of mechanism at *Enc.* I §§194–9 opens with an account of Leibniz's monads or atoms, whose internal states conform to each other owing to a harmony pre-established by the monad of monads, God (§194). This, on Hegel's view, is not a mechanical system, since the monads do not interact at all: it is bare objectivity. Mechanism proper has three phases:

(a)   *Formeller Mechanismus*: Objects or bodies affect and propel each other by pressure and impact. No single body is dominant over the others, so the movements of the bodies have no central focus. The bodies are EXTERNALLY related only: their relations do not affect their essential nature. This corresponds to the first sections of 'Matter and Motion: Finite Mechanics [*Mechanik*]' at *Enc.* II §§262–5.

(b)   *Differenter* (i.e. non-indifferent or biased) *Mechanismus*: One body is central and the others gravitate towards it. This corresponds to 'Fall' at *Enc.* II §§267–9.

(c)   *Absoluter Mechanismus*: Bodies (planets) are related to a central body (the sun); they are themselves centres for lesser bodies that revolve around them (moons). This corresponds to 'Absolute Mechanics' at *Enc.* II §§269–72. Hegel conceives the sun, planets and moons to form a system of INFERENCES in which each term in turn unites the other two.

The category of mechanism applies primarily to inorganic nature. But mechanism essentially consists not in the relations of *physical or material bodies*, but in the *external* RELATIONS of *persistent, independent* objects. Thus the mind is viewed mechanically not only if it is seen as a physical mechanism, reducible to the interrelations of material particles, but if it is seen as a psychical analogue of a physical mechanism, as, e.g., a collection of mental FORCES (faculties), or of ideas related by laws of association analogous to the laws governing the relations of physical bodies (*Enc.* III §455). The mind and life in general are not mechanisms. But the category can apply to certain aspects of organic nature and of mind, especially when their functions are impaired, e.g., while normal digestive processes cannot be understood mechanically, *indigestion* is a reversion to mechanism; memory, reading, etc., need to become *mechanical*; and so on. Non-indifferent mechanism is exemplified not only by bodies falling to the earth, but also by desire and by sociability (*Enc.* I §196). Absolute mechanism applies to the STATE, whose three elements, the individual, his needs and the government, form a social solar system (*Enc.* I §198). The limited applicability of mechanism to organic and spiritual phenomena explains in part its inclusion in the Logic.

2. *Chemismus*, from *Chemie* ('chemistry') and ultimately from the Arabic *al-kimiya*, 'alchemy', means, analogously to *Mechanismus*, (a) the arrangement and interaction of things on chemical principles, and (b) the doctrine that the world as a whole operates on chemical principles. Again, Hegel uses it in sense (a) only. An object in a mechanistic system might in principle exist, he believes, even if it were detached from the system and thus unrelated to other objects. But chemical substances or stuffs are intrinsically related by their OPPOSITION to and affinity for each other. An acid essentially stands in contrast to a base or alkali, and could not exist in isolation. When an acid and a base combine, they neutralize each other to form a salt, losing the properties each previously had. The compound can be broken up again by a process external to it. Hegel was especially interested in the phenomenon of 'elective affinity' (*Wahlverwandtschaft*), which he considers earlier in *SL* under the heading MEASURE and also in *Enc.* II §333. The elements in a compound have an affinity that binds them together. But the affinity of elements for each other varies in strength. Thus if a compound consisting of x and y encounters a substance z, the affinity of x and z may be stronger than the affinity of x and y. Then the original compound will break up, forming a new compound of x and z, and leaving y free. In his novel *Elective Affinities* (1809), Goethe applied this idea to human relations: each of two lovers prove to have a stronger affinity for another person than for each other. For Hegel, like Goethe, chemism is exemplified not only in the relations of chemical substances, but also in the sexual relations of living creatures and in human love and friendship.

3. *Teleologie* (from the Greek *telos* ('end, goal', etc.) and *logos* ('word, reason, doctrine', etc.)) is literally the 'doctrine of PURPOSE or purposiveness', but Hegel applies it primarily to the teleological or goal-directed character of an object or system of objects. Like Kant, he distinguishes between external and internal teleology. In external teleology: (a) The purpose to be realized is not immanent in the objects in which it is to be realized, but is introduced from outside by a purposive agent, whether human or divine. (b) The objects in which the purpose is to be realized are thus PRESUPPOSED by the agent, and

operate, both before and after his intervention, not on teleological principles, but on mechanical or chemical principles. (c) The agent realizes his purpose in them by manipulating their behaviour in accordance with these principles. (d) When the purpose is realized in them, the purpose they serve is not their own, but that of the agent and usually also that of another entity and/or activity: e.g. God made the cork-tree so that we can stop up our bottles (a favourite example of Hegel's, derived from Goethe); I make a boat to sail in, etc.

In internal teleology, by contrast: (a) The purpose is immanent in the object. (b) The object in which the purpose is realized is thus not presupposed, and it operates throughout primarily on teleological principles, governed by its purpose. (But even an internally teleological system presupposes a mechanically and chemically ordered environment.) (c) No external intervention or manipulation is involved. (d) The purpose served by the object is itself and its own activities. Thus internal teleology is exemplified, for Kant and Hegel, by living organisms.

We might expect Hegel to proceed in the Logic from chemism to internal teleology, just as in *Enc.* II chemistry is followed by organic life (§§342ff). But what he describes is rather external teleology, primarily the human agent intervening in mechanical and chemical systems to realize his purpose (*SL*; *Enc.* I §§204–12). The reasons are these: (a) The simpler form of teleology needs to precede the more complex internal teleology. (b) The logical development follows a pattern: in mechanism and chemism the concept is wholly INTERNAL (and thus wholly EXTERNAL) to the objects; in external teleology (but not internal teleology) a gap opens up between the concept (i.e. the purpose) and the object; the closure of this gap by the realization of the purpose leads on to the IDEA, in which the immanence of the concept in the object is first exemplified by LIFE, with its internal teleology.

In *SL*, Hegel argues that mechanism, chemism and teleology are all applicable in their appropriate realms. But they are not simply *gleich gültig* ('equally valid', with a pun on *gleichgültig*, 'INDIFFERENT'): teleology is the TRUTH of mechanism and chemism. Teleology presupposes a mechanically and chemically ordered environment, but in a higher sense mechanism and chemism presuppose teleology: since teleological systems are self-determining and self-explanatory in a way that mechanical and chemical systems are not, the universe must culminate in teleological systems (minds) and must itself form an overarching teleological system in which mechanism and chemism play a necessary, but subordinate part.

mediation and immediacy   The German for '(the)' middle' is *(die) Mitte*. This generates an adjective *mittel* ('middle') and another noun *(das) Mittel* (originally '(the) middle, the thing in the middle', but now 'means, what serves the attainment of a PURPOSE'). It also generates several verbs, especially *mitteln* ('to help someone to, to settle, mediate', e.g. a quarrel), which is now obsolete but has left *mittelbar* ('mediate, indirect') and *unmittelbar* ('immediate, direct'), and *vermitteln* ('to achieve union, mediate; to bring about', etc.). The past participle of *vermitteln, vermittelt* ('mediated, indirect') is used in contrast to *unmittelbar*. Both give rise to abstract nouns, *Vermittlung* ('mediation') and *Unmittelbarkeit* ('immediacy').

In non-Hegelian philosophy, *unmittelbar* is primarily an epistemological term. Immediate CERTAINTY is a certainty that is not mediated by inference or proof, or perhaps even by symbols or concepts. The main representative, for Hegel, of the doctrine of immediate certainty is not Descartes, but F. H. Jacobi, for whom knowledge of, or FAITH in, the reality of the phenomenal and supersensible worlds involved a certainty that neither needs nor admits of proof. This doctrine was opposed by Goethe ('The true is godlike; it does not appear immediately, we must ascertain it from its manifestations') and Hölderlin ('The immediate in the strict sense is impossible for mortals and immortals alike'), as well as by Hegel.

Immediacy also has a religious significance: God may reveal himself *mediately*, i.e. through the workings of nature, or immediately, i.e. by miracles or direct revelation (*Offenbarung*). But the religious significance of *Vermittlung* is more prominent: man cannot approach the divine without an intermediary, whether this be the symbols supplied by the Bible (John Scotus Erigena), a lengthy EDUCATION (Lessing) or Christ himself (especially Nicholas of Cusa). In *PS*, 'the mediator' (*der Vermittler*) for unhappy CONSCIOUSNESS is the priest (IV.B), but in revealed (*offenbare*) RELIGION it is Christ (VII.C). The mediator forms the middle term of an INFERENCE uniting God and man. But any stark OPPOSITION between disparate terms is felt, especially by Hegel, to require mediation: not only God and man, but MIND and body, STATE and individual, etc.

Thus in Hegel *Vermittlung* often refers to the uniting of two terms by a third term, e.g. the uniting of the UNIVERSAL and the INDIVIDUAL in an inference by the PARTICULAR. But *Vermittlung* and *Unmittelbarkeit* are often used more widely. The immediate is unrelated to other things; simple; given; elementary; and/or initial. The mediated, by contrast, is related to other things; complex; explained; developed; and/or resultant. The mediation may be (1) physical (e.g. an acorn is immediate, but the oak tree is mediated by a process of growth); (2) epistemic (e.g. my knowledge of my own existence is immediate or direct, but my knowledge of God's is mediated or inferential); or (3) logical (e.g. pure BEING is immediate, but ESSENCE is mediated by a logical process).

The contrast between mediation and immediacy is itself an opposition that requires mediation, and the result of this, Hegel argues, is that nothing is purely immediate or purely mediated: everything is both at once. For example:

1. An acorn is mediated, as well as immediate, since it is the result of a previous cycle of growth, and the oak is immediate, as well as mediated, since it has a definite present character that can be seen and described without explicit reference to its relations with other things or to the process that led up to it. Something that lacked all immediacy would be nothing but a cross-section of a process or the intersection of a set of relations, with no

intrinsic nature of its own. Something that lacked all mediation would have nothing but an intrinsic nature, with no relations to anything else and no process leading up to it; it would not even have an intrinsic nature, since all DETERMINACY depends on mediation.

2. My knowledge of my own existence is mediated by an education that makes me a SELF-CONSCIOUS being, a philosophical tradition that induces me to focus on my pure I*, my relations with others that enable me to distinguish 'I' from 'you' and 'he', etc. My knowledge of God's existence or of any other inferred information is also immediate, since it is, e.g., knowledge of a definite piece of information, not just a cross-section of a process of inference, and the knowledge can subsequently be recalled and employed without constant recourse to the inference by which it originally arose.

3. Pure being is mediated, since our thinking of it is the culmination of the (non-logical) education described in *PS*, and presupposes a special effort of ABSTRACTION from empirical details. Conversely, essence is also immediate, since not only is it a definite stage of the logical IDEA, it also involves a withdrawal into inner simplicity from the external complexity of QUALITY, QUANTITY and measure.

Although 'mediate' and 'immediate' both apply to everything, Hegel nevertheless draws a distinction between things that are at least relatively immediate, such as the seed and being, and things that are relatively mediated, such as the tree and becoming. Something can be immediate in one of two ways: (1) It may be simply immediate, lacking the relevant type of mediation (e.g. being, the acorn). (2) It may be mediated, but SUBLATE its mediation into immediacy:

(a) The acorn from which the oak emerged, the process of its growth, and nutrition that fostered its growth are sublated in the immediacy of the oak tree; the butterfly newly emerged from its chrysalis has sublated its mediation.
(b) Descartes ABSTRACTED from his education and sublated it into the immediate awareness of his own existence. (From this standpoint he could even doubt that he had had such an education.)
(c) Essence sublates its logical mediation into simple self-IDENTITY.

The sublation of mediation into immediacy is similar to an entity's sublation of its own CONDITIONS. Both processes occur, on Hegel's view, in our knowledge of GOD. God (Jacobi has argued) is unmediated and uncon-ditioned, while our KNOWLEDGE of him is mediated and conditioned; thus either our cognition falls short of God or it degrades him to a mediated entity. The solution, Hegel replies, is that while both God and our cognition of him are mediated, they sublate their mediation into immediacy.

Thus mediation and immediacy form not a dyadic opposition, but a TRIAD: (1) Bare (but still relative) immediacy; (2) mediation; (3) mediated imme-diacy, in which an entity's mediation is taken up into it. This pattern is repeated: the mediated immediacy that concludes one triad is the bare immediacy that opens the next. The triads are also nested within each other:

185

the largest triad, the universe as a whole, forms a circle of three terms (the logical IDEA, NATURE and SPIRIT), each of which in turn serves as bare immediacy, as mediating the other two terms, and as mediated immediacy.

Hegel constantly attacks the doctrine that we have immediate access to the truth, whether by KNOWLEDGE, FEELING or faith: (a) All knowledge, like anything else, is mediated, as well as immediate, at least by education, etc. (b) Relatively immediate knowledge, etc., such as SENSORY certainty (*PS*, I) or Jacobi's immediate knowledge (*Enc.* I §§61ff) is defective: it leads to the impoverishment of the object of knowledge (since determinacy and complexity require mediation) and it implicitly contradicts itself, since its access to objects is intrinsically mediated by, e.g., universal terms such as 'this'. (c) The supposed defects of mediated cognition are dispelled by the sublation of mediation into immediacy.

Hegel's arguments are often obscured by the different levels of mediation and immediacy that come into play: e.g. absolute, wholly unmediated, immediacy (which never occurs), relatively bare immediacy, and mediated immediacy, in which mediation is internalized by the mediated entity. They also seem vitiated by his conflation of apparently distinct types of mediation and immediacy: e.g. physical or CAUSAL, epistemic and logical. (The fact that knowledge of my own existence presupposes various biological and educational mediations may not be thought to impair its status as immediate *knowledge*.) But the coincidence of physical, cognitive and logical processes is essential to Hegel's IDEALISM: absolute knowledge must accurately mirror the structure of the OBJECT known.

memory, recollection and imagination German has several words for 'memory' and 'remember'. The most important in Hegel are *Erinnerung* and *Gedächtnis*:

1. The verb *erinnern* is related to the preposition *in* ('in') and originally meant 'to make (someone) get inside, i.e. become aware of, (something)'. Hence now, as in Hegel's day, it means 'to be reminiscent of, to remind (someone) of (something)'. (It also means 'to criticize adversely, draw unfavourable attention to'.) The reflexive form, *sich erinnern*, thus means 'to remind oneself of, recall, remember (something)'. Like the Greek *anamimnē̄skesthai* ('to recollect'), it suggests the successful outcome, rather than the process, of an attempt to recall or recollect something one knows or has previously encountered. The noun *Erinnerung* means a 'reminder', but also 'memory, recollection'. Plato's doctrine that all learning is the recollection (*anamnēsis*) of things previously known but later forgotten casts a shadow over the idealists' uses of *Erinnerung*: Schelling wrote that the 'Platonic idea that all philosophy is recollection is true in this sense: all philosophy consists in a recollecting of the state in which we were one with NATURE' (*Universal Deduction of the Dynamic Process or of the Categories of Physics*, 1800).

2. The verb *gedenken* is related to *denken* ('to THINK') and means 'to think of, bear in mind; to remember, recollect; to mention', etc. It is less active than *sich erinnern*, and does not suggest an intentional attempt to recall. The noun

Gedächtnis originally meant 'thinking of something, *Erinnerung*', but now means:
  (a) Like the Greek *mnēmē*, the whole stock of experiences, etc., that *can* be recalled, but need not be recalled at the moment.
  (b) The ability to retrieve or recall knowledge and past experiences, and to recognize them as encountered before. (*Gedächtnis* is here close to *Erinnerung*.)
  (c) The ability to remember or memorize things, in the sense of adding them to one's stock of memories, i.e. to one's *Gedächtnis* in sense (a).
There are also two words for imagination:
  3. The verb *einbilden*, from *Bild* ('picture, image', etc.) and *bilden* ('to shape, form, EDUCATE', etc.), originally meant 'to stamp, impress (something) into (the soul)'. Hegel sometimes uses it to mean 'to impress (something) into (something else)', when imagination is not explicitly in play. (Schelling often uses *einbilden* to mean 'inform', and associates imagination with the artist's ability to inform the real or particular with the IDEAL or UNIVERSAL.) But in his day, as now, it usually occurred in the reflexive form, *sich einbilden*, and meant 'to imagine'. *Einbildung* is 'imagination', and *Einbildungskraft* is 'the (power of) imagination'. Kant distinguished the *productive* from the *reproductive Einbildung*: The reproductive imagination forms images (*Bilde*) of perceived objects and combines them according to laws of association. The productive imagination has two functions: (a) It forms a bridge between sensibility and UNDERSTANDING; it unifies the 'manifold of INTUITION' and thus makes EXPERIENCE possible. (b) It creatively transforms the material of nature into works of art.
  4. *Phantasie* ('fancy, imagination'), from the Greek *phantasia* ('imagination, the ability to perceive appearances'), is the usual word for, e.g., a 'lively imagination'. Philosophers (e.g. Schiller) often use it interchangeably with *Einbildung(skraft)*. If a distinction is drawn, *Phantasie* is usually the higher, more creative faculty. Jean Paul, e.g., saw *Einbildungskraft* as simply reproductive and associative (even animals have it, since they dream and fear things), while *Phantasie* 'makes all parts into a whole ... it totalizes everything, brings the absolute and the infinite of reason closer and more vividly before mortal men' (*PA*, §§6, 7). Hegel too distinguishes between the passive (i.e. reproductive and mechanically associative) *Einbildungskraft* and the creative, artistic *Phantasie*, but he often uses the words interchangeably. Translators sometimes distinguish them as 'imagination' (*Einbildungskraft*) and 'fancy' or 'creative/productive imagination' (*Phantasie*).

In *Enc.* III §§451–64 Hegel treats *Erinnerung, Einbildungskraft* and *Gedächtnis* as successively higher phases of *Vorstellung*. (*Vorstellung* is at first used in the wider sense of 'internal REPRESENTATION', but it acquires the sense of 'conception' as the account proceeds.) He stresses what he takes to be the root meanings of the words. Most notably, he takes *erinnern* to mean, not 'remind' or 'be reminiscent (of)', but 'to internalize', while *sich erinnern* is less 'to recall' than 'to internalize, withdraw into, (re)collect, oneself'. The word is often contrasted with (*sich*) *entäussern*, 'to externalize (one-, itself)'. It is often used even when memory is not explicitly in play, especially for an entity's SUBLATION of its CONDITIONS or of its MEDIATION. ESSENCE, e.g., withdraws into itself from the complexity of QUALITY, etc.; SCEPTICISM involves a complete self-internalization. Self-internalization and self-externalization, in accordance with Hegel's view of the INNER and OUTER, are often complementary rather than opposed: a person deepens his inner life, thoughts, etc., to the extent that he externalizes himself in speech, writing, etc. (Often, as in the case of essence, the introduction of *Erinnerung* generates a reference to the past.) Conversely, Hegel continues to use *Erinnerung* for 'recollection', but usually with a suggestion of internalization. He agrees with Plato that learning involves *Erinnerung* ((self-)internalization), but not that it involves *Erinnerung* (recollection). (*Anamnēsis* has no similar suggestion of internalization.)

The recollection of a past event is, in a sense, an internalization of the event: the event is, as it were, in me, rather than at some distance from me in space and time. But to recollect an event, I must at the time of the event have internalized it and acquired a memory of it that can later be recalled; this memory is not so much internalized by my recollection as externalized, dredged up from my memory. Thus Hegel takes *Erinnerung* to be, not primarily recollection, but the internalization of a sensory INTUITION as an image (*Bild*); the image is abstracted from the concrete spatio-temporal position of the intuition, and given a place in the intelligence (which has its own subjective space and time). But the image is fleeting, and passes out of consciousness. The imagination is thus needed to revive or reproduce the image. The imagination is successively reproductive, associative and productive or creative (*Phantasie*).

However creative the imagination may be, its images are still images of intuited objects. Liberation from intuition and image is provided by *Gedächtnis*. Hegel associates this with THOUGHT: the past participle of *denken* ('to think') is *gedacht* ('(having been) thought'), so that *Gedächtnis* has the flavour of 'having-been-thoughtness'. Hence *Gedächtnis*, though it precedes thought itself (*Enc.* III §§465–8) in Hegel's account, is thought-memory, and, since thinking, on Hegel's view, involves LANGUAGE, verbal memory. *Gedächtnis* has three phases: (1) retentive memory, which retains words and their meanings, enabling us to recognize and understand words when we encounter them; (2) reproductive memory, which enables us to utter words on our own account; and (3) mechanical memory, the memorizing of words without regard for their meaning, which Hegel regards as an essential preliminary to thinking. The notion of *Erinnerung*, as the 'internalization' of a word and its meaning, continues to dominate Hegel's account of *Gedächtnis*.

Erinnerung is crucial throughout Hegel's thought. *Gedächtnis* is less so; elsewhere it is not usually restricted to verbal memory. Imagination, as *Phantasie*, plays an important role in Hegel's philosophy of ART, as it did in other aesthetic theories of the time, especially Kant's and Schelling's. Hegel also regarded it as crucial for philosophy, and in his review of Schulze (in *CJP*) rebukes him for suggesting that the philosopher can dispense with it.

mind and soul No single German word covers all the uses of the noun 'mind', but several overlap it. The most notable are *Gemüt*, *Seele* and *Geist*.

1. *Gemüt* originally means the 'totality of one's FEELINGS, SENSATIONS and THOUGHTS', and then the 'seat of one's feelings, etc.'. Eckhart, Paracelsus and Böhme used it for the mind or SPIRIT in general, and also for INNER withdrawal or spiritual inwardness (*Innerlichkeit*). For Leibniz and his followers, *Gemüt* includes both the capacity for thought, or the UNDERSTANDING, and the WILL. Kant (and Schiller) use it in a similarly wide sense, to embrace feelings, sensations and thought: he defines it as the capacity to SENSE (*empfinden*) and think, and says that the forms of INTUITION (SPACE and TIME) lie in the *Gemüt*.

At this stage *Gemüt* was a wider term than the more intellectual *Geist*, but under pressure from *Geist* (and also from the ROMANTICS) the connotation of inner, emotional depth implicit in the mystics' uses of *Gemüt*, but suppressed by the Enlightenment, came to predominate. Thus Fichte claimed that while the French have *Geist* ('*esprit*, wit'), the Germans have *Gemüt* ('soul, heart, (the seat of) large-scale, warm emotions'). Romantics such as Novalis saw *Gemüt* as the source of poetry: 'Poetry is the portrayal of the *Gemüt*, of the inner world in its totality' and 'in the end everything becomes poetry. Does not the world in the end become *Gemüt*?' Hegel uses *Gemüt* in the narrower sense of 'seat of emotion', and associates it especially with AESTHETICS.

2. *Seele* corresponds to the Greek *psuchē*, the Latin *anima* and the English 'soul'. Hegel uses it in several ways:
(a) Occasionally, he refers to the *Weltseele* ('world-soul'), referring to the doctrine (initiated by the Pythagoreans and by Plato's *Timaeus*, and endorsed by the STOICS, Plotinus, Giordano Bruno and Schelling) that the world as a whole is an ORGANISM animated by a single soul. But Hegel does not endorse this view, at least in his later works (*Enc.* III §391).
(b) In Greek thought, especially Plato and Aristotle, the soul is the principle of LIFE. Thus anything alive, animals and men (Plato) and even plants (Aristotle), has a soul. *Psuchē* covers all psychic activities: nutrition and reproduction (Aristotle), perception, emotion, reason (Plato and Aristotle). When the creature dies it loses its soul. (Whether the soul, or some part of it, persists after DEATH was a controversial question.) Hegel endorses this use of *Seele*, and thus ascribes a soul to whatever has life: plants, animals and men. But *Seele* does not, like *psuchē*, cover all psychic activities, only those that men share with plants and with animals: bodily qualities and alterations, sensation, feeling and habit (*Enc.* III §§388–412). It contrasts with CONSCIOUSNESS and spirit (*Geist*). The *Seele* in this sense is not a THING; it is not a separable constituent of the organism; and, like Aristotle, Hegel has no inclination to ascribe immortality to it. It is the middle term between body and spirit (*Enc.* I §34A.).
(c) *Seele* is often used metaphorically for the 'essential, inner side' of an entity that is not literally alive.

(d)   Descartes (and occasionally Plato) regarded the soul as a distinct SUBSTANCE, which is combined with, and can survive the death of, the body. Plato tends to see the soul in this sense as predominantly intellectual or rational; for Descartes it is exclusively intellectual, and animals are soulless machines. Wolff and other Leibnizian rationalists made the soul in this sense the subject of a special study, rational psychology. The soul is the mind (*Geist*) transformed into a *thing*. But the mind is not, on Hegel's view, a thing: it is essentially active, 'absolute actuosity' (*Enc.* I §34A.). Thus he uses *Seele* in this sense only when dealing with the views of others.

(e)   The *schöne Seele* ('beautiful soul') is criticized in *PS*, VI.C.c. He is too conscientious to dirty his hands by acting decisively, but self-righteously condemns the ACTIONS of others as wrong and hypocritical. All action, Hegel argues, entails the loss of innocence. But it is a greater sin to abstain from action and to impute base motives to others, especially to world-HISTORICAL individuals. The concept of the beautiful soul originated in sixteenth-century Spanish mystics (*alma bella*), appears in Shaftesbury and Richardson as 'beauty of the heart' and in Rousseau's *Nouvelle Héloïse* (1761) as the *belle âme*, and was introduced into Germany by Wieland as the *schöne Seele* in 1774. For Schiller it represents an ideal harmony between the moral and aesthetic aspects of a person, between duty and inclination. Book 6 of Goethe's *Wilhelm Meisters Lehrjahre* (*Wm Meister's Apprenticeship*) consists of the 'Confessions of a Beautiful Soul'.

3. *Geist* has a wide range of meaning: *see* SPIRIT. In the sense of 'mind', it tends to indicate the more active and intellectual aspects of the mind. In *Enc.* III Hegel distinguishes the *subjektive, objektive* and *absolute Geist*. Subjective *Geist* is the individual mind. It in turn is divided into three: (a) the soul (the subject of *Anthropologie*); (b) consciousness (the subject of PHENOMENOLOGY of Spirit); (c) *Geist* (the subject of *Psychologie*). (*Seele* and *Geist* denote different levels of psychic activity, while 'consciousness' and *Geist* refer to the same level(s), but from different points of view: phenomenology considers the mind in relation to its intentional OBJECTS, while psychology considers it in itself). Thus in the wider sense subjective *Geist* is equivalent to the wider sense of *Gemüt*, covering all psychic activity. In the narrower sense, (c), it excludes the soul, but still covers a wide range. It is subdivided into the theoretical mind (which Hegel often calls the *Intelligenz*) and the practical mind, with the 'free mind', i.e. the free WILL, thrown in as a briefly considered third term (§§481–2), which leads into objective *Geist*. Theoretical mind includes INTUITION, CONCEPTION (RECOLLECTION, IMAGINATION and MEMORY) and THINKING. Practical mind includes practical feeling, impulses and WILFULNESS, and happiness.

Geist is thus Hegel's main word for 'mind'. It differs from the I* in that, though any *Geist*, in this sense, is an I and any I is a *Geist*, the I is conceived as withdrawn into itself and RELATED to itself, while the Gesit is EXTERNALIZED into a variety of capacities and activities. Hegel constantly attacks the view that the mind consists of a collection of faculties (*Vermögen*), FORCES or POWERS: (1) The various capacities do not simply belong to a single entity, but form a structured hierarchy, each stage of which leads on to the next. (2) The mind is essentially activity: its capacities could not lapse into inactivity all at once. (He considers sleep and dreams at *Enc.* III §398 and A.) (3) The capacities are not distinct from each other: one cannot, for example, engage in significant practical activity without a theoretical conception of one's goal, and, conversely, thinking itself is a practical activity.

morality   All three German words for 'morality' derive from a word for 'CUSTOM': *Ethik* is from the Greek *ethos*, *Moralität* from the Latin *mos* (plural: *mores*), and *Sittlichkeit* from the German *Sitte*. But only in the case of *Sittlichkeit* ('ETHICAL LIFE') does Hegel stress this genealogy: *Ethik* has little significance for him, but is occasionally used to cover both *Sittlichkeit* and *Moralität*. *Moralität* is regularly used for 'individual morality', especially as conceived by Kant.

Hegel shares Kant's beliefs that to be moral is to be rational, that rationality is the central core of one's nature, and that to be moral is thus to be FREE. But he objects to (what he took to be) certain other features of Kant's account: that the rationality that grounds morality is one's own rational thought, rather than the rationality embodied in the institutions of one's society; that there is a sharp OPPOSITION between REASON (or duty) and inclination; that morality is a matter of what one OUGHT to do; and that it involves an endless pilgrimage towards the supreme good. *Moralität* is a higher phase of human development than Greek *Sittlichkeit*, since it enhances our SELF-CONSCIOUSNESS, and, in a modified form, it is an essential feature of the modern STATE. But it must be subordinate to ethical life and confine itself for the most part to the reflective acceptance of the norms and institutions of our society. (In *NL*, *Moralität* is associated primarily with the bourgeoisie.)

Moralität is associated with a number of other notions: WILL; duty (*Pflicht*); the good (*das Gute*), in contrast to the bad or evil (*das Böse*); virtue (*Tugend*), in contrast to vice (*Laster*); RESPONSIBILITY (*Schuld*); conscience (*das Gewissen*); and the 'ought' (*das Sollen*). Hegel treats them in different ways:

(1)   The 'ought' is simply rejected, since for Hegel it is inextricably associated with unmodified individualistic and utopian morality, and has no place in *Sittlichkeit*.

(2)   Some are wholeheartedly accepted, since they have a role in simple *Sittlichkeit*, as well as in the complex modern version: there are, besides moral duties, legal (*rechtliche*) and ethical (*sittliche*) duties, the duties attached to the roles one occupies in a system of ethical life; ethical virtues are required for, and displayed in, the performance of ethical duties, not only of moral duties.

(3)   Some have a more tenuous, but nevertheless secure, position in modern *Sittlichkeit* in virtue of the element of *Moralität* involved in it, though they play no part in *Sittlichkeit as such*: 'The [ethical] Greeks', Hegel says, 'had no conscience', but there is a place for it in the private life of the

191

individual in a modern state. Hegel associates conscience, *Gewissen*, with self-CERTAINTY, an ineliminable feature of modern life. But the genuine conscience, he argues, is the *Gesinnung* to will what is objectively good. *Gesinnung* is one's inner ethical attitude, sentiment or disposition. It can also be a political attitude: the political *Gesinnung* is patriotism (*PR* §268).

Moralität, unlike *Sittlichkeit*, stresses the INNER will and intention of the agent, in contrast to his OUTER conduct and its consequences. Thus in simple Greek *Sittlichkeit*, on Hegel's view, guilt or responsibility is ascribed to an agent (such as Oedipus) for what he does (his *Tat*, 'DEED'), regardless of his knowledge and intentions. In pure *Moralität*, by contrast, one is responsible only for one's intentions and for that aspect of one's deed that one intended (the *Handlung*, 'ACTION'). Hegel acknowledges this *Recht des Wissens* ('RIGHT to know'), but he does not believe that one can disown responsibility for all the unintended and/or unforeseen consequences of one's actions.

Moralität and *Sittlichkeit* similarly differ in their attitude towards the good. The adjective *gut* ('good') contrasts with several words, but the most important here are *böse* and *schlecht*. Their meanings overlap, but *böse* and *das Böse* are more usual for morally 'evil' and 'moral evil', while *schlecht* indicates what is substandard through no fault of its own. Thus Nietzsche wanted to transcend the opposition between *gut* and *böse*, and to replace it with that between *gut* and *schlecht*, which, he believed, was the central contrast in pre-Christian heroic societies and lacked the moralistic associations of *gut–böse*. Hegel anticipated much of Nietzsche's thought on this, but he was more inclined than Nietzsche to allow a place for the *gut–böse* contrast in modern *Sittlichkeit*. But Hegel makes three modifications of the moralistic view of good and evil:

(1) Just as *Moralität* assigns responsibility only for intentions and the will, and for what is willed or intended, so it locates good and evil only, or primarily, in the will and intentions. Kant, for example, argued that the good will is the only unqualified good. Hegel, by contrast, locates them primarily in overt conduct, in part because it is only by outer expression that the will acquires a determinate character, in part because any crime or atrocity might be justified by a good intention or a good reason or GROUND.

(2) *Moralität* tends to see the good as something that *ought* to be achieved, and the present state, whether of an individual person, a society or humanity as a whole, as more or less evil. Hegel, by contrast, believes the good to be realized in the present state of affairs, the ACTUAL.

(3) Ore reason for his belief that the good is already realized is that whereas *Moralität* tends to draw a sharp contrast between good and evil and to hold that the realization of the good requires the complete elimination or defeat of evil, Hegel sees evil as necessarily involved in the good: the good requires the subordination or taming of evil, not its elimination. This doctrine appears at several levels in his thought:

192

(a) It is only possible to be morally good, rather than *innocent*, if one freely chooses the good. But this means that one is also free to choose evil, and if this possibility is eliminated one loses the possibility of being good. (Hegel interprets the myth of the fall as describing an ascent, rather than a fall, since it involves acquisition of the knowledge of good and evil, which is a necessary condition of goodness, in contrast to innocence.)

(b) Our inclinations and passions, which are, for *Moralität*, the root of evil, are not to be combated and eventually extirpated, but canalized into the routines and rituals of *Sittlichkeit*: lust is domesticated to become conjugal love and is satisfied in marriage, etc.

(c) Decisive action involves one's whole personality, passion (*Leidenschaft*) as well as reason, and, as Hegel argues against the beautiful SOUL, it inevitably runs the risk of evil. 'Nothing great in the world has been achieved without passion' (*LPH*).

Hegel is particularly opposed to the moral assessment of historical agents by moral standards. But such assessment is not, as he often implies, a peculiarity of *Moralität*, in contrast to *Sittlichkeit*. It is true that, unlike *Sittlichkeit*, *Moralität*, at least as Kant views it, does not vary over HISTORY, and that it assesses intentions rather than deeds. But the *deeds* of great men often contravene both the *Sittlichkeit* of their own society and the new type of *Sittlichkeit* which they help to establish, not simply Kantian *Moralität*. In the case of great men, Hegel thus transcends the standpoint both of individual morality and of social ethics, and adopts the standpoint of 'world history'. But he supplies no clear criteria for deciding whether a person is to be judged from this standpoint or by more conventional standards.

N

nature and philosophy of nature   *Natur*, from the Latin *natura* and ultimately from *nasci* ('to be born, to arise, originate') corresponds closely to 'nature'. It means 'what has come about or grown without outside help; the creation or world', and, in a secondary sense, 'ESSENCE, character, etc.', as in e.g. 'human *nature*'. 'Nature' in both senses is often contrasted with 'culture' and the 'cultural', and with 'art' and the 'artificial'. 'Nature' in its primary sense is contrasted with 'man' and with what is specifically human, 'SPIRIT' and the 'spiritual'. (In the later nineteenth century, the *Naturwissenschaften* ('natural SCIENCES') were contrasted with the *Geisteswissenschaften* (originally a translation of J. S. Mill's 'moral sciences').)

   Enc. II is devoted to *Naturphilosophie* ('natural philosophy, philosophy of nature'), in contrast to 'logic' (*Enc.* I) and 'philosophy of spirit' (*Enc.* III). The expression *philosophia naturalis* first appears in Seneca, but he, like other ancients, drew no distinction between 'science' and 'philosophy' of nature. They are still conflated in the expression 'natural philosophy', which Newton and his English successors applied to physics and chemistry. But in the eighteenth century Wolff and his followers (including Kant) distinguished *physica speculativa* or philosophy of nature from *physica empirica* or natural science: natural science establishes empirical facts, while philosophy of nature examines general questions concerning nature and general concepts applicable to it. (At *Enc.* I §35 and A., Hegel discusses 'cosmology' as a branch of Wolff's METAPHYSICS.) Kant's *MENS* considers the '*a priori* principles' of natural science and general concepts such as MATTER, FORCE and motion. But Kant does not confine himself to examining the presuppositions of the natural sciences: he also attempts to establish *a priori* such scientific doctrines as that matter consists of the forces of attraction and repulsion.

   Schelling went further than Kant in this respect. In *IPN* he argued that philosophy of nature sets out from intrinsically certain principles and can dispense with any guidance by APPEARANCES (*Erscheinungen*). On Schelling's view, philosophy of nature, unlike the natural sciences, treats nature as living and creative. To express this he adopted the medieval and Spinozist concept of *natura naturans* ('creative nature'), in contrast to *natura naturata* ('created nature'). Nature, like the realm of spirit, consists of stages or levels (*Stufen*), which Schelling calls 'powers' or 'potencies' (*Potenzen*), but these do not follow each other in time. The stages of nature are more or less parallel to those of spirit, and, he believes, 'nature is just intelligence turned into the rigidity of being; its qualities are sensations extinguished to being; bodies are its perceptions, as it were, killed' (*IPN*). Schelling's philosophy of nature had a considerable influence on, e.g., Oken, Steffens, Schopenhauer and Hegel.

Hegel often criticizes Schelling's philosophy of nature, especially for its use of imaginative analogies, but he fully endorses Schelling's claim that nature is 'petrified (or "ossified") intelligence' (*versteinerte Intelligenz*) (*Enc.* I §24A.; *Enc.* II §247A.), and his own enterprise is similar to Schelling's in both its overall purpose and its execution. Philosophy of nature is distinct from philosophy of science: its primary subject-matter is nature as such, not the natural sciences. But neither Schelling nor Hegel claim to study nature independently of the natural sciences. Their claim to derive nature, or general truths about it, *a priori* does not entail that they could have done so if natural scientists had not prepared the material for them (*Enc.* I §12).

The relationship between nature and the logical idea, or between logic and the philosophy of nature, is a controversial matter. At the end of *SL*, the logical IDEA freely 'releases itself' (*sich ... entlasst*, 'lets itself go') or by a free 'resolve' (*Entschluss*) determines itself as the 'EXTERNAL' or 'INTUITIVE' (*anschauende, Enc.* I §244) idea. *Entschluss* is from (*sich*) *entschliessen*, which originally meant 'to open up (it-, oneself)' and the prefix *ent-* still has, in some of its occurrences, the force of separation. (Cf. 'de-, and 'un-'.) But in Hegel's day it meant 'to resolve, decide', and thus his use of the term has anthropomorphic or theological overtones. This transition from logic to nature is quite different from the transitions (*Übergange*, from *übergehen*, 'to go, pass, over') linking categories *within* the Logic. Hence the logical idea does not immediately become LIFE, the stage of nature that is the most obvious counterpart to the highest phase of logic, but returns, as it were, to its beginning and becomes the sheer being of SPACE. It then passes through the phases of MECHANICS (space and TIME, matter and motion, absolute mechanics, viz. the planetary system), physics (passing from light to the chemical process), and organic physics (the earth as an organism and organic life). Each phase passes into its successor in a way similar to that in which categories pass into each other in the Logic. Nature does not, on Hegel's view, have a HISTORY: fossil remains were never alive. But like Schelling, he is constantly on the look-out for spiritual or conceptual significance in such phenomena as light and magnetism. There are several reasons for this:

(1) In accordance with Hegel's overall IDEALISM, nature, though not the product of any *finite* mind, must bear the marks of spirit: it is 'intelligence', albeit 'petrified'.

(2) Philosophy of nature is intended not simply to provide information about nature, but to reclaim it for spirit, to SUBLATE or overcome nature or its ALIENATION from man (or his alienation from nature). Making discoveries about nature and adequately conceptualizing them is only one way of doing this. Another, more satisfactory, way is to show that the products and operations of nature are more mind-like than are the solid atoms and their mechanical interactions in terms of which Newton viewed it.

(3) One aim of philosophy of nature is to show that (and how) the MIND, in

195

particular the mind that observes nature, emerges out of nature. This cannot be done if nature consists only of entities and processes that are entirely alien to the mind, or if we insist on conceptualizing them in ways that are inapplicable to the mind itself. Thus Newtonian physics implicitly postulates an unbridgeable gulf between nature and mind.

The point and purpose of Hegel's philosophy of nature is unclear in several respects:

1. Is its subject-matter simply nature as such or nature as seen by the natural sciences? Hegel's overall programme suggests conflicting answers. The nature that emerges from the logical idea and that *precedes* the emergence of spirit should be simply nature as such, uncontaminated by human thought about it. On the other hand, Hegel could, and would, no more claim to describe nature as such, independently of previous thought about it, than to describe history as such, independently of previous historians. (The cases differ in that there can be no history without contemporaneous historical writing, but the existence of nature does not presuppose that of natural science.) He saw himself as completing the work of scientists, organizing their results into a unified system and occasionally criticizing their conceptual inadequacy. (Unlike Kant, Hegel was not a natural scientist and usually confines himself to supporting one current theory, e.g. Kepler on planetary motions or Goethe on light, against another, e.g. Newtonianism in general.)

2. To what extent are natural phenomena or truths about them NECESSARY or *a priori*, in contrast to CONTINGENT? Hegel often suggests that his procedure is to compare the APPEARANCE (*Erscheinung*) with the conceptual DETERMINA-TION (*Begriffsbestimmung*) (e.g. *Enc.* II §323A.), implying that there is a necessary general scheme of nature, but the details of its realization are contingent. But he gives no clear account of where (or why) the line is to be drawn between the conceptual scheme and the empirical details.

3. As indicated above, philosophy of nature is part of an overall process of sublating or overcoming nature. Hegel is less attracted to nature than Schelling, and tends to see spirit as involving a conflict with nature, rather than a smooth development out of it: he agrees with Hobbes, against Rousseau, that the state of nature was a 'war of all against all', which civilization needed to overcome, and he saw this process reflected in such Greek myths as the battle of the gods against the Titans. But the overcoming of nature involves several distinct strands that he does not clearly differentiate or relate: (a) There is a sense in which nature overcomes itself, at least to the extent that without our assistance it rises from the level of mere space to that of the living animal and its DEATH, the very brink of spirit. (b) Science and philosophy of nature discover that, all along, nature has been less alien than we supposed, when they discover that it contains such mind-like phenomena as light, as well as atoms and earthquakes. (c) THINKING about something, on Hegel's view, *ipso facto* alters it: thus our discoveries about and conceptualization of nature not only show that nature is not wholly alien, but make it less alien. (Science and philosophy reveal the TRUTH of nature in Hegel's, as well as the usual, sense.) (d) Practical activities make nature less

alien by, e.g., transforming it into parks, and by producing artefacts and social groups that insulate us against the rigours of raw nature.

necessity, possibility and contingency *Notwendig* and *Notwendigkeit* mean 'necessary' and 'necessity'. They contrast with *möglich* ('possible') and *Möglichkeit* ('possibility'), from the verb *mögen* ('can, may, might, like', etc.), and with *Zufall* ('chance, accident'), *zufällig* ('fortuitous, contingent') and *zufälligkeit* ('contingency'). In non-Hegelian philosophy, the words are related roughly as follows. If something is possible, it may, or may not, be ACTUAL (*wirklich*). If it is not actual, it is *merely* possible. If it is actual, it may be contingent (i.e. such that it is possible for it not to be actual, as well as to be actual) or necessary (i.e. such that it is not possible for it not to be actual). But what is necessary is not always actual: something may be a necessary (i.e. indispensable) CONDITION of something else, e.g. of the truth of a theorem or of the actuality of a state of affairs, but not be realized (in which case, what it is a condition of cannot be actual, or true, either). Hegel's uses of the words are influenced by Aristotle's contrast between what is actual (*energeiai*) and what is merely potential (*dunamei*). He examines necessity, etc., at length in *SL*. The briefer account in *Enc.* I §§143–9 runs as follows.

1. Hegel begins with formal (or logical) possibility. Something is formally possible, according to the Wolffian logic of the time, if it involves no CONTRADICTION. What is possible is regularly equated with what is thinkable. Hegel's examples are: it is possible that the moon will fall to the earth tonight; it is possible that the Sultan will become the Pope (*Enc.* I §143A.).

Unlike orthodox logicians, who held, e.g., that the sentence 'This is both square and circular' expresses an impossibility, Hegel affirms that everything is formally possible. There are three reasons for this:

(a) The claim that something is formally possible involves ABSTRACTING an entity from its present circumstances (e.g. ignoring facts about the moon which are logically incompatible with its falling to the earth). Someone who claims that it is impossible for something to be both square and circular is not abstracting sufficiently. For even if it is actually square, it is possible for it to be circular.

(b) Hegel is thus concerned with the possibility of events or states of affairs rather than of PROPOSITIONS.

(c) He is concerned, as his examples suggest, with future possibilities: it is possible for this, which is now square, to *become* round.

Not only is everything possible, but conversely, since anything CONCRETE involves OPPOSITION and contradiction (e.g. MATTER involves both attraction and repulsion, *Enc.* I §143A.), everything is formally impossible. Formal possibility is thus, on Hegel's view, a singularly vacuous notion.

2. Orthodox logicians (e.g. Kant) had a notion of formal necessity co-ordinate with that of formal possibility: the formally necessary is that which cannot possibly not be, or whose negation is formally impossible. But Hegel's belief that everything is formally possible deprives him of this notion. Hence he proceeds to the notion of formal actuality, of actuality not in

Hegel's preferred sense, but in the sense of simply being or existing, in contrast to being merely possible. The formally actual is the contingent (*Zufälliges*): it is possible for it not to be, as well as to be. That it is actual is thus a matter of chance (*Zufall*). But the concept of *Zufälligkeit* is complex: it contrasts with what is essential, necessary or intended, but it also suggests dependence on, or being contingent *upon*, something else: 'the *Zufällige* in general is what has its GROUND not in itself, but in an OTHER' (*Enc.* I §145A.). Hegel infers that the contingent is not simply an IMMEDIATE actuality, but also serves as the possibility or condition of a new actuality. (Here, as elsewhere, he exploits the verb *voraussetzen*, 'to PRESUPPOSE', but literally 'to POSIT in advance, pre-posit': the contingent is posited by something else, but it is posited in advance or presupposed.)

3. The conditions (*Bedingungen*) of something and their interaction are the real (*reale*), not simply the formal, possibility of it. It is a formal possibility that there should be a statue, that this block of unshaped marble should be or become a statue; but when the sculptor sets to work on the marble with his chisel, this is the *real* possibility of a statue. But the real possibility of something is also its real actuality, since 'if *all conditions* are present, the THING (*Sache*) must become actual' (*Enc.* I §147). But it is not only actual; it is necessary. This is relative (or hypothetical) necessity, necessity in relation to certain conditions. But since the emergence of the thing from its conditions involves the SUBLATION of those conditions, the sublation of MEDIATION into immediacy, it is also ABSOLUTE or unconditioned necessity. Kant had denied the possibility of anything absolutely necessary in the phenomenal world, but Hegel reinterprets the notion of unconditional necessity, so that it is exemplified by any relatively self-contained and self-sustaining entity that absorbs the conditions of its emergence: a work of art, an ORGANISM, a person, a STATE, etc.

Hegel's account is intended to apply not only to the emergence of entities in the world, but also to human COGNITION. The world presents us with a mass of empirical contingencies. These form the conditions of the work of the natural scientist, but he does not simply accept them as they are: by observation and experiment he extracts their common features or ESSENCE and expresses it in universal LAWS that do not contain low-level empirical terms such as 'stone', but only more general terms such as 'body', 'attraction', 'repulsion'. At a higher level still, Hegelian logic, though conditioned by empirical contingencies as well as by the results of the natural and other sciences, abstracts from these conditions and operates at the level of pure THOUGHT. At this level, Hegel believes, many of the results of the sciences that were originally arrived at empirically can be shown to be necessary (*Enc.* I §12). (Logic, on Hegel's view, involves no contingency: any given category has a unique successor.)

Nevertheless there is, Hegel believes, an ineliminable element of contingency in the world, not only in NATURE (where, e.g., the number of species of parrot is contingent and has to be simply accepted, not derived or explained), but in HISTORY, ART and RIGHT. This is problematic for several reasons:

1. The concept of contingency is unclear: The claim that something is contingent may mean that (a) it is a matter of sheer chance, so that there is no reason for it; (b) there is a reason for it (since, after all, the contingent 'has its ground ... in an other'), but this reason is inaccessible to us; (c) the reason for it is accessible to the natural sciences, but the phenomenon cannot be shown to be necessary and *a priori* by philosophy.

2. Equally unclear is the concept of 'overcoming' contingency (e.g. *überwinden, Enc.* I §145A.). If the contingency of the number of species of parrot cannot be overcome, 'overcoming' must mean 'explaining', either in the sense of showing that, given certain other (non-contingent) facts the number can be neither more nor less than, say, 193, or in the sense of showing that 193 parrot-species serve some PURPOSE that no other number would. But in other senses of 'overcoming contingency', such as abstracting from the parrot-species and doing logic instead, or making them serve some higher purpose by, e.g., eating them or stuffing them and placing them in a museum, their contingency can easily be overcome. The accounts in *SL* and *Enc.* I do not discriminate sufficiently between these different ways in which contingency can be overcome.

3. Hegel's Logic implies that contingency, like other categories, must be exemplified in the world. But he gives no satisfactory account of (a) where the line is to be drawn between the contingent and the non-contingent; (b) why it is to be drawn at that, rather than some other, point; or (c) how the existence of sheer contingencies is compatible with other features of his thought, e.g. his thoroughgoing theism and his denial of any distinct, formless MATTER or CONTENT.

negation and negativity The native German for 'negation' is *Verneinung*, from *verneinen* ('to answer "No" (*nein*) to a question, to deny or contradict an assertion'). Its antonym is *Bejahung* ('affirmation'), from *bejahen* ('to answer "Yes" (*ja*) to a question, to assent to an assertion'). But Hegel usually prefers *Negation*, from the Latin *negare* ('to deny'), with the verb *negieren* ('to negate'), the adjective *negativ*, the adjectival noun (*das*) *Negative* ('(the) negative'), and the noun *Negativität* ('negativity, being negative, the process of negating'). These contrast with *Realität*, with *Affirmation* and *affirmativ*, and with *Position* (used only infrequently), *positiv* and *Positivität*. (*Positivität* usually, and *positiv* often, contrast not with *Negativität* and *negativ*, but with 'rational' or 'natural', and indicate the sheer existence of something, e.g. a LAW or a RELIGION, regardless of its rationality.)

In non-Hegelian philosophy, the concept of negation has several uses. It is applied primarily to the negative JUDGMENT or PROPOSITION: 'The rose is not red.' By extension, it applies to concepts or predicates: 'not red' or 'non-red'. It is also used in mathematics for negative quantities, $-a$, -6, in contrast to $(+)a$, $(+)6$. Negation is also ascribed to things: Kant, e.g., regarded any thing, or quality of a thing, as lying on a continuous scale between *Realität* and *Negation*, between, say, the brightest of reds and a pink that shades off into colourlessness. (Kant used this idea to refute Mendelssohn's proof of the IMMORTALITY of the SOUL, that owing to its simplicity the soul is not liable to destruction by disintegration. But it may, Kant replies, just fade away into nothing.) In the Leibniz–Wolff tradition, to which Kant is indebted here, any FINITE entity involves negation, i.e. none of its qualities is real to the highest degree; only GOD is fully real, with no negation whatsoever. Hegel endorsed Spinoza's doctrine that all DETERMINATION is negation, but he rejected Spinoza's view that REALITY is at bottom a wholly indeterminate SUBSTANCE, since unless substance itself involves negativity the negations constituting determinate entities can come only from an intellect implicitly located outside substance or the ABSOLUTE. Mystics such as Böhme also ascribed negation, like CONTRADICTION, to the nature of things: 'All things consist in the Yes and No.'

Negation and negativity are fundamental to Hegel's thought, but his interpretation of them is novel in several respects:

1. If one thing is the negation of another, then the negation is as determinate as what it negates. This conflicts both with the common view of propositional negation and with Kant's doctrine that the negation of a reality '= 0' (*CPR*, A167; B209). The negation of the proposition 'The rose is red', viz. 'The rose is not red' (or 'It is not the case that the rose is red') is determinate to the extent that it differs from the negation of 'The water is hot' (and thus is not '= 0'), but it is less determinate than the proposition negated by it: it leaves open what colour the rose is, whether it has a colour at all, and even whether there is a rose or not. Again, on Kant's acccount, the negation of red is less determinate than the reality of red: as blank colourlessness it does not differ from the negation of green, or perhaps from the negation of sweetness. Hegel's reply to this is that however fully and unqualifiedly red something is, it still involves negation, since it is not green, not blue, etc., and it is only in virtue of being not green, not blue, etc., that it is red. Thus green, blue, etc., negate or LIMIT red, just as it negates them.

2. In standard two-valued logic (the only formal logic available to Hegel), if something is negated, and the negation is in turn negated, we return to our starting-point: 'It is not the case that it is not the case that the rose is red' amounts to 'The rose is red'. For Hegel, the negation of a negation results in an affirmation, but a different affirmation from that originally negated: the something (*das Etwas*), e.g. (a) red (thing), is negated by the OTHER (*das Andere*), e.g. (a) green (thing), but it also negates it in turn and is thus the negation of the negation. This is not *simply* a return to its original, unnegated status: stage (i) is simply DETERMINATE BEING in general, not a determinate something; stage (ii) is the bifurcation into a something and its negating other; stage (iii) is the something's affirmation, by its negation of the other, of its own intrinsic nature, of the fact that it is more than simply a blank space marked off by the other(s).

3. Hegel discusses positive and negative judgments, but he is not much interested in negation as a feature of judgments. Like the notions of contradiction, INFERENCE, and judgment itself, negation is primarily a characteristic of concepts and things. But *Negation* and *Negativität* retain the active flavour of judgmental negating or denying. Things and concepts are not simply nega-

tive or exclusive, they actively negate each other. As in the case of limit, Hegel tends to conflate the ideas of conceptual and physical negation.

Negation and the negation of negation operate at different levels and in different ways:

(a) A simple (and oversimplified) historical analogue of the dialectic of something and other is this: Before the emergence of Protestantism, Catholicism is just (Western) Christianity as such. It then generates Protestantism, which negates it. Protestantism is not just non-Catholicism, but actively differentiates itself from it and bears the marks of the Catholicism that it negates. Catholicism in turn negates Protestantism, thereby ceasing to be simply Christianity as such and bearing the marks of its active self-differentiation from Protestantism.

(b) An unreflective Catholic and an unreflective Protestant come to reflect on their respective faiths (perhaps owing to their awareness of the difficulty of substantiating either FAITH in opposition to the other). They then lapse from, or negate, their faiths. But each still bears the marks of the faith he negates or SUBLATES: a lapsed Catholic is different from a lapsed Protestant, since such negation is determinate. Subsequently, by further REFLECTION each reacquires the faith he lost: he negates the negation. But neither returns to the unreflective faith he lost: it is now a reflective faith, enriched by the return journey by which it was reached. (Hegel often sees later phases of logic, HISTORY, a LIFE, etc., as the restoration of an earlier phase on a higher level.)

(c) Cases (a) and (b) both involve the attachment of individuals to one of a range of co-ordinate creeds each of which negates the other(s). But the negation of the negation often entails the transcendence of a whole range of co-ordinate negations. Thus the negation of the negation may be (i) an attempt to espouse and savour in turn each of the seemingly endless variety of competing creeds (cf. IRONY); (ii) a withdrawal into oneself, away from all competing creeds and faiths; or (iii) the adoption of a creed which embraces all others and does not negate them, but only their claims to exclusivity or their negations of each other. This type of double negation is INFINITY. Response (i) is, or is governed by, bad infinity, an endless procession of finite entities, each of which negates its predecessor. (ii) is a type of good infinity, since it involves the circular return of something into itself. In the Logic, it appears as being-FOR-ITSELF, exemplified by the self-reflexive I*, which transcends the range of determinate QUALITIES. (iii), also good infinity, appears most prominently in the absolute IDEA which embraces all the THOUGHT-determinations that appear earlier in the Logic. Although Hegel regards (i) and (ii) as necessary historical phases, he prefers (iii) as a response to, e.g., the diversity of apparently competing philosophies.

The pattern of 'simple affirmation–negation–negation of negation' is constantly repeated throughout Hegel's thought, and what is the negation of the negation in one application reappears as the simple affirmation of another application. For example, the first phase of the WILL, its withdrawal into itself and negation of everything determinate (a version of (ii) above), is negated by its adoption of a determinate option, and this in turn is negated by its willing itself.

In the Logic (Doctrine of ESSENCE), the negative and the positive are seen as the paradigm of opposition, a heightened form of negation in which each term is not simply other than the other (as red is other than blue, green, etc.), but *its* other (as north is the other of south). The negative that is opposed to the positive here is distinct from the negative involved in Hegelian negation: the positive negates the negative as much as the negative negates the positive, and is as much negative as positive.

notion *see* CONCEPT

O

object and objectivity (*Das*) *Objekt*, from the Latin *objectum* (the past participle of *objicere*, 'to throw before or over against'), means 'something thrown before, or over against'. It contrasts with 'SUBJECT', 'what is thrown or put under'. From their first occurrence in Duns Scotus until the eighteenth century, 'subject' and 'object' were used in a sense that is the reverse of their modern sense: the 'subject' was the underlying subject of discourse (or object), while the 'object' was what was thrown against or towards it, viz. the subjective conception or predicate. But Wolff gave *Objekt* the sense of 'something thrown before, or over against, the mind', the object of CONSCIOUSNESS, CONCEPTION or KNOWLEDGE. It can also be the object of striving, of a wish or of action. It need not be an existing physical entity: numbers, unicorns or consciousness itself can be the *Objekt* of consciousness or thinking. Kant also uses it in the narrower sense of an object given in experience, a real object: 'Object is that in the concept of which the manifold of a given INTUITION is combined' (*CPR*, B137). *Objekt* is also used in a grammatical sense for the object of a verb in a sentence.

A native German counterpart occurs alongside *Objekt*: from the seventeenth century on, the earlier *Gegenwurf* ('something thrown against') was displaced by *Gegenstand* ('what stands over against'), though at the end of the seventeenth century *Gegenstand* still occurred in the religious sense of a spiritual 'support, resistance' against temptations and afflictions. In Hegel's Swabian dialect it also meant 'obstacle, hindrance', but in philosophical German it meant, like *Objekt*, an 'object (of consciousness, knowledge, action, etc.)' and a '(real) object'. Kant drew no distinction between *Objekt* and *Gegenstand*.

Gegenstand gives rise to *gegenständlich* ('objective') and *Gegenständlichkeit* ('objectivity'). But Hegel, like Kant, usually prefers the derivatives of *Objekt*: *objectiv* ('objective'), *Objektivität* ('objectivity'), and, occasionally, *objektivieren* ('to make into an object, objectify') and *Objektivierung* ('objectification'). (E.g. RELIGION begins with the 'objectification' of the universal, essential nature of things, i.e. its transformation into an objective God.) The general sense of *objektiv* is 'pertaining to a/the object', but its more specific senses are: (1) 'real, actual, being an object' (as in 'objective fact'); (2) 'impartial, directed on the object' (as in an 'objective attitude to the facts'). *Objektivität* has two corresponding senses: (1) 'reality'; (2) 'impartiality'. Objectivity, in the sense of 'impartiality', may be practical as well as cognitive: following, e.g., impersonal rules, in contrast to one's personal whims.

In Hegel *Objekt* differs from *Gegenstand* in three respects: (1) He stresses the etymology of *Gegenstand* more than that of *Objekt*, so that a *Gegenstand* is essentially and immediately an object of knowledge, etc., while an *Objekt* is, at least initially, independent (*Enc.* I §193). A *Gegenstand* is an intentional object, while an *Objekt* is a real object. (2) When an *Objekt* is the object *of* something, it is usually the object of a *Subjekt*, while a *Gegenstand* is the object of knowledge (*Wissen*), consciousness, the I*, etc. (There is no comparable native German version of *Subjekt*.) (3) A FORM of consciousness and its object are, on Hegel's view, interdependent and have a comparable richness and complexity. Thus since the *Objekt* is correlative to the *Subjekt*, and (in the Logic) the subject involves the CONCEPT, the JUDGMENT and the INFERENCE, the *Objekt* must be a complex system of objects (such as the solar system) related by the forms of inference. A *Gegenstand*, by contrast, may be the object of a simple form of consciousness, such as SENSORY CERTAINTY, which is not yet a fully fledged subject. (In *PP*, a *Gegenstand* is a CONCRETE object with many perceptible features, but if I disregard or ABSTRACT from these, what remains is an abstract *Objekt*.)

Thus in *PS* (Intro., etc.), where Hegel is examining the forms of intentional consciousness, from the most rudimentary to absolute knowledge, the object is the *Gegenstand*. But in the Logic, where 'The Object' follows 'The Subjective Concept' (*Enc.* I) or 'Objectivity' follows 'Subjectivity' (*SL*), 'object' and 'objectivity' are *Objekt* and *Objektivität*. The *Objekt*, which passes through the phases of MECHANISM, CHEMISM and TELEOLOGY, displays the 'conceptual DETERMINATIONS' developed in 'the Subjective Concept' (especially a syllogistic structure), but is initially conceived as independent of a cognizing or practical subject. When Hegel poses the (or 'a') problem of knowledge as 'How do we subjects get over to the objects?' (*Enc.* II §246A.), the objects are *Objekte*, not *Gegenstände*, which are intrinsically related to consciousness. (In *PS*, Intro., the object that is real and consequently difficult to reach is not the *Gegenstand*, but *die Sache*, the 'THING, etc.')

In *SL*, Hegel argues that *objektiv* and *Objektivität* have two senses: (i) 'Standing over against the independent concept' or the I, i.e. the 'manifold world in its IMMEDIATE EXISTENCE', which the concept or I must overcome. (Hegel connects this with a 'less determinate sense', in which the *Objekt* is the *Gegenstand* of any 'interest or activity of the subject'.) (ii) 'The IN AND FOR ITSELF, which is free of restriction and opposition', viz. by a subject. The objective in this sense includes rational and necessary theoretical or ethical principles that the subject must simply conform to, rather than overcome or alter, and the object that the subject must COGNIZE, 'free from the additions of subjective REFLECTION'. Mechanism and chemism, on Hegel's account, involve objectivity in sense (ii), while teleology, in which the purpose or concept detaches itself from the object and attempts to determine it, involves objectivity in sense (i). But in fact, there are three stages of objectivity, not simply two: (1) An object that is independent of the subject, in the sense that the subject is left out of account altogether (except in so far as a subject or concept is implicitly presupposed as constituting the object as an object), viz. mechanism and chemism. (2) An object that stands over against a subject and is to be overcome by it, viz. teleology, but also, at the level of the IDEA, the ideas of the true (cognition) and of the good (Kant's and Fichte's MORALITY). (Objectivity in sense (i) above.) (3) An object that has been worked up to NECESSITY and rationality, so that the subject does not need to alter or determine it, but must simply conform to it. This corresponds to the absolute idea, which, on Hegel's view, is both subject and object. It is exemplified by, e.g., someone doing (Hegelian) logic or conforming to the laws and practices of a rational STATE. (Objectivity in sense (ii) above.)

At *Enc.* I §41A.2, Hegel distinguishes *three* senses of *objectiv*: (a) The ordinary sense of 'externally present, in contrast to the merely subjective, imagined, dreamt, etc.'. (b) Kant's sense of 'universal and necessary in contrast to the contingency, particularity, and subjectivity of our sensations'. (c) Hegel's preferred sense of the 'THOUGHTS that are not merely *our* thoughts, but are equally the IN ITSELF of THINGS (*Dinge*) and of the objective (*des Gegenständlichen*) in general.' Sense (a) corresponds to sense (i) above, while sense (ii) above covers both (b) and (c) here. Kant is right, Hegel argues, to think that the CONTINGENCIES of sensation, etc., are objective in only a degenerate sense, in contrast to thoughts or categories, which are UNIVERSAL and necessary, both in the sense that they apply to all objects and in the sense that they do not vary from person to person. But for Kant thoughts are still subjective in sense (c), since he regards them as imposed by us on things, not as constituting their ESSENCE (as Hegel believes).

Hegel's attempts to distinguish different senses of *Objektivität* ignore the distinction between objective attitudes towards things and the objective things themselves. This stems from two doctrines: first, that at the highest level of objectivity, the attitude (or subject) and its object coincide; second, that in general, attitudes and their objects are objective at the same level or to the same degree: if, e.g., I think objectively (viz. rationally and impartially), I discern the objective thoughts that constitute the essence of things, while if I merely sense or perceive, I discern only the lesser objectivity of the sensory qualities of things. But it is not obvious that this correspondence obtains. My sensations may be fleeting and subjective, but this does not entail that the sensory qualities of things (ascertained by collating different sensations of one observer and those of different observers) are equally subjective. Again, in the case of ethical and aesthetic judgments, an objective (impartial) attitude does not guarantee an objective (correct) answer, nor even that there is an objective (correct) answer to be found. In the case of ethics, there is no obvious *object* for the objective attitude to attain to, but Hegel tends to see the LAWS (or the STATE itself) as an object analogous to the object of cognition.

In both *SL* and *Enc.* I, Hegel associates the transition from the 'subjective concept' to the 'object' with the ontological PROOF of God's existence.

opposition *Gegensatz* ('opposite, opposition, contrary, antithesis'), coined in the fifteenth century to translate the Latin *oppositio* (from *opponere*, 'to set, put against'), was originally a legal term meaning 'bringing something forward in opposition in a lawsuit'. It gives rise to an adjective *gegensätzlich* ('opposite, contrary'), but the corresponding verb is *entgegensetzen* ('to set against, oppose, counterpose'). (The root verb is *setzen*, 'to POSIT'.) In addition to *Gegensatz*, Hegel often uses the past participle *entgegengesetzt* ('opposed, opposite') and the noun *Entgegensetzung* ('opposition'). He also uses the Greek-derived eighteenth-century coinage, *Polarität* ('polarity, polar opposition'), and the native *Gegenteil* ('opposite, reverse').

The Greeks tended to view the world as constituted by opposed forces, qualities or substances (e.g. fire–water, the hot–the cold, the wet–the dry). Opposites play an important part in the thought of Anaximander, the Pythagoreans and especially Heraclitus. Heraclitus believed in the essential unity of opposites, and (like Hegel) often found confirmation of this in language: 'The bow [*biòs*] is called life [*bíos*], but its work is DEATH.' Plato and Aristotle analysed change as a passage from one opposite to another. They also tended to regard intermediate things as a mixture of opposites, colours, e.g., as various combinations of black and white.

The idea that opposites coincide in the INFINITE (God) was espoused by Nicholas of Cusa: since God transcends reason, human contrasts and contradictions dissolve in his presence. He gives several mathematical illustrations of this: e.g. as the diameter of a circle is increased the curvature of its circumference decreases; thus if the diameter is increased to infinity, it coincides with a straight line (*On Learned Ignorance*, I. 13ff). Giordano Bruno held that the oppositions and conflicts that occur throughout the universe and our experience of it are sustained and harmonized by the divine unity.

Goethe and the ROMANTICS endorsed the idea that the world essentially involves opposition or polarity. Hamann invoked the principle of the coincidence of opposites against Kant's dichotomies, and the principle is central to Schelling's thought. In his earliest works, Schelling viewed opposites as Fichte did: one opposite (e.g. the I*) POSITS the other (e.g. the non-I). But in his philosophy of IDENTITY, opposites (SUBJECT and OBJECT, SPIRIT and NATURE) emerge from the division of a primordial unity. In *B*, he paraphrases Giordano's claim that 'he who wants to know nature's deepest secrets must observe and contemplate the minimum and maximum values [which, for Bruno, coincide] of contraries and opposites. There is a deep magic in being able to draw out the contrary after one has found the point of union' (*Della causa, principio ed uno* (*On Cause, Principle and Unity*), V, 1584). Schelling (like Hegel) was also influenced by such polar phenomena as magnetism and electricity.

Opposition is also a feature of concepts and propositions: Aristotle distinguished opposite or contrary propositions (e.g. 'All A's are B' and 'No A's are B') from contradictory propositions ('All A's are B' and 'Some A's are not B'). But *Gegensatz* covers both CONTRADICTION (e.g. '(It is) red' and '(It is) not red') and contrariety ('black' and 'white'). Thus in his account of opposition Hegel includes a discussion of the law of the excluded middle or of 'opposition' (*Gegensatz*), as well as of positive and negative numbers (*Enc.* I §119).

Polar opposition is central to Hegel's thought. Its central features are these:

1. A thing has only one opposite: if north is opposed to south, it cannot be opposed to anything else. (This principle was enunciated by Plato and endorsed by Aristotle. Aristotle used it to detect ambiguities in words: if 'sharp' is the opposite of both 'flat' and 'blunt', 'sharp' has two senses.)

2. If two things are opposed, they essentially involve each other and cannot be separated. A physical example of this that occurs throughout his works is the magnet: there cannot be a bar of metal that is magnetized only at one end; if a magnet is sawn in half through its point of indifference or neutrality, the result is not two half-magnets, each with only one magnetic pole, but two complete magnets, since what was the point of indifference is now magnetically polarized; each pole has generated its complementary opposite. As a *general* principle, the inseparability of opposites is more plausibly seen as conceptual, rather than physical: e.g. if a person is (described as) an introvert or a swan is (described as) white, it follows not that the same person is also an extrovert or that the same swan is also black, but that we are ready to apply the words 'extrovert' and 'black', if the need arises, or perhaps that some (other) things are extrovert or black. But Hegel argues, wherever possible, that the conceptual interdependence of opposites means that wherever one of two opposites occurs, they both occur to the same degree: to the extent that a person, or a state of a person, is e.g. INNER, it is to the same extent also OUTER. It is, on his view, absurd to hope to eliminate evil from the world (or even from an individual person), since evil is a necessary condition of the good.

3. In the case of some oppositions, Hegel argues not only that each opposite requires or involves the other, but that each opposite equally is, or becomes, the other. This is particularly true of the positive and the negative: if we represent steps taken to the west by positive numbers and steps to the east by negative numbers, we may equally well represent steps to the west as negative and steps to the east as positive; we can either represent credits as positive and debits as negative, or vice versa, especially since 'credit' and 'debit' are relative terms: one person's credit is another's debit. But what follows from this is that, of any pair of opposites, either may be represented as positive or negative, not that the opposites are the same as each other: it is possible, if unnatural, to represent a person's defects as positive and his merits as negative, but it does not follow that his defects are merits and his merits defects. In *PS*, III, Hegel examines the idea, suggested e.g. by the Sermon on the Mount and by Sophocles' *Antigone*, that there is a world beyond the world of APPEARANCE, in which opposites are reversed, what is right here is wrong there, etc. But he rejects this hypothesis in favour of the unity of opposites in *this* world. (The association of this 'inverted world (*verkehrte Welt*)' with Plato's forms or Kant's THING IN ITSELF is erroneous, since neither of these involves an inversion of the phenomenal world.)

4. Some opposites are distinguishable from each other not intrinsically, but only by their opposition to each other: the north and south poles of magnets

are distinguishable only by the fact that like poles repel each other, while unlike poles attract; if they reversed their polarity, but continued to repel and attract each other as they do now, we would not detect the change. (*PS*, III and *Enc*. II §314 refer to the poles of magnets as 'like-named' and 'unlike-named', rather than 'like' and 'unlike', since there is no *intrinsic* difference between the poles.) But this is not true of all opposites: a change of black things to white and of white things to black would be detectable.

5. Opposites pass over into each other when they reach their extreme point. Nicholas of Cusa's example can be restated in terms of true, rather than false, INFINITY: A circle on the surface of a sphere (e.g. the earth), if enlarged sufficiently, becomes a great circle (whose centre is the centre of the sphere), any arc of which is the shortest distance between its end-points and thus a straight line or geodesic. If I walk far enough to the north, I eventually begin to walk to the south. Movement to the east, conversely, never becomes movement to the west (since east and west are non-polar directions), but it eventually brings me closer to, rather than further from, my starting-point. In *PS*, IV.A., complete mastery over a slave leads to a reversal of the positions of master and slave: the master's refusal to recognize the slave reduces the slave to something whose RECOGNITION of the master is worthless and the master is master over nothing, while, conversely, the slave's obligation to work, etc., confers on him a type of SELF-CONSCIOUSNESS that eludes his master; overwhelming victory becomes defeat, and defeat becomes victory. The tendency of opposed *concepts* to pass over into each other is one of the moving forces of Hegel's DIALECTIC: e.g. pure BEING becomes pure NOTHING, and vice versa. Such reversals involve an intrinsic NEGATIVE unity of the two concepts.

6. Thus for Hegel, unlike Schelling, opposites do not become one in (or emerge from) a neutral ABSOLUTE or point of indifference, but are transformed into each other at their highest points. Their ultimate unification in the absolute IDEA is not blank neutrality, but a CONCRETE TOTALITY or SYSTEM, which SUBLATES opposition, but does not dissolve it.

Hegel's account is marred by a failure to distinguish different types of opposition (e.g. north/south, east/west, red/non-red, black/white, male/female) and different ways in which the opposites entail, become, etc., each other. His thought on opposition is thus sporadically illuminating rather than systematic.

organism, organic *see* LIFE AND LIVING ORGANISMS

ought The verb *sollen* is a modal auxiliary, etymologically related to *Schuld* ('debt, guilt, responsibility', but originally 'obligation') and to the English 'shall'. In contrast to *wollen*, which expresses the will of the agent (as in 'I am going to (*Ich will*) fast'), *sollen* expresses the will of someone or something (e.g. FATE) else (as in 'I am to (*Ich soll*) fast' or 'thou shall(st) (*Du sollst*) not kill'). In contrast to *müssen* ('must'), which suggests that something cannot but occur or be the case, *sollen* leaves open the possibility that it will not occur or is not the case. Hence it often corresponds to 'ought' or 'should'. But it often means 'to be said to, supposed to', as in 'he is said/supposed to be ill', or 'to be going, destined to', as in 'That was (going, destined) to be our last encounter', and so on.

'Ought' or 'the ought' (*das Sollen*) was central to Kant's account of MORALITY: It expresses the moral or rational NECESSITY of an ACTION, not from natural or physical causes, but from a concept of practical reason. It can thus be true only of rational beings that they ought to do something. On the other hand, it can be true only of rational beings who are in part *natural* beings, viz. burdened with desires, etc., not fully under the sway of REASON, that they *ought* to do things, since the will and conduct of a fully rational being would be automatically determined by reason, which would thus not present itself to him as an 'ought' or obligation.

Kant sees the Ought as presenting us with an infinite task, viz. a task that can be completed only at INFINITY: I ought to be perfectly morally good, but however many dutiful actions I perform, I shall never attain this state in a finite period of time. It does not follow that I should abandon my efforts, since I can become ever morally better, just as counting '1, ½, ¼, . . .' brings me ever closer to '0'. Since it would be morally absurd if my efforts were to be cut short by DEATH, it is a 'postulate of pure practical reason' that men are immortal and can continue their moral striving after death. (God and FREEDOM are also such postulates.)

Fichte took over Kant's notion of the ought, and made it the centre of his system. The pure I* POSITS an external world primarily as an arena for its moral striving (*Streben*). The goal of the finite I, of the I that has a non-I over against it, is to restore itself to the status of the pure I, to become a purely rational being whose will and conduct are exclusively determined by reason and morality. But this is an infinite task that it ought to, but will never in fact, complete. Schelling abandoned this feature of Kant's and Fichte's thought, since he rated NATURE and ART more highly than morality: nature is not simply a presupposition of morality, and the perfection of the work of art, together with the fusion of rational purposiveness and raw natural force in the artistic genius, supplies a unifying conclusion to the system of philosophy that the moral imperfection of men cannot, and need not, provide.

Kant's notion of the ought transgresses two central Hegelian principles: (1) It involves a sharp OPPOSITION between what is the case (or ACTUALITY) and what ought to be the case. (2) It involves a bad infinite regress.

1. Hegel rejects any claim that the world, the present state of the world, or the present state of one's own society is radically other than it ought to be, independently of whether the claim generates an infinite regress:
   (a)   Even if such a claim were true, no one is in a position to make it: There is no otherwordly standard against which this world can be assessed; criteria for judging the world or a society must be found within it, and thus cannot substantiate a thoroughgoing rejection of it. The person best able to assess his society as a whole is the philosopher, since he stands at some distance from it and has access

not only to other societies and historical periods, but to the rational structure of things. But he comes on the scene when things are already moving on, and his task is essentially retrospective (and, Hegel argues, reconciliatory).

(b)   No such a claim is ever true, since there can be no radical rift between reason (or the IDEA) and actuality. Hegel fuses together theology (the world is governed by divine PROVIDENCE), metaphysics (it is imbued with THOUGHT and is rationally intelligible), and evaluation (it is good). His idea is not so much that the world at any given stage is impeccable, as that it corrects its own defects in its onward movement and does not need criticism or correction by an external observer.

2. Hegel associates the ought with the notions of LIMIT, RESTRICTION and FINITUDE: A restriction is essentially something that ought to be overcome, and, conversely, if something ought to be the case, this implies a restriction or obstacle that needs to be overcome. Thus the ought is for Hegel not only a moral ought, but is a feature of any infinite regress, e.g. the quantitative regresses of numbers and of SPACE and TIME. But often the ought is a moral ought and implies an endless striving towards the good. As such, Hegel has two main objections to it:

(a)   The ought is an attempt to resolve a CONTRADICTION, between, e.g., my rational self and my sensory, bodily nature, or between rationality and the actual state of the world. But a contradiction cannot be properly resolved by resorting to an infinite regress. It is pointless to embark on an infinite task, since one makes no headway: as soon as one has got the stone to the top of the hill, it rolls back down again.

(b)   The task must be infinite, since moral activity contradictorily *requires* what it attempts to overcome. If I were to subdue completely my animal nature or make the world wholly as it ought to be, my moral activity would cease altogether. Kant and Fichte attempt to postpone this unwelcome outcome by locating it at infinity. But the contradiction still remains.

Neither of these objections is very weighty: an infinite task is pointless if one makes no headway, but Kant's and Fichte's task is not of this type – one continually *improves* oneself (or the world), even if one can never *perfect* it. Hegel ignores the distinction between regresses that converge on a limit and those that do not. Again, it is not unreasonable to aim at a goal, which, if it were reached, would make such activity impossible. It is sensible, e.g., to improve one's skill at chess, even though the interest of chess depends on the imperfections one is trying to overcome and would disappear if one achieved perfection. There is similarly no incoherence in attempting to relieve poverty, even though complete (and improbable) success would undercut one's activity, as long as one does not secretly hope for harvests to fail in order to have scope for munificence.

Hegel (like Aristotle) found it hard to accept that much valuable activity consists in striving for goals, which, once attained, are less valuable than the striving: climbers enjoy trying to reach the top of mountains more than they enjoy *being* at the top of them; we enjoy research and discovery more than the contemplation of our results, etc. But for Hegel it is more satisfying to participate in an on-going social order than to attempt continually to put the world right. Participating in a society or in an established body of knowledge is not wholly static and has some of the attractions of striving, both because a result (e.g. the absolute idea) SUBLATES and preserves the conflicts and OPPOSITIONS that led up to it, and because the status quo or the world as it now is often includes such movements beyond itself as Caesar's and Napoleon's battles. (Caesar, Napoleon and their followers are conceived not as external critics attempting to make the world as it ought to be, but as agents of the onward march of the world SPIRIT.) Nevertheless, DEATH results from a sophisticated contentment with the world.

P

---

people and nation *Volk* means 'people', both in the sense of the 'common people', in contrast to their leaders, and in that of a community united by customs, sentiments and language. It originally meant the 'multitude', especially the mass of the army. But with the rise of nationalism it acquired the sense of a people related by language, customs, culture and history, which may, but need not, be united in a single STATE. It is not sharply distinct in sense from *Nation*, imported in the fourteenth century from the Latin *natio*, which comes from *nasci* ('to be born') and thus indicates a collection of people inhabiting a single area and related by birth. But from the eighteenth century *Nation* acquires political overtones and denotes a community aware of a shared political and cultural heritage and aiming to form a state, even if it does not yet do so.

The concepts *Volk* and *Nation* were influenced by developments in France and especially by Montesquieu, whose *L'Esprit des lois* (*Spirit of the Laws*, 1748) considered the implications of national differences for laws and the constitution. The expression 'spirit of the nation' (*esprit de la nation*) first appears in Montesquieu (whom Hegel mentions with approval in *ETW*, as well as in later works): it is the result of the influence of historical events and of the natural environment on a people's character.

But the German interest in people and nation had several sources: The division of the German people into several states and their humiliation by the French led to an emphasis on the *Volk* or *Nation* and on the desirability of its political unification. Fichte (in *AGN*), Schleiermacher and F. Schlegel all insisted on the importance of the nation-state. The historical interests of Herder and of jurists such as Savigny gave rise to the notion of the *Volksgeist* or 'SPIRIT of a people', which, in contrast to Montesquieu's *esprit de la nation*, is an active, creative, but unconscious, force that moulds a people's history and DESTINY (*Schicksal*). The expression '*Genius* of a *Volk*' appears in this sense in Herder, and *Volksgeist* in *ETW*. Herder and the ROMANTICS stressed INDIVIDUALITY, the differences not only between individual men, but between individual peoples, in contrast to the uniform rationality valued by the Enlightenment. The romantics regarded what is peculiar to a *Volk* as a matter of FEELING rather than REASON. (But at *Enc*. III §394 and A. Hegel considers differences in national character under the heading of the 'natural SOUL' rather than of the 'feeling soul'.) Thus *Volk* combines the ideas of national peculiarity and of the primitive or primordial.

Herder was especially interested in 'folk-poetry' (*Volksdichtung*), poetry which emerges from, and expresses, the vital energy of a people, in contrast to poetry based on foreign models: he regards as folk-poetry such diverse works as the Bible, Homer, Shakespeare and folk-songs. (In *LA* Hegel gives Herder credit for drawing attention to folk-song.) The rediscovery of the ancient songs and legends of the German *Volk* will, Herder argues, contribute to a German literature comparable to that of other European nations, since *Volksdichtung* is nourished by such anonymous material. His views had considerable influence, e.g. on the Grimms.

Volk and compounds containing it occur throughout Hegel's work: *Volksgeist*, *Volksglaube* ('popular FAITH or BELIEF'), *Volkspoesie*, *Volksreligion*, etc. (Some, such as *Völkerrecht*, which is simply the 'law of nations' or 'international law', involve no reference to the *spirit* of a people.) He believed in general that a people has a distinctive character or spirit, which is in part the product of its historical circumstances and natural environment, but which also gives a common flavour to its language, customs, etc., and also to its laws and political constitution. HISTORY is the successive emergence of such *Volksgeiste* on the world stage: each one actualizes itself to its full extent and then, since it is only a limited or restricted fragment of the world-spirit, gives way to its successor.

But Hegel did not share all the views often associated with a stress on the *Volk* and *Volksgeist*. Savigny held, for example, that LAWS begin not with formal legislation, but with the native CUSTOMS of a people. Law, like language, is a result of the organic development of a people. It is, he inferred, a mistake for a legislator to attempt to impose a universal law-code on a people; at most he should codify existing customs. Hegel agreed that the pre-existing customs of a people are a condition of, and set limits to, legislation. But it is essential to the development of a people that it should be given universal, rational laws that go beyond what is implicit in their customs. A law may have arisen in a historically intelligible way from a people's customs and yet be irrational and unjustified (*PR*, §3). There is thus a distinction between the unreflective, uncultivated *Volk* and the reflective, developed *Volk*, with, e.g., a rational law-code. The DEVELOPMENT of the first into the second is not, on Hegel's view, smooth and organic, but requires the ALIENATION from traditional practices that CULTURE essentially involves. It is, for example, crucial to the growth of the German people that their scholarly and scientific works were once produced in French or Latin, that the Bible was translated into German (by Luther) only in the sixteenth century, and that they learn ancient languages.

Hegel's attitude to the *Volk* and *Volksgeist* exemplifies this pattern in other spheres: A state presupposes a *Volk* or *Nation*, with beliefs and institutions shaped by its *Volksgeist*. But the modern state can accommodate, and accord civil RIGHTS to, minorities who do not accept these beliefs and institutions (such as Quakers, Anabaptists and Jews), and it should do so simply because they are *men* (*PR* §270). Art may presuppose folk-art, but it is inappropriate for a modern poet (such as Klopstock) to attempt to do for the Germans what Homer did for the Greeks by reviving Germanic deities and heroes who have no connection with our present life. The enthusiasm displayed in *ETW* for

213

Greek folk-religion, in contrast to Christian positive (or rational) religion, wanes in later years; he is not inclined to favour a belief or practice solely because it is traditional and customary and regardless of its rational content. In *LPH*, Hegel condemns the attempts by, e.g., Schelling and Schlegel to locate deep wisdom in a postulated primeval people, whose memory is preserted in myths and legends. Legends are of little use for history.

In general the *Volk* and *Volksgeist* become less significant the higher up the cultural scale we ascend. The characteristics of a particular people are especially marked on certain ART-forms, such as lyric poetry and Italian opera. They become less significant in the case of RELIGION, and virtually disappear when we come to philosophy, the highest form of ABSOLUTE spirit. The German language, for example, may have certain features which can be exploited for the purposes of logic. But the Logic often uses German words in novel senses and could find similar words and expressions to exploit in other languages. Philosophy and logic present a single, universal system of REASON, that is not confined to any particular *Volksgeist*.

phenomenology The word *Phänomenologie* comes from the Greek *logos* ('word, reason, doctrine, theory', etc.) and *phainomenon* ('APPEARANCE'), which entered German, in the seventeenth century, as *Phänomen*. *Phainomenon* and the corresponding verb, *phainesthai*, are (like 'apparent' and 'appear') ambiguous: (1) 'appearance', 'to appear', in contrast to what is the case; (2) 'what is plain to see', 'to be, become plain to see', both literally and metaphorically. Thus *Phänomenologie* is the study of appearances in either of these two senses.

The word first appears in J. H. Lambert's *NO*. This work has four parts: (1) *Dianoologie* or the doctrine of the laws of thinking; (2) *Alethiologie* or the doctrine of truth in so far as it is opposed to error; (3) *Semiotik* or the doctrine of the designation of thoughts and things; (4) *Phänomenologie* or the doctrine of appearance (*Schein*). The aim of *Phänomenologie* is to 'avoid appearance/ illusion (*Schein*) in order to penetrate to the truth'. But *Schein* is not simply falsity: it is intermediate between TRUTH and falsity. Thus optics discovers laws of perspective which enable us to determine, from the visual *Schein* of a thing, the true nature of the thing, and, conversely, to determine from the nature of a thing what will be its *Schein* from a given perspective. The procedures of optics can be generalized to cover the whole range of *Scheine*: sensory, psychological, moral, the probable (*das Wahrscheinliche*, literally 'the truth-like, verisimilitude'), etc. *Phänomenologie* is thus a 'transcendent optics': it discovers the 'transcendent perspective' by which each type of *Schein* is related to the truth and thus enables us to determine the truth from the *Schein*. The result of this will be not piecemeal information, but a complete system of scientific cognition.

Herder valued Lambert's phenomenology and foresaw a phenomenology of aesthetics: 'since visible beauty is nothing but appearance (*Erscheinung*), there is also a great and complete science of this appearance: an aesthetic phenomenology that awaits a second Lambert' (*Kritische Wälder* (*Critical Woods*), IV, 1769). This work was not published until 1846, but references to a 'phenomenology of the beautiful' occur elsewhere in his writings. His phenomenological accounts of sight, hearing and touch, in relation to painting, music and sculpture, foreshadow parts of *LA*, but have little bearing on *PS*.

Kant's *MENS* consists of four parts: *Phoronomie*, *Dynamik*, *Mechanik* and *Phänomenologie*. *Phänomenologie* considers 'motion and rest merely in relation to the mode of representation or modality, hence as an appearance of the external senses'. It is thus far narrower in scope than Lambert's or Hegel's phenomenology. But Kant's letters to Lambert show that he originally planned a work on phenomenology in Lambert's sense: 'It seems that metaphysics must be preceded by a quite distinct, but merely negative science (*Phaenomenologia generalis*), which will determine the validity and limits of the principles of sensibility, so that they do not confuse judgments about objects of pure reason' (2 September 1770). In a letter to Herz, Kant projected a work entitled *The Limits of Sensibility and Reason*, the first section of which was to be *Die phaenomenologie überhaupt* ('Phenomenology in general') (21 February 1772). The work did not materialize, but *CPR* contains elements of a phenomenological enterprise in the 'Transcendental Aesthetic' (on sensory appearance (*Erscheinung*)) and in the 'Transcendental Dialectic' (on the 'transcendental illusion (*Schein*)'). At *Enc.* III §415, Hegel argues that Kant presents a phenomenology, rather than a philosophy, of spirit, but for the quite different reason that Kant considers the I* in relation to an independent THING IN ITSELF.

Fichte too, in his *Wissenschaftslehre* (*Theory of Knowledge*) of 1804, suggested that a '*Phänomenologie*, a theory of appearance and illusion' (*Erscheinungs-und Scheinlehre*), was needed to complement the *Wissenschaftslehre*. *Wissenschaftslehre* shows that CONSCIOUSNESS is the 'original fact (*Urfaktum*) and source of everything factual (*Faktischen*)'. *Phänomenologie*, conversely, will derive the factual, what (illusorily) appears to be other than consciousness, from consciousness.

Hegel mentions Lambert only to deplore his (in fact considerable) contributions to symbolic logic, but he was no doubt aware of *NO*, and also of Kant's correspondence with him, which was published in 1786. He associates *Phänomenologie* with 'appearance' (*Erscheinung*), rather than with 'illusion' (*Schein*), and with 'SPIRIT'. The 'phenomenology of spirit' is equivalent to the 'doctrine of the appearances of spirit'. But the expression has more than one meaning:

1. Spirit *appears* (or 'goes forth') in so far as it is consciousness of an OBJECT other than itself. *Phänomenologie* in this sense contrasts with *Anthropologie*, the study of the SOUL that is enclosed within itself and not yet conscious of external objects, and with *Psychologie*, the study of spirit as it is intrinsically or IN AND FOR ITSELF, regardless of its relations to objects.

2. But spirit as consciousness or as it appears is not simply one phase of spirit, or one way in which spirit may be viewed. It also involves illusion, in that spirit projects onto objects what is in fact its own doing. The distinct types of object that it encounters and its elevation from one type to the next

are due to intrinsic features of spirit itself, but it sees them as features of the objects. Hence consciousness of objects is not only not the highest way of *viewing* spirit; it is not the highest phase of spirit, but one that it must supersede. (A way of viewing spirit, such as psychology, is itself a phase of spirit: spirit itself must advance if it is to view itself in a more advanced way.)

3. But *PS* is concerned not only with the general illusion involved in consciousness as such, but with the possibility that any given 'form of consciousness' is illusory, that its intentional objects or its conception of objects may not correspond to the actual objects. Hegel proposes to solve this problem not, like Lambert, by considering the relationship between the appearance and the actual object, but by an internal examination of each form of consciousness and of the way in which its intrinsic defects transform it into a different form of consciousness. Hegel and Lambert share the aim of reaching truth by way of appearance. But while for Lambert the truth or falsity of an appearance lies in its relationship to an object distinct from it, for Hegel it lies within appearance itself, and truth is attainable by surveying the breakdown of each appearance into its successor (its proximate truth) until we reach absolute KNOWLEDGE, in which appearances and their intrinsic defects are SUBLATED.

4. Thus the appearance of spirit is not simply its consciousness of an object at any one stage, but its appearance on the scene or its emergence from its humble beginnings in SENSORY CERTAINTY. 'Spirit' has several senses: In a wide sense, it includes even elementary forms of consciousness such as sensory certainty, and in this sense spirit is the subject-matter of *PS* from the start; in a narrower sense, it enters the scene only with interpersonal ETHICAL LIFE (*PS*, VI); in a narrower sense still, spirit is only fully realized when it attains to 'absolute KNOWLEDGE' (*PS*, VIII). Thus what is spirit only in a wider sense is a stage in the appearance or emergence of spirit (in a narrower sense).

Hegel considers the phenomenology of spirit not only in *PS*, but in *Enc.* III. In *Enc.* III it has a far narrower range than in *PS*, covering only consciousness and SELF-CONSCIOUSNESS (with a short section on REASON); it excludes (as well as anthropology and psychology) objective and absolute spirit, which both appear (in a different form) in *PS*. Hegel's lectures at Nuremberg (*PP*) also restrict phenomenology to consciousness and distinguish it from psychology, politics, etc.

Phenomenology of Spirit (1807) The full title of this work is: *System of Science: First Part, the Phenomenology of Spirit* (*System der Wissenschaft: Erster Teil, die Phänomenologie des Geistes*). It was originally conceived as the introductory part of the system which Hegel had had in view in his writings and lectures at Jena. After some false starts, he began in the winter of 1805–6 to write the introduction to his system, which, together with the Logic, was planned to occupy the first volume. But the introduction expanded, and by the summer of 1806 was conceived as a separate part.

The subtitle was originally intended to be '*First Part. Science of the Experience of Consciousness*'; this appeared on some printed copies, and still appears in some modern editions (e.g. Hoffmeister's) between the Preface and the Introduction. The word *Phänomenologie* first appears in Hegel's announcement of his lectures for the winter of 1806–7: '(a) Logic and metaphysics or speculative philosophy, preceded by phenomenology of spirit, according to his forthcoming book, *System of Science* . . .' The original subtitle was then replaced by '*I. Science of the Phenomenology of Spirit*', which appeared between the Preface and the Introduction in some copies of the first edition.

In a brief 'Notice' of his book, Hegel announced that it was to be followed by a second volume, containing 'the system of *Logic* as speculative philosophy and of the two other parts of philosophy, the *Sciences* of *Nature* and of *Spirit*' (*Intelligenzblatt der Jenaer Allgemeinen Literatur-Zeitung*, 28 October 1807). In his Preface to the first edition of *SL* (22 March 1812), Hegel confirms that this was his original plan, but adds that since the Logic has expanded into a separate volume, an account of the two 'real' sciences will follow later. A note added in his revision of *SL* (1831) says that in the second edition of *PS*, to be published 'next Easter' (1832), the title '*System of Science*' will be removed, since the original plan has been superseded by *Enc.* Hegel began revising *PS* for a second edition in the spring of 1831, but he got no further than the first half of the Preface; J. Schulze's edition of 1832, for the posthumous collected *Works*, incorporated these revisions.

PS opens with a long Preface (composed after the rest of the work), which gives a general survey of Hegel's projected system and its relationship to the culture of the time. In his 'Notice', Hegel says that the Preface gives his views on 'the need of philosophy at its present standpoint' and on the 'presumption and plague of philosophical formulae which at present degrades philosophy'. This and other remarks, such as the criticism of the empty ABSOLUTE, are aimed at, among others, Schelling: *PS* was the first public airing of Hegel's differences with him. (But Hegel was much influenced by some of Schelling's other ideas, especially that of a HISTORY (*Geschichte*) of SELF-CONSCIOUSNESS in, e.g., *STI*.)

The Preface (*Vorrede*) is followed by a briefer Introduction (*Einleitung*), in which Hegel explains the problem of COGNITION, to which *PS* is, in part, a response: If the OBJECT of cognition is distinct from cognition itself, how can we be sure that the two conform? Hegel rejects the view (Kant's), that, regarding cognition as a tool, we should examine it before putting it to work on objects, and the view (Lambert's) that, regarding cognition as a medium, we can discover the law of refraction that governs its distortion of the 'ray' from the object. Both views assume, e.g., that cognition can at least supply reliable information about itself. He proposes an examination of CONSCIOUSNESS that is internal to consciousness itself and assesses it by its own standards. Each form of consciousness will be found wanting, and will become the object of the next form of consciousness. Hegel's 'Notice' says that *PS* 'portrays the rise of knowledge (*das werdende* ("BECOMING") *Wissen*)' and 'is to supplant psychological explanations and also the more abstract investigations of the grounding of knowledge'.

The 'Notice' summarizes the main body of the work as follows:

It conceives the various FORMS [*Gestalten*] of the spirit as stations on the way in(to) itself [*Stationen des Weges in sich*], the way by which it becomes pure knowledge or absolute spirit. The main sections of the science, which are in turn subdivided, thus consider: consciousness, self-consciousness, observing and active reason, spirit itself as ethical, cultivated and moral spirit, and finally as religious spirit in its different forms. The wealth of appearances [*Erscheinungen*] of spirit, which at first sight seems chaotic, is presented in its NECESSITY: imperfect appearances dissolve and pass into higher ones that are their proximate TRUTH. They reach the ultimate truth initially in religion, and then in science, the result of the whole.

The original subtitle of *PS*, and the Introduction, imply that *PS*, like the phenomenology section of *Enc.* III, will be concerned solely with consciousness of objects. But its subject-matter expands far beyond consciousness as such into the interpersonal social and historical forms of spirit, which occupy the second half of *PS* (VIff). Here the transitions from one form of spirit to the next bear little relation to the schema outlined in the Introduction. Hegel believes that 'knowledge' is not sharply distinct from our practical activities and attitudes, that it is not an exclusively individual accomplishment but involves a variety of interpersonal relationships, that it, or what we know, is not identical from one historical period to the next, and that what we know in any one historical epoch depends on what happened, both with respect to knowledge and in other respects, in earlier epochs. Thus what was originally intended to supply an introduction to SCIENCE transcends its pedagogic aim to become a more or less complete survey of human CULTURE and history of the world.

But *PS* does not present history in a straightforward way. 'Consciousness' (I–III) is not located in a specific historical epoch. 'Self-consciousness' (IV) proceeds from prehistory (the struggle for RECOGNITION) to Greece and Rome (STOICISM and SCEPTICISM) and medieval Christianity (unhappy consciousness). 'REASON' (V) considers modern science and MORALITY. 'Spirit' (VI) returns to early Greek ETHICAL LIFE and proceeds down to the French Revolution and post-revolutionary morality. 'Religion' (VII) traces religion from ancient Israel and/or Persia down to Christianity. Historical epochs are thus treated as paradigms of phases of thought and culture; often, but not invariably, the logical or systematic order of these phases coincides with the order of their emergence in history.

History was often seen, in Hegel's day, as the result of the emergence and dominance of successively higher psychological faculties, types of reason or phases of religious development. Often the DEVELOPMENT of an individual is held to pass through the same stages as the history of the race. Hegel's intertwining of history, psychology and epistemology is close to Schiller:

Those three MOMENTS [the 'physical' state of nature's domination of man, the 'aesthetic' state of his emancipation from nature, and the 'moral' state of man's mastery over nature] are, in general, three different epochs in the development both of humanity as a whole and in the whole development of an individual man; but they can also be discerned in every individual perception of an object and are, in short, the necessary conditions of every cognition that we obtain through our senses. (*AE*, XXV)

'Absolute knowledge', with which *PS* concludes, is, in part, the knowledge that Hegel himself displays in writing *PS*. It involves an insight into the various forms of spirit and of their interrelationships that no previous form of spirit had, and also an ability to reconstruct the logic, which has, in part, governed the development of spirit portrayed in *PS*. Absolute knowledge has been prepared for by the development of spirit over history, and the individual reader is introduced to it by studying *PS*.

Hegel later expresses some dissatisfaction with the conception and execution of *PS*. What role does *PS* play in his mature system? As a pedagogical *introduction* to the system, it is dispensable, since although Hegel regarded *some* introduction as necessary, he supplies an alternative introduction, the account of the 'attitudes of thought to objectivity' (Leibniz, Wolff et al., Kant and Jacobi) at *Enc.* I §§25–78. Since the system forms a circle, *Enc.* III can also serve as an introduction to *Enc.* I. As an account of the historical route by which humanity attained to absolute knowledge, it is also dispensable, since although Hegel believed some such account to be required, this need is met by *Enc.* III (which, as a record of the development of spirit, is also historical) and by the historical lectures accompanying it. Nevertheless, *PS* is a rich, if chaotic, work that contains material (on sensory certainty, on physiognomy and phrenology, etc.) that does not appear elsewhere in Hegel.

philosophy The Greek *philosophos*, from *philos*, *philein* ('friend', 'to love') and *sophos*, *sophia* ('wise', 'wisdom', etc.) and thus meaning 'lover of wisdom', is said to have been coined by Pythagoras. Originally, it had strong religious and ethical overtones (which persist in Plato's *Phaedo*). But for Aristotle *philosophia* is equivalent to *epistēmē* ('rational knowledge'). In Plato *philosophos* contrasts with *sophistēs*, which originally denoted anyone of high scientific achievements, but later referred to the professional teachers of the Greek enlightenment, whom Socrates and Plato despised, and thus acquired the flavour of 'sophistry' or pseudo-philosophy. But *philosophia* does not, at this stage, contrast with other branches of knowledge. Aristotle divides it or *epistēmē* into three branches: *praktikē* (i.e. ethics and politics), *poiētikē* (i.e. productive, especially of poems), and *theōretikē*. Theoretical philosophy is in turn divided into *prōtē philosophia* or *theologikē* ('first philosophy, theology', which studies both the divine substances and the general features of all beings as such), physics (including cosmology and psychology), and mathematics. The STOICS divided philosophy into physics, ethics and logic.

Under the influence of Plato, Aristotle and the Stoics, the medieval scholastics divided philosophy into METAPHYSICS, including ontology and (natural, but not revealed) THEOLOGY, physics (including cosmology and psychology), and ethics (including politics). With such additions as the theory or 'critique' of knowledge and AESTHETICS (Baumgarten), this division persisted into eighteenth-century Germany. But the growth of the natural and other sciences meant that philosophy needed to be distinguished from them. Hence by Hegel's day 'physics' is replaced by 'philosophy of NATURE' and 'psychology' by 'philosophy of MIND or SPIRIT'. For Hegel philosophy has three main branches: logic, philosophy of nature and philosophy of spirit (*Enc.* I, II and III). The philosophy of spirit includes various other philosophies: the philosophy of RIGHT, the philosophy of HISTORY, aesthetics or the philosophy of ART and the philosophy of RELIGION.

The main German words for 'philosophy', etc., derive from the Greek, via Latin: *Philosoph* ('philosopher') and *Philosophie* were introduced in the late fifteenth century, *philosophisch* ('philosophical') and *philosophieren* ('to philosophize') in the sixteenth century. Native German coinages were relatively unsuccessful: Paracelsus used *Weltweisheit* ('world(ly), secular wisdom') for 'philosophy', in contrast to *Theosophie* ('divine, sacred wisdom') or *Theologie*. This word was common in the eighteenth century as a term for *Philosophie*, and was revived by F. von Schlegel, with the aim of disqualifying philosophy from the discussion of, e.g., religion. In *LHP*, Hegel agrees that the word had a point in so far as it expressed the concern of philosophy for FINITE, worldly matters, in contrast to an otherworldy religion, but argues that since philosophy is also concerned with the divine IDEA and has the same purpose as religion, the term is not appropriate. Fichte attempted to replace *Philosophie* by the native *Wissenschaftslehre* ('theory of science or knowledge'), but conceded that the word had not taken root. Hegel, like many of his contemporaries, refers to philosophy as '(a) SCIENCE' (*Wissenschaft*) and to its branches as '(philosophical) sciences'. But this is intended to convey the systematic character of philosophy, not to replace the word *Philosophie*.

Hegel's brief definitions of philosophy (as, e.g., the 'thinking study of objects', *Enc.* I §2) are, as he admits, usually unilluminating. The meaning of *Philosophie* depends in part on the variety of enterprises with which it contrasts:

1. Philosophy is distinct from EXPERIENCE and the empirical disciplines. In England especially, the word 'philosophy' was applied to empirical disciplines: Newton's physics was regarded as 'natural philosophy' and Newton as a 'philosopher'; scientific apparatus was called 'philosophical instruments'; and statesmen (such as Canning) spoke of the application of philosophical maxims to administration (*Enc.* I §7). (Hegel was especially shocked by an advertisement in an English newspaper: 'The Art of Preserving the Hair, on Philosophical Principles, neatly printed on post 8vo, price seven shillings'.) Some of these matters are not the concern of philosophy in Hegel's sense; they are to be settled by experience. Others (such as Newton's laws or Grotius' work on international law) are too empirical to qualify as philosophy, but are a legitimate concern of philosophy. The philosopher thinks, at a higher level and more systematically, about the concepts involved in them, their presuppositions, their justification, etc. Hegel equivocates between the view that philosophy thinks directly about the objects of other disciplines (thinks, e.g., about NATURE), but thinks about them in a different way, and the view that philosophy thinks about the thinking involved in other disciplines (thinks, e.g., about physics).

2. Philosophy has the same 'CONTENT' as, but differs in 'FORM' from, art and, more especially, religion. Philosophy, like religion, is concerned with God, his creation of the world, etc., but (a) it reaches its conclusions by rational, conceptual thought, rather than by FAITH, authority or revelation; (b) it presents its conclusions in the form of thoughts or concepts, rather than pictorial CONCEPTIONS. Sometimes he stresses the supremely REFLECTIVE character of philosophy: philosophy thinks about religion, but religion cannot think about, or form a conception (*Vorstellung*) of, philosophy. In *LHP* he suggests that philosophy combines the free thinking of the empirical disciplines with the subject-matter of religion: 'It combines both aspects: the Sunday of life, on which man humbly sacrifices himself, and the weekday, on which he stands upright, is the master, and acts for his own interests.'

Hegel was troubled by a problem, which he derived from Schulze's SCEPTICISM: Given that there are so many competing, but internally coherent philosophies, how is one to decide which to adopt? One reply is that to abstain from philosophy for this reason is like refusing to eat apples, cherries, etc., because none of them is *fruit as such* (*Enc.* I §13). But different philosophies are not co-ordinate species, like types of fruit. Apparently distinct philosophies complement each other, and display internal incoherences that can only be resolved by the transition to another philosophy. Higher philosophies (i.e. usually those that appear later in HISTORY) SUBLATE lower ones, embodying the principles that they advanced in isolation. Hegel's own philosophy is the UNIVERSAL philosophy that contains all that is true in earlier philosophies. One sign that a philosophy is higher than another is the ability of the first to reflect on the second in a way in which the second cannot reflect on the first: Hegel's philosophy can reflect not only on itself, but on all other philosophies, and is thus supreme among them. It does not follow that the novice can adopt Hegel's philosophy at once: but if he adopts some lower philosophy, he will, if he thinks hard enough (and with some guidance from Hegel), arrive at Hegel's own system.

Philosophy of Right (1821) (PR)   The full title is: *Foundations of the Philosophy of Right or Natural Right and Political Science in Outline* (*Grundlinien der Philosophie des Rechts oder Naturrecht und Staatswissenschaft im Grundrisse*). Like *Enc.*, it was intended as a textbook to accompany Hegel's lectures and thus consists of numbered paragraphs, which are often brief and obscure. But Hegel added more leisurely 'Remarks' for the general reader, and, in his edition of 1833, E. Gans interspersed 'Additions' from notes on Hegel's lectures. These Additions are reproduced in most subsequent editions and translations. Hegel made extensive notes on the first part of *PR* in his own copy of the work. These were published by Lasson in 1930 and are reprinted in Hoffmeister's 1955 edition of *PR*.

Recht ('RIGHT') has a wider meaning than any English word, and the work covers not only jurisprudence, but moral philosophy and political theory. The contents of *PR* are these:

221

1. A Preface in which Hegel says that the work exemplifies the SPECULA-TIVE method of COGNITION explained and justified in *SL*; affirms, in opposition to the utopian moralizing personified by Fries, that 'what is RATIONAL is ACTUAL and what is actual is rational' and that we should 'recognize reason as the rose in the cross of the present'; and argues that philosophy cannot predict or prescribe the course of future events: 'When philosophy paints its grey in grey, then has a shape of life grown old. By philosophy's grey in grey it cannot be rejuvenated but only understood. The owl of Minerva [or Athena, the Greek goddess of wisdom, associated with the owl] spreads its wings only with the fall of dusk.'

2. An Introduction which explains that the work will develop the IDEA of right out of the CONCEPT of right. The idea of right is the concept of right together with its reality or actualization (*Verwirklichung*). Thus *PR* is not concerned with the merely positive and contingent details of social and political systems, but with their essential, rational structure. The concept of right is, on Hegel's view, the free WILL, and the Introduction describes the three phases of the will as successively more adequate notions of FREEDOM.

The structure of the will, i.e. the concept of right, supplies the framework for the division or CLASSIFICATION of the account of the actualization of the concept: (a) The IMMEDIATE will corresponds to ABSTRACT right; (b) The will reflected back into itself corresponds to MORALITY; (c) The union of (a) and (b) corresponds to ETHICAL LIFE. These three phases are successively more adequate realizations of the concept of right. Thus (a) is the abstract concept of right, analogous to the seed with the concept encoded in it, while (c) (or the final phase of (c), the STATE) is the fully realized concept, the idea, analogous to the fully grown plant. But although certain phases of right are especially associated with particular historical periods (e.g. abstract right with the Roman Empire), they are not historically successive: they are all essential elements or MOMENTS of the modern state, which SUBLATES and includes the central features of earlier political formations.

3. Abstract Right: The will is embodied in an external object, PROPERTY, and is thus a 'person'. This section has three subsections: (i) Property; (ii) Contract; (iii) Wrong. (iii) includes Hegel's main account of PUNISHMENT.

4. Morality: This includes an account of ACTION, and its three subdivisions are: (i) Design (*Vorsatz*) and Responsibility; (ii) Intention and Welfare; (iii) Good and Conscience.

5. Ethical Life: This section occupies more than half the book. Its three main subdivisions are:

(i) The FAMILY: This in turn is divided into (A) Marriage; (B) The Family Capital; (C) The EDUCATION of Children and the Dissolution of the Family (i.e. the dissolution of particular families by the DEATH of parents and the departure of children, not the dissolution of the family as such).

(ii) CIVIL SOCIETY: The three subdivisions are: (A) The SYSTEM of Needs (i.e. the economic system); (B) The Administration of Justice (*Die Rechtspflege*); (C) The Police and the Corporation.

(iii) The state: The subdivisions are: (A) Internal Constitutional Law

(*Das innere Staatsrecht*). (The first section of this deals with the main POWERS (*Gewalten*) or organs of the state: the princely power or crown, the governmental power or executive, and the legislative power. A brief second section deals with 'Sovereignty *vis-à-vis* foreign states' and argues that WAR between states is necessary and inevitable.) (B) International Law, which continues the account of war. (C) World History, a brief account of Hegel's view of HISTORY.

PR employs many concepts that are derived and explained in *SL*, and the TRIADS into which it is structured are usually intended to exemplify one or more logical patterns: (1) concept–reality–idea; (2) UNIVERSAL–PARTICULAR–INDIVIDUAL; (3) IN, FOR, IN AND FOR ITSELF. The family, for example, is universal and in itself, civil society is particular and for itself, and the state is individual and in and for itself. But the structure of the work as a whole does not correspond systematically to that of the Logic.

PR has a wider range and a greater wealth of detail than most comparable works, notably those of Kant (*MM*), and of Fichte (*FNR*). Among its distinctive features are: an attempt to integrate into a single theory *both* freedom of the will *and* social and political freedom; an attempt to sublate reflective, individualist morality into social morality or ethical life; the rejection of a sharp dichotomy between the individual and the state, and an account of the various intermediary institutions that prepare the individual for citizenship; a distinction between civil society and the state, and an account of the role of the economy in society, together with an appreciation of its need for regulation; and an appreciation of the role of warfare in the life of a state, and of the fact that a state is essentially one member of a system of states.

The feature of *PR* that has attracted most attention is the doctrine that everything actual is rational and Hegel's attempt to reconcile his contemporaries to a relatively liberal, but relatively undemocratic and hierarchical modern state. This issue, like that of GOD and RELIGION, divided his followers into 'left' and 'right' Hegelians. (The most renowned left Hegelian, Karl Marx, wrote a penetrating critique of the later parts of *PR*, the *Critique of Hegel's 'Philosophy of Right'*.) The issue involves several distinct questions:

(1) How objectionable is the state Hegel portrays?
(2) Does his portrayal of it imply an endorsement of the existing Prussian state, on which it is loosely modelled? (A. W. Wood argues, in *Hegel's Ethical Thought*, p. 13, that Hegel's rational state 'bears a striking resemblance', in e.g. proposing a constitutional rather than an absolute monarchy, not to the actual Prussian state, but to W. von Humboldt's and K. A. von Hardenberg's plans for a new constitution, drafted in 1819, but never realized.)
(3) Does Hegel's system, especially the DIALECTIC, entail an endorsement of, or 'reconciliation' with, the status quo, or is it (as Marx believed) incompatible with it?
(4) Is the endorsement of the modern state, or the equation of actuality

223

with rationality, intended to exclude future political transformations or only moralistic utopianism?

picture thinking *see* REPRESENTATION AND CONCEPTION

positing and presupposition   The verb *setzen* means 'to make sit' and the reflexive, *sich setzen*, is 'to sit down'. Often it is equivalent to its etymological relative, 'to set', but it occurs in many idioms (e.g. '*put/write* your name on the form'), where 'set' is inappropriate. The past participle, *gesetzt*, is used for 'assuming, supposing (that)' or 'let us assume, suppose (that)'.

The philosophical uses of *setzen* correspond to, and are influenced by, those of the Greek *tithenai*, *tithesthai* (1 'to place', 2 'to affirm, posit, assume'), but the common translation, 'to posit', comes from the past participle, *positus*, of the Latin *ponere* ('to put', etc.). It indicates, primarily (1) the assumption or supposition of a PROPOSITION (*Satz*); (2) the assertion or affirmation of a proposition, in contrast to its denial; (3) the affirmation or postulation of (the existence of) an entity. Fichte (and, under his influence, Schelling) uses *setzen* very frequently in a sense that combines the ideas of the assertion of propositions and the affirmation or positing of entities, and thus of intellectual assent and volitional affirmation or (self-)assertion. What is posited is not simply affirmed to be real, but is thereby made real: The absolute I* exists in virtue of its self-positing or self-assertion, and the non-I is realized by the positing of the I. In Fichte's usage, only a mind posits, and it does so non-temporally.

Setzen, gesetzt ('posited') and *Gesetztsein* ('positedness') occur frequently in Hegel, but not usually (unless he is discussing Fichte) in Fichte's sense. To say that something is *gesetzt* has two implications, either of which may be dominant in a given context. (1) What is *gesetzt* is explicit or set out rather than implicit or IN ITSELF: what is implicit in the seed is *gesetzt* in the plant; homogeneous, empty space is 'only the possibility, not the positedness of juxtaposition or self-EXTERNALITY (*Aussereinander*)' (*Enc.* II §254). (2) What is *gesetzt* is produced by or dependent on something else: the APPEARANCE of ESSENCE, e.g., is *gesetzt*, while DETERMINATE BEING is not. In sense 2, *gesetzt* and *setzen* are often equivalent to 'MEDIATED' and 'to mediate'. Such positing may be either physical or conceptual: the CAUSE (physically) posits the effect, but the effect (conceptually) posits the cause. Something can posit *itself*: in the series of stages of NATURE, e.g., the IDEA 'posits itself as what it is in itself' (*Enc.* II §251).

Setzen forms many compounds: An important one for Hegel is *voraussetzen*, 'to presuppose, require, assume (a thing or proposition)', but literally 'to posit beforehand, in advance (*voraus*)'. Hegel uses several words for 'presupposing' and 'presupposition': *Annahme* ('acceptance, assumption'), *Vorurteil* ('prejudgment, prejudice'), but his favourite is *Voraussetzung*, '(pre)supposition, assumption, (pre)requisite, (pre)condition', but literally 'positing, or what is posited, in advance'. (The Greek counterparts of *voraussetzen* and *Voraussetzung* are *hypotithesthai* and *hypothesis*.)

Hegel was vexed by the problem that philosophy, unlike other sciences, is

224

not entitled to make assumptions or presuppositions, and yet seems inevitably to assume certain concepts, propositions, a method of procedure, etc. (*Enc.* I §1). In part the problem is one of SCEPTICISM: If I can assume something, without PROOF, then someone else can assume, with equal legitimacy, its negation or opposite. But even where scepticism is not an obvious threat, in the case, e.g., of such seemingly self-evident assumptions as Descartes' 'I think' or Fichte's 'I am I', not only are further assumptions (e.g. of a method of procedure) required if we are to get beyond the beginning, but Descartes' and Fichte's ability to make such claims, and our ability to understand them, involve a variety of historical and cultural presuppositions. Hegel is concerned not only to give an account of the world that is invulnerable to scepticism, but a complete account, viz. one that includes an account of the presuppositions of its own emergence and intelligibility.

Hegel has several answers to this problem:

(1) Where possible he attempts to avoid making assumptions; e.g., he refuses to assume LAWS of THOUGHT such as the law of CONTRADICTION. Such assumptions as he makes, e.g. the concept of pure BEING in the Logic or SENSORY CERTAINTY in *PS*, he takes to be virtually empty.

(2) Often (e.g. in *PS* and *SL*) he suggests that it is not he, Hegel, who is developing the subject-matter (*Sache*, 'THING'), but that the subject-matter develops or considers itself, while Hegel and his readers simply watch. It does not follow from this that the subject-matter has no presuppositions, but it does follow that it is not he, Hegel, who is making these presuppositions. (This objective stance is one reason for Hegel's neglect of the distinction between *cognitive* presuppositions and other types of presupposition.)

(3) Hegel holds that the result of a course of DEVELOPMENT involves or SUBLATES the steps that led up to it. Thus, e.g., the absolute IDEA that is the result of logic is not simply the last of a series of distinct categories: it includes being, etc., and (an account of) the method of logic within itself. Since the presuppositions of the result are only elements in it, they are in fact *posited* by the result, but they are posited *in advance*.

(4) He argues that his SYSTEM, and each part of it, forms a circle. This gives more substance to the idea that the presuppositions of the system, or of any part of it, are posited by it, but in advance: pure being, e.g., with which logic begins, is posited by the end of the Logic, the absolute idea, and also by the end of the philosophy of spirit, which is philosophy and thus logic. He also holds that the world as a whole forms such a circle: SPIRIT, which is from one point of view the end or result, posits in advance its own presuppositions, the logical idea and nature.

Positing in advance is similar to the sublation of CONDITIONS and the mediation of mediation into IMMEDIACY. In *SL* and other works Hegel gives several more down-to-earth interpretations of the concept of presupposition:

1. In RECIPROCITY, a SUBSTANCE, A, has an effect posited in it by, and thus

presupposes, the activity of another substance, B. But the positing activity of B is itself the result of the prior activity of A on B. Thus the activity of B is posited in advance by A.

2. (a) The presuppositions of an activity such as eating, e.g., fruit on trees, are not in themselves presuppositions of the activity, but are made into presuppositions by the PURPOSE of the agent. (Cf. the event that is made into, posited as, a *cause* by its effect.) (b) Nor are they strictly necessary for the activity. The agent could utilize other things if this fruit were not available. (By contrast, the road might have become wet, from some other cause, even if it had not rained, but this is not likely.) (c) The fruit does not survive the activity, but is consumed by the agent and becomes a part of him. (Cf. the cause that is used up in its effect.)

3. In HISTORY, the world SPIRIT (or perhaps world historical individuals) is related to its presuppositions as the eater to his fruit: (a) it makes states of affairs and individual people, which are not intrinsically presuppositions of its activity, into presuppositions; (b) it could use other states of affairs or individuals, within certain limits, for the same purpose; (c) the presuppositions are used up, destroyed or sublated, in the activity and its result.

4. Even if men do not literally produce or posit the natural and historical presuppositions of their activities, they take intellectual and practical control of them by conceptualizing and understanding them, and, in the case of nature, by transforming it. They also SUBLATE them, in the sense that they can rise above their natural and historical circumstances, making a pearl of a stone, though not, on Hegel's view, to the extent that one can 'leap beyond one's age' or cease to be a 'child of one's times'.

Hegel thus gives a variety of interpretations to the idea that presupposition is positing in advance. Not all of them are applicable to the presuppositions of Hegel's system: e.g. he makes no serious attempt to argue that logic could begin with something quite different from pure being, utilizing more or less any concept it found available. None of his attempts to avoid or disarm the presuppositions of his own thought is *obviously* successful. His achievement is to propose and explore novel solutions to the problem and to raise such questions as: What presuppositions make it so tempting to try to avoid presuppositions?

proof *Weisen*, originally 'to make aware (*wissend*)', means 'to impart instruction by showing, direct, instruct, expel (i.e. show out)'. The fifteenth century gave rise to *beweisen* ('to show as true or correct, prove') and *Beweis* ('evidence, proof'). From the seventeenth century, these were used by mathematicians for the Latin *demonstrare, demonstratio*, and the Greek *apodeiknunai, apodeixis*, 'to prove', 'proof', in the sense of deriving a proposition from one or more propositions whose truth is accepted, by a procedure which guarantees the truth of the proposition so derived.

The proofs with which Hegel was most familiar were (1) the proofs of Euclidean geometry, and (2) the traditional proofs of GOD's existence, which by Hegel's time had, via Kant, been narrowed down to three: the cosmologi-

226

cal, teleological and ontological proofs. Hegel often mentions a fourth, the proof *ex consensu gentium* (from the consensus of peoples), but shows little interest in Kant's moral proof, in part because he rejected the view of MORALITY on which it depends.

In *PS*, Preface, and *LPEG* (which he was preparing for publication when he died), Hegel makes several criticisms of proofs as commonly conceived:

(1) The premisses are immediately PRESUPPOSED and not proved.
(2) The premisses remain true even after the conclusion has been derived.
(3) A given step in the proof is not fully determined by the preceding step, but is taken only with a view to proving the conclusion: e.g. Euclid's proof of Pythagoras' theorem involves drawing lines whose point becomes apparent only when we reach the end of the proof and see how they help to prove the theorem. Any proposition entails infinitely many other propositions; which one we choose to derive from it depends on our proposed destination, not on the proposition from which we set out.
(4) The premisses and steps of the proof are not involved in the conclusion. The meaning of the theorem is independent of the proof of it. Thus the same theorem admits of several different proofs.
(5) The moves made in the proof are not moves made by the object of the proof, e.g. by the triangles with which the proof is concerned. It is thus an external REFLECTION on the object.

Hegel did not believe that geometry can be substantially remedied in these respects, since it concerns the EXTERNALITY of SPACE. But the proofs of God, the subject-matter of PHILOSOPHY, must be remedied if the proofs are to be accepted:

(1) Philosophy cannot presuppose such truths as the CONTINGENCY of the world (required for the cosmological proof).
(2) The premisses of the proof cannot remain TRUE alongside the conclusion after its derivation, but must be SUBLATED. To suppose, e.g., that the contingency of the world remains true alongside the NECESSITY of God implies that God is one entity alongside the world and that he is dependent on or conditioned by the contingency of the world, just as our knowledge of him is conditioned by it. The MEDIATION of (our knowledge of) God must be sublated into IMMEDIACY.
(3) Unlike a geometrical proof, a philosophical proof cannot presuppose that we know in advance the meaning of the theorem to be proved and of the terms in it. Hence the proof must confer meaning on the theorem and thus cannot be guided by it. Each step of the proof must therefore uniquely determine its successor.
(4) The premisses and steps of the proof must be involved in its conclusion, since (a) they determine its meaning; (b) they cannot persist alongside God, but must be sublated in him; and (c) our rise to (KNOWLEDGE of) God is a phase of God himself.
(5) Since God is INFINITE (i.e. all-encompassing) our knowledge of God is not distinct from God, but a phase of him, his SELF-CONSCIOUSNESS.

227

Thus God himself makes the moves that we make in our proofs. Hence Hegel feels no need to distinguish (e.g. in (2) above) the ontological conditions (of God or the ABSOLUTE) from the epistemological conditions (of our knowledge of him). Ontology and epistemology ultimately coincide.

In *CJ*, Kant had anticipated some of Hegel's views by interpreting the proofs of God not as alternative proofs of the same conclusion, but as proving different aspects of the desired conclusion, as filling out our picture of God: e.g., the cosmological proof establishes that God is a necessary being, but not that he is a PURPOSIVE agent; the teleological proof establishes that he is a purposive agent, but not that he is a moral agent; this is established only by the moral proof. Hegel often interprets the traditional proofs in this way, and criticizes, e.g., the proof *ex consensu gentium* not for the reason that its premisses are false or the argument invalid, but that it results in an excessively thin concept of God, the highest common factor of all religious beliefs. He argues that such traditional proofs impoverish, and are not required for, FAITH, but that such reflection on faith is an inevitable phase of the DEVELOPMENT of SPIRIT. The solution is to think more, not to relapse into unreflective faith.

Kant was commonly supposed to have demolished the proofs of God in *CPR*, leaving room only for a moral faith. Hegel attempted to revive them. But he did so by radically reinterpreting the proofs and the notion of God. He makes several criticisms of Kant's attempt to refute the proofs: e.g. he quibbles over whether what the ontological proof purports to prove is the BEING, EXISTENCE, OBJECTIVITY, etc., of God. Such criticisms are of more relevance to Hegel's reinterpretation of the proofs than to Kant's refutation of the traditional versions.

As infinite, God is not distinct from the world, but is in essence the logical structure of the world, the world itself (NATURE), and man's knowledge of the world (including religion). Thus the ontological proof, on Hegel's view, establishes not the existence of a transcendent entity corresponding to our concept of God, but the realization of the CONCEPT (i.e. the logical structure portrayed in the Logic) in the world. Since the logical structure of the world prefigures its own relationship to the world, the proof also occurs within the Logic, in the transition from the concept to the OBJECT, which foreshadows the move from logic to nature. Similarly the other proofs correspond both to transitions within logic, e.g. from contingency to necessity (the cosmological proof), and to claims about the world, e.g. that its contingencies are overarched by a necessary structure. Thus Hegel does not accept only three proofs: each transition, or at least each TRIAD, in the Logic is in effect a proof of God, and also a step in our elevation to God, once spirit enters the scene and retraces, in a variety of ways, the steps of the Logic. Thus the proofs ultimately express the *Erhebung des Geistes zu Gott*. (This phrase is conveniently ambiguous: (1) 'rise of the spirit to (knowledge of) God'; (2) 'rise of the spirit to (the status of) God'.)

Hegel also criticizes, in *PP* and *SL*, Kant's proofs of antinomies, e.g. of both the FINITUDE of the world and its infinity in space and TIME. In essence, however, Hegel accepts the antinomies, but argues that (1) there are far more than the four that Kant exposed, and (2) antinomies are rooted in the *concepts* of finitude, etc., not in their application to the world or to THINGS IN THEMSELVES. Hegel believes that these proofs, like the proofs of God, concern concepts or THOUGHT-DETERMINATIONS, rather than PROPOSITIONS. His solution to antinomies is thus to argue that antinomial concepts, such as infinity and finitude, essentially involve each other and are both sublated in the infinite concept, the absolute IDEA. But he, like Kant, supplies no adequate answer to the question whether the world is finite or infinite in space and time.

property, possession and person A now defunct verb, related to 'to own' and meaning 'to have, possess', gave rise to the adjective *eigen* (originally 'possessed, taken into possession', now 'own', as in 'my own house'). From this comes *Eigenschaft*, which once meant '(owned) property, possession(s)', but was used by Eckhart for a 'peculiar feature' (*Eigenheit*, the Latin *proprietas*) and by Wolff for an 'attribute, property, the Latin *attributum*'. Hegel uses it only for a 'property (attribute)' of a THING (*Ding*).

Owned property is *Eigentum* (which was also used by Eckhart to translate *proprietas*), everything that is a person's own, which may or may not include his body. (Hegel believes that by cultivating one's mind and body, one takes possession of oneself and becomes one's own property: *PR* §57.) My possessions are also my property, but ownership is distinct from possession, and what I own or my property is distinct from what I possess or have in my possession: property may not be in the possession of its rightful owner. Thus one has a RIGHT or title to one's property, but not necessarily to what is in one's possession. 'To possess' is *besitzen*, which originally meant 'to sit on' something, and *Besitz* is 'possession', both in the sense of what one possesses and in that of having or taking something into one's 'possession'. 'Taking possession', especially (in Hegel) of something not yet owned by anyone else, is *Besitznahme*. *Besitzergreifung* ('taking possession, occupancy') is similar, but suggests physical seizure or grasping (*ergreifen*), which, on Hegel's view, is only one way of taking possession of a thing, alongside forming it and marking it as one's own (*PR* §54ff).

Besitz and *besitzen* display the same ambiguity as 'to possess' and 'possession': Thus Kant distinguishes between 'sensuous' or 'empirical' *Besitz*, i.e. physical possession, and 'legal' or 'intelligible' *Besitz*, i.e. legal ownership (*MM*, I §§1–17). For Hegel, *Besitznahme* of an unowned THING (*Sache*) is the first phase of *Eigentum*. What I take possession of becomes my property, but only because I thereby acquire a right to the thing that is recognized by others.

Whoever owns property is, on Hegel's view, a *Person*, and property can be owned only by a person. *Person* comes from the Latin *persona*, originally an 'actor's mask', hence a 'character in a play', and then a 'person'. In ordinary usage, a *Person* is: (1) a person, in contrast to a thing; (2) a notable or personage; (3) a character in a play; (4) in a disparaging sense, especially a low-class woman. (Sense (4) arises from the fact that personhood is the lowest common denominator of all humans; hence *Person* applies to someone with no other status. It explains why Hegel says that *Person* is an 'expression of contempt', *PS*, VI.A.c; *PR* §35A.) *Person* gives rise to *persönlich* ('personal') and *Persönlichkeit* ('personality, personhood'). Hegel's use of these generally conforms to his use of *Person*, excluding such senses as a '(great, strange, etc.) personality': in respect of their personality, all persons are equal (*PR* §49).

Person has two main specialized uses, which Hegel attempts to relate:

(1)   In philosophy a *Person* is a thinking, rational being. Kant distinguishes three senses of *Person* in this use:
   (a)   A logical SUBJECT or I*, CONSCIOUS of its identity persisting through changes in its states.
   (b)   A real subject, i.e. a persistent SUBSTANCE, conscious of its persistent identity. (Kant argues that I cannot know that I am a person in this sense.)
   (c)   A rational subject, which forms purposes independently of nature, is responsible for its actions and is thus a PURPOSE or end in itself.
(2)   In jurisprudence a *Person* is a subject of legal rights and duties. It includes persons in sense 1 (especially (c)), but also *juristische Personen* ('legal persons'), organizations that contain, but are not themselves, persons in sense 1 ('natural persons'). (*PR* is mainly concerned with legal persons who are also natural persons. But *PR* §46 considers 'artificial' persons and *PR* §169 sees the FAMILY as a person.)
(3)   *Person* also denotes the persons of the Trinity. At the level of RELIGION, Hegel regards GOD as a person, and also as triune. But he does not stress that the three members of the Trinity are themselves persons.

Unlike Kant, Hegel distinguishes *Person* from *Subjekt*, but he does so in two different ways, corresponding to the ambiguity of 'subject'. In one sense, any living thing is a subject, but not a person (*PR* §35A.); in another sense, the *Person* as such is not a *Subjekt*, and becomes one only with the REFLECTION of the WILL into itself characteristic of MORALITY (*PR* §105). *Persönlichkeit* is also distinguished from SELF-CONSCIOUSNESS, but again in different ways: At *PS*, IV.A., an individual (*Individuum*) who has not risked his life may be recognized as a *Person*, but not as an independent self-consciousness, while at *PR* §35, to be a person is more than being self-conscious, since personhood involves an awareness of oneself as an I, while self-consciousness is awareness of oneself as a concrete, determinate being. The relationship of *Person* to *Subjekt* and *Selbstbewusstsein* is thus unstable. But for Hegel, unlike Kant, *Person* is a relatively abstract and meagre characterization of a human being, with a suggestion of merely legal personhood. He associates personhood especially with imperial Rome, whose citizens were reduced to atomic bearers of property rights, lacking the inner depth of the moral *subject* and the substantial ETHICAL LIFE of Greece and the Roman Republic. Personhood is an essential feature of the modern STATE, but its citizens are more than persons.

To be a person, on Hegel's view, is not simply to have a specific situation, needs, desires, etc., but to be able to ABSTRACT from everything peculiar to oneself and think of oneself as an I (*PR*, §35). This is a person in Kant's sense 1(a). To be a person in this sense is not yet to be a moral subject, a person in sense 1(c), but it involves the capacity for rights and entitles one to respect as a person (*PR* §36). The rights are, at this stage, only formal or negative rights: the right not to have one's personhood, and what it entails, infringed (*PR* §38).

The central right of a person, on Hegel's account, is the right to property. The point of property is not to satisfy physical needs: it is to develop or fulfil one's personhood. Personhood as such is, in contrast to the world of nature confronting it, purely subjective: it needs to realize itself in the external world by claiming some portion of it as its own. It thus has a right to do this and to whatever it thus appropriates. Hegel's account of the acquisition of property is thus similar to his account of self-consciousness: the bare I confronted by an alien objective world has to appropriate the world, whether literally or metaphorically, in order to become a fully fledged human being.

Why must a person embody his will in the external world and why should his doing so take the form of appropriation? Why, that is, must a person in sense 1(a) also be, or become, a person in sense 2? Hegel's explicit answers are unsatisfactorily bald and abstract: (1) Since the person is intrinsically INFINITE and UNIVERSAL, the restriction to mere SUBJECTIVITY is 'CONTRADIC-TORY and null'); it must thus actively SUBLATE this restriction and give itself reality, or make external NATURE its own (*PR* §39). (2) As a mere CONCEPT, the person must give itself an outer sphere of its FREEDOM, in order to exist as IDEA (*PR* §41). He does not introduce the idea of RECOGNITION (*Anerkennung*) by other persons until a later stage, contract (*PR* §71), though my inner will alone is not sufficient for the acquisition of property, since the embodiment of my WILL requires recognizability (*Erkennbarkeit*) for others (*PR* §51).

There are two more concrete strands of thought in Hegel:

1. As a bare person (in sense 1(a)), I abstract from everything definite about me, including my own body, so that the external world, including my body, confronts me as wholly alien, undifferentiated in the sense that no portion of it is peculiarly mine. I am nowhere, and everywhere, in this world; there is no place in it for persons on a par with myself, who will recognize, and be recognized by, me. Only by staking out a portion of this world as mine can I achieve a satisfactory intellectual relationship to it, give some content to my vanishingly thin ego, and take my place as one person among others. This line of thought (which is akin to Fichte's) more obviously legitimates the acquisition of property in my body and in items of everyday use than in more extensive holdings.

2. Personhood involves abstracting my bare I from my situation, desires, etc. I interact with external objects in virtue of my desires, etc. But to give content to the idea that I am an I, a person, not simply a collection of desires, activities, etc., I need to stake out an objective counterpart to my bare I, an OBJECT that is related to me simply in virtue of being *mine*, not in virtue of satisfying one of my fleeting desires. This line of thought legitimates the

231

acquisition of an object that is unrelated to my needs, but it is less obvious that it legitimates the acquisition of more than one such object.

In *PR* Hegel considers property in its three phases (taking possession, use and ALIENATION – which involve, respectively, a positive, a negative and an infinite JUDGMENT); contract; and the role of property in CIVIL SOCIETY. He believed in the necessity of personal (private), rather than institutional, property, but held that the state, but only the state, 'may cancel private ownership in exceptional cases' (*PR* §46A). His account of property and of its different types is insightful, but his endorsement of property goes some way beyond his explicit arguments for it.

punishment and crime Hegel was familiar with various attempts to justify punishment. Plato alone presents several theories: that of Protagoras (in the *Protagoras*), that men are punished with a view to the future, not to the past, i.e. in order to deter both the offender and others from future offences; Socrates' theory (in the *Republic*) that to punish a wrongdoer is to benefit him, since it improves his soul; and so on. Hegel was interested in punishment from *ETW* on (where, in *SCF*, he discusses the relationship between punishment and FATE), and was puzzled by the diversity of possible justifications of it. In *NL*, he notes that punishment has a variety of features – it exacts retribution for an offence, it deters, it often improves the offender – and that a merely empirical procedure cannot justify the selection of one of these features as *the* point or PURPOSE of punishment. In *SL* too he notes the arbitrariness with which one feature of the CONCRETE phenomenon of punishment is selected as its GROUND, while others are regarded as contingent accompaniments.

Similar considerations led Nietzsche, in his *Genealogy of Morals* (1887), to the conclusion that 'it is impossible today to say definitely why we inflict punishment: all concepts in which a whole process is semiotically concentrated elude DEFINITION; only what has no HISTORY is definable.' But Hegel believes that it is possible to give a single justification of punishment, in part because punishment is not simply a concrete historical phenomenon, but also part of a SYSTEM of RIGHT, its place in which confers on it a distinct significance, in part because there are, on Hegel's view, strong objections to certain theories of punishment, especially deterrence theories. In *PR* §§82–103, his account runs as follows.

Under the heading of 'Abstract Right', the account of PROPERTY and contract leads to the consideration of wrong (*Unrecht*). Wrong takes three forms: (1) Non-malicious wrong, where the wrongdoer respects right or the LAW, but mistakes its application to a particular case, in a dispute over, e.g., property; wrong of this type gives rise to a civil action for restitution, not to punishment. (2) Fraud, where the wrongdoer respects not right, but at least the APPEARANCE or semblance (*Schein*) of right; though punishment is introduced only later, Hegel concedes that punishment is appropriate for fraud (*PR* §89A.). (3) Coercion (*Zwang*) and crime (*Verbrechen*), in which neither right nor the semblance of it is respected and thus punishment is appropriate. *Verbrechen* comes from *verbrechen*, originally an emphatic form of *brechen* ('to break'), meaning 'to break up, destroy, annihilate', hence 'to break (the peace, an oath or a law)', and now 'to commit (an offence)'. Thus Hegel readily associates crime with damage and destruction.

Why should crimes be punished? Hegel rejects several answers:

(1) Beccaria's view (*On Crimes and Punishments* (1764), II) that the right to punish derives from an original social contract, in which laws and penalities for breaches of them were agreed to, is mistaken, since the STATE does not rest on a contract.

(2) The aim of punishment is not the moral improvement of the offender: such an aim (a) requires an answer to the prior question 'Why is it just (*gerecht*) to punish?', since it is not obviously just to inflict pain on a person without his consent for his moral betterment (*PR* §99), and (b) cannot be realized, since it is impossible to *compel* a person to alter his moral convictions (*PR* §94A.). The free WILL as such cannot, on Hegel's view, be coerced (*PR* §§5, 91). In *LPR*, he distinguishes ecclesiastical penance (*Busse*, related to *besser*, 'better'), which aims at improvement and conversion, from CIVIL (*bürgerliche*) punishment, which does not.

(3) Hegel associates deterrence theory with P. J. A. Feuerbach, who argued, in his *Textbook of Common Penal Law* (1801), that the threat of punishment induces abstention from crime by 'psychological coercion'. The infliction of punishment, if the threat is disregarded, emphasizes the seriousness of the threat and makes it more effective in future. But, Hegel objects, (a) we again need to ask 'What entitles us to issue the threat, and, still more, to punish someone in order to increase its efficacy?'; (b) to threaten someone is to forget that he is free and able to act despite the threat: 'It is to treat a man like a dog instead of with the freedom and respect due to him as a man.' Thus considerations of deterrence may play a part in deciding on the penalty for a given type of offence, but not in justifying punishment in general (*PR* §99A.).

Theories 2 and 3 (and implicitly 1) regard a crime primarily as an 'evil' (*Übel*), not necessarily as a moral evil, but as a 'bad thing' or 'nasty', independently of the fact that it is a breach of right. Right, or laws, are, on this view, to be explained by our desire to avoid or minimize such evils. Punishment is another 'evil' and its infliction can be justified only by its tendency to reduce the first type of evil (*PR* §99). Hegel proceeds in the contrary direction: abstract right (*Recht*) is justified not by its tendency to reduce a certain type of antecedent evil, but by its making human beings into PERSONS, who are susceptible to the 'evil' of crime only in virtue of being persons. What is wrong with crime is thus not that it is unpleasant or inconvenient for its victims, but that it is an *Unrecht*, an attack on right as such, usually in the form of an attack on a particular person or his property. Similarly, although punishment is usually unpleasant or inconvenient for the offender, its central characteristic is that it is a restoration of right, a NEGATION or SUBLATION of the negation or sublation of right represented by the crime. The question to be asked of punishment is thus not 'How is this (second) evil to be justified?', but 'Is it just (*gerecht*)?' The answer to this question is an automatic 'Yes'.

But Hegel does not simply argue that a breach of right or law *ipso facto* justifies the punishment of it. For he agrees with Beccaria that the criminal must consent to his punishment, if it is to be justified (*PR* §100A.). But the criminal consents not by his endorsement of a social contract, but by his criminal act itself: In the *System der Sittlichkeit* (*System of* ETHICAL LIFE, 1802–3), Hegel argues that the wrongdoer's bad conscience provides an IDEAL opposition (*Gegenwirkung*) to, or reversal (*Umkehrung*) of, his crime, which calls for completion by an external 'avenging justice'. But in *PR* he stresses the UNIVERSAL implications of the criminal's rational will rather than his bad conscience. As a rational being, in, e.g., taking someone's property, he does not simply will that the property of *this* particular person be taken by *him*, but wills universally that any person's property should be taken from him and thus that his own property should be taken (*PR* §100). This has the merit of justifying not only the punishment of the criminal, but a penalty that is proportional to his offence (*PR* §§96, 101). For in committing an offence, the criminal wills that a similar, or at least equivalent, act be perpetrated on himself.

For this reason, the crime is intrinsically 'null' and 'CONTRADICTORY' (*PR* §97 and A.): the criminal wills that, e.g., the property he has stolen, and more, should be taken from him. He thus has a right to be punished: to punish him is to treat him as a free and rational person (*PR* §100). The punishment explicitly annuls a crime which is already implicitly null.

Punishment (*Strafe*) is retribution (*Wiedervergeltung*, 'paying back again') and is thus akin to revenge (*Rache*). In his Jena lectures on philosophy of spirit (1805–6), Hegel argues that punishment is 'revenge, but as justice (*Gerechtigkeit*)'. Punishment, unlike revenge, is a proportional response to an acknowledged offence against right, the response, Hegel stresses, of an acknowledged, impartial authority, not of the injured individual or his kinsfolk. Revenge, unlike punishment, can lead to an endless vendetta. (Hegel was influenced by his reading of Aeschylus' *Oresteia*, in which the theme of revenge is prominent, and the establishment of a law-court helps to bring about a resolution and conciliation.) The requirement of a neutral authority, and thus of a 'particular subjective will [viz. that of the judge] that wills the universal as such' and is not simply one party to the dispute, supplies the transition from abstract right to morality (*PR* §103).

Hegel's theory is often welcomed by opponents of utilitarian and deterrence theories of punishment. But it is open to several criticisms:

(1) To raise a stick to a person may be to treat him like a dog, but the more subtle and indirect threat implicit, on Feuerbach's view, in a law can affect only persons, not dogs.

(2) The exclusion of utilitarian considerations from the justification of punishment is not obviously acceptable. Hegel tends to assume that a system of punishment constructed on his theory will also deter criminals. But if this assumption were found to be mistaken, he would be

committed to preferring, e.g., a society with many crimes, all (or most) of which were punished, to a society with few crimes, most of which went unpunished. This preference is not self-evidently correct.

(3) The interpretation and validity of his own theory are uncertain. How should we deal with someone who, e.g., steals or kills on the strength of his real or imagined superiority to others and thus cannot be seen as willing that he should be treated as he treats others?

(4) Hegel's belief that the criminal has a right to be punished and that the theory thus explains why we are obliged (rather than merely *entitled*) to punish him is not clearly substantiated. He perhaps conflates (a) 'To leave a criminal unpunished is to infringe his rights' with (b) 'To inflict pain on a criminal, e.g., solely to deter others, or to leave him unpunished in the belief that he is not responsible for his actions, is to infringe his rights'. (b) does not entail (a).

purpose and purposiveness A *Zweck* was originally a nail in the centre of a target, and hence something aimed at, a goal (*Ziel*). It corresponds to 'purpose' or 'end, aim' and to the Greek *telos*. The adjective *zweckmässig* need not imply that something is designed for a purpose, but only that it serves a purpose or is 'useful, expedient', etc. But for Kant, in *CJ*, an entity is *zweckmässig* if, and only if, its existence and nature cannot be explained except by a 'causality according to CONCEPTS'. This characteristic of an entity is its *Zweckmässigkeit* ('usefulness, purposiveness, TELEOLOGY'). Thus something is *zweckmässig* not if it *serves* a *Zweck*, but if it can only be seen as *produced* by a *Zweck*, since a *Zweck* is the concept of an entity in so far as it contains the GROUND of the ACTUALITY of the entity.

If I form the concept of an action, object or state of affairs and then produce it on the basis of my concept, the concept is the *Zweck*, and the action or entity produced by it, and in accordance with it, is *zweckmässig*. But an entity can, on Kant's view, be *zweckmässig*, even if it is not in fact produced by a *Zweck* or concept: An entity may be such that we cannot explain it except in terms of its concept or purpose, and yet not be the product of a purpose. Kant held that living organisms are of this type: they exhibit *Zweckmässigkeit* without *Zweck*. Their purposiveness is thus SUBJECTIVE in a higher degree than, e.g., the causal relationships of things: causal relations are required for any objective EXPERIENCE, while purposiveness is required only for us to explain the existence and nature of certain items within our experience.

Hegel agreed with Kant that a purpose is a concept. But since he believed that a concept is embedded in things, not simply formed by a (*finite*) mind, he rejected Kant's view that the apparent purposiveness of organisms is without a purpose and thus lacks full OBJECTIVITY. Hegel (like Aristotle and unlike Plato) held that the purpose or *telos* of a thing is inherent in it and does not require a mind or *nous* external to it, which forms or has the purpose. (Both Hegel and Aristotle postulate a cosmic SPIRIT or *nous*, but it does not impose its purposes on things from without.)

This is INNER teleology or purposiveness. But the 'Teleology' section of *SL* and *Enc.* I deals mainly with OUTER teleology, an agent's realization of his purpose in the objective realm. This, Hegel argues, is an INFERENCE (*Schluss*) in which (1) a subjective purpose is united with (2) the objective realm by way of (3) the agent's activity and the means he employs (*Mittel*, 'means', from *Mitte*, '(the) middle' and *mittel*, 'middle, central'). This conforms to Hegel's conception of an inference (or PROOF), since the performance of the inference negates its terms: the purpose, once realized, is no longer merely subjective, the objective realm is no longer merely objective, but informed by the purpose, and the MEDIATING activity (and often the means employed) does not survive the realization of the purpose (*Enc.* I §204).

Each of these terms itself involves three elements or MOMENTS, which in turn form an inference that is a version of the main inference in a particular mode:

1. This is most convincing in the case of the subjective purpose, since Aristotle, in his *Nicomachean Ethics*, had plausibly represented this as a 'practical syllogism', consisting of a universal premiss ('Such-and-such is needed' or 'A thing of this kind is the *telos* and the best'), a particular premiss ('This is a such-and-such, a thing of this kind') and a conclusion that is a decision to act or an action. Hegel has Aristotle's account in mind, but the three terms of his inference are (as usual) non-propositional:

(a) The UNIVERSAL concept as such.

(b) The PARTICULARIZATION of this universal into a determinate CONTENT.

(c) An INDIVIDUAL decision to act, an *Entschluss* (from *entschliessen*, originally 'to unlock, open', now 'to decide, come to a decision').

Hegel makes some play with *schliessen* ('to close, conclude, infer'), *Schluss* ('closure, conclusion', etc.) and their compounds: In a decision the universal joins (*zusammenschliessen*) with itself by way of the particular; *beschliessen* is 'to resolve', but also 'to close, conclude'; to decide (*entschliessen*) is to close off or exclude (*ausschliessen*) other possibilities, and to open oneself up (*aufschliessen*) into objectivity. The contrast between the subjective purpose and objectivity, and the joining of the two, is foreshadowed in the subjective purpose itself: this represents (i) the subjective purpose itself, (ii) the objective state of affairs aimed at, and (iii) the desired unification of the two. The perceived discrepancy between (i) and (ii) leads to the opening up of (iii).

2. The elements of the middle term are:

(a) An external object that is brought under the power of the subject and employed as a means.

(b) The activity of the agent in reducing (a) to a means for his purpose.

(c) The activity of the agent in directing (a) against other objects and using its and their MECHANICAL and CHEMICAL powers to shape them to his purpose.

3. The result of this, the realized purpose, is: (a) externally objective; but (b) POSITED and MEDIATED, rather than IMMEDIATE; and (c) of the same content as the subjective purpose, which, unlike a CAUSE, is preserved in its product.

Outer purposiveness has several defects. Both the subjective and the realized purpose have only a FINITE content: an agent aims at *this* rather than *that*, and his achievement of *this* excludes the achievement of *that*, but the material employed could have been used for *that* rather than *this*, since the purpose is only externally imposed on the material. A purpose realized is not usually a final purpose, but serves in turn as a means to some further end, and this raises the prospect of an INFINITE series of ends, each a means to a further end. Kant resolves this by locating the final end (*Endzweck*), the supreme good, in the unattainable future, as an end that we OUGHT to, but never will, realize. Hegel's solution is inner purposiveness, in which purposes do not proliferate into an endless series, but come round in a circle: each part of a whole, e.g. of an organism, is both end and means for every other part. Moreover, the ends are not externally imposed on the materials of which the organism consists, but is immanent in them: the materials could be used for no other purpose and thus their purpose is not a finite purpose.

Hegel prefers inner to outer purposiveness. But it does not follow that he values living organisms above rational agency, for LIFE is only the simplest form of inner purpose or the IDEA. A higher form is ETHICAL LIFE, the norms and institutions of a society. The purposes of such a society are immanent in it, not imposed from outside. Hegel prefers to see a rational agent as an organic part of such a society, himself and his actions serving as both end and means to other agents and institutions, than as an external MORAL agent, bringing his purposes to bear on an alien and resisting material: our actions maintain the on-going life of our environment, rather than alter it. He holds a similar view of the world as a whole: God is not an external agent imposing his purposes on it and directing it to its final end; he (i.e. the concept) is immanent in it and the good is already realized, but since error is a necessary preliminary to, and constituent of, TRUTH, the realization of the good involves the illusion that the good is not yet realized, as well as the eventual unmasking of this illusion (*Enc.* I §212A.).

Since genuine thought mirrors its OBJECT, Hegel's thought is also teleological: The SYSTEM as a whole, and the parts of it, are often conceived as the realization or DEVELOPMENT of a concept. But he has two distinct models for this: (1) the growth of an organism from a seed; (2) the life of a developed organism. On neither model does Hegel's teleology imply that each step in SCIENCE (like the steps of a geometrical proof) is determined and explicable only by the conclusion of science. A developed organism has no conclusion, only reciprocal purposiveness. The stages of growth of a plant are determined by the concept encoded in its seed, not by its end-state, except in so far as this is implicit in its concept. Model 1 is appropriate for each part of the system as we read it through, since each part has a conclusion (e.g. the absolute idea of the Logic), and each stage is the 'truth' of its predecessor. Model 2 is appropriate for the system as a whole, which forms a circle (of circles) with no conclusion or beginning. One of Hegel's main problems is the reconciliation of model 2 with the apparent rectilinearity of HISTORY.

Q

quality, quantity and measure   The first main section of the Logic, the Doctrine of BEING, is divided into three subsections: Quality, Quantity and Measure:

1. *Qualität* is a sixteenth-century borrowing from the Latin *qualitas*, which in turn comes from *qualis* ('of what sort?'). In ordinary usage it is (a) a degree of excellence ('of poor, good quality', etc.) or (b) overall excellence ('we worry about quality, not quantity'). In philosophy it is an 'attribute'; Hegel equates it with *Bestimmtheit* ('DETERMINACY, determinateness'). The quality of a JUDGMENT is its being positive, negative or infinite. (Hegel tends to conflate this with the judgment's ascribing a quality to something.) Böhme associated *Qualität* with *Qual* ('pain, torment, anguish') and coined the words *Qualierung* and *Inqualierung* to indicate the conflict by which a quality produces and maintains itself. This association has no etymological basis.

In the Logic, *Qualität* is *both* a general heading, covering being, DETERMINATE BEING, and being FOR ITSELF, *and* a phase of determinate being. A quality differs from a PROPERTY (*Eigenschaft*) in that (a) a property is also a power, which has effects on other things (e.g. 'coffee has the property of keeping one awake'), while a quality is more passive; and (b) a property belongs to a THING, which can persist throughout changes in its properties, while an entity is, on Hegel's account, constituted by its quality and cannot survive its loss. Quality in general passes over into quantity by way of being-for-self, which, in being related only to itself and not to anything else, ceases to have a determinate quality and becomes an atom or unit, which in turn generates other atoms or units alongside itself.

2. *Quantität* is a sixteenth-century borrowing from the Latin *quantitas*, which comes from *quantus* ('how big, much, many? As much, etc. as . . .'). The neuter of *quantus*, *quantum*, supplies the (seventeenth-century) German *Quantum*, a specific quantity or an item of a specific quantity. The native *Grösse* ('size, largeness, quantity', from *gross*, 'great, large, big') fluctuates between *Quantität* and *Quantum*; Hegel usually equates it with *Quantum*. The quantity of a judgment is its being UNIVERSAL, PARTICULAR or INDIVIDUAL.

Quantity is traditionally regarded as (a) either discrete (*diskret*) or continuous (*kontinuierlich, stetig*) and as (b) either *extensiv(e)* or *intensiv(e)*:

(a)   The natural numbers (1, 2, 3, 4 . . .) are discrete: if we confine ourselves to this series, there is, e.g., no number between two adjacent terms of the series (between, e.g., 3 and 4). The natural numbers are suitable for counting, e.g. dots on paper or cows in a field: each of the cows is divisible into parts, but this is of no relevance if one is simply counting one's cows. If we add fractions and irrational numbers (e.g. $\sqrt{2}$), the series becomes continuous and is suitable for measuring, e.g., a line or the length of a cow. Hegel regards any quantity or quantum as both continuous and discrete. Whether a quantity is seen as discrete or continuous depends on our viewpoint or interests: there are six (discrete) cows, but placed end to end they stretch for 10 metres; 10 metres is a continuous quantum, further divisible into fractions, etc., of a metre, but it is also a discrete quantum, ten exemplifications of a metre, like the six cows, which remain six discrete cows even if they are placed end to end. Hegel sees this as the solution to Kant's second antinomy, viz. that matter both consists of simple parts and is infinitely divisible: matter, Hegel argues, can be seen either as discrete, consisting of a definite number of parts each of a specific size, or as continuous, divisible *ad infinitum* into ever smaller parts, and so it is both discrete and continuous. (This merely side-steps Kant's problem, which is whether matter is continuous in the sense that it *can*, in principle, be divided *ad infinitum*, or discrete in the sense that it *cannot*.)

(b) A quantity may be extensive (the number of cows in a field, the extension of something in space or the duration of an event in time) or intensive (the strength of a force, the weight of something, the *Grad* or 'degree' of its temperature). Intensive quantity sometimes behaves like extensive quantity: a weight of 2 lb is twice as heavy as one of 1 lb whatever system of measurement we apply, and their joint weight is 3 lb. But sometimes it does not: a pint of water of 90°C is not twice as hot as a pint of water of 45°C, since the ratio of the numerical values of their temperatures will differ on different systems of measurement; if two pints of water, each of 45°C, are mixed, the two pints are of 45°C, not 90°C. Hegel argues that any quantity must be both extensive and intensive, since, e.g., an entity must have not only a size and duration, but also some distinctive quality and thus a certain degree of that quality; and intensive quantity can only be measured by correlating it with an extensive quantity, e.g. temperature with the height of mercury in a tube.

In *SL*, Hegel deals at length with arithmetic and mathematical infinity. He regards arithmetic as a science of the UNDERSTANDING, unsuitable for application to the objects of philosophy. He criticizes Schelling for applying quantitative considerations to the ABSOLUTE, making its bifurcation into nature and spirit depend on the quantitative predominance of the objective over the subjective, or vice versa, and using the mathematical notion of a 'power' (*Potenz*) for a stage of being or development. Nevertheless, he attempts to derive from each other and to systematize the various arithmetical operations. Hegel assumes that mathematics is exclusively concerned with quantity, since he knew nothing of the non-quantitative, but mathematical discipline of topology, though elements of it are implicit in his account of measure.

The *Quantum*, like the qualified something (*Etwas*), involves a LIMIT and quantitative INFINITY consists in the endless overcoming of the limit. The limit of a *Quantum*, unlike that of a something, is 'indifferent' (*gleichgültig*): A something or a quality is bounded by something different from itself (e.g. red differs from green, and a red thing is next to a green thing), but a quantum as such is not bounded by anything that differs from it either in quality or in quantity: an area of, e.g., empty space is bounded by more empty space, so that it is a matter of indifference where the boundary is drawn. Qualitative features are required for non-arbitrary boundaries between things.

The account of quantity concludes with ratio or proportion (*Verhältnis*), the RELATION between two variables, such as x:2x. The values of the variables may be increased indefinitely (e.g. 2:4, 3:6, 4:8...), but their ratio remains the same. This, Hegel argues, is a re-emergence of quality, the enduring feature of an entity, within the sphere of quantity, whose characteristic is that it can be increased or decreased indefinitely. Quality and quantity thus united are measure.

3. (*Das*) *Mass* ('(the) measure') is related to *messen* (originally 'to mark out, stake out (an area)', now 'to measure'). It has a complex history in which it acquired several layers of meaning, often involving different senses of *messen* and its derivatives: (1) the amount assigned (*zugemessen*) to one, the correct quantity, the demarcated area; (b) the way, mode (of doing something); (c) the suitable or fitting (*angemessenes*); (d) moderation, restraint (*Mässigung*). Now it means: 'measure, proportion (*Verhältnis*), dimension, degree (*Grad*), moderation, (weights and) measures'. In its feminine form, *die Mass(e)*, it means (a) a 'measure, litre' of, e.g., beer, and (b) 'moderation, decorum', now especially in such expressions as *über alle Massen* ('immoderately, beyond all bounds'). It occurs in several compounds: *Massregel* ('measure-rule, i.e. a guiding rule, a step or measure taken'); *Massstab* ('measuring stick or rod, scale, standard, criterion'). *Messen* also supplies *Durchmesser* ('through-measurer, i.e. diameter) and *Erdmesser* ('earth-measurer, i.e. geodesic').

Most of these senses and associations appear in Hegel's account of measure, as does the Latin *modus* ('right measure, rule, way, mode', especially the mode of an attribute in Spinoza) and the Greek idea of moderation and of limits whose transgression provokes nemesis. But Hegel's central idea is this: The quality of an entity and its quantity are initially independent of each other. A field may be big or small, while still a field. Water may be hot or cold, while still remaining water. But there are, in both extensive and intensive quantity, limits beyond which quantitative variation produces qualitative change. Living organisms cannot, as in fairy-tales, alter their size while retaining the same shape: a giant with the same shape as a man, but ten times as big, would break his legs, since their width and strength has not increased in proportion to his weight. If everything were to double in size, we would notice the extra weight we were carrying. As an infant increases in size, its head becomes smaller in relation to its body.

But Hegel focuses on cases where qualitative changes, like knots on a piece of string, occur only intermittently in the course of continuous quantitative change: Water, heated sufficiently, becomes steam, and, cooled sufficiently, ice; its undergoing some such qualitative change is essential if we are to *measure* its temperature. This raises the prospect of an endless increase and decrease in, e.g., temperature, 'knotted' at intervals by an infinity of qualitative changes. But Hegel sees the transformation of quality and quantity into each other as pointing to the ESSENCE underlying them.

R

rational, rationality *see* REASON AND UNDERSTANDING

real, reality *see* ACTUALITY; EXISTENCE, REALITY AND DETERMINATE BEING

reason and understanding *Vernunft* ('(faculty of) reason') comes from *vernehmen* ('to perceive, hear, examine, interrogate'), but it has lost its connection with the verb. It generates *vernünftig* ('rational, reasonable', in both an objective and a subjective sense) and *Vernünftigkeit* ('rationality, reasonableness'). It was used by Eckhart, Luther, etc., for the Latin *ratio* (in the sense of '(faculty of) reason', not of 'GROUND'). *Vernunft* is distinct from its French-derived counterparts, *Räsonnement* ('reasoning, argumentation') and *räsonieren* ('to reason, argue') which are often, and in Hegel invariably, derogative: 'specious or sophistical argument from grounds or reasons'. *Vernunft* is also distinct, in Hegel, from derivatives of its Latin equivalent, *ratio*: *Rationalismus*, *rational* and *rationell*. These are usually associated with the rationalism of the Enlightenment, and thus have more in common with *Verstand* than with *Vernunft*.

Verstand ('(faculty of) understanding, intellect') retains its link with its parent verb, *verstehen* ('to understand', etc.), which comes from *stehen* ('to stand') and is thus associated, by Hegel, with fixity rather than fluidity. It gives rise to *verständig* ('intelligent, of the understanding', e.g. '*verständiges* THINKING' in contrast to '*vernünftiges* thinking'). It also enters into *Menschenverstand* (literally 'human understanding', hence 'common sense'), often qualified as *gemeiner* ('common, ordinary') or *gesunder* ('healthy'): Hegel invariably, but especially in *CJP*, regards common sense as uninformed parochial prejudice.

Verstand is used for the Latin *intellectus*. But in Hegel derivatives of *intellectus* (unlike *Verstand*), such as *Intellektualität* ('intellectuality'), *Intellektualismus*, *Intellektualwelt* ('intellectual world'), and *intelligibel* ('intelligible'), are usually associated with the intelligible world of Plato, Neoplatonism and Leibniz, in contrast to the phenomenal world. The exception is *Intelligenz*, which refers to the intelligent MIND in general, including, e.g., MEMORY and IMAGINATION, but often excluding the WILL.

Philosophers have traditionally postulated two intellectual faculties. In Plato, *dianoia* ('discursive reason') lies between perception and *nous* ('mind, intellect') or *noēsis* ('thinking, the activity of *nous*'): *dianoia* deals with mathematics, the more intuitive *nous* with philosophy. In Plato's successors, *nous* is usually the higher faculty and is contrasted with *dianoia*, *logismos* ('calculation, ratiocination', in, e.g., Plotinus), or *pathētikos nous* ('passive (in contrast to active) *nous*', in Aristotle). The higher faculty is often ascribed to God or the gods, and is the divine spark in man, while the lower faculty is peculiar to men, or sometimes shared with other animals. *Nous* brings us into contact with the intelligible order, the cosmic *nous* or the intelligible (*noētos*) world. In contrast to the lower faculty, *nous* often reflects not only on lower faculties and their objects, but on itself, so that it is 'thinking about/of thinking' and identical with its object (Aristotle, Plotinus).

The distinction enters medieval thought, by way, e.g., of Boethius, who distinguished the higher, intuitive *intellectus* or *intelligentia* from the lower, discursive *ratio* or *ratiocinatio*. In medieval thought *intellectus* or *mens* is the higher faculty, and *ratio* the lower. Thus when the distinction was translated into German by Eckhart and other mystics, *Verstand* (*intellectus*) was the higher faculty and *Vernunft* (*ratio*) the lower: *Vernunft* conceptualizes sensory material, while *Verstand* gives non-sensory knowledge of God. But their positions were reversed by Enlightenment thinkers such as Wolff, who had no place for the supersensory, intuitive knowledge of *Verstand*. *Verstand* is still more intuitive than *Vernunft*, but is now connected with CONCEPTS and their application to sensory material: it is the 'faculty of distinctly representing the possible'. *Vernunft* retains its link with INFERENCE and argument: it is the 'faculty of seeing into the connection of truths'.

Kant took over this distinction: *Verstand* is the faculty of concepts and JUDGMENTS (though these are often assigned to the *Urteilskraft*, the ('faculty of) judgment'), and *Vernunft* that of inference. But *Vernunft* also has a higher role: it is the faculty of IDEAS and the source of METAPHYSICAL concepts; it reflects on the knowledge acquired by the understanding and attempts to make it a self-enclosed WHOLE, an attempt which leads it to transgress the LIMITS of EXPERIENCE which reason itself imposes on the understanding.

Goethe too helped to shape the distinction: *Verstand* solves definite, small-scale problems, while *Vernunft* surveys and reconciles OPPOSITES. In contrast to ancient and medieval thinkers, who usually associated the higher faculty (*intellectus*, etc.) with BEING or what is, and the lower (*ratio*, etc.) with BECOMING, Goethe assigns *Vernunft* to what becomes (*das Werdende*) and *Verstand* to what is (*das Gewordene*, 'what has become'): reason is concerned with development, understanding with keeping things as they are for practical purposes. In Jacobi, *Vernunft* becomes again a 'sense for the supersensible': at first he contrasted both *Vernunft* and *Verstand* with the higher faculties of FAITH and FEELING; but later *Vernunft* is equated with faith and is supposed, in contrast to inferential *Verstand*, to give an IMMEDIATE and complete view of the TRUTH. But Schiller's view is close to Hegel's: 'NATURE (SENSE) everywhere unites, the understanding separates everywhere, but reason unites again' (*AE*, XIX).

Hegel's (and Schelling's) conception of *Verstand* and *Vernunft* contains elements of all these views. The essence of *Verstand*, says Schelling, is clarity without depth. It fixes, and isolates from each other, concepts such as INFINITY and FINITUDE. It produces clear analyses and argues deductively. It is thus associated with concepts in the traditional sense, not with the

Hegelian concept that flows over into other concepts and generates its own instantiation. But it is an indispensable first stage of logic and science in general: we cannot, as Jacobi and, at times, Schelling supposed, proceed directly to the truths of reason without a preliminary ABSTRACT understanding of the subject-matter (*Enc.* I §80).

The next stage is that of negative *Vernunft* or DIALECTIC: this exposes the CONTRADICTIONS implicit in the abstractions of the understanding and the tendency of sharply defined opposites to veer into each other (*Enc.* I §81). Finally, SPECULATIVE or positive reason derives a positive result from the collapse of understanding's abstractions: the dialectic of being and NOTHING ends, e.g., in the relative stability of DETERMINATE BEING.

Hegel represents the understanding, and more especially reason, not as operations which we, as external observers, perform on concepts, but as internal to the concepts or SUBJECT-MATTER themselves. Similarly, he regards understanding or *das Verständige*, and reason or *das Vernünftige*, as intrinsic features of entities, and not simply of the concepts we form of them. But understanding and reason are involved in things in two distinct ways:

(1) In temporal DEVELOPMENT, an existing entity (e.g. the Roman Empire) is a product of the understanding, its collapse (often resulting from the sharp separation or isolation from each other of its citizens and institutions, a feature of the understanding) is the work of NEGATIVE reason, and the establishment of a new order (e.g. medieval Europe) on the basis of the old is the work of speculative reason. This new order, when it develops to maturity, itself becomes a stage of understanding and serves as the beginning of a new process of dissolution and restoration.

(2) In non-temporal hierarchies, an existing entity (e.g. persons with abstract property rights) is (seen to be) internally flawed (negative reason), until it is subsumed or sublated in a higher, inclusive whole: ETHICAL LIFE or the STATE (positive reason).

In nature, temporal developments and non-temporal hierarchies do not coincide, since natural events (apart from small-scale events such as the growth of a seed into a plant) are repetitive and cyclical: the ascending levels of NATURE do not succeed each other in TIME. In the realm of SPIRIT, they often coincide, since spirit has a developing HISTORY; but often they do not, since there never were, e.g., persons outside a state.

The objectification of reason and understanding are essential to Hegel's IDEALISM: The processes and ontological hierarchies of nature and spirit are conceived as governed by an immanent understanding and reason that is analogous, in its development, to the understanding and reason of the human mind. Genuine rationality consists in the submission and conformity of *our* reason to the reason inherent in things: In COGNITION we should follow the immanent dialectic of concepts, objects and processes. In practical life, we should conform to the intrinsic rationality of our society, of the ACTUAL. Apparently irrational features of the natural or social worlds are in reality essential elements in an overarching rationality, just as error is not only an essential step on the way to TRUTH, but an essential ingredient in it.

recognition and acknowledgement *Anerkennung* and *anerkennen* overlap the meanings of 'recognition' and 'to recognize', and of 'acknowledgement' and 'to acknowledge', but do not coincide with either pair. *Anerkennen* is a sixteenth-century formation, on the model of the Latin *agnoscere* ('to ascertain, recognize, acknowledge'), and based on the (thirteenth-century) legal sense of *erkennen* ('to judge, find (e.g. a person guilty)'), rather than its older sense of 'to KNOW, COGNIZE'. It thus suggests overt, practical, rather than merely intellectual, recognition.

'To recognize' has five broad meanings in English:

(1)   To identify a thing or person as a particular individual (e.g. Socrates) or as of a certain type (e.g. a lion). One may recognize an individual in virtue of one's past experience of it or, without such experience, in virtue of one's knowledge of some distinguishing feature of it. Similarly, one's recognition of an instance of a type may be due to previous encounters with other cases of the same type or to one's knowledge of some distinctive feature of the type. 'Recognize' in this sense is not replaceable by 'acknowledge': one may recognize someone without acknowledging him. In German it is *erkennen*, or *wiedererkennen* ('to recognize again') if past experience is stressed, but rarely *anerkennen*. (Krug's *Handwörterbuch* gives *Wiedererkennung* as one sense of *Anerkennung*, 'theoretical recognition', but focuses primarily on 'practical recognition'.)

(2)   To realize, e.g., one's error, a truth, that something is so. In so far as the recognition is private, 'acknowledge' cannot be used: one may recognize one's error, but not acknowledge it. This is *erkennen*, rather than *anerkennen*.

(3)   To admit, concede, confess or 'acknowledge' a thing or person to be something. This is *anerkennen*.

(4)   To endorse, ratify, sanction, approve, 'acknowledge' something; to take notice of, acknowledge a thing or person; etc. This is *anerkennen*.

(5)   To take notice of someone in a special way, to honour him. ('He has at last received due recognition/acknowledgement'.) This too is *anerkennen*.

Thus *Anerkennung* involves not simply the intellectual identification of a thing or person (though it characteristically presupposes such intellectual recognition), but the assignment to it of a positive value and the explicit expression of this assignment. Thus in *PS*, IV.A., where Hegel discusses the struggle for recognition, he is not dealing with the problem of 'other minds', of one's epistemological entitlement to regard others as persons (and of others to regard oneself as a person), but with the problem of how one *becomes* a fully fledged person by securing the acknowledgement of others. The epistemological problem of other minds hardly appears as a distinct problem before J. S. Mill. Before then, e.g. in Kant, Fichte and Schelling, the problem of other persons is primarily a practical or moral problem. Other people appear on the scene not in theoretical philosophy, but in practical philosophy, where they are seen as creatures on a par with myself with whom I interact, to whom I owe certain duties and who owe certain duties to me.

245

My intellectual identification of them as persons is less of a problem than how I should behave towards them. Fichte held that the reason for the existence of other people, and the justification for one's belief in them, is primarily moral: others exist to place moral constraints on the conduct of the I* and to give scope for its moral endeavours. Schelling argued that my recognition of others is necessary for my belief in an OBJECTIVE world, a world that is perceived by others, as well as myself, and thus does not require my presence or my awareness of it in order to exist. Hegel's innovation (though it owes much to Hobbes, Rousseau, Schiller, Schelling, etc.) is to regard interpersonal relations as not primarily moral relations, and reciprocal recognition as more than simply a requirement of MORALITY.

In *PS*, IV.A. and *Enc.* III §§430–5, Hegel associates recognition with SELF-CONSCIOUSNESS, but elsewhere it is associated with PERSONhood. *PS*, IV.A. is difficult for several reasons: (i) It attempts to answer not only the question 'What is required for self-consciousness?' but also 'How did social relations originate?' Hence it postulates a near-Hobbesian struggle for recognition. (At *Enc.* III §432A. Hegel concedes that this struggle belongs to the state of nature, and that in a modern STATE recognition is secured by other means.) (ii) It combines in a single narrative a variety of distinct factors, e.g. in order to distinguish himself from his natural condition, his LIFE, the combatant must risk DEATH. But one can knowingly risk death on one's own, with or without the presence of others, and thus with or without their recognition of one's risk. (iii) *Anerkennung* is used in more than one sense: what is required for self-consciousness or personhood is recognition in sense (4) above, acknowledgement as a person, as one person among others. But what the combatant seeks is recognition in sense (5), a special acknowledgement of his worth, in contrast to the other's. This purpose is defeated if recognition is reciprocal. But it is also defeated if it is unilateral, since acknowledgement is worth only as much as the acknowledger; if *he* is not acknowledged by the recipient of his acknowledgement, his acknowledgement is worthless.

Owing in part to the slipperiness of *Anerkennung*, Hegel conflates three distinct questions:

(a) Why does self-consciousness require that I recognize other persons, and am recognized by them, in senses (1) and (2)?
(b) Why does it require that I recognize/acknowledge, and am recognized/acknowledged by, others, in sense (4)?
(c) Why does it require that I am (specially) recognized/acknowledged by others in sense (5)?

But his answers do not depend only on the ambiguity of *Anerkennung*:

(a) To be self-conscious or a PERSON is to be aware of oneself as an I, in contrast to one's bodily and psychological states. It is to be 'reflected into oneself', and not to exist as simply an endless proliferation of, e.g., desires. (Self-consciousness's first attempt to establish itself is to satisfy its desire by consuming one object after another.) But REFLECTION into oneself requires that one is reflected back from something that is seen not simply as an object for one's consumption, but as another self on a par with one's own self. The use of 'I' contrasts with, and thus requires, the use of 'he/she', as well as of 'it'.

(b) Legal personhood clearly involves recognition: appropriate recognition of something as a person is both necessary and sufficient for it to be a person (just as Caligula's appointment of his horse as a consul was necessary and sufficient for it to be a consul), though usually the criteria of natural personhood must be met by an entity to which such recognition is accorded. But why is recognition (4) required for natural personhood or for self-consciousness? Why does my reflection into myself back from another person require that he acknowledge or take notice of me as a person, and not simply that I view him as a person? There are several possible answers:

(i) *Selbstbewusstsein* ('self-consciousness') also means 'self-confidence, self-respect'. Self-respect requires confirmation by others: people who are constantly devalued by others tend to devalue themselves.

(ii) Unless persons recognize each other in sense (4), they lack the evidence on which to recognize each other in senses (1) and (2): To be self-conscious, one must recognize others in senses (1) and (2). But no one can have evidence that one does this unless one also recognizes/acknowledges others in sense (4).

(iii) To recognize others in senses (1) and (2), I must be able to think, and thus (on Hegel's view) to speak a language. But I cannot acquire a language, unless I speak to others, and to speak to others is to recognize them in sense (4). 'I' contrasts with, and requires, 'you'.

(c) Hegel's belief that self-consciousness involves (special) recognition in sense (5) has four sources:

(i) His (plausible) belief that much of our conduct is 'conspicuous', motivated less by the intrinsic value to us of the conduct than by a desire to be seen to be behaving in a certain way and thus to acquire unilateral recognition (5).

(ii) The 'self-assertiveness' sense of *Selbstbewusstsein*.

(iii) His conflation of self-consciousness with the conflict in a Hobbesian state of nature.

(iv) His (plausible) belief that to transcend one's natural self (one's desires, etc.) and to be reflected into oneself as a pure I, one needs to submit to, and be disciplined by, an external agent. (*Zucht*, from *ziehen*, 'to pull, draw', etc., means both 'EDUCATION (*Erziehung*), cultivation', etc., and 'drill, discipline', with associations of PUNISHMENT.) Thus to acknowledge (5) another unilaterally enhances the self-consciousness both of the slave in *PS*, IV.A. and of the child in the modern state.

reflection In Latin *reflectere* and *reflexio* mean 'to bend back' and 'bending back'. *Animum reflectere*, literally 'to bend back the mind', originally meant 'to turn one's own or another's mind away, dissuade from (a course of action)', but later came to mean 'to turn one's thought to, reflect on, something'. In the sixteenth and seventeenth centuries these gave rise to the German *reflektieren* ('to reflect') and *Reflexion*. These have three main senses, acquired by their Latin originals in medieval times:

(1) To bend back or reflect, e.g. sound, heat, and especially light; hence to reflect or mirror an object by reflecting the light-waves from it. *Reflexion* is both the process of reflecting and its product, the reflected image.
(2) To reflect on, consider a matter. Near-equivalents in this sense are *nachdenken* ('to after-think, think over, reflect') and *überlegen*, *Überlegung* ('to consider', 'consideration').
(3) To turn back one's thoughts or attention from objects to oneself, to reflect upon oneself. In Locke and Leibniz, 'reflection' is perception of oneself or attention to what is 'in us'.

(Hegel often uses *Reflexion* and *reflektieren* in connection with RELATIONS: e.g. self-IDENTITY is 'relation (*Beziehung*) to itself, not as IMMEDIATE, but as reflected' (*Enc.* I §115). But he has no word for, and only a rudimentary concept of, a 'reflexive' (*reflexiv*) relation, an expression (*riflessività*) first used by G. Vailati in 1891.)

In *CPR*, A260ff, B316ff, Kant distinguishes transcendental and logical *Überlegung* or *Reflexion*. Logical reflection is a comparison (*Vergleichung*) of concepts to see whether they are the same or different, compatible or conflicting, determinable (MATTER) or DETERMINING (FORM), whether something is internal (analytically involved in) or external (synthetically added) to them. Transcendental reflection asks the same questions, but with an eye to the source of the concepts in our cognition. Leibniz, Kant argued, neglected transcendental reflection on the sensory conditions for the application of concepts and thus succumbed to the '*Amphibolie* ("ambiguity") of the concepts of reflection (*Reflexionsbegriffe*)', e.g. Leibniz argued that if two concepts are exactly similar, they can be exemplified by only one entity (the 'identity of indiscernibles'). This involves an illegitimate transference of the concepts of sameness and difference from their application to concepts to sensory phenomena. The concepts of sameness and difference, compatibility and conflict, INNER and OUTER, and matter and form, concepts that are applicable to other concepts in respect of their intellectual sources, are *Reflexionsbegriffe*. This influenced the second main section of Hegel's Logic, on ESSENCE and the DETERMINATIONS of reflection (*Reflexionsbestimmungen*) that derive from it, which include identity and DIFFERENCE, CONTRADICTION, inner and outer, and form and matter.

In *CJ*, Kant introduced the 'reflective (*reflektierende*) JUDGMENT': it looks for a UNIVERSAL to apply to a given PARTICULAR, while the 'determining judgment' looks for a particular to subsume under a given rule or universal. *Reflexion* also plays a part in Fichte. The I* has two drives that both presuppose and compete with each other: a practical drive to 'fill out the infinite' and a drive to 'reflect upon itself'. Each of these drives limits the other and the conflictual interplay between them generates the feeling of necessity or compulsion that accompanies representations of the supposedly external world, in contrast to our imaginings. Fichte sees reflection on oneself in terms of the reflection of light: the reflective tendency is reflected back off the point at which the practical drive is limited.

In early works, especially *DFS* and *FK*, Hegel is much concerned with *Reflexion* as a method of philosophy and with the *Reflexionsphilosophie* that, on his view, reached its peak in the thought of Kant, Jacobi and Fichte. The characteristics of *Reflexion* are that (1) it does not simply accept what is given and unreflective ways of viewing it, but reflects on them; (2) it ABSTRACTS from them contrasting pairs of general concepts, or OPPOSITES, which it attempts to keep separate, such as faith and reason, finite and infinite, subject and object; and (3) it thus conceives of itself or the reflecting SUBJECT as distinct from and external to the object(s) on which it reflects. *Reflexion* in this sense is akin to UNDERSTANDING, and is contrasted with, e.g., INTUITION, FAITH and SPECULATION. It cannot do justice to the ABSOLUTE, since it is confined to FINITE forms of COGNITION: it places restrictions (*Beschränkungen*) on the absolute, by arguing that it is, e.g., INFINITE and not finite. Hegel often refers to *Reflexion* of this type as 'EXTERNAL (*äussere* or *äusserliche*) *Reflexion*'.

But *Reflexion* is not, on Hegel's view, an unmixed evil:

1. Non-philosophical reflection is an inevitable feature of human advance. It is, for example, by reflection on my FEELINGS and distancing myself from them that I extricate my I or self from my bodily and psychological states and become SELF-CONSCIOUS. By reflection on my desires or drives, I bring order into them, dissociate myself from some of them, and make a rational decision that is more than a response to an immediate urge. Characteristically, *Reflexion* involves going beyond or transcending the object of one's reflection, not simply in the sense that I pass from, e.g., one desire to another, but that I withdraw, or am reflected (like light), into myself and then view my situation from a more elevated vantage point. (The basis for this is laid, Hegel believes, in childhood, when one's desires are frustrated or repressed, so that one is reflected back into oneself.)

2. *Reflexionsphilosophie* is not simply to be rejected in favour of a return to immediate faith or intuition: It is an inevitable stage both in the history of CULTURE and in philosophical thought. The remedy is to reflect further, on, for example, the oppositions which it sets up and attempt to overcome them.

3. *Reflexion* is not only an external activity which we apply to things and concepts: like the understanding, it is immanent in things and concepts themselves. Our *Reflexion* becomes more adequate to the extent that it conforms to the *Reflexion* of our object. But even external *Reflexion* is a phase of the immanent *Reflexion* of objects, for we ourselves and our activities are a phase of the ABSOLUTE.

In the Logic, and especially *SL*, Hegel elaborates 3 in terms of the connection between the reflection of light and mental reflection on an OBJECT. When a ray of light strikes a surface, it is no longer immediate, but reflected. Analogously, when we reflect on an object, we do not leave it as it is or simply proceed through its various qualities and quantities: we view it as the

APPEARANCE (*Schein*) of an underlying essence (*Enc.* I §112A.). Thus *Reflexion* is associated with essence, and with its *Schein(en)*, with an ambiguity parallel to that of *Reflexion*: (a) 'shine, glow; to shine, glow'; (b) 'seeming, semblance, illusion; to seem, etc.'. Thus in *SL, Reflexion* has three phases:

1. POSITING *Reflexion*, by which the essence shines and thus posits a *Schein*. Essence does this because it PRESUPPOSES what it posits: it is only an essence in virtue of positing a *Schein*, just as *Schein* is only *Schein* in virtue of being posited by an essence. Thus essence is reflected into itself by the process of *Reflexion*, just as much as it is reflected outwards into *Schein*. *Reflexion* is thus the 'movement of nothing to nothing, hence the NEGATION that comes together with itself': it *constitutes* the items that it relates. This doctrine depends on Hegel's view (derived from Goethe's *Farbenlehre* (*Doctrine of Colours*), 1810) that light manifests itself as light, and thus becomes strictly light, only when it encounters a LIMIT (*Grenze*), the 'Not (*Nicht*) of light' or a dark surface which reflects it (*Enc.* II §275A.).

2. External *Reflexion* on an object. Hegel argues, against Kant, that such reflection mirrors the immanent reflection of the object: If we look for a universal to apply to an entity, we do not leave the entity as it is in its IMMEDIACY. It is only in virtue of such subsumption that the entity becomes a *particular* (and the universal a *universal*). Correspondingly, the universal essence posits an entity, and thus makes *it* particular and *itself* universal. Thus, in defiance of Kant's contrast between 'determining' and 'reflective' judgment, Hegel concludes with:

3. Determining (*bestimmende*) *Reflexion*, the union of 1 and 2: the SUBJECT's reflection on the object mirrors or reflects the object's immanent reflection. The subject's reflection on the object is immanent to the subject, since the subject is itself an essence which shines in its reflective interplay with the object. The subject's reflection into itself (the pure I) mirrors the object's reflection into itself (the essence), and their *Schein* lies at the interface between them. (At *Enc.* II §275A. Hegel compares the manifestation of light when it impinges on its limit to the I's attainment of self-consciousness through its CONSCIOUSNESS of an alien object.)

Determining *Reflexion* involves the 'determinations of reflection' or 'essentialities' (*Wesenheiten*), pairs of concepts (ranging from identity and difference to the RECIPROCITY of two SUBSTANCES) that are applicable to an essence and its manifestations. Like the subject and object of 3, such pairs shine, or are reflected, into each other and then back into themselves: opposites such as 'positive' and 'negative', like the poles of a magnet, constitute each other. But external reflection attempts to separate them (especially in the 'LAWS of thought'), and it is essential to their nature that they can be treated in this way.

External reflection, despite its integration as a phase of *Reflexion*, continues to be seen as (a) responsible for such illegitimate separations, and (b) as external to its object, making moves that its object cannot make, like the PROOFS of geometry, Kant's external comparison of concepts, or an account of a form of consciousness in terms not available to itself.

relation   German has several words for 'relation(ship)':

1. The verb *beziehen*, like its parent verb *ziehen* ('to pull, draw, lead', etc.), has a wide range of senses ('to obtain, occupy', etc.). It also means 'to apply, relate one thing to another (e.g. a statement to another case)'. From the seventeenth century, the reflexive, *sich beziehen*, was used for 'to make a judicial appeal to', then 'to refer to as evidence', and hence 'to be related, directed to'. The seventeenth-century noun derived from it, *Beziehung*, is the most general word for a relation(ship) or connection between things or persons. *Beziehungen* ('relationships') between persons are cooler, less intimate and more external than a *Verhältnis* between them. (Relationship by blood or marriage is *Verwandtschaft*, 'kinship', from *verwandt*, 'kindred, akin', but it is also used metaphorically of, e.g., 'cognate' words and CHEMICAL 'affinity'.) In *CPR*, Kant uses *sich beziehen* and *Beziehung* for the relationship of a mental entity, especially an INTUITION or a concept, to an OBJECT, rather than for a relation between things. Thus they are close to 'refer' and 'reference'. But in other philosophers of the time (e.g. Krug) *Beziehung* is not sharply distinguished from *Verhältnis* or *Relation*, and is used for any relation between things.

2. The verb *verhalten*, from *halten* ('to hold, keep', etc.), means 'to keep back, hold in, suppress', but the reflexive *sich verhalten* is 'to behave, conduct oneself', with *Verhalten* for 'conduct, behaviour'. But the seventeenth-century *Verhältnis* means (a) a proportion or ratio, e.g. between two numbers or variables; (b) a (cor)relation between two things that are more than loosely connected and stand in a certain ratio to each other, e.g. the relation between body and soul or cause and effect; (c) an intimate relationship between persons; (d) in the plural, *Verhältnisse*, usually 'conditions, circumstances, state of affairs', not (a), (b) or (c). *Verhältnis* is used by Kant for (i) relations between mental or logical entities, such as the relations expressed by the 'concepts of REFLECTION'; (ii) relations between things or events, e.g. a cause and its effect.

3. *Relation*, borrowed from Latin *c.* 1300, first meant 'report, account, reporting', but came to mean 'relation' in the sixteenth century. In logic it was also the 'relation' of a JUDGMENT, viz. the judgment's being categorical, hypothetical or disjunctive. Kant explains this use as referring to the 'relations [*Verhältnisse*] of ... (a) the predicate to the subject, (b) of the GROUND to the consequent, (c) of the divided cognition and the collected terms of the division to one another' (*CPR* A73, B98). The 'categories of *Relation*' derived from these types of judgment (SUBSTANCE and accident, CAUSE and effect, and RECIPROCITY) reappear in *SL* under the heading of 'The Absolute Relation [*Verhältnis*]'.

4. *Zusammenhang* ('coherence, (inter)connection, (inter)connectedness, context'), from *zusammenhangen* ('to hang together', etc.), indicates the logical interconnection of thoughts or ideas, and the close interrelatedness of things, but not personal relations. Unlike 1, 2 and 3, it is not a technical term in logic for a relation, but it can be used, e.g., of the relationship of soul and body.

5. Hegel uses many other terms for relatedness in general and for specific

relations, especially *zusammenschliessen* ('to join closely'), which he associates with *Schluss, schliessen* ('INFERENCE, to infer'), and *Einheit* ('unity'), especially in the expression 'NEGATIVE unity', where the unity of two things consists in the fact that each is constituted by its not being the other.

Hegel uses these terms as follows:

1. *Beziehung* and *sich beziehen* are his most general words for 'relation' and 'to be related'. Any *Verhältnis* is a *Beziehung*, but not every *Beziehung* is a *Verhältnis*. Unlike a *Verhältnis*, a *Beziehung* does not require two distinct terms: an entity can be related to itself. But Hegel found reflexive relations (e.g. self-IDENTITY, SELF-CONSCIOUSNESS) problematic. Properly conceived they involve an ALIENATION of the entity, whereby it goes outside itself into something else and then returns to itself, actively relating itself to itself. Thus *sich beziehen auf* (*sich*, etc.) is used to mean not simply 'to be related to (itself, etc.)', but 'to relate, connect itself to (itself, etc.)'. In so far as something is related to itself, it is relatively independent of, and unrelated to, other things. (But even unrelatedness is, for Hegel, a type of relation.) He is also troubled by 'indifferent' (*gleichgültig*) relations, which make no difference to the related terms, such as likeness and DIFFERENCE (e.g. my being the same height as someone I have never met). Such relations require an 'EXTERNAL comparison (*Vergleichung*)' or 'reflection' by a third party. In genuine relations the terms actively relate themselves to each other. The relation or relating may be negative (e.g. the repulsion of units or atoms of each other), as well as positive (e.g. attraction) (*Enc.* I §97).

2. Hegel uses *Verhältnis* in its full range of meaning, and often uses *sich verhalten* (*zu*) for 'to relate (itself), be related (to)'. Under the heading of 'QUANTITY', *SL* discusses the *quantitative Verhältnis* ('ratio, proportion'), whose three phases are the direct ratio; the inverse ratio; and the ratio of powers (e.g. $x = y^2$). As a (cor)relation, a *Verhältnis* invariably has two terms that are to some degree independent of each other. In *SL* he distinguishes 'ESSENTIAL (*wesentliche*) relation' and 'ABSOLUTE relation'. The terms of an essential relation, though interlinked, are also relatively independent. Thus the first essential relation is that of WHOLE and PARTS, where the whole is conceived as a MECHANICAL aggregate of parts that have a life of their own. The relationship of a FORCE (*Kraft*) and its expression or externalization (*Äusserung*) is closer and more dynamic, since each term tends to change into the other. Closer still is the (cor)relation of INNER and OUTER. In absolute (cor)relation (which is immediately preceded by, and thus involves, absolute NECESSITY) the terms are so closely interdependent that they are regarded as the result of the bifurcation of a single entity and require the external reflection of a third party to distinguish them. Thus the relation of substance to its accidents is virtually identity: each term of the relation is a 'TOTALITY', i.e. is itself the whole relationship; each term 'shines' or APPEARS (*scheinen*) in such a way that each is, like light, nothing but its shining, with no residual underlying THING or substratum. (In his *SL* account of the absolute, which is closely similar to that of substance, Hegel speaks of the absolute's *Auslegung*, 'laying out, interpretation, exposition', of itself.) Causality and reciprocity are also

absolute relations. An absolute relation is almost too close to be a relation at all. (The adjective *relativ* commonly *contrasts* with *absolut*.)

Elsewhere *Verhältnis* is used for close correlations, e.g. the religious relationship of finite SPIRIT to God in *LPR*. This is conceived as the result of an original bifurcation of God, which is eventually repaired in cult or worship (*Kultus*); thus both terms of the relation, and the relation itself, are phases of God. It is also used for the relationship of, e.g., RELIGION to the state, or of ART to religion and PHILOSOPHY, and also for relatively superficial relations such as the relation of 'use', if e.g., religion is regarded as *useful* for political stability.

3. *PP* speaks of the *Relation* of judgments, and of inferences of *Relation*, but the term is not common elsewhere, and *SL* speaks instead of the judgment and inference of 'necessity'.

4. A *Zusammenhang* is the relation between, or relationship of, two or more items. Especially as *innerer* ('inner') *Zusammenhang*, it is tighter than a *Verhältnis*: if, e.g., we see art or religion as having a mere *Verhältnis* of use to, e.g., political life, we extract them from their inner, 'essential' or 'substantial' *Zusammenhang* with other spiritual phenomena. But a *Verhältnis* too can be 'substantial', etc., and then it is as close as a *Zusammenhang*. *Zusammenhang* is sometimes used as a general term for, e.g., the various types of relation between two DETERMINATIONS in the Logic, or for relations such as CONDITIONING, causality, etc. Here *Verhältnis* in its technical sense would be inappropriate.

Three general points deserve notice:

(1) Hegel chose his words carefully: it usually makes a difference which 'relation'-word he uses. But the words often differ in force in different contexts, and resist any single English translation.

(2) Everything, on Hegel's view, is involved in relations, and its intrinsic nature depends on these relations, even if the relations are (especially in the case of GOD) immanent in the thing itself. CONTRADICTIONS arise, in part, from the severance of concepts and things from their relationships.

(3) It is central to his IDEALISM that he conflates the relations between things with the relations between the CONCEPTS applied to (but, for him, immanent in) things. Thus, e.g., the relation between a cause and its effect is not sharply distinguished from the relation between the concept of a cause and that of an effect.

religion, theology and philosophy of religion Hegel's age was an age of deep religious FAITH. Thus any philosopher had to come to terms with religion and assign a place to it in his thought. Herder, e.g., saw religion as the pinnacle of *Humanität* ('humanity'), of the harmonious growth of human powers. In other spheres (e.g. language and literature) he advocated the development of a specifically national culture, but he saw the Christianity of the Gospels as the highest form of religion and thus of *Humanität*. Yet Christianity, although different PEOPLES give it different forms, is a world religion whose imposition on the Germans is responsible for the regrettable loss of their folk-religion and its accompanying customs, legends, etc. (He also regretted Luther's failure to establish a single German religion.) Hegel shared both Herder's Christianity and his nostalgia for folk-religion, but for Greek, rather than German, folk-religion.

Theologie is distinct from *Religion*. From the Greek *theos* ('God') and *logos* ('word, reason', etc.), it means the study of God or of divine things, and Hegel sees it as thoughtful REFLECTION on the truths embodied in religion. But he was discontented with the theology of his time. At least four types of theology met with his disapproval:

(1) The 'rational (*rationelle*) theology' of such Enlightenment thinkers as Wolff, who attempted to prove the existence of God and other religious truths. This takes both too much and too little from religion: it PRESUPPOSES religious REPRESENTATIONS (especially GOD) instead of properly deriving them, and yet it impoverishes the content of religion. It regards God solely as an OBJECT (*Gegenstand*) and does not take account of our union with him (and his union with us) in religion.

(2) Kant's reduction of religion to MORALITY, especially in *RLR*.

(3) Schleiermacher's and Jacobi's view that religion is based on FEELING or IMMEDIATE KNOWLEDGE. On this account, Hegel argues, religion draws lines into empty space.

(4) Historical theology, which simply records the HISTORY of religious doctrines, with no account of their TRUTH or rationality. This theology is concerned only with religion, not with God.

Hegel was a fierce opponent of Catholicism, but rated medieval theology more highly than modern theology: it did justice both to religion and to the philosophical interpretation and justification of it.

In a wide sense, Hegel believes, his whole system (and philosophy in general) is theology, since it (like religion) is concerned with God or the ABSOLUTE. But since religion is also an indispensable mode of access to God, though not the only or the highest mode, there is room in his system for a special study not just of God as such, but of religion: *Religionsphilosophie* or 'philosophy of religion'. *Religionsphilosophie* differs from theology of types 1, 2 and 3 in that it is concerned with religion as such, both as a way of representing God, etc., and as itself a phase in God's DEVELOPMENT, since our religious consciousness and worship is itself a stage in God's SELF-CONSCIOUSNESS. It also involves REASON and the CONCEPT, not simply the UNDERSTANDING. It differs from 4 in that it is concerned with the truth and rationality of religions.

Throughout his career Hegel was aware of a conflict between himself as INFINITE, able to ascend in thought or imagination to a view of, and near-identification with, the absolute or the universe as a whole, and himself as FINITE, restricted to a particular location in the world and to a particular outlook on it. Hegel himself is neither, and both, of these conflicting selves: he is the self that is aware of and contains them both. In *ETW* he tends to restrict philosophy to the finite and to assign the infinite to religion. But he soon came to alter this view, seeing ART, religion and PHILOSOPHY as three progressively more adequate ways of transcending the confines of everyday life and ascending to the absolute. (This emerges more clearly in his 1805–6 Jena lectures on the philosophy of spirit, than in *PS*, where art appears only as a phase of religion, in the Greek 'religion of art'.) Philosophy not only concludes the series; it also gives an account of the whole series, not only of art, religion and philosophy itself, but also of e.g. social and political life, which immediately precedes art in Hegel's arrangement. Thus philosophy, more than religion, integrates the finite and the infinite, assigning to each, and to their various phases, an appropriate place in a rational WHOLE.

In Hegel's accounts of his SYSTEM (*PS*; *Enc.* III, etc.) religion precedes philosophy. Religion temporally precedes philosophy in a given epoch (e.g. the Greeks developed their religion before they produced significant philosophy), and in the life of an individual, who absorbs a religious faith before he engages in philosophical reflection. But religion does not precede philosophy in history: it undergoes a historical development similar to, and more or less contemporaneous with, that of philosophy. Later religions are usually more developed than, and SUBLATE, earlier ones: The 'absolute religion' (Christianity) stands in a similar (all-embracing) relation to earlier religions as Hegel's philosophy does to earlier philosophies.

In some periods (e.g. the Middle Ages) philosophy and religion are closely intertwined, in others (e.g. the Enlightenment) they are separate or even hostile. But in general, Hegel believes, religion and philosophy have the same CONTENT (*Inhalt*), but present it in a different FORM (*Form*, not *Gestalt*), e.g. what Hegel presents, in the higher and more perspicuous form of THOUGHT, as the emergence of the logical IDEA into nature, or the overcoming of our natural urges, etc., is presented by Christianity, in the form of CONCEPTION, as God's creation of the world, or as the DEATH of Christ. It is often not so obvious that religion and philosophy have the same content, as it is that, e.g., a statue and a painting are of the same object and have the same content. The difference of form makes their objects and content seem different. This is why conflicts arise between religion and philosophy, and why philosophy is required to translate the conceptions (or 'metaphors') of religion into conceptual thought. Since philosophy involves conceptual thought, it can reflect upon and interpret religion, while religion cannot reflect on or interpret philosophy or, for that matter, art.

This account raises two questions:

1. Is the claim that philosophy and religion (or Hegel's philosophy and Hegel's religion) have the same content, but a different form, true or plausible? It is not unreasonable, if one accepts both a certain philosophy and a certain religion, to look for some intelligible relation between them, and one alternative is to suppose that the religion and the philosophy are at bottom saying the same thing. The translation of religious into philosophical notions goes back at least to Heraclitus. Plato presented many of his doctrines as interpretations of myths. The Neoplatonists interpreted Greek religion in terms of their own thought. Augustine gave a shamelessly Neoplatonic interpretation of Genesis: 'when I hear people say "Moses

meant this" or "Moses meant that", I think it more truly religious to say "Why should he not have had both meanings in mind, if both are true?" ' (*Confessions*, XII.31). The scholastics developed the doctrine of 'double truth', the truth of faith and the truth of reason: for Aquinas, the two truths supplement each other; for Averroes, Duns Scotus and Ockham, they can conflict; for Hegel, they more or less coincide. But both his general account of the doctrine and his application of it are defective:

(a)   The specification of the forms in which art, religion and philosophy present their content is unsatisfactory. Poetry, Hegel concedes, involves conception, as well as INTUITION. Philosophy too requires conceptions, e.g. the conception of a magnet. His notion of a conception is too fluid and ambiguous to serve its purpose. (Some notions, e.g. SPIRIT, have the role both of a religious conception and of a philosophical thought.)

(b)   Hegel's translation of a religious conception into a philosophical thought is often an arbitrary selection from several equally plausible translations, with no rational procedure for deciding between them.

(c)   Such plausibility as the translations have often depends on dubious interpretations of religions within their own terms, e.g. the virtual elimination of IMMORTALITY from Christianity.

2. If religion has the same content as philosophy, but an inferior form, why is religion needed? Hegel has several replies:

(a)   In some periods, a religion, e.g. early Christianity, presents a truth, e.g. the fundamental freedom and equality of all men, more adequately than contemporaneous philosophy.

(b)   Even when philosophy catches up with religion and presents the same truth in philosophical terms, its doing so presupposes the achievements of religion. In general, the philosophical advances of an epoch or an individual presuppose religious advances.

(c)   Religion is not dispensable even when philosophy has caught up: philosophy is essentially esoteric, neither attractive nor intelligible to most people in its pure form. Religion, by contrast, captures the imagination of the masses, and presents them with deep truths about the universe and their place in it in an attractive form. Even a philosopher need not regard lectures and conferences as an adequate substitute for communal worship.

(d)   Religion serves the purposes of moral and political order, but religion and the political constitution must be in harmony, since man-made laws have little force against the religious conscience: 'It is a modern folly to alter a corrupt ethical system, its constitution and legislation, without changing the religion, to have a revolution without a reformation' (*Enc.* III §552). But the necessity of religion does not lie in its serving some presupposed purpose: religion determines what matters to us and what our purposes are, and is not to be judged by a purpose external to it.

Hegel's philosophy of religion gave rise to much debate after his death. The most significant contributions were made by the 'left'-Hegelians: Strauss

(*The Life of Jesus*, 1835), Feuerbach (*The Essence of Christianity*, 1841) and Marx.

representation and conception The verb *vorstellen*, literally 'to put forward, in front (of)', is used of introducing or presenting something, usually a person, to another person, and of representing something in, e.g., ART (usually in less detail than is implied by *darstellen*, which also means 'to represent, exhibit'). In its reflexive form, *sich vorstellen*, it means 'to (re)present something to oneself, imagine, conceive, picture to oneself'. The product of this activity, the idea, conception or mental picture, is a *Vorstellung*. (In Hegel, (*die*) *Vorstellung* occasionally denotes the possession or employment of conceptions, but the usual term for these is the substantival infinitive, *das Vorstellen*.) The word stresses the subjective mental state of the subject rather than the nature of the represented object; one speaks, e.g., of *his Vorstellung* of God, but of *the* CONCEPT of God.

In philosophy *Vorstellung* has two senses: (1) In a wider sense, it is equivalent to 'idea' in Locke's (but not Hegel's) usage, and covers thoughts, concepts, intuitions, sensations and perceptions. In this sense a *Vorstellung* need not be either universal or pictorial. In translations of Kant, who used the word in this sense, it is often rendered as 'representation'. (2) In a narrower sense, *Vorstellung* contrasts (a) with perception, sensation, and INTUITION, in that it need not involve the presence of the represented object or refer to a definite individual, and (b) with THOUGHT, concept and IDEA (*Idee*), in that it involves an image or a pictorial element. In this sense it is sometimes translated as 'conception' or 'idea'.

Hegel consistently uses *Vorstellung* in the narrow sense, both because he needs a term to contrast with 'concept' (*Begriff*) and to cover those mental items to which he denies the traditional title of 'concept', and because he sees no need for a generic term to capture what sensations, conceptions, concepts, etc., have in common, when these items are, on his view, both distinct, and yet dialectically and hierarchically ordered. His main account of the *Vorstellung* occurs in *Enc.* III §§451–64. The *Vorstellung* is the intermediate stage between intuition (*Anschauung*), the sensory apprehension of individual external objects, and conceptual thought. It involves three main phases, RECOLLECTION, IMAGINATION and MEMORY:

1. *Erinnerung* standardly means 'memory' or 'recollection', but Hegel stresses its root meaning of 'internalization' (*Er-innerung*): when someone recollects something, he internalizes it or makes it his own, and, since the corresponding verb is reflexive (*sich erinnern*, 'to remind oneself (of), recall', but also, for Hegel, 'to internalize, withdrawn into, oneself'), he also withdraws into himself. This occurs by means of an image or picture (*Bild*) of the object, which, unlike the intuition of it, is detached from the externality of space and time, and 'received into the universality of the I' (§452). The image itself is not at this stage universal, but it is not as fully determinate as the intuition. An image is not always conscious: it is in itself or implicit in the 'nocturnal pit' of the mind. At first we become conscious of it only in the presence of the intuited object; my image of a person, e.g., enables me to

257

recognize him when I see him. But after repeated encounters, I can recall the image of a thing even in its absence. This is the *Vorstellung* in its simplest phase: the possession of an image that is *mine* in a way that external objects and intuitions are not.

2. The reproductive imagination differs little from recollection: it simply recalls an image of a previously intuited object, but, unlike recollection, it can do this voluntarily in the absence of the intuited object. The associative imagination, by contrast, reflects upon images and relates them in ways other than those in which the corresponding objects and intuitions are related. Primarily, the imagination forms from images UNIVERSAL conceptions, the conception of redness or of a plant, and these are *Vorstellungen* in the strict sense. The abstraction of such conceptions does not occur simply through the association of ideas or by the constant recurrence of similar intuitions or images, but is controlled by the rational activity of the I* or intelligence. Such conceptions are related to images in much the way that images are related to intuitions: images, though universal and internal in relation to intuitions, are discrete, INDIVIDUAL and EXTERNAL in relation to conceptions. Conceptions are thus *mine*, internal to myself, in a stronger sense than images are.

The third type of imagination, the productive phantasy, associates the universal conception with a sign (*Zeichen*), primarily, but not exclusively, a linguistic sign. The word is itself an intuition, initially a sound, and secondarily a visual intuition, but, unlike ordinary intuitions (and, to a lesser degree, a *symbol*), its association with the conception owes nothing to similarity of content, but is purely arbitrary and WILFUL. The I asserts its power over intuitions by choosing which intuitions, usually produced by itself, to link with its conceptions.

3. Memory (*Gedächtnis*), finally, performs on these intuitive signs an operation similar to those performed by recollection on intuitions and by imagination on images: in familiarizing us with the use of a given sign for a given conception, it converts the sign-intuition into a universal *Vorstellung*, that is, into a word-type, in contrast to a fleeting token. The two conceptions, the conception and the word-type, become one conception. A conception thus requires no non-verbal intuition or image: 'In the name "lion" we need neither the intuition of such an animal nor even the image; the name, when we understand it, is the simple imageless conception. It is in names that we think' (§462). The internalization of the *Vorstellung* is thus complete; it is wholly *mine*.

Hegel next turns to thinking and thoughts (§§465–8), which are distinct from, though systematically related to, representation and conceptions. The differences are these:

(a) The conception is mine; in its early phases, it is SUBJECTIVE, while thinking and the thought are impersonal and objective. But the conception approaches such OBJECTIVITY in its final phase, when the full internalization of the conception involves the dissolution of my subjective and idiosyncratic imagery. In becoming wholly mine, the conception becomes wholly other than mine – a thought.

(b) Conceptions involve thought, but they differ from *pure* thoughts, such as that of QUALITY, in that they are empirical or pictorial, even if they require no mental image. They relate to pure thoughts in two distinct ways: They are, first, empirical specifications of pure thoughts, as, for example, the conception of red is a specification of the thought of quality. Second, they are 'metaphors' of pure thoughts, as the conception of God is a metaphor of the thought of the ABSOLUTE (*Enc.* I §3); RELIGION in general presents, in the form of *Vorstellung*, the absolute that ART presents in the form of intuition and PHILOSOPHY in the form of conceptual thought.

(c) The CONTENT of a conception is isolated from that of other conceptions and is 'given' and IMMEDIATE (*Enc.* I §20; III §455). A thought, by contrast, is connected with, and derived from, other thoughts. By this criterion, a non-empirical category of the UNDERSTANDING, such as CAUSALITY, will be the content of a conception, rather than a thought, if it is acquired and employed in isolation from other categories. Hegel might argue that if the category is isolated from other categories, it is likely to have closer connections, both in its origin and in its content, with sensory intuition and imagery, than if it is a thought; thus the *conception* of causality will differ from the *thought* of it in way (b), as well as (c).

It is unlikely, however, that these three differences will invariably coincide, and the boundary between thoughts and conceptions is not clearly drawn.

right The adjective *recht* has most of the senses of the cognate 'right'. It originally meant 'straight', then 'correct' (*richtig*), and thus 'lawful; just (*gerecht*); ethically good'. (*Die rechte Hand* is 'the right hand', whose use is felt to be correct.) The neuter singular of *recht* becomes the noun (*das*) *Recht*. This means: (1) a right, claim or title; (2) justice (as in, e.g., 'to administer *justice*', 'to have justice on one's side', but not justice as a virtue, viz. *Gerechtigkeit*); (3) 'the law' as a principle, or 'the laws' collectively (as in, e.g., 'Roman law', 'international law (*Völkerrecht*)', not particular LAWS, viz. *Gesetze*). *Recht* corresponds to the Latin *ius*, the French *droit*, and the Italian *diritto*, in contrast to *lex, loi, legge* ('law, *Gesetz*'). But no single English word fulfils this function. *Recht* enters into several compounds, notably *Staatsrecht* ('constitutional law') and *Naturrecht* ('natural law').

In philosophy (e.g. in Kant and Fichte) *Recht* is commonly used for legal norms and institutions, in contrast to *Moralität* ('MORALITY') and *Sittlichkeit* ('ETHICAL LIFE'). Fries developed the idea that *Recht* is concerned only with external conduct, while morality is concerned with one's *Gesinnung* ('disposition'). Hegel often uses *Recht* in this narrower sense, both in *PP*, which precedes *PR*, and in *Enc.* III §§448ff, which follows it. But in *PR*, *Recht* is used in a wider sense, to include *Moralität* and *Sittlichkeit*, along with world HISTORY, as well as *Recht* in the narrow sense (which corresponds to *abstrakte*

Recht at *PR* §§34–104; PROPERTY, contract and wrong, including CRIME and PUNISHMENT). There are several reasons for this:

1. For Kant and Fichte, *Sittlichkeit* is equivalent to *Moralität*, and can thus be appropriately contrasted with *Recht*. But Hegel's redefinition of *Sittlichkeit* means that it now covers much that previously fell under the heading of *Recht*, e.g. laws and *Staatsrecht*. (Even in *Enc.* III, *Rechtspflege*, the 'administration of justice', falls under the heading of *Sittlichkeit* rather than *Recht* as such: §§529ff.) Thus it can no longer be simply contrasted with *Recht*. *Moralität* is intermediate between abstract *Recht* and *Sittlichkeit*: abstract *Recht*, which embodies FREEDOM in an external object, represents the OBJECTIVE side of right, and *Moralität* the SUBJECTIVE side, while *Sittlichkeit* combines subjectivity and objectivity. It is thus natural to include *Moralität* under the heading of *Recht*. In *Enc.* III §§483ff the expression 'objective SPIRIT' covers the same area as *Recht* in *PR*. But this is more natural, when (as in *Enc.* III, but not *PR*) 'objective' spirit is contrasted with 'subjective' and 'ABSOLUTE' spirit.

2. Hegel is continually aware that *Recht* means 'a right', as well as 'right' or '(the) law'. But morality too confers certain rights on an individual, e.g. the right not to be held responsible, either morally or legally, for ACTIONS performed unknowingly. World history owes its inclusion in *Recht* in part to the fact that in world history, the 'world's court of judgment', the 'spirit of the world' exercises its *right*, 'the highest right of all', over finite national spirits (*Volksgeiste*) (*PR* §340).

3. The contrast between morality and right depends in part on the belief that they can conflict with each other, that what is legally permitted, or even required, may be immoral. But, on Hegel's view, morality and right cannot ultimately confict: *moral* criticism of current social and legal arrangements is rarely, if ever, appropriate or rationally tenable. Right may fail to do justice to the moral conscience of its citizens, or be defective in other ways. But these defects are discerned not by the individual moral conscience, but by an examination of the rationality inherent in right itself. Thus *PR* aims to limit the claims of *Moralität* and to integrate it into the SYSTEM of right.

4. In contrast to morality, abstract right is relatively objective. But it also develops the individual into a self-aware PERSON. *Recht* and *Sittlichkeit*, like morality, do not simply regulate the external conduct of individuals who are already fully formed human beings: they form them, by stages, into proper human beings. Thus Fichte was wrong to argue, in *FNR*, that *Recht* involves coercion, while *Moralität* does not: *Recht*, as much as *Moralität*, requires the acquiescence of the individual, and secures it by moulding him to its purposes. *Recht*, *Moralität* and *Sittlichkeit* are thus phases of a single enterprise.

The term *Naturrecht* (introduced by Leibniz for the Latin *ius naturale*, and in contrast to *positives Recht*) occurs in the title of *PR*, as well as *NL*. But Hegel rejected the view customarily associated with the term, viz. that men have certain rights and should be governed by certain laws that are wholly independent of, and can be wholly at odds with, the rights they are accorded and the ways they are governed in ACTUAL societies. He is more sympathetic to the view, descending from Aristotle, that certain general principles can be derived from an examination of man as a social being, and that although these principles for the most part underlie existing social and political arrangements, they can be used for the internal assessment and improvement of a society. But he distinguishes this view from *Naturrecht* as such. At *Enc.* III §502 he argues that *Naturrecht* refers ambiguously to two views, involving two distinct senses of 'NATURE':

(a) If 'nature' is used in contrast to the 'spiritual' and the 'social', *Naturrecht* is a *Recht* that obtains in a state of nature (*Naturzustand*). Then CIVIL SOCIETY and the STATE require the restriction of our natural freedom and rights. But right and rights, Hegel argues, obtain only in society: 'a state of nature is a state of violence and wrong (*Unrechts*)'.

(b) If 'nature' is used for the 'ESSENCE' of right, *Naturrecht* is *Recht* as it is determined by the CONCEPT of right. *Naturrecht* in this sense is not natural in the sense of (a), but social, and is based on the 'free personality'.

Theory (b) is Hegel's own. But even the right of the free personality is a historical product of the Roman Empire and has not beeen realized at all times and places, e.g. in ancient Greece. He rejects (a) not only for its association with a fictional state of nature, but also for its overvaluation of the individual's PARTICULAR WILL. Freedom consists not in being free to do as one likes, but in being a fully developed human being.

In the modern state, individuals have certain 'abstract' or 'formal' rights that are inalienable (*unveräusserlich*) and imprescriptible (*unverjährbar*), rights that constitute my personhood, such as the right not to be enslaved, to acquire and own property, etc. (*PR* §66). Such rights must not be infringed by other persons. But since abstract right is only the lowest of the three phases of *Recht*, abstract rights are not immune to interference from the higher spheres, *Moralität* and *Sittlichkeit*: A person whose life is in immediate danger has a right to another's property, and if he steals it, 'it would be wrong to treat this action as an ordinary theft' (*PR* §127A.). Hegel leaves it unclear whether the thief's right is only a moral right or is (or should be) a legally enforceable right; but a debtor has (on Hegel's view, rightly) a legal, as well as a moral, right to retain such of his creditor's property as he needs to live on (*PR* §127). A state at WAR has the right to require its citizens to sacrifice their lives and property (*PR* §324). Its justification is not that the sacrifice of the rights of some individuals is required for the preservation of the rights of other individuals. For the central purpose of the state is not, on Hegel's view, the protection of the abstract rights (to property, etc.) of its citizens. But since the citizens of a state must also be persons (and since man is essentially free), there are restrictions on the state's right to violate or remove abstract rights: it must not e.g. enslave, or permit the enslavement of, its citizens (or any other human being).

In the sphere of abstract right, the possession of rights entails no duties, except the duty to respect the rights of others, while in ethical life one has (e.g. marital) rights only in so far as one has duties, and vice versa (*PR* §155).

261

S

scepticism and stoicism   Stoicism, epicureanism and scepticism were, on Hegel's view, the three main philosophical tendencies in Greece between Aristotle and Neoplatonism. Hegel considers epicureanism in *LHP*, but regards it as a sensualist, unphilosophical doctrine, inferior to stoicism and scepticism. Thus it does not appear in *PS*, IV.B, where stoicism and scepticism are followed by the unhappy CONSCIOUSNESS (medieval Christianity). (Karl Marx attempted to redress Hegel's injustice to Epicurus in his doctoral dissertation, *The Differences between the Natural Philosophies of Democritus and Epicurus*, 1841.)

Stoicism or the Stoa was founded by Zeno of Citium (in Cyprus) *c*. 300 BC. The name derives from the *Stoa poikilē*, the 'decorated portico' in Athens in which Zeno taught. The school lasted for several centuries, and falls into three periods: the old Stoa (especially Zeno, Cleanthes and Chrysippus); the middle Stoa (especially Panaetius and Posidonius); the late Stoa (especially Seneca, Epictetus and Marcus Aurelius). Hegel was more familiar with the late stoics, since their works survive in quantity, while the earlier periods are known only from later reports and quoted fragments. In *PS*, he is impressed by the fact that one stoic, Epictetus, was a (liberated) slave, while another, Marcus Aurelius, was an emperor (a master).

Stoics believed that the universe was governed by an all-pervading *logos* or reason. This was identified with a rarefied fire, which was present in everything in a more debased form. (Most Stoics believed in the periodic conflagration and re-emergence of the world.) Man's rational soul is a fragment of the divine *logos*; it can thus ascertain the divine purpose and conform to it. Virtue, and happiness, consist only in such conformity. Everything else (health, wealth, etc.) is 'indifferent', neither good nor bad. To attain this state of mind (*apatheia*, 'freedom from emotion, imperturbability'), and thus to live 'in accord with nature' is the goal of life. (These doctrines did not prevent Stoics from holding high office: they often conceived of themselves as actors, distanced from the role that they nevertheless played to good effect.) Greek Stoics, although their aim was mainly ethical, based their ethics on metaphysics, logic, physics and epistemology. (The idea of a *kritērion* of truth derives from stoicism.) But these fields were neglected under the Empire, when stoicism became as much a religion as a philosophy.

In *LHP*, Hegel shows a fair knowledge of the more intellectual aspects of stoicism, but in *PS* he focuses on its attempt to deal with the external world by inner withdrawal. The ethics of stoicism exerted a continuous influence on

262

later thinkers, including (despite his criticisms) Hegel. His view, e.g., that the ACTUAL is rational owes more to stoicism than to plain conservatism. But the beliefs, expressed in *LPH*, that HISTORY is a 'spectacle of passions' and that 'nothing great in the world has been achieved without passion' imply a criticism of the doctrine of *apatheia*.

Greek scepticism (from *skepsis*, 'inquiry, investigation', not 'disbelief' or 'doubt') also had a long history, roughly contemporaneous with that of stoicism. The movement traced its origins to Pyrrho of Elis in the fourth century BC, and our main source for it is the works of Sextus Empiricus, a Greek doctor and sceptic of the third century AD. Sceptics advocated undogmatic inquiry (*skepsis*) and suspension of belief (*epochē*) in contrast to the dogmatism of, e.g., Platonism and stoicism. *Epochē*, they held, produces tranquillity. (In Hegel's day *Skeptizismus* is still contrasted with *Dogmatismus*, but *Kritizismus*, i.e. Kantianism, is often seen as a third alternative.) In the third century BC, under the headship of Arcesilaus, the Academy founded by Plato converted to scepticism and adhered to it for two centuries; it produced such notable sceptics as Carneades and Aenesidemus, who rebelled against what he saw as the residual dogmatism of the Academy. There was controversy in antiquity over the relationship between Pyrrhonism and Academic scepticism. (*LHP* treats the New Academics and scepticism separately, but consecutively.) Ancient scepticism resurfaced in the sixteenth century, and made a significant impact on Montaigne, Pascal, Bayle, etc.

Aenesidemus is said to have formulated the ten *tropoi*, 'modes, ways', of scepticism, which exploit the variations in APPEARANCES, depending on: (1) the animal species; (2) the individual human; (3) the sense or sense-organ (e.g. sight or touch); (4) the circumstances (e.g. drunkenness and sobriety); (5) the position of the object (e.g. in or out of water); (6) the admixture to the object (i.e. the distortion of the object by the medium through which it is sensed, e.g. the warm or cold air through which it is seen); (7) the quantity of the object (e.g. a few silver filings appear black, a lot white); (8) relativity (e.g. Jumbo appears small in relation to other elephants, but big in relation to other animals); (9) the frequency of one's encounters with the object (e.g. one's first earthquake appears more frightful than later ones); (10) one's lifestyle, customs and laws, and one's prior mythical and dogmatic beliefs. In each case the sceptical argument is of the type:

(1) The object appears red to one person, in one set of circumstances, etc., but green to, in, etc., another.
(2) It cannot be both red and green.
(3) There is no reason to prefer one appearance to the other. (This is *isostheneia*, 'equipollence'.)
(4) We cannot affirm that it is red or that it is green, but must suspend belief.

Agrippa later added five modes: (a) In both philosophy and common life there are disputes, with no reason to prefer one opinion to the other. (b) The warrant provided for an opinion in turn requires a warrant, leading to an INFINITE regress. (c) An object appears in relation to the subject and other circumstances; we must suspend judgment on what it is like in itself. (d) Dogmatists avoid an infinite regress by assuming a hypothesis (or PRESUPPO-SITION). (e) Their reasoning often involves a vicious circle, when each of two doctrines requires the warrant of the other (the 'reciprocal mode'). (a) and (c) summarize the original ten modes; (b), (d) and (e) are directed against philosophical dogmatism, e.g. against Aristotle's theory that there are IMME-DIATE axioms that need no PROOF.

Hegel studied Greek scepticism carefully, especially for his review of Schulze in *CJP*. In this review, and later, he regarded ancient scepticism as superior to modern (e.g. Hume, Schulze), mainly because it is more scepti-cal. In particular, while modern sceptics are sceptical about philosophy and about the application of THOUGHTS to sensory phenomena, ancient sceptics attacked sensory phenomena and common-sense beliefs as well. Hegel sees them as allies in his attack on such philosophers of 'common sense' as Krug, who appeal to the 'facts (*Tatsachen*) of CONSCIOUSNESS'. Thus he prefers the ten modes to Agrippa's five, since the ten are aimed at common sense, while the five attack philosophy. (There is considerable controversy over the scope of ancient scepticism, over whether it, or various strands in it, attacked only philosophical dogmas or also the beliefs required for everyday life.)

Hegel is influenced by scepticism at several levels:

(1) His accounts of particular topics (CAUSALITY, the THING, the criterion of TRUTH in *PS*, Intro., etc.) often owe as much to Sextus as to modern philosophers.

(2) Scepticism is a FORM of consciousness in *PS*, where Hegel recognizes the practical, rather than purely epistemological, aim of ancient scepticism, the attainment of tranquillity by *epochē*. His objections to scepticism in *PS* are not compelling: the Sceptics, like the Stoics, had half a millen-nium to think of replies to arguments against them.

(3) Hegel regards his own procedure as sceptical with respect both to forms of consciousness (including SENSORY CERTAINTY) and to DETERMINA-TIONS of THOUGHT (including other philosophies). But his scepticism involves not simply suspension of belief about a position, but the NEGATION of it, a negation which results in the affirmation of a new position. Hegel's procedure is complicated by the fact that his scepti-cism (like that of some Greeks) extends to the LAWS of logic, while his rejection of a position usually depends on a CONTRADICTION in it.

(4) Hegel also attempted to fortify his SYSTEM against sceptical attacks, especially on the basis of Agrippa's five modes. His defences include the following:

   (i) His philosophy is not in dispute with other philosophies distinct from and incompatible with itself: it SUBLATES and thus embraces other philosophies. His reply to an attempt to counterpose another view to his own is: 'I've already said that.' (Against mode (a).)

   (ii) Hegel simply watches 'the THING (*Sache*) itself', viz. forms of consciousness, of thought, etc., develop and criticize themselves, with no contribution from himself. (Against mode (c).)

(iii)   The criterion of truth (which for the sceptic is as disputable as anything else) is thus supplied, and applied to itself, by the form of consciousness, etc., not by Hegel.

(iv)   Presuppositions are made, but are sublated in the circular movement of the SYSTEM. The system does not reason in a circle about a static world distinct from itself, but follows the circular movement of the world itself. Thus it involves both *hypotheseis* and circularity, but no infinite regress. (Against modes (b), (d) and (e).)

Hegel distinguishes scepticism from (especially Cartesian) doubt. *Zweifel* ('doubt') comes from *zwei* ('two'), and implies a continued attachment to the beliefs one doubts and a hope of restoring one's confidence in them. Sceptical doubt is rather despair (*Verzweiflung*), a hopeless abandonment of the position doubted.

science and system   *Wissenschaft*, from *Wissen* ('KNOWLEDGE'), originally meant 'knowledge', but from the sixteenth and seventeenth centuries was used for the Latin *scientia*, '(a) science, an organized, cohesive body of knowledge; the activity of acquiring such knowledge'. It applies to the natural sciences (*Naturwissenschaften*), but is less closely associated than 'science' with the natural sciences and their methods. Thus it is applied more widely than 'science' now is: e.g. the systematic study of ART, RELIGION, HISTORY, ethics, etc., is a *Wissenschaft*. (The word *Geisteswissenschaft* post-dates Hegel, and is a translation of J. S. Mill's 'moral science'.) Hence, it is natural to regard philosophy, as long as it is systematic, as a *Wissenschaft*.

System comes from the Greek *systēma* ('an articulated whole composed of several parts'), which comes in turn from *synistanai* ('to put together, combine', from *sun*, 'with, together', and *histanai*, 'to put, set'). Wolff defined it as 'a collection of truths connected with each other and with their principles'. Kant views a *System* more organically, and associates it closely with *Wissenschaft*. (An art, *Kunst*, such as chemistry, can also be systematic, on Kant's view, but it is practical, while a *Wissenschaft* is theoretical.) A *System* is, for Kant, 'the unity of manifold cognitions under an IDEA. The idea is the rational CONCEPT of the form of a WHOLE, in so far as the concept determines *a priori* both the scope of the whole and the place of the parts in relation to each other' (*CPR* A832, B860). A system is governed by a PURPOSE contained in its concept, and is an articulated whole, not an aggregate of externally related parts. Parts cannot be added or subtracted without impairing the system, but it can grow organically, like a living creature.

Hegel shares this notion of a system and its association with *Wissenschaft*. From his Jena years, he held that philosophy must be systematic and scientific, though he was critical of *Formalismus*, the application of irrelevant and artificial abstract schemata to empirical material (e.g. *PS*, Pref.), and opposed systems, such as Spinoza's, that proceed from presupposed initial DEFINITIONS and axioms. At *Enc.* I §14, he gives two reasons why 'a philosophy without system is wholly unscientific':

1. The object of philosophy, the idea or the ABSOLUTE, itself forms a system: 'The TRUTH is CONCRETE; it unfolds within itself, and gathers and holds itself together in unity' (*Enc.* I §14). To do justice to it, philosophy must mirror its structure. (For Hegel, a system is not, as its derivation suggests, 'put together' by the philosopher: he reveals interconnections intrinsic to it, and puts together only what has been separated by previous thinkers or by CULTURE.)

2. A scientific system ensures that what one chooses to deal with and one's claims about it express more than personal idiosyncrasies: 'Apart from the whole of which it is a MOMENT, a content lacks justification, and is a baseless PRESUPPOSITION, or personal conviction' (*Enc.* I §14). Hegel thus rejects Fichte's view: 'What sort of philosophy one chooses depends on what sort of man one is; for a philosophical system is not a dead piece of furniture that we can accept or reject as we wish; it is animated by the soul of the person who holds it' (First Intro. to *SKW*). System and science, Hegel believes, eliminate such personal factors.

Personal idiosyncrasy in the choice of a system is also excluded by the fact that, on Hegel's view, a system of PHILOSOPHY is not one among several alternative systems: a system is not a philosophy with a 'restricted principle, distinct from other principles; it is the principle of genuine philosophy to contain all particular principles' (*Enc.* I §14). (Some epochs display several distinct philosophies, embodying distinct principles – e.g. STOICISM, Epicureanism and SCEPTICISM in post-Aristotelian Greece – but such a situation is philosophically unsatisfactory, and is to be resolved by a philosophy that combines all such principles.)

Hegel often speaks of philosophy, especially his own philosophy, as '(the) science' (*die Wissenschaft*), seeming to imply that there is only one science. The reason is this: in so far as Hegel's philosophy includes all particular philosophical principles, it is philosophy as such, not *a* philosophy. But philosophy also embraces other sciences in so far as they are genuinely sciences and not simply aggregates of information (e.g. philology), based on WILFULNESS (e.g. heraldry), or positive, in contrast to rational, in their subject-matter (e.g. the taxation system), in their form (e.g. most empirical sciences at present) or in their mode of cognition (e.g. appeals to FEELING, authority, etc.). For a genuine science employs thought-DETERMINATIONS, which since they are FINITE, implicitly transcend the sphere of the science in question and pass over into a higher sphere, i.e. another science. Thus when, e.g., experimental physics and history have purified their concepts sufficiently, they will 'mirror the concept', and fall into place as parts of a single science. Only quasi-sciences or those aspects of science that are irremediably positive will remain outside this science. But that is because they are not genuinely scientific: a genuine science cannot be distinct from other sciences (*Enc.* I §16).

This single science, Hegel argues, will form a circle, and each of the particular sciences that it contains will form a circle, which, since it is a TOTALITY, 'breaks through the barrier of its element and grounds another sphere'. Thus science forms a 'circle of circles' (*Enc.* I §15). The main spheres are logic, philosophy of NATURE and philosophy of SPIRIT, but more specific sciences take their place within these spheres. (*Enc.* does not purport to present the particular sciences in full, but only their starting-points and basic concepts.) The circular structure of science, in contrast to particular sciences and other, earlier philosophical systems, will face no problem of where to *begin*: in principle one can begin at any point, once one has made the decision to philosophize, though some points may be more appropriate for a novice than others (*Enc.* I §17).

Several beliefs underlie Hegel's drive to system: that the world as a whole forms a single, intelligible system that it is our business to discern and reflect; that items and bodies of knowledge, since they share a common rational framework, must be intelligibly related; that the fragments of a system are not wholly intelligible in isolation from each other ('The truth is the whole': *PS*, Pref.); and that only a system on his plan can be epistemologically secure.

Hegel's was an age of philosophical systems, and thus he does not do full justice to the question: Why must philosophy be systematic or scientific? He knew of writers who present their thoughts in an unsystematic form, some of whom he admired (e.g. Diderot, Lichtenberg), and of critics of system such as the ROMANTIC, F. Schlegel: 'It is equally fatal for the mind to have a system and to have none. It will simply have to decide to combine the two' (*Athenaeum Fragments*). But he reserves *LHP* in the main for those philosophers who had (e.g. Aristotle), or might be seen as having (e.g. Plato), a system. Two of Hegel's greatest critics, Nietzsche and Kierkegaard, were also critics of system and science. (Kierkegaard regularly refers to Hegelianism as 'the system', and his *Philosophical Fragments* and *Concluding Unscientific Postscript* announce their anti-Hegelianism in their titles.) Their, and other, objections are these:

(1)   The world is too complex, and our knowledge of it now too vast, to be accommodated in a system.

(2)   A system is limited and restricting: it closes one's mind to alternatives and to new discoveries that cannot be accommodated in the system (Jaspers).

(3)   A system is cognitive and retrospective rather than practical and prospective: it cannot cater for human choices in life and ACTION (Kierkegaard).

(4)   A system is ultimately groundless and essentially expresses the personality of the systematizer (Nietzsche).

(5)   A system cannot accommodate the supreme reflectiveness of the human mind. Such questions as 'Why prefer truth to falsehood?' (Nietzsche) or 'Why have a system?' necessarily arise outside any system.

Hegel would have to concede (1), though (1) does not entail that a system is either impossible or undesirable in principle. He explicitly rejects (2) at *Enc.* I §14. His concern for truth and objectivity would lead him to reject (3), if he has not already dealt with Kierkegaard in his account of the 'unhappy

CONSCIOUSNESS'. He attempts to eliminate the personal factors referred to in (4); his answers to the problem(s) of knowledge are not obviously inferior to Nietzsche's. Hegel's thought and the construction of his system proceed by way of successive REFLECTIONS on the present state of play: it is not obvious that he cannot accommodate the questions raised in (5), even if he did not explicitly do so. (His reflections on truth are no less innovative than Nietzsche's.)

Hegel also uses *System* in a non-technical sense, e.g. for the taxation system, and for CIVIL SOCIETY's 'system of needs' (*PR* §§189ff; *Enc.* III §§524ff).

Science of Logic (*Wissenschaft der Logik*) (1812–16)

SL consists of two 'volumes'. The first, 'The Objective Logic', contains two 'books': the 'Doctrine (*Lehre*) of BEING' (published in 1812) and 'The Doctrine of ESSENCE' (1813). The second volume, 'The Subjective Logic', contains the 'Doctrine of the CONCEPT' and was published in 1816. In 1831 Hegel completed a greatly revised and expanded version of the 'Doctrine of Being', but had no time to revise the rest of *SL*. The Preface to the second edition is dated 7 November 1831, just before his death on 14 November 1831. This edition appeared in 1832, and again in 1834–5 in the posthumous *Works*. Only the second edition of *SL* is translated into English.

The subject-matter of *SL* corresponds to no single traditional discipline, but is an attempt to combine several previously distinct subjects into a single whole. The main antecedents of *SL* are these:

1. In his *Categories*, Aristotle tried to list and define the most general types of predicate applicable to an entity: SUBSTANCE, QUALITY, QUANTITY, RELATION, etc. Plato had attempted a similar task, especially in the *Sophist*, Hegel's favourite Platonic dialogue.

2. In his *De Interpretatione*, Aristotle considered the structure and constituents of the PROPOSITION or JUDGMENT. Plato had again explored this matter, especially in the *Theaetetus* and *Sophist*.

3. Aristotle's *Prior Analytics* deals with the nature and validity of INFERENCES or SYLLOGISMS, while his *Posterior Analytics* deals with PROOF or demonstration and with demonstrative SCIENCE. *Analutika* is Aristotle's word for 'logic'. *Logikē* (*technē*) ('(the art of) logic', from *logos*, 'word, reason', etc.) was first used by the STOICS.

These and other logical works of Aristotle were later called the *Organon*, the 'instrument' of correct thought. (Works entitled 'New Organon', such as Bacon's and Lambert's, are attempts to outdo, or update, Aristotle.)

4. In his *Metaphysics*, Aristotle attempted to justify the LAWS of CONTRADICTION and of the excluded middle. (He assigned them to METAPHYSICS or 'first philosophy', since they apply to all entities.) By Hegel's time the 'laws of THOUGHT' also included the law of IDENTITY and (since Leibniz) the principle of sufficient reason or GROUND.

2, 3, 4 and, in part, 1 made up the subject-matter of the 'FORMAL', 'classical' or 'traditional' logic of Hegel's day. Hegel, like Kant, held that this had made no important advance since Aristotle. (This underrates the medieval and stoic contributions to logic, as well as the mathematical logic that began with Leibniz's 'universal characteristic', and which Hegel thoroughly despises.)

5. Hegel also says that SL incorporates the material of the 'old' METAPHYSICS, which derives from Aristotle (and Plato), but also embraces Leibniz, Spinoza, Wolff, etc. Many of the concepts examined in SL, especially in the 'Doctrine of Essence', were employed by metaphysicians.

6. In the first main section of CPR, the 'Transcendental Doctrine of Elements', Kant defines 'transcendental' logic as the science which, in contrast to formal logic, 'determines the origin, range and objective validity of [a priori] cognitions' (CPR, A57, B81). Transcendental logic falls into two parts: (a) the logic of truth (transcendental analytic), and (b) the logic of ILLUSION (Schein) (transcendental dialectic). In (a) he attempts to systematize and justify the categories (e.g. CAUSALITY) presupposed by OBJECTIVE judgments and EXPERIENCE. In (b) he attempts to curb the SPECULATIVE use of REASON, arguing, e.g., that it leads to antinomies. Many of the concepts considered in (a) and (b) reappear in SL. But Hegel combines analytic and DIALECTIC at every stage of SL, arguing that every concept (except the absolute IDEA) gives rise to antinomies or contradictions. The second main section of CPR, the 'Transcendental Doctrine of Method', which determines the 'formal conditions of a complete system of pure reason' (A708, B735), is also relevant, especially to Hegel's concern for SYSTEM. Hegel's knowledge of, and indebtedness to, Kant were great. But the extent to which his fundamental motivations and procedures are Kantian is still a matter of controversy.

7. SL also explores concepts such as FORCE, polarity or OPPOSITION and INFINITY, which figure not only in metaphysics and THEOLOGY, but also in the natural science and mathematics of the day.

The main contents of SL are these:

1. 'The Objective Logic', opens with the Preface to the first edition. This outlines the general character of SL, the philosophical and cultural context in which it was written, and its relation to PS.

2. The Preface to the second edition considers the relationship of THOUGHT-DETERMINATIONS to LANGUAGE, to the I* and to THINGS. It explains some of the procedures of SL and defends them against misconceptions.

3. The Introduction outlines the 'general concept' of logic, and its relationship to PS, to language, to formal logic and to earlier philosophies, especially Kant's. It then explains the division of logic into the logic of being, of essence and of the concept.

4. Book I, 'The Doctrine of Being', opens with a section entitled 'With what must SCIENCE begin?' This considers the difficulty of a beginning (Anfang) of logic and of philosophy in general, especially since philosophy should have no PRESUPPOSITIONS and also forms a circle. Hegel explains why he does not (like Fichte and the early Schelling) begin with the pure I* (since, e.g., it presupposes a prior cultural and philosophical introduction), but with being. Hegel's claim that SL is the 'exposition of GOD as he is in his eternal essence before the creation of nature and of a finite spirit' (SL, Intro.)

269

is misleading in its suggestion that logic forms the beginning of the SYSTEM, when, since the system forms a circle, it is equally the end (and the middle).

5. *SL*, like Hegel's whole system, consists of TRIADS within triads. A whole triad often has the same title as the first term of the triad, in part because Hegel believes that a (generic) UNIVERSAL specifies itself into a (specific) universal, a PARTICULAR and an INDIVIDUAL. The Doctrine of Being proper falls into three sections. Section I (DETERMINATENESS or QUALITY) considers (a) being (being, NOTHING, BECOMING); (b) DETERMINATE BEING (determinate being, FINITUDE, infinity); and (c) Being-FOR-ITSELF (being-for-itself, one and many, repulsion and attraction). Section II (Magnitude or QUANTITY) covers (a) quantity (pure quantity, continuous and discrete magnitude, and LIMITATION of magnitude); (b) quantum (number, extensive and intensive quantum, and quantitative infinity); and (c) quantitative RELATION or ratio. Section III (MEASURE) covers (i) specific quantity; (ii) real measure; (iii) the becoming of essence.

6. Book II, the 'Doctrine of Essence', also has three sections. Section I (Essence as REFLECTION within itself) covers (a) illusion (*Schein*) (essential and inessential, illusion, reflection); (b) the essentialities or the determinations of reflection (IDENTITY, DIFFERENCE, CONTRADICTION); and (c) GROUND (absolute ground, determinate ground, CONDITION). Section II (APPEARANCE (*Erscheinung*)) deals with (a) EXISTENCE (THING and properties, the constitution of the thing out of MATTERS, the dissolution of the thing); (b) appearance (the LAW of appearance, the appearing world and the world IN ITSELF, dissolution of appearance); and (c) the essential relation (WHOLE and PARTS, FORCE and its expression, OUTER and INNER). Section III (ACTUALITY) covers (a) the ABSOLUTE (the exposition of the absolute, the absolute attribute, the mode of the absolute); (b) actuality (CONTINGENCY, etc., relative NECESSITY, etc., absolute necessity); and (c) absolute relation (SUBSTANCE, CAUSALITY, RECIPROCITY).

7. 'The SUBJECTIVE Logic or the Doctrine of the Concept' has three sections. Section I (Subjectivity) deals with (a) the concept (the universal concept, the particular concept, the individual); (b) the types of JUDGMENT; and (c) the types of INFERENCE. Section II (Objectivity) considers (a) MECHANISM, (b) CHEMISM and (c) TELEOLOGY or PURPOSIVENESS. Section III (the IDEA) considers (a) LIFE; (b) the idea of COGNITION (the idea of the TRUE and the idea of the good); and (c) the absolute idea.

Many 'notes' or 'remarks' (*Anmerkungen*) are interspersed in the main body of *SL*. These mostly deal with the role of a given thought-determination in other philosophies or in science and mathematics. These are usually less difficult than the main text and do much to illuminate it.

Hegel's logic differs from its predecessors in several respects:

(1) Ideally it has a single, necessary and complete structure which leaves the logician with no arbitrary choice about how to begin or to proceed, especially since the logician is (ideally) wholly absorbed in the subject-matter and the thought-determinations develop and criticize *themselves*. (This is not disproved by differences of detail between *SL* and *Enc.* I:

that there is a single correct logic does not entail that any work of Hegel's is the definitive expression of it.)

(2) Logic is 'THINKING about thinking'. The thoughts in terms of which we think about thoughts must figure among the thoughts that we think about. Thus one meaning of the absolute idea is that at the end of *SL* all the thoughts required to think about thoughts have been developed within logic itself. Hegel's logic, unlike Aristotelian and Kantian logic, is in this sense infinite and self-contained.

(3) The fusion of objective and subjective (i.e. formal) logic is secured in part by Hegel's belief that the forms of subjective logic (concept, judgment, inference, as well as truth, dialectic, etc.) constitute the structure of things as much as that of our thought about things. This is an essential aspect of his IDEALISM.

(4) Hegel derives and 'reconstructs' thought-determinations. But he also holds that they constitute the essential logical structure both of the MIND or SPIRIT and of the world. Thus *SL*, unlike formal logic, supplies the necessary logical framework of NATURE, of spirit, and of the relationship between them. It is not a contingent fact that the world displays the logical structure unravelled in *SL*. Thus Hegel attempts, with varying degrees of completeness and success, to structure his other works in accordance with logic.

Hegel's logic is, in intention, wholly *a priori* and requires no appeal to EXPERIENCE. It does not follow that it could have been developed at any earlier period, since it has cultural conditions, which it SUBLATES. The thoughts of *SL* are *implicit* in the human mind at any period, but (unlike Kant) Hegel does not believe that they are *explicit* at every time (or place). The thoughts are unravelled over HISTORY.

self *see* I

speculation, the speculative and metaphysics *Spekulation, spekulativ* and *spekulieren* ('to speculate') come from the Latin *speculatio* ('spying out, reconnoitring; contemplation') and *speculari* ('to spy, observe; to look around'), which in turn descend from *specere* ('to see, look'). (The Latin for a 'mirror' is *speculum*, which gave rise to the German *Spiegel*, 'mirror'). *Spekulieren* developed other senses: 'to count on, rely on; to guess, conjecture', hence, in the eighteenth century, 'to engage in risky commercial ventures'.

Speculatio was used by Boethius for the Greek *theōria* ('contemplation'). Augustine, the scholastics (e.g. Aquinas) and the mystics (e.g. Seuse, Nicholas of Cusa) associate it with *speculum*, and, following St Paul (1 Cor.13: 12), argue that God cannot be seen or known directly, but only in his works or effects, as in a mirror. Thus speculation goes beyond SENSORY EXPERIENCE to the divine or supernatural.

Speculation acquired a derogatory flavour from Luther's attack on scholasticism, and also from Herder's and Goethe's opposition to the Enlightenment. For Kant 'theoretical COGNITION is speculative, if it aims at an OBJECT, or at

271

concepts of an object, to which one cannot attain in any experience. It contrasts with natural [i.e. primarily causal] cognition, which aims only at objects, or predicates of them, that can be given in a possible experience' (*CPR*, A634f, B662f). He associates it with speculative REASON, which is responsible, e.g., for the PROOFS of God's existence.

Fichte, Schelling and Hegel regarded their own thought as speculative, not because it transcended possible experience in Kant's sense, but because the alternatives presented by Kant, transcendent *Spekulation* and natural cognition, are not exhaustive, but leave room for a third alternative, one that Kant himself pursued: reflection on the nature of experience and on the concepts involved in it. Schelling, like the mystics, for a time regarded speculation as involving a unitary vision or INTUITION, but Hegel sees it as a conceptual process.

Hegel does not associate *Spekulation* with the mirror. He is averse to the idea that GOD (or anything else) is inaccessible to direct cognition and can be discerned only in an image; he contrasts speculative philosophy with the philosophy of REFLECTION; and although the reflection of OPPOSITES, and of other DETERMINATIONS of reflection, into each other is involved in *Spekulation*, such reflection is only one phase of 'speculative' logic. He makes little attempt to link the philosophical sense(s) of *Spekulation* with its ordinary senses, but remarks that a matrimonial or a commercial speculation, like philosophical speculation, involves (1) going beyond what is immediately present, and (2) making OBJECTIVE what is initially SUBJECTIVE. But there is no implication of risk or uncertainty in Hegel's philosophical *Spekulation*.

The central feature of *Spekulation* in Hegel's usage is that it unifies opposed, and apparently distinct, thoughts (and things). Thus, in contrast to the analytical UNDERSTANDING, it is akin to the poetic IMAGINATION and to mysticism, but it differs from them in that it is conceptual and presupposes the work of the understanding. It is at odds with the *Dogmatismus* of pre-Kantian metaphysics, which insists on applying only one of a pair of contrasting predicates to objects, insisting, e.g., that the world is *either* FINITE *or* INFINITE, and cannot be both. Speculative thought, by contrast, unifies the two concepts, and thus regards the world as both finite and infinite (*Enc.* I §32A.). The speculative (or the positively rational) is only the third phase of Hegel's thought, contrasting with the understanding, which sets up sharp distinctions, and the negatively rational or DIALECTIC, which breaks them down again (*Enc.* I §§79ff). But since it is the final and most distinctive phase of his thought (and since *Spekulation* also has a wider sense), he often refers to his philosophy and logic, etc., as 'speculative'. *Spekulation*, Hegel insists, is not merely subjective: it SUBLATES the opposition between subjectivity and objectivity, along with other oppositions. It is thus intimately associated with IDEALISM. For the same reason, it is not (as Kant supposed) concerned with the supersensible, in contrast to experience.

In some usages (e.g. Kant's) *Spekulation* is linked to *Metaphysik*. A work of Aristotle's, concerned with 'first philosophy' or 'theology', came to be known as *ta meta ta phusika* ('the work after the *Physics*' in a catalogue). This was taken to mean 'things beyond *phusika*, natural things' and gave rise to the medieval Latin *metaphysica*. This covered the subjects considered in Aristotle's book: (1) the universal features of all beings as such (ontology) and (2) beings that are eternal, unchanging and separate from the world of change (THEOLOGY). Later thinkers, especially Wolff and his followers, added other subjects to the field of metaphysics, such as cosmology and rational psychology, which Aristotle had treated as parts of physics, since he drew no sharp distinction between empirical science and philosophy.

Kant believed that he had disposed of metaphysics in Wolff's sense: ontology is to be replaced by 'transcendental logic', which is an 'analytic' not of beings, but of the pure understanding (*CPR*, A247, B303). Other areas of metaphysics, which advance claims about GOD, the SOUL and the world that transcend all possible experience, are rejected (or at least assigned to moral FAITH), since arguments for such claims are inevitably fallacious and, in some cases, lead to unresolvable antinomies. Metaphysics of this type is a product of *Spekulation* and the speculative use of reason. But Kant did not reject everything that, on his view, fell under the heading 'metaphysics'. At *CPR*, A841–51, B869–79, he gives an inventory of current senses of the word, and in some of these senses he regards himself as a metaphysician. Thus *Metaphysik* appears in the titles of his works on ethics and on nature (*MM* and *MENS*), implying that their treatment is pure or non-empirical, fundamental and systematic. (In his *Handwörterbuch*, Krug criticizes Kant's ethical use of 'metaphysics': Krug equates *Metaphysik* with the 'philosophical theory of cognition'.)

A Jena manuscript of 1804–5, now entitled *Jenenser Logik, Metaphysik und Naturphilosophie*, is divided into three parts: 'Logic', 'Metaphysics' and 'Philosophy of Nature'. In later works Hegel does not assign a separate section to 'metaphysics', but incorporates the material of metaphysics into other disciplines, especially logic: logic 'coincides with metaphysics, the science of things grasped in THOUGHTS' (*Enc.* I §24) and 'constitutes proper metaphysics or pure speculative philosophy' (*SL*, Pref. to 1st edn). In the 1812 Preface to *SL* he remarked that German philosophy and common sense had conspired to produce the 'strange spectacle of a cultured PEOPLE without metaphysics – like an elaborately adorned temple without a holy of holies'. He often criticizes the 'old' or 'former (i.e. Wolffian) metaphysics', not usually for Kant's reasons, but for its 'dogmatism', its 'one-sidedness' and rigid 'either–or' distinctions between concepts that are dialectically or 'speculatively' related (*Enc.* I §§26ff). The sharp contrast between the sensible and supersensible worlds characteristic of pre-Kantian metaphysics, and of Kant himself, is one such opposition that needs to be overcome. Thus Hegel, unlike Kant, attributes such metaphysics to the understanding, not to reason. Its concepts are incorporated into the Logic, and there subjected to a speculative reworking. He is more favourable to ancient metaphysics, especially Neoplatonism, than to Wolffian metaphysics, and attempts to dissociate it from *Schwärmerei*, unreasoned and emotional fantasy. (*Schwarm*, 'swarm', and *schwärmen*, 'to swarm', were applied originally to bees, and then to religious sects in the Reformation. *Schwärmerei* is thus close to 'enthusiasm' as used by, e.g., Locke.)

273

'Metaphysics' is now too indeterminate in sense for us to give an unequivo-
cal and informative answer to the question 'Was Hegel a metaphysician?'
Hegel saw himself as in some sense a metaphysician. But this does not entail
that he reverted, or wished to revert, to pre-Kantian metaphysics. A direct
return to the past is never possible, on Hegel's view: once naive faith (e.g.
that truth can be attained by reflective thought, *Enc.* I §26) has been shaken
by doubt, it can be restored only at a higher, more sophisticated level, not in
its original naivety. Hegel's reservations about the understanding mean that
he cannot advance one principle at the expense of others, but must assign a
place to all significant categories, and that he cannot postulate a supersensible world or a 'Beyond' (*Jenseits*), sharply distinct from the sensible or this
world (*Diesseits*). Thus the least misleading answer is that he is both a
metaphysician and an anti-metaphysician: 'The highest stage and maturity
that anything can attain is that at which its downfall begins.'

spirit   *Geist* is etymologically related to 'ghost', but its range of meaning
corresponds closely to that of 'spirit'. Originally, it meant 'emotion, excite-
ment', but it developed the senses of 'spirit, SOUL, MIND; supernatural being,
ghost'. In Christian times it was influenced by the Latin *spiritus* and the
Greek *pneuma* ('air, breath, spirit') and also *nous* ('mind, intellect'). Later it
fell under the influence of the French *esprit*, and acquired the connotations of
'vivacity', 'wit' and 'genius', in addition to the native German suggestion of
breadth and profundity.

Geist thus has a wide range of meaning:

(1)   The holy spirit, the third person of the Trinity (*der heiliger Geist*, cf.
      spiritus sanctus).
(2)   The spiritual, non-material aspect of man, in contrast, e.g., to the flesh
      or the body.
(3)   A spirit, demon or ghost.
(4)   Vivacity, vitality, liveliness.
(5)   In the plural, 'spirits', as in 'high spirits, restoring one's spirits', etc.
(6)   In chemistry, 'spirit, essence', as in, e.g., *Kampfergeist* ('spirit of
      camphor'), *Weingeist* ('spirit of alcohol'); hence *Geist* is 'alcohol'. This
      accounts in part for Hegel's occasional suggestions that TRUTH in-
      volves intoxication: 'The true is thus the bacchanalian frenzy, in
      which no member is sober' (*PS*, Pref.).
(7)   Mind, intellect, both in general and of an individual. In this sense,
      'mind' is more appropriate than 'spirit', but the adjective *geistig*
      usually requires 'spiritual' rather than 'mental'.
(8)   The mental attitude, spirit, genius, temper of an age (*der Geist der Zeit,
      Zeitgeist*), a PEOPLE (*Volksgeist*), Christianity (*der Geist des Christentums*),
      etc.
(9)   A/the spirit of revenge, contradiction, etc.
(10) The inner meaning or 'spirit' of, e.g., a law, in contrast to its letter.

Geist is not a central concept for Kant, but, in accordance with 4 and 7
above, he sees it as the enlivening or animating principle of the mind (*Gemüt*)

(*Anthropology*, §57; *CJ* §49). It is also what gives life to a work of ART or a conversation, and as such is distinct from wit or *esprit*. In AESTHETICS it is the capacity to present aesthetic IDEAS, to capture the 'quickly passing play of the IMAGINATION' and communicate it to others (*CJ* §49).

Hegel uses *Geist* in a great variety of ways, and in his mature works attempts to systematize its meanings:

(1) In a general sense *Geist* denotes the human mind and its products, in contrast to NATURE and also to the logical idea. Thus *Enc.* III as a whole contains the philosophy of *Geist*.

(2) In a narrower sense, *Geist* is the 'SUBJECTIVE spirit', which covers all individual psychological life, ranging from the 'natural soul' to THINKING and the WILL (*Enc.* III §§387–482).

(3) In a narrower sense still, *Geist* covers the more intellectual aspects of the psyche, ranging from INTUITION to thinking and the will, but excluding, and contrasting with, the soul, FEELING, etc. (*Enc.* III §§440–83). The 'PHENOMENOLOGY of *Geist*' (*Enc.* III §§413–39) covers the same ground, but with a regard for spirit's CONSCIOUSNESS of OBJECTS; in *PS* it also includes OBJECTIVE and ABSOLUTE spirit.

(4) 'Objective spirit' is the common spirit (in sense 8 above) of a social group, embodied in its CUSTOMS, LAWS and institutions (RIGHT), and permeating the character and consciousness of the individuals belonging to the group. It is conceived as the objectification of subjective *Geist* (*Enc.* III §§483–552).

(5) 'Absolute spirit' covers ART, RELIGION and PHILOSOPHY (*Enc.* III §§553–77). Unlike (2) and (4), which are FINITE, it is INFINITE, since in it spirit is (an object) 'for' spirit itself, but also because it reflects upon what is other than, and thus LIMITS or restricts, spirit (*Enc.* III §§386 and A., 563f;. Hegel sees (2), (4) and (5) as, respectively, the CONCEPT of spirit, its REALITY, and the unity of concept and reality (*Enc.* III §385). 'Absolute spirit' has a more theological flavour than (2) or even (4): the spirit that is for spirit is GOD, and thus absolute spirit is the SELF-CONSCIOUSNESS of God. Spirit is also 'absolute' in the sense that it is relatively 'detached' from the social life of a particular community, i.e. (4).

(6) The *Weltgeist* or 'world-spirit' was, in the seventeenth century, the 'worldly' spirit, in contrast to the divine spirit; then it became (e.g. in Thomasius) a cosmic spirit pervading the whole of nature, like the world-SOUL; and finally, in Herder and Hegel, it is the spirit that manifests itself in HISTORY. History is a coherent, rational DEVELOPMENT, because the rise and fall of nations is governed by a single spirit. The *Weltgeist* is thus usually treated under the heading of 'right' or 'objective spirit' (*PR* §§341–60; *Enc.* III §549), but it is also responsible for the development of art, religion and philosophy, and thus of absolute spirit.

(7) The *Volksgeist* ('spirit of a/the people) is similar to (4), but it includes a people's contribution to (5), or at least those aspects of it that are

275

specific to a particular people, and, especially since it, unlike (4), occurs in the plural, is more readily seen as historically relative and transitory. The world-spirit realizes itself in a particular people (e.g. Greece), develops its spirit to the full, and then withdraws from it and turns to another people (e.g. Rome). The spirit of a people survives its withdrawal from the centre of the world-stage, but remains relatively static and can never again make a decisive contribution to world-history.

(8) Hegel speaks of the *Geist der Zeit* ('spirit of the age, time(s)'), rather than the *Zeitgeist*. The mentality, social life and cultural products of a given age, especially within a single people, share a common spirit. An individual is imbued with this spirit and cannot 'leap beyond' his age. Thus the spirit of the age is a phase of the world-spirit. (J. S. Mill's essay, 'The Spirit of the Age' (1831), shows that the concept has appeal beyond the confines of German idealism.)

(9) In religion, God is spirit. But the 'holy spirit' that pours forth from God and inspires and sanctifies man, is the third person of the Trinity. In *LPR*, Hegel conceives it as immanent in the Christian community (*Gemeinde*), and thus as God's self-consciousness. It is the religious analogue of the sphere of *Geist* as a whole, in contrast to the logical idea and nature (1). Hegel gives no priority to the original Christian community: *Geist* in this sense, as in others, develops, and its later phases are higher than earlier ones, e.g. in not requiring the sensory presence of Christ for FAITH.

Hegel views these not as distinct senses of *Geist*, but as systematically related phases in the development of a single *Geist*. This is made possible by three special features of *Geist*: (a) it involves no underlying THING or substratum, but is pure activity; (b) it develops by stages into successively higher forms, primarily by reflection on its current stage; and (c) it takes over, both cognitively and practically, what is other than itself, nature as well as lower levels of *Geist*, and realizes itself in them. The development of *Geist* is sometimes conceived as logical and non-temporal (e.g. in *Enc.* III), sometimes as historical (in the LECTURES).

Although we speak of 'the Greek mind' and of being 'of one mind', as well as of the 'team spirit', 'mind', more than 'spirit', suggests a single centre of consciousness. Thus objective and absolute 'spirit' may be thought to lack the special unity of the subjective 'mind', and the '*world-spirit*' to be simply the rational coherence of history, not a 'mind' whose coherent development explains the coherence of history. But the connotation of 'mind' cannot be wholly excluded from any of Hegel's main uses of *Geist*, for three reasons:

(1) The uses of *Geist* are systematically related, and are so owing to the activity of *Geist* itself. But the paradigmatically active *Geist* is subjective *Geist*, i.e. 'mind' as much as 'spirit'.

(2) The theological background of Hegel's *Geist* suggests that it is a mind, as well as a spirit.

(3) He often personifies the *Weltgeist*: 'the architect of this work of millennia is the one living *Geist*, whose thinking nature it is, to bring to conscious-

ness what it is and, when this has become its OBJECT, to be at once already elevated above it and at a higher stage' (*Enc.* I §13).

Nevertheless, since it is activity, not a thing, and, as truly infinite, is not sharply distinct from the finite, *Geist* cannot simply transcend worldly phenomena, and is hard to distinguish from the logical structure of these phenomena. Hegel's claim that *Geist* is the absolute does not mean that everything is mental or the product of one's own mind, but that: (a) the unified system of THOUGHTS and rational structures that form the core of the (subjective) *Geist* are immanent in nature and in the development of *Geist* itself; and (b) spirit/mind 'overreaches' (*übergreift*) and IDEALIZES what is other than spirit, by its cognitive and practical activities.

state (*Der*) *Staat* was formed from the Latin *status* ('state, condition', etc., from *stare*, 'to stand') in the fifteenth century. It originally meant 'standing, status; condition; way of life; dignity'. In the seventeenth century, it developed the now dominant sense of '(political) state' under the influence of the French *état* (also a descendant of *status*). It retains an older sense of 'pomp, finery, costly expenditure especially by a prince on his court', but it has now lost its other senses. Thus 'state' in the sense of 'condition' is not *Staat*, but *Zustand*, especially in *Naturzustand*, 'state of nature', and 'state' in the sense of 'estate, rank' is *Stand* or *Rang*. (*Stand* and *Zustand* come from *stehen*, 'to stand'.)

But even in its political sense *Staat*, like 'state', has a range of meaning. A state usually involves three elements: (1) a PEOPLE (*Volk*) that is more or less culturally and linguistically homogeneous; (2) a territory occupied by them that is more or less unified (but not necessarily homogeneous) geographically; (3) a political organization, with a central authority that exerts POWER throughout the territory. *Staat* may refer to any one of these, or to all three together. Thus if something is in the interest of the *Staat*, it is in the national interest or the interest of the nation, i.e. of 1, 2 and 3 together, a politically organized people occupying a certain territory. If something happens in the German *Staat*, it happens in the territory. Someone who works for the *Staat* works for the government or in some branch of the *Staat* in sense 3. If a decision is taken *von Staats wegen*, it is taken on a governmental level, i.e. within the higher reaches of sense 3.

Sense 3 generates further ambiguities. First, the power exerted by the central authority can vary in degree: it is relatively restricted both in a federal state (*Bundesstaat*) and in its constituent states. (The territory of a state may also be ill-defined.) Second, 3 usually embraces a wide range of institutions, often hierarchically organized, and *Staat* may cover a wider or narrower range of these. It may, e.g., exclude or include the police force, universities, etc. (As a professor at Berlin, Hegel was an official of the Prussian state.) *Staat* usually includes the government (*Regierung*) as an institution, but it can contrast with a particular government: what is, e.g., in the interests of the *Staat* need not be in the interests of the government. The force of *Staat*, as of other words, often depends on what it is contrasted with, e.g. the individual, the Church, the economy, etc.

277

Hegel uses *Staat* in two senses: (I) A state in contrast to other states, which embraces 1, 2 and 3. He uses *Staat*, e.g., for the Greek *polis*, which was not, on his view, as internally articulated and differentiated as the modern state. (*Polis* means (i) a city, in contrast to the country and villages; (ii) a city-state, including the surrounding countryside and villages. Only (ii) is a *Staat*; (i) is a *Stadt*.) (II) The state, in contrast to other aspects of society, especially the FAMILY and CIVIL SOCIETY. The two senses are related, in that something is a *Staat* in sense (I) if, and only if, it has a *Staat* in sense (II) or, as in the case of a *polis*, something approximating to it.

Some central features of the *Staat* in sense (II) depend on its contrasts with:

(1) Abstract RIGHT: The state protects the rights of PERSONS, but this is not, as, e.g., Locke supposed, its sole or main purpose.

(2) Morality: The state and its actions are not to be assessed by the standards of individual MORALITY.

(3) The family: The state, in contrast to civil society, has a unity comparable to that of the family. But it is not based, like the family, on love and FEELING: 'In the state, feeling disappears; there we are conscious of unity as LAW; there the content must be rational and known to us' (*PR* §158A.). Hence the state, in contrast to the family and civil society, is associated with SELF-CONSCIOUSNESS. The state is held together not by FORCE, but by our 'sense of order', i.e. genuine patriotism (*PR* §268 and A.).

(4) Civil society: The state does not rest, like the commercial transactions of civil society, on a contract. It was not formed by an original contract; it is not, as, e.g., Fichte supposed, a voluntary institution from which one can resign if one wishes; nor is it to be assessed according to its fulfilment of a supposed contract with its citizens (*PR* §§75, 258). Men in a state of nature had no rights or right. But whatever they were (or would be) like in a state of nature has no bearing on the NATURE or ESSENCE of man: the essence of an entity consists in its fully developed condition, not its beginnings. The state is not primarily a device for satisfying our antecedent needs or wishes; it makes us into full human beings: 'The rational end of man is life in the state' (*PR* §75A.) The state is needed, in part, to bring individuals back into unity, out of the dispersal into private interests promoted by civil society. Like de Tocqueville, Hegel saw self-seeking individualism as a constant danger to the community after the collapse of the old, pre-revolutionary order, and held that neither despotism nor a return to the old order can meet the threat, but only a rational political structure with which individuals can identify and which allows some free play to the individualism of civil society.

At *PR* §§257–360 and *Enc.* III §§535–52, Hegel considers the state under three headings: (1) constitutional law (*inneres Staatsrecht*); (2) international law (*äusseres Staatsrecht*); and (3) world-HISTORY:

1. The constitution (*Verfassung*) of the rational state involves three elements or POWERS (*Gewalten*):

(a) The INDIVIDUAL element is the monarch. The office is hereditary, so as to avoid the caprice and the contractual element involved in election. He has the final decision in the appointment of executives and in acts of state such as the declaration of war, but his decisions are guided by expert advice. He is not an absolute, but a constitutional monarch: 'the objective aspect belongs to the law alone, and the monarch's part is merely to set to the law the subjective "I will" ' (*PR* §280A.).

(b) The executive or governmental power (*Regierungsgewalt*) is PARTICULAR in the sense that it subsumes the particular under the universal (*PR* §287), i.e. puts into effect the laws and the decisions of the monarch. It includes the heads of the civil service, judiciary, police, etc. The positions are to be open to anyone of talent.

(c) The UNIVERSAL element is the legislature (*gesetzgebende Gewalt*) (*PR* §§298–320; *Enc.* III §544). The people as a whole (but not peasants and workers) are represented in this branch of the state, not as private individuals, but as members of 'estates' (*Stände*). Estates are professional groups, rather than social or economic classes. Hegel, like Durkheim, sees them as institutions that mediate between atomic individuals and the government, and prepare men for life in the state. There are, on his view, three estates: (i) the hereditary landed gentry, who sit as individuals in an upper house, and (ii) the business class and (iii) the 'universal' class of civil servants (including teachers, etc.), who through their 'corporations' elect representatives to sit in a lower house. (The 'houses' are also called *Stände*.)

2. A state is only a state if it contrasts with, and is related to, other states. States require RECOGNITION by other states, just as PERSONS require recognition by other persons (*PR* §331). Here *Staat* is used primarily in sense (I) above. But sense (II) is also in play, since in its relations with other states the state must, as an *individuelles Subjekt*, be represented by the monarch, who thus commands the armed forces, conducts foreign affairs through ambassadors, makes WAR and PEACE, and concludes treaties (*PR* §329). Right between states takes the form of treaties and of international law (*Völkerrecht, ius gentium*), which is based on custom, rather than a central authority, and is designed to mitigate the conduct of war and make possible the restoration of peace.

3. Any state is eventually swept away by world history, the world's court of judgment (*Weltgericht*, also the 'last judgment (of the world)') (*PR* §340; *Enc.* III §548).

Hegel set a high value on the state, and is reported as saying that it is the 'march of God on earth' (*PR* §258A.). This remark should be read in the light of the following considerations:

(a) He adds that the 'state is no work of ART; it stands on earth and so in the sphere of caprice, chance and error' (*PR* §258A.).

(b) To say that the state is the march of GOD on earth is not to say that it is God, in the sense that it is the height of perfection or that any given state is everlasting. ABSOLUTE SPIRIT is higher, for Hegel, than objective spirit, including the state, and individual states succumb to history.

(c) Hegel rejects the sharp contrast between the state and the individual. The relation between the state and the individual is MEDIATED by a variety of institutions – the family, etc. None of these leave the individual unscathed. They form him into an individual of a certain type. The state makes him a citizen (a *citoyen*, not simply a *Bürger*), who thinks and acts with the state in view. The modern individual is thus a many-tiered being, shaped by the institutions to which he belongs. To insist that the primary value is the individual's FREEDOM to do as he WILL is, on Hegel's view, to overvalue a lower tier of the individual, that associated with abstract right or with civil society. (Hegel does not regard the state as the main threat to freedom even of this type.)

(d) Hegel was influenced by Plato's and Aristotle's organic view of the state, and cannot conceive of a fully human life outside a state, or even outside the particular state into which one was born. (He refers more often to Plato's political doctrines than to Aristotle's, since he believed, incorrectly, that Plato presented a description of the actual Greek *polis*, rather than an IDEAL. But his own views are closer to Aristotle's.) But he allows more scope to SUBJECTIVE freedom than, on his view, the *polis* did. He holds that the modern rational state must include all the significant values embodied in past states, and is thus not, as they often were, 'one-sided'.

subject and subjectivity   In the sixteenth century (*das*) *Subjekt* was borrowed from the Latin *subjectum* (the past participle of *subicere*, 'to throw under') in the sense of the 'subject, theme' of a sentence. But its philosophical uses were also influenced by Aristotle's uses of *to hypokeimenon*, 'that which underlies', for (1) the matter of which something consists or from which it was made; (2) a substance or bearer of attributes; and (3) the logical subject of predicates – but not specifically for the *human* subject. Until the eighteenth century it referred to what exists independently of our knowledge, i.e. the OBJECT. *Subjekt* has only some of the senses of the English 'subject': it occurs only as a noun, and it does not mean a 'dependent, subordinate' or a 'discipline, field'. It is used less frequently than 'subject' for the 'theme' of a painting, novel, piece of music, etc. Where we speak of a 'subject' of, e.g., criticism or of ridicule, German says *Gegenstand* ('object') rather than *Subjekt*. It is also a derogatory term for a 'fellow, character' (cf. PERSON). Its main philosophical uses are:

(1) The subject, substratum or bearer of states and activities. In this sense, it is not clearly distinct from SUBSTANCE.

(2) The grammatical or logical subject of a sentence, PROPOSITION or JUDGMENT, the bearer of predicates.

(3) The subject or bearer of psychological states and processes, the human subject or I*.

(4) The cognitive subject, in contrast to the object of cognition.

(5) The acting subject, the performer of actions and activities, especially, in Hegel, the moral subject.

In the eighteenth century, *Subjekt* generated *subjektiv* and *Subjektivität*. Like the English 'subjective', *subjectiv* was once used for 'actual, essential', i.e. pertaining to a *Subjekt* in sense 1. But by Hegel's time its uses related to *Subjekt* in senses 3, 4 and 5, and were:

(a)   Pertaining to the human subject in general.
(b)   Pertaining to a specific, individual human subject, hence 'personal, idiosyncratic'.
(c)   One-sided, biased, partial.

The senses of *Subjektivität* correspond to those of *subjectiv*.

The use of 'subject' and *Subjekt* in senses 3–5 began in the late seventeenth century, under the impact of Descartes. Hobbes uses *subiectum sensionis* for 'the subject of sensation' (*De corpore*, 25, 3.). In his *Metaphysica* (1739) and *Aesthetica* (1750–8), Baumgarten sometimes uses *subiectum* as a synonym of *obiectum*, e.g. for the subject, i.e. object, of one's business, sometimes for the acting and sensory subject. But he is probably responsible for the modern sense of *subjectivus* ('subjective'), which is well established in Kant (who based his lectures on Baumgarten's *Metaphysica*).

All the traditional senses of *Subjekt* enter into Hegel's use of the term, but sense 1 is more usually expressed by *Substanz*. *Subjekt* contrasts with *Prädikat* (sense 2); with *Substanz* (senses 3–5); and with *Objekt* (sense 4). It is different from *Geist* (SPIRIT): *Geist* embraces or 'overreaches' (*übergreift*) its object, and is not counterposed to it; it similarly develops into and embraces its manifestations (THOUGHTS, FEELINGS, etc.); and it develops into intersubjective structures, into an 'I that is we, and a we that is I' (*PS*, IV). The *Subjekt*, by contrast, is conceived as more withdrawn into itself, as what *underlies*, and is thus counterposed to, the object, the states and activities of the subject, and other subjects. But the distinction is not sharp, and the *Subjekt* develops into *Geist*. Thus while *Geist* is associated with the IDEA, the union of subjectivity and objectivity, *Subjekt* is associated with the CONCEPT (*Begriff*) and thus with the I.

Hegel sees a connection between the sense of *Subjekt* in which it contrasts with *Prädikat* (sense 2) and the sense of 'human subject'. The link is not, on his view, simply that the human subject underlies its states and activities in the way that a grammatical or logical subject underlies its predicates. It is that the *Subjekt*, in both senses, is constituted by the concept. The human subject or I is associated with the concept both because the I is sheerly indeterminate and because it is constituted by conceptual thought. The subject of a sentence is associated with the (or *a*) concept, since in a JUDGMENT such as 'The rose is red', the subject, the rose, is picked out by a concept (that of a rose) – and is, on Hegel's view, constituted by this concept – while the predicate, at least in lower forms of judgment, ascribes to it a contingent feature that is not determined by its concept. But the two types of subject and the two types of concept are not simply *analogous*: Hegel sees the production of judgments as the result of the active self-differentiation and self-specification of the human subject or of *the* concept.

Begriff, in Hegel, is as diverse in meaning as *Subjekt*. But it has three features that help to explain his use of *Subjekt*:

(1)   The/a concept has a non-derivative and primordial unity, and whatever unity a thing has it owes to its concept.

(2)   The/a concept is essentially active: it actively differentiates itself into a subject and an object, into a subject and its predicates (or into UNIVERSAL, PARTICULAR and INDIVIDUAL), and into a diversity of specific *concepts*.

(3)   It actively seeks to restore its unity. The human subject SUBLATES the object both cognitively and practically; the forms of judgment assign to the subject predicates that are successively more adequate to its concept; and the diversity of concepts is brought together into a SYSTEM.

These features of the concept and of the *Subjekt* are as prominent in Hegel's mind when he contrasts *Subjekt* with *Substanz* (e.g. in the claim, in *PS*, Pref., that the ABSOLUTE is subject as well as substance), as are the ideas of human (or divine) consciousness and agency. The absolute as *Subjekt* involves a DEVELOPMENT from simple unity to disunity, and a return to differentiated unity. This, or at least its third stage, requires the cognitive and practical activity of human subjects.

Hegel is sensitive to ambiguities in *Subjekt*, *subjektiv* and *Subjektivität*, especially in their application to the human subject. The main source of ambiguity, on his view, is that *Subjekt* may refer only to the pure, self-reflective I, but it can also include the states, activities, wants, etc., of the I. The states, etc., of the I differ from person to person, and are thus CONTINGENT and *subjektiv* in a derogatory sense. In this sense, a bad painting, a judgment, a resolution of the WILL, etc., may be *subjektiv*, in that it expresses only the private opinions, etc., of its author. The I as such, by contrast, does not vary from person to person and is thus not contingent or arbitrary. This sense of *Subjekt* gives rise to the sense of *subjektiv* and *Subjektivität*, in which Kant's categories are subjective (*Enc.* I §41A.2), or in which *Subjektivität* involves the requirement that one should be able to endorse reflectively what is presented for one's cognitive or practical acceptance (*PR*, §26A.).

Hegel refers to these two types of subjectivity as, respectively, 'bad or FINITE subjectivity' and 'INFINITE subjectivity'; he associates infinite subjectivity with Christianity, since it ascribes such subjectivity to GOD and thus assigns an 'infinite value' to human subjectivity (*Enc.* I §147A.). Kierkegaard adopted the expression 'infinite subjectivity', and, against Hegel, argued, in, e.g., the *Concluding Unscientific Postscript*, that it is 'subjectivity that Christianity is concerned with, and it is only in subjectivity that its truth exists, if it exists at all; objectively Christianity has absolutely no existence.' But the opposition of 'subjectivity' to the similarly ambiguous 'OBJECTIVITY' is alien to Hegel. There are, for him, three (rather than two) broad phases of *Subjektivität*:

(1)   The withdrawal of the subject into itself, as a pure I. This also involves objectivity (in a good sense), owing to, e.g., its association with the concept.

(2)   The manifestation of the subject in a variety of states and activities, both psychological (e.g. OPINIONS, desires) and physical (e.g. ACTIONS, paintings). This involves objectivity, but often in a bad sense, since the objects express only the subjective whims of the subject.

(3)   The rational subject's reclamation of its external objectifications: e.g. its manifestation in, and endorsement of, a rational STATE. Here again subjectivity and objectivity (both in a good sense) coincide.

Hegel would assign Kierkegaard's subjective FAITH to phase (2).

sublation   The verb *heben* is related to 'heave' and originally meant 'to seize, grasp', but now means 'to lift, raise; to remove (especially an adversary from his saddle, hence) to supplant him; to remove (e.g. a difficulty, a contradiction)'. It enters many compounds, the most significant for Hegel being *aufheben* ('to sublate'). *Aufheben* has three main senses:

(1)   'to raise, to hold, lift up'.
(2)   'to annul, abolish, destroy, cancel, suspend'.
(3)   'to keep, save, preserve'.

The reflexive, *sich aufheben*, now has reciprocal force, when numbers or items in an account 'cancel' or 'balance each other', but it was used more widely in Hegel's day, e.g. for someone 'getting up' from his seat, and is used by Hegel for something's sublating *itself*. The noun *Aufhebung* similarly means (1) 'raising up'; (2) 'abolition'; and (3) 'preserving'. (The nominal infinitive, *Aufheben*, occurs in the expression *Aufheben(s) machen*, 'to make a fuss'.)

Usually, *aufheben* is used in only one of these senses on a given occasion. Schiller mostly uses it in sense (2), but in *AE*, XVIII, he comes close to combining all three senses, when he argues that BEAUTY 'combines the two opposed states [viz. of FEELING (*Empfinden*) and THINKING] and thus sublates the OPPOSITION'. But sense (2) predominates, since he adds that 'both states disappear entirely in a third and no trace of the division remains in the whole that they form'. (Cf. *Aufhebung* in *AE*, XXIV.) Hegel regularly uses *aufheben* in all three senses at once, and Schiller, even when he does not use *aufheben*, influenced his usage. Thus Schiller anticipates Hegel's view of the sublation of NATURE: '[Man] does not stop short at what mere nature made of him; he has the capacity to retrace by REASON the steps she took on his behalf, to transform the work of compulsion into a work of his free choice and to elevate physical NECESSITY to moral necessity' (*AE*, III).

A similar ambiguity occurs in the Latin *tollere*, which means (1) 'to raise up' and (2) 'to take up from its place, i.e. to destroy, remove'. Thus, when Cicero said that Octavius was *tollendus* ('to be raised up'), he meant both that he was to be elevated and that he was to be got rid of. The past participle of *tollere* is *sublatus*, and this gave rise to the English verb 'to sublate'. This originally meant 'to remove, take away', but is now obsolete in this sense. It was used by Sir William Hamilton for 'to deny, contradict, disaffirm (a proposition)', in contrast to 'to POSIT'. It was then used by Stirling, in *The Secret of Hegel* (1865), in the sense of both 'destroy' and 'preserve', for Hegel's *aufheben*. The defects of 'sublate' as a rendering of *aufheben* are that *tollere*, as Hegel points out, does not have sense (3), 'to keep, etc.', and that it is not a familiar English word. Thus translators have also used 'supersede', 'abolish', 'cancel', 'sublimate' (Kaufmann), etc. Its closest English counterpart, 'to kick upstairs', is too colloquial to win general approval.

In his explicit accounts of *aufheben*, Hegel refers only to senses (2) and (3), since it is, on his view, of great interest to SPECULATIVE thought that *aufheben* has opposite senses. Both senses, he argues, are implicit in (3), since to preserve something involves removing it from its IMMEDIACY and from its exposure to external influences. There are, he says, several such words in German. He mentions no others in his accounts of *aufheben* (e.g. *Enc.* I §96A.), but he has in mind such words as *Person* (PERSON), 'SUBJECTIVITY', and *Begriff* (CONCEPT), which is associated both with the beginnings of a thing and with its climax. Many English words and phrases have opposite senses: e.g. 'to cleave (to)' (which is etymologically two distinct words), 'to betray (e.g. one's origins)', 'to dispose (of)', 'to go downhill', and 'mirror-image'. This has no general philosophical significance.

When a word has two or more senses, Hegel does not invariably give equal weight to each of its senses on all (or most) occasions of its use. *Aufhebung* responds more fruitfully to this treatment than most other words. But (1) even when one of a word's senses is dominant in Hegel's use, its other senses are usually also in play, i.e. sublated, but not wholly suppressed, and (2) he tends to connect systematically the different senses of, e.g., 'REFLECTION' and 'JUDGMENT'.

Hegel associates *aufheben* with several other words: Thus when something is sublated (*aufgehoben(e)*), it is IDEAL (*ideell*), MEDIATED (or 'reflected'), in contrast to immediate, and a MOMENT of a WHOLE that also contains its opposite. *Aufhebung* is similar to the determinate NEGATION that has a positive result. What results from the sublation of something, e.g. the whole in which both it and its opposite survive as moments, is invariably higher than, or the TRUTH of, the item(s) sublated. Thus despite Hegel's silence on the matter, it is reasonable to see sense (1), 'elevation', as an ingredient in its Hegelian meaning.

Like many other Hegelian terms, *Aufhebung* applies both to concepts and to things. The concepts of BEING and NOTHING are sublated in DETERMINATE BEING, and in general lower DETERMINATIONS in the Logic are sublated into higher ones. Earlier stages of a temporal, DEVELOPMENTAL process are sublated in(to) later stages: e.g. earlier philosophies are both destroyed and preserved in Hegel's philosophy. (One's early beliefs, we might say, are sublated in one's later, more measured beliefs or one's early drafts in one's final draft.) The sublation of a concept in the Logic is compatible with its availability for application to lower types of entity: e.g. MECHANISM is sublated in TELEOLOGY, but it remains applicable to the solar system. But the sublated phases of a temporal process are not usually retrievable in an analogous way.

Hegel often conflates the logical sublation of a concept with the physical sublation of a thing. For example, DEATH is 'the sublation [*das Aufheben*] of the individual [animal] and hence the emergence of the genus, of SPIRIT' (*Enc.* II §376A.). Death physically sublates the individual animal, but the result of this is not the next stage in the physical process, viz. a corpse, but the next stage in the logical process, the genus and, indirectly, spirit. The reasons for such conflations are that (1) sublation proceeds from the lower to the higher, not from, e.g., an animal to a corpse; and (2) Hegel sees a deep connection between the development of concepts and the development of things, which is essential to his IDEALISM.

substance *Substanz* entered German in the Middle Ages from the Latin *substantia*, which in turn comes from *substare* ('to stand under, be under, be present'). Its root meaning is thus similar to that of 'SUBJECT', but it was associated with the Greek *ousia* ('being, substance, etc.', from *einai*, 'to be') rather than with *to hypokeimenon*. Its meanings are close to those of the English 'substance': (1) Stuff, matter, a type of stuff; (2) a persisting, independent thing, in contrast to its dependent 'accidents' (*Akzidenz(en)*), attributes, and/or 'modes'; (3) the persisting ESSENCE of a thing; (4) the essential CONTENT of, e.g., a book, in contrast to its FORM or expression; (5) property, possessions.

The dominant sense of 'substance' in pre-Hegelian philosophy is (2). Descartes defined it as 'a thing that exists in such a way that it needs no other thing for its own existence'. He recognized a thinking and an extended substance, both created by the absolute substance, GOD. Spinoza defined it as 'that which is in itself and is conceived through itself, i.e. that whose concept does not need the concept of another thing, in order to be formed from it.' Believing a plurality of substances to be incompatible with this, and also Descartes', DEFINITION, he argued that there is only one substance. This has an infinity of attributes, but only two are known to us: thought and extension. FINITE things, including people, are 'modes' of these attributes; under the attribute of thought they are IDEAS, under that of extension bodies. Spinoza was revived in the late eighteenth century. Goethe and Herder saw his substance as an organic WHOLE, a totality of vital FORCES. Hegel, by contrast, saw Spinozism as *Akosmismus*, a 'denial of the world', which holds that only God or substance is fully real, while worldly things are only APPEARANCES (*Scheine*). He usually has Spinoza in mind when he uses *Substanz* in a philosophical sense.

Substanz plays a more subdued role in Kant, where its main senses are: (1) A logical subject, in which predicates inhere and which is not a predicate of anything else. (In this sense, the I* is a substance.) (2) A relatively independent thing that persists throughout changes in its accidents. (In this sense, the I or subject is not a substance.) (3) That which persists through 'all change of appearances' and whose 'quantity in nature is neither increased nor diminished' (*CPR*, A182, B224). (In this sense, there is only one substance, viz. MATTER.) Hegel's view of *Substanz* is not much influenced by Kant. But he follows Kant in treating it, in the Logic, as the first term of the TRIAD: substance, CAUSALITY and RECIPROCITY.

In the Logic, Hegel speaks as if there is only one substance. There are several reasons for this: (1) As in his account of the ABSOLUTE, he has in mind Spinoza's doctrine. (2) If, as we initially do, we disregard the diverse and changing accidents of a thing and focus on the bare, underlying substance, the differentiation of distinct substances is problematic. (3) Since a substance generates its own accidents, it is in any case relatively independent of other substances and they do not enter into the initial account of it. The interaction of two or more substances is considered under the heading not of substance, but of reciprocity.

A substance is in constant activity, generating and dissolving its accidents. Substance appears or 'shines' in its accidents and they are its APPEARANCE (*Schein*). But this shining produces not only the accidents, but substance itself: substance is only substance in virtue of producing and dissolving accidents. Thus the accidents are or include substance, just as much as substance includes its accidents.

Hegel regularly contrasts *substance* with the subject (primarily, but not exclusively, the human subject), the concept, and SPIRIT. He argues that the absolute is subject, as well as substance, that substance must become a subject, etc. (e.g. *PS*, Pref.). He has in mind several points:

(1) Spinoza's substance, unlike the Christian God, is not a PERSON or subject, and thus lacks the unity characteristic of a subject (*Enc.* I §151A.).

(2) No adequate explanation is provided of substance's generation of accidents, or of its bifurcation into attributes. Hegel misunderstood Spinoza's definition of an attribute ('that which the intellect knows of substance as constituting its essence') to mean that substance only has attributes in so far as they *appear* to an intellect. But this intellect is either itself a mode of substance, and thus presupposes the bifurcation into attributes, or incoherently located outside substance.

(3) The accidents (or modes) of substance are not themselves genuinely independent subjects. Human beings are no more than modifications of substance.

(4) One reason why the modes are not independent subjects is that this would be, within Spinoza's framework, incompatible with their belonging to a single substance, since Spinoza provides no adequate mechanism for the return of independent entities into substance: he simply claims, in effect, that everything (including himself) is one in the absolute.

On Hegel's view, by contrast, God is (at the level of RELIGION) a person, and (at the philosophical level) the CONCEPT. This explains the emergence of independent subjects. The cognitive, practical and religious activities of these subjects (which amounts to God's SELF-CONSCIOUSNESS) brings them, and other entities, back into unity. (Spinoza arguably anticipated more of this than Hegel acknowledges, in, e.g., his doctrine that the 'intellectual love of the mind for God is a part of the infinite love with which God loves himself'. Hegel discusses this in other contexts, e.g. *Enc.* I §158A., but not in that of substance.)

Hegel's concept of *Substanz* plays an important role in his account of RIGHT and ETHICAL LIFE. A social or political community cannot, as contract theorists imply, consist only of subjects, of individuals who are constantly reflective in their thoughts and deeds. It presupposes a background of unreflective relationships and activities, in which people do not stand out as individual subjects. (Similarly, reflective literary or philosophical discourse presupposes a background of unreflective everyday discourse.) This background is '(the) ethical substance', that which underlies. The ancient Greek city-state was predominantly 'substantial', with subjects emerging only indistinctly. But the modern state has three elements:

(1) A fully substantial background, in which individuals are united by unreflective ties of FEELING and affection, viz. the FAMILY and, at the STATE level, the peasantry.

(2) The emergence of reflective, self-seeking subjects in CIVIL SOCIETY, and also of reflective MORAL subjects.

(3) The reunification of independent subjects in the state, which (unlike civil society) is itself a single subject, represented by a monarch, and (unlike the family) requires the reflective, rational endorsement of its members.

It is, on Hegel's view, only a strong unifying state that allows, far more than the Greek city-state, the emergence of independent subjects; without such a state, society would dissolve into a collection of individuals.

Thus, on Hegel's view, ethical substance, in the form of the modern state, mirrors the universe as a whole. Spinoza's doctrine mirrors the Greek city-state and, on Hegel's view, displays a similar instability.

supersede, supersession *see* SUBLATION

T

thing and subject-matter German has two words for 'thing':

1. *Ding* was originally a legal term meaning 'law-court', and also 'legal case, action', but came to mean 'thing' in general. In philosophy *Ding* traditionally covered 'everything that is possible, whether it is ACTUAL or not' (Wolff). A thing that is possible, but not actual is a *Gedankending* ('thought-thing'). *Unding* ('non-thing') sometimes refers to a *Gedankending*, sometimes to what is not possible (e.g. a square circle). A *Ding* has PROPERTIES (*Eigenschaften*). Wolff distinguished between a thing that subsists independently or FOR ITSELF, i.e. a SUBSTANCE, and a thing that subsists through another thing. The former, e.g. the SOUL, has the source of its changes in itself, an internal FORCE; the latter is only a 'RESTRICTION of what subsists for itself'.

A thing IN ITSELF (*Ding an sich*) is strictly a thing independently of its relationships to other things. But for Kant (like Locke, Lambert, etc.) it was a thing independently of its relationship to the perceiving, etc., SUBJECT. Only APPEARANCES can be known, not things in themselves. Kant purports to make only a 'negative use' of the concept of a thing in itself: it serves as a 'LIMITing concept'. To make a 'positive use' of it is to view it as the object of an intellectual INTUITION, whose existence and nature are as problematic as that of the thing in itself (*CPR*, B307). But Kant often makes a more than negative use of the concept, arguing that appearances must be the appearances of things in themselves and that things in themselves are the GROUND of appearances. The idea that there are unknowable things in themselves was rejected by Jacobi, Fichte and Schelling, as well as by Hegel.

2. *Sache* too was originally a legal term: it meant a 'lawsuit', and was generalized to mean 'thing', and also 'affair, business, matter'. It is often equivalent to 'point' (as in 'to, beside the point') or to the 'heart of the matter'. *Sache* suggests, more strongly than *Ding*, a contrast with *Person*. Thus Kant equated a *Sache* with a 'corporeal thing' (*res corporalis*), and defined it as a thing (*Ding*) that cannot be held responsible for what it does, since it lacks free WILL. Kant follows the distinction in Roman law between (a) a RIGHT to a thing (*ius ad rem*), which entitles one to use a thing (*res, Sache*) and to exclude others from the use of it, and (b) a right to a PERSON (*ius ad personam*), which entitles one to require a person to act, or not to act, in a certain way. (Hegel criticizes the distinction at *PR* §40.)

Hegel uses *Ding* and *Sache* in quite different ways:

1. *Ding* has several uses:

(a) Sometimes it is used in a general sense for contingent, worldly things, including the finite SPIRIT, in contrast to GOD or the absolute NECESSITY (e.g. *LPEG*, XVI).

(b) Related to this is the use of *Ding* in which it is contrasted with *denken* (THINKING) or *Gedanke* (THOUGHT). But the contrast is only superficial. Thought(s) form the ESSENCE of things, and Hegel sees this connection preserved in the similarity of the words: 'Thinking [*das Denken*] is thinghood [*Dingheit*], or thinghood is thinking' (*PS*, VI.B.IIb.). (There is in fact no etymological kinship between *Ding* or 'thing' and *denken* or 'think'.)

(c) In a narrower sense, *Ding* appears as the OBJECT of PERCEPTION in *PS*, II, and as a DETERMINATION of REFLECTION in the Logic (*Enc.* I §§125ff). To regard something as a *Ding* in this sense is only one among several ways of viewing it: one might instead view it as, e.g., a FORCE that manifests itself. A thing necessarily has properties, which, in *PS*, are correlative to our various SENSE organs. Unlike the 'something' (*Etwas*) and its QUALITY, a thing can change its properties without ceasing to EXIST. Thus it 'has', rather than 'is', its properties. The difficulty of accounting for the unity of the thing in view of its diverse properties leads on to the idea that the properties are independent MATTERS (e.g. heat is caloric), that interpenetrate each other's pores. Hegel rejects this theory on both empirical and conceptual grounds at, e.g., *Enc.* I §130 and *Enc.* II §§305A., 334.

(d) Hegel often associates Kant's thing in itself with *Ding* in sense (c), the bearer of properties, and argues that it is unknowable only because, if we ABSTRACT from all the properties (and relations) of a thing, there is nothing left to be known. But often (and more conformably to Kant's intentions) he associates it with *Ding* in sense (b), arguing that things in the sense in which they contrast with thought are in fact the product of thought and that thought is their essence or 'in-itself'. The tenor of Hegel's complex arguments against the unknowable thing in itself is thus not that SPECULATIVE philosophy provides access to entities that eluded Kant and his predecessors, but that the essence of things is their logical structure, open to conceptual and empirical investigation.

Ding is cognate with *bedingen*, *Bedingung* ('to CONDITION', '(a) condition'). Schelling once argued that if, e.g., the I* is seen as conditioned or as having conditions, then it is (mistakenly) regarded as a *thing*. On Hegel's view, Schelling and Kant rightly rejected Descartes' view that the I (or SOUL) is a thing (*Enc.* I §34A.). But it does not follow that it must be unconditioned, since conditions are SUBLATED into what they condition (which is, for Hegel, a *Sache* rather than a *Ding*).

2. In contrast to *Ding*, *Sache* in Hegel has the flavour of 'the thing that matters', 'the real point', in contrast, e.g., to the transitory forms in which it appears or to the interpretations that people put on it. Often it is referred to

289

as *die Sache selbst*, 'the *Sache* itself'. (The pronoun *selbst* does not indicate that the *Sache* is *a* self, a *Selbst*.)

Thus in *PS*, V.C.a, 'The Spiritual Animal Kingdom and Deceit or the "Matter in Hand" itself [*die Sache selbst*]', the *Sache selbst* is the 'work' that an individual produces in accordance with his nature and his aims, and in which he locates his own worth or import. But the *Sache selbst*, viz. the import of his work, need not coincide with, and does not depend primarily on, the agent's aim or intention. Its fate depends on what others do and how they view it. Thus, e.g., the *Sache selbst* is Conan Doyle the creator of Sherlock Holmes, not Conan Doyle the historical novelist, or Columbus's discovery of America, not of a route to India. But the *Sache selbst* need not be located only in the work of an individual. In Greek ETHICAL LIFE, it is the ethical SUBSTANCE, while from the point of view of conscience, it is the SUBJECT himself: what matters for the conscientious person is not the external action or result, but the spirit in which the decision is made (*PS*, VI.C.c).

The *Sache selbst* appears in a variety of contexts in the Logic. In MEASURE, e.g., the *Sache selbst* is the persisting material substance underlying successive quantitative and qualitative changes, e.g. H_2O, in contrast to its solid, liquid and gaseous states. It is also the thing or 'fact' that emerges from its GROUND or conditions (e.g. *Enc.* I §148), and the thing in the CAUSE (*Ursache*, 'original *Sache*') that passes over into the effect (*Enc.* I §153). The INNER and OUTER are different forms of one *Sache*.

Hegel's central use of *die Sache selbst* is to distinguish his own method of COGNITION from cognition which is EXTERNAL to the *Sache selbst*, 'the subject-matter'. His procedure is to absorb himself in the *Sache selbst* and to follow its immanent movement or DEVELOPMENT, without imposing on it his own external REFLECTIONS (*PS*, Pref.; *SL*, Pref. and Intro.; *Enc.* I §23). Here the connotation of 'main thing' and the contrast with the person are in play. Thus Hegel purports in *PS* to be simply watching the self-assessment and development of CONSCIOUSNESS, and in *SL* to be surveying the immanent DIALECTIC of concepts. This is one of his main defences against SCEPTICISM and against the possibility of error. Husserl's slogan *Zu den Sachen selbst!* ('To the things themselves!') was intended to make a similar point.

Sache also occurs in *Tatsache* ('fact'), introduced in the eighteenth century to translate 'matter of fact'. Hegel uses this in a derogatory way, to decry, e.g., Krug's appeal to the 'facts of consciousness'.

thinking and thought   'To think' in German is *denken*. 'Thinking' or '(the activity of) thought' is conveyed by the nominal infinitive, *das Denken*. *Gedanke* is usually not 'thought' as an activity, but '(a) thought' as the product or content of thinking. A *Gedanke* may be either a psychological entity ('His thoughts are confused', 'The thought of his arrival excited me') or an ideal, logical entity ('It is a comforting thought that the actual is rational'). The past participle of *denken* is *gedacht*. Hence Hegel associates it with the cognate *Gedächtnis* (MEMORY, especially of words). *Denken* enters several compounds: especially important for Hegel is *nachdenken* (literally 'to after-think', hence 'to reflect') and *das Nachdenken* ('after-thinking, reflection'). But it is distinct from *reflektieren* and *Reflexion* (REFLECTION), in that it has the favourable connotation of 'thinking over, about' what one has first encountered by, e.g., PERCEPTION or FEELING, and of producing *thoughts* about it (*Enc.* I §2).

In philosophy, as in everyday speech, 'thinking' can cover a wide range of mental activity. Leibniz and his followers regarded all psychical activity as thinking, differing only in its degree of clarity and distinctness. But Parmenides, Plato, etc., sharply distinguished thinking (*to noein* or *noēsis*) from other faculties or activities, especially 'OPINION' (*doxa*) and perception. Against the Leibnizians, Kant distinguished thought sharply from INTUITION (*Anschauung*), and argued that COGNITION requires both thinking and intuition of an OBJECT. Thus while we can think about THINGS IN THEMSELVES, we cannot know about them since they supply no intuitions for our CONCEPTS. Kant (like Krug) held that one can *think* whatever one likes, as long as one does not contradict oneself. The LAW of CONTRADICTION thus has a special status among the *Denkgesetze* ('laws of thought'): a contradictory thought is no thought at all. Hegel rejects this doctrine, and the laws of thought in general, since he holds that thought, like REASON, can neither accept from without, nor assign to itself, LIMITS to its activity which it cannot surmount or think beyond. The discovery and overcoming of contradictions in our thinking plays an essential part in the advance of our thought.

When concepts or categories are not filled out with intuitions, they are, on Kant's view, merely *Gedankenformen* ('forms of thought(s)'). But a more common expression among his successors (e.g. Schleiermacher, Reinhold) is *Denkform* ('thought-form, form of thinking'), in contrast to *Denkstoff* ('material of thought, thinking'). Thought-forms are often equated with the forms of formal logic: e.g. the thought-form 'All S is P' becomes, by the addition of appropriate thought-material, the thought 'All men are mortal'. Hegel equates them with the subject-matter of logic, which includes both Kant's categories and the forms of formal logic: e.g. the thought-form of CAUSALITY is involved in the CONCRETE thought of a stone's breaking glass. Often he uses the word *Denkbestimmung* ('thought-DETERMINATION'), and occasionally *Gedankenbestimmung*, as a near-synonym, but with the additional suggestions of the word *Bestimmung*. He often equates a thought-form or -determination with a thought, since (1) a thought-form is not, on his view, simply the FORM of a thought, but can also be the CONTENT of a thought, and (2) a concrete thought, of a horse or of a stone's breaking glass, is a CONCEPTION (*Vorstellung*), not strictly a thought.

Hegel sometimes equates a thought or thought-form with a concept. More often he distinguishes them, since the concept properly belongs only to the last phase of the Logic. But, like 'concept', 'thought' and 'thinking' are involved in a set of contrasts which Hegel attempts to SUBLATE. They contrast with (1) the I* that thinks or 'has' thoughts; (2) other psychical activities of the I such as perceiving, imagining, etc.; and (3) with the object which I think about:

1. From Plato and Aristotle down to Kant, philosophers have associated the I and its identity with thought, rather than with, e.g., perception, desire

or action, Hegel too insists that the I does not 'have' thoughts or thought-forms, but is identical with, or constituted by, them (*Enc.* I §§20, 24A.1). Apart from the considerations under (2) below, he has two arguments for this. (a) To be an I is to be aware of oneself as an I, and awareness of oneself as an I involves thought, since the I is accessible only by way of pure thinking: the I as such provides no sensory material for perception or conception. (b) I cannot coherently distance myself from my thought(form)s, supposing that they are a tool that I use (like a hammer) or that I might have lacked them (like a desire), since my thinking in these ways of my thoughts and of my relation to them involves the very thoughts from which I attempt to distance myself.

2. Hegel accepts Aristotle's doctrine that what distinguishes man from all other creatures is the ability to think, and infers (invalidly) that 'everything human is human because, and only because, it is produced by thinking' (*Enc.* I §2). Thus thinking is not simply one activity alongside others that we engage in. First, my other activities involve thought. My perceiving a horse as a horse, my conception of a horse, my feeling of the presence of God, etc., involve the thought(-form)s of, e.g., a THING, LIFE, or the ABSOLUTE. No animal, Hegel argues, has a morality or a RELIGION, and this is because, even if morality or religion appear in the form of, e.g., feeling, they essentially involve thought. My feelings, etc., are not imbued with thought from birth, but my development into a full human being and my ability to claim my feelings, etc. (and my body) as my own requires their infusion with thought. This, Hegel believes, is at odds with Kant's doctrine that MORALITY essentially involves a conflict between REASON and our inclinations.

Second, my other activities, my perceiving, desiring, etc., are objects of my thinking in a way in which my thinking is not, conversely, an object of *them*. I can think that I am perceiving, that perception has INDIVIDUALS for its objects, etc., while I cannot perceive that I am thinking or that thinking is of UNIVERSALS. This exemplifies a general principle: Thinking is of, or 'over-reaches' (*übergreift*), what is OTHER than thought. Thinking of this type, especially the extraction of the pure thoughts implicit in feelings, etc., constitutes philosophical thinking, in contrast to the thinking involved in everyday activities.

3. Thinking does not simply contrast with its objects. First, the principle that thought overreaches what is other than thought applies here too. If a thing is individual (in contrast to the universality of thoughts) or even wholly alien to thought or unthinkable, it is nevertheless by thinking that I know this, and 'individual', 'alien to thought', and 'unthinkable' express thoughts, not, e.g., perceptions.

Second, the ESSENCE of things is discerned by thinking, not by perceiving, and constituted by thoughts, not by their external perceptible features that we first encounter. This is so both at the level of the natural sciences (e.g. electricity, discovered by *Nachdenken*, is the essence of lightning) and at the level of philosophy (e.g. the concept is the essence of the I). Thus thoughts are as much OBJECTIVE as SUBJECTIVE.

292

So far Hegel's view of the relation of thought to its objects is similar to Kant's. For Kant too, the thoughts that we apply to intuitions constitute the essence of the resulting things. But Hegel differs from Kant in that he rejects the view that thoughts are imposed by us on intrinsically thought-free intuitions. Thoughts are embedded in things independently of our thinking about them. It is only our thought about the Great Bear that makes it a unity, but, e.g., a horse is a self-determining unity; it is not unified solely by our thought about it. (This seemingly innocuous doctrine plays a part in Hegel's IDEALISM and his belief that the ABSOLUTE is SPIRIT.)

Hegel also differs from Kant in stressing that we can think not only about what is other than thought, but about thought itself. In particular we can (in logic) think about thought(-form)s in terms of thought(-form)s. Such pure thinking needs no external intuitions, and yet is, on Hegel's view, non-arbitrary and constitutes cognition. He associates such thinking with the *noēsis noēseōs* ('thinking of/about thinking') that Aristotle ascribes to God, and Plotinus to the 'true intellect (*nous*)'.

When Hegel says that thought or thinking is INFINITE, he means several things: (1) Thought(-form)s are not sharply distinct from, and bounded by, each other; they are knit together by reason and DIALECTIC. (2) Thought(s) overreach what is other than thought. (3) Thought can think about itself. (4) Thought as a whole has no limits. FINITE thoughts, by contrast, are segments of thought that are (a) treated as distinct from other thoughts; (b) treated as distinct from things; (c) incapable of, or not regarded as, applying to themselves; and/or (d) applicable to, or thoughts *of*, finite entities.

time, space and eternity   Hegel's views on space, time and eternity owe as much to Greek antiquity as to modern philosophers. In the *Timaeus*, Plato saw space (*chōra*) as a 'receptacle' in which the *genesis* ('becoming') of material things (in contrast to the FORMS or IDEAS, on which they are modelled) takes place. In his *Physics*, Aristotle focused on the place (*topos*) occupied by a body: it is not identical with the body, since a body can change its place; it is the 'immediate unmoving LIMIT of the containing body'. In the *Republic*, Plato speaks of the 'upward journey of the soul to the intelligible place [*noēton topon*]'. In later Platonism this became the 'place of the forms', and was sometimes equated with the mind of God. Like Wittgenstein's 'logical space', it is a spatial analogue of 'eternity'.

The distinction between time (*chronos*) and eternity (*aiōn*) is implicit in Parmenides, who denied the occurrence of 'becoming' and thus the past and the future, arguing that everything is simultaneous in the present. In Plato's *Timaeus*, and in Neoplatonism generally, time is a 'moving image [*eikōn*] of eternity'. Eternity characterizes the forms; it is timeless, and excludes the use of verbs in the past and future tenses. Time is identified with the periodic revolution of the heavenly sphere, initiated by the divine demiurge. Plato's *Parmenides* raises puzzles about time, e.g. the status of 'the now' (*to nun*), the punctual instant or present. This dialogue influenced Hegel's treatment of time, as well as Aristotle's.

293

Aristotle's *Physics* questions the reality of time, since the present is vanishingly thin and past and future time do not exist *now*. He rejects the *identification* of time with motion, but associates it closely with motion, especially regular, circular motion: time is 'the number of change with respect to earlier and later'. Since he recognized no transcendent forms, Aristotle ignores the distinction between time and eternity: *aiōn*, even when applied to God, is everlasting duration, not timeless eternity. But the distinction persisted, via Neoplatonic and medieval thought, into modern times.

In Hegel's day, space (*Raum*) and time (*Zeit*) were usually treated together. Four conceptions of them were abroad:

(1) Space and time are each a thing, in which other things are contained. This view was associated with Newton.
(2) Space and time are attributes of things, a view close to Aristotle's.
(3) Space and time are RELATIONS between things, a view initiated by Leibniz.
(4) Space and time are 'forms of our sensibility' and thus 'transcendentally IDEAL'; we impose them on our INTUITIONS. Only phenomena, not THINGS IN THEMSELVES, are in space and time. This was Kant's view.

Kant held that his conception resolves the questions ('antinomies') whether the world is FINITE or INFINITE in space and time: if space and time are merely ideal, the answer is 'Neither'. The view that reality is timelessly eternal (*ewig*) and that time is a form that we impose on it was challenged by Schelling in *The Ages of the World*, written in 1811, but published posthumously. Time, he argued, is not a homogeneous medium, but intrinsic to, and articulated by, the things and events in it: 'everything has its time . . . time is not an external, wild, inorganic principle, but an inner principle in the large and in the small, always whole and organic.' (We might paraphrase this as: By the principle of MEASURE, the nature or QUALITY of a thing determines not only its size, but how long it lasts and the duration of its various phases.) True eternity (*Ewigkeit*), he argues, is 'not the eternity that excludes all time, but the eternity that contains time itself (eternal time) subject to itself. Real eternity is the overcoming of time.' He held, in this period, a similarly anti-Newtonian and anti-Kantian view of space.

Hegel regards space and time as the concern not of logic, but of the philosophy of NATURE, and he discusses them in his Jena lectures on the philosophy of nature and especially in *Enc.* II (§§254–61). His account of them is quite different from Kant's, which he criticizes in *LHP*. Unlike Kant, he views space and time not as forms of sensibility, distinct from the concepts of the UNDERSTANDING, but as the most fundamental manifestations of the CONCEPT in nature. He thus attempts a conceptual derivation of space and time, and of their main features, e.g. the three dimensions of space and of time (past, present and future). But unlike Kant's, his *a priori* derivation does not confine itself to space and time: he goes on to derive conceptually the place (*Ort*) of a body, bodies themselves, and movement. Since he argues that space and time involve each other he is sometimes held to have anticipated

H. G. Wells's and Minkowski's doctrine that time is a fourth dimension. But Hegel's view depends more on such familiar facts as that the measurement of time, and our perception of its passage, require movement in *space*, esp. of the heavenly bodies.

In *Being and Time* (1927), Heidegger argued that Hegel reproduced in its essentials Aristotle's conception of time, and saw time as a homogeneous continuum constituted by the flow of 'the now' (*das Jetzt*), focusing on the time of the natural sciences and ignoring the time of human experience. Kojève and Koyré argued that when Hegel says that time is 'the existing (*daseiende*) concept itself' (*PS*, Pref., etc.), he links 'concept' with the human subject and anticipates Heidegger's view that time is primarily the time of decision and ACTION and that the future is thus prior to the past and the present. But what Hegel in fact means is this: in virtue of their conceptual structure (i.e. the concept) and the CONTRADICTIONS involved in it, FINITE entities DEVELOP, change, pass away and give rise to other entities. Such changes entail time, and without them there would be no time. Hence time is the 'existent concept' (cf. *Enc.* II §258A.). This view is close to Schelling's.

Time is thus intrinsic to finite things and is not a form imposed on them. But Hegel also regards timeless eternity as prior to time. The concept itself and the SPIRIT that ascends to the concept are eternal, not temporal (*Enc.* II §258 and A.). This is why (like Fichte, and Kant in *The End of All Things*, but unlike Schelling) Hegel cannot ascribe genuine IMMORTALITY to spirit.

Enc. II deals mainly with the concept of time involved in the physical sciences, but *Enc.* III contains several comments on the psychology of time-perception (e.g. §448 and A.). In *LPH*, etc., Hegel employs a notion of historical time (and, in *LA*, of the time of, e.g., a piece of music) that is not homogeneous, but articulated into phases or periods: world history is the 'exposition (*Auslegung*, "laying out") of spirit in time'. But he assigns no priority to the future. Philosophy is essentially retrospective, confined to understanding the past and the present. We cannot foresee or prescribe the future, and should thus reconcile ourselves to the present (*Gegenwart*). He agrees with Epicurus that the future is no concern of ours. This doctrine was rejected by Kierkegaard, who insisted that while life is 'understood backwards', it must be 'lived forwards'. But it coheres with Hegel's view that action involves not momentous choices between equally possible alternatives, but conformity to the norms of ETHICAL LIFE.

In '*Ousia* and *Grammē*', Heidegger's account of Aristotle is criticized by Derrida, who argues that both Aristotle's conception of time and its later influence are more complex and multifaceted than Heidegger supposed. The same is true of Hegel's conception of time.

triads Philosophical concepts often take the form of OPPOSITION: MIND–body, SPIRIT–MATTER, noumena–phenomena, good–evil, REASON–desire, SUBJECT–OBJECT, THOUGHT–BEING, etc. One approach to this is dualism, the acceptance that there are two entities or types of entity (Plato, Descartes, etc.). Another is monism, the claim that one opposite is reducible to the other, or that some third entity underlies both. Hegel, like, e.g., Nicholas of

Cusa, Böhme and Schelling, held that philosophy's task is to overcome such oppositions. But oppositions, on his view, are not simply to be dissolved in a blank unity: opposition is an essential factor in LIFE and must be preserved and SUBLATED in the TOTALITY that emerges from it. Thus Hegel is neither a monist nor a dualist. If any number is to be assigned to him, it is the number 3.

Hegel has specific objections to dualism and to monism. The single entity postulated by monism must be wholly indeterminate, since DETERMINACY involves NEGATION. Dualism is both intellectually untidy and epistemologically unstable, since the philosopher must have cognitive access to *both* types of entity: either one of the two entities cognitively overreaches (*übergreift*) the other and is thus not co-ordinate with it, or the philosopher is himself a third type of entity, alongside the other two. (Hegel found this defect in Spinoza's ABSOLUTE or SUBSTANCE. But it also emerges in Plato's dualism of FORMS and phenomena, since the SOUL that knows both realms can belong to neither – a difficulty raised by Plato himself in the *Sophist* and *Parmenides*.)

The triadic structure has a long history. For earlier Greek philosophers, the third term of a triad is usually the mid-point between two opposites. The Pythagoreans viewed things as a balance between opposites, Plato in the *Philebus* sees them as a mixture of the INFINITE and LIMIT, and Aristotle regarded a virtue as a mean between two opposing vices. But the triad is most characteristics of Neoplatonism. Plotinus postulates three *hypostaseis* ('substances'): the one, the intellect and the world soul. Intellect in turn has three phases: being, life and thought. The more systematic Proclus also postulates the being–life–intellect triad, along with many others, but he justifies them by a principle: every CAUSE proceeds to its effect by way of a middle or mean (*meson*). To ensure continuity, the absence of sharp rifts, in the spiritual world, Proclus, like Hegel, requires MEDIATION.

A crucial triad in Proclus, is that of remaining–procession–return. The Neoplatonists were faced with a question that goes back to Parmenides: how do diversity and plurality arise from an original unity? Plotinus answered that it is because everything that is 'complete' tends to reproduce itself, to generate timelessly an inferior likeness of itself. The one is not thereby diminished, but remains as it was, just as a source of light is not diminished by the light it sheds. Plotinus allows for a return to the one (e.g. he describes himself as 'being alone with the alone'), but does not exploit the notion of REFLECTION for this purpose. Proclus sees *proodos* ('going forth, procession, emanation') in terms of the generation of a series of numbers by the unit. This model accommodates the notion of a reversal or return (*epistrophē*) to the *archē* ('beginning, principle'). Every perfect being generates an effect resembling itself, which remains in the cause (since the cause is undiminished), proceeds from it, and returns to the cause (since it desires reunification with the cause, which is like itself, but on a higher plain). This triad is repeated at successive levels. The world is a continuous chain of beings, descending from the one and resembling it to varying degrees. It is a unified, organic WHOLE. Souls ascend, both morally and cognitively, back to the one, thus completing a circular movement.

These doctrines had an immense influence on medieval theology (especially via the *Divine Names*, by a Christian plagiarist purporting to be Dionysius the Areopagite), and on Renaissance and modern thought, especially Scotus Erigena, Eckhart, Böhme, Nicholas of Cusa, Leibniz and Schelling. Erigena, e.g., held that all things proceed from God by an ETERNAL creation, while remaining within the divine nature, and eternally return to God. The doctrine was later given a historical interpretation: HISTORY, for Schelling and Hegel, is God's or SPIRIT's revelation of itself. Hegel studied Plotinus and Proclus thoroughly, and admired them both, though he preferred Proclus to Plotinus. He differs from them in regarding the source of a triadic movement (e.g. BEING) as SUBLATED, rather than preserved in its original purity, but it is restored on a higher plain at the end of the triad, the 'return'. Thus a Hegelian triad, like the Neoplatonic triad, is a return journey, and, as in Proclus, the triadic scheme reappears at successive levels. E. R. Dodds, in his 2nd edition of Proclus' *The Elements of Theology* (Oxford: Clarendon, 1963), argued that Proclus' main fault is his 'assumption that the structure of the cosmos exactly reproduces the structure of Greek logic. ... In form a metaphysic of Being, the *Elements* embodies what is in substance a doctrine of categories: the cause is but a reflection of the "because", and the Aristotelian apparatus of genus, species and differentia is transformed into an objectively conceived hierarchy of entities or forces' (p. xxv). With some qualifications, the same charge has been made, especially by Schelling, against Hegel.

A more immediate source of Hegel's triad is the idea that the third term is the overcoming or synthesis of two opposites. This idea is not conspicuous in the Neoplatonists, but it is prominent in Kant and more especially Fichte. In *CPR*, the categories appear in four groups of three (though in only two of the triads can the first two categories – unity/plurality and reality/negation – be plausibly regarded as opposites), and the 'third category in each case arises from the combination [*Verbindung*] of the second with the first' (*CPR*, B111). Each of the four antinomies (*CPR*, A426ff, B454ff) involves a *Thesis* and an *Antithesis*, but Kant does not present his own solution as a *Synthesis*. ('Synthesis', in Kant, usually refers to the 'synthesis of a/the sensory manifold', and contrasts with 'analysis', not with 'thesis' or 'antithesis'.) Often a third term mediates between two other, disparate terms: the IMAGINATION (*Einbildungskraft*) receives its material from sensibility, but is, like the UNDERSTANDING, spontaneous, and thus mediates between, or combines, the two. The terms 'thesis', 'antithesis' and 'synthesis', and the corresponding triadic movement, pervade Fichte's *SKW*. The initial triad is (1) the self-POSITING of the I*; (2) the counterpositing of the non-I; and (3) the positing of a divisible non-I over against the divisible I. Schelling also favoured triads. The ABSOLUTE manifests itself in two *Potenzen* ('powers, potences'), those of the real (NATURE) and of the IDEAL (SPIRIT), and is itself the indifference betwen the real and the ideal. This pattern is repeated within the resulting terms. Nature involves a real power (matter), an ideal power (light), and a power of indifference (ORGANISM), and so does spirit: knowledge, action, and ART. Each of these terms is again divided and subdivided into three on the same principle.

Hegel does not apply the terms 'thesis', 'antithesis' and 'synthesis' to his own triads, and uses them together only in his account of Kant's triads. But he owes much to Fichte's triadic procedure, and often describes his own procedure as one of overcoming oppositions by DIALECTICAL and SPECULATIVE REASON. This is more appropriate to the first section of the Logic, than to the second, where the movement proceeds by reflection, or to the third, where it proceeds by a DEVELOPMENT, especially of the UNIVERSAL into the PARTICULAR and the INDIVIDUAL, that is reminiscent of Neoplatonism.

Triadic structures in the realms of NATURE and spirit (e.g. the WILL) are often seen in terms of triads from the third part of the Logic, especially universal–particular–individual, the INFERENCES relating them, concept–JUDGMENT–inference, and CONCEPT–REALITY–IDEA. The dominant triad for Hegel is that of spirit itself, which (1) is the self-enclosed I; (2) has an OBJECT opposed to it; and (3) 'overreaches' (*übergreift*) and sublates its object, like 'the light that manifests itself and something else too' (*Enc.* III §413). Spirit overreaches and unifies, while preserving, opposites. Hegel is thus neither a monist nor a dualist; he is not in any straightforward sense an 'idealist' in contrast to a 'materialist', or an adherent of any other '-ism' in contrast to its opposite.

truth, falsity and correctness   The adjective *wahr* ('true') is cognate with the Latin *verus* ('true', etc.) and originally meant 'trustworthy, reliable'. (The English 'true' is cognate with the German *treu*, 'faithful, loyal, dependable, reliable'.) From this come the noun (*die*) *Wahrheit* ('truth') and the adjectival noun *das Wahre* ('the truth, that which is true'). *Falsch*, like the English 'false', is cognate with the Latin *falsus*, and originally meant 'faithless, dishonourable; spurious, deceptive'. This gives rise to (*die*) *Falschheit*, 'falsity, falsehood', and *das Falsche* ('the false', etc.). *Wahr* is close to *richtig*, which is cognate with *Recht* (RIGHT), 'right', and the Latin *rectus* ('straight, correct', etc.), and originally meant 'straight'. It now means 'correct', but overlaps 'real' and 'quite', as in 'a real (quite a) success, fool, etc.'

Wahr and *Wahrheit*, like 'true' and 'truth', apply not only to beliefs, statements, etc., but also to things, as in 'a true artist', a 'true friend', etc. This usage has an ancient pedigree: Plato applied *alēthēs* ('true, undeceptive') and *alētheia* ('truth, undeceptiveness, reality') to things, especially to what is knowable rather than merely opinable. He argued, in the *Republic*, that the supreme FORM, the form of the good, supplies truth to what is known, as the sun illuminates earthly objects. But Aristotle excluded truth from things and confined it to JUDGMENTS: a judgment is true if it says, of what is, that it is, or says, of what is not, that it is not. Syrianus insisted that 'nothing can be strictly true or false except assertion and denial'. Aristotle's definition passed into scholasticism as *adaequatio rerum et intellectus*, 'the agreement of things and the intellect'. But the idea that things, as well as judgments, may be true or false persists in, e.g., St Augustine's *Soliloquies* and in later writers, together with the idea that God is supremely true or (the) truth and confers on other things such truth as they have. In the eighteenth century, truth was closely associated with the LAWS of THOUGHT. A true proposition must conform to the laws of thought, especially the law of CONTRADICTION. At *CPR*, A294,

B350, Kant says that the 'formal element of all truth consists in agreement with the laws of the UNDERSTANDING'.

Hegel uses *wahr* and *Wahrheit* in unusual ways. He rejects Aristotle's usage and regards a judgment such as 'This rose is red' as capable of being *richtig*, but not *wahr*. He applies *wahr* and *Wahrheit* primarily to concepts and to things. But he tends to believe that only GOD or the ABSOLUTE is strictly true. His usage exploits and develops various strands in previous usage:

1. Hegel associates his own use of *wahr* with such locutions as 'true friend' and 'true work of art' (e.g. *Enc.* I §§24A.2, 172A., 214A.). A true friend, he argues, is a friend who conforms to the CONCEPT of a friend and a true work of art is one that agrees with the concept of a work of art. But no FINITE entity fully agrees with its concept. It is entangled in relations to other things which confer on it features that are not determined by its concept. Hence nothing can be strictly true except the WHOLE, that which has no external entanglements and is thus fully in accord with its concept. In the Logic, this is, or is represented by, the absolute IDEA, in which the concept is fully in accord with REALITY.

2. Hegel accepts the view that something can be true only if it is not self-contradictory. But it is not only judgments, beliefs, etc., that can contradict themselves. Even Leibniz and Kant agree that a concept may contradict itself, and thus be, by their own criterion, false. A false friend or a false work of art also contradicts itself, in the sense both that it falls short of or 'contradicts' its concept, and that it is (often, at least) internally discordant. But in fact any finite entity, whether it is a thing or a concept, contradicts itself, at least if it is ABSTRACTED from its RELATIONS with other things or concepts. Thus again, it is only the whole that is strictly true, that which, since it is not finite, SUBLATES the contradictions in its parts.

3. Hegel also accepts the definition of truth as *adaeqatio rerum et intellectus*, but he reinterprets it as, e.g., the 'identity of THINKING and BEING' or the 'agreement of the SUBJECTIVE and the OBJECTIVE'. But full accord between thinking and being is not to be found in a judgment such as 'This rose is red'. My thought about the rose fails to capture the whole truth about the rose, its fragrance, etc., let alone the whole truth about being in general. The rose may be diseased and thus fall short of the concept of a rose that I apply to it, but even if it is healthy and well developed as roses go, it must, as a finite entity, fall short of the concepts I apply to it. Judgments of this type presuppose that I and my thinking are distinct from the OBJECTS of my judgments and thus that, however correct my thinking is, it does not *coincide* with its object. Hegel saw such coincidence of thinking and being, of the subjective and the objective, only in the absolute IDEA, i.e. primarily in the universe as a whole and the concept of it, but also in our pure, logical THINKING, our thought about thought itself.

4. Hegel does not advocate that we cease to make judgments about, e.g., roses. But he does hold that the judgment or PROPOSITION is not an appropriate form for thinking about what is fully true, viz. God, the absolute, the idea, SPIRIT, etc. One reason for this is that the judgment-form implies that

299

the subject of the judgment is a THING, a substratum supporting properties that are not intrinsically connected with each other. But even if a rose is a thing of this type, the absolute, spirit, etc., are not. The THOUGHT-(DETERMINATION)s that constitute their essence do not inhere in a substratum and they are DIALECTICally interconnected.

5. Only the absolute, the idea, etc., is strictly true. But Hegel often refers to a concept, a FORM of CONSCIOUSNESS, a level of nature or a historical stage as the *Wahrheit of* one or more of its predecessors in the conceptual hierarchy or historical process, even if it is not the final stage, not, that is, the 'absolute truth'. Thus PERCEPTION is the truth of SENSORY CERTAINTY; BECOMING is the truth of BEING and NOTHING; TELEOLOGY is the truth of MECHANISM and CHEMISM. This usage involves three ideas:

(a)   If something is the truth of its predecessor, then although it contains contradictions of its own which will subsequently emerge, it resolves, and is free of, the truth-impairing contradiction(s) that its predecessor contained.

(b)   It is, or embodies, the concept that its predecessor strove to realize, but could not adequately realize without changing into something else. One might, analogously, write a draft of an article, but be unable to realize one's intentions or what one has in mind without expanding it into a treatise. (It does not follow that the treatise, when complete, is definitive and will require no changes for its second edition.)

(c)   The truth of the predecessor does not simply supplant it, but contains or sublates what is true *in* it. (The treatise contains what was true in the draft.)

6. The 'truth of' locution coheres with the fact that truth is not simply opposed to error and falsehood. Error (*Irrtum*) or falsehood develops into truth and is sublated in it. Analogously, finite or 'false' entities within the universe are not simply opposed to the true or INFINITE, but sublated in it. Hölderlin held a similar view: 'That alone is the truest truth, in which error too becomes truth, because truth, in its total system, sets it in its time and place.' Thus when Hegel criticizes another philosopher, such as Spinoza or Jacobi, he tends to argue not that his view is false, but that it develops into his own view.

Hegel's conception of truth coheres with several other aspects of his thought:

(1)   The truth of something, whether a thought or a thing, is not sharply distinct from its value or significance. A true work of art is *ipso facto* a good work of art. Conversely, Hegel is loath to concede that a trivial statement (or a statement about the trivial) can be a true statement.

(2)   A piecemeal truth that is framed in terms of an inappropriate conceptual system or scientific theory cannot be strictly true. Hence the primary locus of truth and falsity is the conceptual system or theory within which a judgment is framed, rather than the judgment itself.

(3) The world forms an interconnected SYSTEM, such that no piecemeal thought or judgment can do justice, or be true, *to* it.

(4) There is a deep parallel, and ultimate convergence, between the world and our thought about it. Thus they must both be true (or false) together. (*See* IDEALISM.)

(5) The truth of a philosophy, and its invulnerability to SCEPTICISM, depends not, e.g., on its correspondence to facts, but on its internal coherence and comprehensiveness.

U

universal, particular and individual For each of these, German has a native and a Latin-derived word:

1. (a) *Allgemein* ('general, universal') is literally 'common (*gemein*) to all (*all*)'. It gives rise to (*das/ein*) *Allgemeine* ('(the/a) universal') and (*die*) *Allgemeinheit* ('universality'). (b) In the sixteenth century, *universal*, and in the eighteen, *universell* (via the French *universel*), were derived from the late Latin *universalis*, which comes from *universus* (literally 'turned (*versus*) into one (*unus*)', hence 'universal, embracing, whole', etc.).

Hegel's usual term for 'universal' is *allgemein*. He uses *universell* only occasionally, especially of the universal JUDGMENT in *SL*. (He uses *Universum* in the sense of 'universe, TOTALITY, (whole) world'.)

2. (a) *Besonder* is cognate with the English '(a)sunder', and originally meant 'separated, marked out, special'. It generates *das Besondere* ('the particular'), (*die*) *Besonderheit* ('particularity'), and (*die*) *Besonderung* ('particularizing, particularization, specification'). The link with 'sunder' (*sondern*) is preserved in Hegel's use of the word. (b) *Partikular* and *Partikularität* come from the Latin *pars* ('part, portion, division').

Hegel uses *besonder* more often than *partikular*, but he uses the latter for, e.g., the particular judgment and for particular, i.e. special, interests.

3. (a) *Einzeln* ('singular, single, individual, isolated', etc.) comes from *ein* ('one' and 'a'). This generates *das Einzelne* ('the individual (thing)'), *der Einzelne* ('the individual (man, person)'), (*die*) *Einzelheit* ('singularity', etc., and also 'particular point, detail') and *vereinzeln, Vereinzelung* ('to isolate, individualize', 'isolating, individualization'). (b) The Latin *individuum* ('the indivisible', a translation of the Greek *atomon*) gave rise, in the sixteenth century, to (*das*) *Individuum* ('(the) individual') and *individual*, and, in the eighteenth via French, to *individuell* and *Individualität*. These words carry a stronger suggestion of human individuality and individualism than *einzeln*, etc. But the common expression for 'the individual' in the sense of 'person' is *der Einzelne*, not *das Individuum*.

Hegel usually uses *einzeln*, etc., to contrast with *allgemein*, etc., and *besonder*, etc. But he often uses *Individuum* and *Individualität*, especially for the human individual and individuality, e.g. the 'world-HISTORICAL individual' is *das Individuum*, not *der Einzelne*. He sometimes uses the latinate *singular* for the 'singular' or 'individual' judgment.

The terms had two main uses in the logic of Hegel's day:

1. The distinction between 'universal' and 'particular' corresponds in part to that between the generic (or 'determinable') and the specific (or 'determinate'). A universal (concept, etc.) is a concept that applies to, or a characteristic that inheres in, all entities, or all entities of a given type: e.g. 'coloured'. A particular applies to only some of these entities: e.g. 'red'. ('Universal' and 'particular' are here relative terms: what is, from one point of view, particular, i.e. a specification of a universal, is, from another, a universal, i.e. a general term that can be specified into particulars.) An individual is a single entity: e.g. Socrates.

2. The terms also apply to types of judgment: a universal judgment concerns all entities of a given type: e.g. 'All men are wise'. (Hegel often refers to this type of universality as 'allness', *Allheit*.) A particular judgment concerns some of the entities of a given type: e.g. 'Some men are wise'. An individual judgment concerns an individual: e.g. 'Socrates is wise'. The individual judgment was seen by Kant (*CPR*, A71, B96) and other logicians as similar to the universal judgment, in that the predicate applies to the *whole* of the subject (e.g. Socrates), not just to a part of it, as in the particular judgment. (This, together with the fact that individuality represents unity, in contrast to the 'sundering' of particularity, accounts in part for Hegel's view that individuality is a restoration of universality on a higher level.)

In traditional logic, nothing can be both individual and universal. But in less formal usage an individual can be viewed as universal: Krug argues that a PEOPLE (*Volk*) is, in contrast to other peoples, particular (*etwas Besonderes*), but when viewed as a whole and in contrast to the individuals it contains, it is universal. Hegel uses *allgemein* in a similar way. In *PS*, I, the 'here' and the 'now' are universal, not only because the terms apply to any place and time, but because any area of space referred to as 'here' contains smaller areas that can each be referred to as 'here', and any stretch of time referred to as 'now' contains shorter stretches that are also 'nows'. The I* is universal not only because everyone is an I (*Enc.* I §20), but because it is a 'receptacle' for all one's CONCEPTIONS, etc. (*Enc.* I §24A.1). 'Universal' is thus often close to 'WHOLE', '(all-)encompassing', or 'comprehensive'. Another reason for the universality of the I is that it is 'empty' or INDETERMINATE. Thus Hegel also associates universality with simplicity, indeterminacy or lack of specificity. He sees universality (like the CONCEPT) as developing from indeterminate simplicity into a rich comprehensiveness in which it coincides with individuality. (Cf. the *universaler Mensch*, the 'universal (or "Renaissance") man', the man of comprehensive talents and interests, but also of marked individuality.)

Individuals were often felt to be logically, epistemologically and/or ontologically inferior to universals, especially by adherents of Plato's view that FORMS, IDEAS or universals are prior to individuals. Individuals received more logical respectability from the postulation of individual, as well as universal, forms (Plotinus), of individual essences (Duns Scotus's *haecceitas*, 'thisness'), and of a concept of each individual differing from that of any other individual (Leibniz). Hegel rejects these attempts to give the individual a status equal to, and co-ordinate with, that of the universal. For him, THOUGHT and

LANGUAGE are concerned with universals, and cannot refer to unique individuals, since terms such as 'I', 'this' and 'this individual' are universal terms (*Enc.* I §20). Individuals derive their status from the universality involved in them. He does not, like Spinoza, view individuals as mere accidents of SUBSTANCE.

The Enlightenment saw human individuals as uniformly rational, their individual differences being merely secondary. But Herder and the romantics stressed the unique *Individualität* of, e.g., individual men and works of ART. Hegel acknowledges particular differences between men, but he subordinates them to what men have in common. In respect of their highest faculty, REASON, men do not essentially differ: 'the rational is the high road where everyone travels, where no one is conspicuous' (*PR* §15A.). In society, the sphere of particularity, CIVIL SOCIETY, is subordinate to the individuality of the STATE, in which particular needs and interests are reintegrated and SUBLATED in a more differentiated, comprehensive universality than the simple universality of the FAMILY.

Universality, particularity and individuality are the three MOMENTS of the concept. Hegel rejects the view that universals, particulars and individuals are logically, ontologically or epistemologically sharply distinct from each other. The universal is CONCRETE, not ABSTRACT, and DEVELOPS into, but maintains itself in, the particular and the individual. He argues for this at different levels:

1. The concept of universality develops into those of particularity and individuality (e.g. *Enc.* I §§163–5). It is, e.g., only universal in virtue of contrasting with them. Universality *particularizes* itself into universality, particularity and individuality: universality is thus *both* the universal genus *and* a particular species of this genus, co-ordinate with particularity and individuality. (The operation can be repeated: the particular universal can again particularize itself into the subspecies of universality, particularity and individuality.) He often exploits the idea that a universal genus may be one of its own species: it accounts in part for his use of words such as 'BEING' in a wider and a narrower way. It is akin to the idea that thought 'overreaches' (*übergreift*) what is other than thought.

2. In the Logic in general, universal thought particularizes itself into specific thoughts, and eventually returns to the unity of the absolute IDEA.

3. Universality 'overreaches' particulars and individuals. Individuals can only be described and referred to in universal terms, including '(this) individual'. Universals are embedded in particulars and individuals, constituting their ESSENCE

4. Since universals are embedded in things, things involve the self-differentiation of a universal into particulars and then the reunification of individuality. This may or may not be a temporal process: e.g. an indeterminate, universal seed particularizes itself into a differentiated plant, which then withdraws into individuality by producing a new seed; but at any given time an animal is an indeterminate, universal LIFE that differentiates itself into particular organs, but keeps them united in a single individual.

Throughout Hegel's works, both thoughts and things are seen as exemplifying the TRIADIC, DEVELOPMENTAL pattern of universal–particular–individual: the universal I* particularizes itself into the consciousness of OBJECTS, and then restores its individuality in SELF-CONSCIOUSNESS; the universality of the logical idea particularizes itself into NATURE and is individualized in SPIRIT. The individual that results is as much universal as individual. But it is universal not in the sense of 'simple, indeterminate', but in that of 'all-encompassing, comprehensive': e.g. the diverse, particular philosophies that emerged from the primitive simplicity or universality of thought are embraced by, or sublated in, Hegel's PHILOSOPHY, which is thus universal in a higher sense (*Enc.* I §13). *See* CLASSIFICATION, DEFINITION, NEGATION.

W

war and peace Hegel never fought in a war, but for much of his life European states were at war with each other. Some philosophers had regarded warfare as desirable. Heraclitus affirmed that 'war [but probably more in a metaphorical than a literal sense] is the father of all things', and Machiavelli saw it as necessary, not only for the survival of the state, but also for the 'virtue' of its citizens. Others had regarded it as regrettable, but inevitable. But in the eighteenth century several plans were proposed for a 'perpetual peace', either among European states or over the whole world. The first such proposal was the Abbé de St Pierre's *Project for Perpetual Peace*, written in 1715 and later published in a popular form by Rousseau, along with his own *Judgment on Perpetual Peace* (1756). Both Leibniz (who at one time hoped for a revival of the medieval 'Republic of Christendom', but later accepted the existence of independent nation-states) and Rousseau were critical of the plan, but their doubts concerned the feasibility of perpetual peace, rather than its desirability.

The most famous work on the subject was Kant's *OPP*. Kant argued that perpetual peace (in contrast to the temporary armistice with which hostilities are customarily concluded) is a requirement of practical REASON. It is to be realized gradually by the formation and development of a 'league of nations' (*Völkerbund*), whose members will forswear war against each other. Even if perpetual peace can never be fully achieved, it is, Kant argued, our duty to work towards it to INFINITY. Fichte endorsed Kant's ideal and proposed a similar plan in *FNR*. Krug mentions a fierce critic of perpetual peace and of Kant's plan: Embser, who wrote *The Idolatry of our Philosophical Century. First Idolatry: Perpetual Peace* (1779) and *Refutation of the Perpetual Peace-Project* (1797). But most philosophers welcomed the idea of perpetual peace, even if they doubted the feasibility of Kant's or any other plan.

Hegel too doubted the practicality of Kant's plan: the unanimity of different 'sovereign WILLS' is 'plagued with CONTINGENCY' and thus continually uncertain (*PR* §333). And 'even if a number of states make themselves into a family, this group as an individual must engender an opposite and create an enemy' (*PR* §324A.). But Hegel's main objection to perpetual peace is not that it is unrealizable, but that it is undesirable. Most critics of warfare view it as follows:

Since the purpose of the STATE is simply to regulate men's conduct towards each other, it is in principle possible that there should be only one state, and thus no occasion for warfare between states. But, as it happens, several states have arisen with no immediate prospect of joining into one. It is in principle possible that such states should never engage in warfare. But in practice states tend to encroach on each other's rights, and the only way for a state to defend itself and its citizens against such encroachments is to prepare for, and if necessary resort to, war.

Hegel dissents from this view in three respects:

(1) The state is more than a device for regulating the conduct of its citizens. It makes them into full human beings, and permeates their nature.

(2) Just as there cannot be one free individual alone, but only a multiplicity of them, each recognizing the others, so there cannot be one state alone: 'a state is an individual, and INDIVIDUALITY essentially implies NEGATION' (PR §324A.). A state is essentially a member of a system of states, each RECOGNIZING the others.

(3) War is not simply a response to external accidents, any more than eating is simply an animal's response to the accidental presence of food. Warfare is an essential feature of the state. States are founded by war and preserve themselves by war. External encroachments are merely occasions for war, and how a state responds to them depends on its internal condition, not on the intrinsic nature of the encroachment: a state that has been at peace for a long time is more likely to seek an occasion for war than one that has not (PR §334). A society, like the United States, that has no external enemies to threaten it cannot become a proper state.

Not only must a proper state be able and willing to wage war effectively if the need arises; it must on occasion actually wage war. (It is unlikely, Hegel believes, to remain *ready* to wage war, if it has no external threat and never *actually* wages war.) Thus unlike Kant and Fichte, Hegel holds that the DEATH of a state is more likely to arise from its pacific tendencies than from warfare.

This view appears in *NL*: 'war preserves the ethical health of PEOPLES in their indifference to specific institutions. . . . Just as the blowing of the winds preserves the sea from the foulness that would result from a continual calm, so corruption would result for peoples under continual or indeed "perpetual" peace.' It is repeated at *PR* §324 and argued for at greater length (*PR* §§321–40). The main argument is this: in peace citizens become absorbed in their own affairs and interests, and cease to identify with the state. The state will thus cease to exist as an individual, unless it draws them back into unity by warfare, which requires the citizen to be ready to sacrifice his property and life for the state. Hegel sees this sacrifice as a particular case of the general transience of the FINITE: 'We hear plenty of sermons from the pulpit about the insecurity, vanity and instability of temporal things. . . . But if this insecurity now comes on the scene in the form of hussars with shining sabres and they actualize in real earnest what the preachers have said, then the moving and edifying discourses which foretold all these events turn into curses against the invader' (*PR* §324A.). He also appeals to empirical evidence: e.g. states overcome internal strife by wars abroad (*PR* §324A.).

307

Unlike Hegel, Fichte had no interest in the survival of more than one state, and thus argued that states at war cease to recognize each other and aim at each other's annihilation, i.e. incorporation. It does not follow that a state can treat the enemy population as it likes: civilians in captured territory and prisoners of war must be respected, since they are now subjects of the state that has conquered them. Hegel, by contrast, holds that states continue to recognize each other even in war. They do not aim at each other's annihilation, and war should not be conducted in such a way as to make the restoration of peace impossible (*PR* §338).

Hegel was not an unswerving patriot or a glorifier of violence. He was right to stress the role of conflict in the DEVELOPMENT both of the individual and of humanity as a whole; the deep roots of war in our social arrangements; and the problem of reconciling individualism with communal life. But his view that war is both inevitable and desirable can be challenged in several ways:

(1) One might argue that while human development has so far depended on states with a more than regulatory role, it is neither inevitable nor desirable that it should continue to do so, and that the dispersal of individuals into their private pursuits would be no bad thing. Hegel attacks this view throughout *PR*.

(2) One might argue that a more than regulatory state does not require the existence of other states, and that there might be a single world-state, which fulfils Hegel's conditions for statehood, except with regard to external relations. This view takes issue with the doctrine that 'individuality implies negation', and would need to explain how the allegiance of citizens to such a state could be secured.

(3) One might argue that a system of more than regulatory states does not require warfare:

    (a) If a system of individuals within a state no longer requires individual combat between them, why should a system of states require warfare? Why need negation imply *physical* conflict? Hegel could dispute this parallel: individual citizens can dispense with combat, since they are disciplined by EDUCATION, CIVIL SOCIETY and the state. But states cannot be members of a higher *state*, and, without that, international regulatory institutions lack real power over them.

    (b) Wars between technologically advanced states are now more likely to annihilate than to invigorate them, while wars between technologically advanced and less advanced states are too unequal to invigorate advanced states in the way Hegel intended. The transience of the finite need not commit him to favouring reciprocal annihilation or one-sided carnage: the old function of war could, he might suggest, be fulfilled by alternatives.

(4) Some states do not wage war, whether or not they are (like twentieth-century Switzerland) prepared to do so, and states that do wage war do so to differing extents and with differing degrees of ferocity. There is little evidence that citizens of more warlike states are less self-seeking,

more devoted to public causes and to the well-being of their state, than are those of less warlike states.

Hegel might attempt to curtail the argument by insisting that philosophy is essentially retrospective and has no business to speculate on how things OUGHT to be. But his account of war is not merely retrospective, and the suggestion that warfare will persist indefinitely in its traditional form is no more realistic than the project of perpetual peace.

whole and parts, totality and moments. The adjective *ganz* means 'whole, entire'. It gives rise to the adjectival noun, (*das*) *Ganze* ('(the) whole'). Often *das Ganze* is correlative to (*die*) *Teile* ('(the) parts', and, in the singular, 'share, portion'), which is associated with *teilen* ('to divide, share') and thus suggests that the whole can be divided into parts.

Hegel uses *das Ganze* in two senses:

1. In the Logic, the correlation of whole and parts is the first category of RELATION (*Verhältnis*) (*Enc.* I §135). A whole essentially consists of parts, but this gives rise to a problem: 'the relation of whole and parts is UNTRUE, in so far as its CONCEPT and reality do not correspond to each other. The concept of the whole is to contain parts; but if the whole is POSITED as what it is according to its concept, if it is divided or *parted*, it ceases to be a whole' (*Enc.* I §135A.) Thus a whole and its parts are *both* essentially related to each other *and* independent of each other. In *SL* he regards this CONTRADICTION as the source of Kant's second antinomy, that the world can be proved both to be divisible to INFINITY and to consist of indivisible parts. But Hegel attempts to resolve it, and Kant's antinomy, by turning to the concept of a FORCE and its EXTERNALIZATION.

It does not follow, Hegel argues, that there are no wholes consisting of parts in the world. For THINGS can be untrue, as well as categories. Thus things that 'correspond to this relation are *ipso facto* low and untrue existences' (*Enc.* §135A.). They do not include higher entities such as living ORGANISMS, MINDS or philosophical systems. He often refers to a whole consisting of parts as an *Aggregat* or as *zusammengesetzt* ('put together, composite'). The parts of such a whole are prior to the whole itself, and the whole is fully understood if we understand each of its parts.

2. *Das Ganze* is also used for a whole such as a mind, an organism or SYSTEM, whose parts can either not be removed at all or can be removed only with damage to the part removed and to the remaining parts. (Some wholes can replace parts removed, as a lizard grows a new tail.) Such a whole is not formed by composition (*Zusammensetzung*), but by DEVELOPMENT out of its CONCEPT. The whole is prior to the parts, and the parts can only be understood in terms of the whole. Each part serves the PURPOSE of the whole. Hegel has a whole of this type in mind, when he says: 'The true is the whole. But the whole is only the ESSENCE [or 'entity': *Wesen*] perfecting itself through its development' (*PS*, Pref.). He often speaks of the *Teile* of such a whole, but often prefers some other word, such as *Glieder* ('limbs, members'), *Organe*

('organs') or *Momente* ('moments'), which does not suggest that the parts can be separated.

This concept of a whole appears in Aristotle, mystics such as Böhme, and Kant, especially *CJ*. The distinction between 1 and 2 is similar to the distinction, in Plato's *Theaetetus* and Aristotle's *Metaphysics*, between *to pan* ('the all, total(ity)') of the parts and *to holon* ('the whole'). A *holon*, for Aristotle, is not just the total of its parts, even when they are in position, but has an inner cause of unity, viz. a FORM.

The Latin for *ganz* is *totus*, and this gave rise, in scholastic Latin, to *totalis* ('total') and *totalitas* ('totality'). In the sixteenth century German, these became *total* and *Totalität*. *Totalität* means 'totality', both in the sense of 'completeness, entirety, wholeness' and in that of '(a) totality, whole'. It differs from *Ganzheit* ('wholeness') and *das Ganze* in two respects:

1. It need not suggest the internal articulation characteristic of a whole (at least in sense 2 above), but may amount only to *Allheit* (or *to pan*). Thus Kant speaks of the *absolute Totalität* of the CONDITIONS of conditioned entities, which, he argues, underlies transcendental IDEAS and the SPECULATIVE use of REASON (*CPR*, A407, B434ff). Here the stress is on the (unattainable) completeness, the *Allheit*, of the conditions, not on their systematic interrelations.

2. *Totalität* often stresses more emphatically than *das Ganze* the completeness of the whole, the fact that nothing is left out. A whole must be relatively self-contained and independent of its environment, but it is not difficult to suppose that a whole (e.g. a man) is a part of a larger whole (e.g. a STATE). It is more difficult to suppose that a totality is, in the ordinary sense, a part of a larger totality. A lyric or a tragedy is a whole. But it is not, Hegel argues in *LA*, a totality, since it presents only a fragment of the Greek world. An epic, by contrast, is an *einheitsvolle Totalität* ('fully unified totality'), since it presents the Homeric world in its entirety, as well as the particular actions that take place against that background. But elsewhere he is ready to call any good work of ART a *Totalität*, especially a *Totalität in sich* ('within itself').

Hegel's use of *Totalität* varies. Sometimes it is little more than an aggregate: 'the totality of the reactions [of a chemical to other chemicals] is present only as a sum total [*Summe*], not as INFINITE return to itself' (*Enc.* II §336A.). But often a totality is an all-embracing whole: totalities are entities that 'belong essentially to reason, to the thinking of the intrinsically CONCRETE UNIVERSAL – SOUL, world, GOD' (*Enc.* I §30). The 'principle of totality' forbids us to apply to such an entity one of a pair of OPPOSITE predicates, to the exclusion of the other (*Enc.* I §32A.).

Each part of such a totality is itself the whole: thus each PERSON of the deity is implicitly the whole deity, and each part of Hegel's system is implicitly the whole system (*Enc.* I §15). A simple model of this is the magnet, which, if sawn in half, becomes two complete magnets, each pole having generated its own opposite (*Enc.* II §312A.). A totality usually involves three 'moments', those of universality, PARTICULARITY and INDIVIDUALITY (e.g. *PR* §275 on the princely POWER). The tendency of each part to become the whole is seen in terms of the logical interrelations of universality, particularity and individuality. Since each part of a totality is itself the totality, several (especially three) totalities (e.g. the three parts of Hegel's system) often form a single totality. This coheres with Hegel's idea that the universal is a genus whose species are the universal, the particular and the individual: a totality such as the logical IDEA, whose three parts are respectively universal, particular and individual, can be seen as a *particular* specification of a higher universal (which is just itself in a different guise), and then it is the universal *as such*, alongside the particular (NATURE) and the individual (SPIRIT).

When Hegel stresses the reciprocal entailment and inseparability of the parts of a whole or totality, he often calls them *Moment(e)* ('moment(s)', aspect(s), element(s)'). *Moment* was borrowed in the seventeenth century from the Latin *momentum*, which comes from *movere* ('to move') and means 'moving FORCE, impetus'. It then came to mean:

(1) 'Instant, moment (of time)'. In this sense *Moment* is masculine (*der Moment*). Hegel does not use the word in this sense: he prefers *Augenblick* (literally an 'eye-glance') or *das Jetzt* ('the now').

(2) 'Motive force, decisive factor, essential circumstance'. In this sense *Moment* is neuter (*das Moment*). Hegel's use of *Moment* derives from this.

When Hegel argues, in *SL*, that BEING and NOTHING are moments of DETERMINATE BEING, he connects this use of *Moment* with the lever: 'In the case of the lever, weight and distance from a point are called its mechanical moments owing to the sameness of their effect, despite the fact that they are otherwise very different, since one, the weight, is real, while the other, as a mere spatial determination, the line, is ideal' (Cf. *Enc.* II §261, 265 and A.). A *Moment* is what is 'SUBLATED' (*das Aufgehobene*) or 'IDEAL' (*das Ideelle*). Universality, particularity and individuality are moments of a whole or totality. But more generally, a moment is an essential feature or aspect of a whole conceived as a static system, and an essential phase in a whole conceived as a dialectical movement or process.

will and wilfulness *Wollen* means 'to wish, want, intend, be about to', etc. This gave rise to (*der*) *Wille* ('(the) will'). (*Wahl*, 'choice' and *wählen*, 'to choose', are also cognate with *wollen*.) A now obsolete verb, *kiesen* ('to check, inspect, choose (after checking)'), gave rise to *Kür* ('choice'). (*Kür* now occurs only in the sense of 'free, optional exercise (in sport)'. This is an abbreviation of *Kürübung*, 'optional exercise'.) *Wille* combined with *Kür* to give *Willkür*, which thus originally meant a 'decision, resolve of the will'. *Willkür* developed a derogatory sense: 'caprice, acting as one pleases with no regard for others'. In the late eighteenth century this became its predominant sense in ordinary usage, and it now commonly means 'arbitrariness'. The adjective *willkürlich* means 'arbitrary, high-handed', but its negation, *unwillkürlich*, still means 'involuntary, automatic'.

In philosophy before Hegel, *Willkür* does not usually have a derogatory sense and is not clearly distinct from *Wille*. *Wille* is normally associated with the Latin *voluntas* and is conceived as the capacity to bring about effects in accordance with our ideas or PURPOSES. It is distinct from an impulse (*Trieb*) or a desire (*Begehren, Begierde*), since one may not will to do what one has an impulse or desire to do, and one may will do do what one has no impulse or desire to do. *Willkür* was used by Schottelius in his *Ethica* (1669) for the Latin *vis electiva* ('the power of choice'), and by Wolff for the Latin *arbitrium* ('free(dom of) choice'). It is thus the *Wille* in so far as it chooses between alternatives.

Kant ascribes *Willkür* (but not *Wille*) to animals, and divides it into two types (*CPR*, A534, B562):

(1)   Animal *Willkür* (*arbitrium brutum*) is not only 'pathologically affected' by SENSORY impulses and desires, but 'pathologically necessitated' by them. An animal inevitably acts on its strongest current desire, unless it is externally prevented from doing so.

(2)   Free *Willkür* (*arbitrum liberum*) is also sensory (*sinnlich*), in that it is 'pathologically affected' by impulses, but is not necessitated by them and can choose to act against them, either for its long-term happiness (viz. the best overall satisfaction of its probable future desires, as well as its present desires) or on rational principles that are independent of its desires and impulses altogether.

Since both these types of *Willkür* are described as *sinnlich*, Kant implies that there is a non-sensuous *Willkür*, which is either wholly unaffected by sensory impulses (the 'divine' or 'holy' will) or, though affected by them, regularly ignores them in favour of rational principles. But he usually refers to this as *Wille*, rather than *Willkür*, and reserves 'FREEDOM of *Willkür*' for the ability to pick and choose among one's current impulses or to override them in one's long-term interests.

Wille, in the sense of 'empirical will', is the ability to act on rational principles that are based on one's sensory nature and aim at one's overall happiness. It is thus close to *Willkür* in sense (2) above. Pure, or absolutely free, *Wille*, by contrast, is subject to rational LAWS that are independent of one's desires or happiness.

Schiller uses *Wille* and *Willkür* in a similar way, but the tendency of *Willkür* to mean 'arbitrary caprice', 'doing what one likes', is more marked. Like Kant, Schiller valued 'moral freedom', the ability to transcend one's desires and physical circumstances and to act as a purely rational being. But he was more troubled than Kant by the sharp rift between REASON and desire, and hoped that ART and BEAUTY would promote a type of freedom consisting in the harmonious co-operation of our rational and sensuous natures. Apart from the role assigned to art, this is close to Hegel's view of freedom.

Hegel's main accounts of *Wille* and *Willkür* occur at *Enc.* III §§473–82 and especially at *PR* §§4–28. The *Wille* is essentially free, but it has three main phases, each involving a different phase of freedom:

1. The UNIVERSAL *Wille* is our capacity to ABSTRACT from all our desires, impulses, etc., and to satisfy none of them. This type of freedom is wholly negative and appears, in a pure form, only in such unsatisfactory enterprises

as suicide, oriental mysticism and the destructiveness of the French revolutionary terror. But the ability to abstract from one's desires is an essential ingredient of higher types of freedom.

2. The PARTICULAR *Wille* REFLECTS on its desires and impulses to see which of them it will opt for in order to DETERMINE itself to a particular course of ACTION. Since it can abstract from all its desires, it is not bound, like an animal, to act on any one of them, even the strongest of them, and is thus free to pick and choose between them. This is the freedom of *Willkür*, the 'IMMEDIATE' or 'natural' will, and it is, Hegel argues, what is usually meant by 'freedom of the will'. But it is unsatisfactory, because (a) the will is dependent for its CONTENT on a range of options that are simply *given* to it – I am free to choose which of my desires to fulfil, but I do not choose what desires I have – and (b) none of the options is an appropriate OBJECT (*Gegenstand*) of the will, since, while the will is universal, each of its potential objects is merely particular: if it rests content with one of them, the *Wille* will not fulfil its CONCEPT. (Hegel's view of TRUTH is in play here: the 'reality' or object of the true, or truly free, will must match the concept of the will.) Even if the will aims, not at the satisfaction of a current desire, but at its long-term happiness, the content of its happiness still depends on the content of particular desires that are simply given to it.

3. The INDIVIDUAL will overcomes these problems by willing *itself* or willing freedom as such, thus generating from its own resources an object that is, like itself, universal. The individual will is conceived as a combination of 1 and 2, as a restoration of universality out of particularity. Since the will now has itself as its object and is wholly self-contained, it is entirely free (and also INFINITE).

What Hegel means by 'the will wills itself', etc., is not, as in Kantian MORALITY, that the will generates, by purely rational means, rules for its conduct, but rather this: The will, like the THINKING I* (from which it is not sharply distinct), is essentially rational. An appropriate counterpart to this rationality is to be found, not in raw impulses which come and go as they please on no rational plan, but in the structure of ETHICAL LIFE, which, on Hegel's view, embodies the system of rationality that forms the core of the I. The institutions of ethical life overcome the rift between reason and desire postulated by Kant. Raw urges are transformed into the RIGHTS and duties attached to social roles and thus imbued with rationality. Sexual urges are channelled into marriage, hunger is satisfied at organized and ritualized meals, etc. We achieve liberation from our urges not by disregarding them, but by satisfying them in their cultivated form. We are then not simply fulfilling our parochial whims, but working for the maintenance of the larger whole, the STATE and its subsidiary institutions. Each of us plays, not his own tune, but his part in an orchestra.

The will and its freedom thus form a bridge between society and the individual. The will is the concept of right which, together with the REALITY of right, forms the IDEA of right. The three main parts of *PR* (the abstract right of PROPERTY and PERSON, morality, and ethical life) correspond to the three phases of the will and are stages in the ACTUALIZATION of the free will. Freedom of the will and socio-political freedom are thus deeply interconnected.

Bibliography

TRANSLATIONS OF HEGEL'S WORKS

(Most of the translations contain useful introductions.)

Hegel: Selections, edited by M. J. Inwood (London and New York: Macmillan, 1989) contains excerpts from a wide range of Hegel's works.

Three Essays, 1793–1795, translated by P. Fuss and J. Dobbins (South Bend, IN: Notre Dame University Press, 1984). This contains the 'Tübingen Essay' on religion, the Bern fragments and the 'Life of Jesus'.

Early Theological Writings, translated by T. M. Knox (University of Chicago Press, 1948).

The Difference Between Fichte's and Schelling's System of Philosophy, translated by H. S. Harris and W. Cerf (Albany: State University of New York Press, 1977). This was Hegel's first book, published in 1801. It is also translated by J. P. Surber, as *Difference between the Fichtean and Schellingian Systems of Philosophy* (Atascadero, CA: Ridgeview Press, 1978).

Between Kant and Hegel: Texts in the Development of Post-Kantian Idealism, by G. di Giovanni and H. S. Harris (Albany: State University of New York Press, 1985), translates many of Hegel's pieces in *CJP*, including the 'Relation of Scepticism to Philosophy'. It also translates excerpts from other philosophers of the time: Beck, Maimon, Schulze, Reinhold, Fichte and Schelling.

Faith and Knowledge, translated by W. Cerf and H. S. Harris (Albany: State University of New York Press, 1977).

Natural Law, translated by T. M. Knox, with an introduction by H. B. Acton (Philadelphia: University of Pennsylvania Press, 1977).

System of Ethical Life and First Philosophy of Spirit, translated by H. S. Harris and T. M. Knox (Albany: State University of New York Press, 1979). This is a translation of two manuscripts. The *System der Sittlichkeit* (the title was given to it by Rosenkranz in 1844) is closely connected in subject-matter with *NL* and was probably written in 1802–3. The *First Philosophy of Spirit* is usually assigned to 1803–4. Both manuscripts shed light on the development of Hegel's thought on RIGHT and OBJECTIVE SPIRIT. Hegel still uses much Schellingian vocabulary (e.g. *Potenz*, 'power, potency') that he later abandoned, to express fairly non-Schellingian thoughts.

The Jena System, 1804–5: Logic and Metaphysics, translated by J. Burbidge and G. di Giovanni (Montreal/Kingston: McGill-Queen's University Press, 1986). This is a partial translation (excluding the section on philosophy of nature) of a later manuscript from the Jena period. The assignment of logic and metaphysics to different sections is a distinctive feature of this work. Later, metaphysics is assimilated to logic, and the material here dealt with in the metaphysics section is consigned in part to logic, in part to the philosophy of spirit.

Hegel and the Human Spirit: A Translation of the Jena Lectures on the Philosophy of Spirit (1805–6) with Commentary, by L. Rauch (Detroit: Wayne State University Press, 1983). This is a translation of Hegel's manuscript for his lectures in 1805–6, excluding the section on the philosophy of nature. Like the other Jena manuscripts it sheds valuable light on the development of Hegel's thought.

Hegel's Political Writings, translated by T. M. Knox, with an introduction by Z. A. Pelczynski (Oxford: Clarendon, 1964). This contains most of Hegel's political essays from 1798 to 1831.

PS is translated in full by J. B. Baillie as *Phenomenology of Mind* (2nd edn, London: Allen & Unwin, 1931) and by A. V. Miller as *Phenomenology of Spirit* (Oxford: Clarendon, 1977). Other translations of parts of *PS* appear in *Hegel: Preface and Introduction to the Phenomenology of Mind*, translated by L. S. Stepelevich (New York and London: Macmillan, 1990) and in *Hegel: Selections* above, which contains translations of the Preface, by W. Kaufmann, and of the Introduction, etc., by J. L. H. Thomas.

Philosophical Propaedeutic, translated by A. V. Miller, with an introduction by M. George and A. Vincent (Oxford: Basil Blackwell, 1986). This is a translation of Hegel's notes for his lectures to schoolboys from 1808 to 1811.

The *Science of Logic* is translated in full by W. J. Johnston and L. G. Struthers (London: Allen & Unwin, 1929) and by A. V. Miller (London: Allen & Unwin, 1969). The 'Subjective Logic' is translated by H. S. Macran in *Hegel's Doctrine of Formal Logic* (Oxford: Clarendon, 1912) and *Hegel's Logic of World and Idea* (Oxford: Clarendon, 1929).

The *Philosophy of Right* is translated in full by S. W. Dyde (London: Bell, 1896) and (superbly) by T. M. Knox (Oxford: Clarendon, 1942).

The 1830 edition of *Enc.* I, along with the posthumous Additions, is translated by W. Wallace as *The Logic of Hegel* (Oxford: Clarendon, 1873, 1892). It is reprinted, with an introduction by J. N. Findlay, as *Hegel's Logic* (Oxford: Clarendon, 1975).

The 1830 edition of *Enc.* II, with the Additions, is translated as the *Philosophy of Nature* by M. J. Petry (London: Allen & Unwin, 1970) and by A. V. Miller (Oxford: Clarendon, 1970).

The 1830 edition of *Enc.* III, with the Additions, is translated in full, as the *Philosophy of Mind*, by W. Wallace (Oxford: Clarendon, 1894) and A. V. Miller (Oxford: Clarendon, 1971), and in part by M. J. Petry, as the *Philosophy of Subjective Spirit* (Dordrecht: Reidel, 1978) and *The Berlin Phenomenology* (Dordrecht: Reidel, 1981).

LPH is translated in full by J. Sibree as *Lectures on the Philosophy of History* (London: Bohn, 1858, but frequently reprinted). The Introduction to *LPH* is translated by R. S. Hartman as *Reason in History* (Indianapolis and New York: Bobbs-Merrill, 1953), by H. B. Nisbet as *Lectures on the Philosophy of World History: Introduction: Reason in History*, with an introduction by D. Forbes (Cambridge University Press, 1975), and by L. Rauch as *Introduction to the Philosophy of History* (Indianapolis: Hackett, 1988). Sibree, Hartman and Rauch translate Karl Hegel's 1840 edition. Nisbet translates the Lasson edition of 1917–20, which attempts to distinguish between material from different lecture courses, and between manuscripts in Hegel's own hand and those written by his pupils.

LA is translated in full by F. P. B. Osmaston as *The Philosophy of Fine Art* (London: Bell, 1920) and by T. M. Knox as *Hegel's Aesthetics: Lectures on Fine Art* (Oxford: Clarendon, 1975). The Introduction to *LA* is published separately as *Hegel's Introduction to Aesthetics*, translated by T. M. Knox, with an introduction by C. Karelis (Oxford: Clarendon, 1979). The Introduction to *LA* was also translated (superbly) by B. Bosanquet as *The Introduction to Hegel's Philosophy of Fine Art* (London: Kegan Paul, 1886).

LPR is translated, together with *LPEG*, by E. B. Speirs and J. B. Sanderson as *Philosophy of Religion* (London: Kegan Paul, 1895). P. C. Hodgson has attempted to distinguish material from different courses, which varied considerably. The results of this attempt are:

Christian Religion, translated by P. C. Hodgson (Missoula, MT: Scholars, 1979).

Lectures on the Philosophy of Religion: Vol. I *Introduction and the Concept of Religion* (Berkeley: University of California Press, 1984); Vol. II *Determinate Religion* (Berkeley: University of California Press, 1987); Vol. III *The Consummate Religion* Berkeley: University of California Press, 1985). Translated by P. C. Hodgson, R. F. Brown and J. M. Stewart.

Lectures on the Philosophy of Religion: One Volume Edition: The Lectures of 1827, edited by P. C. Hodgson (Berkeley: University of California Press, 1988).

LHP is translated in full as *Lectures on the History of Philosophy*, by E. S. Haldane and F. Simson (London: Kegan Paul, 1892). The Introduction is translated by Q. Lauer in *Hegel's Idea of Philosophy* (New York: Fordham University Press, 1971) and by T. M. Knox and A. V. Miller as *Introduction to the Lectures on the History of Philosophy* (Oxford: Clarendon, 1985).

Hegel: The Letters, translated by C. Butler and C. Seiler (Bloomington: Indiana University Press, 1984). This translates all of Hegel's surviving letters. It often summarizes, with excerpts, letters *to* Hegel – to which his own letters are often replies – but (unfortunately) does not translate them in full. It contains a wealth of biographical and bibliographical material.

TRANSLATIONS OF OTHER AUTHORS

In this book I have attempted to take account of authors who influenced Hegel's vocabulary and concepts, and I list below some translations of those that are likely to be less familiar to the English reader, but relatively digestible:

J. G. FICHTE

Attempt at a Critique of all Revelation, translated by G. Green (Cambridge University Press, 1978). This was Fichte's first book. It won him fame, since, on its first publication in 1792, Fichte's name was omitted from the title-page and it was widely assumed to be the work of Kant.

Most of Fichte's shorter early works appear in *Early Philosophical Writings*, translated by D. Breazeale (Ithaca, NY and London: Cornell University Press, 1988).

Science of Knowledge (Wissenschaftslehre), translated by P. Heath and J. Lachs (New York: Appleton-Century-Crofts, 1970).

The Science of Rights, translated by A. E. Kroeger (London: Trübner, 1889).

The Vocation of Man, translated W. Smith and R. M. Chisholm (Indianapolis and New York: Bobbs-Merrill, 1956).

Addresses to the German Nation, translated by R. F. Jones, G. H. Turnbull and G. A. Kelly (New York and Evanston: Harper & Row, 1968).

317

J. G. HERDER

Herder on Social and Political Culture, translated by F. M. Barnard (Cambridge University Press, 1969), contains a selection from Herder's voluminous writings on history, language, etc., including *OL*.

God: Some Conversations, translated by F. H. Burkhardt (Indianapolis: Bobbs-Merrill, 1940), conveys the flavour of the nineteenth-century Spinoza revival.

F. HÖLDERLIN

Essays and Letters on Theory, translated by T. Pfau (Albany: State University of New York Press, 1988), contains most of Hölderlin's writings on philosophy and aesthetics.

LESSING

Lessing's Theological Writings, translated by H. Chadwick (London: Black, 1956), contains *EHR*.

F. W. J. VON SCHELLING

The Unconditional in Human Knowledge: Four Early Essays (1794–1796), translated by F. Marti (Lewisburg: Bucknell University Press, 1980), contains four short pieces from Schelling's Fichtean period.

Ideas for a Philosophy of Nature (1797), translated by E. E. Harris and P. Heath, with an introduction by R. Stern (Cambridge University Press, 1988), was Schelling's first publication on *Naturphilosophie*.

System of Transcendental Idealism (1800) translated by P. Heath, with an introduction by M. Vater (Charlottesville: University of Virginia Press, 1978).

Bruno or On the Natural and the Divine Principle of Things (1802), translated by M. Vater (Albany: State University of New York Press, 1984). This dialogue shows the influence of Neoplatonism, represented primarily by Giordano Bruno.

The Philosophy of Art, translated by D. W. Stott, with a foreword by D. Simpson (Minneapolis: University of Minnesota Press, 1989). This contains Schelling's lectures of 1802–3 and 1804–5, which were published by his son in 1859.

On University Studies, translated by E. S. Morgan, with an introduction by N. Guterman (Athens: Ohio University Press, 1966), contains the *Lectures on the Method of University Studies* (1803).

Of Human Freedom, translated by J. Gutman (Chicago: Open Court, 1936). This contains the *Philosophical Inquiries into the Nature of Human Freedom*, published in 1809. M. Heidegger, *Schelling's Treatise on the Essence of Human Freedom* (Athens: Ohio University Press, 1985), is a good commentary on the work, shedding light on Hegel as well as on Schelling.

The Ages of the World, translated by F. de W. Bolman (New York: AMS Press, 1967), was written (but not published) in 1811. It contains some of Schelling's thoughts on TIME.

F. SCHILLER

On the Aesthetic Education of Man in a Series of Letters, translated by E. M. Wilkinson and L. A. Willoughby (Oxford: Clarendon, 1967), supplies both a text and a translation, together with an introduction and commentary. (I have frequently consulted its invaluable Glossary of Schiller's word-usage.)

Naive and Sentimental Poetry and *On the Sublime*, translated by J. A. Elias (New York: Ungar, 1966), contains two seminal aesthetic essays by Schiller.

F. VON SCHLEGEL

Dialogue on Poetry and Literary Aphorisms, translated by E. Behler and R. Struc (University Park and London: Pennsylvania State University Press, 1968), contains many of Schlegel's fragments.

Friedrich Schlegel's Lucinde and the Fragments, translated by P. Firchow (Minneapolis: University of Minnesota Press, 1971), supplies a fuller collection of fragments, including many by A. W. Schlegel, Novalis and Schleiermacher.

German Aesthetic and Literary Criticism: The Romantic Ironists and Goethe, edited by K. Wheeler (Cambridge University Press, 1984), contains short pieces by the Schlegels, Novalis, Tieck, Solger, Richter and Goethe.

C. F. WOLFF

Few of C. F. Wolff's numerous works are translated. The flavour of his writing is adequately represented by his *Preliminary Discourse on Philosophy in General* (1728), translated by R. J. Blackwell (Indianapolis: Bobbs-Merrill, 1963).

WORKS ON HEGEL AND LANGUAGE

THE DEVELOPMENT OF PHILOSOPHICAL GERMAN

E. A. Blackall, *The Development of German as a Literary Language, 1700–1775* (Cambridge University Press, 1959), stops short of Hegel, but gives a superly lucid and learned account of the writers, including philosophers, who helped to shape his linguistic inheritance.

R. Eucken, *Geschichte der philosophischen Terminologie im Umriss* (Leipzig: Veit, 1879), is one of the few general works on the history of philosophical terminology. It covers Greek and Latin terminology, as well as German. It is more useful on Hegel's predecessors than on Hegel himself.

J. Hoffmeister, *Wörterbuch der philosophischen Begriffe* (2nd edn, Hamburg: Meiner, 1955), is an invaluable work by a renowned Hegel scholar.

W. T. Krug, *Allgemeines Handwörterbuch der philosophischen Wissenschaften nebst ihrer Literatur und Geschichte* (2nd edn, Leipzig: Brockhaus, 1832–8), supplies useful information on the standard, non-Hegelian (especially Kantian) uses of words in this period, but is wholly unsympathetic to Hegel and his vocabulary.

HEGEL'S USE OF LANGUAGE

Most works on Hegel say something about his use of language and some contain useful glossaries. But there are relatively few explicit or systematic treatments of the subject:

A. Koyré, 'Note sur la langue et la terminologie hégéliennes', in *Revue philosophique de la France et de l'étranger*, CXII (1931), pp. 406–39, and in A. Koyré, *Études d'histoire et de la pensée philosophique* (2nd edn, Paris: Gallimard, 1971), pp. 191–224. (This also contains 'Hegel à Iéna', pp. 147–89, in which Koyré attributes to Hegel a Heideggerian conception of TIME.)

J. Royce, 'Hegel's terminology', in *Dictionary of Philosophy and Psychology*, ed. J. M. Baldwin (New York: Macmillan, 1901), vol. I, pp. 454–64, gives a systematic account of much of Hegel's logical terminology.

HEGEL'S VIEW OF LANGUAGE

T. Bodammer, *Hegels Deutung der Sprache: Interpretationen zu Hegels Äusserungen über die Sprache* (Hamburg: Meiner, 1969), is one of several German works on this theme. It conveniently summarizes previous works on the subject, covers the whole range of Hegel's works, and is admirably lucid. (Only an elementary knowledge of German is required to make use of it.)

D. J. Cook, *Language in the Philosophy of Hegel* (The Hague: Mouton, 1973) is the only work in English on the subject. Though briefer than Bodammer, it too covers the whole range of Hegel's works and is extremely useful.

J. Derrida, 'The pit and the pyramid: introduction to Hegel's semiology', in J. Derrida, *Margins of Philosophy* (Brighton: Harvester Press, 1982), pp. 69–108, is an interesting critique of Hegel's account of LANGUAGE in *Enc.* III.

GENERAL WORKS ON HEGEL

E. Caird, *Hegel* (Edinburgh and London: Blackwood, 1883) is a good biographical work.

J. M. E. McTaggart, *Studies in Hegelian Cosmology* (2nd edn, Cambridge University Press, 1918), is an exploration by a first-rate philosopher of Hegel's thought on a variety of social, political and religious themes.

W. T. Stace, *The Philosophy of Hegel: A Systematic Exposition* (London and New York: Macmillan, 1924), is a sober examination of the argument of *Enc.* I and *Enc.* III.

H. Marcuse, *Reason and Revolution: Hegel and the Rise of Social Theory* (2nd edn, London: Routledge & Kegan Paul, 1955), is a classic Marxist study of Hegel. Marcuse's earlier work, translated as *Hegel's Ontology and the Theory of Historicity* (Cambridge, MA: MIT Press, 1987), is a Heideggerian reading of Hegel.

J. N. Findlay, *Hegel: A Re-examination* (London: Allen & Unwin, 1958), is a classic work by an analytical philosopher.

F. Copleston, *Fichte to Hegel* (New York: Doubleday, 1965), is vol. VII, Part I, of Copleston's massively learned and superbly lucid *History of Philosophy*.

G. R. G. Mure, *The Philosophy of Hegel* (Oxford: Clarendon, 1965), is an insightful survey of the whole of Hegel's writings.

W. Kaufmann, *Hegel: Reinterpretation, Texts and Commentary* (New York: Doubleday, 1965), is extremely useful both on Hegel's thought and on its background. It contains several excellent translations.

I. Soll, *An Introduction to Hegel's Metaphysics* (University of Chicago Press, 1969), explores Hegel's relationship to Kant with exemplary brevity and lucidity.

A. C. MacIntyre (ed.), *Hegel: A Collection of Critical Essays* (New York: Doubleday, 1972), contains some important articles on Hegel.

C. Taylor, *Hegel* (Cambridge University Press, 1975), is a classic work, which provides detailed commentary on Hegel's main writings, a clear, if controversial, view of his thought and of his place in modern philosophy.

M. Rosen, *Hegel's Dialectic and its Criticism* (Cambridge University Press, 1982), is rigorously critical, especially of Hegel's 'Neoplatonism', and immensely stimulating.

M. J. Inwood, *Hegel* (London: Routledge & Kegan Paul, 1983), attempts to combine criticism with sympathy. It stresses the systematic interconnectedness and the ineradicable ambiguity of Hegel's thought.

P. Singer, *Hegel* (Oxford: Clarendon, 1983), is a lucid, compact account, especially of Hegel's social and political thought.

R. Plant, *Hegel: An Introduction* (2nd edn, Oxford: Basil Blackwell, 1983), relates Hegel's political thought to its intellectual background.

M. J. Inwood (ed.), *Hegel* (Oxford University Press, 1985), contains recent articles on the whole range of Hegel's thought.

T. Rockmore, *Hegel's Circular Epistemology* (Bloomington: Indiana University Press, 1986), explores one of Hegel's epistemological strategems, viz. his insistence that knowledge forms a circle, not a straight line.

D. Lamb (ed.), *Hegel and Modern Philosophy* (London: Croom Helm, 1987), is a good collection, mainly, but not exclusively, on social and political matters.

T. Pinkard, *Hegel's Dialectic: The Explanation of Possibility* (Philadelphia: Temple University Press, 1988), reads *SL* as an attempt to explain the possibility of our basic categories, and applies this interpretation to Hegel's ethical and political views.

R. Pippin, *Hegel's Idealism: The Satisfactions of Self-Consciousness* (Cambridge University Press, 1989), interprets Hegel as an idealist in the Kantian tradition.

M. N. Forster, *Hegel and Scepticism* (Cambridge, MA: Harvard University Press, 1989), surveys Hegel's responses to the epistemological difficulties that he found in the Greek sceptics. It gives a novel (and lucid) account of Hegel's thought.

R. Stern, *Hegel, Kant and the Structure of the Object* (London: Routledge & Kegan Paul, 1990), argues that Hegel, especially in *SL* and *Enc.* II, tries to show that the unity of objects is immanent in them, and is not, as Kant believed, imposed by us on the 'sensory manifold'. It is a lucid, but closely argued book with implications for the whole of Hegel's thought.

HEGEL'S EARLY WRITINGS

G. Lukács, *The Young Hegel: Studies in the Relations between Dialectics and Economics* (London: Merlin, 1975), is a controversial and illuminating work.

W. H. Walsh, *Metaphysics* (London: Hutchinson, 1963), ch. 9, reprinted in Inwood (ed.), *Hegel*, above, gives an excellent brief account of *ETW*.

H. S. Harris, *Hegel's Development: Toward the Sunlight* (Oxford: Clarendon, 1972) and *Night Thoughts (Jena 1801–1806)* (Oxford: Clarendon, 1983), give a scholarly account of Hegel's intellectual development up to the composition of *PS*.

L. Dickey, *Hegel: Religion, Economics and the Politics of Spirit, 1770–1807* (Cambridge University Press, 1987), discusses Hegel's early writings against the background of his native Württemberg.

THE PHENOMENOLOGY OF SPIRIT

A. Kojève, *Introduction to the Reading of Hegel* (New York: Basic Books, 1969) – an abridgement of the French original (1947) – is a classic study that has influenced many subsequent readings of Hegel. It displays the influence of both Marx and Heidegger.

J. Hyppolite, *Genesis and Structure of Hegel's 'Phenomenology of Spirit'* (Evanston, Illinois: Northwestern University Press, 1974) is a learned, thorough commentary.

R. Norman, *Hegel's Phenomenology: A Philosophical Introduction* (London: Sussex University Press, 1976), is an excellent, brief introduction to PS.

H. P. Kainz, *Hegel's Phenomenology, Part I: Analysis and Commentary* (University of Alabama Press, 1976) and *Part II: The Evolution of Ethical and Religious Consciousness to the Absolute Standpoint* (Athens: Ohio University Press, 1983), is an illuminating commentary.

J. N. Shklar, *Freedom and Independence: A Study of the Political Ideas of Hegel's 'Phenomenology of Mind'* (Cambridge University Press, 1976), stresses Hegel's nostalgia for Greece.

J. Robinson, *Duty and Hypocrisy in Hegel's 'Phenomenology of Mind'* (University of Toronto Press, 1977), is a close, analytical examination of one chapter (VI.C) of PS.

M. Westphal, *History and Truth in Hegel's Phenomenology* (New Jersey: Humanities Press, 1979), argues that, on Hegel's account, transcendental SUBJECTIVITY in the sense of Kant and Fichte presupposes a social history.

D. Lamb, *Language and Perception in Hegel and Wittgenstein* (London: Macmillan, 1979) and *Hegel – From Foundation to System* (The Hague: Martinus Nijhoff, 1980) both focus on PS.

C. V. Dudeck, *Hegel's Phenomenology of Mind: Analysis and Commentary* (Washington, DC: University Press of America, 1981), is clear and brief.

M. Westphal (ed.), *Method and Speculation in Hegel's Phenomenology* (New Jersey: Humanities Press, 1982), is an interesting collection of papers on PS.

R. C. Solomon, *In the Spirit of Hegel* (New York: Oxford University Press, 1983), is a clear, insightful account of PS and its background. It includes a discussion of ETW and a useful glossary.

J. C. Flay, *Hegel's Quest for Certainty* (Albany: State University of New York Press, 1984), is useful for its discussion of earlier literature on PS.

D. P. Verene, *Hegel's Recollection: A Study of Images in the 'Phenomenology of Spirit'* (Albany: State University of New York Press, 1985), interprets PS in terms of RECOLLECTION (*Erinnerung*).

E. Tugendhat, *Self-consciousness and Self-determination* (1986), provides a clear, analytical account of the concepts of SELF-CONSCIOUSNESS and self-DETERMINATION in Fichte, Schelling, Hegel, Heidegger, etc.

R. Schacht, *Alienation* (London: Allen & Unwin, 1971), gives an interesting account of Hegel's concept of ALIENATION in PS, its origins and its aftermath.

L. Trilling, *Sincerity and Authenticity* (2nd edn, London: Oxford University Press, 1974), discusses Hegel's account of CULTURE and ALIENATION against its literary background.

J. H. Smith, *The Spirit and its Letter: Traces of Rhetoric in Hegel's Philosophy of Bildung* (Ithaca, NY and London: Cornell University Press, 1988), examines the concept of CULTURE, which is crucial in PS, as well as in Hegel's other writings.

LOGIC

J. M. E. McTaggart, *Studies in the Hegelian Dialectic* (Cambridge University Press, 1896) and *A Commentary on Hegel's Logic* (Cambridge University Press, 1910) combine good philosophy with illuminating, if occasionally eccentric, interpretation.

G. R. G. Mure, *A Study of Hegel's Logic* (Oxford: Clarendon, 1950), is a reliable commentary, mainly on *Enc.* I.

M. Clark, *Logic and System: A Study of the Transition from 'Vorstellung' to Thought in the Philosophy of Hegel* (The Hague: Martinus Nijhoff, 1971), is a useful book on an important topic.

W. E. Steinkraus and K. L. Schmitz (eds), *Art and Logic in Hegel's Philosophy* (New Jersey: Humanities Press, 1980), contains illuminating essays and a full bibliography.

E. E. Harris, *An Interpretation of the Logic of Hegel* (Lanham: University Press of America, 1983), is a useful commentary.

PHILOSOPHY OF NATURE

M. J. Petry's translation of *Enc.* II (*Philosophy of Nature*, London: Allen & Unwin, 1970) includes a valuable commentary.

R. S. Cohen and M. W. Wartofsky (eds), *Hegel and the Sciences* (Dordrecht: Reidel, 1983), is an excellent collection of articles.

R.-P. Horstmann and M. J. Petry (eds), *Hegels Philosophie der Natur: Beziehungen zwischen empirischer und spekulativer Naturerkenntnis* (Stuttgart: Klett-Cotta, 1986), includes some articles in English.

PHILOSOPHY OF SUBJECTIVE SPIRIT: MIND AND ACTION

G. Von Wright, *Explanation and Understanding* (London: Routledge & Kegan Paul, 1971), applies the *SL* account of TELEOLOGY to the theory of action and practical reasoning.

R. J. Bernstein, *Praxis and Action* (London: Duckworth, 1972), examines Hegel's theory of action alongside other accounts.

M. Greene, *Hegel on the Soul: A Speculative Anthropology* (The Hague: Martinus Nijhoff, 1972), is a useful exploration of the earlier part of *Enc.* III.

C. Elder, *Appropriating Hegel* (Aberdeen University Press, 1980), looks for a solution to the mind–body problem in Hegel's Logic.

P. G. Stillman (ed.), *Hegel's Philosophy of Spirit* (Albany: State University of New York Press, 1987), is a collection of papers on various aspects of SPIRIT in *Enc.* III.

W. A. de Vries, *Hegel's Theory of Mental Activity: An Introduction to Theoretical Spirit* (Ithaca, NY and London: Cornell University Press, 1988), stresses Hegel's debt to Aristotle.

PHILOSOPHY OF OBJECTIVE SPIRIT: ETHICS AND POLITICS

H. A. Reyburn, *The Ethical Theory of Hegel: A Study of the Philosophy of Right* (Oxford: Clarendon, 1921), is a good introductory study.

M. B. Foster, *The Political Philosophies of Plato and Hegel* (Oxford: Clarendon, 1935), is an illuminating work.

J. Plamenatz, *Man and Society* (London: Longman, 1963), vol. II, pp. 129–268, analytically examines Hegel's political and historical thought.

G. A. Kelly, *Idealism, Politics and History: Sources of Hegelian Thought* (Cambridge

University Press, 1969), gives a good account of the background to Hegel's thought.

W. H. Walsh, *Hegelian Ethics* (London: Macmillan, 1969), examines Hegel's ethical views in relation to Kant's.

S. Avineri, *Hegel's Theory of the Modern State* (Cambridge University Press, 1972), is a classic work on the subject.

B. Cullen, *Hegel's Social and Political Thought* (Dublin: Gill and Macmillan, 1979), is a useful book.

C. Taylor, *Hegel and Modern Society* (Cambridge University Press, 1979), is an abridgement of Taylor's major work on Hegel.

M. Riedel, *Between Tradition and Revolution: The Hegelian Transformation of Political Philosophy* (Cambridge University Press, 1984), is extremely useful on the background to Hegel's thought.

Z. A. Pelczynski has edited two valuable collections. *Hegel's Political Philosophy* (Cambridge University Press, 1971) covers the whole of Hegel's ethical, political and historical thought, while *The State and Civil Society* (Cambridge University Press, 1984) focuses on the STATE and CIVIL SOCIETY.

D. P. Verene (ed.), *Hegel's Social and Political Thought: The Philosophy of Objective Spirit* (Brighton: Harvester Press, 1980), is a good collection.

L. S. Stepelevich and D. Lamb (eds), *Hegel's Philosophy of Action* (New Jersey: Humanities Press, 1983), covers the whole of Hegel's ethical and social thought.

A. W. Wood, *Hegel's Ethical Thought* (Cambridge University Press, 1990), is a thorough, analytical treatment of Hegel's ethical theory and covers the whole range of his ethical and political thought. It is extremely useful on the background to Hegel.

K. Marx's detailed and pungent commentary on the later sections of *PR* is translated as *Critique of Hegel's 'Philosophy of Right'* (Cambridge University Press, 1970).

PHILOSOPHY OF HISTORY

W. H. Walsh, *An Introduction to the Philosophy of History* (3rd edn, London: Hutchinson, 1967), ch. VII, is an excellent introduction to Hegel's view of history.

B. T. Wilkins, *Hegel's Philosophy of History* (Ithaca, NY: Cornell University Press, 1974), makes judicious use of *SL* to illuminate the philosophy of history.

G. D. O'Brien, *Hegel on Reason and History* (University of Chicago Press, 1975), argues that Hegel presents a history of 'historical consciousness', rather than of historical events.

R. L. Perkins (ed.), *History and System: Hegel's Philosophy of History* (Albany: State University of New York Press, 1984), is a good collection of essays.

F. Nietzsche's early essay, translated as 'On the Uses and Disadvantages of History for Life', in his *Untimely Meditations* (Cambridge University Press, 1983), can be usefully compared with *LPH*.

PHILOSOPHY OF ART

A. and H. Paolucci (eds), *Hegel on Tragedy* (New York; Doubleday, 1962) and H. Paolucci (ed.), *Hegel: On the Arts* (New York: Ungar, 1978), are useful collections of translations from Hegel, with informative introductions. The former also contains

324

A. C. Bradley's 'Hegel's Theory of Tragedy', which first appeared in the *Hibbert Journal*, II (1903–4), but is still worth reading.

D. Simpson (ed.), *German Aesthetic and Literary Criticism: Kant, Fichte, Schelling, Schopenhauer, Hegel* (Cambridge University Press, 1984), contains excerpts from these philosophers, with a useful introduction and notes.

I. Knox, *The Aesthetic Theories of Kant, Hegel and Schopenhauer* (New York: Columbia University Press, 1936), is a good introduction to the subject.

Two general histories of aesthetics, B. Bosanquet, *A History of Aesthetic* (2nd edn, London: Macmillan, 1904) and K. E. Gilbert and H. Kuhn, *A History of Esthetics* (2nd edn, London: Thames & Hudson, 1956), contain interesting chapters on Hegel, as well as on his predecessors.

J. Kaminsky, *Hegel on Art* (Albany: State University of New York Press, 1962), provides a useful account of Hegel's logic and of his relationship to Kant, as well as a good, critical survey of *LA*.

W. E. Steinkraus and K. L. Schmitz (eds), *Art and Logic in Hegel's Philosophy* (New Jersey: Humanities Press, 1980), contains interesting essays and an extensive bibliography.

S. Bungay, *Beauty and Truth: A Study of Hegel's Aesthetics* (Oxford: Clarendon, 1984), surveys *LA* in relation to the Logic.

W. Desmond, *Art and the Absolute: A Study of Hegel's Aesthetics* (Albany: State University of New York Press, 1986), does not survey *LA*, but relates Hegel's aesthetics to the rest of his system and stresses the aesthetic character of his whole philosophy. It compares his views with those of Aquinas, Nietzsche, etc.

PHILOSOPHY OF RELIGION

E. L. Fackenheim, *The Religious Dimension in Hegel's Thought* (Bloomington: Indiana University Press, 1967), is a learned and interesting work.

D. E. Christensen (ed.), *Hegel and the Philosophy of Religion* (The Hague: Martinus Nijhoff, 1970), is a good collection of papers.

B. M. G. Reardon, *Hegel's Philosophy of Religion* (London: Macmillan, 1977), is a good, brief survey of *LPR*.

Q. Lauer, *Hegel's Concept of God* (Albany: State University of New York Press, 1982), considers the subject in relation to the Logic. It endorses Hegel's claim to theological orthodoxy.

W. Jaeschke, *Reason in Religion: The Foundations of Hegel's Philosophy of Religion* (Berkeley: University of California Press, 1990), is a thorough examination both of the background and of the development of Hegel's philosophy of religion. It explores the variations between the different lecture courses of *LPR*, and also the divergence of Hegel's followers into 'Left', 'Right' and 'Centre'.

HISTORY AND PHILOSOPHY

GENERAL

W. H. Walsh, 'Hegel on the History of Philosophy', in *History and Theory*, Beiheft 5 (1965), is a sober account of Hegel's approach to the history of philosophy.

J. O'Malley et al. (eds), *Hegel and the History of Philosophy* (The Hague: Martinus Nijhoff, 1974), contains essays on Hegel's relationships with other philosophers from Plato on, and an extensive bibliography.

ANCIENT PHILOSOPHY

J. G. Gray, *Hegel and Greek Thought* (2nd edn, New York: Harper & Row, 1969), is the only book in English on the subject.

G. R. G. Mure, *An Introduction to Hegel* (Oxford: Clarendon, 1940), examines Hegel's relationship to Aristotle.

M. N. Forster, *Hegel and Scepticism* (Cambridge, MA: Harvard University Press, 1989) is fully abreast of recent work on the Greek sceptics and explores Hegel's relationship to them.

MODERN PHILOSOPHY BEFORE HEGEL

No book has yet appeared in English on Hegel's relationship to Spinoza, but two useful articles are:

F. Copleston, 'Pantheism in Spinoza and the German Idealists', in *Philosophy* (1946); and G. H. R. Parkinson, 'Hegel, Pantheism and Spinoza', in the *Journal of the History of Ideas* (1977).

L. P. Hinchman, *Hegel's Critique of the Enlightenment* (Gainesville: University Presses of Florida, 1984), is a useful book.

W. H. Walsh, *Reason and Experience* (Oxford: Clarendon, 1947), is mainly about Kant, but explores Hegel's criticisms of him.

S. Priest (ed.), *Hegel's Critique of Kant* (Oxford: Clarendon, 1987), contains essays on Hegel's response to every aspect of Kant's thought.

J. Royce, *The Spirit of Modern Philosophy* (Boston and New York: Houghton Mifflin, 1892) and *Lectures on Modern Idealism* (Yale University Press, 1919) are useful guides on the route from Kant to Hegel.

MODERN PHILOSOPHY AFTER HEGEL

L. S. Stepelevich (ed.), *The Young Hegelians: An Anthology* (Cambridge University Press, 1983) is a useful collection.

J. E. Toews, *Hegelianism: The Path toward Dialectical Humanism, 1805–1841* (Cambridge University Press, 1980), is a rich study of the Hegelian movement both before and after Hegel's death.

W. Desmond (ed.), *Hegel and his Critics: Philosophy in the Aftermath of Hegel* (Albany: State University of New York Press, 1989), is a good collection of essays on Hegel's relationship to later thinkers. (Especially noteworthy is G. L. Kline, 'The Use and Abuse of Hegel by Nietzsche and Marx', pp. 1–34.)

K. Löwith, *From Hegel to Nietzsche* (New York: Holt, Rinehart & Winston, 1964) is a classic work by a distinguished German philosopher.

S. Crites, *In the Twilight of Christendom: Hegel vs. Kierkegaard on Faith and History* (Chambersburg: American Academy of Religion, 1972), and N. Thrulstrup, *Kierkegaard's Relation to Hegel* (Princeton University Press, 1980), shed some light on Hegel's relationship to his Danish opponent.

Marx's 1844 manuscripts, which discuss, e.g., ALIENATION, were first translated into English by M. Milligan as *Economic and Philosophic Manuscripts of 1844* (Moscow:

Foreign Languages Publishing House, 1959), and then by T. B. Bottomore in *Karl Marx, Early Writings* (London: Watts, 1963).

S. Houlgate, *Hegel, Nietzsche and the Criticism of Metaphysics* (Cambridge University Press, 1986), argues that Hegel has potent replies to Nietzsche's criticisms of him. Another of Hegel's opponents, Heidegger, wrote about him at some length in *Hegel's Concept of Experience* (New York: Harper & Row, 1970) – which considers the Introduction to *PS*. Heidegger's lectures on *PS* – which do not get beyond the chapter on SELF-CONSCIOUSNESS – are translated as *Hegel's 'Phenomenology of Spirit'* (Bloomington: Indiana University Press, 1988).

J.-P. Sartre, *Being and Nothingness* (New York: Philosophical Library, 1956) was influenced by Hegel – as well as by Heidegger – and often illuminates his thought. As does J.-P. Sartre, *Baudelaire* (New York: New Directions, 1950).

In *Being and Time* (Oxford: Basil Blackwell, 1962), Heidegger criticizes Hegel's account of time in *Enc.* II and the Jena lectures, arguing that it is fundamentally the same as the account originated by Aristotle. (Heideggerian interpreters of Hegel, e.g. Kojève and Koyré, often – and wrongly – attempt to find Heidegger's own future-directed concept of time in Hegel.) '*Ousia* and *Grammē*: Note on a Note from *Being and Time*', in J. Derrida, *Margins of Philosophy* (Brighton: Harvester Press, 1982), finds more diversity in Aristotle's and later accounts of time, including Hegel's, than Heidegger allows. (On Aristotle, see M. J. Inwood, 'Aristotle on the Reality of Time', in R. L. Judson (ed.), *Aristotle's Physics: A Collection of Essays* (Oxford: Clarendon, 1991).)

A. Kojève's lectures on Hegel (*Introduction to the Reading of Hegel*, New York: Basic Books, 1969) provoked a piece by G. Bataille, translated as 'Hegel, Death and Sacrifice', in A. Stoekl (ed.), *On Bataille*, Yale French Studies no. 78 (1990), pp. 9–28. This in turn provoked 'From Restricted to General Economy: A Hegelianism Without Reserve', in J. Derrida, *Writing and Difference* (London: Routledge & Kegan Paul, 1978), pp. 251–77.

Index of foreign-language terms

Note: All terms are German except those specified as Latin ('*L.*'), French ('*F.*'), Greek ('*Gr.*'), Italian ('*I.*'), Spanish ('*S.*') or Arabic. Page numbers in bold refer to the main article(s) in which a given term in the index is discussed.

a priori/a posteriori (L.) 11, 16
Abbild 162
Aberglaube 46f.
Abgrund 115
absehen, Absicht 32
absolut, das Absolute 11, **27**, 181, 190, 310
absolvere, absolutus, absolutum (L.) 27
abstrahere, abstractus (L.) 29
abstrahieren, Abstraktion 29
abstrakt, das Abstrakte 29, 259f.
accidens (L.) 8
adaequatio rerum et intellectus (L.) 298f.
aeternus (L.) 8
affirmativ, Affirmation 199
Afterglaube 46
Aggregat 309
agnoscere (L.) 245
ähnlich 132
aiōn (Gr.) 293
aisthanesthai, aisthēsis (Gr.) 41
Akosmismus 114, 285
Akzidenz, -en 285
al-kimiyā (Arabic) 182
alēthēs, alētheia (Gr.) 298
Alethiologie 214
all, Allheit 138, 302f., 310
allgemein, das Allgemeine, Allgemeinheit 6, 302ff.
alma bella (S.) 190
Amphibolie 248
an 133ff.
an ihm 78, 134
an sich, das Ansich, das Ansichsein 12f., 15, 78, **133ff.**
an und für sich, das Anundfürsich, -sein 6f., 12f., **133ff.**
analytika (Gr.) 268
analytisch/synthetisch 11
anamimnēskesthai (Gr.) 186
anamnēsis (Gr.) 186, 188
anankē (Gr.) 101f.
ander, das Andersein 131, 200

anderheit 9
anerkennen, Anerkennung **245ff.**
anima (L.) 189
animus (L.) 247f.
Anmerkung, -en 270
anmessen, angemessen(es) 240
Annahme 224
anschauen 144, 195
Anschauung 12, 42, 58, **144ff.**, 257, 291
Anthropologie 190, 215
apatheia (Gr.) 262f.
apeiron, to apeiron (Gr.) 139
apodeiknunai, apodeixis (Gr.) 226
Apperzeption 61
arbitrium brutum/liberum (L.) 312
archē (Gr.) 296
Art, -en 56, 176
Artsunterschied 56
Ästhetik 10, 41
ästhetisch 151
atomon (Gr.) 302
attributum (L.) 229
auf den Grund gehen 115
auffassen, das Auffassen 146
aufheben, sich aufheben, aufgehoben(e), Aufhebung 1, 6, 13, **283ff.**, 311
aufschliessen 236
Augenblick 8, 311
aus 142
ausdrucken, Ausdruck 144
Auslegung 252, 295
ausschliessen 236
äusser, das Äussere 36, **142ff.**, 160, 249, 278
ausser 142
ausser sich 133
aussereinander, das Aussereinander 144, 224
äusserlich, Äusserlichkeit 93, **142ff.**, 249
äussern, sich äussern 144
Äusserung 50, 107, 142, 144, 252
Auswicklung 9

329

Bedeutung 145, 153, 157, 165
bedeutungslos 72
bedingen, das Bedingte, Bedingung 50, **117**, 198, 289
Bedürfnis, -se 54
Begehren, Begierde 312
begreifen 58ff.
begrenzen, begrenzt 177
Begriff 10, 11, 13, **58ff.**, 257, 281f., 284
begriffen sein in 58
Begriffsbestimmung 196
begründen, das Begründete 115
bei sich, Beisichsein 80, 133, 136
bejahen, Bejahung 199
bekannt 70, 154
belle âme (F.) 190
beobachten, -de 162
beschaffen, Beschaffenheit 78, 178
beschliessen 236
beschränken, Beschränkung 177, 249
besitzen, Besitz 229ff.
Besitzergreifung 229
Besitznahme 229
besonder, das Besondere, Besonderheit 302ff.
Besonderung 302
besser 233
bestimmen, bestimmt 6, **77ff.**, 151, 173, 250
bestimmter Unterschied 132
Bestimmtheit **77ff.**, 94, 238
Bestimmung 6, 17, 74, **77ff.**, 101, 160, 179, 291
Beweggrund 116
Bewegung 82
beweisen, Beweis **226ff.**
bewusst, Bewusstsein **61ff.**
beziehen, sich beziehen auf 132, **151f.**
Beziehung, -en 132, 248, **151f.**
Bild 157, 162, 187f., 257f.
bilden, Bildung 37, **68ff.**, 187
Bildungsroman 69
biòs/biós (Gr.) 206
böse, das Böse 191ff.
bourg (F.) 53
bourgeois (F.) 53
brechen 233
Bundesstaat 277
Burg 53
Bürger 53f., 280
bürgerliche (Gesellschaft, etc.) **53ff.**, 233
Bürgerrechte 98
Busse 233

causa (L.) 50
Chemie 182
Chemismus **181ff.**
chōra (Gr.) 293
chronos (Gr.) 293
citoyen (F.) 53f., 280

civis (L.) 53
civitas (L.) 54
cogito, ergo sum (L.) 121
communitas civilis sive politica (L.) 54
conceptus (L.) 58
conclusio (L.) 136
concrescere, concretus (L.) 29
connaître (F.) 154
conscientia (L.) 61
contemplatio (L.) 144

da 93
Dame 100
darstellen 257
das Was/das Dass 23
daseiend, ein Daseiendes 94, 114, 295
dasein, das Dasein 12f., 44f., 65, 89, **93ff.**, 137ff., 142
dass 23, 154
Definition 74
Deklaration 74
demonstrare, demonstratio (L.) 226
Denkbestimmung, -en 78f., 291
denken, gedacht, das Denken 186, 188, 289, **290ff.**
Denkform 291
Denkgesetz 63, 160, 291
Denkstoff 291
der, die, das 5
der-, die-, dasselbe 131
dialektikē technē (Gr.) 81
dialegesthai (Gr.) 81
Dialektik **81ff.**
dianoia (Gr.) 242
Dianoologie 214
die Sache selbst 290
Diener 100
Dienst 84
diesseits, das Diesseits 274
different, -er 181
Differenz, differenzieren 131
Ding 95, 117, 205, 229, **288ff.**
Ding an sich 288
Dingheit 289
Diremtion 36
dirimieren, dirimiert 176
diritto (I.) 259
diskret 238f.
Dogmatismus 66, 263, 272
doxa (Gr.) 291
droit (F.) 259
Dualismus 36
Durchmesser 240
Dynamik 215

e(x) consensu gentium (L.) 227f.
eidos (Gr.) 108, 123

eigen, Eigenheit 229
eigenschaft, Eigenschaft 9, 229, 238, 288
Eigentum **229ff.**
eikōn (Gr.) 293
ein und derselbe 131
ein, -er, -e, -es 5, 131
einai (Gr.) 285
einbilden, sich einbilden 187
Einbildung 187
Einbildungskraft 187, 297
Einheit 131, 252
einheitsvolle Totalität 310
Einleitung 217
eins, das Eins 131
Einschachtelung 79
einsehen, Einsicht 47, 154
einteilen, Einteilung 55
Einteilungsglied, -er 56
Einteilungsgrund 56
Einzelheit **302ff.**
einzeln, der, das Einzelne 6, **302ff.**
eirōneia (Gr.) 146f.
eitel, Eitelkeit 149
emboîtememt (F.) 79
empfinden, das Empfundene 103, 145, 189, 283
Empfindsamkeit 104
Empfindung 11, **103ff.**, 145f., 164
Empirie 11, 95f., 118
empirisch 95, 97
Empirismus 95
Ende 15, 139, 177
endlich, Endlichkeit 139, **177ff**
Endursache 50
Endzweck 237
energeiai/dunamei (Gr.) 197
enkyklios (Gr.) 86
ent- 195
entäussern, sich entäussern, Entäusserung **35ff.**, 144, 187
Entfaltung 79
entfremden, sich entfremden, Entfremdung **35ff.**, 103
entgegensetzen, -gesetzt, Entgegensetzung 7, 206
entlassen, sich entlassen, -lässt 195
entschliessen, sich entschliessen, Entschluss 195, 236
entwickeln, Entwicklung 9, 11, **79ff.**
entzweien, entzweite, Entzweiung 36, 173
Enzyklopädie **86ff.**
epistēmē (Gr.) 219
epistrophē (Gr.) 296
epochē (Gr.) 263f.
er- 8, 39, 95, 151
Erdmesser 240
erfahren, Erfahrung 9, 11, **95ff.**, 118
Erfahrungswissenschaft, -en 97
erfüllen 78

ergreifen 229
erhaben, das Erhabene 41
Erhebung 83, 115
Erhebung des Geistes zu Gott 228
erinnern, sich erinnern, Erinnerung 144, 168, **186ff.**, 257
Erkennbarkeit 231
erkennen, das Erkennen 48, 56, **154ff.**, 245
Erkenntnis, -se **154ff.**
erklären, Erklärung 6, 74, 116f.
erleben, Erlebnis 95
Ernst 148
Erregung 52
erscheinen **38ff.**, 62
erscheinende Bewusstsein 62
Erscheinung 8, 11, 35, **38ff.**, 52, 62, 89f., 106, 146, 148, 162, 164, 196, 214ff., 218
erteilen 151
erziehen, Erziehung **68ff.**, 247
esprit (F.) 189, 274
esprit de la nation (F.) 212
essentia (L.) 94
état (F.) 277
Ethik 191
ethos (Gr.) 191
etwas, das Etwas 94, 131, 200, 240, 289, 303
ewig, Ewigkeit 8, 73, 294
existentia (L.) 93ff.
Existenz 12f., 23, **94f.**
existieren 94
experientia (L.) 95
Explikation 74
Exposition 74
exsistere (L.) 13, 93
extensiv 238f.

fahren 44, 95
falsch, das Falsche, Falschheit 298
falsus (L.) 298
familia (l.) 98
Familie **98ff.**
famulus (L.) 98
fari (L.) 101
Fatum 101
festsetzen 7
finden 103
finis (L.) 15
Folge 50, 115
folgen 115
Form **108ff.**, 255
formal, formell 108, 110, 181
Formalismus 108, 165
Fortschritt 11
Frau 5, 100
Fräulein 5
frei, Freiheit 13f., **110ff.**
fremd 35

fühlen 103f.
für 133ff.
für sich, Fürsich, -sein 12f., 15, **133ff.**
für uns 134
fürwahrhalten, das Fürwahrhalten 46, 48

ganz, das Ganze **309ff.**
Ganzheit 310
Gattung 56, 102, 176
Gebärde 158
gebildete Volk 69
Gedächtnis **186ff.**, 258, 290
Gedanke 289, **290ff.**
Gedankenbestimmung 291
Gedankending 288
Gedankenform, -en 291
gedenken **186ff.**
Gefühl 11, **103ff.**, 164
Gefühlsleben 164
gegen 7
Gegensatz **205ff.**
gegensätzlich 206
Gegenstand 7, 8, 61, 87, 164, **203ff.**, 254, 280, 313
gegenständlich, Gegenständlichkeit 203ff.
Gegenteil 206
Gegenwart 295
Gegenwirkung 50, 234
Gegenwurf 63
Gehalt **109**, 164
Geist 14, 73, **189f.**, **274ff.**, 281
Geist, der heiliger 274
Geisteswissenschaft(en) 194, 265
geistig 274
gemein 53, 240, 302
Gemein(d)e 53, 276
Gemeinschaft 53
gemuet 9
Gemüt 9, 165, 171, **189**
genaturte Natur 9
genesis (Gr.) 293
genetische Definition 10
Genius 212
gerecht, Gerechtigkeit 233f., 259
germanisch(e) 171
geschehen 101, 118
Geschichte **118ff.**, 217
Geschick 101, 118
Geselle 53
Gesellschaft **53f.**
Gesellschaftswissenschaft 53
Gesetz., -e 40, **160ff.**, 259
gesetzgeben, -de 279
Gesetzmässigkeit 161ff.
Gesinnung 192, 259
Gestalt, -en 62, **107ff.**, 218, 255
gestalten, Gestaltung 107

Gewalt, -en **106f.**, 223, 278f.
Gewalttätigkeit 106
gewesen 89
gewiss, Gewissheit 46, **154f.**
Gewissen 155, 191f.
Gewohnheit 104, 176
Glaube(n) 37, **46ff.**, 154
glauben **46ff.**
gleich 132
gleichen 132
gleichgültig 108f., 132, 178, 183, 240, 252
Gleichheit 132
Glied, -er 309
Grad 239f.
greifen 58
Grenzbegriff 177ff.
Grenze, -n **177ff.**, 250
grenzen (an) 177
Grenzwert 178
gross, Grösse 238
Grund 10, 11, 50, **115ff.**
gründen (auf) 115
Grundlage 116
Grundsatz 115
gut, das Gute 191ff.

haecceitas (L.) 303
halten 251
handeln 31f.
Handlung **31f.**, 192
heben *283*
heimarmenē (Gr) 101f.
-heit 6, 9
Herr 100
hervorgehen, hervortreten 94
Herz 105
histanai (Gr.) 265
historein, historia (Gr.) 118
Historie **118**
Historiker 118
historisch 97, 118
Historismus 118
holon, to (Gr.) 310
hubris (Gr.) 102
Humanität 18, 69, 253
hypokeimenon, to (Gr.) 280, 285
hypostasis, hypostaseis (Gr.) 296
hypothesis, hypotithesthai (Gr.) 224, 265

Ich, das Ich, besseres Ich **121ff.**
ich, du, er 121
idea (Gr.) 123
ideal 13, 93f., **125ff.**
Ideal **125ff.**
ideale, ideelle Realität 93f.
idealisieren, Idealisierung 126f.
Idealismus **128ff.**

Idealität 93, 126f.
Idee 11, 14, 93, **123ff.**, 128, 257
idée (F.) 123
ideell, das Ideelle 13, **126ff.**, 128, 284, 311
idem (L.) 131
identisch, Identität 131
im Begriff sein 58
im Grunde 115
in 133, 142
in sich 133, 310
in uns 134
Inbegriff 167
indifferent 131
Individualität 302, 304
individuell 279, 302
Individuum 148, 230, 302
individuum (L.) 302
Inhalt **108ff.**, 255
inne(n) 142
inner, das Innere **142ff.**, 223, 278
innerlich, Innerlichkeit **142**, 189
Innigkeit 142
Insichsein 178
instare (L.) 8
intellectus (L.) 9, 242f.
Intellektualismus, Intellektualität, Intellektualwelt 242
intellektuelle Anschauung 12, **144f.**
intelligentia (L.) 243
Intelligenz 157, 190, 242
intelligibel 242
intensiv 238f.
ironia (L.) 147
Ironie **146ff.**
Irrtum 300
isostheneia (Gr.) 263
ius (L.) 259
ius ad personam, ius ad rem (L.) 288
ius gentium (L.) 279
ius naturale (L.) 260

ja 199
jenseits, das Jenseits 40, 274
jetzt, das Jetzt 295, 311
juristische Person(en) 230

Kallistik 41
kallos, kalos (Gr.) 41
Kampfergeist 274
kath'hauto (Gr.) 134
kausal, Kausalität 50
-keit 6
kennen, Kenntnis, -se 154
kiesen 311
Klassifikation, Klassifizierung 55
klassisch, das Klassische 147
Knecht 100

koinōnia politikē (Gr.) 54
konkret, das Konkrete **29**
können 40
kontinuierlich 238f.
Korporation 55
Kraft 10, 50, **106f.**, 162, 252
kritērion (Gr.) 262
Kritik, kritisch, Kritizismus 66, 263
Kultur 11, 69
Kultus 253
Kunst 5, **40f.**, 163, 265
Kunstwerk 7
Kür, -übung 311

Laster 191
leben, das Leben **174ff.**
lebendig, Lebendigkeit 174
Lebensgefühl 104
legge (I.) 259
Lehre 268
Lehrsatz 75
Leidenschaft 193
lex (L.) 259
lex, leges naturae (L.) 160
Liberalität 18
lieb 46
logikē (technē) (Gr.) 268
logismos (Gr.) 242f.
logos (Gr.) 63f., 101f., 115, 182, 214, 254, 262, 268
loi (F.) 259

Macht 65, 83, **105ff.**
Mangel 176
Mann 100
Mass, das Mass, die Mass(e) 160, **240f.**
Mässigung 240
Massregel 240
Massstab 161, 240
Materie 108f.
mechanē (Gr.) 181
Mechanik 181, 215
mechanisch 11
Mechanismus **181ff.**
mein 48
meinen, Meinung **48ff.**
Mensch 5, 100
Menschenrechte 98
Menschenverstand, gemeiner/gesunder 242
menschheit 9
Merkmal, -e 56
meson (Gr.) 296
messen 240
Metamorphose 12
metaphysica (L.) 273
Metaphysik **272ff.**
mitewist 8

Mitte 137, 183, 236
mittel, das Mittel 183, 236
mittelbar 183
mittleren Begriffe 12
mnēmē (Gr.) 187
modus (L.) 240
mögen 197
möglich, Möglichkeit **197ff.**
moira, Moirai (Gr.) 101
Moment, -e **311**
momentum (L.) 311
Monist, Monismus 10
Moralität 12f., 16, 92f., **191ff.**, 259ff.
mos, mores (L.) 13, 191
movere (L.) 8, 311
müssen 208

nachdenken, das Nachdenken 248, 290ff.
nasci (L.) 194, 212
natio (L.) 212
Nation **212ff.**
Nationalökonomie 54
Natur 18, 160, **194ff.**
natura (L.) 9, 194
natura naturans/naturata (L.) 9, 104
Naturgesetz 160
natürlich 160
Naturphilosophie 194
Naturrecht 160, **259ff.**
Naturwissenschaft, -en 194, 265
Naturzustand 261, 277
negare (L.) 199
Negation 199
negativ, das Negative, Negativität, negieren **199ff.**
nehmen 146
nein 199
nemesis (Gr.) 102
nicht, das Nicht 44, 250
Nicht-Ich 121
nichts, das Nichts **44ff.**
Nichtsein 44, 93
noein, to noein (Gr.) 291
noēsis, noēsis noēseos (Gr.) 242, 291, 293
noētos (topos) (Gr.) 243, 293
nomos (Gr.) 160
notio (L.) 58
Notio, Notion 11
notwendig, Notwendigkeit **197ff.**
noumenon (Gr.) 178
nous (Gr.) 242f., 274
nun, to nun (Gr.) 293

Obersatz 137
obicere, objicere (L.) 7, 203
Object, Objekt 8, 102, **203ff.**, 281
objectum (L.) 7, 203
objektiv, Objektivität 190, **203ff.**

objektivieren, Objektivierung 203
offenbar(e), Offenbarung 173, 184
öffentliche Macht 55
öffentliche Meinung 49
oikonomia (Gr.) 53f.
oikos (Gr.) 53
Ökonomie 53
opponere, oppositio (L) 205
ordre du coeur (F.) 105
Organ, -e 309f.
organisch 11f.
Organismus 12
organon (Gr.) 268
Ort 294
ousia (Gr.) 285

paideia (Gr.) 86
pan, to (Gr.) 310f.
pars (L.) 302
partikular, Partikularität 302
pathētikos nous (Gr.) 243
peras (Gr.) 139
Person **229ff.**, 284, 288
persona (L.) 229
persönlich, Persönlichkeit 230
Pflicht 191
phaenomenologia generalis (L.) 215
Phaenomenon, Phänomen 11, 214
phainesthai, phainomenon (Gr.) 214
Phänomenologie 11, **214ff.**, 217f.
phantasia (Gr.) 187
Phantasie 157, 165, **187f.**
philos, philein (Gr.) 219
Philosoph 220
philosophia (Gr.) 194, 219
philosophia naturalis (L.) 194
Philosophie 12, **219ff.**
philosophie de l'histoire (F.) 118
philosophieren, philosophisch 220
philosophos (Gr.) 219
Phoronomie 215
physica empirica, physica speculativa (L.) 194
pneuma (Gr.) 274
Pöbel 55
poētikē (Gr.) 219
Polarität 12, 206
polis (Gr.) 54, 278
politeia (Gr.) 54
politikē oikonomia (Gr.) 54
Polizei 54f.
ponere, positus (L.) 224
Popularität 18
Position 199
positiv 160, 199, 260
Positivität 199
Postwesen 89
Potenz, -en 12, 194, 239, 297

potenzieren 12
Pradikät 281
praktikē (Gr.) 219
pronoia (Gr.) 102f.
proodos (Gr.) 296
proprietas (L.) 229
prōtē philosophia (Gr.) 219
psuchē (Gr.) 189
Psychologie 190, 215

Qual 9, 238
Qualierung, Inqualierung 238
qualis (L.) 238
qualitas (L.) 9, 238
Qualität 77, **238ff.**
quantitas (L.) 238
Quantität **238ff.**
Quantum **238ff.**
quantus, quantum (L.) 238

Rache 234
Rang 277
räsonieren 242
Räsonnement 117, 242
ratio (L.) 9, 242f.
ratiocinatio (L.) 243
rational, rationell 242, 254
Rationalismus 242
Raum, 294
real 13, 93, 126, 198
realis, realitas (L.) 93
Realität **93f.**
recht 259
Recht, -e 160, 192, **221ff.**, 233, **259ff.**, 298
rechtlich(e) 191
Rechtspflege 54, 222, 260
rectus (L.) 298
Rede 158
reell 13, 78, 93, 126
reflectere, animum reflectere (L.) **247f.**
reflektieren 151, 248, 291
reflexio (L.) 247
Reflexion 13f., **247ff.**, 291
Reflexionsbegriff(e) 248
Reflexionsbestimmung, -en 89, 248
Reflexionsphilosophie 249
reflexiv 248
Regel **160f.**
Regelmässigkeit 161
Regierung 277
Regierungsgewalt 279
Reich 161
Relation 251ff.
relativ 253
Religionsphilosophie 254
res (L.) 93, 121, 288
res cogitans (L.) 121

res corporalis 288
respublica (L.) 54
richtig 259, 298f.
riflessività (I.) 248
Roman 147
Romantik **147ff.**
romantique (F.) 147
romantisch 147
Rückkehr 144

Sache 50f., 95, 117, 150, 198, 204, 225, 229, 264, **288ff.**
Satz 14, 63, **152f.**, 224
savoir (F.) 154
Schacht 157
Schädellehre 162
schauen 144
scheiden 131
Schein 11, **38ff.**, 81, 89f., 108, 114, 130, 164, 214f., 232, 250, 269f., 285f.
scheinen **38ff.**, 80, 89f., 250, 252
Schicht 118
schicken 101
Schicksal 17, 85, **101ff.**, 118, 212
schlecht 141, 192
schliessen, Schluss **136ff.**, 236, 252
Schlusssatz 137
schön, das Schöne, Kunstschöne, Naturschöne 6, 7, 39, **40f.**, 163
schöne Seele 69, 190
Schönheit 6, **40f.**
Schranke, -n **177ff.**
Schuld 32, 191, 209
schwärmen, Schwarm, Schwärmerei 273
scientia (L.) 265
Seele 62, 73, 88, **189f.**
Seelenwanderung 71
Sehnsucht 149
seiend, das Seiende 7, 44
sein, das Sein 6f., 14, 39, **44ff.**, 88ff., 93
Sein-für-Anderes 134
selbst, das Selbst 61, 77, 290
Selbstand 9
Selbstbestimmung 77
selbstbewusst, Selbstbewusstsein **61ff.**, 230, 247
Selbstempfindung 104
Selbstgefühl 104
Selbstgewissheit 155
Selbstischkeit 104
Semiotik 214
sensiblitias, sensualitas (L) 145
setzen, sich setzen, gesetzt, das Gesetztsein 7, 12, 40, 50, 152, 160, 206, **224ff.**
sich **133ff.**
singular 302
Sinn **145f.**
sinnlich, das Sinnliche 6, 58, **144ff.**, 312

sinnliche Gewissheit 146
Sinnlichkeit 145
Sitte, -n 13, **91ff.**, 191
Sittengesetz, Sittenlehre 91
sittlich, das Sittliche 68, 92, 191
Sittlichkeit 12f., **91ff.**, 191ff., 259ff.
skepsis (Gr.) 263
Skeptizismus 263
sollen, das Sollen 179, 191, **208ff.**
sondern 302
sophistēs (Gr.) 219
sophos, sophia (Gr.) 219
Sosein 89
Soziologie 53
specere (L.) 271
speculari, speculatio (L.) 271
speculum (L.) 271
Spekulation, Speculation, spekulativ **271ff.**
spekulieren 271
Spiegel 271
spiritus (sanctus) (L.) 274
Sprache, sprechen 158
Staat **277ff.**
Staatsrecht 223, 259f., 278
Stadt 278
Stand, Stände 7, 54, 277, 279
stare, status (L.) 277
stehen 242, 277
stellen 107
stetig 238f.
Stimme 77
stoa poikilē (Gr.) 262
Stoff 108
Strafe 234
streben, das Streben 209
Stufe, -n 194
Sturm und Drang 20
subicere, subiectum (L.) 18, 280
subiectum sensionis (L.) 281
subjectivus (L.) 281
Subjekt 204, 230, 279, **280ff.**
subjektiv, Subjektivität 190, **281ff.**
sublatus (L.) 283f.
substantia (L.) 9, 285
Substanz 281f., **285ff.**
substare (L.) 285
Summe 310
syllogismos (Gr.) 136
Syllogismus 136
syllogizesthai (Gr.) 136
Symbol 157
synaisthēsis hautou (Gr.) 61
synistanai (Gr.) 265
System **265ff.**
systēma (Gr.) 265

ta meta ta phusika (Gr.) 272

tadellos 103
Tat **32**, 103, 192
tätig, Tätigkeit 31
tatlos(e) 103
Tatsache. -n 67, 264, 290
täuschen, Täuschung 38f., 164
technē (Gr.) 40
Teil, -e **309ff.**
teilen 152, 309
Teleologia 10
Teleologie **181f.**
teleologisch 151
telos (Gr.) 182, 235
Theologie 220, 254
theologikē (Gr.) 219
theōrētikē (Gr.) 219
theōria (Gr.) 144, 271
Theorie 96
theos (Gr.) 254
Theosophie 220
Thesis, Antithesis, Synthesis 297
tithenai, tithesthai (Gr.) 224
Tod 71
tollere, tollendus 283f.
Ton 158
topos (Gr.) 293
tot, das Tote 71
total 310
totalis, totalitas (L.) 310
Totalität 117, **310f.**
totus (L.) 310
trennen, Trennung 36
treu 298
Trieb 64, 312
tropos, tropoi (Gr.) 263
Trost 103
Tugend 191

Übel 233
über, über- 146, 240
Übergang(e) 195
übergehen 45, 80, 83
übergreifen 58f., 179, 277, 281, 292, 296, 298, 304
überlegen, Überlegung 248
übersinnlich 146
überwinden 199
um 154
Umkehrung 234
un- 15
unbegrenzt 177
Unbestimmtheit 78
und 50
Unding 288
unendlich, Unendlichkeit **15, 139ff.**, 151
Ungrund 115f.
universaler Mensch 303

universalis (L.) 302
universel (F.) 302
universell, universal 302
Universum 302
universus (L.) 302
unmittelbar, Unmittelbarkeit **183ff.**
Unphilosophie 66
Unrecht 232f., 261
Unterlage 18
Untersatz 137
unterscheiden, sich unterscheiden 131
Unterschied **131f.**
unus (L.) 302
unveräusserlich 261
unverjährbar 261
unwesentlich 89
unwillkürlich 311
ur- 8, 50, 152
Urbild 8
Urgrund 116
Urpflanze 8
Urphänomen 8
Ursache 8, 10, **50ff.**, 290
ursächlich, Ursächlichkeit 50
Ursprung, ursprünglich 7f.
Urteil 8f., 13f., 16f., **151ff.**
urteilen 17, **151ff.**
Urteilskraft 41, 151, 243

verändern, sich verändern, Veränderung 178
Veranlassung 52
Verbindung 86, 297
verbrechen, Verbrechen 232f.
vereinzeln, Vereinzelung 302
Verfassung 278
vergehen, vergangen(e), das Vergehen 90, 178
vergleichen, Vergleichung 132, 248, 252
verhalten, sich verhalten, Verhalten 251f.
Verhältnis, -se 173, 240, **251ff.**, 309
verhängen, Verhangnis 101
verkehren, verkehrte Welt 207
Verkehrung 40
vermitteln, vermittelt **183ff.**
Vermittler 184
Vermittlung **184ff.**
vermögen, Vermögen 10, **106f.**
vernehmen 242
verneinen, Verneinung 199
Vernunft 9, 11, 62, **242ff.**
vernünftig, Vernünftigkeit 16, **242ff.**
Verrücktheit 105
verscheiden 131
verschieden, Verschiedenheit **131ff.**
versöhnen, Versöhnung 37, 69, 103, 161, 174
Verstand 9, 10, 11, 16, **242ff.**
verständig **242ff.**
verstandnisse 9

verstehen 58, 242
versteinerte Intelligenz 195
versus (L.) 302
vertrauen, das Vertrauen 46
verursachen 50
verus (L.) 298
verwandt, Verwandtschaft 251
Verwirklichung 222
Verzweiflung 265
vis electiva (L.) 312
Volk 43, 103, **212ff.**, 277, 303
Völkerbund 306
Völkerrecht 213, 259, 279
Volksdichtung 212f.
Volksgeist **212ff.**, 260, 274ff.
Volksglaube 213
Volkspoesie 213
Volksreligion 84, 213
vollenden, vollendet(e), Vollendung 79, 173
voluntas (L.) 311
von 154
von Grund aus 115
voraus 7, **224ff.**
voraussetzen 7, 198, **224ff.**
Voraussetzung **224ff.**
Vorbegriff 87
Vorrede 217
Vorsatz 32, 221
Vorsehung 102f.
vorstellen, sich vorstellen, das Vorstellen **257ff.**
Vorstellung 10, 42, 48, 58, 76, 121, 128, 145, 173, 187, 221, **257ff.**, 291
Vorurteil 224

wählen, Wahl 311
Wahlverwandtschaft 182
wahr, das Wahre 6, 13f., 146, **298ff.**
Wahrheit **298ff.**
wahrnehmen, Wahrnehmung 16, **146**
wahrscheinlich, das Wahrscheinliche 214
was für ein? 134
Wechselwirkung 50
Weib 5
Weingeist 274
weisen 226
Weltanschauung, -en 144, 166
Weltgeist **275ff.**
Weltgericht 279
Weltseele 189
Weltweisheit 220
werden, das Werden, das Werdende, das Gewordene **44ff.**, 217, 243
Wesen 39, 47, **88ff.**, 309
wesen 88
Wesenheit, -en 89, 250
wesentlich, Wesentlichkeit 89
widersprechen, Widerspruch **63ff.**

337

Wiederentstehung 71
wiedererkennen, Wiedererkennung 245
wiederfinden 70
Wiedervergeltung 234
Wille **311ff.**
Willkür **311ff.**
willkürlich 311
wirken, gewirkt(e) 33, 50
wirklich, Wirklichkeit **33ff.**, 51, 93f., 197
wirksam, Wirksamkeit 33, 50
Wirkung 33, **50f.**
Wirtschaft 54
wissen, das Wissen 48, 68, **154ff.**, 161, 192, 204, 217, 226, 265
Wissenschaft 154f., 163, 220, **265ff.**
Wissenschaftslehre 12, 77, 148, 215, 220
wollen 208, 311
würklicheit 9

Zeichen 157, 258
Zeit 274, 294
Zeitgeist, Geist der Zeit 274, 276
zerreissen, zerrissene, Zerrissenheit 36
Zeugemutter 18

ziehen 247, 251
Ziel 235
zu Grunde gehen, richten 115
zu sich 136
Zucht 70, 247
Zufall 197f.
zufällig, Zufälligkeit **197ff.**
zumessen, zugemessen 240
zureichen(d) 116
zurückkehren 144
zusammen 136
Zusammenhang 163, **251ff.**
zusammenhängen 251
zusammenschliessen 136, 236, 252
zusammensetzen, zusammengesetzt, Zusammensetzung 309
Zusich(selbst)kommen 80
Zustand 277
Zwang 232
Zweck 9, 75, **235ff.**
zweckmässig, Zweckmässigkeit 181, **235ff.**
zwei 36, 265
Zweifel 265
Zwiespalt 36

General index

Note: Page numbers in bold refer to the main article(s) in which a given term in the index is discussed.

Abelard, Peter (1079–1142) 93
Abraham 37
absolute, the absolute 11f., **27ff.**, 42f., 45f., 74f., 90, 94, 102, 113, 116, 122, 128, 145, 152, 198, 200, 217, 228, 239, 249, 252f., 254f., 265, 282, 286, 293, 296f., 299f.
absolute idea 33, 114, **125**, 129f., 201, 205, 208, 225, 229, 299, 304
absolute knowledge 28, 154f., 186, 216, 219
absolute spirit 88, 168, 214, 275, 279f.
abstract, abstraction **29ff.**, 32, 59, 71, 74, 122f., 165, 197, 231, 304, 312f.; *see also* concrete
Achilles 73, 171
acid/alkali 78, 82, 182
acknowledgement **245ff.**
action **31ff.**, 38, 103, 143f., 192, 235f., 260, 267f., 295, 313
actual, actuality **33ff.**, 37, 39, 51, 66, 76, 79f., 90, 93f., 124, 130, 171, 192, 197ff., 209ff., 222ff., 244, 260, 263
Aenesidemus (1st century BC) 263f.
Aeschylus (*c.*525–456 BC) 234
aesthetics **40ff.**, 108, 126, 161, 163ff., 189, 214f., 274f.
Agrippa (of uncertain date) 263f.
Alcibiades (of Athens, 5th century BC) 92
Alexander the Great (356–323 BC) 33, 92, 120, 171
alienation **35ff.**, 42, 68, 69f., 80, 82, 86, 144, 158, 195, 213, 232, 252
America 25, 119, 307
analysis/synthesis 152, 155f., 159f., 297
analytic/synthetic 16, 51, 152
Anaximander (*c.*611–545 BC) 139, 206
animals 55ff., 189, 192, 312
annul, annulment *see* sublation
anthropology 88, 215
Antigone 20, 33, 73, 92, 99f., 149, 207
antinomies 64, 81, 228f., 239, 294, 297, 309

antiquity 147, 166f.; *see also* Greece; Rome
appearance 35, **38ff.**, 44, 62, 89f., 106, 128ff., 146, 161f., 196, 207, 214ff., 224, 249f., 263, 286
a priori/a posteriori 16, 29, 56, 97, 196, 271
arbitrary, arbitrariness *see* will and wilfulness
Arcesilaus (315–240 BC) 263
archaeology 172
architecture 39, 40ff., 161, 166
Aristotle (384–322 BC) 8, 18, 30, 41, 53f., 55, 57, 63, 76, 100, 108f., 123f., 134, 136ff., 166, 168, 174, 189, 197, 206f., 210f., 219, 235ff., 243, 260f., 262, 264, 267, 268ff., 272f., 280, 291ff., 293ff., 296f., 298f., 310
arithmetic 97, 161, 238ff.
art 36, 38f., **40ff.**, 108ff., 124f., 126, 135, 142, 145, 147ff., 151, 161, 163ff., 172, 187f., 209, 212ff., 253, 254f., 265, 274f., 279, 299f., 310, 312
Ast, Georg Anton Friedrich (1778–1841) 168
atheism 46, 114f.
atoms 181, 195, 238, 252
Augustine, Aurelius (354–430) 255f., 271, 298
Averroes (Ibn Rushd, 1126–98) 256

Bacon, Francis (Lord, of Verulam, 1561–1626) 169, 268
Bakunin, Michail (1814–76) 23
Bardili, Christoph Gottfried (1761–1808) 167
Bauer, Bruno (1809–82) 172
Baumgarten, Alexander Gottlieb (1714–62) 10, 41, 219, 281
Bayle, Pierre (1647–1706) 24, 86, 114, 263
beauty 39, **40ff.**, 125, 163ff., 283, 312
Beccaria, Cesare (1738–94) 233f.
becoming **44ff.**, 94, 243
being 39, **44ff.**, 89f., 93f., 122, 225f., 243, 270, 299, 311

339

belief **46ff.**, 113, 263
Berkeley, Bishop George (1684–1753) 108
Bible 5, 17, 184, 213
Blumenbach, Johann Friedrich (1752–1840) 56
Boethius, Anicius Torquatus Severinus (480–524) 8, 243, 271
Böhme [or Boehme], Jakob (1575–1624) 9, 16, 20, 24, 61, 63, 114, 116, 136, 169, 189, 200, 238, 296f., 310
Bonaparte, Napoleon (Napoleon I, 1769–1821) 21f., 33, 101, 120, 211
Bonnet, Charles de (1720–93) 79
Bosanquet, Bernard (1848–1923) 23
Bradley, Francis Herbert (1845–1924) 23
Brucker, Johann Jakob (1696–1770) 167f.
Bruno, Giordano (1548–1600) 140, 189, 206
Buhle, Johann Gottlieb (1763–1821) 168
Burke, Edmund (1728–97) 41
Burckhardt, Jakob Christoph (1818–97) 23

Caesar, Julius (100–44 BC) 33, 120, 211
Caligula (Gaius Julius Caesar Germanicus, 12–41 AD) 247
cancel, cancelation *see* sublation
Canning, George (1770–1827) 220
Carneades (214–129 BC) 263
categories 80f., 81f., 97, 157ff., 177, 183, 251, 259, 268ff., 291, 297, 309
Catholicism/Protestantism 47, 85, 142, 149, 173, 201, 254
Cato, Marcus Porcius (234–149 BC) 149
cause, causality **50ff.**, 73, 111, 141, 162, 224ff., 258f., 285, 290, 296
certainty **154ff.**, 184ff.
change 94, 178, 238ff.
chemism 159, **181ff.**, 204, 236
Christ 72f., 85f., 115, 126, 174, 184, 207, 255, 276
Christianity 9, 21, 37, 42, 46f., 72f., 79, 84ff., 101ff., 113ff., 165f., 173f., 201, 218, 253ff., 276, 282, 286
Chrysippus (*c.*280–206 BC) 262
Cicero, Marcus Tullius (106–43 BC) 283
civil society 43, 47, **53ff.**, 93, 98f., 161, 222f., 232, 268, 278ff., 287, 304
classical art 42f., 147, 166
classification **55ff.**, 132f., 165f.
Cleanthes (331–233 BC) 262
cognition 33, 48, 66, 117, 124f., **154ff.**, 177ff., 198f., 217, 244, 290
colours 199f., 206f.
common sense 66, 242, 264
concept 23, 30, 39, 53, 57f., **58ff.**, 75f., 78f., 79ff., 82, 94, 102, 111f., 113f., 116, 122f., 124f., 127, 129f., 137ff., 141, 144f., 151ff., 164ff., 173f., 175f., 179, 183, 196, 222, 228,

231, 235ff., 243f., 253, 254, 257ff., 265ff., 270, 273, 281f., 286, 291f., 294f., 299, 303f., 309ff., 313
conception 70, 157ff., 221, 255f., **257ff.**, 291; *see also* representation
conclusion **136ff.**
concrete **29ff.**, 32, 122, 165, 232, 265, 304
condition 28f., 34, 50, 95, **117**, 124, 197f., 225, 289, 296, 310
Condorcet, Marie-Jean-Antoine-Nicolas Caritat, marquis de (1743–94) 98
conflict 44f., 308
consciousness **61ff.**, 67f., 69, 95f., 104, 109, 122, 156, 167, 190, 204, 215ff., 250, 264f.
conservatism 35, 149, 263
content 41, 105, **107ff.**, 126, 163ff., 199, 221, 255, 291, 313
contingency 34, 39, 60, 196, **197ff**, 227f.
contradiction 15, **63ff.**, 76, 79f., 81f., 150, 175f., 197, 206, 210, 234, 243, 253, 264, 268, 291, 295, 298ff., 309
Copernicus, Nicholas (1473–1543) 140
corporations 55
correctness 259, **298ff.**
Cousin, Victor (1792–1867) 24, 26
Creon 92, 99
Creuzer, Georg Friedrich (1771–1858) 24, 173
crime 39f., 143, **232ff.**
Critical Journal of Philosophy 21, **65ff.**
criticism, critique **66ff.**, 263
Croce, Benedetto (1866–1952) 23
culture 37f., **68ff.**, 110, 194, 213
custom **91ff.**, 161f., 191, 212ff.

Dante Alighieri (1265–1321) 24, 68
death 30, **71ff.**, 88, 99, 101, 175ff., 178f., 189f., 196, 209, 211, 246, 284f., 307
deed **31ff.**, 103, 192
definition 31, 56, **74ff.**, 77, 147, 265
democracy 57
Democritus (*fl. c.*435 BC) 139
Derrida, Jacques 160, 295
Descartes, René (1596–1650), cartesianism 59, 121, 142, 155, 174, 184f., 190, 225, 265, 281, 285, 289, 295
destiny **101ff.**
determinate being 44ff., 65, **93ff.**, 131, 153, 200, 311
determinateness, determinacy **77ff.**, 94, 133, 134, 173f., 178, 185, 200, 295, 303
determination 14, 17, 74f., **77ff.**, 89f., 102, 110ff., 179, 200, 250, 291
development 44, 57f., 60, 76, **79ff.**, 90, 119, 135, 167, 218f., 237, 244, 284, 298, 304f.
dialectic 55, **81ff.**, 87, 123, 147ff., 157, 169, 223, 244, 272, 298

Diderot, Denis (1713–84) 36, 86, 148, 267
difference 28f., 90, **131ff.**, 248, 252
*Difference between the Systems of Fichte and
   Schelling* 21, 36f.
Dilthey, Wilhelm (1833–1911)) 23, 26
Diogenes Laertius (3rd century AD) 167
Dionysius the Areopagite, pseudo- (uncertain
   date) 297
Dodds, E.R. 297
dogmatism 128, 263f., 272f.
doubt 265
Durkheim, Emile (1858–1917) 53
duty 191, 261

Early Theological Writings 21, 36, 47f., **84ff.**
Echtermeyer, Theodor (1805–1844) 23
Eckhart, Johann (Meister Eckhart,
   c.1260–1327) 9, 44, 58, 115, 140, 144, 189,
   229, 242f., 297
education **68ff.**, 82, 86ff., 98, 119, 247
ego *see* I
electricity 40, 50, 62, 162, 206
Embser, Johann Valentin (1749–83) 306
Empedocles (c.490–430 BC) 72
empirical, empiricism **95ff.**
Encyclopaedia 22, 35, 61ff., **86ff.**, 270f.
Engels, Friedrich (1820–95) 23
England, English 5, 22
Enlightenment 10, 16, 29, 47, 69f., 95, 141,
   147, 154, 171, 174, 212, 242, 254f., 271, 304
Epictetus (c.50–138 AD) 262
Epicurus (341–270 BC) 262, 295
Erdmann, Johann Eduard (1805–92) 23
Erigena, John Scotus (810–77) 184, 297
essence 16, 28, 30, 34, 39, 73, **88ff.**, 94f., 108,
   115f., 131, 205, 241, 250, 270, 278, 289, 292,
   304
estates 279
estrangement **35ff.**, 70
eternity 73, **293ff.**
ethical life 12f., 21, 33, 37, 53ff., 68, **91ff.**, 99,
   107, 110, 191ff., 222f., 230, 237, 244, 259ff.,
   287, 290, 313
Euclid (3rd century BC) 56, 226f.
existence 34, 89, **93ff.**, 113f., 137f., 289
experience 38, 60ff., **95ff.**, 118, 220f., 271ff.
explanation **116f.**
explicit *see* for itself

facts of consciousness 67, 76, 264, 290
faith 37, 40, **46ff.**, 69f., 71, 84ff., 87, 113, 154,
   228, 273f.
Faith and knowledge 48, 68
Fall 102, 193
falsity 214ff., **298ff.**
family 53, 92, **98ff.**, 177, 278ff., 287, 304
fate 17, **101ff.**

feeling **103ff.**, 164, 173, 212, 287
Ferguson, Adam (1723–1816) 54
Feuerbach, Ludwig Andreas (1804–72) 23,
   37, 45, 73, 257
Feuerbach, Paul Johann Anselm von
   (1775–1833) 233f.
Fichte, Johann Gottlieb (1762–1814) 7, 11f.,
   17f., 20ff., 27, 36, 38f., 42, 48, 62, 65ff., 68f.,
   77, 81, 91, 119, 121, 128, 140, 145, 146ff.,
   157, 168f., 178, 189, 205, 206, 209f., 212,
   215, 220, 223, 224f., 231, 245f., 248f., 259ff.,
   266, 269, 272, 278, 288, 295, 297f., 306ff.
finite, finitude 15, 60, 64, 72, 78, 81f., 107,
   113f., 128f., 134, 139ff., 149, 153, 175f.,
   177ff., 200, 237, 254, 266, 293, 294f., 299f.,
   307f.
Fischer, Ludwig (Hegel's son, 1807–31) 21f.
for itself 65, 76, 79f., 94, 131, **133ff.**, 201, 223
force 50, **105ff.**, 142ff., 162, 182, 191, 252,
   309
form 41ff., 44, 81, 105, **107ff.**, 126, 146,
   163ff., 197f., 221, 255, 291ff., 310
Forster, Friederich Christoph (1791–1868)
   22
France, French 5, 22, 37f., 68
freedom 13f., 31, 35, 49, 60, 71, 76, 80, 84f.,
   92f., 94, 100, 101ff., 106f., **110ff.**, 119, 122,
   128, 131, 135, 148f., 191, 222ff., 231, 233,
   260f., 262, 280, 312ff.
French revolution 20ff., 35, 37f., 49, 72, 98,
   112, 148, 171, 218, 313
Fries, Jakob Friedrich (1773–1843) 76, 222,
   259

Galen (Galenos, Claudius, c.129–199 AD)
   137
Gans, Eduard (1798–1839) 22, 170, 221
Gentile, Giovanni (1875–1944) 23
geometry 97, 155, 206, 227f.
Germany, German 5ff., 171, 212ff.
German Constitution 35
Gibbon, Edward (1737–1794) 21
God, gods 9, 15, 19, 27ff., 34f., 36, 38, 45f.,
   46f., 64, 72f., 74f., 79, 83, 84ff., 93f., 96, 99,
   101ff., 107, 109, **113ff.**, 119, 123f.,
   132f., 140f., 144f., 148, 152, 155, 164ff.,
   171f., 173f., 179, 181, 183, 184, 200, 203,
   205, 206, 226ff., 230, 237, 243, 253, 254ff.,
   269f., 272, 275f., 279f., 285f., 294, 297,
   298ff.
Goethe, Johann Wolfgang von (1749–1832)
   5, 20, 21, 24, 36, 41ff., 44, 69, 71, 96, 101,
   108, 143, 147f., 182f., 184f., 190, 196, 206,
   243, 250, 271, 285, 293
good/bad/evil 32f., 37, 40, 192f., 207, 209f.,
   233, 237

341

Göschel, Karl Friedrich (1784–1862) 23, 25, 73, 115
grammar 5ff., 158f.
gravity 181
Greece, Greeks 17, 20f., 24f., 31, 36f., 41ff., 46f., 58, 66, 71, 84ff., 92f., 99f., 101ff., 111, 121, 139f., 146, 161, 163ff., 169, 171, 173f., 191f., 196, 213f., 218, 230, 240, 254, 255, 261, 262ff., 278, 287, 290, 293, 310
Grimm, Jacob (1778–1863) and Wilhelm (1786–1859) 213
Grotius, Hugo (1583–1645) 220
ground 28f., 50, 95, **115ff.**, 192, 232, 290
Gurlitt, Johann Gottfried (1754–1827) 167

Hamann, Johann Georg (1730–88) 20, 22, 25, 95, 145, 157, 206
Hamilton, Sir William (1788–1856) 283
Hardenberg, Karl August von (1750–1822) 223
Harris, William Torrey (1835–1909) 23
Hegel, Christiane Louise (sister, 1773–1832) 20
Hegel, Karl (son, 1813–1901) 169ff.
Hegel, Marie, née von Tucher (wife, 1791–1855) 22
Hegelians, Hegelianism 23, 115, 223, 256f.
Heidegger, Martin (1889–1976) 93f., 295
Heraclitus (c.540–480 BC) 44f., 63, 101, 128, 160, 168, 206, 255, 306
Herder, Johann Gottfried (1744–1803) 7, 11, 17, 20f., 24, 29, 38, 40, 69, 71, 79, 84f., 106, 108, 118f., 145, 157, 159, 163, 169, 173, 212f., 214f., 253f., 271, 275, 285, 304
Herodotus (c.490–425 BC) 171
history 14, 31, 35, 38, 42, 58, 59, 63, 69, 71ff., 74, 80, 82, 91, 92, 102f., **118ff.**, 141, 157, 163, 169ff., 172f., 177, 193, 194f., 212ff., 217ff., 222, 226, 237, 244, 255, 259ff., 271, 275f., 279f., 297
Hobbes, Thomas (1588–1679) 196, 246f., 281
Hoffmann, Ernst Theodor Amadeus (1776–1822) 149
Hoffmeister, Johannes (1907–55) 170, 217, 221
Hogarth, William (1697–1764) 161
Hölderlin, Johann Christian Friedrich (1770–1843) 20f., 25, 43, 72, 84, 102, 152, 184, 300
Homer (probably 8th century BC) 5, 43, 149, 213, 310
Horace (Quintus Horatius Flaccus, 65–8 BC) 164
Hotho, Heinrich Gustav (1802–73) 163
Humboldt, Wilhelm von (1767–1835) 22, 25, 157ff., 223

Hume, David (1711–76) 96, 121, 169, 264
Husserl, Edmund (1859–1938) 290
Hypatia (died 415 AD) 98

I 12, 29, 36, 38, 42, 59f., 61ff., 67, 77, 81, 89, 91, 102, 110ff., **121ff.**, 125, 127, 128ff., 132f., 135f., 145, 148f., 152, 185, 190, 201, 206, 209, 224ff., 230ff., 246f., 248f., 257f., 269, 280ff., 289, 291ff., 295, 297, 303ff., 313
I = I 121f., 132f., 152, 225
idea 34, 44, 81, 87f., 110, **123ff.**, 126f., 128ff., 144f., 149, 165f., 171, 176, 183, 195, 205, 222, 224, 265ff., 310f., 313
ideal, ideality **125ff.**, 128ff., 284, 311
idealism 16, 39, 65, 90, 127, **128ff.**, 139, 186, 195f., 244, 253, 271, 285, 293, 298, 301
identity 27, 45f., 90, 112, 114, 116, 121f., **131ff.**, 145, 152f., 206, 248, 252
illusion **38ff.**, 81, 148f., 164, 214ff.
imagination 157f., 165f., **186ff.**, 257ff.
immediacy/mediation 12, 28, 48, 87, 133, 155, **183ff.**, 198, 225, 227
immortality **71ff.**, 176, 189, 199f., 209, 256, 295
implicit see in itself
in and for itself 80, **133ff.**, 223
in itself 40, 76, 78, 79f., 130, **133ff.**, 142, 205, 223, 224
indifference **131ff.**, 183, 262
individual, -ity, -ism 15, 30, 47, 57, 74, 92, 99, 120, 175ff., 191ff., 212, 223, 287, 292, **302ff.**, 307f., 313; see also universality
inference 129, **136ff.**, 141, 153, 176, 181, 184f., 204, 235f., 243f., 268
infinite, infinity 14f., 41, 52, 64, 71ff., 86, 89, 107, 113, 127, 128, 136, 138, **139ff.**, 149, 151, 175f., 178ff., 201, 206, 208, 209f., 227f., 237, 239ff., 243, 254, 263ff., 271, 275, 277, 282f., 293, 294, 300, 309, 313
inner/outer 16, 34, 78, 107, **142ff.**, 157f., 175f., 188, 192, 290
intellectual intuition 12, 28, **144ff.**
internal/external 82, **142ff.**, 182f., 188, 235ff., 249f., 258, 290
intuition 42f., 58ff., **144ff.**, 157f., 188, 256, 257ff., 272, 293
irony **146ff.**, 165
Islam 101, 171, 173f.

Jacobi, Friedrich Heinrich (1743–1819) 11, 24, 25, 48, 68, 87, 95, 96, 105, 155, 169, 173, 184ff., 219, 243f., 249, 254, 288, 300
Jaeschke, Walter 172
Jaspers, Karl (1883–1969) 267
Jean Paul (Friedrich Richter, 1763–1825) 187
Jena, Jena lectures 21, 54, 58, 65ff., 216f., 234, 255, 273

John Duns Scotus (*c.*1270–1308) 93, 203, 256, 303
Judaism 71, 84ff., 140, 146, 173
judgment 13f., 17, 41, 46, 60, 129, 137ff., **151ff.**, 176, 199f., 232, 248, 251, 268, 280ff., 298ff., 303

Kant, Immanuel (1724–1804) 11, 12ff., 18, 20f., 27, 29, 32, 34, 38ff., 41ff., 48, 51f., 54, 55, 58ff., 61, 63f., 66ff., 71ff., 74ff., 81, 85, 87, 91f., 93, 95ff., 106, 111, 119f., 121, 123ff., 126, 128ff., 134, 137, 140, 144ff., 151f., 155f., 157, 163, 165, 167ff., 174f., 177ff., 182f., 188, 189, 191ff., 194, 196, 197, 199f., 203ff., 206f., 209f., 215, 217, 219, 223, 226ff., 229f., 230ff., 239, 243, 245, 248ff., 251, 254, 257, 259ff., 263, 265, 269ff., 271ff., 274f., 281f., 285, 288f., 291ff., 294f., 297f., 298f., 303, 306f., 309f, 312f.
Kepler, Johannes (1571–1630) 196
Kierkegaard, Søren (1813–55) 23, 33, 82, 95, 150, 267f., 282f., 295
Kingsley, Charles (1819–75) 98
Kleist, Heinrich von (1777–1811) 71, 149
Kleuker, Johann Friedrich (1749–1827) 173
Klopstock, Friedrich Gottlieb (1724–1803) 213
knowledge 27f., 48, 66ff., **154ff.**, 179f., 185f., 217f., 227f., 266ff.
Knox, Sir T. M. 84
Kojève, Alexandre 73, 295
Koyré, A. 295
Krug, Wilhelm Traugott (1770–1842) 25, 66ff., 98, 245, 251, 264, 273, 290, 291, 303, 306

Lambert, Johann Heinrich (1728–77) 11, 214ff., 217, 268, 288
language 5ff., 37, 38, 48, 69f., **157ff.**, 188, 212f., 247, 258, 304
Lasson, Georg (1862–1932) 221
Latin 7ff., 17, 20
law 40, 52, 54, 63, 71, 85, 91, 96, 99, 105, 132, **160ff.**, 198, 213, 233f., 259ff., 268, 298f., 312
laws of nature 160f.
lectures 21f., 120, 160, 221
Lectures on Aesthetics **163ff.**
Lectures on the History of Philosophy **166ff.**
Lectures on the Philosophy of History **169ff.**
Lectures on the Philosophy of Religion **172ff.**
Lectures on the Proofs of the Existence of God **174**, **227f.**
Leibniz, Gottfried Wilhelm (1646–1716) 8ff., 17, 41, 50, 61, 63, 79, 93, 101, 116, 132, 136, 140, 151, 159f., 181, 190, 200, 219, 242, 248, 260, 268f., 291, 294, 297, 303, 306

Lessing, Gotthold Ephraim (1729–81) 5, 20, 24, 69, 71, 119, 147, 184
Leucippus (*fl. c.*440 BC) 139
Lichtenberg, Georg Christoph (1742–99) 267
life 29, 31, 36, 52, 58, 64, 71ff., 79ff., 85f., 124, 162, **174ff.**, 181ff., 235ff., 246, 265, 296, 304
life and death struggle 72, 177, 230, 246f.
light 89, 180, 196, 248ff., 252, 296
limit 139ff., **177ff.**, 200, 210, 240, 291
Locke, John (1632–1704) 54, 248, 257, 273, 288
logic 13ff., 30f., 34f., 42, 45f., 57f., 58ff., 70, 73f., 74ff., 77ff., 80, 82, 87f., 114f., 120, 123, 125, 129f., 132ff., 136ff., 145f., 151ff., 168f., 173f., 176f., 181ff., 195, 197ff., 200, 204f., 214f., 217, 219, 228, 238ff., 264, **268ff.**, 273, 277, 284, 297, 303f.
Longinus, pseudo- (1st century AD) 41
love 29, 36, 58, 85f., 99, 161
Lucretius (*c.*95–55 BC) 160
Luther, Martin (1483–1546) 5, 9, 17, 47, 66, 70, 72, 113, 213, 242, 254, 271

Machiavelli, Nicolò (1469–1527) 306
magnetism 40, 62, 162, 206ff., 250, 310
Malebranche, Nicholas (1638–1715) 79
Marcus Aurelius (121–180 AD, Emperor 161–180 AD) 262
Marheineke, Philipp Konrad (1780–1846) 22, 172, 174
Marx, Karl (1818–83) 23, 38, 223, 257, 262
master and slave 72, 99f., 208, 246f., 262
mathematics 75, 178, 199, 238ff.
matter 74, 106, **107ff.**, 129f., 197, 239
McTaggart, John McTaggart Ellis (1866–1925) 23, 73
meaning 7, 13ff., 48, 145, 157ff., 165
measure 79, 102, 160f., **238ff.**, 290, 294
mechanism 102, 174f., **181ff.**, 204, 236
mediation 12, 28f., 122, 137ff., **183ff.**, 224, 235, 284, 296
memory 157ff., 182, **186ff.**, 257ff., 290
Mendelssohn, Moses (1729–86) 18, 24,, 71, 199f.
metaphysics 25, 269, **271ff.**
Meyerson, Emil (1859–1933) 23
Michelet, Karl Ludwig (1801–93) 23, 166
Middle Ages 123, 140, 171, 219, 243, 254f., 269, 297
Mill, John Stuart (1806–73) 138, 159, 194, 245, 265, 276
mind 27, 30, 39, 52, 60, 80, 106f., 127, 129f., 162, 163ff., 181f., **189ff.**, 195f., 242f., 271, 273ff., 309
Minerva, owl of 222
Minkowski, Hermann (1864–1909) 294

343

moments 284, 304, **309ff.**
monarchy 31, 57, 279
Montaigne, Michel de (1533–92) 263
Montesquieu, Charles-Louis de Secondat,
    baron de (1689–1755) 21, 212
morality 12f., 31ff., 36, 48, 68, 72ff., 84f.,
    91ff., 110, 120, 125, 165, **191ff.**, 205, 208ff.,
    222f., 227f., 230, 234, 245f., 254, 259ff., 292,
    313
Möser, Justus (1720–94) 68
Mosheim, Johann Lorenz von (1695–1765)
    172
music 40ff., 160, 161, 166, 295
mysticism, mystics 9, 20, 115f., 142, 189,
    271f.
mythology 43, 92, 196, 213f.

nation **212ff.**
Natural Law 68, 91f., 307
natural law, rights 160, 260f.
nature 12, 38, 41f., 68, 80, 82, 87f., 111f., 114,
    119, 123, 125, 129f., 142ff., 163ff., 171,
    194ff., 198, 209, 224, 261, 271, 278, 283,
    294f.
necessity 28, 34, 60, 75f., 96, 101ff., 110ff.,
    138, 153, 196, **197ff.**, 205, 227f., 270f.
negation, negativity 14, 39f., 44, 63ff., 72, 78,
    94, 133, 134, 141, 151, 178, **199ff**, 206f.,
    233, 244, 264, 284, 296, 307f.
Neoplatonism 9, 16, 18, 41, 61, 79, 98, 123,
    128, 132, 242f., 255, 262, 273, 293ff., 296ff.
Newton, Isaac (1643–1727) 47, 108, 140f.,
    194ff., 220, 294
Nicholas of Cusa (1401–64) 27, 140, 169,
    184, 206, 208, 271, 295f.
Niethammer, Friedrich Immanuel
    (1766–1848) 59, 65
Nietzsche, Friedrich (1844–1900) 29, 44f.,
    72, 77, 91, 114, 141, 150, 192, 232, 267f.
Nohl, Hermann (1879–1960) 25, 84ff.
not-I, not-self 121ff.; *see also* Fichte; I
nothing **44ff.**, 94, 311
notion *see* concept
Notker Labeo (also called 'Theutonicus',
    c.950–1022) 8
Novalis (Friedrich von Hardenberg,
    1772–1801) 9, 20, 24, 63f., 69, 71, 147f.,
    189

object, objectivity 16, 19, 24, 27, 58ff., 61ff.,
    67, 35, 96, 102, 104, 125, 139, 144, 169,
    181ff., **203ff.**, 215ff., 217, 228, 235ff., 246,
    249f., 254f., 258f., 260, 270f., 275, 280ff.,
    292, 313
O'Brien, G. D. 170
Oedipus 33, 192
Oken, Lorenz (1779–1851) 195

opinion 19, **48f.**, 122
opposition 12, 16, 40, 63ff., 69f., 73, 82, 85f.,
    113, 115, 132, 139, 142f., 145, 147ff., 162,
    165, 182, 184, 191, 202, **205ff.**, 209ff., 243f.,
    248f., 272, 295ff., 310
organism 34, 52f., 60, 102, 107, 108f., 129f.,
    168, **174ff.**, 235ff., 309
other(ness) 58, 110ff., 131ff., 136, 200
ought 140, 179, 191f., **208ff.**, 309

painting 38f., 41f., 166
Panaetius (c.180–110 BC) 262
pantheism 86, 114, 132f., 173
Pappus (*fl. c.*300 AD) 155
Paracelsus (Theophrastus Bombastus von
    Hohenheim. 1493–1541) 9, 95, 189, 220
Parmenides (c.515–after 450 BC) 44, 168,
    291, 296
particular(ity) 15, 29, 57, 93, 175ff., 261,
    302ff., 313; *see also* universality
Pascal, Blaise (1623–62) 105, 263
passion 193, 262f.
Patroklos 73
Paul, St (1st century AD) 271
Paulus, Elisabeth Friederike Caroline
    (1767–1844) 100
peace 73, 119, **306ff.**
Peirce, Charles (1839–1914) 23
people, folk 43, 84ff., 103, **212ff.**, 253f., 275f.,
    277, 303
perception 62, **144ff.**, 289
person 100, 171, **229ff.**, 246f., 260, 286f., 313
Pestalozzi, Johann Heinrich (1746–1827) 69
phenomenology 88, 190, **214ff.**
Phenomenology of Spirit 21, 36ff., 61ff., 67f., 69,
    89, 156, 204, 208, 215f., **216ff.**, 255, 290
phenomenon/noumenon 38f.
Philo Judaeus of Alexandria (c.30 BC–45 AD)
    140
Philosophical Propaedeutic 22, 216
philosophy 43, 86, 87, 166ff., 174, **219ff.**,
    222, 224ff., 227f., 254ff., 264f., 265ff., 272f.,
    305
philosophy of nature 67, 88, **194ff.**
philosophy of religion 172ff., 253ff.
Philosophy of Right 22, 34, 82, **221ff.**, 229ff.,
    232ff., 307f.
phrenology 162
physiognomy 38, 162
picture thinking *see* conception; representation
planets 21, 25, 117, 161, 181
plants 55ff., 79f., 136, 184f., 189
Plato (427–347 BC) 14, 18, 20, 23, 24, 40, 41,
    44, 55, 57, 60, 68, 71, 74, 81, 92f, 98, 111,
    123ff., 126, 128, 134, 139f., 144, 147, 164,
    169, 173, 186ff., 189f., 206f., 219, 232, 235,

242f., 255, 263, 267, 268f., 280, 291, 293, 295f., 298, 303, 310
Plotinus (205–270 AD) 20, 24, 41, 61, 148, 173, 189, 243, 293, 296f., 303
Ploucquet, Gottfried (1716–90) 25
poetry 41f., 160, 166, 212ff., 256
polarity 40, 62, 162, 206ff.
political economy 53f.
politics 35, 101, 105ff., 110ff., 212ff., 221ff., 256, 259ff., 313f.
Polyneikes 73, 99
Posidonius (c.135–51 BC) 262
posit, positing 12, 40, 50, 135, **224ff.**, 250
positivity 47, 84ff., 162, 199
Positivity of the Christian Religion 85
possession **229ff.**
possibility **197ff.**
potential/actual 79f., 134f., 140, 143f., 197
power 82, 99, **105ff.**, 191, 277ff.
practical (reason, etc.) 33, 123f., 190f., 219, 306
presupposition 14, 198, **224ff.**, 250, 264f., 269
Proclus (410–485) 20, 24, 169, 173, 296f.
proof 113ff., 174, 184f., 205, **226ff.**, 250, 264
property **229ff.**, 234, 238, 261, 313
proposition 15, 28, 75, **151ff.**, 199f., 224, 229, 268, 299f.
Protagoras (c.480–410 BC) 232
providence **101ff.**, 119, 210
psychology 39, 61, 88, 190, 215, 295
punishment 31, 39f., 91, 103, 117, 161, **232ff.**, 247
purpose, purposiveness 41, 50, 75, 103, 107, 116, 124, 165, 171, 175, 182f., 226, 230, **235ff.**, 256, 309, 312
Pyrrho of Elis (c.360–270 BC) 263
Pythagoras (c.580–500 BC) 219, 227
pythagoreanism 68, 139, 141, 189, 206, 296

quality 78, 94, 178, **238ff.**
quantity 178, **238ff.**

rabble 55
Ranke, Leopold von (1795–1886) 23, 94
rational(ity) *see* reason
reality 78, **93ff.**, 123f., 126f., 199f.
reason 11ff., 29ff., 34, 36, 44, 62, 69f., 81f., 84ff., 110, 120, 139, 141, 162, 170ff., 175, 191ff., 209f., 222, **242ff.**, 254, 262f., 269ff., 272, 292, 298, 304, 310, 312f.
reciprocity **50ff.**, 225f., 285f.
recognition 62, 71, 135, 208, 231, **245ff.**, 279, 307f.
recollection 144, 168, **186ff.** 257ff.
reflection 39, 89f., 100, 112, 118f., 138, 153,

164, 201, 221, 227, 246f., **247ff.**, 254, 267f., 272, 290, 291, 313
Reinhold, Karl Leonhard (1758–1823) 66f., 167f.
relation 28, 78, 114, 132, 134, 179, 240, 248, **251ff.**, 294, 299, 309
religion 21, 36, 46ff., 64, 69, 79, 84ff., 87, 105, 113ff., 172ff., 213f., **253ff.**, 292
representation 30, 42, 58, 75, 113ff., 123, 128, 157ff., 187f., 221, 254ff., **257ff.**
responsibility **31ff.**, 192
restriction **177ff.**, 210
Richardson, Samuel (1689–1761) 190
right, rights 31, 37, 39f., 54, 93, 94, 98, 213, 221ff., 229ff., 232ff., **259ff.**, 278ff., 288, 313
Rist, Johann (1607–67) 72
romantic art 42f., 166
romanticism 20, 99, 142, **146ff.**, 189, 206, 212, 304
Rome, Romans 25, 31, 37, 40, 42, 55, 76, 85, 92, 101f., 171, 173f., 218, 222, 230, 261, 262
Rosenkranz, Karl (1805–79) 23, 25, 98
Rousseau, Jean Jacques (1712-78) 36, 68, 92, 157, 190, 196, 246, 306
Royce, Josiah (1855–1916) 23
Ruge, Arnold (1802–80) 23
rule **160ff.**, 164
Russell, Bertrand 159f.
Ryle, Gilbert 151

Saint-Pierre, Charles Irénée Castel, abbé de (1658–1743) 306
Sappho (7th–6th centuries BC) 98
Sartre, Jean-Paul (1905–80) 23, 91, 94, 150
Savigny, Friedrich Karl von (1779–1861) 23, 212f.
scepticism 67, 150, 156, 226, **262ff.**, 290, 301
Schacht, Richard 37
Schelling, Friedrich Wilhelm Joseph (1775–1854) 9, 12, 16, 20ff., 27f., 40, 41ff., 63, 69, 79, 82, 95, 102, 116f., 121, 124, 128, 132, 140, 145, 146ff., 163, 165, 168f., 175, 186ff., 189, 194ff., 206ff., 209, 214, 217, 224, 239, 243f., 245f., 269, 272, 286, 288f., 294f., 296f.
Schiller, Johann Christoph Friedrich von (1759–1805) 5, 20, 36, 39, 42, 65, 69f., 71, 120, 124, 165, 187, 189f., 218f., 243, 246, 283, 312
Schlegel, August Wilhelm von (1767–1845) 20, 65, 147ff., 163
Schlegel, Friedrich von (1772–1829) 9, 65, 99, 147ff., 212, 214, 220, 267
Schleiermacher, Friedrich Ernst Daniel (1768–1834) 99, 105, 168, 173, 212, 254
Schopenhauer, Arthur (1788–1860) 25, 67, 114, 124, 195

345

Schottelius (Schottel, Justus Georg, 1612–76) 312
Schulze, Gottlob Ernst (1761–1833) 66ff., 86, 188, 221, 264
Schulze, Johannes (1786–1869) 217
science 45, 48f., 87, 95, 96f., 154f., 163f., 194ff., 198f., 217f., 219f., **265ff**., 268
Science of Logic 22, 87, 89f., **268ff**.
sculpture 39, 40ff., 161, 166
self 104, 254; *see also* I
self-consciousness 37, **61ff**., 71ff., 80, 102f., 105, 111f., 114, 119, 122f., 129f., 131, 135, 141, 168, 170, 175, 217f., 227f., 230, 246f., 249, 254
Seneca, Lucius Annaeus (*c*.4 BC–65 AD) 71, 194, 262
sensation 103ff., **144ff**., 205
sense **144ff**., 164
sensory 58ff., 96, 130, **144ff**., 164f., 205, 257ff., 271, 312
sensory certainty 29, 45, 62, 67, 96, 122, 155, 186, 204, 216, 225, 264
Seuse, Heinrich (1300–66) 271
Sextus Empiricus (*fl.* c.190 AD) 263ff.
Shaftesbury, Anthony Ashley Cooper (1671–1713) 190
Shakespeare, William (1564–1616) 19, 148f., 213
shining **38ff**., 89, 250, 252
Shklar, J. N. 40
slavery 53, 76, 80, 99f., 110f., 247, 261, 262
Smith, Adam (1723–90) 34, 54
society 43, 52f., 53ff., 60
Socrates (469–399 BC) 22, 72, 81, 85, 92, 126, 142, 146ff., 169, 219, 232
Solger, Karl Wilhelm Ferdinand (1780–1819) 22, 25, 146ff.
sophists, sophistry 81f., 169, 219
Sophocles (*c*.496–406 BC) 20, 92, 99, 101ff., 207
soul 57, 62, 69, 73, 88, 104f., 115f., 127f., 157f., 165, 175ff., **189ff**., 212, 262, 296
space 139ff., 195, 293ff.
species and genus 55ff., 75, 175ff., 303f.
speculation, speculative 5, 82, 153, 243, 269, **271ff**., 284, 298, 310
Spinoza, Benedictus de (Baruch Despinoza, 1632–77) 14, 20, 24, 27f., 35, 75f., 78, 114, 128, 141, 200, 240, 265, 269, 285ff., 296, 300, 304
spirit 23, 28f., 31, 33, 34, 36, 38, 42, 52, 72ff., 80, 82, 85, 88, 94, 114, 119f., 122, 129f., 141, 142, 163ff., 168, 170ff., 174, 175ff., 179, 189ff., 194ff., 212ff., 215ff., 235, 244, 256, 260, **274ff**., 281, 293, 297f., 299f.
Spirit of Christianity and its Fate 21, 85f.
state 21, 34f., 37, 53ff., 57f., 68, 73, 92, 98f.,

106f., 111, 117, 119f., 125, 126, 129f., 139, 161, 168, 172, 173, 177, 182, 191, 205, 212f., 222ff., 230ff., 244, 246, 259f., **277ff**., 287, 304, 306ff., 313
Steffens, Henrik (1773–1845) 195
Steuart, Sir James (1712–80) 21, 54
Stirling, James Hutchison (1820–1909) 283
stoicism 35, 71, 101f., 111f., 137, 160, 189, 219, **262ff**., 268f.
Stolberg, Friedrich Leopold, Graf zu 173
Strauss, David Friedrich (1808–74) 23, 115, 172, 256f.
subject, subjectivity 16, 27, 36, 61ff., 67, 89, 93, 100, 114, 121, 125, 128, 139, 142f., 152, 169, 203ff., 230f., 235ff., 250, 258f., 260, 270f. ,275, **280ff**., 285f., 290, 292
subject-matter 14, 19, 22, 81ff., 122, 150, 225, 244, 264, 270, **288ff**.
sublation 13, 14, 28f., 71, 99, 110, 112, 117, 124, 127, 149, 168, 185f., 188, 195f., 198, 201, 208, 221, 225f., 227f., 255, 272, **283ff**., 289, 296f., 299, 311
substance 28, 37, 51, 80, 92, 100f., 106, 122, 200, 225f., 230, 280ff., **285ff**., 290, 296, 304
sufficient reason 116, 160, 268
supersede, supersession *see* sublation
syllogism **136ff**.
symbolic art 41ff., 166
Syrianus of Alexandria (5th century AD) 298
system 11ff., 60, 87, 167f., 217ff., 225, 237, 255f., 264f., **265ff**., 269f., 301, 309, 310f.
System of Ethical Life 234

teleology 116, 175, **181ff**., 204f., 235ff.
Tennemann, Wilhelm Gottlieb (1761–1819) 168f.
Tetens, Johann Nikolaus (1736–1807) 11, 75
Thales (*c*.625–545 BC) 169
theodicy 171
theology 118, 219f., **253ff**., 272f.
Theon of Alexandria (4th century AD) 98
theoretical (reason, etc.) 33, 123f., 190f., 219
thesis–antithesis–synthesis 12, 81, 297f.
thing 16, 94f., 108, 117, 122, 146, 198, 238, **288ff**.
thing-in-itself 39, 95, 128, 134, 178, 207, 215, 288f., 294
thinking, thought 11, 30, 64f., 74ff., 78f., 86, 95ff., 107, 109f., 110, 114, 121ff., 125, 129f., 141, 145f., 160, 168, 188, 196, 205, 220f., 228f., 247, 257ff., 264, 266, 268ff., 273, 277, 289, **290ff**., 299f., 303f., 313
this 122, 186
Tholuck, Friedrich August Gottreu (1799–1877) 173
Thomas Aquinas (*c*. 1225–74) 54, 256, 271
Thomasius, Christian (1655–1728) 9f., 275

Thomson, William 98
Tieck, Ludwig (1773–1853) 147ff.
Tiedemann, Dietrich (1748–1803) 168
time 73, 139ff., **293ff**.
Tocqueville, Alexis de (1805–1859) 278
Tönnies, Ferdinand (1855–1936) 53
totality 166, 252, 266f., 296, **309ff**.
transcendental 248, 269, 273
triads 15, 57, 136, 185f., 201f., 223, 270,
    295ff., 305
Trinity 43, 114, 173f., 230, 274, 276, 310
truth 13f., 33, 63f., 113, 124, 146, 155, 171f.,
    179, 196, 214ff., 237, 244, 254ff., 262ff.,
    265ff., **298ff**., 309, 313

understanding 11ff, 16, 20, 29ff., 36, 44, 51f.,
    62, 64, 81, 131, 141, 159, 162, 175, 239,
    242ff., 259, 270, 272
unhappy consciousness 37, 218, 262, 267f.
universal(ity) 15, 19, 29ff., 31f., 38, 39, 57f.,
    59, 72f., 75, 122, 129, 137ff., 146, 149, 151ff.,
    161f., 166, 175, 205, 221, 223, 234, 235,
    248ff., 257f., 279, 282, 292, 298, **302ff**.,
    310f., 312f.

Vico, Giovanni Battista (1669–1744) 7, 17,
    118, 159, 169
Vischer, Friederich Theodor (1807–1887) 23
Voltaire (François-Marie Arouet,
    1694–1778) 118, 120
Voss, Johann Heinrich (1751–1826) 5, 17

war 73, 223, 261, 279, **306ff**.

Weissenborn, G. F. C. 98
Wells, Herbert George 295
Whewell, William (1794–1866) 17
whole and parts 124, 156, 175ff., 252, 265ff.,
    284, 296, 299, 303, **309ff**.
Wieland, Christoph Martin (1733–1813) 190
wilfulness **311ff**.
will 29, 31, 106f., 110f., 122, 162, 191f., 202,
    222, 230f., 233f., 261, **311ff**.
William of Ockham (c.1285–1347) 256
Winckelmann, Johann Joachim (1717–68)
    163, 165
Wittgenstein, Ludwig 75, 293
Wolff, Christian (1679–1754) 11ff., 58, 61,
    74, 93, 106, 116, 134, 136, 145, 151, 167,
    190, 194, 197, 200, 203, 219, 229, 243, 254,
    265, 269, 273, 288, 312
Wollstonecraft, Mary (1759–97) 98
women **98ff**.
Wood, Allan W. 100f., 223
world (inverted, beyond, etc.) 40, 47, 66,
    124, 162, 207, 273f.
world soul 189, 275, 296
world spirit 103, 120, 129f., 170f., 211, 213,
    226, 275ff.

Yearbooks for Scientific Criticism 22f.

Zeller, Eduard (1814–1908) 169
Zeno of Citium (c. 336–264 BC) 262
Zeno of Elea (c.490–430 BC) 81
Zeus 101f.

DH

193
HEG

5001381748

Printed in the United Kingdom
by Lightning Source UK Ltd.
133396UK00001B/58-87/P